W9-CHS-627

THE
NAMES IN
ROMAN
VERSE

THE
NAMES IN
ROMAN
VERSE

A lexicon and reverse index
of all proper names of history, mythology, and geography
found in the classical Roman poets

DONALD C. SWANSON

THE UNIVERSITY OF WISCONSIN PRESS
Madison | Milwaukee | London   1967

31584

Published by
THE UNIVERSITY OF WISCONSIN PRESS
Madison, Milwaukee, and London

U.S.A.: Box 1379, Madison, Wisconsin 53701
U.K.: 26—28 Hallam Street, London, W.1

Printed in the United States of America by
The Colonial Press Inc.
Clinton, Massachusetts

Library of Congress Catalog Card Number 67—25942

Ita me Juppiter, Juno, Ceres,

Minerva, Lato, Spes, Opis, Virtus, Venus,

Castor, Polluxes, Mars, Mercurius, Hercules,

Summanus, Sol, Saturnus, dique omnes ament.

Plautus, *Bacchides*

PREFACE

This volume presents the results of a project accomplished in part by means of a digital computer. It is one of several projects under way since the spring of 1962, and, although this project is the largest of the group, it is the first to be finished.

The original aim was a bare checklist from which might be made a much-needed reverse index. Over the several years of labor this aim was modified to the present enlarged work.

I wish to thank Mrs. Susan Abrams, who did the able work on the key-punch, and Miss Jill Bryant, who assisted in the research. The Graduate School Research Fund of the University of Minnesota awarded me research grants which provided the necessary supplies and assistance. The School of Business Administration courteously allowed me the use of the UNIVAC solid-state 80 computer and the related facilities in their computer center.

To my wife, Dorothy M. Swanson, I owe the deepest debt, for her great talent in programing the system of coded instructions and in operating the computer itself. She also double-checked the Ovid part of the List.

Donald C. Swanson

University of Minnesota
November 18, 1966

CONTENTS

BIBLIOGRAPHICAL NOTE

For editions and indices of individual poets in classical Latin, see the details in Appendix II ("Sources of the Data"). The series in which most standard editions of Roman poets appear are:

BT	Bibliotheca Teubneriana. Leipzig, Teubner.
Budé	Collection des Universités de France. . . . Paris, Société d'édition "Les Belles Lettres."
Loeb	The Loeb Classical Library. London and Cambridge, Mass.
OCT	Oxford Classical Texts, i.e., Scriptorum Classicorum Bibliotheca Oxoniensis.
Paravia	Corpus Scriptorum Latinorum Paravianum. Torino, Paravia.

The principal collections of poetic fragments or of short and anonymous texts are the following:

MLP	Duff, J. Wight, and Duff, Arnold M. *Minor Latin Poets*. Cambridge, Mass., 1934.
FPL	Morel, Willy. *Fragmenta Poetarum Latinorum epicorum et lyricorum*. Leipzig, Teubner, 1927, BT, revised from E. Baehrens' edition.
W	Warmington, E. H. *Remains of Old Latin*, 4 vols. London and Cambridge, Mass., 1935–40.

The following lexicographical works were used in the preparation of this work:

Forcellini, Egidio, and de Vit, Vincenzo. *Supplementum Onomasticum*. Prati, 1885–87.
Lewis, Charlton, and Short, Charles. *Harpers' Latin Dictionary*. New York, 1879; reprinted as *A Latin Dictionary*, Oxford, 1962.
Quicherat, Louis. *Thesaurus Poeticus Linguae Latinae*. 2nd ed.; Paris, 1875.
Thesaurus Linguae Latinae: Onomasticon. Leipzig, 1907–; *A–D* only.

ABBREVIATIONS

I. GENERAL

abl. ablative
acc. accusative
adj. adjective
adv. adverb
arg. argument
coll(ect). collective
comp. companion
conj. conjecture
conn. connected
const(ell). constellation
cont(em). contemporary
d. daughter
desc. descendant(s)
diff. different
dim(in). diminutive
dub. dubious
E. East, eastern
em. emendation, emended
ep. epithet
esp. especially
f. father
fem. female, feminine
fict. fictitious, fictional
fl. floruit
gen. genitive
fr(ag). fragment[1]
Gk. Greek
h. husband
k. king
leg. legendary
m(asc). masculine[2]

metr(on). metronymic
ms. manuscript
mt. mountain(s)
myth. mythical
N noun
N. North, northern (also in NE, NW)
n(eut). neuter
nom(in). nominative
p. pertaining (to)
patr(on). patronymic
personif. personified, -ication
pl. plural
pref. preface
pr(ol). prologue
r. river
ref. reference, referring (to)
s. son
S. South, southern (also in SE, SW)
sg. singular
t. town or city
tr. tribe or people
v.l. varia lectio
w. wife
W. West, western[3]
* (after entry): adjective
+ second meaning
> changed into
< derived from
- (before entry): missing from Harpers'
x (with numeral): times of occurrence

---

1. "fr." means "friend" on pp. 59, 174, 200 of the List.
2. "m." means "mother" on pp. 29, 49, 96, 114, 161, 276, 296.
3. "W." in references to Lucilius and other early texts means
Warmington's edition.

II. AUTHORS AND TEXTS

AET *Aetna*
AV *Appendix Vergiliana*
CAL Calpurnius Siculus
CAT Catullus
CIC Cicero: <u>Ar</u>. or <u>Arat</u>. (*Aratea*)
COL Columella (Book X)
COM Comic fragments
ENN Ennius: <u>An(n)</u>. (*Annales*)
FPLA Fragmenta poetarum
     latinorum I
FPLB Fragmenta poetarum
     latinorum II
GER Germanicus
GR Grattius Faliscus
HL *Homerus Latinus*
HOR Horace
    <u>AP</u> *Ars Poetica*
    <u>C</u>. *Carmina* (the *Odes*)
    <u>Ep</u>(ist). *Epistulae*
    <u>Epod</u>. *Epodes*
    <u>S</u>. *Sermones*
JUV Juvenal
LP *Laus Pisonis*
LUC Lucan
LUCIL Lucilius
LUCR Lucretius
MAN Manilius
MAR Martial
MLP Minor Latin Poets (5 short
      texts; see Appendix III)
OV Ovid
    <u>AA</u> *Ars Amatoria*
    <u>A</u>(m). *Amores*
    <u>Ep</u>. *Epistulae* (= <u>H</u>.)
    <u>F</u>. *Fasti*
    <u>H</u>. *Heroides* (= <u>Ep</u>.)
    <u>M</u>(et). *Metamorphoses*

<u>P</u>. *ex Ponto*
<u>Rem</u>. *Remedia Amoris*
<u>T(r)</u>. *Tristia*
PER Persius
PET Petronius
PH Phaedrus
PL Plautus
PRIAP *Priapeia*
PROP Propertius
S Statius
    <u>A</u>(ch). *Achilleis*
    <u>S</u>. *Silvae*
    <u>T</u>(h). *Thebais*
SEN Seneca
    <u>A</u>(gam). *Agamemnon*
    <u>HF</u> *Hercules Furens*
    <u>HO</u> *Hercules Oetaeus*
    <u>M</u>(ed). *Medea*
    <u>P</u>(h). *Phaedra*
    <u>Th</u>. *Thyestes*
    <u>Tr</u>. *Troades*
SIL Silius Italicus
TER Terence
    <u>Ad</u>. *Adelphoe*
    <u>And</u>. *Andria*
    <u>H</u>. or <u>Heaut</u>. *Heautontimorumenos*
    <u>Hec</u>. *Hecyra*
    <u>Ph</u>(or). *Phormio*
TIB Tibullus
TR Tragic fragments
V Vergil
    <u>A</u>(en). *Aeneid*
    <u>B</u>. *Bucolics*
    <u>G</u>. *Georgics*
VAL Valerius Flaccus
VAR Varro
    <u>Men</u>(ipp). <u>Sat</u>. *Menippean Satires*

INTRODUCTION

PURPOSE AND PLAN OF THE WORK

This volume contains a factual and analytic compilation of all proper names and their meanings found in classical Latin verse, a reverse index of the same names, and three appendices.

A hundred years ago (or even fifty) an industrious schoolboy could have named the Muses, the Furies, the Fates, and a few of the Pleiades, the Horses of the Sun, the Seven against Thebes, and would not have confused ancient Padua and Vienna with modern Padua and Vienna. Nowadays such a feat of memory would be transferred to other, no less trivial, kinds of data. Perhaps now, indeed, is a strategic time for a new, critical listing of the mass of names to be encountered in Roman poetry.

The proper names (nouns, adjectives, a few adverbs) include those of persons, animals, places, celestial bodies, personifications, and products, whether real or imaginary, as listed in the indices of recent standard editions. Generally omitted are titles of poems and epithets which are in themselves not proper names.[1]

The sources (listed in Appendix II) comprise all classical poets from the beginning of recorded Roman verse (Livius Andronicus, late third century B.C.) to Juvenal in the early second century A.D.; included for the sake of completeness are seven fragment collections and the surviving verse of three prosaists, viz., Cicero, Columella, Petronius. This whole corpus of verse represents about 6,500 pages of Teubner editions and thirty-seven different texts.

The List with the identifications provides a demonstration of the use of the digital computer in conjunction with conventional methods of research.

A. Mode of Preparation

The indices nominum of the several poets and fragment collections were pre-edited so far as this was possible while I was in the initial stages of

---

1. For example, *domina Ditis* (= Proserpina) is listed only as DIS, and *conjunx Neptunia* (= Amphitrite) is listed only as NEPTUNIUS.

the work.[2] An abbreviation was assigned to each text, and the proper names were punched onto IBM data cards. Individual or group print-outs were made on the computer as each batch of cards was finished; adjustments in editing were made as the work progressed. A complete print-out was made twice, with further corrections and modifications. The final print-out was placed, page by page, into a typewriter; the identifications were added manually,[3] as well as other useful information (text location, critical notes). The data as printed out yielded 20,687 linear items, the total resulting not only from the instances of a name in each poet but also from second and third repetitions of a name in a poet, where there is a second or third meaning. However, when all the formal duplications were merged, there remained a total of 7,906 different forms, regardless of meaning or number of texts using the name. A separate computer-program produced the reverse index of names.

The limitations of the "printer" attached to the computer required that certain conventions be adopted in the arrangement of the entries and in the use of abbreviations and special signs. The entry word-size was limited arbitrarily to twenty digits. Therefore, names which are twenty spaces long are written right up to the abbreviations for author. One name (Plautus' Argentumexterebronides) is broken just at the suffix in the List. The following long names are not in the List at all and should be added to the total:

Scytalosagittipelliger COM (*Pall. inc.* 61) ep. of Hercules
—Clutomistaridysarchides PL (*Mil.* 14)
—Thensaurochrysonicochrysides PL (*Capt.* 285)
Publius/Pavus/Tuditanus LUCIL 467 (a tripartite phrasal)

B. How To Use This Book

Sample

1	2	3	4	5	6	7	8
—ANNAEUS/SERENUS			MAR			cont. of Seneca, prefect of guard.	7.45.2
ANNALES	pl.		LUCIL		1	title of Ennius' historical poem	
ANNALES			OV	1	2		
ANNA/PERANNA			VAR			Italic goddess	
ANNA/PERENNA			MAR		1	Italic goddess	
ANNA/PERENNA			OV	1	2		
ANNIANUS			MAR			fictional man	
ANNIBAL	(Hannibal)		LUCIL			the Punic general	
ANNIUS			MAR			fictional	
ANNONA	*S.* 1.6.38		S			goddess of the harvest	

---

2. By this I mean that at no time (before the very end) was I certain of the final appearance or nature of the results. The entire project was characterized by changes, greater and lesser, in details and methods. An announcement of this and other projects was made in *Finite String* 2.2 (February, 1965) 3.

3. Care has been taken to identify all names which occur but once. Harpers', the *Thesaurus*, and other works have been sources of informa-

In column 3 (as here in lines 2, 8, 10) occasional information is added, such as modified nouns next to an adjective, number, gender, text reference (<u>S.</u> underlined is the *Silvae* of Statius) or author reference in the case of a rare name, and variants (like Hannibal in line 8). Additional data are added in column 8 (here: a reference 7.45.2) where space for this is lacking in column 3. The author is abbreviated in column 4. The following code explains the remaining symbols and conventions.

Code

—

This dash before an entry in the List usually denotes its total absence in Harpers' Dictionary; in a very few cases it means that a morphological variant or a meaning is absent from Harpers'. Most of these 1,429 items will be found in one text[4] only, and most are *hapax legomena*; these latter are not specially marked.

*

An asterisk after a form in the List means that it is an adjective and is used to distinguish the entry from a homonymous noun. Thus on the first page of the List, ABYDENUS* is distinguished from the noun ABYDENUS. The alphabetic position of the asterisk in the print-out is between the letters *i* and *j*; therefore some adjectives marked with an asterisk in the List will not be adjacent to the corresponding noun.

/

This slant line in an entry separates two parts of a phrasal name, e.g. ANNAEUS/SERENUS and ANNA/PERENNA in the Sample.

{

A brace joins entries in the List which are merely phonological or morphological variants of the same name,

e.g. { CHIRO
      { CHIRON.

+

The plus-sign indicates a second meaning of a name in addition to the standard or more common meaning. Thus JUPPITER (+ planet) CIC means that Juppiter occurs in two meanings in Cicero, the first one (that of the god) having been previously given.

---

tion, but hundreds of rare names have been identified from the unique contexts themselves.

4. About one hundred names each, in Ovid, Statius, and Silius Italicus, are missing from Harpers' Dictionary. The errors in Harpers' do not bulk large, considering the size of the work itself, and the corrections have been tacitly made in the present work.

em.

This is an all-purpose warning that the form so labelled is either a manuscript variant which has been variously corrected by editors or is an
emendation itself. The reader is advised to consult the critical notes of
the text (and passage) in question. These problems are noted chiefly in
the case of the rarer names, and Appendix I lists many of these.

cf.

This abbreviation usually means that a phonetic or orthographic variant of
an entry exists nearby in the List. For example, DELOS (cf. -us) means
that farther down in the List is DELUS, whose frequencies should be
added to those of DELOS. Similarly with OETA and OETE.

numerals

The numeral in column 5 following author abbreviations indicates the number of different persons or places with the same name, e.g., ABANTIADES
OV 2 2, on page 3. A *1* in this column is a total moved over from column 6
by a grand total. Thus, ABARIS VAL 1 4 means that the name occurs in one
meaning in Valerius and that the total of authors/meanings is four. (Note
the entry ABAS in the List, which has three meanings in two authors each,
so that five authors yield a total of nine authors/meanings.) A name with
no number indicates its occurence in one author alone. Each variant has
its own total.

The identifications are reduced to brief labels; all names are glossed,
even the most obvious. In this matter I have followed Harpers', with an
occasional updating of its English diction. Most adjectives have been
translated with the phrase "p(ertaining) to," even though "pertaining" is
a very rare term in contemporary English. A gloss in parentheses indicates
that the meaning is an exception (often an extension) to the general meaning just given. The authors are listed alphabetically rather than chronologically, and so the historical or semantic sequence is not always
apparent.

Some of the abbreviated labels are not to be taken too literally. Thus
tr(ibe) is not the technical term (Roman *tribus*) but means "people, nation,
race"; *fict(ional)* persons (especially in Martial, Horace, Juvenal) may have
existed (and in most cases their names are commonplace, not mythical),
but there is no hope of identifying what was often intended only as a type
in the first place. *Town*, *river*, and *mountain* are used in the widest
meanings.

In using the Reverse Index (Reversal) one must remember that singulars
and plurals of the same stem, when they both occur, will not be found together, e.g., DRYAS, DRYADES. Similarly, inflectional allomorphs, like
-os/-us or *-a/-e*, and gender distinctions like COUS, COUM, COA will
be found each in its own (reversed) alphabetical position. There are also
some spelling variants: AEGAEON and AEGAEUM, CREO and CREON,
PLIAS and PLEIAS. The user must therefore expect to look in two or three
places for any suffix or word-final. When two identical forms occur

together in the Reversal, one is the adjective (with or without an asterisk). Phrasal names naturally permit only the last half of the name to be reversed.

C. Previous Work and Future Work.

The four dictionaries listed at the end of the Bibliographical Note have been the main reference works for Latin verse and onomastics. No one of them is complete. The *Thesaurus* will eventually be complete, but at present it covers only *A—D*.

In the indices to individual poets or verse collections, there are occasional errors and gaps. Editors often differ on the inclusion in their indices of names like Sol, Curia, Hymenaeus, Eurus, Kalendae, and December. Many indices distinguish *u* from *v*, but very few distinguish *i* from *j*; the fact that the Romans did neither in their alphabet is irrelevant.

Harpers' Dictionary has been taken as the norm, since, although it lacks over 1,400 of the proper names found in verse (and many meanings and citations as well) and was based on nineteenth-century editions of texts, it was very carefully done and has again become easily and cheaply available. I have occasionally differed from the interpretations and readings of Harpers'. The current editions of most verse texts are in standard format and are provided with better readings than before, readings based on more (and older) manuscripts or better collations, and this situation has helped to make the present List, I hope, more accurate and far more complete.

There remain to be done the onomastica of classical prose and of the massive *Corpus Inscriptionum Latinarum (CIL)*. These will be more difficult to handle than verse. First, the texts are bulkier and have been less susceptible to textual improvement. Prose literature is about 250 per cent more extensive than verse; Cicero alone uses about 5,470 different names, and Livy has about 4,500 names, according to my estimate. Secondly, prose is different from verse in having numerous phrasal names which are difficult to edit systematically and awkward to arrange economically and unambiguously on IBM cards. Most of the *CIL* volumes are indexed, but new inscriptions keep accumulating, and only a computer project can profitably merge the entire series of indices into one consistent checklist.

I am publishing separately an essay describing the linguistic nature of the proper names in Roman verse; this will be, in effect, my "Conclusion."

THE
LIST OF
NAMES

Name		Source			Description
ABANTĒUS		OV			p. to Abas (k. of Argos)
ABANTIADAE		S			people of Abantia (Euboea)
ABANTIADES	patr.	OV	2	2	Acrisius; Perseus
ABANTIUS		S			p. to Abantia (Euboea)
ABARIS		OV		1	comp. of Phineus
ABARIS		SIL		1	a soldier of Hannibal
ABARIS		V		1	a Rutulian hero
ABARIS		VAL	1	4	a Cyzican hero
ABAS		HL		1	son of Eurydamas
ABAS		OV		3	a Centaur; an Ethiopian; comp. of Dio-
ABAS		S		1	k. of Argos medes
ABAS		V		3	a king; an Etruscan; a Trojan
ABAS		VAL	1	9	f. of Canthus the Argonaut
-ABASCANTUS	S. 5.1pr.	S			a freedman of Domitian
ABATOS		LUC			island in Nile
ABDERA		OV			town in Thrace
ABDERITANUS	adj.	MAR			p. to Abdera
ABDERITES		COM			a person from Abdera
ABELLA		SIL		1	town in Campania
ABELLA		V	1	2	
ABSYRTOS	3.190	LUC			river in Illyria
ABSYRTUS		OV		1	s. of Aeetes
ABSYRTUS		VAL	1	2	
ABYDENUS		OV			ep. of Leander
ABYDENUS*		OV		1	p. to Abydos
ABYDENUS*		S	1	2	
ABYDOS	fem.	LUC		1	town on Hellespont
ABYDOS		SEN		1	
ABYDOS		V	1	3	
ABYDUS		ENN		1	(masc.: G. 1.207)
ABYDUS		OV		1	
ABYDUS		VAL	1	3	
ACADEMIA	fr. 12.73	CIC		1	Plato's school
ACADEMIA	Q. T. Cic.	FPLR	1	2	a villa of Cicero
ACADEMUS		HOR			a Greek hero
ACAMANS		VAL			Cyclops
ACAMAS		HL		2	a Thracian; a Trojan
ACAMAS		S		3	a Theban; an Argive; an Aetolian
ACAMAS		V	1	6	s. of Theseus and Phaedra
-ACANTHIO	Merc. 112	PL			name of a slave
-ACANTHIS	6.77	CAL		1	a shepherdess
ACANTHIS	4.5.63	PROP	1	2	a procuress
ACARNAN		GR		1	breed of dog
ACARNAN	(in pl.)	OV		1	Acarnanians
ACARNAN		S		1	an Acarnanian
ACARNAN		SIL		1	
ACARNAN		V	1	5	
ACARNAN*		SIL			Acarnanian
-ACASTE	T. 1.529	S			a nurse
ACASTUS		OV		1	s. of Pelias
ACASTUS		SEN		1	
ACASTUS		VAL	1	3	
ACCA		OV		1	Acca Larentia, w. of Faustulus
ACCA		S		1	
ACCA		SIL		1	w. of Satricus (a soldier)
ACCA		V	1	4	friend of Camilla
ACCIUS	(Attius)	FPLA		1	L. Attius, the tragic poet

ACCIUS (Attius)	HOR		1	L. Attius, the tragic poet
ACCIUS	JUV		1	
ACCIUS	LUCIL		1	
ACCIUS	MAR		1	
ACCIUS	OV		1	
ACCIUS	PER	1	7	
-ACERRA 1.28	MAR			fictional person
ACERRAE	SIL		1	town in Campania
ACERRAE	V	1	2	
ACERUNTIA (Ach-)	HOR			town of Apulia (Acherontia)
ACESINUS adj.	VAL			p. to the Acesinus (r. in Crimea)
ACESTA (= Egesta)	SIL		1	t. of Sicily
ACESTA	V	1	2	
ACESTES	JUV		1	k. of Sicily
ACESTES	OV		1	
ACESTES	SIL		1	
ACESTES	V	1	4	
ACHAEI	JUV		1	the Greeks
ACHAEI	OV	1	2	(the Greeks on the Black Sea)
ACHAEMENES	HOR			k. of Persia
ACHAEMENIDES	OV		1	companion of Ulixes
ACHAEMENIDES	V	1	2	
ACHAEMENIUS adj.	GR		1	Persian
ACHAEMENIUS	HOR		1	
ACHAEMENIUS	LUC		1	
ACHAEMENIUS	OV		1	
ACHAEMENIUS	PROP		1	
ACHAEMENIUS	S		1	
ACHAEMENIUS	SIL		1	
ACHAEMENIUS	VAL	1	8	
ACHAETUS	SIL			r. in Sicily
ACHAEUS	OV			a k. of Lydia
ACHAEUS*	LUC		1	Achaean, Greek
ACHAEUS*	LUCR		1	
ACHAEUS*	OV		1	
ACHAEUS*	S		1	
ACHAEUS*	VAL	1	5	
ACHAIA	GR		1	Greece
ACHAIA	OV		1	
ACHAIA	PROP	1	3	
ACHAIAS adj.	OV			Greek (woman)
ACHAICUS adj.	AV		1	Greek
ACHAICUS	HL		1	
ACHAICUS	HOR		1	
ACHAICUS	MAN		1	
ACHAICUS	OV		1	
ACHAICUS	SIL		1	
ACHAICUS	V	1	7	
ACHAIS N	OV			= Achaia
ACHAIS*	OV			Achaean (woman)
ACHAIUS adj.	COL		1	Greek
ACHAIUS	OV		1	
ACHAIUS	V	1	3	
ACHARNAE pl.	S			an Attic deme
-ACHARNEUS Phaedr. 22	SEN			a river (?); em.
ACHATES	OV		1	the friend of Aeneas
ACHATES	SIL		1	river of Sicily

ACHATĒS	V	1	3	friend of Aeneas
ACHELOIAS patr.	OV		1	daughter of Achelous
ACHELOIAS	SIL	1	2	
ACHELOIDES patr. pl.	COL			daughters of Achelous
ACHELOIS Copa 15	AV		1	d. of Achelous
ACHELOIS	OV	1	2	
ACHELOIUS	OV		1	p. to river(-god) Achelous
ACHELOIUS	S		1	= Aetolian
ACHELOIUS	V	1	3	p. to Achelous
ACHELOUS	FPLB		1	river-god
ACHELOUS	OV		1	
ACHELOUS	PROP		1	
ACHELOUS	S		1	
ACHELOUS	SEN	1	5	
ACHERON (cf. -uns)	ENN		1	Underworld (or its river)
ACHERON	HOR		1	
ACHERON	LUC		1	
ACHERON	MAN		1	
ACHERON	OV		1	
ACHERON	PROP		1	
ACHERON	S		1	
ACHERON	SEN		1	
ACHERON	SIL		1	
ACHERON	V		1	(+ the river)
ACHERON	VAL	1	11	
ACHERRAE (Acerrae)	SIL			town of Campania
ACHERUNS (cf. -on)	LUCR		1	the Underworld
ACHERUNS	PL		1	
ACHERUNS	TR	1	3	
ACHERUNTICUS	PL			p. to Acheruns
ACHERUSIS	VAL			cave in Bithynia
ACHERUSIUS adj.	ENN		1	p. to Acheron (-uns)
ACHERUSIUS	LUCR		1	
ACHERUSIUS	SIL	1	3	
ACHILLAS	LUC		1	a general of Ptolemy
ACHILLAS	MAR	1	2	a debauched person
ACHILLES	AET		1	the Greek hero
ACHILLES	CAT		1	
ACHILLES	ENN		1	
ACHILLES	GER		1	
ACHILLES	HL		1	
ACHILLES	HOR		1	
ACHILLES	JUV		1	
ACHILLES	LP		1	
ACHILLES	LUC		1	
ACHILLES	MAR		1	
ACHILLES	OV		1	
ACHILLES	PL		1	(+ any handsome man)
ACHILLES	PROP		1	
ACHILLES	S		1	
ACHILLES	SEN		1	
ACHILLES	SIL		1	
ACHILLES	TR		1	
ACHILLES	V		1	(+ any handsome man)
ACHILLES	VAL	1	19	
ACHILLĒUS	MAR		1	p. to Achilles
ACHILLEUS	OV		1	

ACHILLĒUS	S		1	p. to Achilles
ACHILLEUS	V	1	4	
ACHILLIDES patr.	OV			= Pyrrhus
ACHIVI	CAT		1	= Greeks, Achaeans
ACHIVI	CIC		1	
ACHIVI	ENN		1	
ACHIVI	HL		1	
ACHIVI	OV		1	
ACHIVI	PL		1	
ACHIVI	PROP		1	
ACHIVI	SEN		1	
ACHIVI	TR		1	
ACHIVI	V		1	
ACHIVI	VAL	1	11	
ACHIVUS	HOR		1	a Greek
ACHIVUS	OV		1	
ACHIVUS	S	1	3	
ACHIVUS*	HOR		1	Greek
ACHIVUS*	OV		1	
ACHIVUS*	S		1	
ACHIVUS*	SEN		1	
ACHIVUS*	VAL	1	5	
-ACHORUS (or Acorus)	MAR			a funeral director (3.93.24)
ACIDALIA	V			epithet of Venus
ACIDALIUS adj.	LP		1	p. to Venus
ACIDALIUS	MAR	1	2	
ACILIUS	FPLR			a consul
ACILIUS	JUV	1	2	consul (M'. A. Glabrio, fl. AD 123)
-ACIR em.	S			r. of Lucania (S. 2.6.64)
ACIS	OV		2	r. in Sicily; a river-god
ACIS	SIL	1	3	r. in Sicily
ACME 45.1	CAT			mistress of Septimius
ACMON cf. Agmon	OV			companion of Diomedes
ACMONIDES	OV			Cyclops
-ACOETES	OV		1	friend of Euander
ACOETES	S		1	" "
ACOETES (Pacuvius)	TR		1	comp. of Bacchus
ACOETES Aen. 11.30	V	1	4	an Arcadian
-ACONTEUS M. 5.201	OV		1	a soldier of Perseus
ACONTEUS	S		1	an Arcadian
ACONTEUS	SIL		1	a Spaniard
ACONTEUS	V	1	4	a Latin warrior
-ACONTIUS	OV		1	a lover of Cydippe
ACONTIUS	PRIAP	1	2	
ACONTIZOMENOS	COM			title of a lost comedy
-ACOREUS 8.475	LUC			a Macedonian
ACRAE	SIL			t. of Sicily
ACRAGANTINUS 1.716	LUCR			ep. of Empedocles
ACRAGAS cf. Agr-	GR		1	t. of Sicily (see Agrigentum)
ACRAGAS	OV	1	2	
ACRISIONE	AV			= Danaë (Cat. 9.33)
ACRISIONEUS	COL		1	p. to Acrisius
ACRISIONEUS	OV		1	
ACRISIONEUS	SIL		1	
ACRISIONEUS	V	1	4	
ACRISIONIADES patr.	OV			= Perseus
ACRISIUS	HOR		1	Argive king

ACRISIUS	OV		1	Argive king
ACRISIUS	PET		1	
ACRISIUS	S		1	
ACRISIUS	V	1	5	
ACROCERAUNIA	HOR		1	promontory of Epirus
ACROCERAUNIA	OV	1	2	
ACROCORINTHUS	S			the mt. at Corinth
ACRON	PROP		1	k. of Caenina
ACRON	S		1	a Theban
ACRON	V	1	3	a Greek
− ACROPOLISTIDES	PL			a musician (Epid. 479)
ACROTA	OV			a king of Alba Longa
− ACROTELEUTIUM	PL			a meretrix (Mil. 873)
ACTAEON	MAN		1	grandson of Cadmus
ACTAEON	OV		1	
ACTAEON	SEN		1	
ACTAEON	SIL	1	4	
ACTAEUS = Atticus	AV		1	Attic, Athenian
ACTAEUS	COL		1	
ACTAEUS	OV		1	
ACTAEUS	PET		1	
ACTAEUS	S		1	
ACTAEUS	SEN		1	
ACTAEUS	V		1	
ACTAEUS	VAL	1	8	
ACTIACUS	JUV		1	p. to Actium (t. of Epirus)
ACTIACUS	MAN		1	
ACTIACUS	MAR		1	
ACTIACUS	OV		1	
ACTIACUS	PET		1	
ACTIACUS	PROP	1	6	
ACTIAS adj.	S		1	p. to Actium
ACTIAS adj.	V	1	2	p. to Acte (Athenian)
ACTIUS	AV		1	p. to Actium
ACTIUS	HOR		1	
ACTIUS	MAN		1	
ACTIUS	PROP		1	
ACTIUS	SIL		1	
ACTIUS	V	1	6	
ACTOR	JUV		1	an Auruncan
ACTOR	S		2	an Argive; a Theban
ACTOR	V		2	an Auruncan; comp. of Aeneas
ACTOR	VAL	1	6	a Lapith
ACTORIDAE patr.pl.	OV			Eurytus & Cleatus
ACTORIDES sg.	OV		3	Patroclus; Menoetius; Erithus
ACTORIDES	VAL	1	4	Menoetius (f. of Patroclus)
−ADAMASTUS Aen.3.614	V			f. of Achaemenides
−ADELPHASIUM	PL			a girl (Poen. 154)
ADELPHOE	PL			title of comedy
−ADHERBES 7.601	SIL			Punic hero
−ADIMANTUS em.	OV			(Ellis reads Aphidantus; Ibis 327)
ADMETUS	AV		1	legendary husband of Alcestis
ADMETUS	OV		1	
ADMETUS	PROP		1	
ADMETUS	S		1	
ADMETUS	TIB		1	
ADMETUS	VAL	1	6	

—ADMON	VAL			a Cyzican
ADON (= Adonis)	VAR			mythical prince of Cyprus
ADONEUS N, 29.8	CAT	1		= Adonis (trisyllabic)
ADONEUS	PL	1	2	
ADONIS	GR	1		mythical prince of Cyprus, lover of Venus
ADONIS	OV	1		
ADONIS	PROP	1		
ADONIS	V	1	4	
ADRASTEA Cir. 239	AV			a goddess (of just deserts)
ADRASTEUS	S			p. to Adrastus
ADRASTIS patr.	S			d. of Adrastus (= Argia)
ADRASTUS	HL	1		myth. k. of Argos
ADRASTUS	OV	1		
ADRASTUS	PROP	1		
ADRASTUS	S	1		
ADRASTUS	SEN	1		
ADRASTUS	V	1	6	
ADRIA cf. Hadria	LUC			Adriatic Sea
ADRIACUS cf. Had-	LUC			p. to Adriatic Sea
ADRIATICUM 4.6	CAT			the Sea
—ADRYAS em.	PROP			= Dryas ? (1.20.12)
—AD/PIRUM 1.117.6	MAR			a part of Rome
—ADVOLANS 5.24.6	MAR			a gladiator
—ADYRMACHIDAE 3.279	SIL			Libyan tribe
AEA	VAL	2	2	a nymph; land of Colchis
AEACIDA (= -es)	ENN			= Pyrrhus
AEACIDAE	SEN	1		desc. of Pyrrhus
AEACIDAE	VAL	1	2	
AEACIDEIUS	OV			p. to the Aeacidae
AEACIDES (uterque)	AV	1		Achilles & Ajax
AEACIDES	HL	2		Achilles; Ajax
AEACIDES 8.270	JUV	1		Achilles
AEACIDES	MAN	1		"
AEACIDES	MAR	1		"
AEACIDES	OV	6		descendant; Phocus; Telamon; Achilles,
AEACIDES	PRIAP	1		Achilles Peleus; Pyrhhus.
AEACIDES	S	1		"
AEACIDES	SIL	1		Perseus
AEACIDES	V	3		Achilles; Pyrrhus; Perseus
AEACIDES	VAL	2	20	Peleus; Telamon
AEACIDINUS	PL			p. to Aeacides (Achilles)
AEACIUS	COL			p. to Aeacus
AEACUS	AET	1		s. of Jove & Europa, judge in Hades
AEACUS	ENN	1		
AEACUS	HOR	1		
AEACUS	JUV	1		
AEACUS	MAR	1		
AEACUS	OV	1		
AEACUS	PROP	1		
AEACUS	S	1		
AEACUS	SEN	1	9	
AEAEA	OV	1		island in Tyrrhene Sea
AEAEA dub.	TR	1	2	the island (?)
AEAEUS	OV	1		p. to Aea (in Colchis)
AEAEUS	PROP	1		p. to Aea (reference to Calypso)
AEAEUS	S	1		p. to Aea (ref. to Circe)
AEAEUS	V	1		" "

AEAEUS	VAL	1	5	p. to Aea
AEAS -nt-, m.	LUC		1	r. of Epirus
AEAS	OV	1	2	
AEETAEUS	CAT			p. to Aeetes
AEETES	OV		1	k. of Colchis & f. of Medea
AEETES	PH		1	
AEETES	S		1	
AEETES	SEN		1	
AEETES	SIL		1	
AEETES	TR		1	
AEETES	VAL	1	7	
AEETIAS patr., fem.	OV			= Medea
AEETINE	OV			= Medea
AEETIS Maec. 1.110	AV		1	= Medea
AEETIS	VAL	1	2	
AEETIUS	VAL			p. to Aeetes
-AEFULA C. 3.29.6	HOR			town in Latium
-AEFULANUS 6.74	MAR			fictitious man
AEGAE	LUC		1	town in Cilicia
AEGAE	S	1	2	town on Euboea
AEGAEON	OV		1	sea-god
AEGAEON	S		2	giant; the Aegean Sea
AEGAEON	V	1	4	giant
AEGAEUM	JUV		1	the Aegean Sea
AEGAEUM	MAN		1	
AEGAEUM	MAR		1	
AEGAEUM	OV		1	
AEGAEUM	PER		1	
AEGAEUM	S		1	
AEGAEUM	VAL	1	7	
AEGAEUS adj.	AV		1	p. to the Aegean
AEGAEUS	CIC		1	
AEGAEUS	HOR		1	
AEGAEUS	JUV		1	
AEGAEUS	LUC		1	
AEGAEUS	OV		1	
AEGAEUS	PH		1	
AEGAEUS	PROP		1	
AEGAEUS	S		1	
AEGAEUS	SEN		1	
AEGAEUS	SIL		1	
AEGAEUS	TIB		1	
AEGAEUS	TR		1	
AEGAEUS	V		1	
AEGAEUS	VAL	1	15	
-AEGALEUS T. 12.620	S			mt. in Attica
AEGATES fem. pl.	SIL			islands near Sicily
AEGEUS	CAT		1	k. of Athens & f. of Theseus
AEGEUS	OV		1	
AEGEUS	S		1	
AEGEUS	SEN	1	4	
AEGEUS*	VAR			Aegean (adj.)
AEGIALE	S			d. of Adrastus
AEGIALEUS (Pacuvius)	TR			s. of Aeetes
AEGIDES patr.	OV		2	desc. of Aegeus; Theseus
AEGIDES	S	1	3	= Theseus
AEGINA Cir. 477	AV		1	island south of Attica

AEGINA	OV		2	island; mother of Aeacus
AEGINA	S	1	4	m. of Aeacus
AEGION = Aegium	S			t. in Achaea
AEGIS 7.149	LUC		1	the shield of Minerva
AEGIS	OV	1	2	
-AEGISOS P. 1.8.13f.	OV	2	2	t. in Moesia; founder of the t.
AEGISTHUS	OV		1	s. of Thyestes
AEGISTHUS	SEN		1	
AEGISTHUS	TR	1	3	
AEGIUM cf. Aegion	LUCR			town in Achaea
AEGLE	MAR		1	fictitious woman
AEGLE	V	1	2	a nymph
AEGOCEROS m.	GER		1	sign of the Zodiac
AEGOCEROS	LUC	1	2	
AEGON m.	CAL		1	a shepherd
AEGON	FPLR		1	shepherd
AEGON	S		1	Aegean Sea
AEGON	V		1	shepherd
AEGON	VAL	1	5	Aegean Sea
AEGYPTINI Poen. 1291	PL			the Egyptians
AEGYPTIUS adj.	JUV		1	Egyptian
AEGYPTIUS	LUC		1	
AEGYPTIUS	MAN		1	
AEGYPTIUS	OV		1	
AEGYPTIUS	PL		1	
AEGYPTIUS	SIL		1	
AEGYPTIUS	V		1	
AEGYPTIUS	VAR	1	8	
AEGYPTOS	JUV		1	Egypt
AEGYPTOS	S		1	
AEGYPTOS	V	1	3	
AEGYPTUS	CAT		1	Egypt
AEGYPTUS	LUC		1	
AEGYPTUS	LUCIL		1	
AEGYPTUS	LUCR		1	
AEGYPTUS	MAN		1	
AEGYPTUS	OV		2	(+ k. of Egypt & br. of Danaus)
AEGYPTUS	PL		1	
AEGYPTUS	PROP		1	
AEGYPTUS	S		1	k. of Egypt (br. of Danaus)
AEGYPTUS	SEN	1	11	k. of Egypt
AELIA 6.72	JUV		1	cont. woman
AELIA	MAR	1	2	fict. woman
AELIANUS	MAR	2	2	two friends of MAR
-AELIA/GALLA 3.12.1	PROP			wife of Postumus
AELINON dub.	OV			a dirge
AELIUS	MAR			fict. man
-AELIUS/SEXTUS	ENN			S. Ael. Paetus (cos. 198BC)
AELLO (Met.)	OV	2	2	a dog (3.219); a harpy (13.710)
AEMATHIA (Emathia)	VAL			= Macedonia
AEMILIANI 8.3	JUV			a Roman family
AEMILIANUS N	MAR			fict. man
AEMILIA/VIA	MAR			a road
AEMILIUS	CAT		1	cont. Roman
AEMILIUS	JUV		1	any good lawyer (as type)
AEMILIUS	LUCIL		1	lawyer
AEMILIUS 12.19	MAR		1	fictitious man

AEMILIUS	PROP	1	5	Aem. Paullus (cos. 182 BC)
AEMILIUS* (ludus)	HOR		1	p. to the Aemilian family
AEMILIUS* (pons)	JUV		1	
AEMILIUS* (domus)	MAN		1	
AEMILIUS* (gens)	MAR	1	4	
AENARIA	AET		1	volcanic island (= Ischia)
AENARIA S. 3.5.104	S	1	2	(dub., em. to Denarum)
AENĒA (= Aeneas)	FPLA			the Trojan hero
AENEADAE also sg.	V		1	descendants of Aeneas
AENEADAE	VAL	1	2	
AENEADES as pl.	GER		1	
AENEADES as pl.	LUCR		1	
AENEADES sg.	OV		2	Augustus; the Romans
AENEADES	SIL	1	5	Scipio
AENEAS	AV		1	the Trojan hero of the Aeneid
AENEAS	FPLA		1	
AENEAS	HL		1	
AENEAS	HOR		1	
AENEAS	JUV		1	
AENEAS	LUC		1	
AENEAS	MAN		1	
AENEAS	MAR		1	
AENEAS	OV		1	
AENEAS	PET		1	
AENEAS	PROP		1	
AENEAS	S		1	
AENEAS	SIL		1	
AENEAS	TIB		1	
AENEAS	TR		1	
AENEAS	V		1	
AENEAS	VAR	1	17	
AENEIS fem.	OV		1	title of Vergil's epic
AENEIS	S	1	2	
AENEIUS	LP		1	p. to Aeneas
AENEIUS	OV		1	
AENEIUS	S		1	
AENEIUS	SIL		1	
AENEIUS	V	1	5	
AENĪDAE pl.	VAL			the Cyzicans
AENIDES (= -eades)	V			Ascanius (Aen. 9.653)
AENUS fem.	ENN			town of Thrace
AEOLIA dub., 1.721	LUCR		1	land of Aeolus (god of winds)
AEOLIA 2.14.12	MAR		1	name of a bath-house in Rome
AEOLIA	S		1	land of Aeolus
AEOLIA	V	1	4	land of Aeolus
AEOLIDAE m. pl.	LUC		1	sons of Aeolus
AEOLIDAE	OV		1	
AEOLIDAE	VAL	1	3	
AEOLIDES m. sg.	HOR		1	Sisyphus
AEOLIDES	OV		5	Athamas; Cephalus; Misenus; Salmoneus;
AEOLIDES	S		1	Athamas Sisyphus
AEOLIDES	SIL		1	Podaetus (Siculian hero)
AEOLIDES	V		2	Ulixes; Misenus
AEOLIDES	VAL	1	11	Phrixus
AEOLIS	MAR		1	mother of Canace
AEOLIS	OV	2	3	Canace; Alcyone
AEOLIUS* (vallis)	GR		1	p. to Aeolia

AEOLIUS* (carmen)	HOR		1	p. to Aeolia (Gk. region in Anatolia)
AEOLIUS*	JUV		1	p. to Aeolus or his land
AEOLIUS*	LUC		1	p. to Aeolus
AEOLIUS*	MAR		1	p. to Aeolus
AEOLIUS*	OV		2	p. to Aeolus; p. to the Aeolans
AEOLIUS*	PROP		1	p. to Aeolia
AEOLIUS*	S		1	p. to Aeolus or his land
AEOLIUS*	SEN		1	p. to Aeolus
AEOLIUS*	SIL		1	p. to islands of Aeolus
AEOLIUS*	TIB		1	p. to Aeolus
AEOLIUS*	V		1	p. to Aeolia or the islands
AEOLIUS*	VAL	1	14	p. to Aeolus
AEOLUS	GER		1	god of the winds
AEOLUS	MAR		1	
AEOLUS	OV		1	
AEOLUS	S		2	(= a Theban)
AEOLUS	V		2	(= a Trojan)
AEOLUS	VAL	2	9	(= son of Hellen)
AEPY	S			town of Elis
AEPYTIDES (=Ep-)	V			son of Epytus
-AEPYTIUS T. 9.847	S			Arcadian (adj.)
AEPYTUS (Ep-)	S		1	a Theban
AEPYTUS	V	1	2	a Trojan
-AEQUANUS 5.176	SIL			a soldier
AEQUANUS* (juga)	SIL			p. to mt. near Sorrentum
AEQUI	OV		1	tribe of Latium
AEQUI	SIL		1	
AEQUI dub., Aen. 7.695	V	1	3	
AEQUICOLUS N	OV			one of the Aequi
AEQUICULUS*	SIL		1	Aequian
AEQUICULUS*	V	1	2	
AEROPE	OV		1	wife of Atreus
AEROPE (inc.fab. 132)	TR	1	2	
AESACOS	OV			son of Priam
AESAR	OV			river of Bruttium
AESAREUS	OV			p. to the Aesar
-AESCHINUS Ps. 757	PL		1	fictional banker
AESCHINUS Ad. 26	TER	1	2	a young man
-AESCHRODORA Ps. 196	PL			a meretrix
-AESCHYLEUS adj.	PROP			p. to Aeschylus (2.34.41)
AESCHYLUS	HOR		1	Greek tragedian
AESCHYLUS	MAR	1	2	(fictional man)
AESCULAPIUS	ENN		1	Greek god of medicine
AESCULAPIUS	PL		1	
AESCULAPIUS	PRIAP		1	
AESCULAPIUS	TER	1	4	
-AESEPIUS adj., 3.420	VAL			p. to Aesepus (r. near Cyzicus)
AESERNIA	SIL			t. in Samnium
AESERNINUS	LUCIL			p. to Aesernia
AESIS	SIL	2	2	a king; a river
AESON	OV		1	father of Jason
AESON	S		1	
AESON	VAL	1	3	
AESONIDES patr.	MAR		1	son of Aeson (= Jason)
AESONIDES	OV		1	
AESONIDES	PROP		1	
AESONIDES	VAL	1	4	

AESONIUS		OV	1	p. to Aeson
AESONIUS		PROP	1	
AESONIUS		SEN	1	
AESONIUS		VAL	1 4	
AESOPĬUS		PH		p. to Aesop
AESOPUS	(Juventius 9)	COM	1	(uncertain person)
AESOPUS	(Sueius)	FPLA	1	" "
AESOPUS		HOR	2	cont. actor and his son
AESOPUS		PH	1 5	legendary Gk. fabulist
AESTAS	Met. 2.28	OV		"Summer" personified
-AETHALIDES	1.437	VAL		an Argonaut
-AETHALION	M. 3.647	OV		a sailor
-AETHALIS	P. 2.3.84	OV		island of Elba
-AETHALOS	Ibis 619	OV		myth. k. of Egypt
AETHER m., personif.		LUCR	1	Heaven (s. of Chaos)
AETHER		V	1 2	
-AETHION	M. 5.146	OV		an augur
AETHION	T. 6.443	S	2 3	a horse; a Theban (7.757)
AETHIOPES	pl.	JUV	1	Ethiopians
AETHIOPES		LUC	1	
AETHIOPES		LUCR	1	
AETHIOPES		MAN	1	
AETHIOPES		OV	1	
AETHIOPES		S	1	
AETHIOPES		SEN	1	
AETHIOPES		SIL	1	
AETHIOPES		V	1 9	
AETHIOPIA	(v.l.)	OV	1	Ethiopia
AETHIOPIA		TER	1 2	
AETHIOPS		JUV	1	(any negro)
AETHIOPS		MAR	1 2	an Ethiopian
AETHIOPS*		CAT	1	p. to Ethiopia, Ethiopian
AETHIOPS*		HOR	1	
AETHIOPS*		JUV	1	
AETHIOPS*		OV	1 4	
AETHIOPUS	=-ops	LUCIL		an Ethiopian
AETHŌN		MAR	2	Sun-horse; a fict. person
AETHON		OV	1	Sun-horse
AETHON		V	1 4	Sun-horse
AETHRA		OV	2 2	d. of Oceanus; d. of Pittheus
-AETIA	10.4.12	MAR		title of Callimachus' poem
AETNA		AET	1	the volcano of Sicily
AETNA		HOR	1	
AETNA		LUC	1	
AETNA		LUCIL	1	
AETNA		LUCR	1	
AETNA		MAN	1	
AETNA	(also Aetne)	OV	1	
AETNA		PET	1	
AETNA		PL	1	
AETNA		PROP	1	
AETNA		S	1	
AETNA		SEN	1	
AETNA		SIL	1	
AETNA		TR	1	
AETNA		V	1	
AETNA		VAL	1 16	

AETNAEUS	AET	1	p. to Aetna
AETNAEUS	AV	1	
AETNAEUS	FPLR	1	
AETNAEUS	GR	1	
AETNAEUS	HL	1	
AETNAEUS	LUC	1	
AETNAEUS	LUCR	1	
AETNAEUS	MAR	1	
AETNAEUS	OV	1	
AETNAEUS	PROP	1	
AETNAEUS	S	1	
AETNAEUS	SEN	1	
AETNAEUS	SIL	1	
AETNAEUS	TIB	1	
AETNAEUS	V	1	
AETNAEUS	VAL	1 16	
AETOLI	PL		the people of Aetolia
AETOLIA	OV	1	a region of Greece
AETOLIA	PL	1 2	
AETOLICUS	PL		p. to Aetolia
AETOLIS N	OV		an Aetolian woman
AETOLIUS	HL	1	Aetolian
AETOLIUS	OV	1 2	
AETOLUS	S	1	an Aetolian
AETOLUS	V	1 2	
AETOLUS*	GR	1	p. to Aetolia
AETOLUS*	HL	1	
AETOLUS*	HOR	1	
AETOLUS*	MAR	1	
AETOLUS*	OV	1	
AETOLUS*	PL	1	
AETOLUS*	PROP	1	
AETOLUS*	S	1	
AETOLUS*	SEN	1	
AETOLUS*	SIL	1 10	
AFER	FPLA	1	=Terence, the poet
AFER	HOR	1	Hannibal; Africa
AFER	LUC	1	an African
AFER	MAR	1	fictitious person
AFER	SIL	1 5	an African
AFER*	AV	1	African (usually: North African)
AFER*	HOR	1	
AFER*	JUV	1	
AFER*	OV	1	
AFER*	PET	1	
AFER*	PL	1	
AFER*	PROP	1	
AFER*	S	1	
AFER* G. 3.344	V	1 9	
AFRA	MAR		fictitious woman
AFRANIUS	HOR	1	the comic poet
AFRANIUS	LUC	1 2	L. Afranius (a Pompey supporter)
AFRI	AV	1	Africans
AFRI	JUV	1	
AFRI	MAN	1	
AFRI	SIL	1	
AFRI	V	1 5	

AFRICA	COM		1	North Africa
AFRICA	ENN		1	
AFRICA	HOR		1	
AFRICA	JUV		1	
AFRICA	LUC		1	
AFRICA	MAR		1	
AFRICA	OV		1	
AFRICA	PROP		1	
AFRICA	S		1	
AFRICA	SIL		1	
AFRICA	TIB		1	
AFRICA	V		1	
AFRICA	VAR	1	13	
AFRICANI pl. N	MAR			Scipio as type
AFRICANUS	FPLA		1	Scipio
AFRICANUS	HOR		1	Scipio
AFRICANUS (+ pl.)	MAR	1	3	fict.; as pl. Scipios.
AFRICANUS*	PL			African
AFRICUS	AV		1	South-west wind
AFRICUS	CAL		1	wind
AFRICUS	HOR		1	wind
AFRICUS dub.	PROP		1	wind
AFRICUS	SIL		1	wind
AFRICUS	V		1	wind
AFRICUS	VAL	1	7	wind
AFRICUS*	CAT		1	African
AFRICUS*	HOR		1	
AFRICUS*	PL		1	
AFRICUS*	SIL	1	4	
AGAMEMNO	ENN		1	legendary k. of Mycenae
AGAMEMNO	PL		1	
AGAMEMNO	S		1	
AGAMEMNO	SEN		1	
AGAMEMNO	TR	1	5	
AGAMEMNON	HL		1	
AGAMEMNON	HOR		1	
AGAMEMNON	JUV		1	
AGAMEMNON	LUCIL		1	
AGAMEMNON	OV		1	
AGAMEMNON	PROP	1	6	
AGAMEMNONIDES patr.	JUV			desc. of Agamemnon
AGAMEMNONIUS	MLP		1	p. to Agamemnon
AGAMEMNONIUS	OV		1	
AGAMEMNONIUS	PROP		1	
AGAMEMNONIUS	SEN		1	
AGAMEMNONIUS	SIL		1	
AGAMEMNONIUS	V	1	6	
AGANIPPE	CAT		1	prophetic spring of Boeotia
AGANIPPE	JUV		1	
AGANIPPE	OV		1	
AGANIPPE	V	1	4	
AGANIPPEUS	PROP			p. to Aganippe
AGANIPPIS fem. adj.	OV			p. to Aganippe (or to the Muses)
-AGAPENOR (line 175)	HL			s. of Ancaeus, the Arcadian hero
-AGATHINUS 9.38.1	MAR			a wily character
AGATHOCLES	PL			king (of Sicily?)
AGATHOCLĒUS	SIL			p. to Agathocles

AGATHYRNA	SIL			town of Sicily
AGATHYRSI	JUV		1	a N. Balkan people
AGATHYRSI	V	1	2	
AGAUE	AV		1	the Bacchant mother of Pentheus
AGAUE	HOR		1	
AGAUE	JUV		1	
AGAUE	LUC		1	
AGAUE	OV		1	
AGAUE	S		1	
AGAUE	SEN		1	
AGAUE	TR	1	8	
- AGELADAS m. (line 30)	COL			an artist
- AGELAUS	HL			a Trojan
AGENOR	MAR		1	king of Phoenicia
AGENOR	OV		1	
AGENOR	S		1	
AGENOR	SEN		1	
AGENOR	SIL		1	
AGENOR	V		1	
AGENOR	VAL	1	7	
AGENOREUS	GER		1	p. to Agenor
AGENOREUS	MAR		1	
AGENOREUS	OV		1	
AGENOREUS	S		1	
AGENOREUS	SIL		1	
AGENOREUS	VAL	1	6	
AGENORIDAE pl.	S		1	desc. of Agenor (Cadmus, Perseus)
AGENORIDAE	SIL	1	2	" "
AGENORIDES sg. m.	OV		2	Cadmus; Perseus
AGENORIDES	VAL	1	3	s. of Agenor
AGIS -id-, m.	V			a Lycian hero
AGLAIE (Cat. 11.60)	AV			one of the Graces
AGLAUROS fem.	OV			d. of Cecrops
AGMON = Acmon	V			comp. of Aeneas
AGNALIA pl. n.	OV			Roman festival (also Agonalia)
AGONALIS	OV			p. to the Agnalia
AGONIA n. pl.	OV			= Ag(o)nalia
AGONIUM	OV			a feast
-AGORASTOCLES	PL			a young man (Poen. 205)
AGRAGAS (Acr-) m.	SIL		1	town of Sicily
AGRAGAS	V	1	2	
-AGRE M. 3.212	OV			name of a dog
-AGREUS T. 6.887	S			a hero
AGRIGENTINUS	PL			p. to Agragas
-AGRION dub. 310W	LUCIL			(unknown form)
AGRIPPA m.	HOR		1	M. Vipsanius Agrippa
AGRIPPA 6.158	JUV		1	the k. of Judaea
AGRIPPA 1.798	MAN		1	M. Vips. Agr.
AGRIPPA	MAR		1	" "
AGRIPPA F. 4.49	OV		1	mythical son of Tiberinus
AGRIPPA	SEN		1	M. Vips. Agr.
AGRIPPA	V	1	7	" " "
AGRIPPINA	JUV			Agrippina minor, fl. 65 AD
AGRIPPINA	SEN	1	2	wife of Germanicus
AGRIUS	OV			son of Parthaon
-AGROECUS	FPLA			title of a comedy
AGYIEUS	HOR			ep. of Apollo

Entry	Author			Description
−AGYLLE 5.17	SIL			the nymph of Lake Trasimenus
−AGYLLEUS Th. 6.812	S			son of Hercules
AGYLLĪNUS	V			p. to Agylle
−AGYRĪNUS 14.207	SIL			p. to Agyrium (t. of Sicily)
−AGYRTES M. 5.148	OV		1	legendary patricide
AGYRTES T. passim	S	1	2	an Argive
AIACES pl.	HL			the two Ajaxes
AIAX	ENN		1	son of Telamon
AIAX also pl.	HL		1	son of Oileus
AIAX	HOR		2	s. of Oileus; s. of Telamon
AIAX	JUV		1	s. of Telamon
AIAX	OV		2	both Ajaxes
AIAX Capt. 615	PL		1	s. of Telamon
AIAX A. 1.470 & 501	S		1	both Ajaxes
AIAX	SEN		2	both
AIAX	SIL		2	both
AIAX	TR		1	s. of Telamon
AIAX	V		1	s. of Oileus
AIAX 127.10	VAR	1	16	s. of Telamon
ALABANDA	JUV			town in Caria
ALABANDIUS	GR			p. to Alabanda
ALABIS m.	SIL	2	2	s. of Hasdrubal; r. in Sicily
−ALAEUS T. 12.622	S			p. to Alae (an Attic deme)
−ALALCOMENAEUS T. 7	S			p. to a town in Boeotia (ref. to Minerva)
ALANI	LUC		1	the Alans (an eastern people)
ALANI	SEN		1	
ALANI	VAL	1	3	
ALANUS	LUC		1	p. to the Alans
ALANUS	MAR		1	
ALANUS	MLP	1	3	
ALASTOR	OV			comp. of Sarpedon
−ALATREUS T. 7.300	S			s. of Lapithaon
ALATRIOS Capt. 883	PL			town (fictional?)
−ALAUDA 12.58	MAR			fict. man
ALAZON m.	PL		1	title of comedy
ALAZON	VAL	1	2	r. of Albania (near the Caspian)
ALBA = Alba Longa	JUV		1	ancient t. of Latium
ALBA	LUC		1	
ALBA	MAR		1	
ALBA	OV		2	(+ k. of Alba, M. 14.612)
ALBA	PROP		1	
ALBA	S		1	
ALBA	SIL		1	
ALBA	TIB		1	
ALBA	V		1	
ALBA	VAL	1	11	
−ALBANA/PORTA 3.497	VAL			fictional place
ALBANUM (sc. praedium)	FPLA		1	a villa
ALBANUM	JUV		1	a wine
ALBANUM	MAR	2	4	villa; wine
ALBANUS (mons)	CIC		1	p. to Alba (Longa)
ALBANUS	HOR		1	
ALBANUS	JUV		1	
ALBANUS	LUC		1	
ALBANUS	LUCIL		1	
ALBANUS	MAR		1	
ALBANUS	OV		1	

ALBANUS		PROP	1	p. to Alba (Longa)
ALBANUS		S	1	
ALBANUS	also N	SIL	2	(+ a hero)
ALBANUS		TR	1	
ALBANUS		V	1	
ALBANUS		VAL	1 14	Albanian (on the Caspian)
ALBA/LONGA		ENN	1	ancient t. in Latium
ALBA/LONGA		OV	1	
ALBA/LONGA		TIB	1	
ALBA/LONGA		V	1 4	
ALBESIS	as n. pl.	LUCIL		shields (of the Albenses)
-ALBINA 3.130		JUV		contemporary woman
ALBINOVANUS		OV		poet-friend of Ovid (C. Pedo Alb.)
ALBINUS		HOR	1	a loan-shark
ALBINUS		LUCIL	1	Sp. Post. Albinus
ALBINUS		MAR	1 3	fictional person
ALBIS m.		LUC	1	r. in Germany (= Elbe)
ALBIS	Med. 374	SEN	1 2	
ALBIUS		HOR	2 2	two contemporaries
-ALBUCIUS	S. 2.1, 2.2	HOR	2	two contemporaries
ALBUCIUS	87W	LUCIL 1	3	Titus Albucius
ALBULA		MAR	1	the Tiber r. (poetic name); pl.: a spring
ALBULA		OV	1	
ALBULA		S	1	
ALBULA		SIL	1	
ALBULA		V	1 5	
ALBUNEA		HOR	1	fountain-nymph at Tibur
ALBUNEA		V	1 2	
ALBURNUS		LUCIL	1	port (and mt.) in Lucania
ALBURNUS		V	1 2	mt. in Lucania
ALCAEUS		HOR	1	Lesbian poet
ALCAEUS	Ep. 15.29	OV	1 2	
ALCANDER		OV	1	Trojan comp. of Aeneas
ALCANDER		V	1 2	
-ALCANOR	A. 9.672,10.33	V	2 2	a Trojan; a Latin
ALCATHOE	M. 7.443	OV		fortress of Megara
ALCATHOUS		AV	1	s. of Pelops & k. of Megara
ALCATHOUS		HL	1	
ALCATHOUS		OV	1	
ALCATHOUS		S	1	
ALCATHOUS		V	1 5	
-ALCE	M. 3.217	OV		a dog
ALCEDONIA n.pl.		PL		a calm part of the winter
-ALCESIMARCHUS		PL		a young man (Cist. 102)
-ALCESIMUS		PL		a senex (Cas. 515)
ALCESTIS		AV	1	the wife of Admetus
ALCESTIS		JUV	1	
ALCESTIS		MAR	1 3	
-ALCETIDES	T. 12.744	S		three brothers
-ALCIDAMAS	M. 7.369	OV	1	hero of Cea
ALCIDAMAS	T. passim	S	1 2	Spartan boxer
ALCIDES	patr.	AV	1	desc. of Alceus, i.e. Hercules
ALCIDES		GER	1	
ALCIDES		HOR	1	
ALCIDES		LUC	1	
ALCIDES		MAR	1	
ALCIDES		OV	1	

ALCIDES		PRIAP	1	Hercules
ALCIDES		PROP	1	
ALCIDES		S	1	
ALCIDES		SEN	1	
ALCIDES		SIL	1	
ALCIDES		TIB	1	
ALCIDES		V	1	
ALCIDES		VAL	1 14	
ALCIMEDE		OV	1	d. of Autolycus and m. of Jason
ALCIMEDE		S	1	
ALCIMEDE		VAL	1 3	
ALCIMEDON	M. 3.618	OV	1	a sailor
ALCIMEDON		V	1 2	a wood-carver
− ALCIMEON (Accius 78)		TR		= Alcmaeon, s. of Amphiaraus
− ALCIMUS		MAR	2 2	a slave; a contemporary
ALCINOUS		HOR	1	leg. k. of the Phaeacians
ALCINOUS		JUV	1	
ALCINOUS		MAR	1	
ALCINOUS		OV	1	
ALCINOUS		PRIAP	1	
ALCINOUS		PROP	1	
ALCINOUS		S	1	
ALCINOUS		V	1 8	
− ALCIPPE	3.31	CAL	1	a shepherdess
ALCIPPE	B. 7.14	V	1 2	female slave
ALCITHOE	7.12	JUV	1	title of Paccius' poem
ALCITHOE		OV	1 2	d. of Minyas
ALCMAEONIUS		PROP		p. to Alcmaeon
− ALCMAN	S. 5.3.153	S		the Greek poet
ALCMENA		LUCIL	1	d. of Electryon
ALCMENA		OV	1	
ALCMENA		S	1	
ALCMENA		SIL	1 4	
ALCMENE		FPLR	1	
ALCMENE		PROP	1	
ALCMENE		SEN	1 3	
− ALCON	Cul. 67	AV	1	sculptor
ALCON		CAL	1	shepherd
ALCON		HOR	1	slave
ALCON		MAR	1	doctor in Rome
ALCON	M. 12.683	OV	1	artisan
ALCON		S	1	Sicyonian warrior
ALCON	B. 5.11	V	1 7	shepherd
ALCUMENA	= Alcm-	PL		d. of Electryon
ALCUMEUS	= Alcm-	PL		s. of Amphiaraus
ALCYONE	= Halc-	CIC	1	d. of Aeolus
ALCYONE		GER	1	
ALCYONE	Met. passim	OV	1	
ALCYONE		S	1	
ALCYONE		SEN	1	
ALCYONE		V	1 6	
ALECTO	cf. Allecto	SIL		one of the Furies
ALEIUS	adj.	OV		p. to Ale in Lycia
ALEMON		OV		a Greek, f. of Myscelus
ALEMONIDES patr.		OV		= Myscelus (founder of Croton)
ALES		CIC	1	Jove's messenger
ALES		PROP	1 2	= Amor

−ALETES	S		1	a Theban
ALETES	V	1	2	comp. of Aeneas
ALEUAS (Ibis)	OV			tyrant of Larissa & f. of Scopas
ĀLEUS* fr. 20.1	CIC		1	p. to Elis
ĀLEUS* = Eleūs	PL		1	
ĂLEUS*	S	1	3	ep. of Minerva
ALEXANDER	ENN		1	Paris of Troy
ALEXANDER	FPLA		1	Magnus of Macedon
ALEXANDER	HL		1	Paris
ALEXANDER	HOR		1	Magnus
ALEXANDER	JUV		1	
ALEXANDER	LUC		1	
ALEXANDER	LUCR		1	Paris
ALEXANDER	OV		1	Magnus
ALEXANDER	PL	2	10	Magnus; Paris
⌠ALEXANDRĒA	HOR			town in Egypt
⌡ALEXANDRĪA 3.11.33	PROP			
ALEXANDRĪNUS	PL			p. to Alexandria
−ALEXIRHOE M. 11.763	OV			a nymph
−ALEXIS 4.75	CAL		1	a shepherd
ALEXIS 298	COL		1	"
ALEXIS	MAR		1	young slave
ALEXIS	PROP		1	shepherd
ALEXIS B. 2.1	V	1	5	"
−ALFENUS 30.1	CAT		1	contemporary male
ALFENUS S. 1.3.130	HOR	1	2	
−ALFIUS Epod. 2.67	HOR		1	a loan-shark
ALFIUS (Alph-)	MAR	1	2	unknown contemporary
ALGIDUS	HOR		1	mt. in Latium
ALGIDUS	S	1	2	mt.
ALGIDUS* 10.30.6	MAR		1	p. to the mt.
ALGIDUS* F. 6.722	OV		1	
ALGIDUS*	SIL	1	3	
ALIDENSIA n.pl.	LUCR			full dress of Ali(n)da (in Caria?)
ALIDENSIS Capt. 880	PL			p. to Ali(n)da
ALIS =Elis	PL			t. of Achaia
ALLECTO fem.	OV		1	one of the Furies
ALLECTO	V	1	2	
−ALLEDIUS 5.118	JUV			a contemporary man
ALLIA	LUC		1	stream in Latium
ALLIA	OV		1	
ALLIA	SIL		1	
ALLIA	V	1	4	
ALLIFAE	SIL			t. in Samnium
ALLIFANA n. pl.	HOR			type of drinking bowls
ALLIFANUS	SIL			p. to Allifae
−ALLIUS 68.41	CAT		1	friend of CAT
ALLIUS	SIL	1	2	an Apulian soldier
ALLOBROGES	CIC			Gaulish tribe
ALLOBROGICI 8.13	JUV			Gaulish tribe
ALLOBROX sg. for pl.	HOR			the Gauls
ALLOBROX* 7.214	JUV			p. to the Allobroges
ALMO m.	LUC		1	stream in Latium
ALMO	MAR		2	stream; a contemporary
ALMO	OV		1	stream
ALMO	S		1	
ALMO	SIL		1	

ALMO <u>A</u>. 7.532	V		1	(a Latin warrior)
ALMO	VAL	1	8	stream
ALOEUS	LUC			a giant
ALOIDAE patr.	AV		1	sons of Aloeus, i.e. Otus & Ephialtes
ALOIDAE	OV		1	
ALOIDAE	S		1	
ALOIDAE	V		1	
ALOIDAE	VAL	1	5	
ALPES fem. pl.	CAT		1	the Alps
ALPES	FPLB		1	
ALPES	GR		1	
ALPES	HOR		1	
ALPES also sg.10.152	JUV		1	
ALPES also sg.	LUC		1	
ALPES (sg. <u>AA</u> 3.156)	OV		1	
ALPES	PET		1	
ALPES	S		1	
ALPES	SIL		1	
ALPES	TIB		1	
ALPES	V		1	
ALPES	VAL	1	13	
ALPHEIAS fem.	OV			fountain-nymph (=Arethusa)
−ALPHENOR <u>M</u>. 6.248	OV			s. of Niobe
ALPHEOS cf. Alpheus	LUC		1	river & river-god, lover of Arethusa
ALPHEOS	SEN		1	
ALPHEOS	SIL		1	
ALPHEOS	VAL	1	4	
ALPHESIBOEA	PROP			wife of Alcmaeon
ALPHESIBOEUS	CAL		1	shepherd
ALPHESIBOEUS	V	1	2	herdsman
ALPHEUS = Alpheos	MAR		1	river(-god)
ALPHEUS	OV		1	
ALPHEUS	S		1	
ALPHEUS	TR		1	
ALPHEUS	V	1	5	
ALPINUS adj.	FPLB		1	Alpine
ALPINUS	HOR		1	
ALPINUS	LUC		1	
ALPINUS	MAN		1	
ALPINUS	OV		1	
ALPINUS	S		1	
ALPINUS	SIL		1	
ALPINUS	V	1	8	
ALSIUM	SIL			t. of Etruria
−ALSUS <u>A</u>. 12.304	V			a Latin warrior
ALTHAEA	OV		1	m. of Meleager
ALTHAEA	SEN	1	2	
ALTINAS adj.	GR			p. to Altinum
ALTINUM	MAR			t. in NE Italy
ALUMENTO m.	TR			= Laomedon
ALYATTES m. sg.	HOR			k. of Lydia
AMADRYADES (Hama-)	CAT			wood-nymphs
AMALTHEA <u>F</u>. 5.115	OV		1	name of a Naiad
AMALTHEA	TIB	1	2	the Cumaean sibyl
AMANUS	LUC		1	mt. in Syria
AMANUS	SIL		1	
AMANUS	VAL	1	3	

AMARYLLIS -id-, fem.	CAL		1	shepherdess
AMARYLLIS	OV		1	
AMARYLLIS	V	1	3	
-AMARYNCIDFS em.	HL			a warrior
AMASENUS	V			r. in Latium
AMASIS m.	LUC			a king of Egypt
-AMASTRA 14.267	SIL			t. in Sicily
AMASTRIACUS	OV			p. to Amastris (t.)
AMASTRIS fem.	CAT		1	t. in Paphlagonia
AMASTRIS masc.	VAL	1	2	a Scythian
-AMASTRUS A. 11.673	V		1	a Trojan
AMASTRUS	VAL	1	2	a Cyzican
AMATA	OV		1	mother of Lavinia
AMATA	V	1	2	
AMATHŪS -ūnt-, fem.	CAT		1	t. of Cyprus
AMATHUS	OV		1	
AMATHUS	V	1	3	
AMATHUSIA	AV		1	ep. of Venus (of Amathus)
AMATHUSIA	CAT		1	
AMATHUSIA	OV	1	3	
AMATHUSIACUS	OV			p. to Amathus
AMAZON	MAR		1	legendary warrior woman
AMAZON	OV		1	
AMAZON	SEN		1	
AMAZON also pl.	V		1	
AMAZON	VAL	1	5	
AMAZONES pl.	S			
AMAZONICUS	MAR			p. to the Amazons
AMAZONIDES pl.	VAL			Amazons
AMAZONIS	MAR		1	title of poem by Marsus
AMAZONIS also pl.	PROP		1	Amazon
AMAZONIS	V	1	3	
AMAZONIUS	HOR		1	p. to Amazons
AMAZONIUS	OV		1	
AMAZONIUS	S		1	
AMAZONIUS	SEN		1	
AMAZONIUS	SIL		1	
AMAZONIUS	V	1	6	
-AMBENUS 6.85 & 251	VAL	2	2	a Scythian; a mt.
AMBITIO personif.	PER		1	"Canvassing"
AMBITIO	PL	1	2	
AMBRACIA	ENN		1	town of Epirus
AMBRACIA	OV	1	2	
AMBRACIUS	LUC		1	p. to Ambracia (or to Actium)
AMBRACIUS	OV		1	
AMBRACIUS	S		1	
AMBRACIUS	SIL	1	4	
AMBROSIUS N	JUV		1	a flutist at Rome
AMBROSIUS	VAL	1	2	a Cyzican
-AMEANA 41.1	CAT			woman cont.
AMENANUS	OV			river in Sicily
AMENANUS*	OV			p. to the Amenanus
AMERINA n.pl.	S			a fruit (of Ameria)
AMERĪNUS	SIL		1	p. to Ameria (in Umbria)
AMERINUS	V	1	2	
-AMILLUS 7.62.1	MAR			fictional person
AMINNĔUS (-inē-)	V			p. to Aminaea (in Picenum)

AMITERNĪNUS	COL			p. to Amiternum (Sabine t.)
AMITERNUS	MAR	1		p. to Amiternum
AMITERNUS	SIL	1		
AMITERNUS	V	1	3	
AMMIANUS	MAR			fictional person
AMMON cf. Hammon	OV	2	2	Juppiter; a Cephenian boxer
AMMONIACUS	OV			Libyan
AMNES pl.: 1.106, 2.537	VAL			"Rivers" personif.
AMNIS	CIC	1		constellation
AMNIS	GER	1		
AMNIS	MAN	1		
AMNIS Met. passim	OV	1	4	a god
AMOEBEUS	OV			Athenian harpist
− AMOENUS 12.66	MAR			unknown contemporary
AMOR	AV	1		"Love", "Cupid"
AMOR	CAT	1		
AMOR	LUCR	1		
AMOR	MAR	1		
AMOR	MLP	1		
AMOR also pl.	OV	1		
AMOR	PET	1		
AMOR	PL	1		
AMOR	PRIAP	1		
AMOR also pl.	PROP	1		
AMOR	SEN	1		
AMOR	TIB	1		
AMOR	TR	1		
AMOR	V	1		
AMOR	VAR	1	15	
AMORES	OV		1	title of his poem
AMORES also sg.	S		1	"Cupids"
AMORES	VAL	1	3	
AMORGUS fem.	SIL			island in the Sporades
− AMPELISCA Rud. 235	PL			a girl
AMPELOS	OV			boy loved by Bacchus
AMPHIARAUS	OV		1	legendary Greek prophet
AMPHIARAUS	PROP		1	
AMPHIARAUS	S	1	3	
AMPHIAREIADES patr.	OV			= Alcmaeon
AMPHIARĒUS	PROP			p. to Amphiaraus
AMPHIDAMAS	VAL			an Argonaut
−AMPHIGENIA T. 4.178	S			town in Messenia
AMPHILOCHUS Rem. 455	OV		1	son of Amphiaraus
AMPHILOCHUS Acc. 289	TR	1	2	
−AMPHIMACHUS	HL	2	2	two heroes at Troy
AMPHIMEDON	OV			a Libyan hero
AMPHINOMUS	AET			a Sicilian hero
AMPHION	HOR	1		k. of Thebes and s. of Antiope
AMPHION	JUV	1		
AMPHION	MAR	1		
AMPHION	OV	1		
AMPHION	PROP	1		
AMPHION	S	1		
AMPHION	SEN	1		
AMPHION	V	1		
AMPHION	VAL	1	9	
AMPHIONIUS adj.	PROP		1	p. to Amphion

AMPHIONIUS	S		1	p. to Amphion
AMPHIONIUS	SEN		1	
AMPHIONIUS	SIL	1	4	
AMPHISA (= -ss-)	LUC			t. of central Greece
AMPHISSUS	OV			s. of Apollo
AMPHITRITE	AV		1	wife of Neptune
AMPHITRITE	CAT		1	= the sea
AMPHITRITE	COL		1	wife of Neptune
AMPHITRITE	OV	1	4	" " " (+ Sea, M. 1.14)
AMPHITRUO	PL			title of comedy
AMPHITRYON	LUCIL		1	king of Thebes
AMPHITRYON	OV		1	
AMPHITRYON	S		1	
AMPHITRYON	SEN	1	4	
AMPHITRYONIADES	CAT		1	= Hercules (patr.)
AMPHITRYONIADES	LUC		1	
AMPHITRYONIADES	OV		1	
AMPHITRYONIADES	PET		1	
AMPHITRYONIADES	PROP		1	
AMPHITRYONIADES	S		1	
AMPHITRYONIADES	SIL		1	
AMPHITRYONIADES	V		1	
AMPHITRYONIADES	VAL	1	9	
-AMPHĪUS	HL			brother of Adrastus
AMPHRYSIACUS	S			p. to Amphrysus
AMPHRYSIUS	OV		1	p. to Amphrysus (Apollo story)
AMPHRYSIUS	V	1	2	
AMPHRYSOS	LUC			r. in Thessaly
AMPHRYSUS	COL		1	
AMPHRYSUS	OV		1	
AMPHRYSUS	V	1	3	
AMPSANCTUS A. 7.565	V			a lake in Samnium
-AMPSIGURA Poen. 1065	PL			a Punic woman
AMPYCIDES patr.	OV		1	= Mopsus
AMPYCIDES	VAL	1	2	
AMPYCUS	OV			a priest of Ceres
AMPYX	OV	2	2	a Lapith; comp. of Phineus
AMULIUS	FPLA		1	son of Procas (of Alba)
AMULIUS	OV		1	
AMULIUS	SIL		1	
AMULIUS	TR	1	4	
AMUNCULAE em.	COM			= Amyclae
AMYCLAE	GR		1	a town of Laconia
AMYCLAE	LUCIL		1	
AMYCLAE	MAR		2	(+ t. of Latium)
AMYCLAE	OV		1	
AMYCLAE	S		1	
AMYCLAE	SEN		1	
AMYCLAE	SIL		2	(+ t. of Latium)
AMYCLAE	TR		1	
AMYCLAE	V		1	a town of Latium
AMYCLAE	VAL	1	12	a town of Laconia
AMYCLAEUS	AV		1	p. to Amyclae, i.e. Spartan
AMYCLAEUS	MAR		1	
AMYCLAEUS	OV		1	
AMYCLAEUS	S		1	
AMYCLAEUS	SIL		1	

AMYCLAEUS	V		1	p. to Amyclae
AMYCLAEUS	VAL	1	7	
-AMYCLAS 5.520, 539	LUC			fict. boatman
-AMYCLE 4.5.35	PROP			slave of Cynthia
AMYCLIDES patr.	OV			= Hyacinth
AMYCUS	OV		1	a Centaur
AMYCUS	V		2	a Trojan hero; a Bebrycian hero
AMYCUS	VAL	1	4	a son of Neptune
-AMYDON 3.69	JUV			town in Macedonia
AMYMONE	OV		1	a fountain at Argos
AMYMONE	PROP		1	daughter of Danaus
AMYMONE	S		1	d. of Danaus
AMYMONE	VAL	1	4	fountain at Argos
AMYNTAS	CAL		1	a shepherd
AMYNTAS	HOR		1	(unknown man from Cos)
AMYNTAS	MAR		1	shepherd
AMYNTAS	S		1	Boeotian hero
AMYNTAS	V	1	5	shepherd
AMYNTIADES patr.	OV			= Philip of Macedon
AMYNTOR	OV		1	k. of the Dolopes
AMYNTOR	S	1	2	an Argive
AMYNTORIDES patr.	OV			= Phoenix, comp. of Achilles
-AMYROS	VAL			river in Thessaly
AMYTHAON	OV		1	k. of Pylos & f. of Melampus
AMYTHAON	S		1	" "
AMYTHAON	VAL	1	3	a Lemnian
AMYTHAONIUS	COL		1	p. to Amythaon
AMYTHAONIUS	PROP		1	
AMYTHAONIUS	S		1	
AMYTHAONIUS	TIB		1	
AMYTHAONIUS	V	1	5	
ANACHARSIS 3, pr.52	PH			a historical Scythian
ANACREON	HOR			the Greek lyric poet
-ANACTORIE Ep. 15.17	OV			a girl of Lesbos
-ANACTORIUM Poen.87	PL			a town (?)
-ANACTORIUS 15.299	SIL			p. to Anactorium
ANAGNIA	SIL		1	town of Latium
ANAGNIA	V	1	2	
ANAPHE	OV			island in the Cretan Sea
ANAPUS	OV		1	river of Sicily
ANAPUS (or -is)	SIL	2	3	river; hero
ANAUROS	LUC			river in Thessaly
ANAUSIS	VAL			a Scythian
ANAXAGORAS	LUCR			philosopher of Clazomenae
ANAXARCHUS	OV			philosopher of Abdera
ANAXARETE	OV			Cyprian girl
ANCAEUS	GR		1	a son of Neptune
ANCAEUS	OV		1	myth. Arcadian
ANCAEUS	S		1	an Argonaut from Arcadia
ANCAEUS	SEN		1	"
ANCAEUS	VAL	1	5	"
ANCARIUS (-ch-)	LUCIL			= Q. Ancarius (?) (262M)
-ANCHEMOLUS 7.235	JUV		1	a warrior of Turnus & desc. of Rhoetus
ANCHEMOLUS A. 10.389	V	1	2	
-ANCHIALE	FPLB			a woman
-ANCHIALUS cf. Anci-	MAR		1	fictitious person (11.94.8)
ANCHIALUS T. 1.10.36	OV	1	2	town of Thrace

ANCHISA (= -es)	FPLA			father of Aeneas
ANCHISES	ENN	1		
ANCHISES	HL	1		
ANCHISES	HOR	1		
ANCHISES	JUV	1		
ANCHISES	LUC	1		
ANCHISES	OV	1		
ANCHISES	SIL	1		
ANCHISES	V	1	8	
ANCHISĒUS	V			p. to Anchises
ANCHISIADES patr.	SIL	1		= Aeneas
ANCHISIADES	V	1	2	
ANCIALUS Liv.Andr.	TR			son of Neoptolemus
ANCISES =Anchises	TR			father of Aeneas
ANCŌN fem.	CAT	1		town of Picenum
ANCON	JUV	1		
ANCON	LUC	1		
ANCON 8.436	SIL	1		
ANCON	VAL	1	5	promontory of Pontus
ANCUS (Martius)	ENN	1		a legendary k. of Rome
ANCUS	HOR	1		
ANCUS	JUV	1		
ANCUS	LUCR	1		
ANCUS	MAR	1		
ANCUS	OV	1		
ANCUS	V	1	7	
ANDRAEMON	HL	1		f. of Thoas & k. of Aetolia
ANDRAEMON	MAR	1		a horse
ANDRAEMON	OV	2	4	f. of Thoas; husband of Dryope
-ANDRAGORAS	MAR			fictional man
ANDRIA	TER			title of his comedy, "Lady of Andros"
ANDRIUS*	TER			p. to the island Andros
ANDROGEON (cf. -eos)	PROP			son of Minos
ANDROGEONĒUS	CAT			p. to Androgeon
ANDROGEŌS	OV		1	a Cretan, s. of Minos
ANDROGEOS	V	2	3	a Cretan; a Trojan
ANDROMACHA	ENN		1	d. of Ƀetion & w. of Hector
ANDROMACHA	FPLA		1	
ANDROMACHA	PROP		1	
ANDROMACHA	SEN	1	4	
ANDROMACHE	HL		1	
ANDROMACHE	JUV		1	
ANDROMACHE	MAR		1	
ANDROMACHE	OV		1	
ANDROMACHE	V	1	5	
ANDROMEDA	CIC		1	d. of Cepheus & Cassiope; also const.
ANDROMEDA	HOR		1	
ANDROMEDA	MAN		2	
ANDROMEDA	MAR		1	
ANDROMEDA	OV	1	6	
ANDROMEDE	GER		1	
ANDROMEDE	PROP	1	2	
-ANDRON em.	LUCIL			unknown man
ANDROS fem.	JUV		1	island in the Cyclades
ANDROS	OV	1	2	
ANDRUS	TER			
-ANEMORIA T. 7.347	S			town of Phocis

ANGITIA	SIL		1	sister of Medea
ANGITIA	V	1	2	
ANGUIS	CIC		1	constellation
ANGUIS	GER		1	
ANGUIS	MAN		2	Hydra; dragon
ANGUIS	OV		1	constell.
ANGUIS	SEN		1	
ANGUIS	SIL		1	
ANGUIS	V	1	8	
ANGUITENENS	CIC		1	constellation (cf. Ophiuchus)
ANGUITENENS	MAN	1	2	
ANIEN = Anio	OV		1	river in Latium
ANIEN	S		1	
ANIEN	SIL		1	
ANIEN	V	1	4	
ANIENICOLA	SIL			resident on the Anio
ANIENUS = Anio	PROP		1	the river in Latium
ANIENUS	S	1	2	
ANIENUS*	PROP		1	p. to the Anio r.
ANIENUS*	S		1	
ANIENUS*	TIB		1	
ANIENUS*	V	1	4	
ANIGROS	OV			river in Elis
ANIMULA	PL			town in Apulia
ANIO (-iēn-)	ENN		1	river of Latium (cf. Anien, Anienus)
ANIO	HOR		1	
ANIO	LUC		1	
ANIO	OV		1	
ANIO	PROP	1	5	
ANIUS	OV		1	legendary priest of Delos
ANIUS	V	1	2	
ANNA (Perenna)	OV		3	sister of Dido; a woman of Bovillae
ANNA	SIL		1	sister of Dido
ANNA	V	1	5	sister of Dido
-ANNAEUS/SERENUS	MAR			cont. of Seneca, prefect of guard. 7.45.2
ANNALES pl.	LUCIL		1	title of Ennius' historical poem
ANNALES	OV	1	2	
ANNA/PERANNA	VAR			Italic goddess
ANNA/PERENNA	MAR		1	Italic goddess
ANNA/PERENNA	OV	1	2	
ANNIANUS	MAR			fictional man
ANNIBAL (Hannibal)	LUCIL			the Punic general
ANNIUS	MAR			fictional
ANNONA S. 1.6.38	S			goddess of the harvest
ANNUS M. 2.25	OV			personification of the year
ANSER Tr. 2.435	OV			a minor Roman poet (time of Cicero)
ANTAEUS	JUV		1	a giant of Libya
ANTAEUS	LUC		1	
ANTAEUS	MAR		1	
ANTAEUS	OV		1	
ANTAEUS	PL		1	
ANTAEUS	PROP		1	
ANTAEUS	SEN		1	
ANTAEUS	SIL		1	
ANTAEUS A. 10.561	V	1	9	(a Latin warrior)
- ANTAMONIDES Poen.1322	PL			a Punic soldier
ANTANDROS fem.	OV		1	town in the Troad

ANTANDROS fem.	V	1	2	t. in the Troad
ANTECANIS	CIC			constellation
ANTEMNA sg.	SIL			town of the Sabines
ANTEMNAE	V			
ANTENOR	HL	1		a Trojan hero
ANTENOR	HOR	1		
ANTENOR	OV	1		
ANTENOR	SEN	1		
ANTENOR	SIL	1		
ANTENOR	V	1	6	
ANTENOREUS	LUC	1		p. to Antenor
ANTENOREUS	MAR	1		
ANTENOREUS	SIL	1	3	
ANTENORIDES patr.	HL	1		desc. of Antenor
ANTENORIDES	SIL	1		
ANTENORIDES	V	1	3	
-ANTERASTILIS	PL			a girl (Poen. 203)
ANTHEDON fem.	OV	1		town in Boeotia
ANTHEDON	S	1	2	
ANTHEDONIUS adj.	S			p. to Anthedon
-ANTHEMIO em.	HL			?
-ANTHEUS T. 10.544	S	1		an Argive
ANTHEUS A. 1.181	V	1	2	a Trojan
ANTHRAX	PL			a cook
ANTICATONES	JUV			title of Caesar' lost work
ANTICLEA Pacuv. 247	TR			mother of Ulixes
ANTICYRA	HOR	1		three towns in Greece
ANTICYRA	JUV	1		t. in Phocis
ANTICYRA	OV	1		" " "
ANTICYRA as pl.	PER	1	4	hellebore as product of Anticyra
-ANTIDAMAS Poen. 955	PL			a Punic
-ANTIGENES B. 5.89	V			a shepherd
ANTIGONA	TR			d. of Oedipus
ANTIGONE	JUV	1		" " "
ANTIGONE Met. 6.93	OV	1		d. of Laomedon
ANTIGONE 2.8.21	PROP	1		d. of Oedipus
ANTIGONE	S	1		
ANTIGONE	SEN	1	5	
ANTILOCHUS	HL	1		Greek hero at Troy
ANTILOCHUS	HOR	1		
ANTILOCHUS	JUV	1		
ANTILOCHUS	OV	1		
ANTILOCHUS	PROP	1		
ANTILOCHUS	S	1		
ANTILOCHUS	TR	1	7	
ANTIMACHUS	CAT	1		Greek epic poet
ANTIMACHUS	OV	1		a centaur
ANTIMACHUS Aul. 779	PL	1		fict. character
ANTIMACHUS	PROP	1	4	Greek poet
-ANTINOUS Ep. 1.92	OV	1		suitor of Penelope
ANTINOUS	PROP	1	2	
ANTIOCHUS	HOR	1		king of Syria
ANTIOCHUS	JUV	1		
ANTIOCHUS	MAR	1		
ANTIOCHUS	PL	1	4	
ANTIOPA	PER	1		title of Pacuvius' tragedy
ANTIOPA (Pac. 1)	TR	1	2	mother of Amphion

ANTIOPE	MAR		1	fict. woman
ANTIOPE	PROP		1	m. of Amphion
ANTIOPE	SEN	1	3	an Amazon killed by Theseus
ANTIPHATES	HOR		1	k. of the Laestrygones
ANTIPHATES	JUV		1	
ANTIPHATES	OV		1	
ANTIPHATES	S		1	
ANTIPHATES	SIL		1	
ANTIPHATES	TIB		1	
ANTIPHATES	V	1	7	
ANTIPHILA	COM		1	a girl
ANTIPHILA em.	PL		1	
ANTIPHILA	TER	1	3	
− ANTIPHO	COM		1	a comic character
ANTIPHO	PL		1	senex
ANTIPHO	TER	1	3	a young man
− ANTIPHUS	HL		3	three different heroes
ANTIPHUS	S	2	5	two heroes (a Theban; an Argive)
ANTIPOLITANUS	MAR			p. to Antipolis (t. in S. Gaul)
ANTISSA	OV			t. in Lesbos
− ANTISTIUS/RUSTICUS	MAR			husband of Nigrina (9.30)
ANTIUM	HOR		1	town of the Volsci
ANTIUM	MAR		1	
ANTIUM	OV	1	3	
ANTIUS N	CAT			an unknown Roman
− ANTIUS* em.	S			p. to Antium (t. in Latium) S.1.3.89
ANTONIUS	FPLᴿ		1	Marcus Ant., the triumvir
ANTONIUS	HOR		2	(+ Iullus A.)
ANTONIUS	JUV		2	(+ C. Ant. Hybrida)
ANTONIUS	LUC		3	(+ C.A. & M.A. avus)
ANTONIUS	MAR		2	(+ A. Saturninus)
ANTONIUS	OV		1	
ANTONIUS	PROP		1	
ANTONIUS A. 8.685	V	1	13	
ANTONIUS/MUSA	HOR			a doctor
− ANTORES A. 10.778	V			comp. of Evander
− ANTULLA 1.114	MAR			d. of F. Tellesphorus
ANUBIS	COM		1	dog-headed k. of Egypt
ANUBIS	JUV		1	
ANUBIS	OV		1	
ANUBIS	PROP		1	
ANUBIS A. 8.698	V	1	5	
− ANUS	FPLA			title of a comedy
ANXUR usually n.	ENN		1	town of Latium
ANXUR	HOR		1	
ANXUR	LUC		1	
ANXUR m.	MAR		1	
ANXUR	S		1	
ANXUR	SIL		1	
ANXUR A. 10.545	V		1	a Rutulian
ANXUR	VAL	1	8	a Scythian
ANXURUS	V			p. to Anxur (t.)
ANYTUS	HOR		1	an accuser of Socrates
ANYTUS T. 5.12.12	OV	1	2	
− AON T. 8.475	S			a Theban (hero)
AONES adj.	V			Boeotian
AONIA	S		1	the region of Boeotia

AONIA		V	1	2	Boeotia
AONIDES	fem. pl.	FPLB		1	the Muses
AONIDES	7.58	JUV		1	
AONIDES		MAR		1	
AONIDES	M. 5 & 6	OV		1	
AONIDES	masc.	S		1	ep. of Eteocles
AONIDES	fem. 11.463	SIL	1	6	Muses
AONII		S			Boeotians
AONIS	as pl.	S			Muse(s)
AONIUS	N	OV			ep. of Hercules
AONIUS*		CAT		1	p. to Boeotia
AONIUS*		FPLB		1	
AONIUS*		LP		1	
AONIUS*		MAR		1	
AONIUS*		OV		1	
AONIUS*		PROP		1	
AONIUS*		S		1	
AONIUS*		SEN		1	
AONIUS*		SIL		1	
AONIUS*		VAL	1	10	
AORNOS	(a Greek form)	V			=Avernus
APELLA	m.	HOR		1	a Jew
APELLA	(=-es)	PL	1	2	famous Greek painter
APELLES		HOR		1	
APELLES		OV		1	
APELLES		PROP		1	
APELLES		S	1	4	
APELLEUS		MAR		1	p. to Apelles
APELLEUS		PROP		1	
APELLEUS		S	1	3	
APENNINICOLA		SIL			resident of the Apennines
APENNINIGENA		OV			born in the Apennines
APENNINUS	cf. App-	SIL			mt. range of central Italy
APER		MAR			a contemporary (pun on 'boar')
-APESAS	T. 3x	S			mt. of the Argolid
APHAEA		AV			ep. of Britomartis
APHAREIUS	adj.	OV			p. to Aphareius (k. of Messenia)
APHAREUS	M. 12.341	OV			a Centaur
APHELIOTES	cf. Apel-	CAT			a wind
-APHIDAS	M. 12.317	OV			a Centaur
APHIDNA	F. 5.708	OV			town in Laconia
APHIDNAE		SEN			town in Attica
-APHIDNUS	A. 9.702	V			a Trojan
APHRODISIA	n.pl.	PL			festival of Venus
APICIUS		JUV		1	the famous epicure
APICIUS		MAR	2	3	(+ fict. man)
APIDANOS		LUC			river in Thessaly
APIDANUS		PROP		1	
APIDANUS		VAL	1	2	
APIS		LUC		1	ox-god of Egypt
APIS		OV		1	
APIS		S	1	3	
-APOECIDES	Epid. 202	PL			a senex
APOLLINARIS		MAR			= Domitius, a friend
APOLLINARIS*		HOR			p. to Apollo
APOLLINĔUS		LP		1	p. to Apollo
APOLLINEUS		MAR		1	

APOLLINĔUS	OV		1	p. to Apollo
APOLLINEUS	PRIAP		1	
APOLLINEUS	S		1	
APOLLINEUS	SIL	1	6	
APOLLO	AV		1	the god
APOLLO	CAL		1	
APOLLO	COM		1	
APOLLO	ENN		1	
APOLLO	FPLA		1	
APOLLO	HL		1	
APOLLO	HOR		1	
APOLLO	JUV		1	
APOLLO	LUC		1	
APOLLO	LUCIL		1	
APOLLO	MAR		1	
APOLLO	MLP		1	
APOLLO	OV		1	
APOLLO	PET		1	
APOLLO	PH		1	
APOLLO	PL		1	
APOLLO	PRIAP		1	
APOLLO	PROP		1	
APOLLO	S		1	
APOLLO	SIL		1	
APOLLO	TER		1	
APOLLO	TIB		1	
APOLLO	TR		1	
APOLLO	V		2	(+ a ship, A. 10.171)
APOLLO	VAL	1	26	
APOLLODORUS	MAR			Greek author
-APOLLODOTUS 5.21	MAR			a rhetor
APONUS	LUC		1	a spring near Padua
APONUS	MAR		1	
APONUS	SIL	1	3	
APPENNINICOLA	V			resident in the Apennines
APPENNINUS	FPLB		1	mt. range in central Italy
APPENNINUS	HOR		1	
APPENNINUS	LUC		1	
APPENNINUS	OV		1	
APPENNINUS	PER		1	
APPENNINUS	PET		1	
APPENNINUS	V	1	7	
APPIA sc. via	HOR		1	the road from Rome's Porta Capena
APPIA	MAR		1	
APPIA	OV		1	
APPIA	S	1	4	
APPIA/VIA	PROP			
APPIAS (-ad-)	OV			ep. of nymph of Aqua Appia
APPIUS	ENN		1	Appius Claudius Caecus
APPIUS	HOR		1	
APPIUS 6.385	JUV		1	(Appius as type of family)
APPIUS 5.68ff.	LUC		1	App. Claudius Pulcher (the Pompey man)
APPIUS F. 6.203	OV		1	writer (App. Claudius)
APPIUS	SIL	3	8	three different men
-APRES m. sg., 6.638	VAL			a Colchian
APRILIS (mensis)	HOR		1	April, p. to April
APRILIS	MAR		1	

APRILIS N & adj.	OV		1	April
APRILIS 4.5.35	PROP	1	4	
APSUS 5.462f.	LUC			river of Illyria
APULA	JUV		1	an Apulian girl
APULA	S	1	2	
APULI	PL			people of Apulia
APULIA	HOR		1	region of S. Italy
APULIA	JUV		1	
APULIA	LUCIL		1	
APULIA	MAR		1	
APULIA	PL	1	5	
APULICUS em., adj.	HOR			p. to Apulia
-APULIDA	LUCIL			= Apulia
APULUS	HOR		1	an Apulian (man)
APULUS	LUC		1	
APULUS	SIL	1	3	
APULUS*	HOR		1	Apulian, p. to Apulia
APULUS*	JUV		1	
APULUS*	LUC		1	
APULUS*	MAR		1	
APULUS*	OV		1	
APULUS*	PER		1	
APULUS*	SIL	1	7	
AQUA fr. 34.179	CIC			constellation
AQUAE/BAIAE	PROP			Waters of Baiae (in Campania)
AQUARIUS	CIC		1	sign of the Zodiac (Water-Bearer)
AQUARIUS	COL		1	
AQUARIUS	FPLB		1	
AQUARIUS	GER		1	
AQUARIUS	HOR		1	
AQUARIUS	LUC		1	
AQUARIUS	MAN		1	
AQUARIUS	OV	1	8	
AQUA/MERCURII	OV			a fountain of the Via Appia
-AQUICULUS A. 9.684	V			a Rutulian
AQUILA	CIC		1	constellation
AQUILA	MAN	1	2	
AQUILEIA	MAR		1	town of N.E. Italy
AQUILEIA	SIL	1	2	
AQUILO	AET		1	North Wind
AQUILO	CIC		1	
AQUILO	HOR		1	
AQUILO	LUC		1	
AQUILO	OV		2	(+ husband of Orithyia)
AQUILO	PROP		1	
AQUILO	S		1	
AQUILO	SEN		1	
AQUILO	SIL		1	
AQUILO	TR		1	
AQUILO 4.432	VAL	1	12	(husband of Orithyia)
AQUILONIUS	PROP		1	p. to Aquilo (husband of Or.)
AQUILONIUS	S		1	
AQUILONIUS	VAL	1	3	
AQUINAS	HOR		1	p. to Aquinum
AQUINAS	SIL	1	2	
AQUINUM	JUV		1	town in Latium
AQUINUM	SIL	1	2	

AQUINUS as pl.	CAT		1	a bad poet
AQUINUS 1.93	MAR		1	a primipilarius
AQUINUS 6.201	SIL	1	3	comp. of Marius
AQUITANUS	TIB			p. to Aquitania in SW Gaul
– AQUITES 6.295	VAL			a priest of the river Phasis
ARA	CIC		1	constellation "Altar"
ARA	MAN		1	
ARA	OV	1	3	
ARABARCHES	JUV			an Egyptian customs officer
ARABES	CAT		1	the Arabs
ARABES	HOR		1	
ARABES	LUC		1	
ARABES	MAN		1	
ARABES	OV		1	
ARABES	PET		1	
ARABES	PL		1	
ARABES	SIL		1	
ARABES	VAL	1	9	
ARABI A. 7.605	V			Arabs
ARABIA	PL		1	Arabia
ARABIA	PROP	1	2	
ARABICE adv.	PL			in Arabic fashion
ARABICUS	PL			Arabian, Arabic
ARABIUS	PROP			Arabian, Arabic
ARABS also pl.	LUC		1	Arab
ARABS also adj.	MAR		1	
ARABS adj. & pl.N	PROP		1	
ARABS N, adj., pl.	S		1	
ARABS also pl.	SEN		1	
ARABS	TIB		1	
ARABS	V	1	7	
ARABUS N 15.693	SIL			(name of a Roman soldier)
ARABUS* Cir.	AV		1	Arabic, Arabian
ARABUS*	LUCIL		1	
ARABUS*	PL	1	3	
– ARACHNAEUS 4.136	MAN			p. to Arachne
ARACHNE	JUV		1	legendary girl of Colophon
ARACHNE	OV	1	2	
⎧ ARACINTHUS	V			mt. of Attica
⎨ ARACYNTHUS	PROP		1	
⎩ ARACYNTHUS	S	1	2	
ARADUS	LUCR		1	island-town off Phoenicia
ARADUS	SIL	1	2	
ARAE A. 1.109	V			shoals in Mediterranean
ARAR masc.	LUC		1	river in Gaul (= the Saone)
ARAR	SIL		1	
ARAR	TIB		1	
ARAR	V	1	4	
– ARA/MAXIMA F. 1.581	OV		1	legendary altar built at Rome by Hercules
ARA/MAXIMA 4.9.67	PROP		1	
ARA/MAXIMA A. 8.271	V	1	3	
ARATEUS	FPLR			p. to Aratus
ARATUS	GER		1	the Greek poet
ARATUS	OV		1	
ARATUS	S	1	3	
– ARAURICUS 3.403	SIL			tr. of Spain
ARAXES masc.	LUC		1	river in Armenia

ARAXES		PROP	1	river in Armenia
ARAXES		S	1	(inhabitant)
ARAXES		SEN	1	
ARAXES		TIB	1	
ARAXES		V	1 6	
− ARBACUS	3.362	SIL		town of Celtiberia (?)
ARBELA		SIL		town in Sicily
ARBUSCULA		HOR		a woman mime
ARCADES	pl.	MAN	1	Arcadians, people of Arcadia
ARCADES		OV	1	(breed of dog)
ARCADES	(+ adj.)	PRIAP	2	
ARCADES		SEN	1	
ARCADES		TR	1	
ARCADES		V	1	
ARCADES		VAR	1 8	
ARCADIA		FPLA	1	region in the Peloponnesus
ARCADIA		HOR	1	
ARCADIA		OV	1	
ARCADIA		PER	1	
ARCADIA		S	1	
ARCADIA		SIL	1	
ARCADIA		V	1 7	
ARCADICUS	(asellus)	COL	1	Arcadian
ARCADICUS	(juvenis)	JUV	1	
ARCADICUS	(asinus)	PL	1 3	(i.e. stupid)
ARCADIUS		GR	1	Arcadian
ARCADIUS		LUCR	1	
ARCADIUS		MAR	1	
ARCADIUS		OV	1	
ARCADIUS		PROP	1	
ARCADIUS		S	1	
ARCADIUS		SEN	1	
ARCADIUS		SIL	1	
ARCADIUS		V	1	
ARCADIUS		VAL	1 10	
− ARCANUS	8.72.3	MAR		a magistrate of Narbonne
ARCAS		LUC	2	Arcadian (soldier); Mercury
ARCAS		MAR	2	" "
ARCAS		OV	3	s. of Jove and Callisto; Ancaeus; Lycaon
ARCAS		S	3	Mercury; Aconteus; Parthenopaeus
ARCAS		V	1	an Arcadian
ARCAS		VAL	2 13	Arcadia (1.36); a star (5.370)
ARCAS*		MAR	1	Arcadian
ARCAS*		OV	1	
ARCAS*		S	1	
ARCAS*		SEN	1	
ARCAS*		SIL	1	
ARCAS*		V	1	
ARCAS*		VAL	1 7	
− ARCENS A. 9.583		V		a Sicilian
− ARCERA		FPLR		a constellation (Big Dipper)
⌠ARCESILAS		PER		Greek philosopher
⌡ARCESILAUS		HL		
ARCESIUS		OV		father of Laertes
− ARCETIUS A. 12.459		V		a Rutulian
− ARCHELOCHUS		HL		son of Antenor
− ARCHEMORUS 2.34.36		PROP	1	son of Lycurgus

ARCHEMORUS <u>T</u>. passim	S		1	son of Lycurgus
ARCHEMORUS 17.426	SIL	1	3	
– ARCHESTRATA <u>Curc</u>. 643	PL			a nurse
ARCHIACUS adj.	HOR			p. to Archias, a wood-worker
– ARCHIBULUS <u>Asin</u>.116	PL			fict. banker
– ARCHIDEMIDES <u>Bac</u>.258	PL		1	an Ephesian
ARCHIDEMIDES <u>Eun</u>.327	TER	1	2	a senex
– ARCHIDEMUS <u>Asin</u>. 865	PL			unknown character
– ARCHIGENES 6.236	JUV			a doctor
– ARCHILIS <u>Truc</u>. 130	PL			a mid-wife
ARCHILOCHUS	HOR			the Greek poet
– ARCHIPPUS <u>A</u>. 7.752	V			an Umbrian
– ARCHONIDES <u>H</u>. 1065	TER			a senex
– ARCHYLIS <u>And</u>. 228	TER			aged female slave
ARCHYTAS	HOR		1	Greek philosopher (Pythagorean)
ARCHYTAS	PROP	1	2	
ARCILOCUS (Archi-)	LUCIL			the Greek poet
ARCITENENS (Arqui-)	SIL			ep. of Apollo
ARCTOE (Gk. pl.)	MAN	2	2	const. (Big Dipper; Little Dipper)
ARCTOPHYLAX	CIC		1	const. (Boötes)
ARCTOPHYLAX	GER		1	
ARCTOPHYLAX	LUC		1	
ARCTOPHYLAX	MAN		1	
ARCTOPHYLAX	OV	1	5	
ARCTOS	GER		1	const. (Big Dipper)
ARCTOS	HL		1	the North
ARCTOS	HOR		1	const. (also North Wind)
ARCTOS	LUC		1	const. (people of the north)
ARCTOS	MAN		1	const.
ARCTOS	MAR		1	the North
ARCTOS	OV		1	const.
ARCTOS	PROP		1	const.
ARCTOS	S		1	const. (also the North)
ARCTOS	SEN		1	const.
ARCTOS	SIL		1	const.
ARCTOS	V		1	const.
ARCTOS	VAL	1	13	const. (also the North)
ARCTOUS	FPLR		1	northern, boreal
ARCTOUS	MAR		1	
ARCTOUS	S		1	
ARCTOUS	SIL		1	
ARCTOUS	VAL	1	5	
ARCTURUS	CIC		1	star
ARCTURUS	COL		1	
ARCTURUS	GER		1	
ARCTURUS	HOR		1	
ARCTURUS	MAN		1	
ARCTURUS	OV		1	
ARCTURUS	PL		1	
ARCTURUS	S		1	
ARCTURUS	V	1	9	
ARCTUS = -os	CIC	2	2	const. (Big Dipper; Little Dipper)
ARCUS	CIC		1	Bow (of the const. Archer)
ARCUS	GER	1	2	
ARDEA	FPLA		1	town of Latium
ARDEA	MAR		1	
ARDEA	OV		1	

ARDEA	SIL		1	town of Latium
ARDEA	V	1	5	
ARDOR T. 4.662	S			personif. "Eagerness"
ARECTEUS̄ (= -aeus)	TIB			Babylonian (?)
− ARELLIUS S. 2.6.78	HOR			cont. rich man
− ARENE T.̄ 4.81	S		1	town of Messenia
ARENE ‾1.463	VAL	1	2	mother of Lynceus
AREOPAGITAE pl.	ENN			the court at Athens
− AREOS M̱. 12.310	OV			a Centaur
ARES	LUCIL		1	= Mars, god of war
ARES	VAL	1	2	
ARESTORIDES patr.	OV			= Argus
ARETE 51.6	PRIAP			queen of the Phaeacians
ARETHUSA	OV		1	fountain at Syracuse
ARETHUSA	PROP		1	(pseudonym)
ARETHUSA	SIL		1	fountain
ARETHUSA	V	1	4	
ARETHUSIS adj.	OV			p. to Arethusa
ARETHUSIUS adj.	SIL			p. to Arethusa
−ARETULLA 8.32	MAR			sister of a cont. exile
ARGANTHONIACUS	SIL			p. to a k. of Tartessus
ARGANTHUS	PROP			mt. in Mysia
ARGEI	ENN		1	Roman cult statues
ARGEI	OV	1	2	
−ARGENTARIA (Polla)	S			wife of Lucan (S̱. 2, pref. 24)
ARGENTUMDONIDES	PL			a comic "sponger"
ARGENTUMEXTEREBRONI-	PL			" " "
ARGESTES -DES	OV			NW wind
ARGĒUS	AV		1	p. to the town Argos
ARGEUS	HOR		1	
ARGEUS	MAR		1	
ARGEUS	OV		1	
ARGEUS	S	1	5	
ARGI pl. (= Argos)	OV		1	town of Argolid
ARGI	PL		1	
ARGI	S		1	
ARGI	SIL		1	
ARGI	V		1	
ARGI	VAL	1	6	
ARGIA	S			d. of Adrastus
ARGILETANUS	MAR			p. to Argiletum
ARGILETUM (in tmesis)	MAR		1	a part of Rome
ARGILETUM	V	1	2	
− ARGIODUS M̱. 3.224	OV			a dog
− ARGIPUS Ṯ. 9.266	S			an Argive
ARGIVI	CAT		1	Argives, Greeks
ARGIVI	ENN		1	
ARGIVI	HOR		1	
ARGIVI	MAN		1	
ARGIVI	PL		1	
ARGIVI	SEN		1	
ARGIVI	V	1	7	
ARGIVUS	CAT		1	an Argive (Greek)
ARGIVUS	S		1	
ARGIVUS	VAL	1	3	
ARGIVUS*	AV		1	Argive, Greek
ARGIVUS*	CAT		1	

ARGIVUS*	HL	1	Argive, Greek
ARGIVUS*	HOR	1	
ARGIVUS*	MAR	1	
ARGIVUS*	OV	1	
ARGIVUS*	PROP	1	
ARGIVUS*	S	1	
ARGIVUS*	SEN	1	
ARGIVUS*	SIL	1	
ARGIVUS*	TR	1	
ARGIVUS*	V	1	
ARGIVUS*	VAL	1 13	
ARGO fem.	AV	1	the ship of the Argonauts
ARGO	CIC	1	(constellation)
ARGO	ENN	1	
ARGO	LUC	1	
ARGO	MAN	1	(constellation)
ARGO	OV	1	
ARGO	PROP	1	
ARGO	S	1	
ARGO	SEN	1	
ARGO	SIL	1	
ARGO	V	1	
ARGO	VAL	1	
ARGO	VAR	1 13	
ARGOLICUS	AET	1	p. to Argos, Argolic
ARGOLICUS	AV	1	
ARGOLICUS	CIC	1	
ARGOLICUS	HL	1	
ARGOLICUS	LUC	1	
ARGOLICUS	MAR	1	
ARGOLICUS	OV	1	
ARGOLICUS	S	1	
ARGOLICUS	SEN	1	
ARGOLICUS	SIL	1	
ARGOLICUS	V	1	
ARGOLICUS	VAL	1 12	
ARGOLIDES fem. pl.	S		Argive women (T. passim)
ARGOLIS* fem. adj.	OV		Argive
ARGONAUTAE	HOR	1	the crew of the Argo
ARGONAUTAE	MAR	1	
ARGONAUTAE	S	1 3	
ARGOS n. (cf. Argi)	HOR	1	capital of the Argolid
ARGOS	LUC	1	(whole of Greece)
ARGOS	OV	1	city
ARGOS	S	1	
ARGOS	SEN	1	
ARGOS	TR	1	
ARGOS 1.359	VAL	1 7	
ARGŌUS	AV	1	p. to the ship Argo
ARGOUS	GER	1	
ARGOUS	HOR	1	
ARGOUS	MAR	1	
ARGOUS	PROP	1	
ARGOUS	S	1	
ARGOUS	VAL	1 7	
ARGUS	LUC	1	warrior of Massilia
ARGUS	MAR	1	guardian of Io

ARGUS	OV		1	guardian of Io
ARGUS	PH		1	builder of the Argo
ARGUS	PL		1	guardian
ARGUS	PROP		2	guardian; steersman
ARGUS	S		2	guardian; an Argive
ARGUS	V		2	guardian; guest
ARGUS	VAL	3	14	guardian; two heroes
ARGUS*	PL			= Argivus*
ARGYNNUS	MAR		1	slave-boy
ARGYNNUS	PROP	1	2	legendary boy
ARGYRIPA	SIL		1	town in Apulia
ARGYRIPA	V	1	2	
ARGYRIPPUS	PL			a young man
ARIADNA	CAT		1	d. of Minos (became const.)
ARIADNA	OV		1	
ARIADNA	PROP		1	
ARIADNA	SEN	1	4	
ARIADNAEUS	GER		1	p. to Ariadne (as const.)
ARIADNAEUS	MAN		1	
ARIADNAEUS	OV	1	3	
ARIADNEUS	CAT			
–ARIASMENUS 6.103	VAL			a Scythian
ARICIA	COL		1	town of Latium
ARICIA	HOR		1	
ARICIA	LUC		1	
ARICIA	MAR		1	
ARICIA	OV		1	
ARICIA	SIL		1	
ARICIA	V		1	(> a nymph)
ARICIA	VAL	1	8	
ARICINUS	HOR		1	p. to Aricia
ARICINUS	JUV		1	
ARICINUS	MAR		1	
ARICINUS	OV		1	
ARICINUS	S	1	5	
ARIES	CIC		1	const. (Ram)
ARIES	FPLR		1	
ARIES	GER		1	
ARIES	LUC		1	
ARIES	MAN		1	
ARIES	OV	1	6	
ARIMASPUS sg.	LUC			tr. of N. Europe
–ARIMES (or Arines)	VAL			a Colchian (6.638)
ARIMINENSIS	HOR			p. to Ariminum
ARIMINUM	LUC			t. of Umbria
–ARINASPI (Arim- ?)	VAL			"Scythian" tr. (6.131)
ARION	MAR		1	legendary bard
ARION	OV		1	
ARION	PROP		1	(a talking horse)
ARION	S		2	bard; horse
ARION	SIL		1	bard
ARION	V	1	7	bard
ARIONIUS	OV		1	p. to Arion (bard)
ARIONIUS	PROP	1	2	
ARIS	SIL			Phoenician leader
ARISBA cf. Arisbe	V			town in the Troad
–ARISBAS 3.668	SIL			a Carthaginian

ARISBE = Arisba	LUC			town in the Troad (3.204)
ARISTAEUS	OV		1	s. of Apollo & patron of agriculture
ARISTAEUS	S		1	
ARISTAEUS	SIL		1	
ARISTAEUS	V	1	4	
−ARISTAGORAS 42.1	PRIAP			an overseer
ARISTARCHUS	HOR		1	Gk. grammarian
ARISTARCHUS	OV		1	" "
ARISTARCHUS	PL	1	3	the poet
ARISTIDES	OV	2	2	the Athenian; Milesian poet
ARISTIPPUS	HOR		1	philosopher
ARISTIPPUS	LUCIL	1	2	
ARISTIUS	HOR			friend of Horace: Fuscus A.
−ARISTOCRATES	LUCIL			comic figure
ARISTOPHANES	HOR			the Greek comic poet
−ARISTOPHONTES	PL			a young man (Capt. 527)
ARISTOTELES	JUV		1	the Gk. philosopher
ARISTOTELES	VAR	1	2	
−ARIUS 3.281	LUC			Persian tr.
ARIUSIUS	SIL		1	= Chian (with ref. to wine)
ARIUSIUS	V	1	2	
ARMENIA	JUV		1	the region of E. Anatolia
ARMENIA	LUC		1	
ARMENIA	MAN		1	
ARMENIA	S		1	
ARMENIA	VAL	1	5	
ARMENII	MAR		1	the people of Armenia
ARMENII	S		1	
ARMENII	TIB	1	3	
ARMENIUS	HOR		1	an Armenian
ARMENIUS	LUC		1	
ARMENIUS	OV	1	3	
ARMENIUS* (prunus)	COL		1	Armenian (apricot)
ARMENIUS*	HOR		1	Armenian
ARMENIUS*	JUV		1	
ARMENIUS*	LUC		1	
ARMENIUS*	OV		1	
ARMENIUS*	PROP		1	
ARMENIUS*	SEN		1	
ARMENIUS*	TIB		1	
ARMENIUS*	V	1	9	
−ARMES 6.350	VAL			a Scythian
−ARMILLATUS 4.53	JUV			an informer
ARMIPOTENS 7.78, N	S			ep. of Mars
ARNA em., Cul. 14	AV		1	town of Lycia
ARNA	SIL	1	2	Umbrian town
ARNE	OV		1	legendary woman
ARNE	S	1	2	town of Boeotia
ARNUS	SIL			river in Etruria
−ARON 5.590	VAL			a warrior
ARPI	MAR		1	town of Apulia
ARPI	SIL		1	
ARPI	V	1	3	
ARPINAS N	JUV		2	Cicero; Marius
ARPINAS 8.401	SIL	1	3	=Arpinum (or its people)
ARPINUS	MAR			p. to Arpinum, i.e. Ciceronian
ARQUITENENS	CIC		1	const. "Archer"

ARQUITENENS	MAN		1	const.
ARQUITENENS	OV		1	ep. of Apollo
ARQUITENENS	S		1	
ARQUITENENS	TR	1	5	
ARRETĪNUS (= -r-)	MAR		1	p. to Arretium
ARRETINUS	TIB	1	2	
ARRETIUM	PER		1	town in Etruria
ARRETIUM em.	PL		1	
ARRETIUM	SIL	1	3	
ARRIA	MAR		1	wife of Caecina Paetus
ARRIA 4.1.89	PROP	1	2	another woman
-ARRIUS 84.2	CAT		1	a lawyer
ARRIUS S. 2.3.86	HOR	1	2	Q. Arrius, a friend
ARRUNS	LUC		1	Etruscan seer
ARRUNS	V	1	2	
ARS	OV			title of OV's poem
ARSACIDES patr.	LUC		1	desc. of Arsaces (k. of Parthia)
ARSACIDES	SIL	1	2	
ARSACIUS adj.	MAR			Parthian
-ARSES _ 7.598	SIL			Punic soldier
ARSINOE	CAT		1	sister of Ptolemy Philadelphus
ARSINOE	LUC		1	
ARSINOE	VAL	1	3	
-ARSINOUS	HL			a Trojan
ARTACIE	TIB			fountain in Campania
-ARTAMO Bac. 799	PL			a slave (cf. Artemo)
ARTAXATA n. pl.	JUV			a town in Armenia
-ARTEMIDORUS	MAR	2	2	two contemporaries
-ARTEMO	LUCIL			a fict. man
- ARTEMONA	PL			a matrona
- ARTORIUS 3.29	JUV			cont. man
ARTOTROGUS	PL			a parasite
ARUPĪNUS adj.	TIB			p. to Arrupium (t. of Illyria)
ARVERNI	LUC			a Gaulish tribe
- ARVIRAGUS 4.127	JUV			k. of Britain
ASBOLUS	OV			Actaeon's dog
-ASBYTE 2.58	SIL			a heroine
-ASBYTES A. 12.362	V			a Trojan
ASCALAPHUS	HL		1	a hero
ASCALAPHUS	OV	1	2	s. of Acheron & Orphne
ASCANIUS	HL		1	s. of Aeneas
ASCANIUS	OV		1	" " "
ASCANIUS	PROP		1	river (or lake) in Bithynia
ASCANIUS	S		1	s. of Aeneas
ASCANIUS	SIL		1	a Campanian
ASCANIUS	TIB		1	s. of Aeneas
ASCANIUS	V	2	8	s. of Aeneas; river in Bithynia
-ASCHETOS T. 4.204	S			name of a horse
-ASCLEPIUS S.3, pr. 25	S			a cont. man
ASCLUM = Asculum	SIL			town of Picenum
ASCRA	OV			town in Boeotia
ASCRAEUS	OV			ep. of Hesiod
ASCRAEUS*	AV		1	p. to Ascra, Boeotian (i.e. Hesiodic)
ASCRAEUS*	COL		1	
ASCRAEUS*	OV		1	
ASCRAEUS*	PROP		1	
ASCRAEUS*	S		1	

ASCRAEUS*	SIL		1	p. to Ascra
ASCRAEUS*	V	1	7	
-ASCULEUS adj., 2.469	LUC			p. to Asc(u)lum
ASELLUS	LUCIL			a man
ASIA	AV		1	Asia Minor (Anatolia)
ASIA	CAT		1	
ASIA	FPLA		1	
ASIA	HOR		1	
ASIA	JUV		1	
ASIA	LUC		1	
ASIA	LUCIL		1	
ASIA	MAN		1	
ASIA	MAR		1	
ASIA	OV		1	
ASIA	PH		1	
ASIA	PL		1	
ASIA	PROP		1	
ASIA	S		1	
ASIA	SEN		1	
ASIA	SIL		1	
ASIA	TER		1	
ASIA	TR		1	
ASIA	V		1	
ASIA	VAL	1	20	
ASIANUS	JUV			p. to Asia (Minor)
ASIATICUS (sc. poma)	COL		1	Asiatic apples, i.e. peaches
ASIATICUS	FPLA	1	2	p. to Asia Minor
-ASILAS A. 10.175	V	2	2	an Etruscan; (A. 9.571 a Trojan)
-ASILUS 14.149	SIL			an Etruscan soldier
ASILUS*	SIL			Umbrian
ASINA m.	HOR			a cognomen of Vinnius (unknown cont.)
ASINARIA	PL			title of a comedy
-ASINE em. 8.195	LUC			(unknown place)
ASIS = Asia, M. 5.648	OV		1	Asia Minor
ASIS 4.1.25	PROP	1	2	Assisi ?
ASIUS	HL		1	a Trojan
ASIUS	V	1	2	
ASIUS*	CAT		1	p. to Asia
ASIUS*	V	1	2	Lydian
ASOPIADES patr.	OV			grandson of Asopus (= Aeacus)
ASOPIS	OV	2	2	Aegina (woman); Evadne
ASOPIS*	S			Boeotian
-ASOPIUS T. 7.723	S			p. to Asopus
ASOPOS 6.374	LUC			river of Boeotia
ASOPUS Am. 3.6.33	OV		1	
ASOPUS	PROP		1	
ASOPUS	S	2	4	(+ a god)
ASPER	MAR			fictional person
-ASPIS 3.244	SIL			= Clupea, t. of N. Africa
ASSARACUS	ENN		1	Trojan king
ASSARACUS	HOR		1	
ASSARACUS	JUV		1	
ASSARACUS	LUC		1	
ASSARACUS	OV		1	
ASSARACUS	SEN		1	
ASSARACUS	SIL		1	
ASSARACUS	TR		1	

ASSARACUS	V	1	9	Trojan king
ASSYRIA 3.2.24	TIB			Assyria, the region of Mesopotamia
ASSYRII	OV			people of Assyria
ASSYRIUS	HOR			a Syrian
ASSYRIUS*	AV		1	Assyrian
ASSYRIUS*	CAT		1	
ASSYRIUS*	COL		1	
ASSYRIUS*	HOR		1	
ASSYRIUS*	JUV		1	
ASSYRIUS*	LUC		1	
ASSYRIUS*	MAR		1	
ASSYRIUS*	OV		1	
ASSYRIUS*	S		1	
ASSYRIUS*	SEN		1	
ASSYRIUS*	SIL		1	
ASSYRIUS*	TIB		1	
ASSYRIUS*	V		1	
ASSYRIUS*	VAL	1	14	
ASTACIDES patr.	OV		1	= Menalippus
ASTACIDES	S	1	2	
ASTACUS	CAL			a gardener (pastoral person)
-ASTAPHIUM Truc. 93	PL			a maid
ASTERIE Cul. 15	AV		1	= Delos
ASTERIE	HOR		1	a maiden
ASTERIE	OV	1	3	d. of Coeus
ASTERION	S		1	river in the Argolid
ASTERION	VAL	1	2	an Argonaut
-ASTERIS S. 1.2.197	S			pseudonym of Violentilla
-ASTEROPE	CIC		1	a Pleiad
-ASTEROPE	GER	1	2	
ASTRAEA	JUV		1	goddess of justice
ASTRAEA	LUC		1	const. Virgo
ASTRAEA	MLP		1	goddess
ASTRAEA	OV		1	goddess
ASTRAEA	S		2	goddess; const.
ASTRAEA	SEN		1	goddess
ASTRAEA	VAL	1	8	goddess
ASTRAEUS	GER			a Titan
ASTRAEUS*	GER		1	p. to the Titan
ASTRAEUS*	OV	1	2	
-ASTREUS M. 5.144	OV		1	comp. of Phineus
ASTUR 4.8; sg. for pl.	LUC		1	the Asturian(s)
ASTUR	MAR		1	
ASTUR	SIL		1	
ASTUR (Astyr)	V	1	4	an Etruscan warrior
ASTURICUS	JUV		1	Asturian (in Spain)
ASTURICUS	SIL	1	2	
-ASTURIUS em. 4.298	LUC			Asturian
ASTUR*	MAR		1	Asturian
ASTUR*	SIL	1	2	
ASTUTIA Caec. 229	COM			"Cunning" (personif.)
-ASTYAGES M. 5.203	OV		1	comp. of Phineus
ASTYAGES T. 9.253	S	1	2	an Argive
ASTYANAX	MAR		1	son of Hector
ASTYANAX	OV		1	
ASTYANAX	S		1	
ASTYANAX	SEN		1	

ASTYANAX	V	1	5	son of Hector
ASTYLIDES patr.	GR			= Hagnon
ASTYLOS	OV			a centaur (soothsayer)
ASTYLUS	CAL			a shepherd
− ASTYOCHE T. 3.171	S			a Theban woman
ASTYPALAEA	OV			island in Sporades
ASTYPALEIUS adj.	OV			p. to the island
− ASTYR 3.334	SIL			soldier of Memnon
− ASYLUM A. 8.342	V			place on Capitoline
ASYLUS	JUV		1	gladiator
ASYLUS	MAR	1	2	fictitious person
ATABULUS	HOR			a hot sirocco
ATALANTA	OV		2	Boeotian princess; d. of Iasius
ATALANTA	S		1	" "
ATALANTA	TR	1	4	" "
ATALANTAEUS	MAN			p. to Atalanta
ATALANTEUS	S			
ATALANTIADES metr.	S			= Parthenopaeus
− ATARNITES Ibis 317	OV			Hermias, tyrant of Atarna
ATAX	LUC		1	river in S. Gaul
ATAX	TIB	1	2	
ATELLA	SIL			Oscan town in Campania
ATELLANA	JUV			primitive farce
− ATESTINUS 3.38.5	MAR			cont. lawyer
ATESTINUS*	MAR			p. to Ateste (Venetic town)
ATHAMAN or -nus, adj.	PROP			p. to Epirus
ATHAMANES	OV			tr. of Epirus
ATHAMANIA	GR			Epirus
ATHAMANTEUS	MAR		1	p. to Athamas
ATHAMANTEUS	OV		1	
ATHAMANTEUS	S	1	3	
ATHAMANTIADES patr.	OV			= Palaemon
ATHAMANTIS	OV		1	= Helle
ATHAMANTIS	PROP	1	2	
ATHAMAS	LUC		1	son of Aeolus
ATHAMAS	OV		1	
ATHAMAS	S		1	
ATHAMAS	VAL	1	4	
− ATHAS 4.19.8	MAR			a racer
ATHENAE	AET		1	town of Attica
ATHENAE	AV		1	
ATHENAE	CAT		1	
ATHENAE	COM		1	
ATHENAE	ENN		1	
ATHENAE	FPLA		1	
ATHENAE	HOR		1	
ATHENAE	JUV		1	
ATHENAE	LUC		1	
ATHENAE	LUCIL		1	
ATHENAE	LUCR		1	
ATHENAE	MAN		1	
ATHENAE	MAR		1	
ATHENAE	OV		1	
ATHENAE	PH		1	
ATHENAE	PL		1	
ATHENAE	PROP		1	
ATHENAE	S		1	

ATHENAE		SEN	1	town of Attica
ATHENAE		SIL	1	
ATHENAE		TER	1	
ATHENAE		TR	1 22	
ATHENAEUS		HL	1	p. to Athens
ATHENAEUS		LUCR	1 2	
-ATHENAGORAS	8.41	MAR		fictional
ATHENIENSES		COM		people of Athens
ATHENIENSIS adj.		PL		Athenian
ATHESIS		SIL	1	river of N. Italy
ATHESIS		V	1 2	
ATHIS v.l.		OV		a son of Limnate
ATHOS		AV	1	mt. in Macedonia
ATHOS		CAT	1	
ATHOS		GER	1	
ATHOS		JUV	1	
ATHOS		LUC	1	
ATHOS	as pl.	LUCIL	1	= Athones (Athoses)
ATHOS		OV	1	
ATHOS		S	1	
ATHOS		SEN	1	
ATHOS		SIL	1	
ATHOS		V	1	
ATHOS		VAL	1 12	
-ATHYR	1.412	SIL		Punic warrior
-ATII	A. 5.568	V		Roman gens (in pl.)
ATILIUS		AV	1	Roman gens
ATILIUS		FPLA	1	a poet
ATILIUS		MAR	1 3	Roman gens
ATINA		MAR	1	town in Latium
ATINA		SIL	1	
ATINA		V	1 3	
ATINAS	A. 12.661	V		a Latin warrior
ATLANS	=Atlas	MAR	2	mt.; god
ATLANS	T. 1.98	S	1	god
ATLANS	HO passim	SEN	1	god
ATLANS		VAL	1 5	god
ATLANTES		FPLA		people of Libya
ATLANTĒUS		HOR	1	p. to Atlas
ATLANTEUS		LUC	1	
ATLANTEUS		LUCR	1	
ATLANTEUS		OV	1	
ATLANTEUS		S	1 5	
ATLANTIACUS		CAL	1	p. to Atlas
ATLANTIACUS		SIL	1 2	
ATLANTIADES m.sg.		OV	2	Mercury; Hermaphroditus
ATLANTIADES		S	1	Mercury
ATLANTIADES fem.pl.		SIL	1 4	the Pleiades
ATLANTIAS	68.23	PRIAP		d. of Atlas (Calypso)
ATLANTICUS		HOR	1	p. to mt. Atlas
ATLANTICUS		MAR	1	
ATLANTICUS		SIL	1 3	
ATLANTIDES patr.		COL	1	daughters of Atlas
ATLANTIDES HF 11		SEN	1 2	
ATLANTIS		LUC	1	= Pleiad (Electra)
ATLANTIS F. 4.31		OV	1	= Electra
ATLANTIS		SIL	1	= Electra

ATLANTIS	also pl.	V	1 4	= Electra
ATLANTIS*		GER	1	p. to Atlas (or mts.)
ATLANTIS*		LUC	1	
ATLANTIS*		OV	1	
ATLANTIS*		TIB	1 4	
ATLAS	cf. Atlans	ENN	1	mt. in NW Africa (Inc. 43V)
ATLAS		FPLA	1	god
ATLAS	264	GER	1	mt.
ATLAS		HOR	1	god
ATLAS		JUV	2	mt.; a dwarf
ATLAS	1.555	LUC	1	mt.
ATLAS		OV	2	mt.; son of Juppiter
ATLAS	3.22.7	PROP	1	mt.
ATLAS	T. 8.315	S	1	mt.
ATLAS		SIL	4	mt.; god; two warriors
ATLAS		TR	1	god
ATLAS		V	1 17	mt.
ATRACIDES	M. 12.209	OV		= Caeneus of Thessaly
ATRACIS	patr.	OV		= Hippodamia
ATRACIS*		OV		ep. of Hippodamia
ATRACIUS		PROP	1	p. to Atrax
ATRACIUS		S	1	Thessalian
ATRACIUS		VAL	1 3	
-ATRECTUS	1.117.13	MAR		a book-dealer in Rome
ATREUS		HOR	1	legendary son of Pelops & k. of Argos
ATREUS		JUV	1	
ATREUS		MAR	1	
ATREUS		OV	1	
ATREUS		S	1	
ATREUS		SEN	1	
ATREUS		TR	1 7	
ATRIA	sc. Licinia	OV		a law-court
-ATRIANUS	3.93.9	MAR		p. to Atria (t. of Venetum?)
ATRIDA	(= -es) m.	PET	1	a son of Atreus
ATRIDA		PROP	1 2	
ATRIDAE		MAR	1	the sons of Atreus (Agamemnon, Menelaus)
ATRIDAE		PL	1	
ATRIDAE		TR	1 3	
ATRIDES		AV	1	a son of Atreus
ATRIDES		HL	2	(both sons)
ATRIDES		HOR	2	(both sons)
ATRIDES		JUV	3	(both sons) + Domitian
ATRIDES		LP	1	
ATRIDES		MAN	1	
ATRIDES		OV	2	(both sons)
ATRIDES		PROP	1	
ATRIDES		S	1	
ATRIDES		SEN	1	
ATRIDES		SIL	1	
ATRIDES		V	1 17	
ATRIUM/LIBERTATIS		OV		Chapel of Liberty in Rome
ATRIUM/VESTAE		OV		residence of the Vestals
ATROPOS		MAR	1	one of the three Fates
ATROPOS		S	1	
ATROPOS		SIL	1 3	
ATTA	Ep. 2.1.79	HOR		Q. Atta (dramatist?)
ATTALICUS		AV	1	p. to Attalus (+ Pergamean)

ATTALICUS	HOR		1	p. to Attalus
ATTALICUS	PROP		1	
ATTALICUS	SIL	1	4	
ATTALUS	HOR		1	a k. of Pergamum
ATTALUS	MAR		1	(fictional)
ATTALUS	OV		1	k. of Pergamum
ATTALUS	PL	1	4	" " "
ATTHIDES pl., T.12.53ᵇ	S			Attic women
ATTHIS adj.	GER		1	Attica
ATTHIS	LUCR		1	
ATTHIS also pl.	MAR		1	Philomela
ATTHIS	OV		1	a friend of Sappho
ATTHIS	SEN	1	5	an Athenian woman
ATTHIS*	MAR			Attic, Athenian
ATTICA	COM		2	region of central Greece
ATTICA	VAR	1	3	
-ATTICILLA 12.79	MAR			unknown cont. woman
ATTICON n.sg.	LUCIL			an Attic coin
ATTICUS	JUV		1	Ti. Claudius Atticus
ATTICUS	MAR		2	two cont. men
ATTICUS	OV		1	friend of Ovid
ATTICUS Mil.arg. 2.4	PL		1	fictitious Athenian
ATTICUS T. & S. passim	S	1	6	an Athenian
ATTICUS*	AV		1	p. to Attica, Athenian
ATTICUS* (Caec.263*)	COM		1	
ATTICUS*	HOR		1	
ATTICUS*	MAR		1	
ATTICUS*	OV		1	
ATTICUS*	PH		1	
ATTICUS*	PL		1	
ATTICUS*	PROP		1	
ATTICUS*	S		1	
ATTICUS*	SEN		1	
ATTICUS*	TER		1	
ATTICUS*	TR		1	
ATTICUS*	VAR	1	13	
ATTIS = At(t)ys	CAT		1	legendary Phrygian shepherd
ATTIS	FPLB		1	
ATTIS	MAR		1	
ATTIS	OV		1	
ATTIS	PER		1	
ATTIS	S		1	
ATTIS	SEN	1	7	
ATTIUS = Accius	PER			Labeo Attius (early tragedian)
ATURUS	LUC			river in Aquitania
ATYS	S		1	a Delphian
ATYS	V	1	2	a young Trojan
AUCHATAE m.pl.	VAL			Scythian tr.
-AUCHUS 6.60	VAL			a Cimmerian
AUFIDIA 3.70	MAR			fict. woman
AUFIDIUS S. 2.4.24	HOR		1	a glutton
AUFIDIUS 9.25	JUV		1	famous lawyer
AUFIDIUS	MAR	1	3	" "
AUFIDIUS/LUSCUS	HOR			a scribe
AUFIDUS	HOR		1	river in Apulia
AUFIDUS	LUC		1	
AUFIDUS	SIL		1	

AUFIDUS	V	1	4	river in Apulia
AUFIDUS* 10.170	SIL			p. to the Aufidus river
‑AUFILENA 110.1	CAT			a girl from Verona
‑AUFILENUS 100.1	CAT			a man from Verona
AUGE	OV		1	d. of Aleus the Arcadian
AUGE	S		1	
AUGE	SEN	1	3	
‑AUGEUS (stabulum)	SEN			p. to Augias (the stable in Hercules' story)
AUGUSTA	JUV		1	Messalina
AUGUSTA	SEN	1	2	Agrippina
AUGUSTA/JULIA	OV			=Livia (F. 1.536)
‑AUGUSTUM/FORUM	OV			a Roman forum adorned by Augustus (F.5.552)
AUGUSTUS	AV		1	Octavian
AUGUSTUS	GER		1	" (?)
AUGUSTUS	HOR		1	"
AUGUSTUS	JUV		1	(unspecified)
AUGUSTUS	MAN		1	Octavian
AUGUSTUS	MAR		3	Octavian; Domitian; Nerva
AUGUSTUS	OV		2	Octavian; the month
AUGUSTUS	PH		1	Octavian
AUGUSTUS	PROP		1	"
AUGUSTUS	S		2	Octavian; Domitian
AUGUSTUS	SEN	1	15	Nero
AUGUSTUS*	CAL		1	p. to Augustus (Octavian) or the month
AUGUSTUS*	HL		1	
AUGUSTUS*	JUV		1	
AUGUSTUS*	MAN		1	
AUGUSTUS*	MAR		1	
AUGUSTUS*	OV		1	
AUGUSTUS*	PROP		1	
AUGUSTUS*	SEN	1	8	
AUGUSTUS/CAESAR	V			Octavian (A. 6.792)
AULESTES A. 10.297	V			an Etruscan ally of Aeneas
AULIS fem.	CIC		1	port-town of Boeotia
AULIS	HL		1	
AULIS	HOR		1	
AULIS	LUC		1	
AULIS	LUCR		1	
AULIS	MAN		1	
AULIS	OV		1	
AULIS	PROP		1	
AULIS	S		1	
AULIS	SEN		1	
AULIS	V	1	11	
AULON masc.	HOR		1	valley in Calabria
AULON	MAR		1	
AULON	VAL	1	3	
AULUS (a praenomen)	HOR		1	two contemporaries
AULUS	LUC	1	2	two soldiers
‑AUNUS A. 11.700	V			a Ligurian
AURA M. 7.856	OV			"Breeze" personified
‑AURELIA	JUV			a rich lady
AURELIUS	CAT			a cont. man
AURIGA	CIC		1	constellation
AURIGA	GER		1	"
AURIGA Am. 3.12.37	OV	1	3	Phaethon
AURORA	AV		1	goddess "Dawn" (also Orient)

AURORA	CAT		1	"Dawn" (the East)
AURORA	CIC		1	
AURORA	FPLA		1	
AURORA	FPLB		1	
AURORA	HL		1	
AURORA	JUV		1	
AURORA	LUC		1	
AURORA	MAN		1	
AURORA	MLP		1	
AURORA	OV		1	
AURORA	PROP		1	
AURORA	S		1	
AURORA	SEN		1	
AURORA	SIL		1	
AURORA	TIB		1	
AURORA	TR		1	
AURORA	V		1	
AURORA	VAL		1	
AURORA	VAR	1	20	
AURUNCA	JUV		1	town of Campania
AURUNCA	SIL	1	2	
AURUNCI	V			people of Aurunca
- AURUNCULEIA (Junia)	CAT			the bride of Manlius (61.86)
AURUNCUS	JUV		1	p. to Aurunca
AURUNCUS	V	1	2	
AUSONES pl.	S			the Italic peoples (poetic archaism)
AUSONIA	LUC		1	Italy, esp. S. Italy (poetic term)
AUSONIA	OV		1	
AUSONIA	S		1	
AUSONIA	SIL		1	
AUSONIA	V		1	
AUSONIA	VAL	1	6	
AUSONIDAE m. pl.	LUC		1	Italians (or S. Italians)
AUSONIDAE	SIL		1	
AUSONIDAE	V	1	3	
AUSONII	V			Italians
AUSONIS adj.	OV		1	Italian
AUSONIS	SIL	1	2	
AUSONIUS	S		1	an Italian
AUSONIUS	SEN		1	
AUSONIUS	SIL		1	
AUSONIUS	VAL	1	4	
AUSONIUS*	HOR		1	Italian, Italic
AUSONIUS*	LP		1	
AUSONIUS*	LUC		1	
AUSONIUS*	MAR		1	
AUSONIUS*	OV		1	
AUSONIUS*	PROP		1	
AUSONIUS*	S		1	
AUSONIUS*	SIL		1	
AUSONIUS*	V	1	9	
AUSTER	AET		1	the South Wind
AUSTER	CAT		1	
AUSTER	CIC		1	
AUSTER	FPLB		1	
AUSTER	GR		1	
AUSTER	HL		1	

AUSTER		HOR	1	South Wind
AUSTER		JUV	1	
AUSTER		LUC	1	
AUSTER		LUCR	1	
AUSTER		MAN	1	
AUSTER		OV	1	
AUSTER		PROP	1	
AUSTER		S	1	
AUSTER		SEN	1	
AUSTER		SIL	1	
AUSTER		TIB	1 17	
AUTOLOLES	pl.	LUC	1	tr. in Mauretania
AUTOLOLES		SIL	1 2	
AUTOLYCUS	8.59.4	MAR	1	leg. thief (s. of Mercury)
AUTOLYCUS		OV	1	
AUTOLYCUS		PL	1	
AUTOLYCUS	5.114	VAL	1 4	s. of Deimachos of Trikka & comp. of
AUTOMEDON		JUV	1	type of charioteer Hercules
AUTOMEDON		OV	1	Charioteer of Achilles
AUTOMEDON		V	1 3	" "
AUTONOE		JUV	1	d. of Cadmus & m. of Actaeon
AUTONOE		OV	1	
AUTONOE		S	1	
AUTONOE		SIL	1 4	
AUTONOEIUS	adj.	OV		p. to Autonoe
AUTUMNUS		COL	1	The Fall as god; season of harvest
AUTUMNUS		HOR	1	
AUTUMNUS		LUCR	1	
AUTUMNUS		OV	1	
AUTUMNUS		S	1 5	
AUXILIUM	Cist. 154	PL		a god (by personification)
AUXIMON	(or -um)	LUC		town in Picenum
AVARITIA		PER	1	"Greed" personified
AVARITIA	Pers. 555	PL	1 2	
-AVEIA	8.518	SIL		town of the Vestini
-AVENS	6.167	SIL		Umbrian soldier
AVENTINUS		ENN	1	hill in Rome
AVENTINUS		HOR	1	
AVENTINUS		JUV	1	
AVENTINUS		MAR	1	
AVENTINUS		OV	2	(+ k. of Alba)
AVENTINUS		SIL	1	
AVENTINUS		V	1 8	(+ s. of Hercules, A.7.657)
AVENTINUS*		MAR	1	p. to the Aventine hill
AVENTINUS*		OV	1	
AVENTINUS*		PROP	1	
AVENTINUS*		S	1 4	
AVERNA	n. pl.	LUCR	1	Tartarus (Underworld or its lake)
AVERNA		OV	1	
AVERNA		V	1 3	
AVERNALIS		HOR	1	p. to Avernus
AVERNALIS		OV	1	
AVERNALIS		PROP	1	
AVERNALIS		S	1 4	
AVERNUS = Averna		LUC	1	lake near Cumae (or the Underworld)
AVERNUS		MAR	1	
AVERNUS		OV	1	

AVERNUS	PROP		1	lake near Cumae (or the Underworld)
AVERNUS	S		1	
AVERNUS	SEN		1	
AVERNUS	SIL		1	
AVERNUS	TR		1	
AVERNUS	V		1	
AVERNUS	VAL	1	10	
AVERNUS*	LUCR		1	pertaining to Averna (Avernus)
AVERNUS*	OV		1	
AVERNUS*	SIL		1	
AVERNUS*	V		1	
AVERNUS*	VAL	1	5	
-AVIDIENUS/CANIS	HOR			a notorious miser (S.2.2.55)
AVIS	CIC		1	constellation
AVIS	GER		1	
AVIS	OV	1	3	
AVITUS	MAR			Avitus Stertinius (a friend of MAR)
AXENUS	OV			Pontus Euxinus (the Black Sea)
AXIS	GER			the North Pole
AZAN	S			Arcadian tribe
-AZORUS em.	GR			breed of dog
BABYLO	TER			the city on the Euphrates
BABYLON	LUC		1	
BABYLON	LUCIL		1	
BABYLON	MAN		1	
BABYLON	MAR		1	
BABYLON	OV		1	
BABYLON	PROP		1	
BABYLON	S		1	
BABYLON	SIL	1	8	
BABYLONIACUS	MAN			Babylonian
BABYLONICUS	COM		1	Babylonian
BABYLONICUS	LUCR		1	
BABYLONICUS	PET		1	
BABYLONICUS	PL	1	4	
BABYLONIENSIS	PL			Babylonian
BABYLONIUS	HOR		1	Babylonian
BABYLONIUS	LUC		1	
BABYLONIUS	LUCR		1	
BABYLONIUS	OV		1	
BABYLONIUS	PL		1	
BABYLONIUS	PROP	1	6	
-BACCARA 6.59	MAR			fictional
BACCHA	OV		1	a female follower of Bacchus
BACCHA	PROP		1	
BACCHA	SEN	1	3	
BACCHAE pl.	HOR		1	band of followers
BACCHAE	LUC		1	
BACCHAE	PL		1	
BACCHAE	TR	1	4	
BACCHANAL	PL			festival-place (for Bacchus)
BACCHANALIA n.pl.	JUV			festival of Bacchus
BACCHANS sg.	VAR			a Bacchant
BACCHANTES pl.	OV			Bacchantes, devotees of Bacchus
BACCHEIS adj.	S			p. to Bacchis (Corinthian dynast)
BACCHEIUS	V			p. to Bacchus
BACCHĒUS	CAL		1	p. to Bacchus

BACCHĒUS	COL		1	p. to Bacchus
BACCHEUS	OV		1	
BACCHEUS	S	1	4	
BACCHIADAF m. pl.	OV			Corinthian dynasty
BACCHICUS	ENN		1	p. to Bacchus
BACCHICUS	MAR		1	
BACCHICUS	OV		1	
BACCHICUS	S		1	
BACCHICUS	TR	1	5	
BACCHIS	PL		1	a meretrix
BACCHIS	TER	1	2	"
BACCHĪUS	HOR			name of a gladiator
BACCHUS	AET		1	the god of wine/the vine
BACCHUS	AV		1	
BACCHUS	COL		1	
BACCHUS	ENN		1	
BACCHUS	FPLB		1	
BACCHUS	GER		1	
BACCHUS	HL		1	
BACCHUS	HOR		1	(+ vine; wine)
BACCHUS	LUC		1	
BACCHUS	LUCR		1	
BACCHUS	MAN		1	
BACCHUS	MAR		1	(vine)
BACCHUS	MLP		1	
BACCHUS	OV		1	
BACCHUS	PET		1	
BACCHUS	PH		1	
BACCHUS	PL		1	
BACCHUS	PRIAP		1	
BACCHUS	PROP		1	
BACCHUS	S		1	
BACCHUS	SEN		1	
BACCHUS	SIL		1	
BACCHUS	TIB		1	
BACCHUS	TR		1	
BACCHUS	V		1	
BACCHUS	VAL	1	26	
BACTRA n.pl.	HOR		1	capital of Bactria (an Iranian region)
BACTRA	LUC		1	
BACTRA	MAN		1	
BACTRA	PROP		1	
BACTRA	S		1	
BACTRA	SIL		1	
BACTRA	V	1	7	
BACTRIUS adj.	OV			Bactrian
BACTROS	LUC			a river of Bactria
BAEBIUS	FPLA		1	(unknown Roman)
BAEBIUS	LUC	1	2	M. Baebius, killed by Marius
BAETICA	S			a province of Spain
BAETICOLUS	SIL			a resident on the r. Baetis
BAETICUS 3.77.81	MAR			a man's name
BAETICUS*	JUV		1	p. to Corduba (or S. Spain)
BAETICUS*	MAR		1	
BAETICUS*	SIL	1	3	
BAETIGENA	SIL			born near the Baetis r.
BAETIS m.	CAL		1	river in S. Spain (=Guadalquivir)

BAETIS		LUC	1	river in S. Spain
BAETIS		MAR	1	
BAETIS		S	1	
BAETIS		SEN	1	
BAETIS		SIL	1 6	
-BAGAS	2.14	SIL		a soldier of Hannibal
-BAGASUS	5.410	SIL		a soldier of Hannibal
-BAGESUS	10.459	SIL		a soldier of Hannibal
BAGOUS		OV		a guard of women (type)
BAGRADA	m.	LUC	1	river in Zeugitana (Africa)
BAGRADA		S	1	
BAGRADA		SIL	3 5	
BAIAE		HOR	1	resort-town near Naples (& any spa)
BAIAE		JUV	1	
BAIAE		MAR	1	(spa)
BAIAE		OV	1	
BAIAE		PROP	1	
BAIAE		S	1	
BAIAE		SIL	1	
BAIAE		TIB	1	(spa)
BAIAE		V	1 9	
BAIANUS		HOR	1	p. to Baiae
BAIANUS		JUV	1	
BAIANUS		MAR	1	
BAIANUS		S	1 4	
BAIUS		HOR	1	p. to Baiae
BAIUS		SIL	1 2	
-BALARUS	3.378	SIL		leader of the Vettones
BALATRO		HOR		Servilius Balatro (cont. parasite)
-BALBINUS	S.1.3.40	HOR		(unknown man)
BALBUS		CAT	1	a cont. widower
BALBUS		MAR	1 2	(unknown cont.)
BALEARICUS		COM	1	p. to the Balearic islands
BALEARICUS		MAN	1	
BALEARICUS		OV	1	
BALEARICUS		S	1 4	
BALEARIS*		LUC	1	p. to the Balearic islands
BALEARIS*		S	1	
BALEARIS*		V	1 3	
BALIARIS	N sg.	SIL		resident of the Balearic islands
BALIARIS*		SIL		Balearic
BALLIO		PL		a leno
BALLIONIUS		PL		p. to Ballio, the leno
BALLONITI		VAL		a Scythian tribe
BANDUSIA		HOR		fountain near Venusia
-BANIURA	3.303	SIL		tribe of Mauretania
BANTINUS		HOR		p. to Bantia (t. of Apulia)
BAPTAE	m. pl.	JUV		priests of Cottyto
BARCAEI		V		the people of Barce
BARCAEUS adj.		SIL		p. to Barce
BARCAS		SIL		son of Belus (Punic god)
BARCE		SIL	2	town in Libya; Punic woman
BARCE		V	1 3	the nurse of Sichaeus
BARDAICUS adj.		JUV		p. to the Bardaei (in Illyria)
BAREA	m.	JUV		a Roman cognomen
BARINE		HOR		a maiden
-BARISAS -nt-, 6.557		VAL		a Scythian

BARIUM	HOR			town in Apulia
BARRUS	HOR			a vain man
- BASILUS 7.145	JUV		1	cont. lawyer
BASILUS	LUC	1	2	officer with J. Caesar
- BASSA passim	MAR			fictional person
BASSAREUS	FPLR		1	ep. of Bacchus
BASSAREUS	HOR	1	2	
BASSARICUS	PROP			ep. of Bacchus
BASSARIDES pl.	S		1	Bacchantes
BASSARIDES	SEN	1	2	
BASSARIS	FPLR		1	a Bacchant
BASSARIS	PER	1	2	
BASSUS	HOR		1	(unknown Roman)
BASSUS	MAR		2	friend; unknown
BASSUS	OV		1	poet
BASSUS	PER		1	Caesius Bassus (a friend)
BASSUS	PROP	1	6	friend
BASTERNAE	OV			Scythian tribe
-BATARNAE 6.96	VAL			unknown tribe
BATAVI	LUC			tribe of Holland (Germanic)
BATAVUS	JUV		1	p. to Batavia (= Holland)
BATAVUS	MAR		1	
BATAVUS	SIL	1	3	
BATHYLLUS	HOR		1	a Samian boy
BATHYLLUS	JUV		1	pantomime
BATHYLLUS	PER		1	"
BATHYLLUS 5.7.5	PH	1	4	"
BATO	OV			Dalmatian insurgent
-BATON 14.452	SIL			Punic pilot
-BATRACHOMACHIA (em.)	MAR			title of poem 14.183: "Frog War"
BATRACHOMYOMACHIA	S			title of parody
-BATTARUS (Dirae)	AV			unknown cont.
BATTIADAE m. pl.	SIL			the people of Cyrene
BATTIADES m. sg.	CAT		1	ep. of Callimachus the poet
BATTIADES	OV		1	
BATTIADES	PET		1	
BATTIADES	S	1	4	
BATTUS	CAT		1	a king of Cyrene
BATTUS	OV		2	king; a herdsman (M. 2.688)
BATTUS	SIL	1	4	king
BATULUM	SIL		1	town of the Samnites
BATULUM	V	1	2	
-BATUS 4.239	SIL			a Gaulish soldier
BAUCIS	OV		1	myth. wife of Philemon
BAUCIS	PER	1	2	
BAULI	MAR		1	town near Baiae (in Campania)
BAULI 12.156	SIL	1	2	town near Baiae
BAVIUS	FPLR		1	a stupid poet
BAVIUS	V	1	2	" "
BEBRIACUM (or Bed-)	JUV			town in N. Italy
BEBRYCIA	VAL			= Bithynia
BEBRYCIUS	LUC		1	p. to Bebrycia
BEBRYCIUS	S		1	p. to king Bebryx
BEBRYCIUS	SIL		1	
BEBRYCIUS	V		1	p. to Bebrycia
BEBRYCIUS	VAL	1	5	
BEBRYX	S		1	king of Bebrycia

BEBRYX	SIL		1	(another king)
BEBRYX	VAL	1	3	k. of Bebrycia
BELGA m.	LUC			a Belgian national
BELGICUS adj.	PROP		1	Belgian
BELGICUS	SIL		1	
BELGICUS	V	1	3	
BELIAS fem., HO 960	SEN			desc. of Belus
BELIDAE pl. m.	FPLB		1	= Danaus & Aegyptus (or the Phoenicians)
BELIDAE	S	1	2	" " "
BELIDES fem. pl.	JUV		1	the Danaids
BELIDES	OV		1	"
BELIDES m. sg.	SIL		1	= Barcus, the Carthaginian
BELIDES A. 2.82	V	1	4	= Palamedes, the hero
BELLA pl., HF 695	SEN			"War" as personification
{ BELLEROPHON	JUV			the hero, s. of Glaucus
{ BELLEROPHON(TES)	HOR		1	
(BELLEROPHONTES	MAN	1	2	
BELLEROPHONTĒUS	PROP			
BELLIPOTENS	S			Mars (but: T. 2.716 refers to Minerva)
BELLONA	CAL		1	goddess of War
BELLONA	HOR		1	
BELLONA	JUV		1	
BELLONA	LUC		1	
BELLONA	MAR		1	
BELLONA	OV		1	
BELLONA	PET		1	
BELLONA	PL		1	
BELLONA	S		1	
BELLONA	SEN		1	
BELLONA	SIL		1	
BELLONA	TIB		1	
BELLONA	V		1	
BELLONA	VAL	1	14	
BELLOROPHON	PL			the hero, s. of Glaucus (Bac. 810)
BELLUM A. 6.279	V			War, personified
BELUS	OV		1	k. of the Persians
BELUS	S		1	k. of Egypt
BELUS	SIL		1	ancestor of Dido
BELUS	V	1	4	" "
BENACUS A. 10.205	V			lake in N. Italy (=Garda)
BENEVENTANUS	JUV			p. to Beneventum
BENEVENTUM	HOR			t. in Samnium
BERECYNTHIA (-ti-)	OV			= Cybele
BERECYNTHIUS	FPLB		1	p. to Cybele
BERECYNTHIUS	MAR	1	2	
BERECYNTIADES	OV			=Atthis ? (Ibis 506)
BERECYNTIUS (-th-)	HOR		1	p. to Cybele
BERECYNTIUS	OV		1	
BERECYNTIUS	PER		1	
BERECYNTIUS	S		1	p. to mt. Berecyntus (in Phrygia)
BERECYNTIUS	V	1	5	p. to mt. Berecyntus
BERENICIS	LUC		1	region of Cyrene
BERENICIS	SIL	1	2	
BEROE	OV		1	a nurse
BEROE	V	2	3	an Oceanid; w. of Doryclus
BERONICĒ (=Bere-)	JUV			d. of king Agrippa
BERONICĒUS	CAT			p. to Berenice (of Egypt)

−BERYAS 14.152	SIL			a Punic hero
BERYTUS em.	AV			t. in Syria (Maec. 19)
− BESSA Tr. 848	SEN			t. in Locris
BESSI	OV		1	Thracian tribe
BESSI	VAL	1	2	
BESSUS	LUC			Thracian tribesman
BESTIUS	HOR		1	a crude miser
BESTIUS	PER	1	2	" "
BIANOR	V			hero of Mantua; cf. Bienor
−BIBULA 6.142	JUV			unknown woman
BIBULUS	FPLA		1	M. C. Bibulus
BIBULUS	HOR		2	(+ his son)
BIBULUS	SIL	1	4	C. Publicius Bibulus
BICORNIGER	OV			ep. of Bacchus
−BIENOR M. 12.345	OV		1	a centaur
BIENOR	VAL	1	2	a Cyzican
BILBILIS	MAR			town in Spain
BIONEUS	HOR			p. to Bion, the philosopher
− BIRRIUS S. 1.4.69	HOR			a robber
BISALTA	GR			breed of horse
BISALTAE	V		1	Thracian tribe
BISALTAE	VAL	1	2	
BISALTIS	OV			= Theophane (d. of Bisaltes)
−BIS/COMPRESSA	FPLA			title of comedy
BISTONES	LUC		1	Thracian tribe
BISTONES	S		1	
BISTONES	SEN		1	
BISTONES	SIL		1	
BISTONES	VAL	1	5	
BISTONIA	VAL			Thrace
BISTONIDES	S			Thracian women
BISTONIS	AV		1	a Thracian woman
BISTONIS	HOR	1	2	
BISTONIS*	OV			Thracian
BISTONIUS	AV		1	Thracian
BISTONIUS	LUC		1	
BISTONIUS	LUCR		1	
BISTONIUS	OV		1	
BISTONIUS	PROP		1	
BISTONIUS	S		1	
BISTONIUS	SIL	1	7	
−BITHUS S. 1.7.20	HOR			gladiator
BITHYNIA	CAT		1	region of NW Anatolia
BITHYNIA	FPLR		1	
BITHYNIA	MAN	1	3	
BITHYNICUS N	MAR			fict. man
BITHYNIS A. 3.6.25	OV			a Bithynian woman
BITHYNUS adj.	CAT		1	Bithynian
BITHYNUS	HOR		1	
BITHYNUS	JUV		1	
BITHYNUS	VAL	1	4	
BITIAS	MAR		1	a Trojan
BITIAS	SIL		1	Punic warrior
BITIAS	V	2	4	a Tyrian; a Trojan
BITTIS	OV			a woman loved by poet Philetas
− BITTO	LUCIL			a witch
−BITURIX 1.423	LUC			member of the Gallic tr.

BLAESIANUS	MAR			p. to Blaesus
BLAESUS	MAR	1		Velleius Blaesus
BLAESUS	S	1	2	" "
BLANDITIAE 10.72.1	MAR		1	"Flattery" personified
BLANDITIAE AA 1.2.35	OV	1	2	
BLEPHARO Amph. 951	PL			a comic character
BOCCAR or -cch-	JUV			a Numidian
BOCCHUS	SIL			Ethiopian leader
BOEBE	OV			t. in Thessaly
BOEBEIS	LUC	1		lake in Thessaly
BOEBEIS	PROP	1		
BOEBEIS	VAL	1	3	
BOEBEIUS	VAL			Thessalian
BOEOTI	HL	1		the people of Boeotia
BOEOTI	LUC	1	2	
BOEOTIA	FPLA	1		(title of comedy)
BOEOTIA	OV	1		region of Greece
BOEOTIA Merc. 647	PL	1	3	
BOEOTIUS	GR	1		p. to Boeotia, Boeotian
BOEOTIUS	OV	1		
BOEOTIUS	PROP	1		
BOEOTIUS	S	1		
BOEOTIUS	SEN	1		
BOEOTIUS	VAL	1	6	
BOEOTUS N	HOR			a Boeotian man (Ep. 2.1.244)
BOEOTUS*	HL	1		Boeotian, p. to Boeotia
BOEOTUS*	OV	1		
BOEOTUS*	S	1		
BOEOTUS*	SEN	1	4	
BOETHUS Cul. 67	AV			(uncertain meaning)
BOGUS (Bogud?)	SIL			a Punic bard
BOII	SIL			a Celtic tribe
BOIUS (& Boia)	PL			members of the Boii tr.
BOLA	V			t. in Latium
BOLANUS N	HOR	1		unknown man
BOLANUS S. 5.2.37	S	1	2	Vettius Bolanus
BONA/COPIA M. 9.88	OV			goddess of Plenty
BONA/DEA	OV		1	the Good Goddess (of women)
BONA/DEA (in tmesis)	TIB	1	2	
BONA/DIVA	OV			the Good Goddess
BONA/FORTUNA	COM		1	goddess of Luck
BONA/FORTUNA	PL	1	2	
BONONIA	MAR		1	t. in N. Italy
BONONIA	SIL	1	2	
BONONIENSIS	CAT			p. to Bononia
BOOTES	AET	1		constellation
BOOTES	CAT	1		
BOOTES	CIC	1		
BOOTES	FPLB	1		
BOOTES	GER	1		
BOOTES	JUV	1		
BOOTES	LUC	1		
BOOTES	MAN	1		
BOOTES	MAR	1		
BOOTES	OV	1		
BOOTES	PROP	1		
BOOTES	S	1		

BOOTES	SEN		1	constellation
BOOTES	V		1	
BOOTES	VAL	1	15	
BOREAS	AET		1	North Wind (or the North, generally)
BOREAS	AV		1	
BOREAS	CAT		1	
BOREAS	COL		1	
BOREAS	FPLB		1	
BOREAS	HOR		1	
BOREAS	LUC		1	
BOREAS	MAN		1	
BOREAS	MAR		1	
BOREAS	OV		2	(+s. of r. Strymon)
BOREAS	PROP		1	
BOREAS	S		1	
BOREAS	SEN		1	
BOREAS	SIL		1	
BOREAS	V		1	
BOREAS	VAL	1	17	
BOREUS adj.	OV			North(ern) Pole (Tr. 4.8.41)
BORYSTHENES	MLP			an Alan warrior
BORYSTHENIDAE	PROP			residents on r. Borysthenes(Sarmatia)
BORYSTHENIUS adj.	OV			p. to the river
BOSPHORIUS adj.	OV			p. to the Bosphorus
BOSPHOROS	VAL			the strait at Byzantium
BOSPHORUS	OV		1	
BOSPHORUS	PROP	1	2	
BOSPOROS	LUC		1	
BOSPOROS	PET	1	2	
BOSPORUS	HOR			
BOSTAR m.	SIL			a Punic name
BOTERDUM	MAR			a town in Spain
BOVARIA n. pl.	PROP			market in Rome
BOVIANIUS	SIL			p. to Bovianum (t. in Samnium)
BOVILLAE	MAR		1	town in Latium
BOVILLAE	OV		1	
BOVILLAE	PER		1	
BOVILLAE	PROP	1	4	
BRANCHUS	S			s. of Apollo
BRAURON	S			t. in Attica
BRENNUS	FPLB		1	Gaulish leader (387 BC)
BRENNUS	PROP		1	
BRENNUS	SIL	1	3	
-BREUCUS 4.233	SIL			Gaulish soldier
BREUNI	HOR			Rhaetian tribe
BRIAREUS	LUC		1	myth. 100-armed giant
BRIAREUS	OV		1	
BRIAREUS	S		1	
BRIAREUS	SEN		1	
BRIAREUS	SIL		1	
BRIAREUS	V	1	6	
BRIGANTES	JUV			British tribe
BRIMO	PROP		1	ep. of Proserpina
BRIMO	S	1	2	
BRISAEUS*	PER			ep. of Bacchus (=old-fashioned)
BRISEIS patr.	HL		1	Hippodamia
BRISEIS	HOR		1	

BRISEIS	MAR		1	Hippodamia
BRISEIS	OV		1	
BRISEIS	PROP		1	
BRISEIS	S		1	
BRISEIS	SEN	1	7	
BRITANNI	CAT		1	Britons
BRITANNI	GR		1	(breed of dogs)
BRITANNI	JUV		1	
BRITANNI	LUC		1	
BRITANNI	MAR		1	
BRITANNI	MLP		1	
BRITANNI	OV		1	
BRITANNI	SEN		1	
BRITANNI	V	1	9	
BRITANNIA	CAT		1	Britain
BRITANNIA	MAR		1	
BRITANNIA	PROP	1	3	
BRITANNICUS	JUV		1	s. of Claudius
BRITANNICUS	SEN	1	2	
BRITANNICUS*	JUV			p. to Britannia
BRITANNUS	HOR		1	British
BRITANNUS	JUV		1	
BRITANNUS	LUC		1	
BRITANNUS	PROP		1	
BRITANNUS	S		1	
BRITANNUS	TIB	1	6	
BRITO (-tt-)	MAR			a Briton (of Brittany)
BRITOMARTIS	AV			Cretan nymph
BRITTANNI	LUCR			Britons
BRITTONES pl., 15.124	JUV			Britons
BRIXIA	AV		1	town of N. Italy
BRIXIA	CAT	1	2	
-BROMIA	FPLB		1	a girl
BROMIA	PL	1	2	a slave-girl
BROMIUS	AV		1	ep. of Bacchus
BROMIUS	CAL		1	
BROMIUS	ENN		1	
BROMIUS	JUV		1	
BROMIUS	LUC		1	
BROMIUS	MAR		1	
BROMIUS	OV		1	
BROMIUS	PL		1	
BROMIUS	S		1	
BROMIUS	SEN	1	10	
BROMIUS*	VAR			Bacchic
BROMUS	OV			name of a centaur
BRONTES	OV		1	Cyclops
BRONTES	S		1	
BRONTES	V	1	3	
BROTEAS	OV	3	3	a Lapith; twin brother of Ammon; s. of
BROTES (-ont-?)	VAL			(?) Vulcan
BRUGES + Phryges	ENN			Phrygians
BRUGIUS + Phry-	ENN			Phrygian
BRUMA	LUCR		1	Winter, personified
BRUMA	S	1	2	
BRUNDISIUM	ENN		1	town of Calabria
BRUNDISIUM	HOR		1	

BRUNDISIUM	LUC		1	town of Calabria
BRUNDISIUM	SIL	1	4	
BRUTI (-tt-)	LUC			tribe of S. Italy
BRŪTIUS (-tt-)	CAL			p. to Bruttium in S. Italy
BRUTTAX or -as	ENN		1	Bruttians
BRUTTAX	LUCIL	1	2	
-BRUTTIANUS 4.23.5	MAR			author of Greek epigrams
BRUTTIDIUS	JUV			Bruttidius Niger, the historian
BRUTTIUS	SIL			a Bruttian
BRUTTIUS*	COL		1	p. to Bruttium or the Bruttii
BRUTTIUS*	JUV		1	
BRUTTIUS*	PER		1	
BRUTTIUS*	S		1	
BRUTTIUS*	SEN		1	
BRUTTIUS*	SIL	1	6	
BRUTUS	FPLR		1	L. Junius
BRUTUS	HOR		1	M. Junius
BRUTUS	JUV		3	L. Junius; M. Junius; another
BRUTUS	LUC		3	D. Junius; L. Junius; M. Junius
BRUTUS	MAN		1	L. Junius
BRUTUS	MAR		2	L. Junius; M. Junius
BRUTUS	OV		4	L.J.B.; M.J.B.; D.J.B.C.; a fr. of Ovid
BRUTUS	PER		1	M. Junius
BRUTUS	PROP		1	L. Junius
BRUTUS	S		2	fr. of Cicero; expeller of kings
BRUTUS	SEN		1	M. Junius
BRUTUS	SIL		2	L.J.B. Collatinus; a Roman soldier
BRUTUS	V	1	23	L. Junius
BUBASIS adj.	OV			p. to Bubassus (t. of Caria)
BUBASTIS	OV			a goddess of Egypt
BUBASTIUS	GR			p. to Bubastis
-BUCCO 11.76.2	MAR			fictional man
-BULLATIUS Ep.1.11.1	HOR			fictional man
-BUMBOMACHIDES	PL			comic character (Mil. 14)
BUPALUS	HOR			Greek sculptor
-BURADO 4.55.23	MAR			town of Spain
-BURDIGALA 9.32.6	MAR			town of Gaul
BURIS	OV			town of Achaia
-BURNUS 16.559	SIL			Iberian hero
BURRUS	ENN		1	Pyrrhus of Epirus
BURRUS	MAR	1	2	son of Parthenius
BUSIRIS	OV		1	king of Egypt
BUSIRIS	S		1	
BUSIRIS	SEN		1	
BUSIRIS	V	1	4	
- BUTA 5.540	SIL			Roman minstrel
BUTES	OV		1	son of Pallas
BUTES	S		1	an Aetolian
BUTES	SIL		1	Punic warrior
BUTES	V		2	a Trojan; a Bebrycian
BUTES	VAL	1	6	an Argonaut
{BUTHROTOS fem.	OV			town of Epirus (M. 13.72)
{BUTHROTUM	V			" "
- BUTRA Epist.1.5.26	HOR			a contemporary
BUTUNTI	MAR			town of Calabria
BUXENTIUS	SIL			p. to Buxentum (t. in Lucania)
BYBLIS	MAR		1	leg. girl, in love with Caunus

BYBLIS	OV	1	2	leg. girl, in love with Caunus
-BYRRIA And. 301	TER			a young man
BYRSA	SIL		1	the citadel of Carthage
BYRSA	V	1	2	
BYZACIUS adj.	SIL			p. to Byzacium (t. in Tunisia)
BYZANTIACUS	S			p. to Byzantium
BYZANTION	LUC			town on the Bosporus
BYZANTIUS	HOR		1	p. to Byzantium
BYZANTIUS	OV	1	2	
-BYZERES m.pl., 5.152	VAL			nomadic group
-BYZES or Byces	VAL			a lake near Maeotis (6.68)
CABIRI	TR			Pelasgian gods
CACISTUS (Vid., pers.)	PL			name of a fisherman
CACUS	JUV		1	legendary robber-giant
CACUS	MAR		1	
CACUS	OV		1	
CACUS	PROP		1	
CACUS	S		1	
CACUS	V	1	6	
-CADMAEUS (= -ēus)	TIB			p. to Cadmus
CADMEIDES pl.fem.	SEN			daughters of Cadmus
CADMEIS patr.	OV	2	2	Ino; Semele
CADMEIS*	AV		1	p. to Cadmus (or his desc.)
CADMEIS*	OV		1	
CADMEIS*	TR	1	3	
CADMEIUS	S		1	Cadmean, p. to Cadmus
CADMEIUS	VAL	1	2	
CADMEUS	AV		1	Cadmean, p. to Cadmus
CADMEUS	LUC		1	
CADMEUS	MAR		1	
CADMEUS	PROP		1	
CADMEUS	S		1	
CADMEUS	SEN		1	
CADMEUS	SIL		1	
CADMEUS	VAL	1	8	
CADMOGENA (Semela)	TR			daughter of Cadmus (Acc. 642)
CADMUS	FPLB		1	the Phoenician, king of Tyre
CADMUS	HOR		2	(a slave; an executioner)
CADMUS	LUC		1	the Phoenician
CADMUS	MAR		1	
CADMUS	OV		1	
CADMUS	PROP		1	
CADMUS	S		1	
CADMUS	SEN		1	
CADMUS	SIL		1	
CADMUS	VAL	1	11	
CADUCIFER	OV			ep. of Mercury
CAECILIANUS N	MAR			an unknown cont.
CAECILIUS	CAT		1	a friend of CAT
CAECILIUS	HOR		1	the comic poet
CAECILIUS	LUCIL		1	" "
CAECILIUS	MAR		2	a friend; fictional man
CAECILIUS	TER	1	6	the poet
CAECILIUS/METELLUS	COL			consul 251 BC (developed a lettuce)
CAECILIUS/STATIUS	FPLA			the early Roman comic poet
CAECUBUM also pl.	HOR		1	a wine (from Latium)
CAECUBUM also pl.	MAR	1	2	

CAECULUS		V		son of Vulcan
-CAEDICIANUS	1.118	MAR		fictional man
-CAEDICIUS	13.197	JUV		a Roman gens name
-CAEDICUS A. 9.362		V		name of an Etruscan
-CAELIA	7.30	MAR		fictional woman
CAELIUS		CAT	1	a friend from Verona
CAELIUS		FPLA	1	unknown man
CAELIUS		HOR	1	a robber
CAELIUS		LUCIL	1	unknown
CAELIUS		MAR	2	mountain; fictional man
CAELIUS		OV	1 7	mt.
-CAELIUS/NUMERIUS		LUCIL		(a grammatical example)
CAELUM n.		CIC	1	"Heaven" personified
CAELUM		OV	1	
CAELUM		V	1 3	
CAELUS m.		ENN		
CAENEUS		OV	1	s. of Elatus, a hermaphrodite
CAENEUS		S	1	
CAENEUS		V	2 4	(+ a Trojan)
CAENINA		OV		town in Latium
CAENINUS		PROP		p. to Caenina
CAENIS fem. (= -neus)		OV		Caeneus, with change of gender and sex
-CAERATEUS adj.		AV		Cretan (Cir. 113)
CAERE n.		SIL	1	town of Etruria
CAERE		V	1 2	
-CAERELLIA (Cer- ?)		MAR	2 2	two cont. women (4.20, 4.63)
CAERES adj.		HOR		p. to Caere
CAERETANUM as pl.		MAR		a wine
CAERETANUS		MAR		p. to Caere
-CAERULUS N (Cat.10)		AV		an inn-keeper
-CAERUS T. 6.502		S		a horse of Amphiaraus
CAESAR (Cat., Maec.)		AV	2	Julius (?); Augustus (Octavian)
CAESAR		CAL	2	Julius; Nero
CAESAR		CAT	1	Julius
CAESAR		FPLA	1	Julius
CAESAR		FPLB	3	Julius; Augustus; Tiberius
CAESAR		HOR	2	Julius; Augustus
CAESAR		JUV	7	
CAESAR		LUC	2	Julius; Nero
CAESAR		MAN	2	Augustus; Tiberius
CAESAR		MAR	9	
CAESAR		MLP	1	Hadrian
CAESAR		OV	4	Julius; Augustus; Germanicus; Tiberius
CAESAR		PER	1	Caligula
CAESAR		PET	1	Julius
CAESAR	2.5.7	PH	1	Tiberius
CAESAR		PROP	2	Julius; Augustus
CAESAR		S	3	Julius; Nero; Domitian
CAESAR		SEN	1	Julius
CAESAR		SIL	1	Julius
CAESAR		V	2 48	Julius; Augustus
CAESARES pl.		LUC	1	the Caesars
CAESARES		OV	1 2	
CAESARĔUS		CAL	1	p. to Caesar, Caesarian
CAESAREUS		FPLB	1	
CAESAREUS		LP	1	
CAESAREUS		LUC	1	

CAESARĔUS	MAR		1	p. to Caesar, Caesarian
CAESAREUS	MLP		1	
CAESAREUS	OV		1	
CAESAREUS	S	2	9	
CAESARIANI	MAR			adherents of Caesar
CAESARIANUS	MAR	2	2	p. to Augustus (10.73.4); imperial
-CAESARIS/FORUM 1.117	MAR			= Forum Julium (or Palladium) in Rome
CAESAR/AUGUSTUS	HOR			Octavian
CAESAR/GERMANICUS	OV			s. of Drusus & adopted s. of Tiberius
CAESAR/TIBERIUS	PH			emperor Tiberius (2.5.7)
-CAESENNIA (v.l.)	JUV			a rich man (6.136)
CAESIUS	CAT		1	a poet
CAESIUS	MAR	1	2	unknown cont.
CAESIUS/SABINUS	MAR			a friend of MAR
CAESO (Titin. 107)	COM		1	unknown
CAESO 3.377	SIL	1	2	a Spanish leader
CAESONIA	JUV		1	wife of Caligula
CAESONIA	MAR		1	wife of Rufus
CAESONIA	PER	1	3	wife of Caligula
CAESONIUS/MAXIMUS	MAR			friend of Seneca
-CAETRONIUS 14.86	JUV			name of a Roman gens
CAIANUS = Gaianus	S			p. to Caligula
CAICUS	LUC		1	river of Mysia
CAICUS	OV		1	" "
CAICUS	SIL		1	a Saguntine
CAICUS	V		2	r. of Mysia; comp. of Aeneas
CAICUS	VAL	1	6	a Colchian
CAIETA	JUV		1	town in Latium
CAIETA	MAR		1	nurse of Aeneas
CAIETA	OV		1	" "
CAIETA	SIL		1	town in Latium
CAIETA	V	2	6	nurse of Aeneas; town in Latium
CAIETANUS N	MAR			fictional person
CAIUS = Gaius	MAR			a Roman praenomen
CALABER (poetic sg.)	SIL			= the Calabrians
CALABER*	HOR		1	Calabrian, p. to Calabria
CALABER*	LUC		1	
CALABER*	MAR		1	
CALABER*	OV		1	
CALABER*	PER		1	
CALABER*	S		1	
CALABER*	SIL		1	
CALABER*	V		1	
CALABER*	VAL	1	9	
CALABRIA	HOR			a region of S. Italy
CALACTE	SIL			town of Sicily
CALAIS m.	HOR		1	(a young contemporary)
CALAIS	OV		1	myth. son of Boreas
CALAIS	PROP		1	
CALAIS	S		1	
CALAIS	SEN		1	
CALAIS	SIL		1	
CALAIS	VAL	1	7	
CALAMIS m.	OV		1	a Greek sculptor
CALAMIS	PROP	1	2	
CALATIA	SIL			town in Campania
CALAUREA	OV			island of Poros

CALCAS = Calchas	TR			legendary Greek prophet
CALCHAS	CIC		1	
CALCHAS	HL		1	
CALCHAS	OV		1	
CALCHAS	PET		1	
CALCHAS	PL		1	
CALCHAS	PROP		1	
CALCHAS	S		1	
CALCHAS	SEN		1	
CALCHAS	SIL		1	
CALCHAS	V	1	10	
CALCHEDON = Chalc-	SEN			the Greek name for Carthage
CALEDONII	MAR			a tribe of N. Scotland
CALEDONIUS	LUC		1	p. to this tribe, the Caledonians
CALEDONIUS	MAR		1	
CALEDONIUS	S		1	
CALEDONIUS	SIL		1	
CALEDONIUS	VAL	1	5	
CALENUM	JUV			the wine of Cales
CALENUS	FPLR		1	husband of Sulpicia
CALENUS	MAR		2	h. of Sulpicia; an unknown
CALENUS	SIL	2	5	a Roman; a Campanian
CALENUS*	HOR		1	p. to Cales
CALENUS*	VAR	1	2	
CALES pl.	HOR		1	t. in Campania
CALES P. 4.10.47	OV		1	(river, in Bithynia?)
CALES also sg.	SIL		1	t. in Campania
CALES	V	1	4	
CALETI	TR			Gaulish tribe
CALIDONIA (=Calyd-)	COM			= Atalanta
-CALIDORUS Ps. 35	PL			a young man
CALLAECI = Gallaeci	GR			tribe of Spain
CALLAECIA or Gall-	SIL			region of W. Spain
CALLAICUS or Gall-	MAR		1	p. to the Callaeci
CALLAICUS	OV		1	
CALLAICUS	SIL	1	3	
-CALLIAS Trin. 916	PL			fictional man
-CALLICHORUS 5.75	VAL			(legendary?) river in Paphlagonia
CALLICLES	PL	2	2	two different senes
CALLIDAMATES	PL			a young man
CALLIDEMIDES	PL		1	comic character
CALLIDEMIDES	TER	1	2	" "
-CALLIFO cf. -ph-	COM			??
CALLIMACHUS	HOR		1	the Alexandrian (Gk.) poet
CALLIMACHUS	MAR		1	
CALLIMACHUS	OV		1	
CALLIMACHUS	PROP		1	
CALLIMACHUS	S	1	5	
-CALLIMARCHUS Tr. 917	PL			fictional person
CALLINICUS	PL			a comic character
-CALLIODORUS	MAR			fictional
CALLIOPA (-a)	SEN			the Muse of Epic
CALLIOPE	AV		1	
CALLIOPE	COL		1	
CALLIOPE	FPLR		1	
CALLIOPE	HL		1	
CALLIOPE	HOR		1	

CALLIOPE	JUV	1		the Muse of Epic
CALLIOPE	LP	1		
CALLIOPE	LUCR	1		
CALLIOPE	MAR	1		
CALLIOPE	MLP	1		
CALLIOPE (& -ea)	OV	1		(+ Poetry)
CALLIOPE	PROP	1		
CALLIOPE	S	1		
CALLIOPE	SIL	1		
CALLIOPE	V	1	15	(all the muses)
CALLIOPEA = -e	PROP		1	Muse of Epic
CALLIOPEA	V	1	2	
CALLIPHO	PL			a senex
CALLIPOLIS	SIL			town of Sicily
CALLIPPUS	PL			fict. man
CALLIRHOE	CAL	1		shepherdess
CALLIRHOE	PER	1	2	a meretrix
CALLIRRHOE	OV	1		d. of Achelous
CALLIRRHOE	S	1	2	Athenian fountain
CALLISTO	CAT	1		a nymph, d. of king Lycaon
CALLISTO	FPLA	1		
CALLISTO	OV	1		
CALLISTO	PROP	1	4	
CALLISTRATUS	MAR			fictional person
- CALLISTUS 5.64.1	MAR			a contemporary
CALOCISSUS	MAR			a cup-bearer
CALOR	LUCR			"Summer" personified
CALPE	JUV	1		Gibraltar
CALPE	LUC	1		
CALPE	PROP	1		
CALPE	SEN	1		
CALPE	SIL	1		
CALPE	VAL	1	6	
- CALPETANUS N	MAR			unknown person (6.94)
- CALPETUS F. 4.46	OV	1		king of Alba
CALPETUS T. 10.319	S	1	2	a Theban
CALPURNIUS	MAR			fictional person
CALPURNIUS* (domus)	LP			p. to a Calpurnius
CALPURNIUS/PISO	LUCIL			member of a famous Roman family
- CALPUS (Calpys)	LP			son of Numa
CALVINA	JUV			a notorious woman
CALVINUS	JUV	1		a friend (poet?)
CALVINUS	MAR	1	2	a bad poet
CALVUS	CAT	1		L. Licinius Calvus, the poet
CALVUS	FPLR	1		
CALVUS	HOR	1		
CALVUS	MAR	1		
CALVUS	OV	1		
CALVUS	PROP	1	6	
- CALYBE A. 7.419	V			priestess of Juno
- CALYBITA Copa 25	AV			priest of Cybele (?)
- CALYCE em., H. 18.133	OV			d. of Hecation
- CALYDNA Tr. 839	SEN			Aegean island
CALYDON	LUC	1		town in Aetolia
CALYDON	MAR	1		
CALYDON	OV	1		
CALYDON	PL	1		

CALYDON	S		1	town in Aetolia
CALYDON	SEN		1	
CALYDON	SIL		1	
CALYDON	V		1	
CALYDON	VAL	1	9	
CALYDONEUS	MAN			p. to Calydon
CALYDONIA (or adj.?)	TR			= Calydon
CALYDONIDES fem.pl.	S			women of Calydon
CALYDONIS	OV			a woman of Calydon (esp. Deianira)
CALYDONIUS	GR		1	p. to Calydon
CALYDONIUS	HL		1	
CALYDONIUS	MAR		1	
CALYDONIUS	OV		1	
CALYDONIUS	PL		1	
CALYDONIUS	S		1	
CALYDONIUS	SEN	1	7	
CALYMNE	OV			island near Rhodes
CALYPSO	FPLA		1	nymph of Ogygia
CALYPSO	OV		1	
CALYPSO	PRIAP		1	
CALYPSO	PROP		1	
CALYPSO	TIB		1	
CALYPSO	TR	1	6	
CAMARINA	SIL			town of Sicily
CAMBYSES	LUC		1	son of Cyrus (k. of Persia)
CAMBYSES	PROP	1	2	
CAMENA also pl.	FPLA		1	a muse (of song, poetry)
CAMENA	HOR		1	(+ poem)
CAMENA	OV		1	(+ poem)
CAMENA	PER		1	
CAMENA	PROP		1	
CAMENA	SEN	1	6	
CAMENAE	AV		1	the muses
CAMENAE	CAL		1	
CAMENAE	JUV		1	
CAMENAE	LUCIL		1	
CAMENAE	MAR		1	
CAMENAE	S		1	
CAMENAE	TIB		1	
CAMENAE	V	1	8	
-CAMERE F. 3.582	OV			a region in Bruttium
-CAMERINA F. 4.447	OV		1	a town of Sicily
CAMERINA A. 3.701	V	1	2	
CAMERINI	JUV			typical aristocrats (of gens Sulpicia)
CAMERINUS 8.38	JUV		1	Ser. Sulpicius Cam., an early consul
CAMERINUS	OV	1	2	an epic poet (cont.)
CAMERIUS	CAT			a friend
CAMERS also pl.	SIL		1	a man from Camerinum
CAMERS	V	1	2	a Rutulian
CAMILLA	V			Volscian heroine
CAMILLI pl. of -us	GR		1	type of Roman hero
CAMILLI	MAR	1	2	
CAMILLUS	AV		1	M. Furius Camillus, captor of Veii
CAMILLUS	FPLA		1	(Flaminius Camillus?)
CAMILLUS	HOR		1	M. Furius Camillus
CAMILLUS 2.154	JUV		1	" " "
CAMILLUS also pl.	LUC		1	" " "

CAMILLUS	also pl.	MAN		1	M. Furius Camillus
CAMILLUS	also pl.	MAR		1	" " "
CAMILLUS		OV		1	L. Furius Camillus
CAMILLUS	also pl.	PROP		1	M. Furius Camillus
CAMILLUS	pl.	S		1	(M.F.C. as type of hero)
CAMILLUS		SIL		1	M. Furius Camillus
CAMILLUS	A. 6.825	V	1	12	M. Furius Camillus
-CAMONIUS/RUFUS	6.85	MAR			a friend of MAR
CAMPANI		ENN			the people of Campania
CAMPANIA		JUV		1	the region S. of Latium
CAMPANIA		OV		1	
CAMPANIA		PROP		1	
CAMPANIA		SIL		1	
CAMPANIA		TIB	1	5	
CAMPANICUS		PL			p. to Campania
CAMPANS		PL			p. to Campania
CAMPANUS		HOR		1	a Campanian
CAMPANUS		SIL	1	2	
CAMPANUS*		HOR		1	p. to Campania
CAMPANUS*		LUC		1	
CAMPANUS*		LUCIL		1	
CAMPANUS*		MAR		1	
CAMPANUS*		S		1	
CAMPANUS*		SIL		1	
CAMPANUS*		V	1	7	
-CAMPESUS	5.593	VAL			heroic figure
CAMPUS		HOR		1	the Campus Martius in Rome
CAMPUS		LUC		1	
CAMPUS		MAN		1	
CAMPUS		OV		1	
CAMPUS		PROP		1	
CAMPUS		SIL	1	6	
-CAMPUS/MINOR	55.3	CAT			field in Rome (uncertain location)
-CANACE	11.91	MAR		1	fictitious person (slave)
CANACE	T. 2.384	OV	1	2	daughter of Aeolus
CANACHE	M. 3.217	OV			name of a dog
CANCER		AV		1	sign of the Zodiac ("Crab")
CANCER		CIC		1	
CANCER		FPLR		1	
CANCER		GER		1	
CANCER		LUC		1	
CANCER		MAN		1	
CANCER		OV		1	
CANCER		PROP		1	
CANCER		S		1	
CANCER		SIL	1	10	
-CANCHLUS	v.l.	GER			= Cancer, sign of Zodiac
CANDAVIA		LUC			a section of Illyria
-CANDIDUS	12.38	MAR			fictional man
CANENS		OV			d. of Janus and w. of Picus
CANICULA		HOR		1	constellation
CANICULA		MAN		1	
CANICULA		OV		1	
CANICULA		PER	1	4	
CANIDIA		HOR			a witch
CANINIUS		CIC			the consul
CANIS		CIC		1	constell. (usually Canis Major)

CANIS	GER		1	constell.
CANIS	HOR		1	
CANIS	LUC		1	
CANIS	MAN		1	
CANIS	OV		1	
CANIS	PROP		1	
CANIS	TIB		1	
CANIS	V	1	9	
CANIUS	MAR	2	2	a poet; a friend
CANIUS/RUFUS	MAR			the poet
CANNA	FPLA			= river Aufidius
CANNAE	JUV		1	town of Apulia
CANNAE	LUC		1	
CANNAE	MAN		1	
CANNAE	MAR		1	
CANNAE	SIL	1	5	
CANNENSIS	PROP		1	p. to Cannae
CANNENSIS	S	1	2	
CANOPĪUS adj.	CAT			p. to Canopus
CANOPOS	LUC		2	Egypt; a star
CANOPOS	MAN	1	3	a star
CANOPUS	COL		1	island in Nile
CANOPUS	GR		1	
CANOPUS	JUV		1	
CANOPUS	OV		1	
CANOPUS	PROP		1	
CANOPUS	S		1	
CANOPUS	SIL		1	
CANOPUS	V	1	8	
CANTABER	HOR		1	Spanish tr. (in Cantabria)
CANTABER	JUV		1	
CANTABER	LUC		1	
CANTABER	SIL	1	4	
CANTABRICUS	HOR			p. to Cantabria (region in Spain)
CANTHARA	PL		1	a woman
CANTHARA	TER	1	2	"
-CANTHARUS 9.9	MAR			contemporary man
CANTHUS	CAL		1	a shepherd
CANTHUS	SIL		1	an Argonaut
CANTHUS	VAL	1	3	"
-CANUS 4.5.8, 1.80	MAR	2	2	a musician; fictional
CANUSINA fem.	MAR			wool garment of Canusium
CANUSINATUS 9.22.9	MAR			dressed in a woolen Canusina
CANUSINUS pl. as N	HOR		1	the people of Canusium
CANUSINUS	JUV		1	p. to Canusium
CANUSINUS	SIL	1	3	
CANUSIUM	HOR			town in Apulia
CAPANEIUS	S			p. to Capaneus
CAPANEUS	OV		1	s. of Hipponous & Astynome
CAPANEUS	PROP		1	
CAPANEUS	S	1	3	
CAPANĒUS*	S			p. to Capaneus
CAPELLA fem.	MAN		1	star (in Auriga)
CAPELLA	OV	2	3	star; a friend-poet (m.)
CAPELLIANA	MAR			a dish (?)
CAPENA (sc. porta)	JUV		1	gate in Rome
CAPENA	MAR		1	

CAPENA	PROP	1	3	gate in Rome
CAPENAS adj.	SIL			p. to Capena (t.) or the gate
CAPENUS adj.	V			p. to Capena
CAPER	MAN		1	star (in Auriga)
CAPER	SIL	1	2	
-CAPEREUS =Caphareus	TR			mt. in Euboea
CAPETUS	OV		1	king of Alba
CAPETUS	S	1	2	an Argive
CAPHAREUS (Capher-)	OV		1	mt. in Euboea
CAPHAREUS	VAL	1	2	" "
CAPHAREUS*	OV		1	p. to Caphareus
CAPHAREUS*	PROP	1	2	
CAPHEREUS	AV		1	mt. in Euboea
CAPHEREUS	S		1	
CAPHEREUS	SEN		1	
CAPHEREUS	SIL		1	
CAPHEREUS	V	1	5	
CAPHERIDES adj., pl.	SEN			p. to Caphareus
CAPITO (Fonteius)	HOR		1	lieutenant of Anthony
CAPITO (Cossutianus)	JUV	1	2	son-in-law of Tigellinus (8.93)
CAPITOLIA pl.	JUV		1	the Capitol in Rome
CAPITOLIA	LUC		1	
CAPITOLIA	LUCIL		1	
CAPITOLIA	OV		1	
CAPITOLIA	PET		1	
CAPITOLIA	PROP	1	6	
CAPITOLINI 2.145	JUV			cognomen of the Manlii
CAPITOLINUS N	MAR			the jester of Trajan (10.101.3)
CAPITOLINUS*	CIC		1	p. to the Capitoline or the Capitol
CAPITOLINUS*	JUV		1	
CAPITOLINUS* 4.28	MAN		1	
CAPITOLINUS*	MAR		1	
CAPITOLINUS*	OV		1	
CAPITOLINUS*	S		1	
CAPITOLINUS* 3.86	SIL	1	7	
-CAPITOLINUSPETILLIUS	HOR			unknown man (S. 1.4.94)
CAPITOLIUM	HOR		1	the Capitol in Rome
CAPITOLIUM	MAR		1	
CAPITOLIUM	PL		1	
CAPITOLIUM	S		1	
CAPITOLIUM	SIL		1	
CAPITOLIUM	V	1	6	
CAPITONES pl.	PL			type of parasites
CAPITO/FONTEIUS	HOR			lieutenant of Anthony & consul 33BC
CAPPADOCAE	MAR			lettuce from Cappadocia
CAPPADOCES	JUV		1	people of Cappadocia
CAPPADOCES	LUC		1	
CAPPADOCES	MAN		1	
CAPPADOCES	MAR		1	
CAPPADOCES	PER	1	5	
CAPPADOCIA	PL			a region of Anatolia
CAPPADOCUS adj.	COL			p. to Cappadocia
CAPPADOX	HOR		1	a Cappadocian
CAPPADOX	PL	1	2	name of a leno
CAPRA	CIC		1	a star (in Auriga)
CAPRA	GER		1	
CAPRA	HOR	1	3	

CAPREAE	JUV		1	island off Naples (= Capri)
CAPREAE	OV		1	
CAPREAE	S		1	
CAPREAE	V	1	4	
CAPRICORNUS	AV		1	a sign of the Zodiac
CAPRICORNUS	CIC		1	
CAPRICORNUS	FPLB		1	
CAPRICORNUS	GER		1	
CAPRICORNUS	HOR		1	
CAPRICORNUS	MAN		1	
CAPRICORNUS	OV		1	
CAPRICORNUS	PROP	1	8	
-CAPRIUS S. 1.4.66	HOR			a cont. lawyer
CAPUA	COL		1	town of Campania
CAPUA	HOR		1	
CAPUA	LUCIL		1	
CAPUA	PL		1	
CAPUA	SIL		1	
CAPUA	V	1	6	
CAPYS	ENN		1	father of Anchises
CAPYS	OV		2	(+ k. of Alba)
CAPYS	S		1	comp. of Aeneas
CAPYS	SIL		2	" " (+ a warrior of Aricia)
CAPYS or Capis (Acc.)	TR		1	father of Anchises
CAPYS	V	2	9	friend of Aeneas; king of Alba
CARALIS fem.	FPLB		1	town of Sardinia (+ modern Cagliari)
CARALIS	SIL	1	2	
CARAMBIS	VAL			promontory in Paphlagonia
CARBO	FPLA		1	a man's name (in a pun)
CARBO 2.548	LUC		1	M. Papirius Carbo
CARBO	LUCIL	1	3	C. Papirius Carbo
CARCHEDONIUS adj.	COM		1	Carthaginian
CARCHEDONIUS	PET		1	
CARCHEDONIUS	PL	1	3	
CARCINOS (Gk. form)	LUC			constell. (Cancer)
-CARDUAE 4.55	MAR			town of Spain
CARES m. pl.	MAN		1	the Carians
CARES	MAR		1	
CARES	OV		1	
CARES	PL		1	
CARES	V	1	5	
-CARESUS 6.192	VAL			a Scythian
-CARFINIA 2.69	JUV			a moecha
CARIA	MAN		1	country or province in Anatolia
CARIA	PL		1	
CARIA	TER	1	3	
CARICAE	S			figs (of Caria)
CARINAE	HOR		1	a quarter of Rome
CARINAE	V	1	2	
-CARIO Mil. 1397	PL			name of a fict. cook
-CARMANUS adj.	LUC			p. to a Persian tribe
-CARME Cir. 220	AV			a nurse, d. of Phoenix
-CARMEIUS 5.582	VAL			a warrior
-CARMELUS 7.662	SIL			a Roman soldier
CARMENTALIS adj.	V			p. to Carmentis
CARMENTIS	OV		1	mother of Evander & goddess of prophecy
CARMENTIS	SIL		1	

CARMENTIS	V	1	3	mother of Evander & goddess of prophecy
CARMENTIS/PORTA	OV			gate in Rome
CARNA	OV			goddess of domesticity
CARNEADES	LUCIL			the Stoic philosopher
CARNUTIS 1.7.12	TIB			a Gaulish tribe (sg. for ethnic pl.)
CARPATHIUS	AV		1	p. to island Carpathus (or to its sea)
CARPATHIUS	HOR		1	
CARPATHIUS	JUV		1	
CARPATHIUS	LUCIL		1	
CARPATHIUS	OV		1	
CARPATHIUS	PROP		1	
CARPATHIUS	S		1	
CARPATHIUS	SIL		1	
CARPATHIUS	V	1	9	
-CARPOPHORUS 6.199	JUV		1	name of an actor
CARPOPHORUS Sp. 15	MAR	1	2	fictional (?)
CARPUS	MAR	2	2	two contemporaries
CARRHAE	LUC			town of Mesopotamia
CARSEOLANUS adj.	OV			p. to Carseoli
CARSEOLI	OV			town of Latium
CARTEIA	SIL			town in Spain
CARTHAEUS or -eus	OV			p. to Carthaea (t. on Cea)
CARTHAGINIENSIS	ENN		1	p. to Carthage
CARTHAGINIENSIS	PL	1	2	
CARTHAGO cf. Kar-	AV		1	the town in N. Africa
CARTHAGO	HOR		1	
CARTHAGO	JUV		1	
CARTHAGO	LUC		1	
CARTHAGO	LUCR		1	
CARTHAGO	MAN		1	
CARTHAGO	OV		1	
CARTHAGO	PL		1	
CARTHAGO	PROP		1	
CARTHAGO	SIL	2	11	(+ New Carthage)
-CARTHALO 1.406;15.450	SIL	2	2	a Punic; a Libyan
CARTHEIUS = -aeus	OV			p. to Carthaea (t. on Cea)
CARUS 1.36	JUV		1	Metius Carus, an informer
CARUS	MAR		3	" " (+ 2 fictional men)
CARUS	OV	1	5	poet-friend
CARYBDIS cf. Char-	AV		1	whirlpool opposite Scylla
CARYBDIS	CAT	1	2	
CARYSTEUS	OV			p. to Carystos
CARYSTOS	LUC		1	town on Euboea
CARYSTOS	MAR		1	
CARYSTOS	S		1	
CARYSTOS	SEN	1	4	
CARYSTUS	PL		1	
CARYSTUS	TIB	1	2	
CARYUS adj.	S			p. to Caryae (t. in Laconia)
CASCA m.	SIL			a Roman soldier
CASCELLIUS	MAR	2	2	two contemporaries
CASCELLIUS/AULUS	HOR			cont. lawyer
CASILINUS adj.	SIL			p. to Casilinum (t. in Campania)
CASINA	PL			a maid
CASINAS adj.	LUCIL			p. to Casinum
CASINUM	SIL			town of Latium
CASINUS	PL			a fict. man

CASINUS*	SIL			p. to Casinum
CASIUS adj.	LUC			p. to a mt. in Syria
-CASMILLA A. 11.543	V			mother of Camilla
CASPERIA	SIL	1		Sabine town
CASPERIA	V	1	2	
CASPIACUS (porta)	S			a mt. pass in Cilicia
CASPIADAE	VAL			people of the Caspian region
-CASPIAS HO 145	SEN			p. to the Caspian Sea
CASPIUM	HOR			the Caspian Sea
CASPIUS	LUC	1		Caspian
CASPIUS	MAN	1		
CASPIUS	OV	1		
CASPIUS	S	1		
CASPIUS	SEN	1		
CASPIUS	V	1		
CASPIUS N	VAL	1	7	a Caspian native
CASPIUS*	VAL			Caspian
CASSANDRA	JUV	1		the prophetess, d. of Priam
CASSANDRA	LUCIL	1		
CASSANDRA	OV	1		
CASSANDRA	PH	1		
CASSANDRA	SEN	1		
CASSANDRA	V	1	6	
CASSANDREUS	OV			p. to Cassandrea, t. in Macedonia
CASSIANUS N	MAR			a friend of Martial
CASSIEPIA	CIC	1		constell.
CASSIEPIA	GER	1		
CASSIEPIA	MAN	1	3	
CASSIOPE (same as -ia)	MAN	1		constell.
CASSIOPE	OV	1		wife of Cepheus
CASSIOPE	PROP	1	3	port on Corcyra
CASSIOPEA	AV			constell.
CASSIUS (Pomp. 15)	COM	1		(uncertain meaning)
CASSIUS	HOR	2		two contemporaries
CASSIUS	JUV	1		C. Cass. Longinus (assassin of Caesar)
CASSIUS	LUC	1	5	" " "
CASSIUS/GAIUS	LUCIL			C. Cassius Sabaco (?)
-CASSIUS/PARMENSIS	HOR			C. C. Long., murderer of Caesar
CASTALIA	AV	1		a spring at Delphi
CASTALIA	COM	1		(a girl)
CASTALIA	FPLB	1		the spring
CASTALIA	HOR	1		
CASTALIA	S	1		
CASTALIA	SEN	1		
CASTALIA	TR	1		
CASTALIA	V	1	8	
CASTALIS adj. & N	MAR			Castalia(n)
CASTALIUS	SIL			ancestor of Imilce
CASTALIUS*	COL	1		p. to the spring of Castalia
CASTALIUS*	LUC	1		
CASTALIUS*	MAR	1		
CASTALIUS*	OV	1		
CASTALIUS*	PROP	1		
CASTALIUS*	S	1		
CASTALIUS*	SEN	1		
CASTALIUS*	SIL	1		
CASTALIUS*	TIB	1	9	

CASTOR	AV	1	myth. brother of Pollux
CASTOR	CAT	1	
CASTOR	HOR	2	(+ a gladiator)
CASTOR	JUV	1	
CASTOR	MAR	2	(+ a fict. man)
CASTOR	OV	1	
CASTOR	PL	1	
CASTOR	PROP	1	
CASTOR	S	1	
CASTOR	SEN	1	
CASTOR	SIL	1	
CASTOR	V	1	(a Trojan)
CASTOR	VAL	1 15	
CASTOREUS adj.	SEN		p. to Castor
CASTRANUS adj.	MAR		p. to Castrum Inui
-CASTRICUS 6.43	MAR		a poet-friend
CASTRUM sc. Inui	OV	1	town of the Rutuli in Latium
CASTRUM " "	SIL	1 2	"
CASTRUM/INUI	V		"
CASTULO	SIL		town of Spain
CASUS T. 8.421	S		"Chance" personified
CATAGELASIMUM	PL		name of a parasite
⎰CATAMEITUS	PL		= Ganymede
⎱CATAMITUS	TR		
CATANE = Catina	SIL		town of Sicily
CATIA	HOR		contemporary woman
CATIANUS	MAR		fictional man
CATIENA	JUV		cont. woman
CATIENUS as pl.	HOR		a type of actor
CATILINA	FPLB	1	the famous conspirator
CATILINA	JUV	1	(as a type)
CATILINA	LUC	1	
CATILINA	MAR	1	
CATILINA	SIL	1	
CATILINA	V	1 6	
⎰CATILLUS	S	1	the founder of Tibur
⎪CATILLUS	SIL	1	
⎨CATILLUS	V	1 3	
⎩CATILUS	HOR		
CATINA	FPLB		town in Sicily
CATINENSIS	JUV		p. to Catina
CATIUS	HOR		an Epicurean author
CATO	CAT	1	friend of Catullus
CATO	FPLA	1	M. Porcius Cato
CATO	FPLB	1	Valerius Cato, poet
CATO	HOR	3	M.P.C.; Val.C.; a philologist
CATO 2.40	JUV	1	M.P.C. (Censorius)
CATO	LUC	2	Censorius; Uticensis
CATO	LUCIL	1	(uncertain)
CATO	MAN	2	Censorius; Uticensis
CATO	MAR	2	Cato Younger; a type
CATO	MLP	1	(Cato as type)
CATO	OV	1	Val. Cato, the poet
CATO 3.45	PER	1	Uticensis
CATO	PET	1	"
CATO 4.7.21	PH	1	unknown cont.
CATO	S	1	Uticensis

CATO	SIL		2	Uticensis; Censorius
CATO A. 6.841	V	1	23	Censorius
CATONES pl.	FPLB		1	the Cato family
CATONES 1.313	LUC		1	
CATONES 5.106	MAN		1	
CATONES	MAR	1	4	(as types)
CATONIANUS adj.	MAR			p. to Cato
CATTUS = Chattus	S			a German
-CATULLA 2.49	JUV		1	a cont. woman
CATULLA 8.54	MAR	1	2	" "
CATULLIANUS	MAR			p. to Catullus
CATULLUS	CAT		1	the poet (Q. Valer. Catullus)
CATULLUS	FPLB		1	
CATULLUS	HOR		1	
CATULLUS	JUV		3	(+ two contemporaries)
CATULLUS	MAR		3	(+ two contemporaries)
CATULLUS	OV		1	
CATULLUS 2.25.4	PROP		1	
CATULLUS 3.6.41	TIB	1	12	
CATULUS	JUV		2	Q. Lutatius Catulus (consul 242 BC)
CATULUS	LUC		2	
CATULUS	MAR	1	5	
-CATUS 3.586	LUC		1	a Roman soldier
CATUS 4.139	SIL	1	2	" "
CAUCASEUS	PET		1	p. to Caucasus mountains
CAUCASEUS	S		1	
CAUCASEUS	VAL	1	3	
CAUCASIUS	OV		1	
CAUCASIUS	PROP		1	
CAUCASIUS	SIL		1	
CAUCASIUS	V	1	4	
CAUCASOS	S			the Caucasus mt. range
CAUCASUS	CIC		1	
CAUCASUS	HOR		1	
CAUCASUS	OV		1	
CAUCASUS	PROP		1	
CAUCASUS	SEN		1	
CAUCASUS	SIL		2	(+ a name of a horse)
CAUCASUS	V		1	
CAUCASUS	VAL	2	10	(+ a Colchian)
CAUDINAE/FAUCES	SIL			narrow pass near Caudium
CAUDINAE/FURCAE	LUC			
CAUDINUS	SIL			name of a Bruttian soldier
CAUDINUS*	COL		1	p. to Caudium
CAUDINUS*	GR	1	2	
CAUDIUM	HOR			a town of the Samnites
CAULO	V			town in Bruttium (= Colonia)
CAULON M. 15.705	OV			
CAUNIAE	COL			figs (of Caunos)
CAUNOS	S			town in Caria
CAUNUS	OV		1	
CAUNUS	SIL	1	2	
CAURINUS	GR			p. to Caurus
CAURUS cf. Corus	COL		1	the North-west Wind
CAURUS	GR		1	
CAURUS	SIL	1	3	
-CAYCI = Chauci	LUC			a Germanic tribe (1.463)

CAYCUS = Caicus	SEN			river in Mysia
CAYSTER = Caystros	PROP			river in Lydia
CAYSTRIUS adj.	OV			p. to the Cayster (Caystros)
CAYSTROS	OV		1	river in Lydia
CAYSTROS	V	1	2	
CAYSTRUS	MAR		1	
CAYSTRUS	SIL	1	2	
CEA cf. Cia	OV		1	island of Ceos in the Cyclades
CEA	V	1	2	
CEBENNAE pl., 1.435	LUC			mountain in Gaul
CEBRENIS patr.	OV		1	d. of Cebren, i.e. Hesperie
CEBRENIS	S	1	2	
CECROPIA	CAT			ep. of Athens
CECROPIDAE m.pl.	OV		1	Athenians (poetic patr.)
CECROPIDAE	S		1	
CECROPIDAE	SIL		1	
CECROPIDAE	V	1	4	
CECROPIDES m.sg.	JUV		1	any aristocratic type
CECROPIDES	OV	1	2	ep. of Theseus, k. of Athens
CECROPIS fem. patr.	JUV		1	any Athenian woman
CECROPIS	OV	2	3	= Aglauros; (pl.) Procne & Philomela
CECROPIS*	OV			Attic, Athenian
CECROPIUS	AET		1	Attic, Athenian
CECROPIUS	AV		1	
CECROPIUS	CAT		1	
CECROPIUS	HOR		1	
CECROPIUS	JUV		1	
CECROPIUS	LP		1	
CECROPIUS	LUC		1	
CECROPIUS	MAR		1	
CECROPIUS	OV		1	
CECROPIUS	PL		1	
CECROPIUS	PRIAP		1	
CECROPIUS	PROP		1	
CECROPIUS	S		1	
CECROPIUS	SEN		1	
CECROPIUS	SIL		1	
CECROPIUS	V		1	
CECROPIUS	VAL	1	17	
CECROPS	FPLB		1	leg. king of Athens
CECROPS	LUCR		1	
CECROPS	OV		1	
CECROPS	VAL	1	4	
CEFALUS (= -ph-)	TR			a mythical person
CELADON	OV	2	2	comp. of Phineus; a Lapith
-CELADUS 7.215	JUV			a teacher
CELAENAE	LUC		1	town of Phrygia
CELAENAE	OV		1	
CELAENAE	S	1	3	
CELAENAEUS	MAR		1	p. to Celaenae
CELAENAEUS	S	1	2	
-CELAENEUS (trisyll.)	VAL			a god of the underworld
CELAENO	CIC		1	a Pleiad
CELAENO	GER		1	"
CELAENO	JUV		1	(a greedy woman)
CELAENO	OV		1	a Pleiad
CELAENO	V		1	a Harpy

CELAENO	VAL	1	6	a Harpy
CELEMNA	V			town of Campania
– CELENNIA M. 15.704	OV			a promontory in Bruttium
CELER	MAR		?	two contemporary men
CELER F. 4.837	OV		1	fictional man
CELER	S	1	4	Maecius Celer
CELEUS	OV		1	leg. king of Eleusis
CELEUS	S		1	
CELEUS	V	1	3	
CELMIS m.	OV			one of the Corybantes
CELSUS	HOR		1	C. Albinovanus, a friend of HOR
CELSUS	JUV		1	A. Cornelius Celsus, a rhetor
CELSUS	OV	1	3	friend of Ovid
CELSUS/ALBINOVANUS	HOR			friend of Horace
CELTAE m.	GR		1	(a breed of dog)
CELTAE	LUC		1	the Celts
CELTAE	MAR		1	
CELTAE	SIL	2	5	(+ the Celtiberians)
CELTIBER	CAT			a Celtiberian (of Spain)
CELTIBERIA	CAT			region of Spain, inhabited by Celts
CELTIBER*	MAR			p. to the Celtiberians
CELTICUS	SIL			Celtic, Gaulish (of N. Italy, in this case)
CENAEUS adj.	OV		1	Euboean
CENAEUS	SEN	1	2	
CENCHREAE	OV			a harbor of Corinth
CENCHREIS	OV			wife of Cinyras
CENCHREUS adj.	S			p. to Cenchreae
CENSORINUS	HOR			a friend of HOR
CENTAUREUS	AV		1	p. to Centaurs
CENTAUREUS	HOR		1	
CENTAUREUS	S	1	3	
CENTAURI	LUC		1	myth. people (half-human, half-equine)
CENTAURI	MAR		1	
CENTAURI	S		1	
CENTAURI	SEN		1	
CENTAURI	V	1	5	
CENTAURICUS	PROP		1	p. to Centaurs
CENTAURICUS	S	1	2	
CENTAUROMACHIA	PL			a fictitious country
CENTAURUS	CIC		1	constellation
CENTAURUS	GER		1	"
CENTAURUS	HOR		1	a Centaur (specifically Chiron)
CENTAURUS also pl.	LUCR		1	"
CENTAURUS	MAN		2	two different constellations
CENTAURUS also pl.	OV		1	a Centaur
CENTAURUS also pl.	PROP		1	"
CENTAURUS also pl.	SIL		1	Chiron
CENTAURUS fem.	V	1	10	name of a ship
–CENTENIUS 12.463	SIL			a Roman
–CENTORES 6.151	VAL			Scythian tribe
CENTURIPAE	SIL			town in Sicily
CEPHALIO dub.	OV		1	?? (A. 1.13.31)
CEPHALIO	PL	1	2	(unknown)
CEPHALLANES	SEN			residents of Cephallenia
CEPHALLENES	SIL			
CEPHALO	LUCIL			nickname of C. Cossius
CEPHALOEDIAS*	SIL			p. to Cephaloedis (t. in Sicily)

CEPHALUS		MAR		1	mythical person
CEPHALUS		OV	1	2	" "
CEPHEIS patr.		GER		1	const. Andromeda
CEPHEIS		MAN		1	
CEPHEIS		OV	1	3	
CEPHEIUS cf. -eus		OV		1	p. to Cepheus
CEPHEIUS		PROP	1	2	
CEPHENES pl.		OV			Ethiopian tribe
CEPHENUS adj.		OV			Cephenian, i.e. Ethiopian
CEPHEUS N		CIC		1	k. of Ethiopia (> constell.)
CEPHEUS		GER		1	const.
CEPHEUS		MAN		1	
CEPHEUS		OV		1	
CEPHEUS 1.375		VAL	1	5	an Argonaut
CEPHEUS* cf. -eius		OV		1	p. to Cepheus
CEPHEUS*		PROP	1	2	
CEPHISIAS adj.		OV			p. to Cephisus
CEPHISIS		OV			p. to Cephisus
CEPHISIUS		OV			ep. of Narcissus
CEPHISOS		LUC			river in Phocis
CEPHISUS		OV		2	(+ r. in Attica)
CEPHISUS		S	1	3	
CERAMBUS		OV			myth. person, changed into beetle
-CERAMNUS 6.550		VAL			a Scythian
CERASTAE		OV			myth. horned people on Cyprus
CERAUNIA n.pl.		LUC		1	mountain in Epirus
CERAUNIA		OV		1	
CERAUNIA		PROP		1	
CERAUNIA		S		1	
CERAUNIA		SIL		1	
CERAUNIA		V		1	
CERAUNIA		VAL	1	7	
CERAUNUM		GR			mt. in Epirus
CERAUNUS		PROP			p. to Ceraunia
CERBEREUS		LUCR		1	p. to Cerberus
CERBEREUS		OV		1	
CERBEREUS		S		1	
CERBEREUS		SIL	1	4	
CERBERUS		AV		1	multi-headed monster
CERBERUS		HOR		1	
CERBERUS		LUC		1	
CERBERUS		LUCR		1	
CERBERUS		OV		1	
CERBERUS		PROP		1	
CERBERUS		S		1	
CERBERUS		SEN		1	
CERBERUS		SIL		1	
CERBERUS		TIB		1	
CERBERUS		V	1	11	
_ CERCOBULUS (v.l.)		PL			fictional person (Trin. 1020)
CERCOPES		OV			tribe of Pithecusa
CERCYO		OV			robber
CERCYON		S			"
CERCYONEUS adj.		OV			p. to Cercyon
CERDO		MAR			a shoe-repair man
CEREALIA n.pl.		OV			festival of Ceres
CEREALIS N		MAR			Julius Cerealis (18.48)

CEREALIS*	OV		1	p. to Ceres
CEREALIS*	S		1	
CEREALIS*	V	1	3	
CERES	AET		1	goddess of grain; also grain itself
CERES	AV		1	
CERES	CAL		1	
CERES	CAT		1	
CERES	COL		1	
CERES	COM		1	
CERES	ENN		1	
CERES	FPLA		1	
CERES	GER		1	
CERES	GR		1	
CERES	HOR		1	
CERES	JUV		1	
CERES	LUC		1	
CERES	LUCIL		1	
CERES	LUCR		2	(+ a girl's name)
CERES	MAN		1	
CERES	MAR		1	
CERES	OV		1	
CERES	PET		1	
CERES	PL		1	
CERES	PRIAP		1	
CERES	S		1	
CERES	SEN		1	(grain, food; rites: HF 845)
CERES	SIL		1	
CERES	TER		1	
CERES	TIB		1	
CERES	V		1	
CERES	VAL		1	
CERES	VAR	1	30	
CERILLAE	SIL			town in Bruttium
-CERINTHUS S. 1.2.81	HOR		1	infamous contemporary
CERINTHUS 3.9.11	TIB	1	2	unknown pseudonym
CERRETANA	MAR			a ham (from Spain)
CERRETANI	SIL			tribe of Spain
- CERRINIUS 8.18	MAR			a poet-friend
- CERVIUS	HOR	2	2	two contemporaries
- CERYLUS 1.67	MAR			fictional man
- CESSAEUS em., 6.130	VAL			p. to a Scythian tribe
- CESTOS 1.92; 50.18	MAR	2	2	two slaves
CETHEGI	LUC			the Cethegus family
CETHEGUS	FPLR		1	comp. of Catiline
CETHEGUS	HOR		1	the orator
CETHEGUS	JUV		1	comp. of Catiline
CETHEGUS	LUC		1	" "
CETHEGUS	SIL		1	Samnite leader
CETHEGUS	V	1	6	a Rutulian
CETO	LUC		1	wife of Phorcus
CETO em., 2.317	VAL	1	2	??
CETOS n.?	MAN			constellation
CĒUS	HOR		1	p. to Cea
CEUS	OV	1	2	
CEYX	OV		1	son of Ceyx (next)
CEYX	SEN	1	2	king of Trachis
CHAEREA masc.	PL		1	fictional man

CHAEREA m.	TER	1	2	fict. young man
-CHAEREMON 11.56	MAR			cont. philosopher
-CHAERESTRATUS 5.25	MAR		1	fictional person
CHAERESTRATUS 5.162	PER		1	" "
CHAERESTRATUS	PL	1	3	" " (Asin. 865)
-CHAERIBULUS Epid. 68	PL			a young man
-CHAERIPPUS 8.95	JUV			a Cilician (?)
CHALCEDON fem.	LUC			town in Bithynia
CHALCIDICUS	COL		1	p. to Chalcis
CHALCIDICUS	LUC		1	
CHALCIDICUS	S		1	
CHALCIDICUS	SIL		1	
CHALCIDICUS	V		1	
CHALCIDICUS	VAL	1	6	
CHALCIOPE	OV		1	wife of Phrixus
CHALCIOPE	VAL	1	2	
CHALCIS	LUC		1	town on Euboea
CHALCIS	PL		1	
CHALCIS	S		1	
CHALCIS	SEN	1	4	
CHALCODONII em.	AV			the people of Chalcis
CHALDAEI	JUV		1	the people of Assyria
CHALDAEI	LUCR	1	2	
CHALDAEUS	JUV		1	Chaldaean, Assyrian
CHALDAEUS	LUC	1	2	
-CHALĪNUS Cas. 104	PL			name of a slave
CHALYBEIUS adj.	OV			p. to the Chalybes
CHALYBES pl.	CAT		1	a people of Anatolia
CHALYBES	MAR		1	
CHALYBES	V		1	
CHALYBES	VAL	1	4	
CHAON m.	V			a son of Priam
CHAONI	GR			a breed of horses
CHAONIA	V			a tribe or nation of Epirus
CHAONIS adj.	OV		1	p. to Chaonia
CHAONIS	SEN	1	2	
CHAONIUS	LUC		1	p. to Chaonia
CHAONIUS	OV		1	
CHAONIUS	PROP		1	
CHAONIUS	S		1	
CHAONIUS	SEN		1	
CHAONIUS	SIL		1	
CHAONIUS	V		1	
CHAONIUS	VAL	1	8	
CHAOS n., 6.696	LUC		1	Underworld (also darkness, primitive cosmo
CHAOS	OV		1	
CHAOS	S		1	
CHAOS	SEN		1	
CHAOS	V		1	primitive cosmos; a god
CHAOS	VAL	1	6	Underworld
CHARADRUS fem.	S			town in Syria
CHARAXUS	OV	2	2	a Lapith; brother of Sappho
CHARES m.	PL			a fictitious name (Trin. 922)
CHARICLO	OV			a nymph
-CHARIDEMUS 6.31	MAR	2	2	two contemporaries
-CHARĪNUS 1.77	MAR		1	a contemporary
CHARINUS Merc. 128	PL		2	two different young men

CHARĪNUS <u>Andr</u>. 305	TER	1	4	a young man
–CHARISIANUS 6.24	MAR			a contemporary
CHARITES pl., <u>F</u>.5.219	OV			the Graces (cf. Gratia, Gratiae)
–CHARMENION 10.65.2	MAR			a cont. sissy
CHARMIDES	PL			comic figure
CHARON	AV		1	the ferryman in the Underworld
CHARON	SEN		1	
CHARON	SIL		1	
CHARON	TIB		1	
CHARON	V	1	5	
–CHAROPEIUS adj.	S			p. to Charops (<u>T</u>. 5.159)
–CHAROPĪNUS 5.50	MAR			a contemporary
–CHAROPS <u>M</u>. 13.260	OV			Trojan killed by Ulixes
CHARYBDIS	HOR		1	the Whirlpool (cf. Scylla); anything dangerous
CHARYBDIS	JUV		1	
CHARYBDIS	LUC		1	
CHARYBDIS	LUCR		1	
CHARYBDIS	MAN		1	
CHARYBDIS	OV		1	
CHARYBDIS	PROP		1	
CHARYBDIS	S		1	
CHARYBDIS	SEN		1	
CHARYBDIS	SIL		1	
CHARYBDIS	TIB		1	
CHARYBDIS	V	1	12	
CHATTI (Catti)	JUV		1	a Germanic tribe
CHATTI	MAR	1	2	
–CHATTICUS adj.	MAR			p. to the Chatti (14.26.1)
CHELAE	CIC		1	constellation (part of Scorpio)
CHELAE	GER		1	
CHELAE	LUC		1	
CHELAE	MAN	1	4	
CHELIDONIUS* (fici)	COL			a type of figs
–CHERSIDAMAS <u>M</u>. 13.259	OV			son of Priam
CHIA fem. sg.	CAL		1	Chian figs
CHIA	HOR		1	
CHIA	MAR	1	3	
CHIMAERA	HOR		1	a hybrid, fiery monster
CHIMAERA	LUCR		1	
CHIMAERA	MAR		1	
CHIMAERA	OV		1	
CHIMAERA	SEN		1	
CHIMAERA	SIL		1	(name of a ship)
CHIMAERA	TIB		1	
CHIMAERA	V	2	9	(+ name of a ship)
CHIMAEREUS Cul. 14	AV			p. to mt. Chimaera (in Lycia)
CHIMAERIFER	OV			parent of Chimaera
–CHIMERINOS 9.13.2	MAR			fictional person
–CHINEUS dub.,adj.	CAT			?? (67.32)
CHIONE	JUV		1	a meretrix
CHIONE	MAR		1	"
CHIONE	OV	1	3	d. of Daedalion
CHIONIDES	OV			ep. of Eumolpus
CHIOS fem., cf. -us	GER		1	(constellation)
CHIOS	HOR		1	island in Aegean
CHIOS	LUC		1	
CHIOS	LUCIL		1	

CHIOS	S	1	5	island in the Aegean
CHIRO = Chiron	TR			a learned Centaur and a god of healing
CHIRON	CAT		1	
CHIRON	COL		1	
CHIRON	GER		1	
CHIRON	JUV		1	
CHIRON	LUC		2	(+ a star)
CHIRON	OV		1	
CHIRON	PROP		1	
CHIRON	S		1	
CHIRON	SEN		2	(+a star)
CHIRON	V		1	
CHIRON	VAL	1	13	
CHIUM	HOR			wine of Chios
CHIUS	CIC			constell. (= Scorpio)
CHIUS*	COL		1	p. to island Chios (and its wine)
CHIUS*	HOR		1	
CHIUS*	MAR		1	
CHIUS*	OV		1	
CHIUS*	PL		1	
CHIUS*	PROP		1	
CHIUS*	TIB		1	
CHIUS*	VAR	1	8	
-CHLIDE Am. 3.7.23	OV			a woman
CHLOE	HOR		1	a maiden
CHLOE	MAR	1	2	fictional girl
CHLOREUS	V			a Trojan
CHLORIS	HOR		2	a Greek woman; a crone
CHLORIS	OV		1	ep. of Flora
CHLORIS	PROP	1	4	the mistress of PROP
CHOASPES m.	SIL		1	river in Persia
CHOASPES	TIB		1	
CHOASPES	VAL	1	3	
CHOATRAE	LUC		1	Scythian tribe
CHOATRAE	VAL	1	2	
CHOERILUS	HOR			a Greek poet
CHREMES	HOR		1	a miserly type (in comedy & satire)
CHREMES	LUCIL		1	
CHREMES	PL		1	
CHREMES	SIL		1	(Punic soldier)
CHREMES	TER	2	6	a senex; a young man
-CHRESTILLA 8.43	MAR			fictional
-CHRESTILLUS 11.90	MAR			"
-CHRESTINA 2.31	MAR			"
-CHRESTUS 7.55; 9.27	MAR			"
CHROMIS m.	OV		2	comp. of Phineus; a Centaur
CHROMIS	S		1	Centaur
CHROMIS	SIL		1	a Saguntine
CHROMIS	V	2	6	a Satyr; a Trojan
-CHROMIUS	HL		2	two heroes at Troy
CHROMIUS M. 13.257	OV	1	3	a Lycian
-CHRYSALUS Bacc. 243	PL			a slave
CHRYSAS m.	SIL			river of Sicily
CHRYSE	OV		1	town of Mysia
CHRYSE	SEN	1	2	
CHRYSEIS patr.	HL		1	Astynome, d. of Chryses
CHRYSEIS	OV	1	2	

CHRYSES	HL		1	priest of Apollo (in the Troad)
CHRYSES	LUCIL		1	
CHRYSES	OV		1	
CHRYSES	PRIAP		1	
CHRYSES	S	1	5	
CHRYSIPPUS	HOR		1	Stoic philosopher
CHRYSIPPUS	JUV		1	
CHRYSIPPUS	PER	1	3	
CHRYSIS fem.	COM		1	fictional
CHRYSIS	PER		1	"
CHRYSIS	PL		1	" (a copa)
CHRYSIS	TER	1	4	" (a meretrix)
CHRYSOGONUS	JUV			cont. citharist
-CHRYSOPOLIS Pers.506	PL			fictional town
CHTHONIUS	OV		1	a Centaur
CHTHONIUS	S	1	2	one of the Sparti
CIA =Cea	PH			island in the Cyclades
CIBYRATICUS adj.	HOR			p. to Cibyra (t. in Caria)
CICERO	CIC		1	the famous orator-politician
CICERO	FPLR		1	
CICERO	JUV		1	
CICERO	LP		1	
CICERO	MAR		1	
CICERO	PET	1	6	
CICIRRUS	HOR			a nickname (= ?)
CICONES	AV		1	Thracian tribe
CICONES	OV		1	
CICONES	PROP		1	
CICONES	SIL		1	
CICONES	TIB		1	
CICONES	V	1	6	
CICUTA m.	HOR			cont. loan-shark
CILICES	JUV		1	the people of Cilicia
CILICES	LUC		1	
CILICES	MAN		1	
CILICES	MAR		1	
CILICES	OV		1	
CILICES	S		1	
CILICES	TIB	1	7	
CILICIA	PL		1	province (region) in SE Anatolia
CILICIA	TER	1	2	
CILICIUS	MAR			p. to Cilicia
CILISSA adj.	OV		1	p. to Cilicia
CILISSA adj.	PROP	1	2	
CILIX 4.121	JUV		1	(a gladiator)
CILIX	LUC		1	a Cilician
CILIX	MAR		1	"
CILIX	PL	1	4	(a slave)
CILIX*	AV		1	Cilician, p. to Cilicia
CILIX*	LUCR		1	
CILIX*	MAR		1	
CILIX*	OV		1	
CILIX*	SIL	1	5	
CILLA	OV		1	town in the Troad
CILLA	SEN	1	2	
CILNIUS	SIL			an Arretine man
CIMBER	LUC		1	a German man

CIMBER	MAN		1	a German man
CIMBER	OV		1	
CIMBER	SIL	1	4	(a Roman soldier)
CIMBRI	JUV		1	a Germanic tribe
CIMBRI	LUC		1	
CIMBRI	PROP	1	3	
⎧CIMINIUS or -nus	V			lake in Etruria
⎩CIMINUS	SIL			" " "
CIMMERII	OV		1	a cave people (near Naples)
CIMMERII	TIB		1	
CIMMERII	VAL	1	3	
CIMMERIUS	AV		1	p. to this people
CIMMERIUS	OV		1	
CIMMERIUS 10.132	S		1	p. to a Thracian tribe
CIMMERIUS	SIL		1	p. to the cave-people
CIMMERIUS	VAL	1	5	p. to a Thracian tribe
CIMOLUS	OV			an island in the Cyclades
CINARA	HOR		1	a Greek girl
CINARA	PROP	1	2	
CINGA	LUC			a river in Spain
CINGULUS adj.	SIL			p. to Cingulum (t. in Picenum)
CINNA m.	CAT		1	the poet (C. Helvius Cinna)
CINNA	FPLR		1	poet
CINNA	LUC		1	L. Cornelius Cinna (assassin)
CINNA	MAR		2	poet; fictional
CINNA	OV		1	poet
CINNA	SIL		1	L. Corn. Cinna
CINNA	V	1	8	poet
CINNAE pl.	LUC			type of cruelty
-CINNAMUS	MAR	3	3	three different contemporaries
CINYPHIUS	GR		1	p. to Cinyps (hence African)
CINYPHIUS	LUC		1	
CINYPHIUS	MAR		1	
CINYPHIUS	OV		1	
CINYPHIUS	S		1	
CINYPHIUS	SEN		1	
CINYPHIUS	SIL		1	
CINYPHIUS	V	1	8	
CINYPS	LUC		1	river of Libya
CINYPS	SIL	1	2	
CINYRA m.	V			Ligurian chieftain
CINYRAEUS	LUC			p. to Cinyras
CINYRAS	OV	2	2	k. of Assyria; k. of Cyprus
CINYREIUS	COL		1	p. to Cinyras
CINYREIUS	OV	1	2	
CINYRĒUS = -eius	S			p. to Cinyras
CIPUS	OV			leg. Roman praetor
CIRCA cf. Circe	PL			myth. d. of the Sun (Epid. 604)
CIRCAEUS	HOR		1	p. to Circa (Circe)
CIRCAEUS	LUC		1	
CIRCAEUS	OV		1	
CIRCAEUS	PROP		1	
CIRCAEUS	SIL		1	
CIRCAEUS	V		1	
CIRCAEUS	VAL	1	7	
CIRCE	FPLA		1	myth. d. of the Sun
CIRCE	HOR		1	

CIRCE	JUV		1	mythical d. of the Sun
CIRCE	MAR		1	
CIRCE	OV		1	
CIRCE	PET		1	
CIRCE	PRIAP		1	
CIRCE	PROP		1	
CIRCE	S		1	
CIRCE	SIL		1	
CIRCE	TIB		1	
CIRCE	V		1	
CIRCE	VAL	1	13	
⎧CIRCEI	HOR			town in Latium
⎨CIRCEII	JUV		1	
⎩CIRCEII	MAR	1	2	
CIRCUS	CAT		1	Circus Maximus, the racecourse in Rome
CIRCUS	OV		2	C. Maximus; C. Flaminii (in Campus Martius)
CIRCUS	S	1	4	(unspecified)
CĪRIS (Ciris)	AV			a fabulous bird; also title of the poem
CIRRHA	JUV		1	town in Phocis
CIRRHA	LUC		1	
CIRRHA	MAR		1	
CIRRHA	S		1	
CIRRHA	SIL	1	5	
CIRRHAEUS	JUV		1	p. to Cirrha
CIRRHAEUS	LUC		1	
CIRRHAEUS	S		1	
CIRRHAEUS	SEN		1	
CIRRHAEUS	SIL	1	5	
CIRTA (m.)	SIL			a Phoenician hero
CISSEIS patr.	V			ep. of Hecuba
CISSEUS	TR		1	leg. king of Thrace
CISSEUS	V	2	3	(+ a Rutulian)
CITHAERON	COL		1	mountain in Boeotia
CITHAERON	OV		1	
CITHAERON	PROP		1	
CITHAERON	S		1	
CITHAERON	SEN		1	
CITHAERON	TR		1	
CITHAERON	V		1	
CITHAERON	VAL	1	8	
-CITRIO Cas. III.6	PL			fictional cook
CIUS = Chius	LUCR			cloth of Chios (as n.pl.)
CIVIS	MAR			a lawyer (fict.?)
-CIZIGES T. 2.110	OV			Scythian tribe
-CLADUS or -ius	MAR			cont. banker (2.57.7)
CLANIS	OV		2	a Centaur; a comp. of Phineus
CLANIS	SIL		1	river in Etruria
CLANIS	VAL	1	4	Centaur
CLANIUS	SIL		2	river in Campania; Roman soldier
CLANIUS	V	1	3	river in Campania
-CLARANUS 10.21.2	MAR			a grammarian
CLARIUS	OV		1	ep. of Antimachus of Colophon, the poet
CLARIUS	S		1	ep. of Apollo
CLARIUS	V	1	3	" " "
CLARIUS*	OV		1	p. to Claros
CLARIUS*	VAL	1	2	
CLAROS fem.	OV			town in Ionia

Name	Ref.	Source			Description
CLARUS m., A. 10.126		V			a Lycian warrior
– CLASSICUS 2.69		MAR			a contemporary
– CLASSIUS (-ia?)		PL			p. to Amazons (comic formation, Curc.445)
CLAUDIA		MAR	2		a friend of MAR; a fict. woman
CLAUDIA		OV	1		Claudia Quinta, leg. Roman matron
CLAUDIA		PROP	1		"
CLAUDIA		S	2		" (+ wife of Statius)
CLAUDIA		SEN	1		Claudia Octavia, d. of Emperor Claudius
CLAUDIA		SIL	1		a heroine
CLAUDIA A. 7.708		V	1	9	the Claudian tribe
CLAUDIANUS adj.		MAR			p. to Emperor Claudius
– CLAUDIA/PEREGRINA		MAR			wife of A. Pudens (4.13)
CLAUDIA/PORTICUS		MAR			colonnade by the temple to Claudius
CLAUDIA/QUINTA		OV			leg. Roman matron, granddaughter of Ap.C.
– CLAUDIA/RUFINA		MAR			a British woman (11.53) Caecus
CLAUDIUS		HOR	1		emperor Tiberius
CLAUDIUS 5.147		JUV	1		emperor Claudius
CLAUDIUS 1.795		MAN	1		Appius Cl. Caecus (?)
CLAUDIUS 1.20.4		MAR	1		emperor Claudius
CLAUDIUS		OV	2		Claudius Marcellus; Appius Cl. Caecus
CLAUDIUS 4.9.39		PROP	1		M. Cl. Marcellus, maior
CLAUDIUS		S	1		emperor Claudius
CLAUDIUS Oct. 38		SEN	1		" "
CLAUDIUS 13.149		SIL	1	10	Cl. Asellus, a Roman
CLAUDIUS*		HOR		1	p. to the Claudian family
CLAUDIUS*		SEN	1	2	
CLAUDIUS/NERO		HOR			the emperor Tiberius
CLAUSUS		OV		1	Attus Clausus, founder of the Claudii
CLAUSUS		SIL		1	" "
CLAUSUS		V	1	3	a Sabine warrior
CLAVIGER		OV			ep. of the god Janus
CLAZOMENAE fem.pl.		HOR		1	town in Ionia
CLAZOMENAE		PH	1	2	
– CLEADAS 7.637		SIL			a Sidonian
CLEANTHES as pl.		JUV			statue of Cleanthes, the Stoic
CLEANTHEUS adj.		PER			Stoic
– CLEARETA Asin. 751		PL			a lena
CLEMENS		MAR			fictional man
CLEMENTIA		CAL	1		"Kindness" personified
CLEMENTIA		MAR	1		
CLEMENTIA		S	1	3	
– CLEOBULA Curc. 643		PL			mother of Planesium
– CLEOMACHUS		COM	1		fict. boxer
CLEOMACHUS Bac.589		PL	1	2	a soldier
CLEONAE		OV		1	town in Argolis
CLEONAE		S		1	
CLEONAE		SEN	1	3	
CLEONAEUS		LUC		1	p. to Cleonae
CLEONAEUS		MAR		1	
CLEONAEUS		S		1	
CLEONAEUS		SEN		1	
CLEONAEUS		SIL		1	
CLEONAEUS		VAL	1	6	
CLEOPATRA		JUV		1	queen of Egypt
CLEOPATRA		LUC		1	
CLEOPATRA		MAR		2	(+ fict. woman)
CLEOPATRA		S		1	

CLEOPATRA		VAL	1	6	
-CLEOSTRATA Cas.393	PL			a matrona
CLERUMENOE Gk. pl.	PL			title of Diphilus' comedy
CLINIA m.	COM		1	a type in comedy
CLINIA	PL		1	
CLINIA	TER	1	3	
CLINIADES patr.	OV			= Alcibiades
CLIO	AV		1	the Muse of history
CLIO	HOR		1	
CLIO	JUV		1	
CLIO	MLP		1	
CLIO	OV		1	
CLIO	S		1	
CLIO G. 4.341	V		1	(a daughter of Ocean)
CLIO	VAL	1	8	Muse of history
CLIPEA cf. Clupea	ENN			town in Africa
-CLITE 3.11	VAL			wife of Cyzicus
-CLITIPHO H. 209	TER			a young man
CLITOR T. 4.289	S			river in Arcadia
CLITORIUS	OV			p. to the Clitor
CLITUMNUS	JUV		1	river in Umbria
CLITUMNUS	PROP		1	
CLITUMNUS	SIL		1	
CLITUMNUS	V	1	4	
CLITUMNUS*	S			p. to the Clitumnus
CLOACINA	PL			ep. of Venus
CLOANTHUS	V			comp. of Aeneas
CLODIA (sc. Via)	OV			a road going north from Rome
CLODIA/VIA P.1.8.44	OV			"
CLODIUS	JUV			P. Clodius Pulcher, cont. of Caesar
CLOELIA	MAN		1	legendary Roman maiden
CLOELIA	SIL		1	
CLOELIA	V	1	3	
CLOELIUS	SIL			Roman hero
-CLONIS T. 7.712, 369	S	2	2	a Theban; an Abantian
CLONIUS	HL		1	a Boeotian
CLONIUS	S		1	a Theban
CLONIUS	V	1	3	comp. of Aeneas
CLONUS	V			an artist
CLOTHO	HL		1	one of the Fates (the Spinner)
CLOTHO	JUV		1	
CLOTHO	OV		1	
CLOTHO	S		1	
CLOTHO	SEN		1	
CLOTHO	SIL	1	6	(+ "Life", 5.404)
CLUENTIUS	V			a Roman gens name
CLUPEA cf. Clipea	LUC			town in N. Africa
CLUSINUS	HOR		1	p. to Clusium
CLUSINUS	MAR		1	
CLUSINUS	SIL		1	
CLUSINUS	V	1	4	
CLUSIUM	V			town of Etruria
CLUSIUS F. 1.130	OV			ep. of the god Janus
-CLUVIA 2.49	JUV			cont. woman
-CLUVIENUS 1.80	JUV			cont. poet
CLYMENE	OV		1	wife of Merops
CLYMENE	V	1	2	daughter of Ocean

CLYMENEIUS	OV			p. to Clymene
-CLYMENEUS S. 1.2.124	S			p. to Clymene
CLYMENUS	OV		2	ep. of Pluto; comp. of Phineus
CLYMENUS	VAL	1	3	an Argonaut
CLYTAEMESTRA	JUV		1	daughter of Tyndarus
CLYTAEMESTRA	PROP	1	2	
CLYTAEMNESTRA	OV			
CLYTEMESTRA	FPLR			
CLYTEMNESTRA	SEN		1	
CLYTEMNESTRA	TR	1	2	
CLYTIE	OV			daughter of Ocean
CLYTIUS	FPLR		1	an Argonaut
CLYTIUS	OV		1	a comp. of Phineus
CLYTIUS	SIL		1	a Macedonian
CLYTIUS	V	1	4	a Trojan
CLYTOS	OV			son of Pallas (the hero)
CLYTUS	MAR		1	fict. person
CLYTUS	OV	1	2	comp. of Phineus
CNIDIUS adj., cf. Gn-	HOR			p. to Cnidos
CNIDOS cf. Gn-	HOR		1	town in Caria
CNIDOS	PRIAP	1	2	
CNIDUS	CAT		1	
CNIDUS	OV		1	
CNIDUS	PL	1	3	
CNOSIUS (Gn-), adj.	FPLR			p. to Cnossos (Gnossos)
COA n. pl.	HOR		1	silks (of Cos)
COA	OV	1	2	"
-COASTES 6.155	VAL			a Scythian warrior
COCALIDES	SIL			daughter of Cocalus
COCALUS	OV			leg. king of Sicily
COCCEIUS	HOR			Cocc. Nerva (consul 39 BC)
COCLES	JUV		1	the leg. Horatius Cocles
COCLES	MAN		1	
COCLES	PROP		1	
COCLES	SIL		1	
COCLES	V	1	5	
-COCLITES Curc. 393	PL			(comic, punning hybrid)
COCYTHOS = Cocytos	SIL			myth. river in Underworld
COCYTIUS	V		1	p. to Cocytos
COCYTIUS	VAL	1	2	
COCYTOS	S		1	myth. river in Underworld
COCYTOS	V	1	2	
COCYTUS	HOR		1	
COCYTUS	JUV		1	
COCYTUS	PET		1	
COCYTUS	SEN	1	4	
CODRUS	FPLR		1	a bad poet
CODRUS	HOR		1	the last Athenian king
CODRUS	V		1	a bad poet
CODRUS	VAL	1	4	a Lemnian
COELALETAE	VAL			Scythian tribe
COELICUS = Caelicus	S			Celestial
-COERANOS M. 13.257	OV			myth. hero, son of Iphitus
COEUS	FPLA		1	a Titan
COEUS	OV		1	
COEUS	PROP		1	
COEUS	V		1	

COEUS	VAL	1	5	a Titan
COLAPHUS	PL			name of a slave
COLAX	TER			title of a comedy
-COLAXES 6.48	VAL			chief of the Bisaltae
COLCHI pl. of -us	AET		1	Caucasian tribe
COLCHI	CAT		1	
COLCHI	ENN		1	
COLCHI	LUC		1	
COLCHI	MAR		1	
COLCHI	OV		1	
COLCHI	PET		1	
COLCHI	S		1	
COLCHI	SEN		1	
COLCHI	TR		1	
COLCHI	VAL	1	11	
COLCHICUS	HOR		1	p. to the Colchi
COLCHICUS	SEN	1	2	
COLCHIDES N, pl.	MAR		1	Colchians (10.4.2)
COLCHIDES adj. pl.	VAL	1	2	p. to the Colchi
COLCHIS	AET		1	Medea (in all texts)
COLCHIS	AV		1	
COLCHIS	ENN		1	
COLCHIS	GER		1	
COLCHIS	HOR		1	
COLCHIS	JUV		1	
COLCHIS	LUC		1	
COLCHIS	MAN		2	(+ the country)
COLCHIS	MAR		1	
COLCHIS	OV		2	(+ the country)
COLCHIS	PROP		1	
COLCHIS	S		1	
COLCHIS	SEN		1	
COLCHIS	VAL	2	17	(+ the country)
COLCHIS*	LUC		1	Colchian or Medean
COLCHIS*	MAN		1	
COLCHIS*	S	1	3	
COLCHUS	HOR			a Colchian
COLCHUS*	HOR		1	p. to the country Colchis
COLCHUS*	MAR		1	
COLCHUS*	OV		1	
COLCHUS*	PROP		1	
COLCHUS*	SEN	1	5	
COLLABUS	PL			a character in comedy
COLLATIA	OV		1	town in Latium
COLLATIA	SIL	1	2	
COLLATIA/PORTA	OV			= Porta Collatina (F. 2.785)
COLLATINUS	OV		1	p. to Collatia
COLLATINUS	V	1	2	
COLLINA/PORTA	LUC		1	a gate in Rome
COLLINA/PORTA	OV	1	2	
COLLINUS	MAR		1	a poet
COLLINUS	SIL	1	2	a Roman soldier
COLLINUS*	JUV		1	p. to hills of Rome (or the Gate)
COLLINUS*	PROP	1	2	
-COLLYBISCUS Poen.170	PL			a steward
-COLONIA 17.1	CAT			town near Verona
COLOPHON m.	HOR		1	town in Ionia (Lydia)

COLOPHON	LUC	1	2	town in Ionia (Lydia)
COLOPHONIACUS	AV			p. to Colophon
COLOPHONIUS	OV			p. to Colophon
COMATA sc. Gallia	LUC			Gaul proper
COMBE	OV			mother of the Curetes
COMETES m. sg.	OV		1	a Lapith
COMETES	VAL	1	2	father of Asterion
COMINIUS	CAT			cont. man
COMMAGENUS	JUV			p. to Commagene (province in Syria)
COMMODITAS Mil.1134	PL			personification of "Good Luck"
COMMORIENTES	FPLA		1	title of a comedy
COMMORIENTES	TER	1	2	
COMOEDIA	FPLA			"Comedy" personified
COMPITALIA n.pl.	COM			festival for the Lares
COMUM	CAT			town in N. Italy
CONCANUS sg.	HOR		1	Spanish tribe
CONCANUS	SIL	1	2	
CONCORDIA	JUV		1	the Goddess (or her temple)
CONCORDIA	MAR		1	
CONCORDIA	OV		1	
CONCORDIA	PET		1	
CONCORDIA	S	1	5	
CONDALIUM	FPLA			title of a comedy
-CONDYLUS 5.78.30	MAR			name of a slave
-CONE 3.200	LUC			town on the Ister
CONFIDENTIA Most.350	PL			"Assurance" personified
CONGEDUS	MAR			river in Spain
CONGRIO	PL			a cook
CONON	CAT		1	the Hellenistic astronomer
CONON	PROP		1	
CONON	V	1	3	
CONSUALIA n.pl.	FPLA			festival of Consus
CONSUS F. 3.199	OV			Italic deity of fertility
CONTEREBROMNIUS	PL			comic ep. of Libya
COPIA personif.	HOR		1	"Plenty"
COPIA	PL	1	2	
COPTOS fem.	JUV		1	town in Egypt
COPTOS	S	1	2	
CORA	LUC		1	town in Latium
CORA	PROP		1	
CORA	SIL		1	
CORA	V	1	4	
-CORACINUS 4.43	MAR			fictional man
CORALLI	OV		1	tribe of Moesia
CORALLI	VAL	1	2	
CORANUS	HOR		1	contemporary man
CORANUS	JUV		1	
CORANUS	MAR	1	3	
-CORAS A. 7.672	V			a hero from Tibur
CORAX	PL			name of a slave
-CORBULO 3.251	JUV		1	contemporary man
CORBULO S. 5.2.35	S		1	Cn. Domitius C.
CORBULO 14.408	SIL	1	3	captain in Marcellus' fleet
CORCYRA	ENN		1	island in Ionian Sea
CORCYRA	LUC	1	2	
CORCYRAEUS	JUV		1	p. to Corcyra
CORCYRAEUS	MAR		1	

CORCYRAEUS		OV	1 3	p. to Corcyra
-CORDALIO	Capt. 657	PL		slave-name
- CORDALUS	Capt. 735	PL		a freedman
CORDUBA		MAR	1	town in Spain
CORDUBA		SIL	1 2	
CORDUS	1.2	JUV	1	poet
CORDUS	8.715	LUC	1	a soldier of Pompey
CORDUS		MAR	2 4	two contemporaries
-CORESUS	6.39.21	MAR		fictional
CORFINIUM		LUC	1	town of the Paeligni
CORFINIUM		SIL	1 2	
- CORIENDRUS	Men. 295	PL		a comic figure
CORINNA		MAR	1	pseudonym of Ovid's mistress
CORINNA		OV	1	" " "
CORINNA		PROP	1	Greek poetess
CORINNA		S	1 4	Greek poetess
CORINTHIACUS adj.		OV		p. to Corinth
CORINTHIARIUS		FPLR		(a brass-worker)
CORINTHIENSIS adj.		PL		p. to Corinth
CORINTHIUS adj.		AV	1	p. to Corinth
CORINTHIUS		MAR	1	
CORINTHIUS		SEN	1	
CORINTHIUS		TER	1 4	
CORINTHOS fem.		JUV	1	the Greek city
CORINTHOS		MAR	1 2	
CORINTHUS		AV	1	
CORINTHUS		ENN	1	
CORINTHUS		HOR	1	(also: vase)
CORINTHUS		JUV	1	
CORINTHUS		MAN	1	
CORINTHUS		OV	1	
CORINTHUS		PL	1	
CORINTHUS		PROP	1	
CORINTHUS		S	1	
CORINTHUS		SEN	1	
CORINTHUS		TER	1	
CORINTHUS		V	1 12	
- CORNELIA	6.167	JUV	1	mother of the Gracchi
CORNELIA	2.349	LUC	1	wife of Pompey
CORNELIA	11.104.17	MAR	1	mother of the Gracchi
CORNELIA		PROP	1 4	daughter of Scribonius
CORNELI/FORUM		MAR		town in Cisalpine Gaul (3.4.4)
CORNELIUS		CAT	1	a contemporary
CORNELIUS		LUCIL	1	a type
CORNELIUS		MAR	1 3	a contemporary
-CORNELIUS/CETHEGUS		ENN		consul in 204 BC (Ann. 300 W)
-CORNELIUS/PUBLIUS		LUCIL		Scipio (254 W)
CORNICULANUS adj.		OV		p. to Corniculum (t. of Latium)
CORNIFICIUS	38.1	CAT	1	poet-friend (Quintus Corn.)
CORNIFICIUS		LUCIL	1	a type
CORNIFICIUS	T.2.436	OV	1 3	poet (Quintus Cornelius)
CORNIGER		MAN		ep. of Aries (const.)
CORNUTUS		PER	1	Annaeus Cornutus, freedman of Seneca
CORNUTUS		TIB	1 2	a friend of Tibullus
COROEBUS		HL	1	a Trojan, leg. s. of Mygdon
COROEBUS		OV	1	
COROEBUS		S	1	

COROEBUS	V	1	4	a Trojan, leg. son of Mygdon
CORONA	CIC		1	constellation (crown of Ariadne)
CORONA	GER		2	" (+ Southern Crown)
CORONA	MAN		1	"
CORONA	OV	1	5	
CORONEUS	OV			king of Phocis
CORONI (v.l., M.13.698)	OV			= Coronae (daughters of Orion)
CORONIA (= -eia)	S			town of Boeotia
CORONIDES	OV			= Aesculapius
CORONIS	OV			mother of Aesculapius
CORSICA	JUV			the island
CORSICUS adj.	MAN		1	p. to Corsica
CORSICUS	MAR		1	
CORSICUS	OV		1	
CORSICUS	SEN	1	4	
CORSUS adj.	MAR		1	Corsican, p. to Corsica
CORSUS	OV	1	2	
CORTONA	SIL			town of Etruria
CORTYNIUS (= Gor-)	S			p. to Gortyn (town on Crete)
CORUS cf. Caurus	JUV		1	North-west Wind
CORUS	LUC		1	
CORUS	S		1	
CORUS	SEN		1	
CORUS	SIL	1	5	
CORVINI	LUC			a Roman family
CORVINUS	HOR		1	= Messala
CORVINUS	JUV		2	a friend; a contemporary
CORVINUS	MAN		1	early Roman hero
CORVINUS	SIL	1	5	a Roman soothsayer
CORVUS	CIC		1	constellation "Crow"
CORVUS	GER		1	
CORVUS	OV	1	3	
CORYBANTES pl.	GER		1	the priests of Cybele
CORYBANTES	HOR		1	
CORYBANTES	OV		1	
CORYBANTES	SEN	1	4	
CORYBANTIUS adj.	V			p. to the Corybantes
CORYBAS	JUV		1	a priest of Cybele
CORYBAS	MAR	1	2	
CORYCIDES pl.	OV			daughters of Plistus
CORYCIUM Maec.133	AV			Corycian (saffron?)
CORYCIUS	AV		1	p. to a cave on Parnassus (the Muses)
CORYCIUS em.	FPLB		1	
CORYCIUS S.2.4.68	HOR		1	p. to Corycus (town in Cilicia)
CORYCIUS	JUV		1	"
CORYCIUS	LUC		1	"
CORYCIUS	MAR		1	"
CORYCIUS	S		1	Parnassan
CORYCIUS	V	1	8	Cilician
CORYDON	CAL		1	a shepherd
CORYDON	COL		1	
CORYDON	JUV		1	
CORYDON	PROP		1	
CORYDON	V	1	5	
-CORYMBUS T. 8.548	S			friend of the Muses
CORYNAEUS	V			a Trojan hero
-CORYPHAEUS 8.62	JUV			a horse

CORYTHUS	OV		3	a Lapith; a Libyan; a son of Paris
CORYTHUS	SIL		1	the founder of Cortona
CORYTHUS	V		1	town in Etruria (later Cortona)
CORYTHUS	VAL	1	6	a Cyzican warrior
COSAE pl. = Cosa	V			town of Etruria
-COSCONIA 11.55.5	MAR			the wife of Urbicus (cont.)
COSCONIUS	MAR			a writer of epigrams
COSMIANUM	MAR			an unguent (perfume)
COSMIANUS	MAR			p. to Cosmus
COSMUS	JUV		1	a perfume-maker
COSMUS	MAR	2	3	(+ fict. man)
COSSUS	JUV		2	two contemporaries
COSSUS	MAN		1	A. Cornelius Cossus
COSSUS fr. 3	OV		1	
COSSUS	PROP		1	
COSSUS	V	1	6	
COSSYRA	SIL			island near Sicily
COSYRA	OV			
COTHON	SIL	2	2	a Punic soldier; a pilot
-COTILUS 2.70	MAR			fictional man
COTISO	HOR			king of the Dacians
COTTA	CIC		1	consul in 200 BC
COTTA	ENN		1	"
COTTA	FPLR		1	(unknown)
COTTA	JUV		1	Ovid's patron
COTTA	LUC		2	trib. plebis; legatus
COTTA	MAR		3	three fictional men
COTTA	OV	1	10	patron; C. Maximus
COTTAE P. 4.16.43	OV			the Cotta family
COTUS cf. Cotys	LUCIL			king of the Odrysii (in Thrace)
COTYS	LUC		1	"
COTYS	OV		1	"
COTYS	VAL	1	3	a Cyzican
COTYTIA cf. -tt-	HOR			festival of Cotyto
COTYTO	JUV			a Greek goddess of lustfulness
COTYTTIA n.pl.	AV			festival of Cotyto (Cat. 5.19)
COUM	HOR		1	the wine of Cos
COUM	PER	1	2	"
COUS as N, T 1.6.2	OV		1	ep. of Philetas, the Gk. poet
COUS = Cos	S	1	2	the Aegean island
COUS*	HOR		1	p. to Cos, island in the Aegean
COUS*	JUV		1	
COUS*	LUC		1	
COUS*	OV		1	
COUS*	PROP		1	
COUS*	TIB	1	6	
CRAGOS	OV			mt. in Lycia
CRAGUS	HOR			
CRANE = Carna	OV			Roman goddess of domesticity
CRANNON fem.	CAT			town of Thessaly
CRANTOR	HOR		1	Greek philosopher
CRANTOR	OV		1	legendary hero
CRANTOR	SIL	1	3	Punic ship's captain
CRASSI	SIL			youths in Fabius' army
CRASSICIUS (-itius)	FPLR			a grammarian
CRASSUS	FPLA		1	(pun on the family name)
CRASSUS C. 3.5.5	HOR		1	M. Licinius Crassus dives, triumvir

CRASSUS	JUV	1	M. Licinius Crassus (as wealthy type)
CRASSUS	LUC	2	M.L.C.; his son P. L. Crassus
CRASSUS	LUCIL	1	L. Crassus, consul 131 BC
CRASSUS	MAR	2	M.L.C.; a fictional Crassus
CRASSUS	OV	1	M.L.C. (triumvir)
CRASSUS	PER	1	M.L.C.
CRASSUS	PET	1	M.L.C.
CRASSUS	PROP	1	M.L.C.
CRASSUS	VAR	1 13	M.L.C.
CRASTINUS	LUC		a soldier of Caesar
CRATAEIS (Ciris)	AV	1	mother of Scylla
CRATAEIS M. 13.749	OV	1	Scylla (or her mother)
CRATER	GER	1	constellation "Bowl"
CRATER	MAN	1	
CRATER	OV	1 3	
CRATERA	CIC		
CRATERUS	HOR	1	a cont. doctor
CRATERUS	PER	1 2	" "
CRATES (Mallotes)	FPLR		Greek grammarian
CRATHIS m.	OV		river of S. Italy
CRATINUS	HOR	1	Greek comic writer
CRATINUS	PER	1	" " "
CRATINUS	PL	1	(a young man)
CRATINUS	TER	1 4	(a senex)
CREDULITAS M. 12.59	OV		personification of "Credulity"
-CREMEDON 6.194	VAL		an Albanian (i.e. Caucasian) warrior
CREMERA	JUV	1	a river in Etruria
CREMERA	OV	1	
CREMERA	SIL	1 3	
-CREMETAON T.7.712	S		a Theban
CREMONA	AV	1	town in N. Italy
CREMONA	MAR	1	
CREMONA	SIL	1	
CREMONA	V	1 4	
-CRENAE 8.503	SIL		a place in Phrygia (?)
CRENAEUS N	OV	1	a Centaur
CRENAEUS N	S	1	son of Faunus
CRENAEUS N	VAL	1 3	a Cyzican warrior
CREO	PL	1	leg. king of Corinth
CREO	SEN	2 3	
CREON	HOR	1	
CREON	OV	1	
CREON	S	1 3	
-CREPEREIUS/POLLIO	JUV		cont. bankrupt (9.6)
CRES cf. pl. Cretes	OV	1	a Cretan
CRES	SIL	1	
CRES	TIB	1	
CRES	V	1 4	
CRESIUS	CAL	1	Cretan, p. to island Crete
CRESIUS	GER	1	
CRESIUS	OV	1	
CRESIUS	S	1	
CRESIUS	SEN	1	
CRESIUS	V	1 6	
CRESSA (nota, adj.)	HOR	1	Cretan (C. 1.36.10)
CRESSA 10.327	JUV	1	ep. of Phaedra
CRESSA	OV	2	ep. of Ariadne; ep. of Aerope

CRESSA adj.	PROP	1		Cretan
CRESSA S. 2.6.25	S	1		ep. of Ariadne
CRESSA Oed. 489	SEN	1		Cretan (adj.)
CRESSA also adj.	V	1	8	a Cretan woman (A. 5.285); adj. G. 3.345
CRESSA*	OV			Cretan
CRESSIUS = Cresius	OV			Cretan, p. to Crete
CRETA	CAT	1		the island (cf. also creta 'chalk')
CRETA	GR	1		
CRETA	HOR	1		
CRETA	JUV	1		
CRETA	LUC	1		
CRETA	LUCR	1		
CRETA	MAN	1		
CRETA	MAR	1		
CRETA	OV	1		
CRETA	PL	1		
CRETA	S	1		
CRETA	SEN	1		
CRETA	V	1	13	
CRETAEUS	AV	1		Cretan, p. to Crete
CRETAEUS	FPLA	1		
CRETAEUS	GER	1		
CRETAEUS	HL	1		
CRETAEUS	MAN	1		
CRETAEUS	OV	1		
CRETAEUS	PROP	1		
CRETAEUS	SEN	1		
CRETAEUS	V	1	9	
CRETANI	PL			the people of Crete
CRETE = Creta	PRIAP			island
CRETENSES	ENN			the Cretans
CRETES	CAT	1		the Cretans
CRETES	LUC	1		
CRETES	SEN	1	3	
-CRETHEIUS adj., 2.611	VAL			p. to Cretheus
-CRETHEUS T. 9.307	S	1		a Theban hero
CRETHEUS A. 9.774	V	1		a Trojan bard
CRETHEUS 1.42	VAL	1	3	father of Aeson
-CRETHIDES patr.	VAL			Aeson (f. of Jason) (6.609)
-CRETHO	HL			son of Diocles
CRETICUS N	JUV	1		a cont. man (one of the Metelli)
CRETICUS N, 7.90	MAR	1	2	a contemporary
CRETICUS* (mare)	HOR	1		the Cretan Sea
CRETICUS*	SEN	1	2	Cretan
CRETIS	OV			a Cretan woman
CREUSA	OV		2	d. of Erechtheus; d. of Creon
CREUSA	PROP	1		d. of Creon & wife of Jason
CREUSA	S	1		"
CREUSA	SEN	1		"
CREUSA	V	1	6	(wife of Aeneas)
CRINISUS	V			river in Sicily
-CRINNUS Trin. 1020	PL			fictional person
CRISEUS	FPLR			p. to Crisa in Phocis, hence Phocean
CRISPINUS	HOR	1		Plotius Cr., minor Roman Stoic
CRISPINUS	JUV	1		an Egyptian slave, offical under Domitian
CRISPINUS	MAR	1		" "
CRISPINUS 5.126	PER	1		a bath-keeper

CRISPINUS	S.5.2	S		1	Vettius Crispinus, s. of Bolanus
CRISPINUS	Oct. 731	SEN		1	Rufrius Cr., husband of Poppaea
CRISPINUS	15.345	SIL	1	7	T. Quinctius Cr., a consul
CRISPUS		FPLA		1	= Sallust, the Roman historian
CRISPUS		FPLR		1	(unknown)
CRISPUS	4.81	JUV		1	Vibius Cr., orator & consul (83 AD)
CRISPUS		MAR	4	7	four different men
CRISPUS/SALLUSTIUS		HOR			the Roman historian
CRISTA m.		SIL			an Umbrian man
CRITIAS		SIL			a tyrant of Athens
CRITO		TER	2	2	senex; lawyer
CRITON		MAR			a doctor
−CRIXUS	4.148	SIL			a Celt
−CROBIALUS	5.102	VAL			town in Paphlagonia
CROCALE		CAL		1	shepherdess
CROCALE		OV	1	2	comp. of Diana
−CROCOTIUM	Stich.150	PL			a maid
CROCUS		OV			a young man
CROESUS		CAT		1	leg. king of Lydia (symbol of wealth)
CROESUS		CIC		1	
CROESUS		HOR		1	
CROESUS		JUV		1	
CROESUS		LUC		1	
CROESUS		MAN		1	
CROESUS	also pl.	MAR		1	
CROESUS		OV		1	
CROESUS		PROP		1	
CROESUS		S		1	
CROESUS		SIL	1	11	
−CROMNA	5.105	VAL			town in Paphlagonia
CROMYON m.		OV			town in Megaris
−CRONIUS adj.		FPLA		1	p. to Cronos (= Saturn)
CRONIUS N , 7.87.4		MAR		1	fictional man
CRONIUS or Clonius		V	1	3	a warrior (A. 10.749)
CROTON		OV		1	Gk. town in Bruttium
CROTON		SIL	1	2	
CROTOPIADES patr.		OV			= Linus (leg. bard)
−CROTOPUS	T. 1.570	S			king of the Argives
CROTOS		COL			constell. (Sagittarius)
CROTUS		MAR			contemp. man
CRUCISALUS		PL			comic character
CRURIFRAGIUM		PL			name of a slave
CRUSTUMERI		V			town of the Sabines
−CRUSTUMIUM	2.406	LUC		1	river in Umbria
CRUSTUMIUM	8.366	SIL	1	2	town of the Sabines
CRUSTUMIUS adj.		V			p. to Crustumium
CTESIPHO		TER			a young man
CULEX		MAR		1	title of a poem
CULEX		S	1	2	
CUMAE cf. Cyme		AET		1	Gk. town in Campania
CUMAE		COL		1	
CUMAE		ENN		1	
CUMAE		HOR		1	
CUMAE		JUV		1	
CUMAE		LUCR		1	
CUMAE		OV		1	
CUMAE		S		1	

CUMAE	SIL		1	Greek town in Campania
CUMAE	V	1	10	
CUMAEUS	OV		1	p. to Cumae
CUMAEUS	PRIAP		1	
CUMAEUS	PROP		1	
CUMAEUS	V	1	4	
CUMANUS	FPLR		1	p. to Cumae
CUMANUS	LUC		1	
CUMANUS	MAR		1	
CUMANUS	S		1	
CUMANUS	SIL		1	
CUMANUS	TIB		1	
CUMANUS	VAR	1	7	
CUNCTATOR	SIL			ep. of Q. Fabius Maximus, the dictator
CUPAVO	V			name of a Ligurian warrior
CUPENCUS	SIL		1	a soldier of Hannibal
CUPENCUS	V	1	2	Sabine priest
CUPIDINES cf. Cupido	CAT		1	"Loves"
CUPIDINES	HOR		1	
CUPIDINES	MAR	1	3	
CUPIDINEUS adj.	MAR		1	p. to Cupid, god of Love
CUPIDINEUS	OV	1	2	
CUPIDO	CAT		1	the god of Love
CUPIDO	COM		1	
CUPIDO	HOR		1	
CUPIDO	MAN		1	
CUPIDO	MAR		1	
CUPIDO	OV		1	
CUPIDO	PET		1	
CUPIDO	PL		1	
CUPIDO	PRIAP		1	
CUPIDO	PROP		1	
CUPIDO	SEN		1	
CUPIDO	SIL		1	
CUPIDO	TIB		1	
CUPIDO	V		1	
CUPIDO	VAL	1	15	
CUPIENNIUS (Libo)	HOR			a friend of Augustus
CUPRA = Cyprus?	FPLR		1	island of Cyprus (?)
CUPRA	SIL	1	2	town of Picenum
CUPRUS = Cyprus	COM			the island
CURA C. 3.1.40	HOR		1	"Sorrow" personified
CURA	S	1	2	
CURAE pl.	SIL		1	"Sorrows"
CURAE	V	1	2	
CURCULIO	PL			a parasite
-CURCULIONIUS adj.	PL			p. to Curculio (Mil. 13)
CURENSIS or Forensis	OV			p. to Cures (or Forum) (F. 3.94)
CURES pl.	OV		2	t. of the Sabines; its inhabitants
CURES	PER		1	town of the Sabines
CURES	PROP		2	(+ Quiris, inhabitant)
CURES	S		1	
CURES	SIL		1	
CURES	V	1	8	
CŪRETES m. pl.	LUCR		1	ancient Cretans
CURETES	MAR		1	
CURETES	OV		1	

CŪRETES	S		1	ancient Cretans
CURETES	SEN		1	
CURETES	SIL		1	
CURETES	V	1	7	
CURETICUS	CAL		1	p. to the Curetes
CURETICUS	SIL	1	2	
CURETIS adj.	OV			p. to the Curetes
CŪRIA 1.62	CAL		1	Roman senate-house
CURIA 4.1.11, 4.4.13	PROP	1	2	
CURIATIUS	MAR			leg. Roman hero
-CURICTES 4.406	LUC			islanders in the Adriatic
CURII = Curiatii	JUV		1	leg. Alban gens
CURII	LUC		1	
CURII	MAR	1	3	
CURIO	LUC		1	C. Scribonius Curio, an ex-Pompey man
CURIO	SIL	1	2	a leader of the Picentians
CURIUS _Cul_. 367	AV		1	C. Dentatus, leg. general
CURIUS	FPLR		1	(a dice-player)
CURIUS	HOR		1	the general
CURIUS	JUV		1	" "
CURIUS as pl.	MAN		1	the family
CURIUS	MAR		1	the general
CURIUS	PROP		1	= Curiatius
CURIUS	SIL	1	8	the general
- CURTILLUS S. 2.8.52	HOR			a contemporary
CURTIUS _Cul_.	AV		1	M. Curtius, leg. Roman figure
CURTIUS	JUV		1	a lawyer
CURTIUS	PROP	1	3	M. Curtius
CURTIUS* (lacus)	OV			a stagnant lake in the Roman Forum
-CURVII (fratres)	MAR			(Lucanus & Tullus) (5.28.3)
-CYAMUS _Truc_. 583	PL			name of a slave
CYANE	JUV		1	contemporary entertainer
CYANE	OV		1	fountain-nymph of Syracuse
CYANE	SIL	1	3	" "
CYANEAE	JUV		1	= Symplegades (islands)
CYANEAE	OV		1	
CYANEAE	S	1	3	
CYANEE	OV			a nymph, m. of Caunus
CYANEUS	AV		1	p. to Cyaneae
CYANEUS	LUC		1	
CYANEUS	MAR		1	
CYANEUS	S		1	
CYANEUS	VAL	1	5	
CYBEBA cf. Cybele	SEN			fertility goddess (= Mater Magna)
CYBEBE	FPLR		1	
CYBEBE	LUC		1	
CYBEBE	PH		1	
CYBEBE	S		1	
CYBEBE	V	1	5	
CYBELE	AV		1	fertility goddess
CYBELE	CAT		1	(mt. in Phrygia)
CYBELE	COL		1	goddess
CYBELE	JUV		1	
CYBELE	MAR		1	
CYBELE	OV		2	(+ mt.)
CYBELE	S		1	
CYBELE	SEN		1	

CYBELE	SIL	1	goddess
CYBELE	VAL	1 11	
CYBELEIUS	OV	1	p. to Cybele
CYBELEIUS	S	1 2	
CYBELUS m.	V		mt. in Phrygia
CYCLADES pl.	AV	1	islands in the Aegean
CYCLADES	CAT	1	
CYCLADES	HOR	1	
CYCLADES	MAN	1	
CYCLADES	OV	1	
CYCLADES	S	1	
CYCLADES	V	1 7	
CYCLAS sg.	JUV	1	one of the Cyclades
CYCLAS	SEN	1	
CYCLAS	SIL	1 3	
CYCLOPES pl.	AET	1	myth. tribe of giants
CYCLOPES	JUV	1	
CYCLOPES	OV	1	
CYCLOPES	S	1	
CYCLOPES	VAL	1 5	
CYCLOPEUS	V		p. to the Cyclops (sg. or pl.)
CYCLOPIUS	SEN	1	p. to the Cyclops
CYCLOPIUS	SIL	1 2	
CYCLOPS	AV	1	a one-eyed giant, esp. Polyphemus
CYCLOPS	FPLA	1	
CYCLOPS	FPLB	1	
CYCLOPS	HOR	1	
CYCLOPS	LUC	1	
CYCLOPS	LUCIL	1	
CYCLOPS	MAR	1	
CYCLOPS	OV	1	
CYCLOPS	SEN	1	
CYCLOPS	SIL	1	
CYCLOPS	V	1	
CYCLOPS	VAL	1 12	
CYCNEIUS	OV		p. to Cycnus
CYCNUS	JUV	1	an Ethiopian (slave?)
CYCNUS	MAN	1	constellation
CYCNUS	SEN	1 3	son of Neptune
- CYDAS 10.83.8	MAR		a contemporary
- CYDIMUS T. 5.227	S		a Lemnian
CYDIPPE	OV	1	the mistress of Acontius
CYDIPPE	V	1 2	a Nereid
CYDNUS	OV	1	a river of Cilicia
CYDNUS 3.338, 14.434	SIL	2	an Iberian leader; a Punic soldier
CYDNUS	TIB	1 4	
CYDON	S	1	a Cydonian (of Crete)
CYDON	SEN	1	
CYDON	SIL	1	
CYDON	V	2 5	(+ son of Phorcus)
CYDONEA	MAR		a town of Crete
CYDONES pl.	LUC	1	the Cydonians
CYDONES	S	1 2	
CYDONEUS	OV	1	Cydonian, Cretan
CYDONEUS	S	1	
CYDONEUS	SIL	1 3	
CYDONIA = -ea, pl.	OV		a fruit, the quince

CYDONIUM	PROP		quince
CYDONIUS	HOR	1	Cydonian, Cretan
CYDONIUS	V	1 2	
-CYDRO or Cydno	OV		friend of Sappho (H.15.17)
-CYDRUS 3.192	VAL		a Cyzican
-CYGNEIS patr.	HL		ep. of Helen
CYGNUS cf. Cycnus	GER	1	a constellation
CYGNUS	OV	2	son of Sthenelus; son of Neptune
CYGNUS Men. 854	PL	1	father of Tithonus (by poetic error)
CYGNUS	S	1	name of a horse
CYGNUS	V	1 6	father of Cupavo
-CYLINDRUS Men. 218	PL		a cook
CYLLAROS	OV	1	a Centaur
CYLLAROS	SEN	1	horse of Castor
CYLLAROS	VAL	1 3	horse of Pollux
CYLLARUS	MAR	1	horse of Castor
CYLLARUS	S	1	" "
CYLLARUS	V	1 3	horse of Pollux
CYLLENE	COL	1	mt. in Arcadia
CYLLENE	GER	1	
CYLLENE	MAR	1	
CYLLENE	OV	1	
CYLLENE	PRIAP	1	
CYLLENE	S	1	
CYLLENE	SIL	1	
CYLLENE	V	1 8	
CYLLENEUS adj.	CAT	1	p. to Cyllene
CYLLENEUS	HOR	1	
CYLLENEUS	OV	1 3	
CYLLENIS adj.	LUC	1	p. to Cyllene (or to Mercury)
CYLLENIS	OV	1	
CYLLENIS	SIL	1 3	
CYLLENIUS 1.662	LUC	1	ep. of Mercury
CYLLENIUS	MAN	2	Mercury
CYLLENIUS	OV	1	
CYLLENIUS T. 7.34	S	1	
CYLLENIUS	SIL	1	
CYLLENIUS	V	1 7	
CYLLENIUS* Cir. 102	AV	1	p. to Cyllene or to Mercury
CYLLENIUS*	CIC	1	
CYLLENIUS*	GER	1	
CYLLENIUS*	MAN	1	
CYLLENIUS*	OV	1	
CYLLENIUS*	PET	1	
CYLLENIUS*	S	1	
CYLLENIUS*	SIL	1	
CYLLENIUS*	V	1	
CYLLENIUS*	VAL	1 10	
CYMAEUS	SIL	1	p. to Cyme (in Aeolis)
CYMAEUS	V	1	
CYMAEUS	VAL	1 3	
CYME cf. Cumae	S	1	town of Aeolis
CYME	SIL	1 2	
-CYMELUS M. 12.454	OV		a Lapith
CYMODOCE	S	1	a Nereid
CYMODOCE	SIL	1	
CYMODOCE	V	1 3	

CYMODOCĒA		V		a Nereid
CYMOTHOE		PROP	1	a nymph
CYMOTHOE		SIL	1	
CYMOTHOE		V	1	
CYMOTHOE		VAL	1 4	
CYNAPSES	P. 4.10.49	OV		a river (in Thrace?)
CYNICI		JUV		the Cynic philosophers
CYNICUS		HOR	1	a Cynic
CYNICUS	P. 1.3.67	OV	1 2	
CYNICUS*	Lab. 37	COM	1	p. to Cynic (philosophy)
CYNICUS*		PET	1 2	
CYNOSURA		CIC	1	a constellation (Little Bear)
CYNOSURA		GER	1	
CYNOSURA		LUC	1	
CYNOSURA		MAN	1	
CYNOSURA	F. 3.107	OV	1	
CYNOSURA		S	1	(town of Arcadia)
CYNOSURA		SEN	1	constell.
CYNOSURA		SIL	1	
CYNOSURA		VAL	1 9	
CYNOSURIS	adj.	GER	1	p. to Little Bear
CYNOSURIS		OV	1 2	
CYNTHIA		FPLB	1	ep. of Diana (Luna)
CYNTHIA		HOR	1	
CYNTHIA		JUV	1	
CYNTHIA		LUC	1	
CYNTHIA		MAR	1	(pseudonym of PROP's friend)
CYNTHIA		OV	2	Diana; PROP's friend
CYNTHIA		PET	1	Luna
CYNTHIA		PROP	1	mistress of PROP (= Hostia)
CYNTHIA		S	1	Luna
CYNTHIA		SEN	1	Diana
CYNTHIA		SIL	1	Diana
CYNTHIA		VAL	1 13	Luna
CYNTHIUS		AV	1	ep. of Apollo
CYNTHIUS		HOR	1	
CYNTHIUS		MLP	1	
CYNTHIUS		OV	1	
CYNTHIUS		PROP	1	
CYNTHIUS		V	1 6	
CYNTHIUS*		PRIAP	1	p. to Cynthos or to Apollo
CYNTHIUS*	3.4.50	TIB	1 2	
CYNTHOS		AET		mt. on Delos (with shrine to Apollo)
CYNTHUS		OV	1	
CYNTHUS		S	1	
CYNTHUS		SIL	1	
CYNTHUS		V	1 4	
CYPARISSOS	T. 7.344	S		a place (?)
CYPARISSUS		MAR	1	myth. youth
CYPARISSUS		OV	1 2	" "
CYPASSIS	fem. sg.	OV		Ovid's mistress
-CYPERUS	8.16	MAR		fictional man
CYPRIA		TIB		epithet of Venus
CYPRIS	(Florus)	MLP		Venus
CYPRIUS		ENN	1	p. to Cyprus
CYPRIUS		HOR	1	
CYPRIUS		OV	2	

CYPRIUS		SEN	1 5	p. to Cyprus
CYPROS cf. -us		COL	1	the island in the eastern Mediterranean
CYPROS		LUC	1	
CYPROS		MAN	1	
CYPROS		MAR	1	
CYPROS		SIL	1 5	
CYPRUS		HOR	1	
CYPRUS		OV	1	
CYPRUS		PL	1	
CYPRUS		TER	1	
CYPRUS		V	1 5	
CYPSELIDES (Ciris)		AV		= Periander
CYRENAE cf. Cyrene		AV	1	town of Libya
CYRENAE		CAT	1	
CYRENAE		LUC	1	
CYRENAE		PL	1 4	
CYRENAEUS		LUC	1	p. to Cyrene (-ae)
CYRENAEUS		PROP	1	
CYRENAEUS		SIL	1 3	
CYRENE cf. Cyrenae		MAN	1	town of Libya
CYRENE		S	1	a fountain in Thessaly
CYRENE		SIL	2	town; nymph
CYRENE		V	1 5	nymph
CYRENENSIS		PL		p. to Cyrene (the town)
-CYRIS 6.80		VAL		a Scythian
CYRNEUS		V		p. to Cyrnus (Corsica)
CYRNUS		SIL	1	a Spaniard
CYRNUS		VAL	1 2	a Colchian
CYRRHA cf. Cirrha		GR		town in Phocis
-CYRTAS 6.39.17		MAR		fictional man
CYRUS		GR	1	Persian king
CYRUS		HOR	2	(+ a youth)
CYRUS		LUC	1	
CYRUS 3.7.141		TIB	1 5	
CYTAEI		VAL		people of Colchis
-CYTAEINE 1.1.24		PROP		Medea
CYTAEIS		PROP		Medea
CYTAEUS adj.		VAL		Colchian
CYTHERA n.pl.		LUC	1	island in the Aegean
CYTHERA		OV	1	
CYTHERA		V	1	
CYTHERA		VAL	1 4	
CYTHEREA fem. sg.		AV	1	ep. of Venus
CYTHEREA		GER	1	(planet Venus)
CYTHEREA		HL	1	Venus
CYTHEREA		HOR	1	
CYTHEREA		MAN	1	
CYTHEREA		MAR	1	
CYTHEREA		OV	1	
CYTHEREA		PROP	1	
CYTHEREA		S	1	
CYTHEREA		SIL	1	
CYTHEREA		TIB	1	
CYTHEREA		V	1	
CYTHEREA		VAL	1 13	
CYTHEREIA		OV		Venus
CYTHEREIAS adj.		OV		p. to Venus

CYTHEREIS		MAN	1	Venus
CYTHEREIS		OV	1 2	
CYTHEREIUS		GER	1	p. to Venus
CYTHEREIUS		HL	1	
CYTHEREIUS		MAR	1	
CYTHEREIUS		OV	1	
CYTHEREIUS		S	1	
CYTHEREIUS		SIL	1 6	
CYTHERĒUS		HOR		p. to Venus
CYTHERIACUS		FPLR	1	p. to Cythera
CYTHERIACUS		MAR	1	
CYTHERIACUS		OV	1 3	
CYTHNOS	fem.	OV		island in the Cyclades
CYTHNUS		AV		
CYTISORUS		VAL		son of Phrixus
CYTORIACUS	adj.	OV		p. to Cytorus
CYTORIUS	adj.	AV	1	p. to Cytorus
CYTORIUS		CAT	1 2	
CYTOROS		V	1	mt. & town in Paphlagonia
CYTOROS		VAL	1 2	
CYTORUS		CAT		
CYZICOS	fem.	OV	1	town in Mysia (Propontis)
CYZICOS		PRIAP	1 2	
CYZICUS		PROP	1	
CYZICUS	m.	SIL	1	king of the Dolopes
CYZICUS		VAL	1 3	
DACI		HOR	1	a Balkan tribe (of modern Rumania)
DACI		LUC	1	
DACI		MAR	1	
DACI		SIL	1 4	
DACICUS		JUV		a coin of Domitian
DACUS		HOR	1	a Dacian
DACUS		LUC	1	
DACUS		MAR	1	
DACUS		S	1	
DACUS		SIL	1	
DACUS		V	1 6	
DACUS*		JUV	1	p. to the Dacians or Dacia
DACUS*		MAR	1	
DACUS*		S	1 3	
DAEDALĒUS		HOR	1	p. to Daedalus
DAEDALEUS		SEN	1	
DAEDALEUS		SIL	1 3	
DAEDALION		OV		brother of Ceyx
− DAEDALIS	Rud. 1164	PL		= Attica
− DAEDALĪUS	adj.	COL	1	p. to Daedalus
DAEDALIUS	2.14.8	PROP	1 2	
DAEDALOS		MAR		myth. builder & inventor
DAEDALUS		HOR	1	
DAEDALUS		JUV	1	
DAEDALUS		OV	1	
DAEDALUS		SEN	1	
DAEDALUS		SIL	1	
DAEDALUS		V	1	
DAEDALUS		VAL	1 7	
DAEMONES	m.sg.	PL		a senex
− DAEMONIE	2.897	MAN		sign of the Zodiac (5th place)

– DAEMONIUM 2.938	MAN			sign of the Zodiac (4th place)
DAHAE	LUC		1	a Scythian tribe
DAHAE	SEN		1	
DAHAE	SIL		1	
DAHAE	V		1	
DAHAE	VAL	1	5	
–DALMATA m.sg.	MAR			a Dalmatian (10.78.8)
DALMATIA	OV		1	country on the coast of Illyria
DALMATIA	S	1	2	
DALMATICUS cf. Del-	LUC		1	p. to Dalmatia
DALMATICUS	S	1	2	
DALMATUS* (montes)	S			p. to Dalmatia
DAMA m.	HOR		1	name of a slave
DAMA m.	MAR	1	2	fictional
–DAMACRĪNUS adj.	VAR			(unknown meaning)
DAMALIS	HOR			a maiden
DAMASCENA n.pl.	MAR			prunes (from Damascus)
⎧DAMASCOS	LUC			town of Syria
⎨DAMASCUS	COL		1	
⎩DAMASCUS	S	1	2	
DAMASICHTHON	OV			son of Amphion and Niobe
DAMASIPPUS	HOR		1	a contemporary
DAMASIPPUS	JUV	1	2	an actor
–DAMASUS T.8.494	S			an Argive
DAMOETAS m.sg.	FPLB		1	a shepherd
DAMOETAS	V	1	2	
DAMON	V			a goat-herd
DANAË	AET		1	Argive princess & m. of Perseus
DANAE	HOR		1	
DANAE	LUC		1	
DANAE	MAR		1	
DANAE	OV		1	
DANAE	PET		1	
DANAE	PROP		1	
DANAE	S		1	
DANAE	SEN		1	
DANAE	TER		1	
DANAE	V	1	11	
DANAEIUS adj.	OV		1	p. to Danae (i.e. Perseus)
DANAEIUS	S	1	2	
DANAI	FPLB		1	the Greeks (esp. of the Trojan era)
DANAI	HL		1	
DANAI	LUCR		1	
DANAI	MAN		1	
DANAI	OV		1	
DANAI	PET		1	
DANAI	PROP		1	
DANAI	S		1	
DANAI	SEN		1	
DANAI	SIL		1	
DANAI	TR		1	
DANAI	V		1	
DANAI	VAL	1	13	
DANAIDAE m.pl.	SEN			the Greeks
DANAIDES fem.pl.	PH			daughters of Danaus
DANAIS sg. fem.	SEN			a d. of Danaus
DANAUS	FPLB		1	leg. king of Argos

DANAUS	HOR		1	leg. king of Argus
DANAUS	OV		1	
DANAUS	PROP		1	
DANAUS	S		1	
DANAUS	TIB	1	6	
DANAUS*	OV		1	p. to Danaus, i.e. Greek
DANAUS*	PROP		1	
DANAUS*	S		1	
DANAUS*	V	1	4	
⎰DANUBIUS	OV		1	the river Danube
⎱DANUBIUS	VAL	1	2	
⎰DANUVIUS	HOR		1	
⎱DANUVIUS	SEN	1	2	
DAPHNE	MAR		1	d. of the river-god Peneus
DAPHNE	OV		1	
DAPHNE	PET		1	
DAPHNE	S	1	4	
-DAPHNEUS T. 8.453	S			mythical hero
DAPHNIS	CAL		1	a shepherd
DAPHNIS	MAR		1	(friend of MAR)
DAPHNIS	OV		1	shepherd
DAPHNIS	PROP		1	shepherd
DAPHNIS	SIL		2	two shepherds
DAPHNIS	V	1	7	shepherd
-DARAPS 6.66	VAL			a Scythian
DARDANIA Cul. 323	AV		1	(country of Dardanus, i.e.) Troy
DARDANIA	OV		1	town on Hellespont
DARDANIA	PH		1	Troy
DARDANIA	SIL		1	"
DARDANIA	V	1	5	"
-DARDANICUS or -ius	COL			p. to Dardanus, i.e. magic (10.358)
DARDANIDES fem. pl.	HL		1	Trojan women
DARDANIDES	OV		1	
DARDANIDES	SIL		1	
DARDANIDES m. sg.	V	1	4	= Aeneas (pl.: Trojans)
DARDANII	SIL			Trojans
DARDANIS adj.	MAR		1	Trojan
DARDANIS	OV		1	
DARDANIS	SEN		1	
DARDANIS	V	1	4	(= Creusa)
DARDANIUS Att.523	TR		1	a Trojan
DARDANIUS A. 12.14	V	1	2	
DARDANIUS*	CAT		1	Trojan
DARDANIUS*	ENN		1	
DARDANIUS*	HL		1	
DARDANIUS*	LUC		1	
DARDANIUS*	MAR		1	
DARDANIUS*	OV		1	
DARDANIUS*	PROP		1	
DARDANIUS*	S		1	
DARDANIUS*	SIL		1	
DARDANIUS*	V		1	
DARDANIUS*	VAL	1	11	
DARDANUS	OV		1	ancestor of the Trojans
DARDANUS	SEN		1	
DARDANUS	SIL		2	(+ Aeneas)
DARDANUS	TR		1	

DARDANUS	V	1	6	ancestor of the Trojans
DARDANUS*	HL		1	Dardanian, Trojan
DARDANUS*	HOR		1	
DARDANUS*	OV		1	
DARDANUS*	PROP		1	
DARDANUS*	S		1	
DARDANUS*	SEN		1	
DARDANUS*	SIL		1	
DARDANUS*	V	1	8	
DARES m.sg.	HL		1	legendary boxer
DARES	V	1	2	
⎰DARĒUS	OV	2	2	two Persian kings
⎱DARĪUS	PL			king of Persia
‑DASIUS 2.52, 6.70.6	MAR		2	two contemporaries
DASIUS 13.32	SIL	1	3	an Arpine man
DATIS m.	VAL			a Scythian
DAUCIUS adj.	V			p. to Daucus (a Rutulian)
DAULIADES fem.pl.	AV			Procne & Philomela
DAULIAS fem. sg.	CAT			Procne
DAULIAS*	OV		1	p. to Daulis
DAULIAS*	SEN	1	2	
DAULIS fem.	OV		1	town of Phocis
DAULIS	S		1	
DAULIS	SEN	1	3	
DAUNIACUS	SIL			p. to Daunus
DAUNIAS ‑ad‑, fem.	HOR			Apulia, region of S. Italy
DAUNIUS adj.	HOR		1	Apulian
DAUNIUS	OV		1	
DAUNIUS	SIL		1	
DAUNIUS	V	1	4	
DAUNUS	HOR		1	leg. king of Apulia
DAUNUS	OV		1	
DAUNUS	S		1	
DAUNUS	SIL		2	
DAUNUS	V	1	6	
⎧DAVOS	TER			a slave (type)
⎪DAVUS	COM		1	
⎨DAVUS	HOR		2	
⎪DAVUS	PER		1	
⎩DAVUS	PL	1	5	
‑DEA 2.916	MAN			sign of the Zodiac (third place)
DECEMBER N & adj.	CAL		1	month name
DECEMBER	HOR		1	(also: the whole past year)
DECEMBER	JUV		1	
DECEMBER	OV		1	
DECEMBER	S	1	5	
‑DECEO fem., Men. 736	PL			a maid
DECI = Decii	MAN			the legendary Roman family
DECIANUS	MAR			a Stoic philosopher from Emerita
DECII cf. Deci	AV		1	father & son (legendary Romans)
DECII	JUV		1	
DECII	S		1	
DECII	SIL		1	
DECII	V	1	5	
DECIMUS	MAR			a contemporary
DECIUS	HOR		1	a legendary Roman
DECIUS	LUC		1	

DECIUS	LUCIL		1	a legendary Roman
DECIUS	PROP		1	
DECIUS	SIL	1	5	
DECOR m., T. 2.287	S		1	"Charm"
DECOR 3.8.8	TIB	1	2	"Glory"
DECUS n., 15.99	SIL			"
-DEGIS 5.3	MAR			a Dacian ambassador
DEIANIRA	OV		1	d. of Oeneus
DEIANIRA	SEN	1	2	
DEIDAMIA	OV		1	d. of Lycomedes (of Scyros)
DEIDAMIA	PROP		1	
DEIDAMIA	S	1	3	
-DEILEON -nt-, 5.114	VAL			an Argonaut & follower of Hercules
-DEILOCHUS T. 2.608	S			a Theban
DEIONIDES patr.	OV			Miletus, s. of Deione & Apollo
DEIOPEA	V			a nymph, attendant on Juno
DEIOTARUS	LUC			king of Armenia (at time of Caesar)
DEIPHOBE	V			d. of Glaucus & priestess of Apollo
DEIPHOBUS	HL		1	son of Priam & husband of Helen
DEIPHOBUS	HOR		1	
DEIPHOBUS	MAR		1	(generic type of adulterer)
DEIPHOBUS	OV		1	
DEIPHOBUS	PROP		1	
DEIPHOBUS	SEN		1	
DEIPHOBUS	V	1	7	
-DEIPYLE T. passim	S			wife of Tydeus
DELIA em., Cat. 1.1	AV		1	ep. of Diana, moon goddess
DELIA	MAN		1	
DELIA	OV		2	(+ friend of Tibullus)
DELIA	PRIAP		1	
DELIA	S		1	
DELIA	TIB		2	(+ pseudonym of Plania)
DELIA B. 3.67, 7.29	V	1	9	(also a shepherdess)
DELIACUS adj.	PET			p. to Delos
DELIUS N	COL		1	ep. of Apollo
DELIUS	OV		1	
DELIUS	PET		1	
DELIUS	S		1	
DELIUS	TIB		1	
DELIUS	VAL	1	6	
DELIUS*	AV		1	p. to Delos, i.e. to Apollo or Diana
DELIUS*	CAT		1	
DELIUS*	FPLA		1	
DELIUS*	HOR		1	
DELIUS*	OV		1	
DELIUS*	PH		1	
DELIUS*	S		1	
DELIUS* (vates)	SIL		1	
DELIUS*	V		1	
DELIUS*	VAL	1	10	
-DELLIUS or Gellius	HOR			cont. Roman (C. 2.3.4)
DELMATICUS cf. Dal-	HOR			Dalmatian
DELOS fem., cf. Delus	AET		1	island in the Cyclades
DELOS	AV		1	
DELOS	HOR		1	
DELOS	MAN		1	
DELOS	MAR		1	

DELOS	OV		1	island in the Cyclades
DELOS	PROP		1	
DELOS	S		1	
DELOS	SEN		1	
DELOS	TIB		1	
DELOS	V	1	11	
DELPHI m.pl.	CAT		1	shrine in Phocis
DELPHI	HOR		1	
DELPHI	JUV		1	
DELPHI	OV		1	
DELPHI	PH		1	
DELPHI	PL		1	
DELPHI	PRIAP		1	
DELPHI	S		1	
DELPHI	SEN		1	
DELPHI	TR	1	10	
DELPHICA (sc. mensa)	MAR			a dressing table
DELPHICĒ adv.	VAR			'in the fashion of the oracle'
DELPHICUS	HL		1	ep. of Apollo
DELPHICUS	OV		1	
DELPHICUS	PET	1	3	
DELPHICUS*	COL		1	p. to Delphi (or to Apollo)
DELPHICUS*	ENN		1	
DELPHICUS*	HOR		1	
DELPHICUS*	LUC		1	
DELPHICUS*	LUCR		1	
DELPHICUS*	OV		1	
DELPHICUS*	PET		1	
DELPHICUS*	SEN		1	
DELPHICUS*	TIB	1	9	
DELPHĪN	GER		1	constellation "Dolphin"
DELPHIN	OV	1	2	
DELPHINUS	CIC		1	
DELPHINUS	GER		1	
DELPHINUS	MAN	1	3	
DELPHIS	MAR			the Pythian priestess at Delphi
DELPHIS*	TR			p. to Delphi
-DELPHIUM Most. 343	PL			a meretrix
DELTOTON	CIC		1	constellation "Triangle"
DELTOTON	GER		1	
DELTOTON	MAN	1	3	
DELUS = Delos	LUC		1	island in the Cyclades
DELUS	LUCIL		1	
DELUS	SIL	1	3	
-DEMAENETUS	LUCIL		1	fictional person
DEMAENETUS Asin.104	PL	1	2	a senex
DEMARCHUS	PL			an Aetolian
DEMEA m.	COM		1	a character in comedy
DEMEA	TER	1	2	a senex
DEMETRIUS	HOR		2	a slave; a musician
DEMETRIUS	JUV		1	comic actor
DEMETRIUS	MAR		1	MAR's secretary
DEMETRIUS 5.1.1	PH		1	Demetrius of Phaleron, the philosopher
DEMETRIUS Bac.912, frag	PL	1	6	" (?)
DEMIPHO	PL		1	a senex
DEMIPHO	TER	1	2	a young man
-DEMOCOON	HL			a son of Priam

DEMOCRITUS	COM		1	Greek philosopher (of Abdera)
DEMOCRITUS	HOR		1	
DEMOCRITUS ⌀	JUV		1	
DEMOCRITUS	LUCR		1	
DEMOCRITUS	MAR	1	5	
DEMODOCUS	FPLR		1	Phaeacian bard
DEMODOCUS	OV		1	" "
DEMODOCUS	V	1	3	Arcadian comp. of Aeneas
DEMOLEON	OV			a Centaur
DEMOLEOS	V			a Greek warrior at Troy
_DEMONASSA	TR			d. of Eriphyle
DEMOPHILUS	PL			Greek comic poet
DEMOPHOON Cul. 131	AV		1	son of Theseus
DEMOPHOON	OV		1	
DEMOPHOON	PROP		2	(+ pseud. of a friend)
DEMOPHOON	V	1	5	comp. of Aeneas
DEMOSTHENES	JUV		1	the Greek orator
DEMOSTHENES	PET		1	
DEMOSTHENES	PL		1	
DEMOSTHENES	PROP	1	4	
_DENTO 5.44	MAR			fictional
DEOIS fem., metron.	OV			Proserpina
DEOIUS adj.	OV			sacred to Deo (= Demeter)
_DERCEITA em., 1.49.17	MAR			river of Spain
_DERCENNUS A. 11.850	V			legendary Latin king
DERCETIS	OV			Syrian goddess
_DERCYLON	GR			Arcadian hunter
DEUCALION	GER		1	s. of Prometheus & h. of Pyrrha
DEUCALION	JUV		1	
DEUCALION	LUCIL		1	
DEUCALION	MAN		1	
DEUCALION	MAR		1	
DEUCALION	OV		1	
DEUCALION	PROP		1	
DEUCALION	SEN		1	
DEUCALION	V		1	
DEUCALION	VAL	1	10	(an Argonaut)
DEUCALIONEUS	COL		1	p. to Deucalion
DEUCALIONEUS	LUC		1	
DEUCALIONEUS	OV	1	3	
DEUS	MAN			position in the Zodiac
DEXAMENUS Ibis 462	OV			a Centaur
_DEXIONE Ibis 468	OV			d. of Aesculapius
_DEXTER 7.27.3	MAR			a friend of MAR
DIA	CAT		1	island (later called Naxos)
DIA	OV	1	2	"
_DIABOLUS Asin. 634	PL			a young man
_DIADUMENOS 3.65	MAR			a "puer"
DIALIS (also N?)	OV			p. to Juppiter
DIANA	AV		1	the goddess (cf. Luna)
DIANA	CAT		1	
DIANA	CIC		1	
DIANA	COM		1	
DIANA	ENN		1	
DIANA	GR		1	
DIANA	HOR		1	
DIANA	JUV		1	

DIANA	LUC	1	
DIANA	LUCIL	1	
DIANA	MAN	1	
DIANA	MAR	1	
DIANA	OV	1	
DIANA	PL	1	
DIANA	PRIAP	1	
DIANA	PROP	1	
DIANA	S	1	
DIANA	SEN	1	
DIANA	SIL	1	
DIANA	TER	1	
DIANA	TIB	1	
DIANA	V	1	
DIANA	VAL	1	
DIANA	VAR	1 24	
DIANIUS adj.	GR	1	p. to Diana
DIANIUS	OV	1 2	
DIAPONTIUS	PL		fict. (pun on transmarinus)
-DIAULUS 1.30.47	MAR		fictional doctor
DICARCHĒUS	S		a resident of Puteoli
DICARCHĒUS*	S	1	p. to Dicarchus
DICARCHEUS*	SIL	1 2	
DICARCHIS	PET		= Puteoli
-DICARCHITAE	LUCIL		the people of Puteoli
DICARCHUS	S		= Puteoli (t. near Naples)
-DICEA dub., Mil. 436	PL		(false reading for Glycera)
DICTAEUS T. 3.481	S		ep. of Juppiter
DICTAEUS*	AV	1	p. to mt. Dicte (i.e. Cretan)
DICTAEUS*	CAL	1	
DICTAEUS*	GER	1	
DICTAEUS*	LUC	1	
DICTAEUS*	LUCR	1	
DICTAEUS*	MAR	1	
DICTAEUS*	OV	1	
DICTAEUS*	S	1	
DICTAEUS*	SEN	1	
DICTAEUS*	SIL	1	
DICTAEUS*	V	1 11	
DICTYNA Cir. 304	AV		= Britomartis (nymph)
DICTYNNA	FPLA	1	Diana
DICTYNNA	FPLB	1	title of Poem by Val. Cato
DICTYNNA	OV	1	Diana
DICTYNNA	S	1	
DICTYNNA	SEN	1	
DICTYNNA	SIL	1	
DICTYNNA	TIB	1 7	
DICTYS	OV	2	a sailor; a Centaur
DICTYS	S	1 3	legendary fisherman
DIDIUS	OV		T. Didius, a consul
DIDO	ENN	1	queen of Carthage (cf. Elissa)
DIDO	MAR	1	
DIDO	OV	1	
DIDO	PRIAP	1	
DIDO	SIL	1	
DIDO	V	1 6	
DIDYMAEUS adj.	S		p. to Didyma (town in Ionia)

DIDYMAON	V		1	legendary artisan
DIDYMAON	VAL	1	2	a hero
DIDYME	OV			island off Lycia
-DIDYMUS	MAR	2	2	two fictional men
DIDYMUS* 12.43.3	MAR			p. to a Didymus (slave-dealer)
DIES Bac. 255	PL		1	"Day" personified
DIES T. 1.97	S	1	2	
DIESPITER (archaic)	HOR		1	Juppiter
DIESPITER	PL	1	2	"
DIGENTIA	HOR			Sabine river
DINDYMA n.pl.	COL		1	mt. in Mysia (also -on, -us)
DINDYMA	OV		1	
DINDYMA	SIL		1	
DINDYMA	V		1	
DINDYMA	VAL	1	5	
DINDYMENE	CAT		1	the goddess Cybele
DINDYMENE	HOR		1	
DINDYMENE	MAR	1	3	
DINDYMON = -a	S			mt. in Mysia
DINDYMUS = -a	CAT		1	mt. in Mysia
DINDYMUS	MAR		2	two contemporaries
DINDYMUS	OV		1	mt.
DINDYMUS	PROP	1	5	mt.
-DINIA m., Asin. 866	PL			a senex
-DINIARCHUS Truc. 122	PL			a young man
DINOMACHE	PER			mother of Alcibiades
DIODORUS	MAR		2	two contemporaries
DIODORUS	PL	1	3	a dancer
DIOMEDEAE (fabulae)	JUV			title of an epic poem
DIOMEDES	AV		1	s. of Tydeus & hero before Troy
DIOMEDES	COM		1	
DIOMEDES	FPLA		1	
DIOMEDES	HL		1	
DIOMEDES	HOR		1	
DIOMEDES	LUCR		1	
DIOMEDES	OV		1	
DIOMEDES	S		2	(+ a Thracian hero)
DIOMEDES	SEN		1	
DIOMEDES	SIL		1	
DIOMEDES	V	1	12	
DIOMEDEUS	MAR		1	p. to Diomedes
DIOMEDEUS	OV		1	
DIOMEDEUS	S	1	3	
DIONAEUS	COL		1	p. to Dione (Venus)
DIONAEUS	HOR		1	
DIONAEUS	S		1	
DIONAEUS	V	1	4	
DIONE	CAT		1	ep. of Venus
DIONE	OV		1	
DIONE	PFT		1	
DIONE	S		1	
DIONE	SIL		1	
DIONE	VAL	1	6	
DIONYSIA n.pl.	PL		1	festival of Dionysus
DIONYSIA	TER		1	
DIONYSIA	VAR	1	3	
DIONYSIUS N	HOR			name of a slave

DIONYSUS	PL		1	Bacchus, god of wine
DIONYSUS	TR	1	2	
-DIORES m. sg.	HL		1	a Trojan
DIORES A. 5.297	V	1	2	"
-DIOXIPPUS A. 11.574	V			a Trojan
DIPHILUS	JUV		1	(unknown)
DIPHILUS	PL		1	the Gk. comic poet
DIPHILUS	TER	1	3	
DIPSAS Am.1.8.2, fem.	OV		1	an old woman
DIPSAS m.	VAL	1	2	a Colchian
-DIPSUS -nt-, (v.l.)	LUC			river in Cilicia (8.255)
DIRAE	S		1	the Furies
DIRAE also sg.	V		1	
DIRAE	VAL	1	3	
DIRCA = Dirce	PL			wife of Lycus, killed by bull (Ps. 199)
DIRCAEUS	HOR		1	p. to Dirce (hence Theban, Boeotian)
DIRCAEUS	LUC		1	
DIRCAEUS	PROP		1	
DIRCAEUS	S		1	
DIRCAEUS	SEN		1	
DIRCAEUS	TR		1	
DIRCAEUS	V	1	7	
DIRCE	LUC		1	a fountain at Thebes
DIRCE	OV		1	
DIRCE cf. Dirca	PROP		1	(wife of Lycus; became fountain)
DIRCE	S		1	fountain
DIRCE	SEN	1	5	"
-DIRCETIS T. 7.298	S			a nymph
DIS cf. Ditis	AET		1	god of the Underworld
DIS	AV		1	
DIS	COL		1	
DIS	GR		1	
DIS	HL		1	
DIS	LUC		1	
DIS	MAN		1	
DIS	MAR		1	
DIS	MLP		1	
DIS	OV		1	
DIS	PROP		1	
DIS	S		1	
DIS	SEN		1	(=Orcus, the Underworld)
DIS	SIL		1	
DIS	TIB		1	
DIS	V		1	
DIS	VAL	1	17	
DISCORDIA n.pl.	CAL		1	"Discord, Strife"
DISCORDIA fem.	ENN		1	
DISCORDIA	HOR		1	
DISCORDIA	PET		1	
DISCORDIA	S		1	
DISCORDIA	SIL		1	
DISCORDIA	V		1	
DISCORDIA	VAL	1	8	
DISCUS	TER			name of a freedman
DITIS archaic form	GER		1	god of the Underworld (cf. Dis)
DITIS	PET	1	2	
-DITIS/JANUA 2.951	MAN			a place in the Zodiac

DIUS/FIDIUS	PL			ep. of Juppiter (Asin. 23)
DIVA/BONA	OV			= Bona Dea, goddess of women
-DOCILIS Epist.1.18.19	HOR			name of a gladiator
DODONA	LUC	1		town and sacred grove in Epirus
DODONA	OV	1		
DODONA	PROP	1		
DODONA	S	1		
DODONA	SEN	1		
DODONA	V	1	6	
DODONAEUS	OV	1		p. to Dodona
DODONAEUS	V	1	2	
DODONE cf. Dodona	AET	1		town & grove in Epirus
DODONE	PRIAP	1	2	
DODONIS adj.	OV	1		p. to Dodona
DODONIS	SIL	1		
DODONIS	VAL	1	3	
DOLABELLA	JUV			notorious plunderer of provinces
- DOLICHAON A. 10.696	V			a Trojan
- DOLIONIUS adj., 5.7	VAL			Cyzican
DOLON	AV	1		a Trojan
DOLON	HL	1		
DOLON	OV	1		
DOLON	V	1	4	
DOLOPEIUS	VAL			p. to the Dolopes
DOLOPES m.pl.	LUC	1		legendary tribe of Thessaly
DOLOPES	OV	1		
DOLOPES	S	1		
DOLOPES	SIL	1		
DOLOPES	V	1	5	
-DOLOPS HO 125	SEN			river in Thessaly (?)
DOLOR	S	1		"Anguish" personified
DOLOR	SIL	1	2	
DOLUS A. 4.5	PH	1		"Ruse, Treachery" personified
DOLUS	VAL	1	2	
-DOMATOR 3.7.116	TIB			Illyrian chieftain (?)
DOMITIANUS N	MAR			the emperor
DOMITIUS	JUV	1		father of Nero
DOMITIUS	LUC	1		L. Ahenobarbus Dom.
DOMITIUS	MAR	1		Apollinaris, a friend
DOMITIUS	SEN	1	4	father of Nero
DONAX	TER			name of a slave
-DONNUS P. 4.7.29	OV			a Celtic chieftain
DONUSA	V			an island in the Aegean
DONYSA	AV			
DORCEUS	OV	1		name of a dog
DORCEUS	S	1		an Arcadian
DORCEUS	VAL	1	3	a Cyzican
DORCIUM	COM	1		a woman slave
DORCIUM Phor. 152	TER	1	2	" "
-DORDALUS Pers. 482	PL			a leno
DORIAS m.	TER			name of a slave
DORICUS adj.	HL	1		Doric, Dorian
DORICUS	JUV	1		
DORICUS	MAN	1		
DORICUS	OV	1		
DORICUS	PROP	1		
DORICUS	S	1		

DORICUS	SEN		1	Doric, Dorian
DORICUS	TR		1	
DORICUS	V		1	
DORICUS	VAL	1	10	
DORIO m.	TER			a leno
-DORION 6.352	LUC		1	a place in Thessaly
DORION T. 4.182	S	1	2	town in Messenia
DORIPPA	PL			a female character
DORIS	GER		1	province in Greece
DORIS	JUV		1	a girl
DORIS	OV		1	d. of Ocean
DORIS	PROP		1	d. of Ocean
DORIS	S		1	the Sea
DORIS	V	1	6	the Sea
DORIS*	AV		1	Doric, Dorian
DORIS*	LUC		1	
DORIS*	SEN	1	3	
DORIUS	HOR			Doric, Dorian
-DOROZANTES 4.5.21	PROP			an Oriental tribe
-DORUS dub., 64.287	CAT		1	Doric, Dorian
DORUS dub., 3.9.44	PROP		1	Doric, Dorian
DORUS	TER	1	3	a comic character
DORYCLUS	V		1	husband of Beroe
DORYCLUS	VAL	1	2	a Lemnian
DORYLAS 2.96	CAL		1	shepherd
DORYLAS	OV		2	comp. of Phineus; a Centaur
DORYLAS	S		1	a Theban
DORYLAS	SIL	1	5	son of Mopsus
DOSSENNUS	COM		1	a stock character in comedy
DOSSENNUS	HOR	1	2	
DOTO -ūs, fem.	V		1	sea-nymph
DOTO	VAL	1	2	
-DRACES m.sg.	SIL			Punic soldier (15.467)
DRACO	CIC		1	a constellation
DRACO	FPLB		1	
DRACO	MAN	2	4	two constellations
DRANCAEUS	VAL			p. to the tribe Drancae (of Persia)
-DRANCES A. 11.122	V			a Latin messenger
DREPANE	SIL			town of Sicily
DREPANUM	S		1	town of Sicily
DREPANUM	V	1	2	
DRIMO (Drymo), fem.	V			sea-nymph
DROMAS -ad-, m.	OV			name of a dog
DROMO -on-, m.	PL		1	name of a slave
DROMO	TER	1	2	" "
DRUENTIA	SIL			river in S. Gaul
DRUSI Maec. 2.4	AV		1	a Roman family
DRUSI	LUC		1	
DRUSI	MAR		1	
DRUSI	V	1	4	
DRUSUS	HOR		1	Nero Claudius Drusus
DRUSUS	JUV		2	brother of Drusus; pl.
DRUSUS	OV		2	father of Germanicus; s. of Tiberius
DRUSUS	SEN	1	6	Livius Drusus
DRYADES fem.pl.	AV		1	class of wood-nymphs
DRYADES	CAL		1	
DRYADES	OV		1	

DRYADES	PET		1	wood-nymphs
DRYADES	PRIAP		1	
DRYADES	PROP		1	
DRYADES	S		1	
DRYADES	V	1	8	
DRYANTIADES m.sg.	OV			ep. of Lycurgus (of Thrace)
DRYAS -ad-, fem.sg.	MAR		1	a wood-nymph
DRYAS -nt-, m. sg.	OV		2	f. of Lycurgus; a Lapith
DRYAS -nt-, T. passim	S		1	a king of Tanagra
DRYAS fem., also pl.	SEN		1	wood-nymph(s)
DRYAS -nt-, Naevius	TR	1	6	f. of Lycurgus & k. of Thrace
-DRYASPES or Dyrapses	OV			a river in Scythia (P. 4.10.53)
DRYOPE	OV		1	a nymph
DRYOPE	S		1	a Theban woman
DRYOPE	V		1	nymph
DRYOPE	VAL	2	5	two different nymphs
DRYOPES m. pl.	LUC		1	tribe of Epirus
DRYOPES	S		1	
DRYOPES	V	1	3	
DRYOPS sg.	OV		1	an Epirote
DRYOPS	V	1	2	
-DUCARIUS 5.645	SIL			leader of the Boii
DUILIUS	SIL			Roman general, victor over Carthaginians
⎰DULICHIA fem.sg.	PROP			legendary island
⎱DULICHIUM	OV		1	
⎩DULICHIUM	V	1	2	
DULICHIUS	AV		1	p. to Dulichium (or to Ulixes)
DULICHIUS	HL		1	
DULICHIUS	MAR		1	
DULICHIUS	OV		1	
DULICHIUS	PRIAP		1	
DULICHIUS	PROP		1	
DULICHIUS	S		1	
DULICHIUS	SIL		1	
DULICHIUS	V	1	9	
DURIUS	SIL	3	3	river of Spain; two Spanish heroes
DURRACHIUM cf. Dyr.	CAT			town of Illyria
DYMANTIS patr.	OV			= Hecuba
DYMAS -nt-, m.	OV		1	father of Hecuba
DYMAS	S		1	an Arcadian
DYMAS	V		1	a Trojan
DYMAS	VAL	1	4	(legendary figure)
DYME	S			town in Achaia
DYRRACHIUM cf. Dur.	LUC			town of Illyria
-DYSPARIS H.13.43	OV			evil Paris (a Greek coinage)
EARINUS cf. Eiar.	S			name of a slave
-EBOSIA S.1.6.15	S			one of the Balearic islands (= Iviza)
EBRIETAS personif.	SIL			comp. of Pleasure (15.96)
EBUSUS cf. Ebosia	MAN		1	one of the Balearic islands (=Iviza)
EBUSUS 3.362	SIL		1	" " "
EBUSUS (Ebysus)	V	1	3	name of a Trojan
ECBATANA n.pl.	LUCIL			town of Persia
-ECHECLUS M.12.450	OV		1	a Centaur
ECHECLUS T.10.314	S		1	a Theban
ECHECLUS 3.138	VAL	1	3	a Cyzican
ECHECRATES Ibis 293	OV			a descendant of Hercules
-ECHEMMON	HL		1	a son of Priam

ECHEMMON or Eth-	OV	1	2	an Arabian hero (M. 5.163)
ECHIDNA	OV	2	2	Lernean hydra; monster m. of Cerberus
ECHIDNĒUS adj.	OV			p. to Echidna
ECHINADES pl.	LUC		1	islands in the Ionian Sea
ECHINADES	OV	1	2	
ECHINAS sg.	S			one of these islands
ECHION	JUV		1	a musician
ECHION	OV		2	an Argonaut (s. of Mercury); f. of Pentheus
ECHION	S		1	one of the Sparti
ECHION	TR		1	father of Pentheus
ECHION	VAL	1	6	an Argonaut
ECHIONIDES m., patr.	OV		1	= Pentheus
ECHIONIDES	S	1	2	
ECHIONIUS	HOR		1	p. to Echion (or Cadmus)
ECHIONIUS	LUC		1	
ECHIONIUS	OV		2	(+ p. to Thebes)
ECHIONIUS	S		1	
ECHIONIUS	V		1	
ECHIONIUS	VAL	1	7	
ECHO -ūs, fem.	OV		1	a wood-nymph
ECHO	SEN	1	2	
ECUS = Equus	CIC		1	constellation
ECUS	MAN	1	2	
-EDONES Cir. 165	AV			a Thracian tribe
EDONI	HOR			a Thracian tribe
EDONIS fem. sg.	LUC		1	a Bacchante
EDONIS	OV		1	
EDONIS	PROP		1	
EDONIS	SIL	1	4	
EDONUS*	OV		1	Thracian
EDONUS*	S		1	
EDONUS*	SEN		1	
EDONUS*	V		1	
EDONUS*	VAL	1	5	
EËTION	OV		1	k. of Thebes (& f. of Andromache)
EETION	SEN	1	2	
EETIONĒUS	OV			p. to Eëtion
EGERIA	ENN		1	a nymph (wife of Numa)
EGERIA	HOR		1	
EGERIA	JUV		1	
EGERIA	MAR		1	
EGERIA	OV		1	
EGERIA	S		1	
EGERIA	SIL		1	
EGERIA	V		1	
EGERIA	VAL	1	9	
EGESTAS	SIL		1	"Need" personified
EGESTAS	V	1	2	
EGNATIUS	CAT			an enemy of CAT
EIARINOS Cf. Ear-	MAR			a slave name
EISOCRATIUS = Iso-	LUCIL			a follower of Isocrates
ELATEIUS	OV			p. to Elatus (a Lapith)
ELATIA	PL			a town of Phocis
ELECTRA	CIC		1	a Pleiad
ELECTRA	GER		1	"
ELECTRA	HOR		1	daughter of Agamemnon
ELECTRA	JUV		1	" "

ELECTRA	OV		?	a Pleiad; title of a tragedy
ELECTRA	PROP		1	d. of Agamemnon
ELECTRA	SEN		1	" "
ELECTRA	SIL		1	a Pleiad
ELECTRA	V	1	10	"
- ELECTRAE T.8.356	S			a gate of Thebes
ELECTRIUS adj.	VAL			p. to Electra (d. of Agam.)
ELECTRUS	PL			father of Alcmene
{ ELEGĒA personif.	S			"Elegy"
{ ELEGEIA	OV			
ELELEIDES fem. pl.	OV			Bacchae
ELELEUS	OV			ep. of Bacchus
ELEPHANTIS	MAR		1	a Greek poetess
ELEPHANTIS	PRIAP	1	?	
ELĒUS	GR		1	p. to Elis (region in Peloponnesus)
ELEUS	HOR		1	
ELEUS	LUC		1	
ELEUS	OV		1	
ELEUS	PROP		1	
ELEUS	S		1	
ELEUS	SEN		1	
ELEUS	SIL		1	
ELEUS	TIB		1	
ELEUS	V		1	
ELEUS	VAL	1	11	
ELEUSIN fem.	OV		1	town of Attica (Eleusis)
ELEUSIN	S		1	
ELEUSIN	SEN	1	3	
ELEUSĪNUS	V			p. to Eleusis
ELEUSIUM	PL			name of a flute-girl
ELIAS adj.	V			p. to Elis (or to Olympia)
ELICIUS	OV			ep. of Juppiter
ELIS cf. Alis	HL		1	region in western Peloponnesus
ELIS	OV		1	
ELIS	PROP		1	
ELIS	S		1	
ELIS	SEN		1	
ELIS	V		1	
ELIS	VAL	1	7	
- ELISOS T.8.766	S			a river of Attica
ELISSA	JUV		1	= Dido, queen of Carthage
ELISSA	OV		1	
ELISSA	S		1	
ELISSA	SIL		1	
ELISSA	V	1	5	
ELISSAEUS	SIL			Punic, Carthaginian
- ELISSON T.4.52	S			river of Sicyonia
ELĪUS = Elēus	FPLB			p. to Elis
ELPENOR	JUV		1	comp. of Ulixes
ELPENOR	MAR		1	
ELPENOR	OV	1	3	
- ELYMUS M.12.460	OV		1	a Centaur
ELYMUS T.5.207	S		1	a Lemnian
ELYMUS or Helymus	V	1	3	a Trojan
ELYSII	LUC		1	the Elysian fields (in Hades)
ELYSII	MAR	1	2	
ELYSIUM	AV		1	the Underworld

ELYSIUM	MAR		1	the Underworld
ELYSIUM	S		1	
ELYSIUM	SEN		1	
ELYSIUM	SIL		1	
ELYSIUM	V		1	
ELYSIUM	VAL	1	7	
ELYSIUS	FPLB		1	p. to Elysium
ELYSIUS	LUC		1	
ELYSIUS	MAR		1	
ELYSIUS	OV		1	
ELYSIUS	PROP		1	
ELYSIUS	S		1	
ELYSIUS	SEN		1	
ELYSIUS	SIL		1	
ELYSIUS	TIB		1	
ELYSIUS	V	1	10	
EMATHIA	CAT		1	= Macedonia
EMATHIA	LUC		1	
EMATHIA	V	1	3	
EMATHIDES fem.pl.	OV			the Pierides
-EMATHION M. 5.100	OV		1	an aged hero
EMATHION A. 9.571	V	1	2	a Rutulian
EMATHIS adj.	LUC			Thessalian
EMATHIUS adj.	AV		1	Macedonian
EMATHIUS	FPLB		1	
EMATHIUS	LUC		1	
EMATHIUS	LUCIL		1	(Thracian)
EMATHIUS	OV		1	Macedonian
EMATHIUS	S		1	
EMATHIUS	SIL	1	7	
EMERITA	MAR			town in Spain
- EMODA or Emeda, 6.143	VAL			region or mt. (?)
EMPEDOCLES	HOR		1	Greek philosopher
EMPEDOCLES	LUCR	1	2	
EMPORIAE	SIL			town of Spain
EMPOROS	PL			title of Philemon's comedy
-ENAESIMUS M. 8.362	OV			father of Hippocoon
ENCELADOS	AET			a giant
ENCELADUS	HOR		1	"
ENCELADUS	LUC		1	
ENCELADUS	OV		1	
ENCELADUS	PROP		1	
ENCELADUS	S		1	
ENCELADUS	SEN		1	
ENCELADUS	SIL		1	
ENCELADUS	V	1	8	
ENCHELIAE	LUC			tribe of Illyria
-ENCOLPOS 1.31	MAR			name of a slave
ENDYMION m.	JUV		1	a handsome young man of Caria
ENDYMION	MAR		1	
ENDYMION	OV		1	
ENDYMION	PROP	1	4	
⎧ENGONASIN	MAN			constellation (Hercules)
⎩ENGONASIS	CIC			
ENGYON n.	SIL			town of Sicily
ENIPEUS	HOR		1	a Roman youth
ENIPEUS	LUC		1	river in Thessaly

ENIPEUS	OV		1	river-god
ENIPEUS	PROP		1	
ENIPEUS	V		1	
ENIPEUS	VAL	1	6	
ENISPE	S		1	town of Arcadia
ENISPE	SEN	1	2	
ENNA = Henna	SEN			town in Sicily
ENNAEUS = Hennaeus	S			p. to Enna
ENNIUS	ENN		1	Q. Ennius, early Roman poet
ENNIUS	FPLA		1	
ENNIUS	HOR		1	
ENNIUS	LUCIL		1	
ENNIUS	LUCR		1	
ENNIUS	MAR		1	
ENNIUS	OV		1	
ENNIUS	PER		1	
ENNIUS	PROP		1	
ENNIUS	S		1	
ENNIUS	SIL		1	
ENNIUS	TER		1	
ENNIUS	VAR	1	13	
-ENNOMOS M.13.260	OV			king of Mysia
ENNOSIGAEUS	JUV			ep. of Neptune
ENSIS	VAL			constellation (part of Orion)
ENTELLA	SIL			town of Sicily
ENTELLUS	MAR		1	scribe of Domitian
ENTELLUS	V	1	2	legendary Sicilian boxer
-ENYEUS T. 11.50	S			an Argive
ENYO -ūs	LUC		1	Greek goddess of war; cf. Bellona
ENYO	MAR		1	
ENYO	PET		1	
ENYO	S		1	
ENYO	SIL		1	
ENYO	VAL	1	6	
EOS	LUC		1	East, Orient
EOS	OV		1	Dawn (cf. Aurora)
EOS	SEN	1	3	"
EŌUS	AV		1	an Oriental
EOUS	FPLB		1	morning-star (planet Venus)
EOUS	OV		2	an Oriental; sun-horse
EOUS	PROP		1	an Oriental
EOUS	S		1	morning-star
EOUS	SIL		1	
EOUS	V		1	
EOUS 7.22	VAL	1	9	
EŌUS*	CAT		1	eastern, oriental
EOUS*	COL		1	
EOUS*	FPLB		1	
EOUS*	GR		1	
EOUS*	HOR		1	
EOUS*	MAR		1	
EOUS*	OV		1	
EOUS*	S		1	
EOUS*	SIL		1	
EOUS*	TIB		1	
EOUS*	V		1	
EOUS*	VAL	1	12	

EPAPHUS	OV		1	Egyptian god
EPAPHUS	S	1	2	
{EPEOS	HL		1	builder of the Trojan horse
{EPEOS	V	1	2	
{EPEUS	OV			
EPHESIUS	PL			p. to Ephesus
{EPHESOS fem.	LUC		1	town of Ionia
{EPHESOS	MAR	1	2	
{EPHESUS	HOR		1	
{EPHESUS	PL	1	2	
EPHIALTES Cul.234	AV			myth. son of Aloeus
EPHYRAEUS	OV		1	p. to Ephyre
EPHYRAEUS	S		1	
EPHYRAEUS	SIL	1	3	
EPHYRE	LUC		1	= Corinth
EPHYRE	OV		1	
EPHYRE	S		1	
EPHYRE	SIL		1	
EPHYRE	V	1	5	
-EPHYREIACUS em.	PET			Corinthian (119.9)
EPHYREIADAE m.pl.	S			Corinthians
EPHYREIUS	V			Corinthian
EPHYREUS	LUC		1	Corinthian
EPHYREUS	PROP	1	2	
EPICHARMUS	HOR			Greek philosopher
EPICUROS	PRIAP			Greek philosopher
EPICURUS	HOR		1	
EPICURUS	JUV		1	
EPICURUS	LUCIL		1	
EPICURUS	LUCR		1	
EPICURUS	PET		1	
EPICURUS	PROP	1	6	
EPIDAMNIENSIS	PL			p. to Epidamnus
EPIDAMNIUS	PL			p. to Epidamnus
{EPIDAMNOS fem.	LUC			town of Epirus (= Dyrrachium)
{EPIDAMNUS	PET		1	
{EPIDAMNUS	PL	1	2	
EPIDAURIUS N	OV			ep. of Aesculapius
EPIDAURIUS*	HOR		1	p. to Epidaurus
EPIDAURIUS*	OV		1	
EPIDAURIUS*	PROP		1	
EPIDAURIUS*	S	1	4	
EPIDAURUS fem.	PL		1	town of Argolis
EPIDAURUS	S		1	
EPIDAURUS	SEN		1	
EPIDAURUS	V	1	4	
EPIDICAZOMENOS	TER			title of Greek comedy
EPIDICUS	COM		1	character in comedy
EPIDICUS	PL	2	3	title of comedy; name of slave
EPIGNOMUS	PL			a young man
EPIMETHIS patr.	OV			= Pyrrha
EPIROS fem., cf. -us	MAN		1	region of NW Greece
EPIROS	S		1	
EPIROS	V	1	3	
EPIROTA = -tes, m.	FPLB			Q. Caecilius Epirota
EPIROTICUS	SIL			p. to Epirus
EPIRUS cf. Epiros	CIC		1	region in NW Greece

EPIRUS	LUC		1	region in NW Greece
EPIRUS	OV		1	
EPIRUS	SIL	1	4	
-EPISTROPHUS	HL	2	2	two different heroes
EPISTULA (sc.Heroidum)	OV			title of Ovid's poem (AA 3.345)
EPITRAPEZIOS	S			a statue of Hercules
EPĪUS = Epēus	PL			builder of the Trojan horse
EPONA	JUV			goddess of horses (Celtic?)
-EPOPEUS M. 3.619	OV		1	a sailor of Acoetes
EPOPEUS T. 5.225	S	1	2	a Lemnian
-EPPIA 6.104	JUV			a contemp. woman
EPULO A. 12.459	V			a Rutulian
EPYTUS	OV			king of Alba
EQUIRRIA n.pl.	OV			horse-races
ERASĪNUS	OV		1	river of Argolis
ERASINUS	S		1	
ERASINUS	SEN	1	3	
ERATO	MLP		1	muse of lyric poetry
ERATO	OV		1	
ERATO	S		1	
ERATO	V	1	4	(any muse)
EREBĒUS	OV			p. to the Underworld (Erebus)
-EREBOIS Cul. 202	AV			p. to Erebus
EREBUS	LUC		1	the Underworld (or its god)
EREBUS	OV		1	
EREBUS	PET		1	
EREBUS	S		1	
EREBUS	SEN		1	
EREBUS	SIL		1	
EREBUS	TR		1	
EREBUS	V		1	
EREBUS	VAL	1	9	
ERECHTHĔUS	CAT		1	king of Athens
ERECHTHEUS	OV		1	" "
ERECHTHĒUS N	PROP	1	3	any Athenian
ERECHTHĒUS*	CAT		1	Athenian, Attic
ERECHTHEUS*	OV		1	
ERECHTHEUS*	S	1	3	
ERECHTHIDES as pl.	OV			Athenians
ERECHTHIS patr.	OV	2	2	Orithyia; Procris
ERECTHEUS*	AV		1	Athenian, Attic
ERECTHEUS*	MAN	1	2	
ERETRIA	PL			town on Euboea
ERETUM	V			town of the Sabines
-ERGASILUS Capt. 138	PL			a parasite
-ERGENNA m., 2.26	PER			an Etruscan
ERGETIUM (or -tum)	SIL			town of Sicily (14.258)
-ERGĪNUS T. 9.305	S		1	a Theban
-ERGINUS 1.415	VAL	1	2	an Argonaut
-ERIBOTES 1.402	VAL			an Argonaut
-ERICETES A. 10.749	V			a Trojan
ERICHTHO cf. Erictho	OV			a witch
ERICHTHONIUS	OV		2	king of Athens; k. of Troy
ERICHTHONIUS	SIL	1	3	king of Troy
ERICHTHONIUS*	AV		1	Athenian
ERICHTHONIUS*	GER		1	"
ERICHTHONIUS*	OV		1	Trojan

ERICHTHONIUS*	PROP	1	4	Athenian
ERICTHO cf. Erichtho	LUC			a Thessalian witch
ERICTHONIUS	V			king of Athens
ERIDANUS	CIC		1	constellation
ERIDANUS	GER		1	"
ERIDANUS	LUC		1	river Padus (Po) in N. Italy
ERIDANUS	MAN		1	
ERIDANUS	OV		1	
ERIDANUS	PROP		1	
ERIDANUS	SEN		1	
ERIDANUS	SIL		1	
ERIDANUS	V		1	
ERIDANUS	VAL	1	10	
-ERIGDUPUS M. 12.453	OV			a Centaur
ERIGONE	AET		1	daughter of Icarius (& a constellation)
ERIGONE	COL		1	
ERIGONE	MAN		1	
ERIGONE	MAR		1	
ERIGONE	OV		1	
ERIGONE	PRIAP		1	
ERIGONE	S		1	
ERIGONE	TIB		1	
ERIGONE	V	1	9	
ERIGONEIUS	OV			p. to Erigone
ERINNYS sg.	SIL			one of the Furies
ERINYES pl.	PROP		1	the Furies
ERINYES	SEN	1	2	
ERINYS sg.	AV		1	one of the Furies
ERINYS	JUV		1	
ERINYS	LUC		1	
ERINYS	LUCIL		1	
ERINYS	OV		1	
ERINYS	PET		1	
ERINYS	S		1	
ERINYS	V		1	
ERINYS	VAL	1	9	
ERIPHYLA	JUV		1	wife of Amphiareus
ERIPHYLA	OV		1	
ERIPHYLA	PROP	1	3	
ERIPHYLAEUS	S			p. to Eriphyla
ERIPHYLE = -a	V			w. of Amphiareus
EROS	MAR	2	2	two contemporaries
-(EROTION fem., 5.34	MAR			slave of MAR
{EROTIUM	COM		1	a girl
(EROTIUM Men. 173	PL	1	2	a meretrix
ERROR	OV		1	Foolishness, personified
ERROR	SEN		1	
ERROR	SIL	1	3	
ERUCIUS	FPLR			a porter
ERYCINA	CAT		1	ep. of Venus
ERYCINA	HOR		1	
ERYCINA	OV		1	
ERYCINA	SEN	1	4	
ERYCĪNUS	LUC		1	p. to Eryx
ERYCINUS	PROP		1	
ERYCINUS	S		1	
ERYCINUS	V	1	4	

ERYMANTHĒUS	VAL			p. to mt. Erymanthus
ERYMANTHIAS	S			p. to Erymanthus
ERYMANTHIS	OV		1	p. to Erymanthus
ERYMANTHIS	S	1	2	
ERYMANTHĪUS	CIC		1	p. to Erymanthus
ERYMANTHIUS	S		1	
ERYMANTHIUS	SIL	1	3	
ERYMANTHUS	AV		1	mountain in Arcadia
ERYMANTHUS	HOR		1	
ERYMANTHUS	MAR		1	
ERYMANTHUS	OV		2	(+ river in Arcadia)
ERYMANTHUS	S		1	
ERYMANTHUS	SEN		1	
ERYMANTHUS	V		1	
ERYMANTHUS	VAL	1	9	
-ERYMAS A. 9.702	V			a Trojan
-ERYMUS 3.194	VAL			a Cyzican
ERYSICHTHON	OV			son of Triopas (k. of Thessaly)
ERYTHĒA	PROP			island at Cadiz
ERYTHEIS	OV			Erythean
ERYTHĪA 5.106	VAL			a town (fict.?)
ERYTHIUS	SIL			p. to Erythea
ERYTHRAE	S			town in Boeotia
ERYTHRAEUS adj.	MAR		1	p. to Erythrae
ERYTHRAEUS	S		1	
ERYTHRAEUS	TIB	1	3	
-ERYTUS M. 5.79	OV			son of Actor
ERYX	AV		1	mt. of Sicily
ERYX	LUC		1	"
ERYX	MAR		1	hero
ERYX	OV		3	mt.; comp. of Phineus; s. of Venus
ERYX	S		2	mt.; a Theban
ERYX	SEN		2	mt.; hero
ERYX	SIL		1	mt.
ERYX	V		?	son of Venus; t. of Sicily
ERYX	VAL	1	14	mt.
ESQUILIAE	HOR		1	a hill of Rome
ESQUILIAE	JUV		1	
ESQUILIAE	MAR		1	
ESQUILIAE	PROP	1	4	
ESQUILĪNUS adj.	HOR			p. to Esquiline Hill
ESQUILIUS	OV			" " " "
ESQUILLIAE (-1-)	OV			a hill of Rome
-ESSEDONIUS cf. Iss-	LUC			a Scythian
ETEOCLES	S			son of Oedipus
-ETEONOS T. 7.266	S			town of Boeotia
ETESIAE	CIC		1	North winds
ETESIAE	SEN	1	?	
ETRURIA	ENN		1	a region N. of Latium
ETRURIA	V	1	2	
ETRUSCI	HOR		1	people of Etruria, Etruscans
ETRUSCI	V	1	2	
ETRUSCUS	AV		1	an Etruscan
ETRUSCUS	CAT		1	
ETRUSCUS	MAR		1	
ETRUSCUS	S		1	
ETRUSCUS	SIL		1	

ETRUSCUS	V	1	6	an Etruscan
ETRUSCUS*	CIC		1	p. to Etruria, Etruscan
ETRUSCUS*	HOR		1	
ETRUSCUS*	JUV		1	
ETRUSCUS*	LUC		1	
ETRUSCUS*	MAR		1	
ETRUSCUS*	MLP		1	
ETRUSCUS*	OV		1	
ETRUSCUS*	PROP		1	
ETRUSCUS*	S		1	
ETRUSCUS*	TIB		1	
ETRUSCUS*	V	1	11	
EUADNE	OV		1	wife of Capanaeus; a nymph
EUADNE	PROP		1	
EUADNE	S		1	
EUADNE	V	1	4	
– EUAGRUS M. 12.290	OV			a Lapith
EUAN cf. Euhan	LUCR			ep. of Bacchus
EUANDER	HOR		1	son of Carmenta
EUANDER	JUV		1	
EUANDER	OV		1	
EUANDER	PROP		1	
EUANDER	S		1	
EUANDER	TR		1	
EUANDER	V	1	7	
EUANDRIUS	S		1	p. to Euander
EUANDRIUS	SIL		1	
EUANDRIUS	V	1	3	
– EUANTHE em.	OV			d. of Asopus (Am. 3.6.41)
– EUANTHES A. 10.702	V			a Phrygian at Troy
– EUARCHUS 6.102	VAL			river in Anatolia
– EUBIUS T. 2.46	OV			writer of Milesian tales
EUBOEA	HL		1	island in the Aegean
EUBOEA	OV		1	
EUBOEA	S	1	3	
EUBOEUS adj.	S			p. to Euboea
EUBOICUS adj.	AV		1	p. to Euboea
EUBOICUS	LP		1	
EUBOICUS	LUC		1	
EUBOICUS	MAN		1	
EUBOICUS	MAR		1	
EUBOICUS	OV		1	
EUBOICUS	PL		1	
EUBOICUS	PROP		1	
EUBOICUS	S		1	
EUBOICUS	SEN		1	
EUBOICUS	SIL		1	
EUBOICUS	V		1	
EUBOICUS	VAL	1	13	
EUBOIS	S			p. to Euboea
– EUCHIOS (Euh-), 424	COL			ep. of Bacchus
EUCLIDES	MAR			a contemporary man
– EUCLIO Aul. 26	PL			a senex
– EUCTUS 8.6.1	MAR			a doctor
EUDOXUS	LUC			Greek philosopher
EUENINUS	OV			p. to river Euenos
EUENOS	LUC		1	river in Aetolia

EUENOS	SEN	1	2	river of Aetolia
EUENUS	OV		1	"
EUENUS	PROP	1	2	king of Aetolia
EUGANĔUS	JUV		1	p. to a tribe of N. Italy
EUGANEUS	LUC		1	
EUGANEUS	MAR		1	
EUGANEUS	SIL	1	4	
EUHADNE cf. Euadne	MAR			wife of Capaneus
-EUHAEMON	HL			father of Eurypylus
EUHAN cf. Euan	OV		1	ep. of Bacchus
EUHAN	S	1	2	
EUHIAS	HOR			a Bacchante
-EUHIPPUS T. 2.258	S			an Arcadian hero
EUHIUS	COL		1	ep. of Bacchus
EUHIUS	HOR		1	
EUHIUS	LUCR		1	
EUHIUS	OV		1	
EUHIUS	S	1	5	
-EUIPPE M. 5.303	OV			wife of Pierus of Pella
-EULOGUS 6.8.5	MAR			a contemporary
-EUMACHUS 4.371	SIL			a son of Xanthippus
EUMAEUS	S			the swine-herd of Ulixes
EUMEDES	OV		1	father of Dolon
EUMEDES	V	1	2	
-EUMELIS S. 4.8.49	S			= Naples
EUMELUS M. 7.390	OV		1	father of Botres
EUMELUS	V	1	2	friend of Aeneas
EUMENIDES fem.pl.	CAT		1	the Furies
EUMENIDES	HOR		1	
EUMENIDES	JUV		1	
EUMENIDES	LUC		1	
EUMENIDES	LUCIL		1	
EUMENIDES	OV		1	
EUMENIDES	PROP		1	
EUMENIDES	SEN		1	
EUMENIDES	V		1	
EUMENIDES	VAL	1	10	
EUMENIS fem. sg.	S		1	a Fury
EUMENIS	SIL	1	2	
EUMOLPUS	OV			son of Musaeus
-EUNAEUS T. 7.649	S			a Theban priest
-{EUNEOS T. 5.713	S			son of Jason
{EUNEUS A. 9.666	V			a Trojan
-EUNOMIA Aul. 780	PL			a matrona
EUNUCHUS	TER			title of TER's comedy
-EUPHEMUS	HL		1	leader of the Cicones
EUPHEMUS 4.8.7	MAR		1	a hotel manager
EUPHEMUS 1.365	VAL	1	3	an Argonaut
EUPHORBUS	OV			a Trojan
EUPHRANOR	JUV			Greek artist
EUPHRATES	JUV		1	the river in Mesopotamia
EUPHRATES	LUC		1	
EUPHRATES	MAN		1	
EUPHRATES	OV		1	
EUPHRATES	PROP		1	
EUPHRATES	S		1	
EUPHRATES G. 1.509	V	1	7	(residents along the river)

-EUPLOEA	S. 2.2.79	S		an island off Cumae
EUPOLIS		HOR	1	Athenian comic poet
EUPOLIS		OV	1	
EUPOLIS		PER	1 3	
EURIPIDES		FPLA	1	Athenian tragic poet
EURIPIDES		PL	1 2	
EURIPUS		LUC	1	the strait between Boeotia & Euboea
EURIPUS		S	1	
EURIPUS		SEN	1	
EURIPUS		SIL	1	
EURIPUS		VAL	1 5	
EUROPA	cf. Europe	CAT	1	the continent
EUROPA		ENN	1	
EUROPA		LUC	1	
EUROPA		MAN	2	(+ the heroine)
EUROPA		MAR	1	
EUROPA		OV	1	
EUROPA		PROP	1	
EUROPA	and -e	S	2	(+ the heroine)
EUROPA	and -e	SEN	1	the heroine (d. of Agenor)
EUROPA	Attius 501	TR	1	continent
EUROPA		V	1	"
EUROPA		VAL	1 14	"
EUROPAEUS	(Minos)	OV		p. to Europe, the girl
EUROPE	cf. Europa	AET	1	the heroine (d. of Agenor)
EUROPE		GER	1	"
EUROPE		HOR	2	(+ continent)
EUROPE		JUV	1	
EUROPE		MAR	1	
EUROPE		OV	1	
EUROPE		PROP	1	
EUROPE		SIL	2 10	continent; name of a ship (14.568)
EUROTA =	-tas, m.	TR		river of Laconia
EUROTAS	m.	AET	1	river of Laconia
EUROTAS		CAT	1	
EUROTAS		MAR	1	
EUROTAS		OV	1	
EUROTAS		PROP	1	
EUROTAS		S	1	
EUROTAS		SEN	1	
EUROTAS		SIL	1	
EUROTAS		V	1	
EUROTAS		VAL	1 10	
EURUS		AET	1	the SE Wind
EURUS		AV	1	
EURUS		CAL	1	
EURUS		COL	1	
EURUS		FPLA	1	
EURUS		FPLB	1	
EURUS		HL	1	
EURUS		HOR	1	
EURUS		JUV	1	
EURUS		MAN	1	(East Wind)
EURUS	also pl.	OV	1	SE or E. Wind, the East
EURUS		PROP	1	SE Wind
EURUS	also pl.	S	1	
EURUS		SEN	1	

EURUS		SIL	1	SE Wind
EURUS		TIB	1	
EURUS	also pl.	V	1	
EURUS		VAL	1 18	(wind in general)
-EURYALE	5.612	VAL		an Amazon
EURYALUS		HL	1	friend of Diomedes
EURYALUS		JUV	1	a gladiator
EURYALUS		OV	2	king of Thessaly; a friend of Nisus
EURYALUS		S	1	friend of Nisus
EURYALUS		V	1 6	" "
-EURYBATES Ep. 3.9		OV	1	herald of Agamemnon
EURYBATES A. 411		SEN	1 2	
EURYDAMAS		OV	1	= Hector
EURYDAMAS		SIL	1 2	a Saguntine
EURYDICA		ENN		a slave
EURYDICE		AV	1	the wife of Orpheus
EURYDICE		FPLB	1	
EURYDICE		MAR	1	
EURYDICE		OV	1	
EURYDICE		S	1	
EURYDICE		SEN	1	
EURYDICE		V	1 7	
EURYLOCHUS		OV		comp. of Ulixes
-EURYMACHUS H. 1.92		OV		suitor of Penelope
EURYMEDON m.		PROP	1	a giant
EURYMEDON		S	1	a son of Faunus
EURYMEDON		SIL	1 3	a Saguntine
EURYMENAE		VAL		town of Thessaly
EURYMIDES m.sg.		OV		ep. of Telemus
EURYNOME		OV	1	daughter of Ocean
EURYNOME		VAL	1 2	wife of Codrus
-EURYNOMUS M. 12.310		OV		a Centaur
EURYPYLUS		ENN	1	son of Euaemon
EURYPYLUS		HL	1	" "
EURYPYLUS		OV	2	" " ; s. of Hercules
EURYPYLUS		PROP	1	son of Hercules (& k. of Cos)
EURYPYLUS		V	1 6	son of Euaemon
-EURYSACES		TR		title of play
EURYSTHEUS		CIC	1	king of Mycenae
EURYSTHEUS		MAR	1	
EURYSTHEUS		OV	1	
EURYSTHEUS		S	1	
EURYSTHEUS		SEN	1	
EURYSTHEUS		V	1	
EURYSTHEUS		VAL	1 7	
EURYSTHEUS*		S		p. to Eurystheus
- EURYTHAS (?) 16.473		SIL		a Spaniard
-EURYTIDES A. 10.499		V		father of Clonus
EURYTION m.		OV	1	= Eurytus, the Centaur
EURYTION		PROP	1	"
EURYTION		S	1	a Theban
EURYTION		V	1	a Trojan
EURYTION		VAL	1 5	an Argonaut
EURYTIS patr.		OV		= Iole
EURYTUS		OV	2	father of Iole; a Centaur
EURYTUS		SEN	1	an Argonaut
EURYTUS		VAL	1 4	an Argonaut

EUTERPE	HOR		1	the muse of music
EUTERPE	MLP	1	2	
-EUTHYNICUS Cas.1014	PL			a young man
-EUTHYNOUS fr. 48T	CIC			philosopher (?)
EUTRAPELUS	HOR		1	nickname of P. Volumnius
EUTRAPELUS	MAR	1	2	fictional
-EUTYCHOS 6.68	MAR			a young man
EUTYCHUS 3, prol.2	PH		1	a freedman (?)
EUTYCHUS Merc. 474	PL	1	2	a young man
EUXINUS	MAN		1	the Black Sea
EUXINUS	OV		1	
EUXINUS	SEN	1	3	
EUXINUS*	OV			p. to the Black Sea
EUXINUS/PONTUS	LUC			the Black Sea
EVADNE cf. Euadne	OV			
-EXADIUS M. 12.266	OV			a Lapith
-EXAERAMBUS Asin.436	PL			a vintner
-EXOMATAE 6.144	VAL			Sarmatian tribe
EXPERIENTIA line 427	GR			"Experience" personified
FABARIS cf. Farfarus	V			river of Latium
FABIA	HOR			a Roman gens
FABIANUS	MAR			fictional man
FABII	AV		1	Roman family
FABII	JUV		1	
FABII	MAR		1	
FABII	OV		1	
FABII	SIL		1	
FABII	V	1	6	
FABIUS	HOR		1	unknown Stoic
FABIUS	JUV		2	Q. Fabius; P. Fabius
FABIUS	MAN		1	Q. Maximus Fabius
FABIUS	MAR		1	F. Quintilianus
FABIUS	OV		1	Q. Max. Fabius
FABIUS	PROP		1	Q. Max. Fabius
FABIUS	SIL	2	9	founder of gens; Q. Maximus
FABIUS*	OV		1	p. to a Fabius or the Fabii
FABIUS*	PROP		1	
FABIUS*	SIL	1	3	
-FABIUS/VEIENTO	FPLR			political figure of first century AD
FABRATERIA	JUV		1	town in Latium
FABRATERIA	SIL	1	2	
FABRICII	LUC			a Roman gens
FABRICIUS	HOR		1	C. Fabr. Luscinus (the hero)
FABRICIUS	JUV		2	(+ Fab. Veiento)
FABRICIUS	LUC		1	
FABRICIUS	MAN		1	
FABRICIUS	MAR		2	(+ a centurion)
FABRICIUS	V	1	8	
FABRICIUS* (pons)	HOR			p. to a Fabricius
-FABULLA 2.68	JUV		1	cont. woman
FABULLA 1.64	MAR	1	2	cont. woman
FABULLINUS	MAR			fictional man
FABULLUS	CAT		1	a friend
FABULLUS	MAR	2	3	two contemporaries
FACELINUS adj.	LUCIL			ep. of Diana (cf. Phacelina)
FACUNDIA S. 5.3.90	S			"Eloquence" personified
-FADUS 5.565	SIL		1	a Roman soldier

FADUS	A. 9.344	V	1 2	a Rutulian
-FAEDRIA	cf. Phaed-	COM		a male character
-FAENIUS/TFLESPHORUS		MAR		cont. (f. of Antulla)
-FAESIDIUS	13.32	JUV		a lawyer
FAESULA	sg.	SIL		town of Etruria
FALACER		ENN		an early Italic hero
FALERNUM		CAT	1	the wine of Campania
FALERNUM		COL	1	
FALERNUM		HOR	1	
FALERNUM		JUV	1	
FALERNUM		LUC	1	
FALERNUM	also pl.	MAR	1	
FALERNUM		PER	1	
FALERNUM		PET	1	
FALERNUM		PROP	1 9	
FALERNUS	N	SIL	1	a legendary farmer
FALERNUS	pl. 2.1.27	TIB	1 2	jars of Wine
FALERNUS*	(vinum)	COM	1	Falernian (in Campania); ref. to wine
FALERNUS*		HOR	1	
FALERNUS*		JUV	1	
FALERNUS*	(musta)	MAR	1	
FALERNUS*		OV	1	
FALERNUS*		PH	1	
FALERNUS*		PROP	1	
FALERNUS*		S	1	
FALERNUS*		SIL	1	
FALERNUS*		TIB	1	
FALERNUS*		V	1 11	
FALISCI		GR	1	a people of Etruria
FALISCI		OV	1	
FALISCI		SIL	1	
FALISCI		V	1 4	
FALISCUS	adj.	MAR	1	p. to Falerii (t. of Etruria)
FALISCUS		OV	1 2	
FAMA		HOR	1	"Rumor" personified
FAMA		MAR	1	
FAMA		OV	1	
FAMA		PET	1	
FAMA		PROP	1	
FAMA		S	1	
FAMA		V	1	
FAMA		VAL	1 8	
FAMES		OV	1	"Greed" personified
FAMES		PL	1	
FAMES		V	1 3	
FANNIUS		HOR	1	a vain poet
FANNIUS		LUCIL	1	C. Fannius (consul)
FANNIUS		MAR	2 4	two contemporaries
FARFARUS	cf. Fabaris	OV	1	a stream (tributary of Tiber)
FARFARUS		SIL	1 2	a Roman soldier
FAS	1.792	VAL		"Retribution"
FASTI	T. 2.549	OV		title of OV's poem
FATA	n.pl.	MAR	1	the Fates (cf. Parcae)
FATA		PH	1	
FATA		S	1 3	
FATUM	sg. of Fata	GR	1	Fate or a Fate
FATUM		HOR	1	

FATUM	PROP	1	3	Fate
FAUNI	ENN		1	wood-land deities (cf. Panes)
FAUNI	LUCIL		1	
FAUNI	LUCR		1	
FAUNI	VAL	1	4	
FAUNIGENA	SIL			ep. of river Arno
FAUNUS	CAL		1	leg. son of Picus & an Italic deity
FAUNUS	GR		1	
FAUNUS	HOR		1	
FAUNUS	MAR		1	
FAUNUS	MLP		1	
FAUNUS	OV		1	
FAUNUS	PRIAP		1	
FAUNUS	PROP		1	
FAUNUS	S		1	
FAUNUS	SIL		1	
FAUNUS	V	1	11	
FAUSTA	HOR			daughter of Sulla
-FAUSTĪNUS 1.25	MAR			a rich friend of MAR
FAUSTITAS	HOR			goddess of fertility
FAUSTULUS F. passim	OV			legendary shepherd
FAUSTUS	JUV		1	contemporary playwright
FAUSTUS	MAR	2	3	two contemporaries
FAVENTIA	SIL			town of Umbria
FAVENTĪNUS	MAR			contemporary loan-shark
FAVONIUS	CAT		1	West Wind (cf. Zephyrus)
FAVONIUS	CIC		1	
FAVONIUS	HOR		1	
FAVONIUS	OV		1	
FAVONIUS	S		1	
FAVONIUS	SEN	1	6	
FAVOR 10.50.2	MAR			"Good-will, Fortune" personified
-FELIX 2.888	MAN			part of Zodiac (cf. Fortuna)
FENESTELLA/PORTA	OV			a gate of Rome
FERALIA n.pl.	OV			feast of the Dead (February)
FERENTINATIS adj.	COM			p. to Ferentinum
FERENTINUM	HOR			town in Latium
FERENTĪNUS as pl. N	SIL			the people of Ferentinum
FERETRIUS	PROP			ep. of Juppiter
FERONIA	HOR		1	goddess of Fertility (cf. Faustitas)
FERONIA	SIL		1	
FERONIA	V	1	3	
FESCENNIA	MAR			fictional woman
FESCENNĪNUS	CAT		1	p. to Fescennia (t. of Etruria)
FESCENNINUS	HOR		1	
FESCENNINUS	SEN		1	
FESCENNINUS	V	1	4	
FESTUS	MAR			friend of Domitian
FIBRENUS	SIL	2	2	river of Latium; an Etruscan
FICEDULENSES	PL			(comic formation): fict. tribe
FICELIAE	MAR			place near Nomentum
FIDENA sg.	SIL		1	town of Latium
FIDENA	V	1	2	
FIDENAE pl.	HOR		1	(same) town of Latium
FIDENAE	JUV		1	
FIDENAE	MAR		1	
FIDENAE	PROP	1	4	

FIDENTĪNUS N	MAR			a plagiarist
FIDES -ei	CAT	1		goddess of Honor
FIDES -is, sg.	CIC	1		constellation "Lyre"
FIDES	COL	1		Honor
FIDES	HOR	1		constell.
FIDES 1.115	JUV	1		Honor
FIDES	MAN	1		constell.
FIDES 12.6.3	MAR	1		Honor
FIDES	PET	1		
FIDES Aul. passim	PL	1		
FIDES	S	1		
FIDES	SEN	1		
FIDES	SIL	1		
FIDES	V	1	13	
FIDIUS F. 6.213	OV			ep. of Juppiter (cf. Dius/Fidius)
FIDUCIA T. 6.371	S			"Confidence" personified
FIGULUS 1.639	LUC			P. Nigidius Fig., philosopher
FIMBRIA 2.124	LUC			C. Flavius Fimbria
FIRMANUS adj.	CAT			p. to Firmum (t. in Picenum)
FISCELLUS	SIL			Sabine mountain
FLACCI	LUCIL			a family (Roman?)
- FLACCILLA 5.34.1	MAR			mother of Martial (?)
FLACCUS	FPLR	1		Q. H. Flaccus, the poet
FLACCUS	HOR	1		
FLACCUS	JUV	1		(or his poetry)
FLACCUS	MAR	3		(+ two contemporaries)
FLACCUS	OV	1		L. Pomponius Flaccus, friend of Ovid
FLACCUS	PER	1	8	Horace
FLAMINIA (sc. via)	JUV	1		Flaminian Way (Rome to Ariminum)
FLAMINIA	MAR	1	2	
FLAMINIA/VIA	MAR	1		
FLAMINIA/VIA	OV	1	2	
FLAMINIUS	OV	1		C. Flaminius (consul)
FLAMINIUS	SIL	1	2	"
FLAMINIUS*	MAR	1		p. to Flaminius (or the Flam. Way)
FLAMINIUS*	S	1	2	
FLAVINA	SIL			town of Etruria
FLAVINIUS	SIL	1		p. to Flavina
FLAVINIUS	V	1	2	
FLAVIUS	CAT	1		a friend of Catullus
FLAVIUS	HOR	1		a man from Venusia
FLAVIUS	JUV	1		the emperor Domitian
FLAVIUS also adj.	MAR	1	4	Roman gens (esp. the Flavian dynasty)
FLAVIUS*	S			p. to Flavius or the family
- FLAVUS 10.104	MAR			friend of Martial
FLETUS 13.582	SIL			"Lament" personified
FLORA	CAL	1		the Italic goddess of flowers & springtime
FLORA	JUV	2		
FLORA	LUCR	1		
FLORA	MAR	1		
FLORA	OV	1		
FLORA	VAR	1	7	
FLORALES (sc. ludi)	MAR			floral games (I, pref.)
FLORALIA n.pl.	MAR	1		festival of Flora
FLORALIA	PER	1	2	
FLORALICIUS	MAR			p. to festival of Flora
FLORALIS	ENN	1		p. to Flora (or her festival)

FLORALIS	JUV		1	p. to Flora (or her festival)
FLORALIS	OV	1	3	
FLORUS	HOR		1	Julius Florus, the orator
FLORUS	MLP	1	2	poet (see Duff, MLP, p. 423)
–FLUMEN Arat. 144	CIC			constellation Eridanus
FLUMINA	MAN		1	constellation
FLUMINA	OV	1	2	"
FOLIA fem. sg.	HOR			a witch of Ariminum
FONS Stichus 699	PL			god of the fountain
–FONTANUS P 4.16.35	OV		1	a poet
FONTANUS 5.540	SIL	1	2	soldier of Fregellae
FONTEIUS	JUV			F. Capito (consul 67 AD)
FORENTUM	HOR			town in Apulia
FORMIAE	HOR		1	town in Latium
FORMIAE	MAR	1	2	
FORMIANUS	CAT		1	p. to Formiae
FORMIANUS	HOR		1	
FORMIANUS	MAR	1	3	
FORMIDO A. 13.335)	V			"Terror" personified
FORNACALIA n.pl.	OV			festival of Fornax
FORNACALIS (dea)	OV			p. to Fornax
FORNAX	OV			goddess of ovens
FORS	HOR		1	goddess of Luck
FORS	OV		1	
FORS	PET		1	
FORS	S		1	
FORS	SIL		1	
FORS	TIB	1	6	
FORS/FORTUNA	COL		1	goddess of Luck
FORS/FORTUNA	TER	1	2	
FORTUNA	COM		1	goddess of Luck
FORTUNA	ENN		1	
FORTUNA	FPLB		1	
FORTUNA	HOR		1	
FORTUNA	JUV		1	
FORTUNA	MAN		2	(+ Zodiacal region)
FORTUNA	MAR		1	
FORTUNA	MLP		1	
FORTUNA	OV		1	
FORTUNA	PET		1	
FORTUNA	PH		1	
FORTUNA	PL		1	
FORTUNA	S		1	
FORTUNA	SEN		1	
FORTUNA	SIL		1	
FORTUNA	TER		1	
FORTUNA	TIB		1	
FORTUNA	TR		1	
FORTUNA	V		1	
FORTUNA	VAL		1	
FORTUNA	VAR	1	22	
FORTUNA/FORS	LUCIL		1	=Fors/Fortuna
FORTUNA/FORS	OV	1	2	
–FORTUNATUS 2.14.11	MAR			a bath-keeper
FORULI	SIL		1	Sabine town
FORULI	V	1	2	
FORUM (sc. Romanum)	PROP			the Roman Forum

FORUM/APPI	HOR			town in Latium
FORUM/CORNELI	MAR			town in N. Italy
FREGELLAE	SIL			town in Latium
FREGENAE	SIL			town in Etruria
FRENTANUS	SIL			= Frentani tribe
FRIGUS M. 8.790	OV			"Chill" personified
-FROEGIA Att. 178	TR			= Phrygia
FRONTINUS	MAR			consul/writer/friend
FRONTO	JUV		1	T. Catius Fronto (?)
FRONTO	MAR	3	4	father of Martial; two contemporaries
FRUGES Turp. 102	COM			= Phryges
FRUSINO	JUV		1	town in Latium
FRUSINO	SIL	1	2	
FUCINUS	MAR		1	lake in Latium
FUCINUS	SIL		1	
FUCINUS	V	1	3	
-FUFICULENUS 2.74.7	MAR			a loan-shark
FUFIDIUS	HOR			" "
FUFIUS	HOR			an actor
FUGA A. 9.719	V		1	"Panic" personified
FUGA 6.181	VAL	1	2	
FULGINIA	SIL			town of Umbria
FULVIA	FPLR		1	wife of M. Antony
FULVIA	MAR	1	2	"
FULVIUS	HOR		1	a gladiator
FULVIUS	SIL	2	3	consul; praetor
-FUNDANIUS S. 1.10.42	HOR			a comedian
FUNDANUM	MAR			a wine of Fundi
FUNDANUS	MAR		1	p. to Fundi (and its wine)
FUNDANUS	OV	1	2	
FUNDI	HOR		1	town of Latium
FUNDI	SIL	1	2	
FURIA also pl.	MAR		1	a Fury
FURIA frag. #4	OV	1	2	a woman's name (in a pun)
FURIAE	CIC		1	the Furies (cf. Dirae)
FURIAE	GR		1	
FURIAE	HOR		1	
FURIAE	JUV		1	
FURIAE	LUCR		1	
FURIAE	OV		1	
FURIAE	S		1	
FURIAE	SEN		1	
FURIAE	SIL		1	
FURIAE	V		1	
FURIAE	VAL		1	
FURIAE	VAR	1	12	
FURINALIS N	ENN			priest of Furina (unknown goddess)
FURIUS	CAT		1	(unknown)
FURIUS	FPLA		1	L. Furius
FURIUS	HOR		1	Fur. Bibaculus
FURIUS	MAR		1	fictional
FURIUS	OV	1	5	M. Junius Camillus
FURNIUS	HOR		1	a friend of Horace
FURNIUS	SIL	1	2	a Roman soldier
FUROR	HOR		1	"Anger" personified
FUROR	OV		1	
FUROR	PET		1	

FUROR	S		1	"Anger"
FUROR	SIL		1	
FUROR	V		1	
FUROR	VAL	1	7	
FUSCINUS	JUV			friend of Juvenal
FUSCUS	HOR		1	a friend of Horace
FUSCUS	JUV		2	Cornelius Fuscus; a lawyer
FUSCUS	MAR	2	5	two contemporaries
FUSCUS/ARISTIUS	HOR			friend of Horace
-GABAR	SIL			a Punic warrior (9.387)
GABBA	JUV		1	a witty person
GABBA	MAR	1	2	" "
GABII	HOR		1	town of Latium
GABII	JUV		1	
GABII	LUC		1	
GABII	OV		1	
GABII	PROP		1	
GABII	V	1	6	
GABINIA	MAR			fictional woman
GABINUS	LUC		1	p. to Gabii
GABINUS	OV		1	
GABINUS	SIL		1	
GABINUS	V	1	4	
GADES fem.pl.	COL		1	Phoenician town in Spain
GADES	HOR		1	
GADES	JUV		1	
GADES	LUC		1	
GADES	LUCR		1	
GADES	MAR		1	
GADES	PRIAP		1	
GADES	S		1	
GADES	SIL	1	9	
-GADILLA 7.87.7	MAR			fict. woman (v.l. of Glaucilla)
GADITANUS as n.pl.	JUV		1	songs of Gades
GADITANUS	MAR	2	3	fictional person
GADITANUS*	MAR			p. to Gades
GAETULIA	SIL			region of NW Africa
GAETULICUS	FPLR		1	agnomen of Cn. Cornel. Lentulus
GAETULICUS	JUV		1	"
GAETULICUS	MAR	1	3	"
GAETULUS	LUC		1	a Gaetulian national
GAETULUS	SIL	1	2	
GAETULUS*	HOR		1	p. to Gaetulia
GAETULUS*	JUV		1	
GAETULUS*	MAR		1	
GAETULUS*	OV		1	
GAETULUS*	S		1	
GAETULUS*	SEN		1	
GAETULUS*	SIL		1	
GAETULUS*	V	1	8	
GAIUS cf. Caius	CAT		1	a common praenomen (10.30)
GAIUS	LUCIL		1	C. Lucilius (himself)
GAIUS passim	MAR	1	3	a common praenomen
GALA m.	SIL			Punic soldier
GALAESUS cf. Galesus	HOR		1	river of SE Italy
GALAESUS	MAR		2	river; a Saguntine
GALAESUS	SIL		1	a Saguntine

GALAESUS	V	2	6	river in SE Italy; a rustic
GALANTHIS	OV			attendant of Alcmene
GALATAE m.pl.	LUC			Celts of Galatia
GALATEA	AV		1	a maiden
GALATEA	HOR		1	friend of Horace
GALATEA	MAR		2	maiden; contemporary woman
GALATEA	OV		1	a Nereid
GALATEA	PROP		1	"
GALATEA	S		2	a heroine; contemporary
GALATEA	SIL		1	nymph
GALATEA	V		2	nymph; shepherdess
GALATEA	VAL	1	12	nymph
GALBA m.	FPLR		1	the emperor (68-69 AD)
GALBA	HOR		1	a lawyer (?)
GALBA	JUV		2	the emperor; a portrait
GALBA	SIL	1	5	an Etruscan leader
GALESUS cf. Galaesus	PROP		1	river of S. Italy
GALESUS	S	1	2	"
GALLA	JUV		1	a contemporary woman
GALLA	MAR	1	2	"
GALLAE	CAT			castrated priests of Cybele
GALLI	ENN		1	Gauls
GALLI	FPLR		1	
GALLI	HOR		2	(+ Galatians)
GALLI	LUC		2	(+ priests of Cybele)
GALLI	OV		2	(+ priests)
GALLI	PET		1	
GALLI	PH		1	priests
GALLI	PROP		1	Gauls
GALLI	SIL	1	12	"
GALLIA	AV		1	Gaul (in wide or narrow sense)
GALLIA	CAT		1	
GALLIA	COL		1	
GALLIA	COM		1	
GALLIA	ENN		1	
GALLIA also pl.	FPLR		1	(+ the two Gauls)
GALLIA	HOR		1	
GALLIA	JUV		1	
GALLIA	LUC		1	
GALLIA	MAN		1	
GALLIA	MAR		1	
GALLIA	OV		1	
GALLIA	SIL		1	
GALLIA	TIB	1	14	
GALLICANUS	CAT		1	Gaulish, Gallic
GALLICANUS	MAR	1	2	
GALLICUS N	JUV		1	a prefect of Rome
GALLICUS	MAR		1	fictional man
GALLICUS 3.13.54;	PROP		2	Gaulish; p. to r. Gallus (at Troy, 2.13.48)
GALLICUS	S	1	5	a friend, Rutilius G. Valens
GALLICUS*	AV		1	Gaulish, p. to Gaul
GALLICUS*	CAT		1	
GALLICUS*	HOR		1	
GALLICUS*	JUV		1	
GALLICUS*	LUC		1	
GALLICUS*	MAR		1	(+ p. to Galli, priests)
GALLICUS*	OV		2	

GALLICUS*	PET	1	Gaulish, p. to Gaul
GALLICUS*	PL	1	
GALLICUS*	SIL	1	
GALLICUS*	TR	1 12	
GALLINA	HOR		a gladiator
GALLINARIUS adj.	JUV		(silva): a forest near Cumae
-GALLIO P. 4.11.1	OV	1	a friend of Ovid
GALLIO S. 2.7.32	S	1 2	brother of Seneca the Younger
-GALLITTA 12.99	JUV		fictional woman
GALLIUS	JUV		a friend of Juvenal
GALLONIUS	HOR	1	P. Gallonius, the epicure
GALLONIUS	LUCIL 1	2	
GALLUS	CAT	1	an unknown contemporary
GALLUS	CIC	1	the Roman poet, C. Corn. G.
GALLUS	COM	1	a Gaul
GALLUS	FPLR	2	a Gaul; the poet
GALLUS	GR	1	breed of dog
GALLUS	JUV	1	a lawyer
GALLUS	MAR	5	a priest of Cybele; 4 contemporaries
GALLUS	OV	2	the poet; river of Phrygia
GALLUS	PRIAP	1	(ambiguous)
GALLUS	PROP	3	three contemporaries
GALLUS	S	1	a contemporary
GALLUS (B.X; A.)	V	2 21	a Gaul; the poet
GALLUS*	JUV	1	Gaulish
GALLUS*	MAR	1 2	
GANGARIDAE	V	1	a tribe of E. India
GANGARIDAE	VAL	1 2	
GANGES m. sg.	GR	1	river of India
GANGES	JUV	1	
GANGES	LUC	1	
GANGES	MAN	1	
GANGES	OV	1	
GANGES	S	1	
GANGES	SEN	1	
GANGES	SIL	1	
GANGES	V	1 9	
GANGETICUS	LUC	1	p. to the Ganges, Indian
GANGETICUS	MAR	1	
GANGETICUS	OV	1	
GANGETICUS	SEN	1	
GANGETICUS	SIL	1 5	
GANGETIS -idis	OV		Indian
GANYMEDES	GER	1	handsome son of Laomedon
GANYMEDES	HOR	1	
GANYMEDES	JUV	1	
GANYMEDES	LUC	2	(+ Egyptian eunuch)
GANYMEDES	MAR	1	(also a type)
GANYMEDES	OV	1	
GANYMEDES	V	1 8	
GANYMEDEUS	LP	1	p. to Ganymedes, the youth
GANYMEDEUS	MAR	1 2	
-GARADUS 7.601	SIL		a Punic soldier
GARAMANS = -as	SEN		a tribesman of the Garamantes
GARAMANTES	LUC	1	African tribe
GARAMANTES	V	1 2	
GARAMANTICUS	SIL		p. to the Garamantes

GARAMANTIS adj.	LUC		1	p. to the Garamantes
GARAMANTIS	SIL		1	
GARAMANTIS	V	1	3	
GARAMAS cf. Garamans	LUC		1	a Garamantian
GARAMAS	SIL	1	2	
-GARAMUS 2.110	SIL			a Punic soldier
GARGANUS	GR		1	mountain in Apulia
GARGANUS	HOR		1	
GARGANUS	LUC		1	
GARGANUS	SIL		2	(+ a horse of Scipio)
GARGANUS	V	1	6	
GARGANUS*	HOR		1	p. to mt. Garganus
GARGANUS*	SIL	1	2	
GARGAPHIE	OV		1	valley in Boeotia
GARGAPHIE	S	1	2	
GARGARA n.pl.	OV		1	= Mt. Ida (in Troad)
GARGARA	S		1	
GARGARA	SEN		1	
GARGARA	V		1	
GARGARA	VAL	1	5	
-GARGARON = -a	GER			mt. Ida (in Troad)
-GARGENUS 5.137	SIL			a king of the Boii
GARGETTIUS	S			ep. of Epicurus, the philosopher
-GARGILIANUS 3.30	MAR			fictional man
GARGILIUS	HOR		1	a hunter
GARGILIUS	MAR	1	2	a contemporary
-GARGONIUS S. 1.2.27	HOR			contemporary orator
-GARRICUS 9.48	MAR			fictional man
GARUNNA	TIB			river of Gaul
GAUDIA (mala) pl.	V		1	criminal Delight (A. 6.279)
GAUDIA 6.179	VAL	1	2	" "
GAUDIUM Bac. 115	PL			Delight
-GAULUM 14.274	SIL			an island
GAURANUS adj. (ostrea)	JUV		1	p. to Gaurus
GAURANUS (mons)	S	1	2	
GAURUS	JUV		1	mountain in Campania
GAURUS	LUC		1	
GAURUS	MAR		1	
GAURUS	S		1	
GAURUS	SIL	1	5	
GAZA	LUC			town in Palestine
GELA m.	OV		1	river in Sicily
GELA f.	SIL		1	town in Sicily
GELA	V	1	3	" "
-GELAS 6.208	VAL			a Scythian
-GELASIMUS Stich.150	PL			a parasite
-GELESTA 10.85	SIL			a Moor
GELLIA	MAR			fictional woman
GELLIANUS	MAR			fictional man
GELLIUS	CAT		1	rival for Lesbia
GELLIUS	MAR	1	2	fictional
GELONI	GR		1	Scythian tribe
GELONI	HOR		1	
GELONI	LUC		1	
GELONI	SEN		1	
GELONI	VAL	1	5	
GELONUS	S		1	a Gelonian

GELONUS sg. for pl.	V	1	2	the Gelonians
GELOUS adj.	V			p. to Gela
GEMELLUS	MAR			fictional man
-GEMINEI/LENONES	FPLA			title of comedy
GEMINI	CIC	1		constell. Twins (Castor, Pollux)
GEMINI	FPLB	1		
GEMINI	GER	1		
GEMINI	LUC	1		
GEMINI	MAN	1		
GEMINI	OV	1		
GEMINI	PER	1	7	
GEMINUS (221M)	LUCIL			M. Servilius Geminus, trib. mil.
-GENABOS fem., 1.440	LUC			town in Gaul (= Genabum)
GENAUNI	HOR			Alpine tribe (Germanic?)
-GENETAEUS 5.147	VAL			ep. of Juppiter
GENITALIS	HOR			ep. of Diána Lucina
GENIUS	HOR	1		personal (tutelary) deity of the Romans
GENIUS	PL	1		
GENIUS	TIB	1	3	
-GENTIUS	LUCIL			contemporary boy
-GENUMANUS	FPLB			= Cenomanus (?)
GENUSUS	LUC			river of Illyria
-GENYSUS 3.114	VAL			a Cyzican
GERAESTUS 1.456	VAL			town of Euboea
GERMANI	FPLB			the people of Germany
GERMANIA	HOR	1		Germany
GERMANIA	MAN	1		
GERMANIA	MAR	1		
GERMANIA	OV	1		
GERMANIA	V	1	5	
GERMANICUS N	FPLB	1		Germ. Caesar, s. of Drusus
GERMANICUS	JUV	1		a coin of Domitian
GERMANICUS	MAR	1		Domitian
GERMANICUS	OV	1		G. Caesar
GERMANICUS	S	1		Domitian
GERMANICUS	SIL	1	6	"
GERMANICUS*	MAR	2	2	p. to Domitian
GERMANUS	JUV	1		a German national
GERMANUS	MAR	1	2	
GERMANUS*	LUC	1		p. to Germany or the Germans
GERMANUS*	MAR	1		
GERMANUS*	OV	1		
GERMANUS*	PER	1		
GERMANUS*	PET	1		
GERMANUS*	S	1	6	
-GERUS 6.67	VAL			a river flowing into Maeotis
GERYON = -nēs	CAL	1		leg. king of Spain
GERYON	OV	1		
GERYON	SEN	1	3	
GERYONACEUS	PL			p. to Geryon
GERYONĒS cf. Geryon	HOR	1		leg. king of Spain
GERYONES	LUCR	1		
GERYONES	MAR	1		
GERYONES	PROP	1		
GERYONES	SIL	1		
GERYONES	V	1	6	
-GESANDER 6.303	VAL			a legendary hero

-GESSITHOUS 6.637	VAL			a Colchian
-GESTAR 2.327, 4.627	SIL	2	2	two Punic soldiers
GETA	OV		1	a Getan
GETA	PL		1	= the slave Cyamus
GETA	S		1	a contemporary Roman
GETA	TER	1	4	a slave
GETAE	HOR		1	a Thracian tribe
GETAE	MAR		1	
GETAE	OV		1	
GETAE	PROP		1	
GETAE	S		1	
GETAE	SEN		1	
GETAE	SIL		1	
GETAE	TIB		1	
GETAE	V		1	
GETAE	VAL	1	10	
GETES cf. Geta	LUC		1	a Getan
GETES	OV		1	
GETES also pl.	S	1	3	
GETES*	OV			p. to the Getae
GETICE adv.	OV			in Getan (i.e. Thracian) language
-GETICUM T. 5.13.1	OV			region (Thrace)
GETICUS	JUV		1	p. to the Getae
GETICUS	LUC		1	
GETICUS	MAR		1	
GETICUS	OV		1	
GETICUS	S		1	
GETICUS	SEN		1	
GETICUS	SIL		1	
GETICUS	V		1	
GETICUS	VAL	1	9	
GETULUS* = Gaetulus	COL			Moorish
-GIDDENIS Poen. 898	PL			a nurse
GIGANTES	AET		1	the Giants, mythical race
GIGANTES	CIC		1	
GIGANTES	FPLA		1	
GIGANTES	HOR		1	
GIGANTES	LUCR		1	
GIGANTES	MAN		1	
GIGANTES	MAR		1	(title of poem)
GIGANTES also sg.	OV		1	
GIGANTES	PET		1	
GIGANTES	PROP		1	
GIGANTES also sg.	S		1	
GIGANTES	SEN		1	
GIGANTES	SIL	1	13	
GIGANTEUS	AV		1	p. to the Giants
GIGANTEUS	HOR		1	
GIGANTEUS	MAR		1	
GIGANTEUS	OV		1	
GIGANTEUS	PROP		1	
GIGANTEUS	S	1	6	
GIGAS sg.	MAR			a Giant
-GILLO 1.40	JUV			cont. legacy-hunter
-GISGO 2.111, 16.675	SIL	2	2	two Punics
-GLAGUS 16.561	SIL			an Iberian
-GLAPHYRA	FPLB		1	a meretrix

-GLAPHYRA	11.20.3	MAR	1	2	fictional woman
-GLAPHYRUS	6.77	JUV		1	a citharist
GLAPHYRUS	4.5.8	MAR	1	2	
-GLAUCIA	6.28	MAR			a freedwoman
-GLAUCIAS	S.2.1.1	S			a boy
-GLAUCIS (or Graugis)		PROP			??
GLAUCUS		HL		1	Lycian general at Troy
GLAUCUS		HOR		1	
GLAUCUS		MAR		1	
GLAUCUS		OV		2	son of Minos; a fisherman
GLAUCUS	Asin.751	PL		1	fictional
GLAUCUS		PROP		1	sea-god
GLAUCUS		S		1	" "
GLAUCUS		V		4	" " (+3 legendary figures)
GLAUCUS		VAL	2	14	" " (+a Cyzican)
-GLISAS -nt-		S			town of Boeotia (T. 7.307)
GLORIA		HOR		1	"Fame" personified
GLORIA		MAR		1	
GLORIA	15.98	SIL	1	3	
GLYCERA pseudonym		HOR		2	mistress of Horace; of Tibullus
GLYCERA		MAR	2	4	mistress of Menander; fictional
-GLYCERANUS	Ein.2.7	MLP			a shepherd
GLYCERIUM		TER			a female character
GLYCON m.sg.		HOR		1	a wrestler
GLYCON	5.9	PER	1	2	contemporary actor
-GLYMPICUS		GR			breed of dog
-GLYPTUS	2.45	MAR			fictional
GNATHO		LUCIL		1	(fictional character)
GNATHO		TER	1	2	a parasite
GNATHONICUS as pl.		TER			followers of Gnatho
GNATIA = Egnatia		HOR			town in Apulia
GNIDIUS cf. Cn-		MAR			p. to Gnidos
GNIDOS cf. Cn-		LUC			town in Caria
GNOSIA		TIB			= Ariadne
GNOSIACUS		OV		1	p. to Gnosus
GNOSIACUS		S		1	
GNOSIACUS		SEN	1	3	
GNOSIAS		OV			= Ariadne
GNOSIAS*		OV			Cretan
GNOSIS		OV		1	ep. of Ariadne
GNOSIS		S	1	2	
GNOSIS* em.		OV			Cretan (Ibis 556)
GNOSIUS cf. Cn-		AV		1	p. to Cnosos (i.e. Cretan)
GNOSIUS		CAT		1	
GNOSIUS		COL		1	
GNOSIUS		HOR		1	
GNOSIUS		LP		1	(a Cretan)
GNOSIUS		MAN		1	
GNOSIUS		MAR		1	
GNOSIUS		OV		1	
GNOSIUS		PROP		1	
GNOSIUS		S		1	
GNOSIUS		SEN		1	
GNOSIUS		V	1	12	
GNOSOS cf. Cnossos		LUC			town of Crete
GOLGI pl.		CAT			town of Cyprus
-GONGYLION	3.84.2	MAR			fictional person

−GONOESSA Tr. 840	SEN			town in Greece
GORGE	OV		1	sister of Meleager
GORGE T. 5.207	S	1	2	Lemnian woman
−GORGINES m.sg.	PL			a fisherman (Vid. 54)
GORGO fem., cf. Gorgon	GER		1	mythical d. of Phorcus (3 in number)
GORGO	JUV		1	
GORGO	MAN		1	
GORGO	MAR		1	(i.e. Medusa)
GORGO	OV		1	(i.e. Medusa)
GORGO	SIL		1	
GORGO	V		1	
GORGO	VAL	1	8	
GORGON cf. Gorgo	LUC		1	
GORGON	PROP		1	
GORGON	S		1	
GORGON	SEN	1	4	
GORGONEUS	JUV		1	p. to the Gorgons (or to Medusa)
GORGONEUS	LUC		1	
GORGONEUS	MAN		1	
GORGONEUS	OV		1	
GORGONEUS	PROP		1	
GORGONEUS	S		1	
GORGONEUS	SEN		1	
GORGONEUS	SIL		1	
GORGONEUS	V		1	
GORGONEUS	VAL	1	10	
GORTYN	VAL			town of Crete
GORTYNA	LUC		1	
GORTYNA	SIL	1	2	
GORTYNIACUS adj.	OV			p. to Crete, Cretan
GORTYNIS adj.	LUC		1	Cretan
GORTYNIS	SEN	1	2	
GORTYNIUS	AV		1	Gortynian, Cretan
GORTYNIUS	CAT		1	
GORTYNIUS	FPLR		1	
GORTYNIUS	SIL		1	
GORTYNIUS	V	1	5	
GRACCHI	JUV		1	brothers (Tiberius & Gaius)
GRACCHI	LUC		1	
GRACCHI	MAN		1	
GRACCHI	SEN		1	
GRACCHI	SIL	1	5	
GRACCHUS	HOR		1	C. Gracchus (orator)
GRACCHUS	JUV		1	a salic priest
GRACCHUS	MAR		1	T. Sempronius G.
GRACCHUS	SIL		2	T.S.G. (consul); T.S.G. Longus (error)
GRACCHUS	V	1	6	one of the Gracchi family
−GRACCUS P. 4.16.31	OV			a poet
GRADIVUS	GER		1	ep. of Mars
GRADIVUS	JUV		1	
GRADIVUS	LUC		1	
GRADIVUS	MAN		1	
GRADIVUS	OV		1	
GRADIVUS	S		1	
GRADIVUS	SEN		1	
GRADIVUS	SIL		1	
GRADIVUS	V		1	

GRADIVUS	VAL	1	10	ep. of Mars
GRADIVVICOLA m.	SIL			a worshipper of Mars
GRAEA	S			town of Boeotia
GRAECE adv.	COM		1	in Greek (language)
GRAECE	JUV		1	
GRAECE	LUCIL		1	
GRAECE	MAR		1	
GRAECE	PER		1	
GRAECE	PL		1	
GRAECE	TER	1	7	
GRAECI	CIC		1	the Greeks
GRAECI	COL		1	
GRAECI	ENN		1	
GRAECI	FPLB		1	
GRAECI	HOR		1	
GRAECI	JUV		1	
GRAECI	OV		1	
GRAECI	PER		1	
GRAECI	PH		1	
GRAECI	TER	1	10	
GRAECIA	AV		1	Greece
GRAECIA	CIC		1	
GRAECIA	ENN		1	
GRAECIA	FPLA		1	
GRAECIA	GER		1	
GRAECIA	GR		1	
GRAECIA	HL		1	
GRAECIA	HOR		1	
GRAECIA	JUV		1	
GRAECIA	LP		1	
GRAECIA	LUC		1	
GRAECIA	MAN		1	
GRAECIA	OV		1	
GRAECIA	PH		1	
GRAECIA	PL		1	
GRAECIA	PROP		1	
GRAECIA	S		1	
GRAECIA	SEN		1	
GRAECIA	SIL		1	
GRAECIA	TR		1	
GRAECIA	V		1	
GRAECIA	VAL		1	
GRAECIA	VAR	1	23	
- GRAECINUS P. passim	OV			a friend of Ovid
GRAECULUS N	JUV		1	a Greek-ling (social-climber in Rome)
GRAECULUS adj.	MAR	1	2	
GRAECUS	HOR			a Greek man
GRAECUS*	AV		1	Greek
GRAECUS*	CAT		1	
GRAECUS*	COM		1	
GRAECUS*	FPLA		1	
GRAECUS*	HOR		1	
GRAECUS*	JUV		1	
GRAECUS*	LUCIL		1	
GRAECUS*	MAR		1	
GRAECUS*	OV		1	
GRAECUS*	PL		1	

GRAECUS*	PROP	1	Greek
GRAECUS*	TER	1 12	
GRAI cf. Graii	AV	1	Greeks
GRAI	CAT	1	
GRAI	CIC	1	
GRAI	COM	1	
GRAI	ENN	1	
GRAI	GER	1	
GRAI	LUC	1	
GRAI	MAN	1	
GRAI	PER	1	
GRAI	PH	1	
GRAI	PROP	1 11	
GRAII cf. Grai	FPLA	1	Greeks
GRAII	GR	1	
GRAII	HOR	1	
GRAII	OV	1	
GRAII	SEN	1	
GRAII	TR	1	
GRAII	VAL	1 7	
GRAIIUGENAE m.	LUCR		Greeks
GRAIUGENA	S	1	a Greek
GRAIUGENA (Pacuv.)	TR	1	
GRAIUGENA	V	1 3	
GRAIUGENAF	VAL		Greeks
GRAIUS	AV	1	a Greek
GRAIUS	CAT	1	
GRAIUS	OV	1	
GRAIUS	S	1	
GRAIUS	SIL	1	
GRAIUS	TR	1	
GRAIUS also pl.	V	1	
GRAIUS	VAL	1 8	
GRAIUS*	AET	1	Greek
GRAIUS*	AV	1	
GRAIUS*	COL	1	
GRAIUS*	ENN	1	
GRAIUS*	HL	1	
GRAIUS*	HOR	1	
GRAIUS*	JUV	1	
GRAIUS*	LP	1	
GRAIUS*	LUC	1	
GRAIUS*	LUCR	1	
GRAIUS*	MAN	1	
GRAIUS*	MAR	1	
GRAIUS*	OV	1	
GRAIUS*	PER	1	
GRAIUS*	PET	1	
GRAIUS*	PROP	1	
GRAIUS*	S	1	
GRAIUS*	SEN	1	
GRAIUS*	SIL	1	
GRAIUS*	TIB	1	
GRAIUS*	V	1	
GRAIUS*	VAL	1 22	
GRANĪCUS	OV		river of Phrygia
GRANIUS	LUCIL		Q. Granius, a crier

GRATIA coll.sg.	OV		1	the Graces (M. 4.629)
GRATIA sg.	S	1	2	a Grace
GRATIAE	HOR			the Graces
-GRATIANA n.pl.	MAR			vases (4.39.6)
GRATTIUS P. 4.16.34	OV			a poet
-GRAVII 1.235	SIL			Spanish tribe
GRAVISCAE	SIL		1	town of Etruria
GRAVISCAE	V	1	2	
-GRIPUS Rud. 934	PL			a fisherman
GROSPHUS	HOR		1	a Siculian
GROSPHUS	SIL	1	2	"
-GRUMIO Most. 51	PL			a slave
GRYLLUS	MAR			a bath-keeper
-GRYNEUS M. 12.260	OV			a Centaur
GRYNEUS*	V			p. to Grynia (t. in Aeolia)
-GRYPUS S. 4.9.15	S			Plotius Grypus, cont.
-GUBERNACLUM Arat.137	CIC			constellation "Rudder"
-GUNEUS	HL			Acarnanian leader
GURGES/FABIUS 6.266	JUV			Q. F. Maximus Gurges (consul 292 BC)
GYARA n.pl. & fem.sg.	JUV			island of the Cyclades
-GYAREUS 3.600, dissyll.	LUC			obscure sailor in Civil War
GYAROS cf. Gyara, fem.	OV		1	island of the Cyclades
GYAROS	S		1	
GYAROS	V	1	3	
GYAS m.	OV		1	100-armed giant
GYAS	S		1	
GYAS	SEN		1	
GYAS	SIL		1	
GYAS	V	2	6	(a Latin hero; a Trojan)
GYGAEUS (lacus)	PROP			p. to Gyges, i.e. Lydian
GYGES m. sg.	HOR		2	a Roman youth (ȳ); a giant (y̆)
GYGES F. 4.593	OV		1	a giant (cf. Gyas)
GYGES	V	1	4	a Trojan hero
GYLIPPUS	TIB		1	Spartan general
GYLIPPUS	V	1	2	an Arcadian
GYMNASIUM fem.	PL			a Gk. girl
GYNDES m.sg.	TIB			river of Assyria
HADRANUM 14.250	SIL			town of Sicily
HADRIA m.	CAT		1	Adriatic Sea
HADRIA	HOR		1	
HADRIA	OV		1	
HADRIA	PROP		1	
HADRIA	S		1	
HADRIA	SEN		1	
HADRIA fem.	SIL	1	7	town of Picenum
HADRIACUS	JUV		1	p. to Adriatic
HADRIACUS	MAN		1	
HADRIACUS	OV		1	
HADRIACUS	PROP		1	
HADRIACUS	SIL		1	
HADRIACUS	V	1	6	
HADRIANUS adj.	HOR			p. to the Adriatic
HAEDI	CIC		1	double star in Auriga
HAEDI	GER		1	
HAEDI	MAN		1	
HAEDI	OV		1	
HAEDI	S		1	

HAEDI		V	1	6	double star in Auriga
HAEDUS	sg.	HOR		1	" "
HAEDUS		MAN		1	
HAEDUS	2.26.56	PROP	1	3	
HAEMON		OV		1	son of Creon
HAEMON		PROP		1	
HAEMON		S		1	
HAEMON		V	1	4	(a Rutulian)
HAEMONIA		HOR		1	poetic name for Thessaly
HAEMONIA		OV		1	
HAEMONIA		S		1	
HAEMONIA		VAL	1	4	
HAEMONIDAE	m.pl.	VAL			the Argonauts
HAEMONIDES	m.sg.	LUC		1	a Thessalian
HAEMONIDES		S		1	
HAEMONIDES		V	1	3	
HAEMONIS	fem.sg.	OV			a Thessalian woman
HAEMONIUS	adj.	GR		1	p. to Haemonia, Thessalian
HAEMONIUS		LUC		1	
HAEMONIUS		OV		1	
HAEMONIUS		PROP		1	
HAEMONIUS		S		1	
HAEMONIUS		SEN		1	
HAEMONIUS		SIL		1	
HAEMONIUS		TIB		1	
HAEMONIUS		VAL	1	9	
HAEMUS		GER		1	mt. in Thrace
HAEMUS		HOR		1	
HAEMUS		JUV		1	(an actor)
HAEMUS		LUC		1	mt. in Thrace
HAEMUS		MAR		1	
HAEMUS		OV		1	
HAEMUS		S		1	
HAEMUS		SEN		1	
HAEMUS		SIL		1	
HAEMUS		V		1	
HAEMUS		VAL	1	11	
-HAGES m.sg., 3.191		VAL			a Cyzican
-HAGNA	S. 1.3.40	HOR			mistress of Balbinus
-HAGNIADES	m.sg.	VAL			= Tiphys (2.48)
-HAGNON	m.sg.	GR			Boeotian hunter
HALAESA		SIL			Halaesa, town of Sicily
HALAESUS		COL		1	river in Sicily
HALAESUS		SIL		1	an Argolian
HALAESUS	cf. Halesus	V	1	3	son of Agamemnon
HALCYONES	pl.	SEN			(cf. Alcyon)
HALCYONEUS	cf. Alc-	OV			p. to Alcyon
HALESUS	cf. Halae-	OV	2	2	son of Agamemnon; a Lapith
HALIACMON		S			an Argive
HALIARTOS		S			town of Boeotia
-HALISCA	Cist. 637	PL			a maid
-HALIUS	M. 13.258	OV		1	a Trojan
HALIUS	A. 9.767	V	1	2	"
HALYS		CIC		1	river in Anatolia
HALYS		LUC		1	
HALYS		OV		1	
HALYS		S		1	(a Theban)

HALYS	V		1	(a Trojan)
HALYS	VAL	2	7	river in Anatolia; a Cyzican
HAMADRYADES fem.pl.	AV		1	a class of wood-nymphs
HAMADRYADFS	OV		1	
HAMADRYADFS	PROP	1	3	
HAMADRYAS sg.	S			a wood-nymph
HAMILCAR	SIL			H. Barca, the father of Hannibal
HAMILLUS	JUV			a teacher
HAMMON	JUV		1	a god (or his shrine) in Libya
HAMMON	LUC		1	
HAMMON	LUCR		1	
HAMMON	PET		1	
HAMMON	S		1	
HAMMON	SIL		3	(+ a ship-name; a Libyan)
HAMMON	V		1	
HAMMON	VAL	1	10	
-HAMPSAGORAS 12.345	SIL			a Trojan
-HAMPSICUS 7.671	SIL			a Punic soldier
HANNIBAL	ENN		1	the famous Punic general
HANNIBAL	FPLR		1	
HANNIBAL	HOR		1	
HANNIBAL	JUV		1	
HANNIBAL	LUC		1	
HANNIBAL	MAN		1	
HANNIBAL	MAR		1	
HANNIBAL	PROP		1	
HANNIBAL	S		1	
HANNIBAL	SIL		1	
HANNIBAL	VAR	1	11	
HANNO Poen., passim	PL			a Punic man
HANNON	SIL	2	2	two different generals
HARMONIA	OV		1	a Gk. goddess, wife of Cadmus
HARMONIA	S	1	2	
-HARPAGIDES (-asides?)	OV			p. to Caria (Ibis 547)
HARPALUS	OV			name of a dog
HARPALYCE	V			a Thracian heroine
-HARPALYCUS A.11.675	V			a Trojan
HARPAX	PL			a slave name
-HARPE 16.365; 2.117	SIL		2	a mare; comp. of Asbyte
HARPE 6.375	VAL	1	3	an Amazon
HARPOCRATES	CAT			(Egyptian god of silence) as type
HARPYIA trisyll.	OV		1	(one of Actaeon's hounds)
HARPYIA	SEN		1	a Harpy (myth. bird-woman)
HARPYIA	V	1	3	
HARPYIAE pl.	HOR		1	myth. bird-women
HARPYIAE	MAR		1	
HARPYIAE	OV		1	
HARPYIAE	PET		1	
HARPYIAE	VAL	1	5	
HASDRUBAL	HOR		1	son of Hamilcar
HASDRUBAL	MAN		1	" "
HASDRUBAL F. 6.770	OV		1	son of Gisco
HASDRUBAL	SIL	3	6	three diff. Punics
HEAUTON/TIMORUMENOS	TER			title of TER's comedy
HEBE	CAT		1	goddess of youth
HEBE	MAR		1	
HEBE	OV		1	

HEBE	PROP		1	
HEBE	S		1	
HEBE	SEN		1	
HEBE	VAL	1	7	
HEBRAEUS adj.	S			Hebrew, Palestinian
HEBRUS	AV		1	river of Thrace
HEBRUS	GER		1	
HEBRUS	GR		1	
HEBRUS	HOR		2	(+name of a youth)
HEBRUS	OV		1	
HEBRUS	PH		1	
HEBRUS	S		2	(+ a Theban)
HEBRUS	SEN		1	
HEBRUS	SIL		1	
HEBRUS	TIB		1	
HEBRUS	V		2	(+ a Trojan)
HEBRUS	VAL	3	17	(+ two heroes)
-HECABE Gk., cf. Hecuba	HL		1	wife of Trojan Priam
HECABE 3.76.4	MAR	1	2	a type of old woman
HECALE	OV		1	kindly old woman of legend
HECALE	PET	1	2	" " "
-HECATAEON dub.	OV			father of Calyce (H. 18.133)
HECATAEUS or -eius	S			p. to Hecate
HECATE	HOR		1	d. of Perses & goddess of magic (often
HECATE	LUC		1	identified with Diana)
HECATE	OV		1	
HECATE	S		1	
HECATE	SEN		1	
HECATE	TIB		1	
HECATE	V		1	
HECATE	VAL	1	8	
-HECATEBELETES (Gk.)	FPLB			an epithet of Apollo
HECATEIS adj.	AV		1	p. to Hecate (Diana)
HECATEIS	OV		1	
HECATEIS	S	1	3	
HECATEIUS	OV		1	p. to Hecate
HECATEIUS Ach.1.447	S	1	2	
HECTOR	AET		1	the Trojan hero
HECTOR	AV		1	
HECTOR	COM		1	
HECTOR	ENN		1	
HECTOR	FPLA		1	
HECTOR	FPLB		1	
HECTOR	GER		1	
HECTOR	HL		1	
HECTOR	HOR		1	
HECTOR	JUV		1	
HECTOR	MAN		1	
HECTOR	MAR		1	
HECTOR	OV		1	
HECTOR	PL		1	
HECTOR	PRIAP		1	
HECTOR	PROP		1	
HECTOR	S		1	
HECTOR	SEN		1	
HECTOR	SIL		1	
HECTOR	TR		1	

HECTOR	V	1	21	the Trojan hero
HECTOREUS	AV		1	p. to Hector
HECTOREUS	HL		1	
HECTOREUS	HOR		1	
HECTOREUS	LUC		1	
HECTOREUS	MAR		1	
HECTOREUS	OV		1	
HECTOREUS	PROP		1	
HECTOREUS	S		1	
HECTOREUS	SEN		1	
HECTOREUS	SIL		1	
HECTOREUS	V	1	11	
HECUBA cf. Hecabe	ENN		1	the wife of Priam
HECUBA	MAR		1	
HECUBA	OV		1	
HECUBA	PL		1	(name of a dog)
HECUBA	SEN		1	
HECUBA	TR		1	
HECUBA	V	1	7	
HECYRA	FPLA		1	title of a comedy
HECYRA	TER	1	2	
-HEDYLUS 1.46	MAR			fictional person
HEDYMELES	JUV			a musician
-HEDYTIUM Ps. 187	PL			a meretrix
-HEGEA Pers. 824	PL			a saltator
-HEGIO Capt. 138	PL		1	a senex
HEGIO Ad., Phor.	TER	2	3	two different senes
HELENA cf. Helene	CAT		1	d. of Leda and wife of Menelaus
HELENA	ENN		1	
HELENA	FPLR		1	
HELENA	HOR		1	
HELENA	LUCIL		1	
HELENA	OV		1	
HELENA	PL		1	
HELENA	PRIAP		1	
HELENA	PROP		1	
HELENA	S		1	(also allusion to H. as star)
HELENA	SEN		1	
HELENA	TR		1	
HELENA	V	1	13	
HELENE = Helena	HL		1	d. of Leda
HELENE	MAR	1	2	
-HELENOR A.9.544	V			a Trojan
HELENUS	HL		1	a Trojan prophet, s. of Priam
HELENUS	OV		1	
HELENUS	PROP		1	
HELENUS	SEN		1	
HELENUS	V	1	5	
HELERNUS	OV			a woods along the Tiber
HELIACUS adj., 1.217	MAN			p. to the Sun
HELIADES fem.pl.	AV		1	daughters of the Sun
HELIADES	JUV		1	
HELIADES	MAR		1	
HELIADES	OV		1	
HELIADES	S	1	5	
HELICAON	MAR			son of Antenor
-HELICAONES T. 8.476	S			Thebans

HELICAONIUS	MAR			p. to Helicaon, i.e. Paduan
HELICE (Gk.)	AFT	1		constellation Great Bear (Big Dipper)
HELICE	CIC	1		
HELICE	GER	1		
HELICE	GR	1		
HELICE	LUC	1		
HELICE	MAN	1		
HELICE	MAR	1		
HELICE	OV	2		(+ town of Achaia)
HELICE	SEN	1		town of Achaia
HELICE	VAL	1	11	constellation
HELICON m.	GER	1		mt. in Boeotia, home of the Muses
HELICON	HOR	1		
HELICON	LUCR	1		
HELICON	MAN	1		
HELICON	MAR	1		
HELICON	MLP	1		
HELICON	OV	1		
HELICON	PER	1		
HELICON	PROP	1		
HELICON	S	1		
HELICON	SIL	1		
HELICON	V	1	12	
HELICONIADES	LUCR			the Muses
HELICONIDES	PER			the Muses
HELICONIS adj.	S			p. to the Muses, Heliconian
HELICONIUS	CAT	1		p. to the Muses, Heliconian
HELICONIUS	OV	1		
HELICONIUS	S	1	3	
HELIODORUS	HOR	1		a rhetorician
HELIODORUS	JUV	1	2	a surgeon
- HELIUS 5.24.5	MAR			a gladiator
- HELIX M. 5.87	OV	1		comp. of Phineus
HELIX 6.570	VAL	1	2	a hero
HELLAS	HOR			a woman
HELLE	COL	1		leg. d. of Athamas & Nephele
HELLE	GER	1		
HELLE	LUC	1		
HELLE	MAR	1		
HELLE	OV	1		
HELLE	PROP	1		
HELLE	S	1		
HELLE	SEN	1		
HELLE	TR	1		
HELLE	VAL	1	10	
HELLESPONTIACUS	AV	1		p. to the Hellespont
HELLESPONTIACUS	MAN	1		
HELLESPONTIACUS	OV	1		
HELLESPONTIACUS	PET	1		
HELLESPONTIACUS	V	1	5	
HELLESPONTIUS	CAT			p. to the Hellespont
HELLESPONTUS	AV	1		a strait (the Dardanelles)
HELLESPONTUS	CAT	1		
HELLESPONTUS	ENN	1		
HELLESPONTUS	LUC	1		
HELLESPONTUS	OV	1		
HELLESPONTUS	SIL	1	6	

-HELOPS	M. 12.334	OV	1	a Centaur
HELOPS	T. 12.746	S	1 2	a Theban
HELORIUS	(Tempe)	OV		p. to Helorus
HELORUS		SIL	1	river in Sicily
HELORUS		V	1 2	"
-HELOS	T. 4.181	S		town of Elis
HELVIDIŪS	5.36	JUV		Helv. Priscus, a Stoic banished by Nero
HELVINA/CERES		JUV		the goddess Ceres
-HELYMUS	14.46	SIL		a Trojan hero
-HENIOCHE	5.357	VAL		the nurse of Medea
HENIOCHI		LUC	1	a Sarmatian tribe
HENIOCHI		VAL	1 2	
HENIOCHUS		MAN	1	constellation; cf. Auriga
HENIOCHUS	Th. 1049	SEN	1 2	Sarmatian tribesman
HENIOCHUS*		OV		p. to the Hen. tribe
HENNA	cf. Enna	OV	1	town of Sicily
HENNA		SIL	1 2	
HENNAEUS		COL	1	p. to Henna
HENNAEUS		LUC	1	
HENNAEUS		OV	1	
HENNAEUS		PRIAP	1	
HENNAEUS		SIL	1 5	
HERACLEAE	(fabulae)	JUV		a lost epic (1.52)
HERACLITUS		AET	1	the Greek philosopher
HERACLITUS		LUCR	1 2	
-HERAS	6.78.3	MAR		cont. doctor
HERBESOS	fem.	SIL		town of Sicily
HERBESUS	m.	V		a Rutulian
HERCĒUS		LUC	1	ep. of Juppiter
HERCEUS	(-eius)	OV	1	(Ibis 282)
HERCEUS		SEN	1 3	
HERCULĀNĔUS adj.		PL		p. to Hercules (Truc. 562)
HERCULES		COM	1	the god of brute strength
HERCULES		HL	1	
HERCULES		HOR	1	
HERCULES		JUV	1	
HERCULES		LUC	1	
HERCULES		LUCR	1	
HERCULES		MAR	1	(+ a statue: 9.43.44)
HERCULES		OV	1	
HERCULES		PER	1	
HERCULES		PH	1	
HERCULES		PL	1	
HERCULES		PRIAP	1	
HERCULES		PROP	1	
HERCULES		S	1	
HERCULES		SEN	1	
HERCULES		SIL	1	
HERCULES		TER	1	
HERCULES		TR	1	
HERCULES		V	1	
HERCULES		VAL	1 20	
HERCULĔUS		COL	1	p. to Hercules, Herculean
HERCULEUS		HOR	1	
HERCULEUS		JUV	1	
HERCULEUS		LUC	1	
HERCULEUS		MAR	1	

HERCULĔUS	OV	1		p. to Hercules
HERCULEUS	PET	1		
HERCULEUS	PL	1		
HERCULEUS	PROP	1		
HERCULEUS	S	1		
HERCULEUS	SEN	1		
HERCULEUS	SIL	1		
HERCULEUS	V		1	
HERCULEUS	VAL	1	14	
HERDONIA	SIL			town of Apulia
HERE	ENN			goddess of heirs
– HERIUS 54.2	CAT	1		Marrucinian praenomen
HERIUS 17.452	SIL	1	2	Roman hero from Teate
HERMAPHRODITUS	MAR		1	son of Hermes and Aphrodite
HERMAPHRODITUS	OV	1	2	
HERMARCHUS	JUV			an unknown person
– HERMEROS 10.83.8	MAR			unknown
HERMES	JUV		1	a statue
HERMES	MAR	2	3	a doctor; a gladiator
HERMINIUS	SIL		1	a Roman name
HERMINIUS	V	1	2	a Trojan
– HERMIO (fr.inc.10)	PL			unknown character
HERMIONE	MAR		1	(cont. or fictional)
HERMIONE	OV		1	daughter of Menelaus
HERMIONE	PROP		1	
HERMIONE	SEN		1	
HERMIONE	V	1	5	
HERMIONĒUS Ciris 471	AV			p. to Hermione
– HERMOCRATES 6.53.4	MAR			fict. doctor
HERMOGENES	HOR		1	Herm. Tigellius, a bad poet
HERMOGENES	MAR	1	2	fictional character
HERMOGENES/TIGELLIUS	HOR			a bad poet
HERMUS	LUC		1	river in Aeolis (W. Anatolia)
HERMUS	MAR		1	
HERMUS	S		1	
HERMUS	SEN		1	
HERMUS	SIL		1	
HERMUS	V	1	6	
HERNICA (sc. saxa)	S			region in Latium
HERNICUS (as N)	JUV		1	= the Hernici (collective sg.)
HERNICUS	OV		1	p. to the Hernici (tr. of Latium)
HERNICUS	SIL		1	
HERNICUS	V	1	4	
HERO fem.	OV			sweetheart of Leander
HERODES m.sg.	HOR		1	king of Judaea
HERODES	MAR		1	fict. doctor
HERODES	PER	1	3	king of Judaea
HEROIDES fem.pl.	S			legendary heroines (& title of OV's poem)
HEROPHILE	TIB			a priestess of Apollo
HERŌUS	LUC			p. to Hero (the girl)
HERSE	OV			d. of Cecrops
– HERSES T. 7.737	S			a charioteer
⎰HERSILIA	MAR		1	wife of Romulus
⎱HERSILIA	SIL	1	2	
⎰HERSILIE	OV			
HERULUS = Herilus	V			king of Praeneste
HESIODUS	AV		1	the Greek poet

HESIODUS		MAN	1 2	the Greek poet
HESIONA		AV	1	d. of Laomedon
HESIONA		HL	1	
HESIONA		VAL	1 3	
HESIONE		LUC	1	d. of Laomedon
HESIONE		MAR	1	
HESIONE		OV	1	
HESIONE		SEN	1	
HESIONE		V	1 5	
HESPERIA		ENN	1	the Western Land
HESPERIA		HOR	1	Italy or Spain
HESPERIA		LUC	1	Italy
HESPERIA		MAN	1	
HESPERIA	F. 1.498	OV	1	
HESPERIA		PET	1	
HESPERIA		SIL	1	
HESPERIA		V	1	
HESPERIA		VAL	1 9	
HESPERIDES	fem.pl.	AV	1	myth. daughters of Hesperus
HESPERIDES		JUV	1	
HESPERIDES		LUC	1	
HESPERIDES		LUCR	1	
HESPERIDES		MAN	1	
HESPERIDES		MAR	1	
HESPERIDES		OV	1	
HESPERIDES		PRIAP	1	
HESPERIDES		PROP	1	
HESPERIDES		S	1	
HESPERIDES		SEN	1	
HESPERIDES		SIL	1	
HESPERIDES		V	1 13	
HESPERIE	M. 11.769	OV		a nymph
HESPERIUS	adj.	AV	1	western
HESPERIUS		FPLB	1	
HESPERIUS		HOR	1	
HESPERIUS		LUC	1	
HESPERIUS		MAR	1	
HESPERIUS		OV	1	
HESPERIUS		PROP	1	
HESPERIUS		S	1	
HESPERIUS		SEN	1	
HESPERIUS		SIL	1	
HESPERIUS		V	1	(Italic)
HESPERIUS		VAL	1 12	
HESPEROS		AV	1	Evening Star (West)
HESPEROS		GER	1	
HESPEROS		MAN	1	
HESPEROS		S	1	
HESPEROS		SIL	2 6	(+ a soldier of Gades)
HESPERUS		AET	1	Evening Star
HESPERUS		CAT	1	
HESPERUS		COL	1	
HESPERUS		FPLB	1	
HESPERUS		HL	1	
HESPERUS		OV	1	
HESPERUS		SEN	1	
HESPERUS		V	1 8	

HESUS (= **E**sus)	LUC			a Gaulish deity
HIARBAS = Iarbas	SIL	3	3	three Punic warriors
HIBER	HOR		1	a Spaniard
HIBER	LUC		1	
HIBER	SIL		1	
HIBER	VAL	1	4	river of Spain (i.e. the Spaniards)
HIBERES (or -i)	CAT			Spaniards
HIBERI	LUC		1	"
HIBERI	MAR		1	
HIBERI	S		1	
HIBERI	V	1	4	
HIBERIA	HOR		2	Spain; Caucasus
HIBERIA 7.232	LUC		1	Spain
HIBERIA	S		1	Spain
HIBERIA	VAL	1	5	Caucasus
HIBERIACUS adj.	SIL			Spanish, Iberian
HIBERICUS	HOR			Spanish, Iberian
HIBERINA	JUV			a Spanish woman
-HIBERIS 4.59	SIL			Hiberia (Spain)
HIBERUS 4.23	LUC		1	river of Spain
HIBERUS	SIL		4	river of Spain; three diff. men
HIBERUS	VAL	1	6	an Iberian (of the Caucasus)
HIBERUS*	CAL		1	Iberian, Spanish
HIBERUS*	CAT		1	
HIBERUS*	COL		1	
HIBERUS*	HOR		1	
HIBERUS*	LUC		1	
HIBERUS*	LUCIL		1	
HIBERUS*	MAR		1	
HIBERUS*	OV		1	
HIBERUS*	PET		1	
HIBERUS*	PROP		1	
HIBERUS*	S		1	
HIBERUS*	SEN		1	
HIBERUS*	SIL		1	
HIBERUS*	V		1	
HIBERUS*	VAL		1	
HIBERUS*	VAR	1	16	
HICETAONIUS	V			p. to Hicetaon (s. of Laomedon)
HIEMES pl.	S			"Storms"
HIEMPS (Hiems)	LUCR			"Storm"
HIEMPSAL	SIL			a Nasamonian
HIEMS	OV		1	"Storm"
HIEMS	SIL		1	
HIEMS	V	1	3	
{HIERO	PL			son of Hierocles
HIERON	SIL			
-HIERUS 9.103.3	MAR			a young slave
HILAIRA	PROP			daughter of Leucippus
HILARUS	MAR			a steward
HILURICUS adj.	PL			Illyrian
HILURIUS adj.	PL			Illyrian
HIMELLA	V			Sabine river
HIMERA n.pl.	OV		1	town in Sicily
HIMERA fem.sg.	SIL	1	2	river of Sicily
-HIMILCO 14.394	SIL			a Punic
- HIPPALMOS (**E**upal-)	OV			comp. of Meleager (**M**. 8.360)

HIPPARIS m.	SIL			river of Sicily
–HIPPASIDES T. 7.355	S			= Naubolos
HIPPASOS	OV			a Centaur
HIPPASUS	OV		1	son of Eurytus
HIPPASUS	VAL	1	2	a Centaur
HIPPO m.	SIL			town of Numidia
HIPPOCOON	OV		1	Calydonian hunter
HIPPOCOON	V	1	2	comp. of Aeneas
HIPPOCRATES	MAR			fictional doctor
HIPPOCRENE	GER		1	fountain near Helicon
HIPPOCRENE	OV	1	2	
HIPPODAMAS	OV			father of Perimele
HIPPODAME	MAR		1	d. of Oenomaus & wife of Pelops
HIPPODAME M. XII	OV		1	
HIPPODAME	V	1	3	
HIPPODAMEA	ENN			
HIPPODAMIA	GER		1	
HIPPODAMIA H. passim	OV		1	(d. of Adrastus)
HIPPODAMIA	PROP		1	
HIPPODAMIA	TR		1	
HIPPODAMIA	VAL	1	5	
HIPPODAMUS	S			ep. of Castor
HIPPOLYTA	PL			the Amazon
HIPPOLYTE	HOR		1	(wife of Adrastus)
HIPPOLYTE	OV		1	the Amazon
HIPPOLYTE	PROP		1	
HIPPOLYTE	S		1	
HIPPOLYTE	SEN		1	
HIPPOLYTE	V	1	6	
HIPPOLYTUS	HOR		1	son of Theseus & Hippolyte
HIPPOLYTUS	JUV		1	
HIPPOLYTUS	MAR		1	
HIPPOLYTUS	OV		1	
HIPPOLYTUS	PH		1	
HIPPOLYTUS Cap. 733	PL		1	(an artisan)
HIPPOLYTUS	PROP		1	son of Theseus
HIPPOLYTUS	S		1	
HIPPOLYTUS	SEN		1	
HIPPOLYTUS	V	1	10	
– HIPPOMEDON T. 1.44	S			one of the "7"
HIPPOMENEIS	OV			= Limone
HIPPOMENES	AV		1	conqueror of Atalanta
HIPPOMENES	OV		1	
HIPPOMENES	PRIAP		1	
HIPPOMENES	S	1	4	
–HIPPONIUS adj.	GR			Bruttian
– HIPPONOUS Ibis 472	OV			a man
HIPPOTADES patr.	OV		1	Aeolus (grandson of Hippotes)
HIPPOTADES	S		1	
HIPPOTADES	V		1	
HIPPOTADES	VAL	1	4	
– HIPPOTES	TR			a hero
HIPPOTHOUS	OV			son of Cercyon
HIRPINUS cf. Irpinus	JUV		1	a breed of horse
HIRPINUS	MAR	1	2	" "
HIRPINUS*	SIL			p. to the Hirpini tr. (Samnites)
– HIRPINUS/QUINCTIUS	HOR			unknown man

– HIRRUS 10.222	JUV			a bad guardian
– HISBO **A.** 10.384	V			a Rutulian
HISPAL n., = Hispalis	SIL			town of S. Spain
HISPANĒ adv.	ENN			in (a) language of Spain
HISPANI	PL			the Iberians
HISPANIA	JUV	1		Iberia, Spain
HISPANIA	LUC	1		
HISPANIA	MAN	1		
HISPANIA	MAR	1		
HISPANIA	SIL	1		
HISPANIA	TIB	1	6	
HISPANIENSIS	MAR			p. to Spain (Iberia)
HISPANUS	GR	1		p. to Spain
HISPANUS	HOR	1		
HISPANUS	LUC	1		
HISPANUS	MAN	1		
HISPANUS	MAR	1		
HISPANUS	OV	1		
HISPANUS	SIL	1	7	
HISPELLAS adj.	SIL			p. to Hispellum
HISPELLUM	SIL			town of Umbria
HISPO 2.50	JUV			an indecent person
HISPULLA	JUV			a woman's name
HISTER cf. Ister	JUV		2	river Danube; Pacuvius (legacy hunter)
HISTER	LUC	1		river
HISTER	MAR	1		(resident on Danube)
HISTER	OV	1		
HISTER	S	1		
HISTER	SEN	1		
HISTER	SIL	1		
HISTER	TR	1		
HISTER	V	1		
HISTER	VAL	1	11	
HISTER/PACUVIUS	JUV			legacy hunter (12.111-112)
HISTRI	ENN	1		people of Istria (in Illyria)
HISTRI	LUC	1		
HISTRI	PL	1	3	
HISTRUS*	MAR			p. to the Hister river (or to Istria?)
– HODITES **M.** 5.97,12.457	OV	2	2	a Centaur; Cephenus
– HOMERĒUS (Cat. 14a.2)	AV			Homeric
HOMERIACUS	PRIAP			Homeric
HOMERICUS	JUV			Homeric
HOMERONIDES	PL			(comic) imitator of Homer
HOMERUS	AV	1		the leg. Greek poet
HOMERUS	ENN	1		
HOMERUS	HL	1		
HOMERUS	HOR	1		
HOMERUS	JUV	1		
HOMERUS	LUCIL	1		
HOMERUS	LUCR	1		
HOMERUS	MAR	1		
HOMERUS	OV	1		
HOMERUS	PRIAP	1		
HOMERUS	PROP	1		
HOMERUS	S	1		
HOMERUS	TIB	1	13	
HOMOLE	V			mt. in Thessaly

HOMOLOIDES sc. portae	S			Homoloian gate at Thebes
HONOR personified	MAR	1		goddess of Esteem, Respect
HONOR	OV	1		
HONOR	PL	1		
HONOR	SIL	1	4	
HONOS	HOR		1	
HONOS	PROP	1	2	
- HOPLEUS T. passim	S			Tydeus' attendant
HORA	ENN		1	= Hersilia, wife of Romulus
HORA	OV		1	"
HORA	VAL	1	3	a nymph
HORAE	OV		1	goddesses of the Seasons
HORAE	S		1	
HORAE	V		1	
HORAE	VAL	1	4	
HORATIUS	ENN		1	the hero, Horat. Cocles
HORATIUS	FPLR		1	Flaccus, the lyric poet
HORATIUS	HOR		1	"
HORATIUS	JUV		1	"
HORATIUS	LP		1	"
HORATIUS	MAN		1	the hero
HORATIUS	MAR		2	heroes (brothers)
HORATIUS	OV		1	Flaccus, the poet
HORATIUS	PROP	1	10	the hero
HORATIUS*	AV		1	p. to the Horatian family
HORATIUS*	MAN	1	2	
- HORMUS 2.15	MAR			fictional person
- HOROS 4.1.78	PROP			an astrologer
HORTENSIUS	CAT		1	Quintus Hortensius Hortalus, the orator
HORTENSIUS	LUC		1	" "
HORTENSIUS	LUCIL		1	(unknown)
HORTENSIUS	OV	1	4	a poet
HORTINUS adj.	V			p. to Hortanum (t. of Etruria)
HOSTILIUS	LUCIL			L. Host. Tubulus
- HOSTUS 12.347, 1.437	SIL	2	2	a Sard; a Saguntine
HYACINTHIA n.pl.	OV			festival of Hyacinth
HYACINTHUS	JUV		1	leg. handsome Spartan youth
HYACINTHUS	MAR		1	
HYACINTHUS	OV	1	3	
HYACINTUS	LUCIL			
HYADES pl. fem.	CIC		1	group of stars in const. Taurus
HYADES	GER		1	
HYADES	HOR		1	
HYADES	MAN		1	
HYADES	OV		1	
HYADES	V		1	
HYADES	VAL	1	7	
HYALE	OV			a nymph
HYAMPOLIS	S			town of Phocis
HYANTEUS	MAR		1	p. to the Hyantes (Boeotians)
HYANTEUS	OV		1	
HYANTEUS	S	1	3	
HYANTIUS	OV		1	p. to the Hyantes
HYANTIUS	S	1	2	
HYAS -nt-, sg.m.	OV		1	son of Atlas
HYAS -d-, sg. fem.	S	1	2	a Hyad (const.)
HYBLA	COL		1	mt. in Sicily (with adjoining town)

HYBLA	LUC		1	mt. in Sicily
HYBLA	MAR		1	
HYBLA	OV		1	
HYBLA	S		1	
HYBLA	SEN		1	
HYBLA	SIL		1	
HYBLA	V	1	8	
HYBLAEUS	CAL		1	p. to Hybla
HYBLAEUS	LUC		1	
HYBLAEUS	MAR		1	
HYBLAEUS	S		1	
HYBLAEUS	SIL		1	
HYBLAEUS	V	1	6	
HYDASPES	HOR		2	river in India; a slave-name
HYDASPES	LUC		1	the river
HYDASPES	PET		1	
HYDASPES	S		1	
HYDASPES	SEN		1	
HYDASPES	V	2	8	(+ comp. of Aeneas)
HYDRA	CIC		1	constellation (cf. Anguis)
HYDRA	GER		1	"
HYDRA	HOR		1	mythical snake
HYDRA	MAN		1	constell.
HYDRA	MAR		1	snake
HYDRA	S	1	6	snake
HYDROCHOOS	CAT		1	constellation "Aquarius"
HYDROCHOOS	GER	1	2	
HYDROS	GER			constellation (Water-snake)
HYDRŪS -nt-, fem.	LUC			town of Calabria
-HYEMPSA 16.461	SIL			Punic soldier
HYGĪA	MAR			Gk. goddess of Health
HYGĪNUS	MAR			a cont. doctor
-HYLA fem.	AET			forest in Cyprus
HYLACTOR	OV			a hound of Actaeon
HYLAEUS	HOR		1	a Centaur
HYLAEUS	OV		2	Centaur; dog
HYLAEUS	S		1	Centaur
HYLAEUS	V	1	5	Centaur
HYLAEUS*	PROP		1	p. to the Centaur
HYLAEUS* (gens)	VAL	1	2	
HYLAS m.	JUV		1	a handsome youth, comp. of Hercules
HYLAS	MAR		3	the youth; a slave; contemporary
HYLAS	OV		1	the youth
HYLAS	PROP		1	
HYLAS	S		1	
HYLAS	SEN		1	
HYLAS	V		2	(a dog, B. 8.107)
HYLAS	VAL	1	11	
-HYLE T. 7.267	S			town of Boeotia
HYLES	OV			a Centaur
HYLEUS	OV			a hunter (of Calydon)
-HYLEUS* M. 13.684	OV			born in Hyla
HYLLEUS (-1-)	PROP			Illyrian tribe
HYLLUS	MAR		1	a contemp. man
HYLLUS	OV		1	son of Hercules by Deianira
HYLLUS	S		1	"
HYLLUS	SEN		1	"

HYLLUS	V	1	5	a Trojan
HYLONOME	OV			wife of Cyllarus the Centaur
HYMEN (Cul. 247)	AV		1	god of marriage
HYMEN	CAT		1	
HYMEN	OV		1	
HYMEN	PL		1	(also wedding song)
HYMEN	S		1	
HYMEN	SEN	1	6	wedding
HYMENAEUS	CAT		1	wedding or song
HYMENAEUS	LUCR		1	song; (pl.) wedding
HYMENAEUS	MAR		1	god of marriage
HYMENAEUS	OV		1	god & hymn
HYMENAEUS	PH		1	(a youth dressed as Hymen)
HYMENAEUS	PL		1	god
HYMENAEUS	PROP		1	god
HYMENAEUS	SEN		1	wedding
HYMENAEUS	SIL		1	god
HYMENAEUS	TER		1	hymn
HYMENAEUS	V	1	11	god; (pl.) wedding
HYMENAEUS*	SIL			p. to Hymen
HYMETTIUS	HOR		1	p. to Hymettus
HYMETTIUS	MAR		1	
HYMETTIUS	OV	1	3	
HYMETTOS	MAR		1	mountain near Athens
HYMETTOS	SIL	1	2	
HYMETTUS	COL		1	
HYMETTUS	HOR		1	
HYMETTUS	JUV		1	
HYMETTUS	OV		1	
HYMETTUS	S		1	
HYMETTUS	SEN		1	
HYMETTUS	VAL	1	7	
HYMNIS	LUCIL			pseudonym of a woman
HYPAEPA n.pl.	OV		1	town of Lydia
HYPAEPA	PET	1	2	
HYPANIS m.	OV		1	river in Sarmatia
HYPANIS	PROP		1	"
HYPANIS	S		1	an Argive
HYPANIS	V		2	river; a Trojan
HYPANIS	VAL	2	7	river; a Colchian
HYPERBOREUS	CAT		1	p. to a tribe vaguely in N. Europe
HYPERBOREUS	HOR		1	
HYPERBOREUS	JUV		1	
HYPERBOREUS	LUC		1	
HYPERBOREUS	MAR		1	
HYPERBOREUS	OV		1	
HYPERBOREUS	S		1	
HYPERBOREUS	V		1	
HYPERBOREUS	VAL	1	9	
-HYPERENOR T. 8.493	S			an Argive
HYPERIA	VAL			fountain in Thessaly
HYPERION	AV		1	(f. of Sun), the Sun
HYPERION	CIC		1	
HYPERION	COL		1	
HYPERION	COM		1	
HYPERION	ENN		1	
HYPERION	FPLB		1	

HYPERION	OV		1	the Sun (or father of the Sun)
HYPERION	S	1	8
- HYPERIONIDES 5.471	VAL			= Aeetes
HYPERIONIS patr.	OV			= Aurora
HYPERIONIUS	S		1	p. to Hyperion
HYPERIONIUS	SIL		1
HYPERIONIUS	VAL	1	3
⎰HYPERMESTRA	OV			a daughter of Danaus
⎱HYPERMESTRE	PROP		
-HYPETAON 6.637	VAL			a Colchian
- HYPNUS 11.36.5	MAR			fict. person
HYPSA 14.227	SIL			river in Sicily
- HYPSAEA S. 1.2.91	HOR			a certain Plotia
HYPSEUS	OV		1	guest of the hero Perseus
HYPSEUS	S	1	2	= Asopus (?)
HYPSIPYLE	OV		1	queen of Lemnos
HYPSIPYLE	PER		1
HYPSIPYLE	PROP		1
HYPSIPYLE	S		1
HYPSIPYLE	VAL	1	5
HYPSIPYLEUS	OV			p. to Hypsipyle
-HYPSISTAE T. 8.356	S			a gate of Thebes
- HYPSO 1.367	VAL			mother of Deucalion
HYRCANI	CAT		1	a tribe on the Caspian
HYRCANI	SIL	1	2
HYRCANIA 3.268	LUC			the country of the Hyrcani
HYRCANIUS	SEN			p. to the Hyrcani
HYRCANUS	AV		1	p. to the Hyrcani
HYRCANUS	GR		1
HYRCANUS	LUC		1
HYRCANUS	LUCR		1
HYRCANUS	MAR		1
HYRCANUS	PET		1
HYRCANUS	PROP		1
HYRCANUS	S		1
HYRCANUS	SEN		1
HYRCANUS	SIL		1
HYRCANUS	V		1
HYRCANUS	VAL	1	12
HYRIE	OV			town (& lake) in Boeotia
HYRIEUS trisyllabic	OV			father of Orion
HYRIEUS*	OV			p. to Hyrieus
HYRTACIDES patr.	OV		1	= Nisus
HYRTACIDES	V	1	2
HYRTACUS	V			father of Nisus
IACCHUS	CAT		1	ep. of Bacchus (wine)
IACCHUS	COL		1
IACCHUS	LUCR		1
IACCHUS	MAN		1
IACCHUS	OV		1
IACCHUS	PROP		1
IACCHUS	S		1
IACCHUS	SEN		1
IACCHUS	SIL		1
IACCHUS	V		1
IACCHUS	VAL	1	11
IADER	LUC			town of Illyria

IAERA	V		a Nereid
-IAHON Poen. 1065	PL		fictional man
-IALMENIDES T. 10.510	S		a Theban
-IALMENUS T. 10.305	S		a Theban
IALYSIUS adj.	OV		p. to Rhodes, Rhodian
IANTHE M. 9.715	OV		daughter of Telestes
-IANTHIS	MAR		pseudonym of Violentilla (6.21)
IAPETIONIDES patr.	OV		= Atlas
IAPETUS	HOR	1	a Titan
IAPETUS	OV	1	
IAPETUS	S	1	
IAPETUS	SIL	1	
IAPETUS	V	1	
IAPETUS	VAL	1 6	
IAPYDIA	TIB		region of Illyria
IAPYGIA	OV		region of S. Italy
IAPYGIUS adj.	SIL		p. to Iapygia
IAPYS adj.	V		p. to the Iapydes of Illyria
IAPYX	HOR	1	NW wind (from Apulia)
IAPYX	OV	1	son of Daedalus
IAPYX	S	1	the wind
IAPYX	SIL	1	son of Daedalus
IAPYX	V	2	wind; a Trojan
IAPYX	VAL	1 7	wind
IAPYX*	OV	1	Iapygian
IAPYX*	SIL	1	
IAPYX* A. 11.247, 678	V	1 3	
IARBA m.	OV		the king of Mauretania
IARBAS	JUV	1	
IARBAS	V	1 2	
IARBITA	HOR		a Mauretanian
IARDANIS patr.	OV		= Omphale
-IAS 1.34.7	MAR		a meretrix
IASIDES patr.	GER	1	ep. of Cepheus
IASIDES	S	2	an Argive; (as fem.pl.) Argive women
IASIDES	V	1 4	= Palinurus
IASION Iasius	OV		son of Juppiter and Electra
IASIS	PROP		= Atalanta
IASIUS	OV	1	son of Juppiter and Electra
IASIUS	S	1	an Argive
IASIUS	V	1 3	son of Juppiter
IASIUS*	VAL		p. to Iasius, i.e. Argive
IASON	GER	1	the Greek hero, s. of Aeson
IASON	HOR	1	
IASON	JUV	1	
IASON	OV	1	
IASON	PL	1	
IASON	PROP	1	(title of poem)
IASON	S	1	
IASON	SEN	1	
IASON	VAL	1 9	
IASONIDAE pl., patr.	S		sons of Jason
IASONIUS	OV	1	p. to Argo (Jason's ship)
IASONIUS	PROP	1	
IASONIUS	S	1 3	
IAXARTES	VAL		a river of Asia
IAZYGES	VAL		a Sarmatian tribe

IAZYX also pl.	OV			a Sarmatian tribe
IBER = Hiber	LUC			(also a spelling in other authors)
IBIS	OV			title of his little poem
IBYCUS	HOR		1	(unknown Roman)
IBYCUS	S	1	2	the Greek lyric poet
ICADION =Icadius	LUCIL			a robber (pirate)
ICARIA	LUC			island in the Icarian Sea
ICARIOTIS patr.	AV		1	= Penelope
ICARIOTIS	PROP	1	2	
ICARIOTIS*	OV			p. to Penelope
ICARIS patr.	OV			= Penelope
ICARIUM	MAN		1	part of the Aegean Sea
ICARIUM	OV	1	2	
ICARIUS	OV		1	father of Penelope
ICARIUS	S	1	2	father of Erigone
ICARIUS*	HOR		1	p. to Icarus or Icarius
ICARIUS*	OV		1	
ICARIUS*	PROP		1	
ICARIUS*	S		1	
ICARIUS*	SIL	1	5	
ICARUS	GER		1	son of Daedalus
ICARUS	HOR		2	" " ; an island
ICARUS	OV		2	" " ; f. of Penelope
ICARUS	PROP		1	son of Oebalus
ICARUS	SEN		1	son of Daedalus
ICARUS	SIL		1	son of Mopsus
ICARUS	TIB		1	son of Oebalus
ICARUS	V	1	10	son of Daedalus
ICCIUS	HOR			a friend of Horace
ICELOS	OV			son of Somnus
ICHNOBATES	OV			name of a dog
ICHNUSA	SIL			Sardinia
IDA cf. Ide	AV		1	mountain in Phrygia
IDA	CAT		1	
IDA	HL		1	
IDA	HOR		1	
IDA	MAR		3	mt. in Phrygia; mt. in Crete; a monster
IDA	OV		2	two mts.
IDA	PET		1	mt. in Phrygia
IDA	PROP		1	
IDA	S		1	mt. in Crete
IDA	SIL		1	mt. in Crete
IDA	TR		1	(unspecified mt.)
IDA	V		3	two mts.; a nymph
IDA	VAL	1	18	mt. in Phrygia
IDAEUS N	HL		1	a Trojan herald
IDAEUS	MAR		1	Ganymede
IDAEUS	V	2	4	two Trojans
IDAEUS*	AV		1	p. to Mt. Ida (Crete or Phrygia)
IDAEUS*	FPLB		1	
IDAEUS*	GR		1	
IDAEUS*	HL		1	
IDAEUS*	HOR		1	
IDAEUS*	JUV		1	
IDAEUS*	LUCR		1	
IDAEUS*	MAN		1	
IDAEUS*	OV		2	(Trojan; Cretan)

IDAEUS*	PET	1	p. to mt. Ida
IDAEUS*	PROP	1	
IDAEUS*	S	1	
IDAEUS*	SEN	1	
IDAEUS*	SIL	1	
IDAEUS*	TIB	1	
IDAEUS*	V	1	
IDAEUS*	VAL	1 18	
IDALIE	OV		ep. of Venus
-IDALIS 3.204	LUC		Cyprus
IDALIUM	CAT	1	town of Cyprus
IDALIUM	LUC	1	
IDALIUM	V	1	
IDALIUM	VAL	1 4	
IDALIUS	AV	1	p. to Idalium
IDALIUS	OV	1	
IDALIUS	PROP	1	
IDALIUS	S	1	
IDALIUS	SIL	1	
IDALIUS	V	1	
IDALIUS	VAL	1 7	
IDAS	CAL	1	a shepherd
IDAS	OV	3	son of Aphareus; comp. of Diomedes;
IDAS	PROP	1	son of Aphareus Cephenus
IDAS	S	1	son of Aphareus
IDAS	V	1	a Trojan
IDAS	VAL	1 8	an Argonaut
-IDASMENUS 6.196	VAL		a Scythian
IDE cf. Ida	GER	1	a mt. (unspecified)
IDE	S	1	mt. in Phrygia
IDE	SEN	1 3	mt. in Phrygia
IDMON	OV	1	father of Arachne
IDMON	S	1	legendary doctor
IDMON Med. 652	SEN	1	a prophet, killed by Mopsus
IDMON	SIL	1	a Rutulian
IDMON	V	1	"
IDMON	VAL	1 6	an Argonaut
IDMONIUS adj.	OV		p. to Idmon
IDOMENEUS	CAT	1	king of Crete
IDOMENEUS	HL	1	
IDOMENEUS	HOR	1	
IDOMENEUS	OV	1	
IDOMENEUS	V	1 5	
IDUMAEUS	MAR	1	p. to Idume, i.e. Palestinian
IDUMAEUS	S	1	
IDUMAEUS	SIL	1	
IDUMAEUS	V	1 4	
IDUME	LUC	1	a section of Palestine
IDUME	S	1	
IDUME	VAL	1 3	
IDUS pl.	HOR	1	the Ides of the month
IDUS	OV	1	
IDUS	PROP	1	
IDUS	SIL	1 4	
IDYIA	OV		mother of Medea
IDYMAEUS (Idum-)	JUV		p. to Idume
IDYME (Idume)	SIL		section of Palestine

−IERTES	5.259	SIL		Punic man
−IETAS	14.271	SIL		town of Sicily
IGNAVIA	Poen. 846	PL	1	"Sloth" personified (also **Pers**.850)
IGNAVIA	T. 10.90	S	1 2	
IGNIPOTENS		HL	1	ep. of Vulcan
IGNIPOTENS		V	1 2	
IGUVIUM		SIL		town of Umbria
ILERDA		HOR	1	town of Spain
ILERDA		LUC	1	
ILERDA		SIL	1 3	
−ILERDES	16.566	SIL		a Spaniard
−ILERTES	3.255	SIL		an African
ILIA		ENN	1	= Rhea Silvia, m. of Romulus & Remus
ILIA		HOR	1	
ILIA		MAR	1	
ILIA		OV	1	
ILIA		S	1	
ILIA		SIL	1	
ILIA		TIB	1	
ILIA		V	1 8	
ILIACUS		CAT	1	p. to Ilium, Trojan
ILIACUS		HL	1	
ILIACUS		HOR	1	
ILIACUS		JUV	1	
ILIACUS		LUC	1	
ILIACUS		MAN	1	
ILIACUS		MAR	1	
ILIACUS		MLP	1	
ILIACUS		OV	1	
ILIACUS		PROP	1	
ILIACUS		S	1	
ILIACUS		SEN	1	
ILIACUS		SIL	1	
ILIACUS		V	1	
ILIACUS		VAL	1 15	
ILIADES	fem.pl.	HL	1	Trojan women
ILIADES	" "	JUV	1	" "
ILIADES	m. sg.	OV	3	Ganymede; Romulus; Remus
ILIADES	fem.pl.	SEN	1	Trojan women
ILIADES		V	1 7	" "
ILIAS		JUV	1	the Iliad
ILIAS		LUCIL	1	
ILIAS		MAR	1	
ILIAS		OV	2	(also: Helen)
ILIAS		PER	1	
ILIAS		PET	1	
ILIAS		PRIAP	1	
ILIAS	also pl.	PROP	1 9	
ILION	cf. Ilium	HL	1	Troy
ILION		HOR	1	
ILION		PROP	1	
ILION		S	1	
ILION		SIL	1	
ILION		TIB	1 6	
ILIONA		HOR		title of a tragedy
ILIONE		V		daughter of Priam
ILIONEUS		OV	1	son of Niobe

ILIONEUS	V	1	2	a Trojan
ILIOS fem., cf. Ilius	GER		1	Troy
ILIOS	OV	1	2	
-ILISOS P. 13	SEN			a river in Attica
ILITHYIA cf. Ily-	HOR		1	goddess of birth
ILITHYIA	OV	1	2	
ILIUM cf. Ilion	COM		1	Troy
ILIUM	OV		1	
ILIUM	PH		1	
ILIUM	PL		1	
ILIUM	SEN		1	
ILIUM	V	1	6	
ILIUS fem., cf. Ilios	HOR		1	Troy
ILIUS	PL		1	
ILIUS	PROP		1	
ILIUS	TR		1	
ILIUS	V	1	5	
ILIUS*	HOR			Trojan
ILLYRIA also pl.	PROP			region in NW Balkans
ILLYRIAE Tr. 1.4.19	OV			the two Illyrias (Gk. & Roman)
ILLYRICUS	HOR		1	Illyrian, p. to Illyria
ILLYRICUS	JUV		1	
ILLYRICUS	LUC		1	
ILLYRICUS	MAN		1	
ILLYRICUS	OV		1	
ILLYRICUS	PROP		1	
ILLYRICUS	S		1	
ILLYRICUS	SEN		1	
ILLYRICUS	SIL		1	
ILLYRICUS	V	1	10	
ILLYRII	ENN			p. of Illyria
ILLYRIS adj.	LUC		1	Illyrian
ILLYRIS	MAN		1	
ILLYRIS also N	OV		1	
ILLYRIS	SIL	1	4	
ILUS	OV		1	son of Tros
ILUS	SIL		1	" "
ILUS	TR		1	" "
ILUS	V		2	a Rutulian; a Trojan
ILUS	VAL	1	6	son of Tros
ILVA	OV		1	island (Elba)
ILVA	SIL		1	
ILVA	V	1	3	
ILYTHYIA cf. Ili-	AV			goddess of birth
-IMAON A. 10.424	V			a Rutulian
IMBRASIDES	HL		1	= Piros, Thracian chieftain (?)
IMBRASIDES also pl.	V	1	2	= Lades
IMBRASUS	V			a Lycian comp. of Aeneas
-IMBREUS M. 12.310	OV			a Centaur
IMBROS	VAL			island in N. Aegean
IMBRUS	TER			
-IMILCE 3.91	SIL			wife of Hannibal
-IMPETUS 7.47	S			comp. of Mars, personified
INACHIA	HOR			a girl
INACHIDAE m.pl.	S			Argives
INACHIDES m.sg.	OV		2	Epaphus; Perseus
INACHIDES fem.pl.	S	1	3	Argive women

INACHIS	patr.	MAR	1	Io
INACHIS		OV	2	Io; Isis
INACHIS		PROP	1	Io
INACHIS		S	1	Io
INACHIS		VAL	1 6	Io
INACHIS*		AV	1	p. to Inachus
INACHIS*		OV	1 2	
INACHIUS		LUC	1	p. to Inachus, i.e. Greek
INACHIUS		OV	1	
INACHIUS		PET	1	
INACHIUS		PROP	1	
INACHIUS		S	1	
INACHIUS		SEN	1	
INACHIUS		SIL	1	
INACHIUS		V	1	
INACHIUS		VAL	1 9	
INACHUS		HOR	1	leg. king of Argos
INACHUS	M. & Am.	OV	1	river in Argolid
INACHUS		S	2	king; river
INACHUS		SEN	1	river
INACHUS		TR	1	river
INACHUS		V	2	king; river
INACHUS		VAL	1 9	river
INACHUS*		S		Greek
INARIME		LUC	1	island off Naples
INARIME		OV	1	
INARIME		S	1	
INARIME		SEN	1	
INARIME		SIL	1	
INARIME		V	1	
INARIME		VAL	1 7	
-INCITATUS	10.76.9	MAR		a circus-driver
INDI	cf. Indus	AV	1	the people of India
INDI		CAT	1	
INDI		HOR	1	
INDI		JUV	1	
INDI		LUC	1	
INDI		MAR	1	
INDI		OV	1	
INDI		PROP	1	
INDI		S	1	
INDI		SEN	1	
INDI		SIL	1	
INDI		TIB	1	
INDI		VAL	1 13	
INDIA		CAT	1	the country in Asia
INDIA		HOR	1	
INDIA		LUC	1	
INDIA		LUCR	1	
INDIA		MAN	1	
INDIA		OV	1	
INDIA		PL	1	
INDIA		PROP	1	
INDIA		S	1	
INDIA		SEN	1	
INDIA		TIB	1	
INDIA		V	1 12	

-INDIBILIS	16.564	SIL		a Spaniard
INDICUS		COM	1	Indian, p. to India
INDICUS		FPLB	1	
INDICUS		HOR	1	
INDICUS		JUV	1	
INDICUS		MAR	1	
INDICUS		OV	1	
INDICUS		PET	1	
INDICUS		PRIAP	1	
INDICUS		PROP	1	
INDICUS		S	1	
INDICUS		SEN	1	
INDICUS		TER	1 12	
INDIGES	sg. (-et-)	OV	1	a class of Roman cult-heroes
INDIGES		TIB	2	
INDIGES		V	1 4	(Aeneas)
INDILIGENTIA		PL		"Indifference" personified (Pers. 557)
INDUS		HOR	1	an Indian (in general)
INDUS	11.125	JUV	1	
INDUS		LUC	2	; the Indus river
INDUS		MAR	1	
INDUS		OV	2	; the Indus river
INDUS	14.3.10	PROP	1	
INDUS		SEN	1	(river)
INDUS		TIB	1	
INDUS		V	2 12	; an Ethiopian
INDUS*		AV	1	Indian, p. to India
INDUS*		CAT	1	
INDUS*		LUC	1	
INDUS*		MAR	1	
INDUS*		OV	1	
INDUS*		PET	1	
INDUS*		PROP	1	
INDUS*		S	1	
INDUS*		SIL	1	
INDUS*		V	1 10	
INFAMIA	15.97	SIL		"Disgrace" personified
INIURIA	Pers. 558	PL		"Injustice" personified
INO		HOR	1	leg. daughter of Cadmus
INO		OV	1	
INO		PROP	1	
INO		S	1	
INO		SEN	1	
INO		VAL	1 6	
-INOIDES	dub. Tr.363	SEN		p. to Ino
INOPIA	Trin., prol.	PL		"Need" personified
-INOPIS	-id-, Am.3.6.41	OV		a spring on Delos
INOPUS	5.104	VAL		" "
INOUS		OV	1	p. to Ino
INOUS		S	1	
INOUS		SEN	1	
INOUS		V	1	
INOUS		VAL	1 5	
INSANIA	M. 4.485	OV	1	"Madness" personified
INSANIA		VAR	1 2	
INSIDIAE		PET	1	"Ambush" personified
INSIDIAE		S	1	

INSIDIAE	SIL		1	"Ambush" personified
INSIDIAE	V	1	4	
-INSTANTIUS/RUFUS	MAR			patron of Ovid
INSULA (TIBERINA)	OV			island in Tiber at Rome (M. 15.740)
INVIDIA	OV		1	"Envy" personified
INVIDIA	PH		1	
INVIDIA	PL		1	
INVIDIA	S	1	4	
IO	HOR		1	legendary daughter of Inachus
IO	JUV		1	
IO	MAR		1	
IO	OV		1	
IO	PL		1	
IO	PROP		1	
IO	S		1	
IO	SIL		1	
IO	TR		1	
IO	V		1	
IO	VAL	1	11	
IOCASTA	S		1	mother of Oedipus
IOCASTA	SEN	1	2	
IOLAUS	OV		1	comp. of Hercules
IOLAUS	SIL	1	2	
IOLCIACUS	AV		1	p. to Iolcos
IOLCIACUS	OV		1	
IOLCIACUS	PROP	1	3	
IOLCOS fem.	COL		1	port-town of Thessaly
IOLCOS	HOR		1	
IOLCOS	LUC		1	
IOLCOS	MAN		1	
IOLCOS	SEN		1	
IOLCOS	VAL	1	6	
IOLE	OV		1	daughter of Eurytus
IOLE	PROP		1	(slave of Cynthia)
IOLE	SEN	1	3	daughter of Eurytus
IOLLAS	CAL		1	a shepherd
IOLLAS	MAR		1	fictional
IOLLAS	V	2	4	a shepherd; a Trojan
ION or Isis? dub.	OV		1	?? (Ibis 620)
ION	S	1	2	leg. founder of Ionia
IONES	MAR			the Ionians
IONIA	MAN		1	Gk. region of W. Anatolia
IONIA	OV		1	
IONIA	PL		1	
IONIA	PROP	1	4	
IONIACUS	OV			Ionian, Ionic
IONICUS	HOR		1	Ionian, Ionic
IONICUS	MAR		1	
IONICUS	PL	1	3	
IONIUM	MAN		1	Ionian Sea, W of Greece
IONIUM	OV		1	
IONIUM	PER		1	
IONIUM	S		1	
IONIUM	V		1	
IONIUM	VAL	1	6	
IONIUS	CAT		1	Ionic, Ionian
IONIUS	HOR		1	

IONIUS	JUV	1	Ionic, Ionian
IONIUS	LUC	1	
IONIUS	LUCR	1	
IONIUS	OV	1	
IONIUS	PROP	1	
IONIUS	S	1	
IONIUS	SEN	1	
IONIUS	SIL	1	
IONIUS	TR	1	
IONIUS	V	1	
IONIUS	VAL	1 13	
-IONOS 6.402	LUC		king of Thessaly
-IOPAS A. 1.740	V		Punic bard
-IOPE 2.28.51	PROP		a heroine
IPHIANASSA	LUCR		= Iphigenia
IPHIAS	OV		= Evadne
IPHICLUS	OV	1	an Argonaut
IPHICLUS	PROP	1	son of Phylacus
IPHICLUS	VAL	1 3	an Argonaut
-IPHIDAMAS	HL		son of Antenor
IPHIGENIA	JUV	1	daughter of Agamemnon
IPHIGENIA	OV	1	
IPHIGENIA	PROP	1	
IPHIGENIA	SEN	1 4	
IPHINOE	VAL		a woman of Lemnos
IPHINOUS	OV	1	a Centaur
IPHINOUS	S	1 2	a Theban
IPHIS -id-, -i-	OV	2	d. of Ligdus; Cyprian youth
IPHIS	S	1	an Argive
IPHIS	VAL	1 4	an Argonaut
IPHITIDES patr.	OV		son of Iphitus
IPHITUS	S	1	leader of the Phoceans
IPHITUS	V	1	a Trojan
IPHITUS	VAL	1 3	an Argonaut
-IPSITHILLA 32.1	CAT		a meretrix
IRA	S	1	"Rage"
IRA	VAL	1 2	
IRAE	SIL	1	"Rage"
IRAE	V	1	
IRAE	VAL	1 3	
IRIS -id-	HL	1	goddess of the rainbow & divine messenger
IRIS	MAN	1	
IRIS	MAR	1	
IRIS	OV	1	
IRIS	S	2	(+ name of a horse)
IRIS	SEN	1	
IRIS	SIL	1	
IRIS	V	1	
IRIS	VAL	2 11	(a river, flowing into the Black Sea)
-IRON m.: 3.111, 6.201	VAL	2 2	a Cyzican; a Scythian
IRPINI =Hirpini	SIL		people of S. Italy
IRPINUS	SIL		name of a Roman soldier
IRPINUS*	SIL		p. to the (H)irpini
IRUS	CAT	1	Homeric beggar (or generic poor man)
IRUS	MAR	1	
IRUS	OV	1	
IRUS	PROP	1 4	

ISAEUS		JUV		cont. rhetorician
- ISALCAS	5.289	SIL		a Cinyphian
ISARA		LUC		river of Gaul
ISAURAE	F. 1.593	OV		a tribe in Anatolia
ISAURUS		LUC		river in Picenum
ISCHOMACHE		PROP		daughter of Atrax
ISIACUS		JUV	1	p. to Isis
ISIACUS		MAN	1	
ISIACUS		OV	1 3	
-ISINDIUS	(-idius)	OV		an Egyptian (Ibis 619)
ISIS		JUV	1	Egyptian goddess
ISIS		LUC	1	
ISIS		OV	1	
ISIS		PROP	1	
ISIS		S	1	
ISIS		TIB	1 6	
ISMARA n.pl., cf. -us	LUCR		1	mountain in Thrace
ISMARA		PROP	1	
ISMARA		S	1	
ISMARA		V	1 4	
ISMARIUS		CAT	1	p. to Ismara, i.e. Thracian
ISMARIUS		MAR	1	
ISMARIUS		OV	1	
ISMARIUS		PROP	1	
ISMARIUS		S	1	
ISMARIUS		SEN	1 6	
ISMARUS cf. -a		V	2 2	mt. in Thrace; a Lydian
ISMENE		S		daughter of Oedipus
ISMENIAS m.		VAR		a Theban flutist
ISMENIS patr.		OV	1	a Theban woman
ISMENIS		S	1 2	
ISMENIS*		SEN		Theban
ISMENIUS		OV	1	p. to Ismenus (Theban)
ISMENIUS		S	1 2	
ISMENOS		S	1	river of Boeotia
ISMENOS		SEN	1 2	
ISMENUS		OV	2 2	(+ son of Niobe)
ISSA		MAR		a dog
ISSE		OV		daughter of Macareus
-ISSEDONIUS adj., 6.750	VAL			p. to the Essedones (in E. Europe)
ISTER cf. Hister		HOR		the river Danube
ISTHMIACUS adj.		S	1	p. to Isthmos
ISTHMIACUS		SIL	1 2	
ISTHMIUS adj.		HOR	1	p. to Isthmos
ISTHMIUS		S	1 2	
ISTHMOS		AV	1	the neck of land at Corinth
ISTHMOS		LUC	1	
ISTHMOS		PROP	1	(strait of Dardanelles)
ISTHMOS		S	1	of Corinth
ISTHMOS		SEN	1	
ISTHMOS		SIL	1	
ISTHMOS		VAL	1 7	
ISTHMUS		OV	1	
ISTHMUS		TR	1 2	
ITALI		CAT	1	the peoples of Italy
ITALI		SIL	1 2	
ITALIA		GR	1	Italy

ITALIA	HOR	1	Italy
ITALIA	JUV	1	
ITALIA	LUC	1	
ITALIA	LUCIL	1	
ITALIA	LUCR	1	
ITALIA	MAN	1	
ITALIA	MAR	1	
ITALIA	OV	1	
ITALIA	PROP	1	
ITALIA	SEN	1	
ITALIA	SIL	1	
ITALIA	V	1 13	
ITALICUS N	HL		Baebius Italicus, the poet
ITALICUS*	OV	1	p. to Italy, Italic, Italian
ITALICUS*	PL	1	
ITALICUS*	S	1 3	
ITALIDES fem. pl.	MAR	1	Italian women
ITALIDES	SIL	1	
ITALIDES	V	1 3	
ITALIS adj.	OV	1	Italian
ITALIS	S	1 2	
ITALUS collect. sg.	S	1	= Romani
ITALUS A. 7.178	V	1 2	ancient king of Italy
ITALUS*	AV	1	Italic, Italian
ITALUS*	FPLA	1	
ITALUS*	HOR	1	
ITALUS*	LUCR	1	
ITALUS*	MAR	1	
ITALUS*	OV	1	
ITALUS*	PER	1	
ITALUS*	PROP	1	
ITALUS*	S	1	
ITALUS*	SIL	1	
ITALUS*	V	1 11	
ITHACA	FPLA	1	the island of Ulixes
ITHACA and -e	HOR	1	
ITHACA	OV	1	
ITHACA	SEN	1	
ITHACA	V	1 5	
ITHACE	TIB		
ITHACENSIS	HOR	1	Ithacan, i.e. Ulixes
ITHACENSIS	TR	1 2	
ITHACESIUS	S	1	Ithacan
ITHACESIUS	SIL	1 2	
ITHACUS	AV	1	ep. of Ulixes
ITHACUS	HL	1	
ITHACUS	JUV	1	
ITHACUS	MAN	1	
ITHACUS	MAR	1	
ITHACUS	OV	1	
ITHACUS	PROP	1	
ITHACUS also pl.	S	1	
ITHACUS	SEN	1	
ITHACUS	SIL	1	
ITHACUS	V	1 11	
ITHACUS*	OV	1	Ithacan
ITHACUS*	PROP	1	

ITHACUS*	SIL	1	3	Ithacan
-ITHEMON 5.546	SIL			captain of the Autololes
ITHOME	S			town of Messenia
ITONAEI	S			people of Itone
ITONE fem.	S			town in Boeotia
ITONUS m.	CAT			" "
ITURAEUS	V			p. to a port of Syria
ITYLUS	CAT			son of Zethus
ITYRAEI	LUC			a people of Syria
ITYRAEUS cf. Itur-	LUC			p. to a port of Syria
ITYS	AV		1	son of Procne
ITYS	HOR		1	
ITYS	MAR		1	
ITYS	OV		1	
ITYS	PROP		1	(son of Philomela)
ITYS	S		1	(a Theban)
ITYS	SEN		1	son of Procne
ITYS	V		1	(a Trojan)
ITYS	VAL	1	9	(a Cyzican)
IULEUS	LUC		1	p. to the Julian gens
IULEUS	MAR		1	Alban; Caesarian
IULEUS P. 1.1.46	OV		1	Roman gens (Julian)
IULEUS	PROP	1	4	Augustan
IULI	CAL		1	inhabitants of Troy
IULI	S		1	Aeneas' followers
IULI	VAL	1	3	the family of Aeneas
IULUS	JUV		1	son of Ascanius
IULUS	LUC		1	son of Aeneas (Ascanius)
IULUS	MAR		1	Ascanius
IULUS	OV		1	
IULUS	PROP		1	
IULUS	SIL		1	
IULUS	V	1	7	son of Ascanius
IXION	AET		1	leg. king of the Lapiths
IXION	HOR		1	
IXION	OV		1	
IXION	PH		1	
IXION	PROP		1	
IXION	S		1	
IXION	SEN		1	
IXION	TIB		1	
IXION	V	1	9	
IXIONIDAE pl.	LUC			the Centaurs
IXIONIDES m.sg.	OV		1	ep. of Perithous
IXIONIDES	PROP	1	2	
⎰IXIONIOS	LUCIL			p. to Ixion
⎱IXIONIUS	V			
JANALIS	OV			p. to Janus
JANI	HOR			4 arched passages in Rome
JANICULUM	MAR		1	the hill in Rome
JANICULUM	OV		1	
JANICULUM	SIL		1	
JANICULUM	V	1	4	
JANIGENA m.	OV			son of Janus
JANITOR	SIL			ep. of Cerberus
JANUS	FPLA		1	the Italic god (of beginnings of things)
JANUS	HOR		1	

JANUS		JUV	1	Italic deity (of beginnings of things)
JANUS		LUC	1	
JANUS		LUCIL	1	
JANUS		MAR	1	
JANUS		OV	1	
JANUS		PER	1	
JANUS		PL	1	
JANUS		S	1	
JANUS		SIL	1	
JANUS		V	1 12	
JOCUS	personified	FPLA	1	"Jest"
JOCUS		HOR	1	
JOCUS		PL	1	
JOCUS		S	1 4	
JOVIS	archaic nomin.	COM	1	Juppiter, chief Roman god
JOVIS		ENN	1	
JOVIS		HL	1	
JOVIS		TR	1 4	
JUBA	m.	HOR	1	king of Numidia
JUBA		LUC	1	
JUBA		OV	1	
JUBA		SIL	1 4	
JUDAEA		JUV	1	region of Palestine
JUDAEA		LUC	1 2	
JUDAEI		HOR	1	the Jews, people of Judaea
JUDAEI		JUV	1 2	
JUDAEUS	also pl.	MAR		a Jew; Jews
JUDAEUS*		HOR	1	Jewish
JUDAEUS*		MAR	1	
JUDAEUS*		OV	1 3	
JUDAICUS		JUV		Jewish
JUGULAE		MAN	1	two stars in Cancer
JUGULAE		PL	1 2	two stars in Orion
JUGURTHA		FPLB	1	king of Numidia
JUGURTHA		HOR	1	
JUGURTHA		LUC	1	
JUGURTHA		PROP	1	
JUGURTHA		SIL	1 5	
⎧ JUGURTHĪNUS		FPLA	1	p. to Jugurtha
⎪ JUGURTHINUS		HOR	1	
⎨ JUGURTHINUS		OV	1 3	
⎩ JUGURTINUS		LUCIL		
JULIA		JUV	1	daughter of Titus
JULIA		LUC	1	daughter of Julius Caesar
JULIA		MAR	2	d. of Titus; d. of Caesar
JULIA	(sc. lex)	S	1	(a law on adultery)
JULIA	Oct. 944	SEN	1 6	daughter of Drusus
JULIANUS 3.25.2		MAR		a contemporary
JULIUS		HOR	1	unknown cont.
JULIUS	11.36	MAR	1	C. J. Proculus
JULIUS		OV	1	Caesar
JULIUS		PET	1	"
JULIUS		V	1 5	the Julian gens
JULIUS*		HOR	1	p. to the Julian family (etc.)
JULIUS* (mensis, lex)		JUV	1	
JULIUS*		MAN	1	
JULIUS*		MAR	1	

JULIUS*	OV		1	p. to the Julian gens
JULIUS* (rostra)	PROP		1	
JULIUS*	S		1	
JULIUS*	V	1	8	
JULIUS/CERIALIS	MAR			friend and poet
JULIUS/FLORUS	HOR			cont. writer
JULIUS/MARTIALIS	MAR			a friend
JULIUS/PROCULUS	MAR			"
JULIUS/RUFUS	MAR			"
JULLUS	HOR			praenomen of Antonius
-JUNCUS 15.27	JUV			a consul suffectus
JUNIA or Vinia? dub.	CAT			cont. woman
JUNIUS	ENN		1	the month of June
JUNIUS F. passim	OV	1	2	" "
-JUNIUS/CŌNGUS	LUCIL			a legal writer
JUNO	AV		1	goddess of women & marriage, w. of Jove
JUNO	CAT		1	
JUNO	CIC		1	
JUNO	ENN		1	
JUNO	FPLA		1	[NOTE: Juno infer(n)a
JUNO	GER		1	= Proserpina]
JUNO	HL		1	
JUNO	HOR		1	
JUNO	JUV		1	
JUNO	LUC		1	
JUNO	MAN		1	
JUNO	MAR		1	
JUNO	OV		1	
JUNO	PET		1	
JUNO	PH		1	
JUNO	PL		1	
JUNO	PRIAP		1	
JUNO	PROP		1	
JUNO	S		1	
JUNO	SEN		1	
JUNO	SIL		1	
JUNO	TIB		1	
JUNO	TR		1	
JUNO	V		1	
JUNO	VAL	1	25	
JUNONALIS F. 6.63	OV			p. to Juno (the month of June)
JUNONICOLA m./fem.	OV			a devotee of Juno
JUNONIGENA	OV			ep. of Vulcan
JUNONIUS	OV		1	p. to Juno
JUNONIUS	S		1	
JUNONIUS	SIL		1	
JUNONIUS	V		1	
JUNONIUS	VAL	1	5	
JUNO/LUCINA	PL		1	Juno as protectress of women in labor
JUNO/LUCINA	TER	1	2	
JUPITER cf. Jovis	FPLA		1	the chief Roman god (= Heaven)
JUPITER	SIL	1	2	
JUPPITER	AET		1	
JUPPITER	AV		1	[NOTE: Juppiter Stygius
JUPPITER	CAL		1	= Pluto]
JUPPITER	CAT		1	
JUPPITER	CIC		2	(+ the planet)

JUPPITER		COL	1	the chief Roman god
JUPPITER		COM	1	
JUPPITER		ENN	1	
JUPPITER		FPLB	1	
JUPPITER		GER	1	
JUPPITER		HL	1	
JUPPITER		HOR	1	
JUPPITER		JUV	1	
JUPPITER		LUC	2	(+ the planet)
JUPPITER		LUCIL	1	
JUPPITER		LUCR	1	
JUPPITER		MAN	2	(+ the planet)
JUPPITER		MAR	1	(at 4.8.12 = Domitian)
JUPPITER		OV	1	
JUPPITER		PER	1	
JUPPITER		PET	1	
JUPPITER		PH	1	
JUPPITER		PL	1	
JUPPITER		PRIAP	1	
JUPPITER		PROP	1	
JUPPITER		S	1	
JUPPITER		SEN	1	
JUPPITER		TER	1	
JUPPITER		TIB	1	
JUPPITER		TR	1	
JUPPITER also Stygius		V	1	
JUPPITER		VAL	2	(+ the planet)
JUPPITER		VAR	1 37	
JUSTINA		MAR		fictional woman
JUSTINUS		MAR		fictional man
JUSTITIA		GER	1	"Justice" personified
JUSTITIA	C. 1.24.6	HOR	1	
JUSTITIA	P. 3.6.24	OV	1	
JUSTITIA		PET	1	
JUSTITIA	S. 5.3.90	S	1	
JUSTITIA	Oct. 398	SEN	1	
JUSTITIA	G. 2.474	V	1 7	
JUTURNA		OV	1	a spring in Rome
JUTURNA		S	1	" "
JUTURNA		V	1 3	a nymph of the spring
-JUVATUS 12.24.4		MAR		friend of Martial
JUVENALIS		MAR		D. Jun. Juvenalis, the satirist
JUVENIS		MAN		constellation (Aquarius)
JUVENTA	M. 7.241	OV		goddess of Youth
JUVENTAS (-tat-)		HOR		goddess of Youth
-JUVENTIUS 48.1		CAT		a young Roman (Juv. Thalna?)
JUVERNA		JUV		Ireland
KALENDAE		CAL	1	the first of the month
KALENDAE		COL	1	
KALENDAE		COM	1	
KALENDAE		OV	1 4	
KARISTIA n.pl. (Char-)		OV		family festival
KARTHAGO or Carthago		V		the famous Punic capital
-LABARUS 4.232		SIL		a Gaulish soldier
LABDACIDES patr.		S	1	= Polyneices; (as pl.) Thebans
LABDACIDES		SEN	1 2	Polyneices
LABDACIUS adj.		S		p. to Labdacus

LABDACUS	S		1	king of Thebes
LABDACUS	SEN	1	2	
LABEO	HOR		1	Antistius Labeo (?)
LABEO	PER		1	Attius Labeo
LABEO	PET	1	3	Antistius Labeo, a lawyer
LABERIUS	HOR		1	D. Laberius, writer of mimes
LABERIUS	MAR	1	2	fictitious
LABICANUS	MAR			p. to Labicum
LABĪCI	SIL		1	the people of Labicum
LABĪCI	V	1	2	
LABĪCUM	SIL			town of Latium
-LABICUS 5.565	SIL			a Roman soldier
LABIENUS	LUC		1	T. Labienus, Caesar's legate
LABIENUS	MAR		1	fictional
LABIENUS	SIL	1	3	T. Labienus, of Cingulum
⎰LABOR S. 1.5.11	S			"Toil"
⎱LABOS A. 6.277	V			" (in Hades)
-LABRAX Rud. 344	PL			a leno
LABROS M. 3.224	OV			name of a dog
-LABULLA dub., 4.9	MAR			fict. woman
-LABULLUS 11.24	MAR			fictional man
LABYRINTHĒUS	CAT			p. to the Labyrinth
-LABYRTAS 7.87.9	MAR			a young slave
LACAENA	HOR		1	Laconian (Spartan) woman
LACAENA	MAR		1	= Leda
LACAENA	OV		1	= Helen
LACAENA	PROP		1	= "
LACAENA also adj.	S		1	Laconian (Spartan) woman
LACAENA	SEN		1	=Helen & Clytemnestra
LACAENA	V		1	=Helen
LACAENA	VAL	1	8	=Clytemnestra
LACAENA*	HOR		1	Spartan, Laconian
LACAENA*	TR		1	
LACAENA*	V	1	3	
LACEDAEMON	HOR		1	Sparta
LACEDAEMON	MAR		1	
LACEDAEMON	OV		1	
LACEDAEMON	V	1	4	
LACEDAEMONIUS adj.	ENN		1	Spartan
LACEDAEMONIUS	GR		1	
LACEDAEMONIUS	HOR		1	
LACEDAEMONIUS	JUV		1	
LACEDAEMONIUS	LUC		1	
LACEDAEMONIUS	MAR		1	
LACEDAEMONIUS	OV		1	
LACEDAEMONIUS	PET		1	
LACEDAEMONIUS	S		1	
LACEDAEMONIUS	V	1	10	
LACERTA 7.114	JUV			name (?) of a "red" jockey
LACHES	COM		1	character in comedy
LACHES	TER	1	2	a senex
LACHESIS	HL		1	one of the three Fates
LACHESIS	JUV		1	
LACHESIS	MAR		1	
LACHESIS	OV		1	
LACHESIS	S		1	
LACHESIS	SEN	1	6	

-LACHNE M. 3.222	OV			name of a dog
LACINIUM	LUC			promontory in SE Italy
LACINIUS adj.	OV		1	p. to Lacinium
LACINIUS	V	1	2	p. to Lacinium (i.e. Juno)
LACON	HOR		1	a Spartan; breed of dog
LACON	MAR		1	a Spartan
LACON	OV		1	breed of dog
LACON	S		1	= Alcidamas, the Spartan boxer
LACON	SIL		1	a Spartan
LACON	VAL	1	6	= Pollux
LACONES	CIC		1	Spartans
LACONES	MAR		1	Castor & Pollux
LACONES	PL		1	Spartans
LACONES	PROP		1	"
LACONES	S	1	5	"
LACONICUS	HOR		1	Spartan
LACONICUS	PL	1	2	
LACONIS adj.	OV			Laconian (Spartan)
LACON*	SIL			"
LACTEUS cf. Via/Lac.	CIC			the Milky Way
LACTEUS/ORBIS	GER			" "
LADAS m.	CAT		1	a runner (time of Alexander the Great)
LADAS	JUV		1	
LADAS	MAR		1	
LADAS	MLP	1	4	(a shepherd)
-LADES A. 12.343	V			a Lycian
-LADMUS 1.397	SIL			a Punic
LADON	CAL		1	a pastoral musician
LADON	MAR		1	boatman on Tiber
LADON	OV		2	river of Arcadia; a dog
LADON	S		1	ep. of Pollux
LADON	V	1	6	an Arcadian, comp. of Aeneas
-LAECANIA 5.43	MAR			fictional woman
LAELAPS	OV			name of a dog
-LAELIA 5.75	MAR			fictional
LAELIUS	FPLA		1	C. Laelius, fr. of Scipio
LAELIUS	HOR		1	" "
LAELIUS 14.195	JUV		1	prefect of the camp (?)
LAELIUS	LUC		1	D. Laelius, politician
LAELIUS	LUCIL		1	C. Laelius, minor writer
LAELIUS	MAR		1	fictitious
LAELIUS	SIL	1	7	friend of Scipio
LAELIUS/DECUMUS	LUCIL			Dec. Laelius
LAENAS 5.98	JUV		1	a legacy-hunter
LAENAS F. 5.330	OV		1	M. Popilius Laenas
LAENAS 15.447	SIL	1	3	a Roman soldier
-LAERNUS = Lernus?	FPLB			??
LAERTES	MAR		1	father of Ulixes
LAERTES	OV		1	
LAERTES	SEN		1	
LAERTES	SIL		1	
LAERTES	TR	1	5	
LAERTIADES patr.	HOR		1	Ulixes (Ulysses)
LAERTIADES	LP		1	
LAERTIADES	MAN		1	
LAERTIADES	OV		1	
LAERTIADES	S		1	

LAERTIADES	TR	1	6	Ulixes
LAERTIUS in vocative	FPLA			Ulixes
LAERTIUS*	AV		1	Laertian, Ithacan, p. to Ulixes
LAERTIUS*	HL		1	
LAERTIUS*	OV		1	
LAERTIUS*	S		1	
LAERTIUS*	SIL		1	
LAERTIUS*	V	1	6	
LAESTRYGON sg.	AV		1	primitive tr. of Italy & Sicily
LAESTRYGON	OV		1	
LAESTRYGON	SIL	1	3	
LAESTRYGONES pl.	JUV		1	primitive tribe of Italy & Sicily
LAESTRYGONES	TIB	1	2	
LAESTRYGONIUS	HOR		1	p. to the Laestrygones
LAESTRYGONIUS	OV		1	
LAESTRYGONIUS	SIL	1	3	
–LAETINUS 3.43	MAR			fictional man
LAETITIA M. 12.60	OV		1	"Joy" personified
LAETITIA Capt. 864	PL	1	2	
LAETORIA	MAR			fictional woman
LAETORIUS	MAR			type of rich man
–LAEVIA 1.71.1	MAR			fictional woman
–LAEVINA 1.62	MAR			" "
LAEVINUS	HOR		1	P. Val. Laevinus
LAEVINUS	MAR		1	fictional man
LAEVINUS	SIL	2	4	two Roman soldiers
LAEVIUS	LUCIL			(unknown man)
LAEVUS	LUC			a soldier of Cato
LAGAEUS	MAR			p. to Lagus, i.e. Egyptian
LAGEUS	LUC		1	
LAGEUS	SIL		1	
LAGEUS	VAL	1	3	
LAGUS	JUV		1	father of Ptolemy I
LAGUS	LUC		1	
LAGUS	SIL		1	
LAGUS	V	1	4	(a Rutulian)
LAIADES	OV			= Oedipus
LAIS	MAR		2	Corinthian courtesan; a fict. woman
LAIS	OV		1	"
LAIS	PROP	1	4	"
LAIUS	S		1	father of Oedipus
LAIUS	SEN	1	2	
LALAGE	HOR		1	a girl
LALAGE	MAR		1	a girl
LALAGE	PRIAP		1	a meretrix
LALAGE	PROP	1	4	a slave-girl of Cynthia
LALETANIA	MAR			a region of Spain
LALETANUS adj.	MAR			p. to Laletania
LAMIA m.	HOR		2	a cognomen; a friend Aelius Lamia
LAMIA fem.	LUCIL	1	3	an old woman
LAMIAE m.pl., 4.154	JUV			cognomen of the Aelian gens
LAMPADIO	COM		1	character in comedy
LAMPADIO	PL	1	2	a slave
LAMPADISCUS	PL			a slave
–LAMPADIUM 4.1165	LUCR			a girl's name
–LAMPETIDES M. 5.111	OV			a bard
LAMPETIE	OV		1	sister of Phaethon & d. of the Sun

LAMPETIE	PROP	1	2	sister of Phaethon
LAMPIA	S			town of Arcadia
LAMPON m.	SIL			name of a horse
LAMPSACIUS	MAR			p. to Lampsacus
LAMPSACUS fr.1.2	CAT		1	town in Mysia
LAMPSACUS	OV		1	
LAMPSACUS	PRIAP		1	
LAMPSACUS	VAL	1	4	
LAMPUS	S			a Theban
LAMUS	HOR		1	myth. Latin ruler
LAMUS	OV		1	son of Hercules
LAMUS	S		1	a Theban
LAMUS	SIL		2	myth. Latin king; a horse
LAMUS	V	1	6	a Rutulian
LAMYRUS	S		1	a Theban
LAMYRUS	V	1	2	a Rutulian
-LANGIA T. passim	S			fountain in Sicyonia
-LANGON 9.50.5	MAR			a statue
LANIGER	MAN			constellation (Aries, the Ram)
LANUINUS	CAT		1	p. to Lanuvium
LANUINUS	COM	1	2	
LANUVINUS	HOR			
LANUVIUM	OV		1	town of Latium
LANUVIUM	PROP		1	
LANUVIUM	SIL	1	3	
LAOCOON cf. Iaucoon	PET		1	son of Priam & priest of Apollo
LAOCOON	V	1	2	
LAODAMIA	OV		2	d. of Acastus; d. of Alexander (of Epirus)
LAODAMIA A. 6.447	V	1	3	d. of Acastus & w. of Protesilaus
LAOMEDON	HOR		1	father of Priam
LAOMEDON	MAR		1	
LAOMEDON	OV		1	
LAOMEDON	PET		1	
LAOMEDON	PROP		1	
LAOMEDON	TR		1	
LAOMEDON	VAL	1	7	
LAOMEDONTEUS	MAR		1	p. to Laomedon, i.e. Trojan
LAOMEDONTEUS	OV		1	
LAOMEDONTEUS	SIL		1	
LAOMEDONTEUS	V		1	
LAOMEDONTEUS	VAL	1	5	
LAOMEDONTIADES	JUV		1	= Priam (patr.)
LAOMEDONTIADES	SIL		1	Trojans (10.629)
LAOMEDONTIADES & pl.	V	1	3	Priam; (pl.) Trojans
LAOMEDONTIUS	V			p. to Laomedon
LAPITHA sg., cf.-es	PROP			a Lapith (one of a leg. tribe)
LAPITHAE pl.	AV		1	leg. & primitive tr. of Thessaly
LAPITHAE	HOR		1	
LAPITHAE	MAR		1	
LAPITHAE	OV		1	
LAPITHAE	S		1	
LAPITHAE	SEN		1	
LAPITHAE	V	1	7	
LAPITHAEUS adj.	OV			p. to the Lapiths
-LAPITHAON T. 7.297	S			a boy (ultimately f. of Alatreus)
LAPITHEIUS adj.	OV			p. to the Lapiths
LAPITHES sg., 6.399	LUC		1	a Lapith (or the founder of the race)

LAPITHES sg., also pl.	VAL	1	2	a Lapith
LĂR (and pl. Lăres)	CAL	1		protective Roman god(s)
LAR	HOR	1		" " "
LAR or Lars	OV	1		(see Lars, below)
LAR	PL	1		protective god (and = hearth)
LAR	PROP	1		
LAR	SEN	1		(= domus)
LAR	TIB	1	7	
LĂRA	OV			a Naiad
LARENTALIA n.pl.	OV			festival for Acca Larentia
LARENTIA	OV			Acca Larentia, wife of Faustulus
LARES pl.	COM	1		protective gods
LARES	JUV	1		
LARES	OV	1		
LARES	PER	1		
LARES	VAR	1	5	
LARGA	JUV			a bad woman contem.
LARGUS	OV			a poet
-LARIDES A. 10.391	V			a Rutulian hero
-LARĪNA Ā. 11.655	V			comp. of Camilla
LARINAS as N	SIL			native of Larinum
LARINAS*	SIL			p. to Larinum (a Samnite town)
LARISA (-ss-)	HOR	1		town of Thessaly
LARISA	LUC	1		
LARISA	S	1	3	
⎧LARISAEUS	CAT	1		p. to Larissa
⎪LARISAEUS	S	1	2	
⎨LARISSAEUS	OV	1		
⎩LARISSAEUS	V	1	2	
LARIUS	CAT	1		lake in N. Italy, now Como
LARIUS	V	1	2	
LARIUS*	CAT	1		p. to Larius
LĂRŌNIA	JUV	1		fict. woman
LARONIA	MAR	1	2	
LARS -rt-, fr. 3	OV			L. Tolumnius, k. of Veii
-LARTIUS Bac. 946	PL	1		= Laertius (Ulixes)
LARTIUS	TR	1	2	"
-LARUS 4.234, 16.49	SIL	2	2	a Gaul; a Cantabrian
-LATAGUS Ā. 10.697	V	1		a Trojan
LATAGUS 5.584, 6.572	VAL	1	2	a Colchian
LATERANI	JUV			a Roman family
LATERANUS	JUV	1		Plautius Lateranus
LATERANUS	SIL	1	2	a Roman soldier
LATIALIS 1.64	CAL	1		p. to Latium
LATIALIS	S	1	2	
LATIARIS 1.198	LUC	1		p. to Latium (i.e. Roman)
LATIARIS or -alis	OV	1	2	" " " (populus; M. 15.481)
-LATIA/VIA 9.64.2	MAR			Appian Way (?)
LATII 16.286	SIL			Romans
LATĪNA (sc. via)	JUV		1	road beginning at the Porta Latina
LATINA	S	1	2	"
LATINAE (sc. feriae)	CIC	1		festival of the Latin allies
LATINAE	HOR	1		
LATINAE	JUV	1		
LATINAE	LUC	1	4	
LATĪNĒ adv.	COM	1		in Latin (language)
LATINE	OV	1		

LATĪNE adv.	PL	1	in Latin (language)
LATINE	PRIAP 1	4	
LATĪNI	CIC	1	the Latins, peoples of Latium
LATINI	ENN	1	
LATINI	PROP	1	
LATINI	S	1	
LATINI	SIL	1	
LATINI	V 1	6	
LATĪNUS (Afran.28)	COM	2	a k. of Laurentum; a mime
LATINUS S. 1.10.27	HOR	1	a king
LATINUS	JUV	1	the mime
LATINUS	MAR	1	the mime
LATINUS	OV	2	the king; a son of Faunus
LATINUS	SIL	2	the king; a Roman soldier
LATINUS	V 1	10	the king
LATINUS*	FPLA	1	Latin, p. to Latium
LATINUS*	FPLR	1	
LATINUS*	HOR	1	
LATINUS*	JUV	1	
LATINUS*	LUC	1	
LATINUS*	LUCR	1	
LATINUS*	MAR	1	
LATINUS*	OV	1	
LATINUS*	PER	1	
LATINUS*	PH	1	
LATINUS*	S	1	
LATINUS*	SEN	1	
LATINUS*	SIL	1	
LATINUS*	TER	1	
LATINUS*	V	1	
LATINUS*	VAR 1	16	
LATIUM	ENN	1	region of W. Central Italy
LATIUM	FPLR	1	
LATIUM	GR	1	
LATIUM	HOR	1	
LATIUM	JUV	1	
LATIUM	LUC	1	
LATIUM	OV	1	
LATIUM	PH	1	
LATIUM	PRIAP	1	
LATIUM	S	1	
LATIUM	SIL	1	
LATIUM	V 1	12	
- LATIUM/FORUM 10.37.2	MAR		
LATIUS	FPLR	1	p. to Latium, Latian, Latin, Roman
LATIUS	GER	1	
LATIUS	JUV	1	
LATIUS	LUC	1	
LATIUS	MAN	1	
LATIUS	MAR	1	
LATIUS	OV	1	
LATIUS	PROP	1	
LATIUS	S	1	
LATIUS	SIL	1	
LATIUS	VAL 1	11	
LATMIUS	CAT	1	p. to Latmus (mt. of Caria)
LATMIUS	OV	1	

LATMIUS	S		1	p. to Latmus (mt. of Caria)
LATMIUS	VAL	1	4	
LATOIS cf.Letois	OV		1	ep. of Diana
LATOIS	S	1	2	
LATOIUS cf. Letoius	OV			ep. of Apollo
LATONA (= Gk. Leto)	AV		1	mother of Apollo and Diana
LATONA	FPLA		1	
LATONA	HL		1	
LATONA	HOR		1	
LATONA	JUV		1	
LATONA	MAR		1	
LATONA	OV		1	
LATONA	PL		1	
LATONA	S		1	
LATONA	SEN		1	
LATONA	TIB		1	
LATONA	V		1	
LATONA	VAL	1	13	
LATONIA	CAT		1	Diana
LATONIA	GER		1	
LATONIA	OV		1	
LATONIA	S		1	
LATONIA	SIL		1	
LATONIA	V		1	
LATONIA	VAL	1	7	
LATONIGENA pl.	OV		1	Apollo & Diana
LATONIGENA Agam.320	SEN	1	2	
LATONIUS	COL		1	p. to Latona (& Apollo, Diana, etc.)
LATONIUS	FPLA		1	
LATONIUS	OV		1	
LATONIUS	S		1	
LATONIUS	SIL		1	
LATONIUS	TIB		1	
LATONIUS	V	1	7	
LATŌUS	HOR		1	ep. of Apollo
LATOUS	OV	1	2	
LATŌUS* M. 6.274	OV		1	p. to Latona
LATOUS* (or Letōus)	S	1	2	(S. 1.2.220)
−LATREUS M. 12.463	OV			name of a centaur (dissyllabic)
LATRIS 4.7.75	PROP		1	a woman's name (slave of Cynthia)
LATRIS m., 6.121	VAL	1	2	a Scythian
− LATRONIUS 14.534	SIL			a Roman sailor
− LATTARA 11.47, m.	MAR			fictional man
LAUCON = Laocoon	PET			son of Priam & priest of Apollo
LAUDAMIA = Laodamia	CAT			daughter of Acastus
LAUDES pl.	SIL			"Praise" personified (15.98)
LAUDICE = Laodice	OV			leg. woman (Ep. 18.135)
LAURENS sc. aper	HOR		1	breed of wild boar
LAURENS	SIL	2	3	a Campanian soldier; a Roman soldier
LAURENS* (ager, aper)	JUV		1	p. to Laurentum
LAURENS* (aper)	MAR		1	
LAURENS*	OV		1	
LAURENS* (bella)	SIL		1	(i.e. Roman)
LAURENS* (castrum)	TIB		1	
LAURENS* (arva)	V	1	6	
LAURENTES pl.	OV		1	people of Laurentum
LAURENTES	S		1	

LAURENTES	V		1	people of Laurentum
LAURENTES	VAL	1	4	
LAURENTINUS	LUC		1	p. to Laurentum
LAURENTINUS	MAR	1	2	
LAURENTIS* (terra)	ENN			p. to Laurentum
LAURENTIUS	V			p. to Laurentum
LAURENTUM	LUC		1	town in Latium
LAURENTUM	V	1	2	
LAUREOLUS	JUV		1	legendary robber
LAUREOLUS	MAR	1	2	
LAURUS	MAR		1	fictional person
LAURUS	SIL	1	2	a Roman soldier
LAŪS m., 17.441	SIL			a Bruttian soldier
LAUSUS	MAR		1	a friend of Martial
LAUSUS	OV		1	son of Numitor
LAUSUS	S		1	an Etruscan warrior
LAUSUS	V	1	4	son of Mezentius
LAVERNA	COM		1	goddess of thieves
LAVERNA	HOR		1	
LAVERNA	LUCIL		1	
LAVERNA	PL	1	4	
LAVINIA	OV		1	leg. d. of Latinus & wife of Aeneas
LAVINIA	S		1	
LAVINIA	SIL		1	
LAVINIA	V	1	4	
LAVINIUM	OV		1	town of Latium
LAVINIUM	TIB		1	
LAVINIUM	V	1	3	
LAVINIUS	LUC		1	p. to Lavinium
LAVINIUS	OV		1	
LAVINIUS	SIL		1	
LAVINIUS	V	1	4	
- LAVINUM N, 12.71	JUV			= Lavinium, town
- LAVINUS* or -ius	PROP			p. to Lavinium (2.34.64)
LEAENA	PL			an old woman
LEANDRIUS	SIL			p. to Leander
LEANDROS	MAR		1	Leander, lover of Hero
LEANDROS	OV	1	2	
LEARCHĒUS	OV			p. to Learchus
LEARCHUS	OV		1	myth. son of Athamas
LEARCHUS	S		1	
LEARCHUS	VAL	1	3	
LEBADĒA	S			town of Phocis
LEBEDUS fem.	HOR			town of Ionia
LEBYNTHOS fem.	OV			island in the Sporades
LECHAEUM	PROP		1	port of Corinth
LECHAEUM	S	1	2	
LECHAEUS adj.	GR			p. to Lechaeum
LEDA	AET		1	d. of Thestius & mistress of Jove
LEDA	AV		1	
LEDA	GER		1	
LEDA	HOR		1	
LEDA	JUV		1	
LEDA	LUCIL		1	
LEDA	MAN		1	
LEDA	MAR		2	
LEDA	OV		1	

LEDA	PH		1	d. of Thestius
LEDA	PROP		1	
LEDA	SEN		1	
LEDA	SIL		1	
LEDA	V		1	
LEDA	VAL	1	16	
LEDAEUS	GER		1	p. to Leda, i.e. Spartan
LEDAEUS	LUC		1	p. to Castor & Pollux
LEDAEUS	MAR		1	Spartan
LEDAEUS	OV		1	p. to Castor & Pollux
LEDAEUS	S		1	Spartan
LEDAEUS	SIL		1	Spartan or Amyclaean, etc.
LEDAEUS	V	1	7	p. to Leda
- LEITUS 5.8.12	MAR			a manager of spectacles
LELEGEIS adj.	OV			Lelegean (i.e. Asianic)
LELEGEIUS	OV			"
LELEGES pl.	LUC		1	prehistoric tribe in Gk. world
LELEGES	OV		1	
LELEGES	V		1	
LELEGES	VAL	1	4	
LELEX M. 8.312,568	OV	2	2	two obscure kings
LEMANNUS (lacus)	LUC			lake Geneva
LEMNIA T. 5.588	S			ep. of Hypsipyle (queen of Lemnos)
LEMNIACUS	MAR		1	p. to Lemnos
LEMNIACUS	S	1	2	
LEMNIAS adj.	OV		1	Lemnian (woman), i.e. Hypsipyle
LEMNIAS	S	1	2	
LEMNICOLA	OV			= Vulcan
LEMNIENSIS	PL			p. to Lemnos
- LEMNISELENIS Par.196	PL			a meretrix
LEMNIUS N, M 4.185	OV		1	= Vulcan
LEMNIUS S.4.6.49	S	1	2	"
LEMNIUS*	OV		1	p. to Lemnos
LEMNIUS*	PL		1	
LEMNIUS*	S		1	
LEMNIUS*	TR		1	
LEMNIUS* (pater)	V	1	5	(ref. to Vulcan)
LEMNOS fem.	S		1	Aegean island
LEMNOS	SEN		1	
LEMNOS	VAL	1	3	
LEMNUS	OV		1	
LEMNUS	PL		1	
LEMNUS	PRIAP		1	
LEMNUS	TER	1	4	
LEMURES m.pl.	HOR		1	ghosts of the dead
LEMURES	OV		1	
LEMURES	PER	1	3	
LEMURIA n.pl.	OV			festival in honor of the dead (cf.Remuria)
LENAEUS	HOR		1	Bacchus
LENAEUS	OV		2	" (+ ep. of a king)
LENAEUS	V	1	4	"
LENAEUS* (pater)	COL		1	Bacchic, of Bacchus
LENAEUS*	S		1	
LENAEUS* (pater)	TIB		1	
LENAEUS*	V	1	4	
LENTULUS	JUV		2	P. Cornelius L.; a mime
LENTULUS	LUC		3	P. Cornelius; L. Cornelius; P. Sura

LENTULUS	PET		1	L. Cornelius L.
LENTULUS	SIL	2	8	L. Cornelius; a Roman soldier
LEO	CAT		1	constell.
LEO	CIC		1	
LEO	FPLB		1	
LEO	GER		1	
LEO	HOR		1	
LEO	LUC		1	
LEO	MAN		1	
LEO	OV		1	
LEO	PROP		1	
LEO	S	1	10	
- LEODOCUS 1.358	VAL			an Argonaut
LEONIDA m.	PL			a slave
LEONTEUS	HL		1	son of Coronus
LEONTEUS	S	1	2	a Theban
LEONTĪNI F. 4.467	OV			town of Sicily
LEONTĪNUS	SIL			p. to Leontini
LEONTIUM	COM			a girl (in comedy)
-LEOPREPIDES Ibis 510	OV			= Simonides
LEPIDI pl.	JUV		1	a Roman family
LEPIDI	LUC	1	2	
LEPIDUS	HOR		1	Q. Aemilius L.
LEPIDUS 6.265 & 8.9	JUV		1	L. Caec. M.; the family name
LEPIDUS 2.547	LUC		1	M. Aemilius L.
LEPIDUS	PROP	1	4	"
-LEPĪNUS line 131	COL			mt. near Signia (in Latium)
LEPONTICUS	SIL			p. to Lepontii (tr. in N. Italy)
- LEPOS S. 2.6.72	HOR			a pantomime
LEPTIS	LUC		1	town of N. Africa
LEPTIS (Magna)	S		1	
LEPTIS	SIL	1	3	
LEPUS	CIC		1	a constellation
LEPUS	GER		1	
LEPUS	MAN	1	3	
LERNA	CIC		1	a swamp near Argos (in story of the
LERNA	MAR		1	Hydra & Hercules)
LERNA	OV		1	
LERNA	PROP		1	
LERNA	S		1	
LERNA	SEN		1	
LERNA	SIL		1	
LERNA	V		1	
LERNA	VAL	1	9	
LERNAEUS	COL		1	p. to Lerna
LERNAEUS	LUC		1	
LERNAEUS	LUCR		1	
LERNAEUS	OV		1	
LERNAEUS	PROP		1	
LERNAEUS	S		1	(i.e. Greek)
LERNAEUS	SEN		1	
LERNAEUS	SIL		1	
LERNAEUS	V	1	9	
LESBIA	CAT		1	mistress of Catullus (= Clodia)
LESBIA	MAR		2	" (+ a fictional woman)
LESBIA	OV		1	"
LESBIA Merc. 647	PL		1	town or island ? (poetic error)

LESBIA	PROP		1	mistress of Catullus
LESBIA	TER	1	7	a girl's name
LESBIAS	OV			a Lesbian woman
LESBIS	OV			" "
LESBIS*	OV			p. to Lesbos
LESBIUM	HOR			wine of Lesbos
LESBIUS N	CAT		1	= Clodius (brother of Clodia)
LESBIUS	HOR		1	p. to Lesbos (and to Sapphos, Alcaeus)
LESBIUS	OV		1	
LESBIUS	PL		1	
LESBIUS (vina)	PROP		1	
LESBIUS	SEN	1	6	
-LESBONICUS Trin.359	PL			a young man
LESBOS fem.	HOR		1	Aegean island off Mysia
LESBOS	LUC		1	
LESBOS	OV		1	
LESBOS	PET		1	
LESBOS	SEN		1	
LESBOS	V		1	
LESBOS	VAL	1	7	
LESBŌUS adj.	HOR			Lesbian (lyric)
LETHAEA	OV			wife of Olenus (myth.)
LETHAEUS	AV		1	p. to Lethe (in Hades), soporific
LETHAEUS	CAT		1	
LETHAEUS	COL		1	
LETHAEUS	HOR		1	
LETHAEUS	LUC		1	
LETHAEUS	MAR		1	
LETHAEUS	OV		1	
LETHAEUS	PROP		1	
LETHAEUS	S		1	
LETHAEUS	SEN		1	
LETHAEUS	SIL		1	
LETHAEUS	TIB		1	
LETHAEUS	V		1	
LETHAEUS	VAL	1	14	
LETHE	LUC		1	Lethe (in Hades; amnesic region)
LETHE	MAR		1	
LETHE	OV		1	
LETHE	S		1	
LETHE	SEN		1	
LETHE	SIL		1	
LETHE	VAL	1	7	
-LETHES ? 16.476	SIL			river of Spain
-LETHON 9.355	LUC			river of Libya
-LETOIDES (= lat-)	S			= Apollo (T. 1.663)
LETOIS metronymic	OV			= Diana
LETOIUS	OV			= Apollo
-LETŌUS dub, = Latous	SEN			p. to Latona (Oct. 230)
LETUM personification	PET		1	"Death, Annihilation"
LETUM	S		1	
LETUM	V		1	
LETUM	VAL	1	4	
LEUCA	LUC			town in Calabria
LEUCADIA dub, N or adj.	PL		1	meaning? (Curc. 485)
LEUCADIA	PROP	1	2	mistress of Varro Atacinus
LEUCADIUS	LUC		1	p. to Leucadia (island in Ionic Sea)

LEUCADIUS	OV		1	p. to island Leucadia (Leucas)
LEUCADIUS	PL		1	
LEUCADIUS	PROP	1	4	
LEUCAS 8.241, dub.	JUV		1	island in Ionian sea
LEUCAS	LUC		1	"
LEUCAS	OV		2	" ; promontory
LEUCAS	S		1	"
LEUCAS	SEN	1	6	promontory (= Leucata)
LEUCASPIS	V			comp. of Aeneas
LEUCATA	ENN		1	promontory on Leucas
LEUCATA 15.302	SIL	1	2	"
LEUCATE	V			"
-LEUCE 1.13	CAL			a shepherdess
-LEUCESIUS	FPLA			ep. of Juppiter
LEUCIPPIS patron.	OV		1	d. of Leucippus
LEUCIPPIS	PROP	1	2	
LEUCIPPUS	OV			f. of Phoebe & Hilaira
LEUCON	HL		1	a friend of Ulixes
LEUCON	OV	2	3	a k. of Pontus; a dog
LEUCONICUM	MAR			a wool
LEUCONICUS	MAR			p. to the Leucones (Gaulish tr.)
-LEUCONOE C. 1.11.2	HOR		1	fictional girl
LEUCONOE M. 4.168	OV	1	2	a d. of Minyas
LEUCOSIA	OV		1	an island off Lucania
LEUCOSIA	SIL	1	2	
LEUCOTHEA	AV		1	= Ino, a sea-goddess
LEUCOTHEA	OV		1	"
LEUCOTHEA	S	1	3	= Aurora
LEUCOTHOE	OV		1	d. of Orchamus
LEUCOTHOE	PROP	1	2	= Ino
LEUCUS coll. sg.	LUC			a tribe in Gaul
LEXANOR m.	VAL			Scythian warrior
LIBANUS	PL			name of a slave
-LIBAS Am. 3.7.24	OV			mistress of Ovid
LIBER	AET		1	Bacchus, god of wine; wine
LIBER	CAT		1	
LIBER	COM		1	
LIBER	ENN		1	
LIBER	GER		1	
LIBER	GR		1	
LIBER	HOR		1	
LIBER	LUCIL		1	
LIBER	LUCR		1	
LIBER	MAN		1	
LIBER	MAR		1	(a friend of MAR)
LIBER	MLP		1	
LIBER	OV		1	
LIBER	PL		1	
LIBER	PRIAP		1	
LIBER	PROP		1	
LIBER	S		1	
LIBER	SEN		1	
LIBER	SIL		1	
LIBER	TER		1	
LIBER	TIB		1	
LIBER	TR		1	
LIBER	V		1	

LIBER	VAL	1	Bacchus, god of wine
LIBER	VAR	1 25	
LIBERA	OV		Ariadne (as wife of Bacchus)
LIBERALIA	COM		festival of Liber
LIBERTAS	OV	1	goddess of Liberty, with temple in Rome
LIBERTAS	PL	1 2	
LIBETHRIDES fem.pl.	V		the Muses (B. 7.21)
LIBITINA	HOR	1	goddess of corpses
LIBITINA	JUV	1	
LIBITINA	MAR	1	
LIBITINA	PH	1 4	
LIBO (Roman cognomen)	CAT	1	a friend of Caesar
LIBO	HOR	1	L. Scribonius Libo
LIBO	LUC	1	"
LIBO 4.11.31, as pl.	PROP	1	the family
LIBO	SIL	1 5	a Roman soldier
LIBRA	FPLB	1	the constellation
LIBRA	GER	1	
LIBRA	HOR	1	
LIBRA	LUC	1	
LIBRA	MAN	1	
LIBRA	OV	1	
LIBRA	PER	1 7	
LIBURNA	JUV	1	type of Illyrian galley
LIBURNA	SIL	1 2	
LIBURNAE pl.	HOR	1	
LIBURNAE 3.534	LUC	1 2	
LIBURNI 4.530	LUC	1	tribe of Illyria
LIBURNI	V	1 2	
LIBURNICUS	MAR		p. to the Liburni
LIBURNUS	JUV	1	a Liburnian slave
LIBURNUS	MAR	1 2	a Liburnian
LIBURNUS*	LUC	1	Liburnian
LIBURNUS*	PROP	1 2	
LIBYA cf. Libye	AV	1	large region of N. Africa, west of Egypt
LIBYA	CAT	1	
LIBYA	ENN	1	
LIBYA	HOR	1	
LIBYA	JUV	1	
LIBYA	MAN	1	
LIBYA	PET	1	
LIBYA	PL	1	
LIBYA	PROP	1	
LIBYA	SEN	1	
LIBYA	SIL	1	
LIBYA	V	1	
LIBYA	VAL	1 13	
LIBYCI	SIL		people of Libya
LIBYCUM (mare)	S		the Libyan Sea
LIBYCUS	AV	1	p. to Libya or to N. Africa generally
LIBYCUS	FPLB	1	
LIBYCUS	GR	1	
LIBYCUS	HL	1	
LIBYCUS	HOR	1	
LIBYCUS	LUC	1	
LIBYCUS	MAN	1	
LIBYCUS	MAR	1	

LIBYCUS		OV	1	p. to Libya
LIBYCUS		PET	1	
LIBYCUS		PROP	1	
LIBYCUS		S	1	
LIBYCUS		SEN	1	
LIBYCUS		SIL	1	
LIBYCUS		V	1	
LIBYCUS		VAL	1 16	
LIBYE	cf. Libya	FPLA	1	region of N. Africa
LIBYE		JUV	1	
LIBYE		LUC	1	
LIBYE		MAR	1	
LIBYE		OV	1	
LIBYE		S	1	
LIBYE		SIL	1 7	
LIBYS		LUC	1	a Libyan (national)
LIBYS		MAR	1	
LIBYS	M.5.75, 3.617	OV	2	; name of a sailor
LIBYS		S	1	
LIBYS		SEN	1	
LIBYS		SIL	1	
LIBYS		VAL	1 8	
-LIBYSCUS v.l., 418		COL		Libyan (figs)
LIBYS*		AV	1	Libyan, African
LIBYS*		MAR	1	
LIBYS*		OV	1	
LIBYS*		SIL	1 4	
LIBYSSA adj.		CAT	1	Libyan (7.3)
LIBYSSA		LUC	1	
LIBYSSA		SIL	1	
LIBYSSA		VAR	1 4	
LIBYSTĪNUS		CAT		Libyan
LIBYSTIS		V		Libyan
LICENTIA C. 1.19.3		HOR		"Wantonness" personified
LICHAS		MAR	1	assistant of Hercules
LICHAS		OV	1	
LICHAS		S	1	(a Theban)
LICHAS		SEN	1	
LICHAS A. 10.315		V	1 5	(a Latin)
LICINIANUS		MAR		a lawyer-friend of MAR
LICINIUS		CAT	1	the poet Calvus
LICINIUS		FPLA	1	"
LICINIUS		HOR	1	L. L. Murena (?)
LICINIUS		LUCIL 1 4		author of a law
LICINIUS* (lex)		FPLA		a law
LICINIUS/SURA		MAR		consul in 102 AD
LICINUS		HOR	1	a rich freedman
LICINUS		JUV	1	
LICINUS		MAR	2	(+ a fict. man)
LICINUS		PER	1 5	
-LICYMNIA C. 2.12.13		HOR	1	pseudonym of Terentia, w. of Maecenas
LICYMNIA A. 9.546		V	1 2	a slave-woman
-LICYMNIUS adj.		S		p. to Tiryns (T. 4.734)
LIGAUNUS		SIL		tribe of Gaul
LIGDUS (cf. Lygdus)		OV		husband of Telethusa
LIGĒA		V		a wood-nymph
-LIGEIA 10.90		MAR		fictional woman

LIGER	SIL		1	a Roman bard
LIGER	TIB		2	river in Gaul (=Loire)
LIGER	V	1	4	a Latin
LIGUR cf. Ligus	CAT		1	a Ligurian
LIGUR	LUC	1	2	
LIGURES	MAR		1	the Ligurians, people of NW Italy
LIGURES	OV		1	
LIGURES	S		1	
LIGURES	SIL	1	4	
LIGURĪNUS N	HOR		1	name of a young man
LIGURINUS	MAR	1	2	fict. man
LIGURĪNUS*	GR			p. to Liguria (in NW Italy)
LIGURRA	MAR			a woman
LIGUS	SIL		1	a Ligurian
LIGUS also pl.	V	1	2	
LIGUS*	PER		1	Ligurian
LIGUS*	SIL	1	2	
LIGUSTICUS	JUV			Ligurian
LILAEA	S			town of Phocis
-LILAEUS 14.489	SIL			a Punic sailor
LILYBAEŌN 14.75	SIL			town in Sicily
LILYBAEUM	OV			
LILYBAEUS	LUC			p. to Lilybaeon
LILYBEIUS	V			p. to Lilybaeon
- LIMNAEE M. 5.48	OV			a nymph
- LIMON S. 2.2.82	S			island near Cumae
LIMONE	OV			d. of Hippomenes
LIMYRE	OV			river & town in Lycia
LINDUS fem.	SIL			town on Rhodes
LINGONES pl.	LUC			Gaulish tribe
LINGONICUS adj.	MAR			p. to the Lingones
LINGONUS	MAR			a Lingonian (of the Lingones)
LINOS	MAR			son of Terpsichore & Apollo
LINUS	MAR		1	fictional man
LINUS Ibis 478	OV		1	son of Psamathe & Apollo
LINUS 3, prol. 57	PH		1	son of Calliope (?)
LINUS	PL		1	son of Terpsichore
LINUS	PROP		1	" "
LINUS	S		1	son of Psamathe & Apollo
LINUS	V	1	7	son of Terpsichore
LIPARAE cf. sg. -e	LUCIL			the Aeolic Islands
LIPARAEUS	HOR		1	p. to Lipare (-ae)
LIPARAEUS	JUV	1	2	
LIPARE	SIL		1	an Aeolic island (near Sicily)
LIPARE	V		1	
LIPARE	VAL	1	3	
LIPARO	PL			king of Syracuse
LIRIOPE	OV			a nymph
LIRIS m.	HOR		1	river of Latium
LIRIS	LUC		1	
LIRIS	MAR		1	
LIRIS	S		1	
LIRIS	SIL		1	
LIRIS	V	1	6	
LISSUM	LUC			town in Illyria
LITERNUM	OV		1	town in Campania
LITERNUM	SIL	1	2	

LITERNUS	S		1	p. to Liternum
LITERNUS	SIL	1	2	
LIVIA Maec. 2.31	AV		1	wife of Augustus
LIVIA	OV		1	
LIVIA Oct. 941	SEN	1	3	
-LIVIA/PORTICUS	OV			portico on Esquiline, built by Augustus (consul)
LIVIUS	ENN		1	
LIVIUS	HOR		1	L. Andronicus, the poet
LIVIUS	MAN		1	M. Salinator (?)
LIVIUS	MAR		1	T. Livius, historian
LIVIUS	SEN		1	Livius Drusus
LIVIUS	SIL	1	6	M. Salinator
LIVIUS* (arbos, 414)	COL			(the fig-tree) of Livia
LIVOR	OV		1	"Malice" personified
LIVOR	PH		1	
LIVOR	SIL	1	3	
LIXUS	OV		1	river of Thrace
LIXUS	SIL	2	3	river of Mauretania; a Punic soldier
LOCRI	HL		1	tribe of Greeks
LOCRI	S		1	tribe of Bruttium
LOCRI 11.20	SIL		1	tribe of Greeks (or t.?)
LOCRI Accius 49	TR		1	a town of Narycium
LOCRI	V	1	5	a Greek tribe
LOCRIS dub., 66.54	CAT		1	ep. of Arsinoe
LOCRIS Ibis 350	OV	1	2	" "
LOLLIUS	AV		1	a governor of Gaul
LOLLIUS	HOR	2	3	" " ; a magistrate
-LONGARENUS S.1.2.67	HOR			notorious fornicator
LONGINUS	JUV			C. Cassius Longinus
LOTIS	OV			a nymph (changed into the lotus-plant)
LOTOPHAGI	OV			leg. African tribe
LUBENTIA cf. Lib-	PL			goddess of Delight
LUCA	LUC			town in Etruria
LUCAGUS	V			Etruscan hero
LUCANI	JUV			people of S. Italy
LUCANIA	GR		1	region of S. Italy
LUCANIA	HOR	1	2	
LUCANICA fem.	MAR		1	sausage from Lucania
LUCANICA	S	1	2	
LUCANUS	HOR		1	a Lucanian
LUCANUS	JUV		1	the poet Lucan
LUCANUS	MAR		2	the poet; a minor contemp.
LUCANUS	S	1	5	the poet
LUCANUS*	CAL		1	p. to Lucania
LUCANUS*	HOR		1	
LUCANUS*	LUCIL		1	
LUCANUS*	MAR		1	
LUCANUS*	OV		1	
LUCANUS*	S		1	
LUCANUS*	SIL	1	7	
-LUCAS 10.139	SIL		1	son of Crista
LUCAS A. 10.561	V	1	2	a Latin hero
LUCENSIS	MAR			p. to Luca
LUCERES	OV		1	early Etruscan(-Roman) tribe
LUCERES	PROP	1	2	
LUCERIA	HOR		1	town of Apulia
LUCERIA	LUC	1	2	

LUCETIUS	V			ep. of Juppiter
LUCIFER m.	AET	1		the Morning-star (= planet Venus)
LUCIFER	AV	1		
LUCIFER	CIC	1		
LUCIFER	COL	1		
LUCIFER	FPLR	1		
LUCIFER	HL	1		
LUCIFER	LUC	1		
LUCIFER	MAN	1		
LUCIFER	OV	2		(+ son of Aurora & Cephalus)
LUCIFER	PROP	1		
LUCIFER	S	1		
LUCIFER	SEN	1		
LUCIFER	SIL	1		
LUCIFER	TIB	1		
LUCIFER	V	1		
LUCIFER	VAL	1	17	
-LUCILIADES	LUCIL			descendant of Lucilius
LUCILIUS	HOR	1		C. Lucilius, the satirist
LUCILIUS	JUV	1		
LUCILIUS	LUCIL	1		
LUCILIUS	MAR	1		
LUCILIUS	PER	1	5	
LUCINA	CAT	1		goddess of childbirth
LUCINA	HOR	1		
LUCINA	MAR	1		
LUCINA	MLP	1		
LUCINA	OV	1		
LUCINA	PL	1		
LUCINA	PROP	1		
LUCINA	S	1		
LUCINA	SEN	1		
LUCINA	TIB	1		
LUCINA	V	1	11	
LUCIUS dub.,Cat.13.35	AV	1		unknown man
LUCIUS Tit. 179	COM	1		"
LUCIUS 362 (Marx)	LUCIL	1		"
LUCIUS	MAR	1	4	"
-LUCIUS/COTTA	LUCIL			consul 119 BC
-LUCIUS/JULIUS 1.107	MAR			friend of Martial (in tmesis)
LUCRETIA	JUV	1		d. of Sp. Lucretius
LUCRETIA	MAR	1		(as type of good wife)
LUCRETIA	OV	1		
LUCRETIA	SIL	1	4	
LUCRETILIS	HOR			mt. in Sabine country
LUCRETIUS	OV	1		the poet
LUCRETIUS	S	1		" "
LUCRETIUS	SEN	1	3	the father of Lucretia
LUCRINA n.pl.	MAR	1		oysters from Lucrine lake
LUCRINA fem. sg.	SIL	1	2	= Dione
LUCRINUS sc. lacus	MAR	1		lake in Campania
LUCRINUS	S	1		
LUCRINUS	SIL	1		
LUCRINUS	V	1	4	
LUCRINUS*	HOR	1		p. to the lake, its oysters, etc.
LUCRINUS*	JUV	1		
LUCRINUS*	MAR	1		

LUCRINUS*	PET		1	p. to the Lucrine lake
LUCRINUS*	PROP		1	
LUCRINUS*	S		1	
LUCRINUS*	VAR	1	7	
− LUCRIO Mil. 843	PL			slave-boy
− LUCRIS Per.624	PL			a virgo
LUCTUS	OV		1	"Grief" personified
LUCTUS	S		1	
LUCTUS	SIL		1	
LUCTUS	V	1	4	
LUCULLUS	HOR		1	L. Licin. Lucullus, the rich man
LUCULLUS dub.,2.5.9	PH	1	2	
LUCUS* (boves)	FPLA		1	elephants
LUCUS*	LUCR		1	
LUCUS*	SEN		1	
LUCUS*	SIL	1	4	
LUCUSTA	FPLR		1	a notorious poisoner (a woman)
LUCUSTA	JUV	1	2	
LUDUS	FPLA		1	"Jest" personified
LUDUS	PL	1	2	
LUGUDUNENSIS	JUV			p. to Lugdunum (t. of S. Gaul)
LUNA	AV		1	Moon-goddess (often = Diana)
LUNA	CAT		1	
LUNA	CIC		1	
LUNA	ENN		1	
LUNA	FPLA		1	
LUNA	FPLR		1	
LUNA	HL		1	
LUNA	HOR		1	
LUNA	JUV		1	
LUNA	LUC		1	
LUNA	MAN		1	
LUNA	MAR		2	(+ t. in Etruria)
LUNA	OV		1	
LUNA	PER		1	
LUNA	PL		1	
LUNA	PROP		1	
LUNA	S		2	(+ t. in Etruria)
LUNA	SEN		1	
LUNA	SIL		2	(+ t. in Etruria)
LUNA	TIB		1	
LUNA	V		1	
LUNA	VAL		1	
LUNA	VAR	1	26	
LUNARIS	OV			Lunar (of the Moon)
LUNENSIS	MAR			p. to Luna (town)
LUPERCAL n.	OV		1	cave on Palatine
LUPERCAL	V	1	2	
LUPERCI	OV		1	priests of Lupercus
LUPERCI	V	1	2	
LUPERCUS	COL		1	the Roman equivalent of Pan
LUPERCUS	JUV		1	a priest of Lupercus
LUPERCUS	MAR		1	fict. man
LUPERCUS 4.1.26,93	PROP		2	Fabius Lupercus; the son of Arria
LUPERCUS	S	1	6	a priest of Lupercus
LUPUS	HOR		1	a consul
LUPUS	LUCIL		2	(a fish); an unknown man

LUPUS		MAR		3	three contemporaries
LUPUS	P. 4.16.26	OV		1	a poet
LUPUS		PER	1	8	L. Cornel. Lent. Lupus
‑ LUSCIUS		FPLA			an early Roman poet
LUSITANUS		SIL			a Lusitanian
LUSITANUS*		SIL			p. to Lusitania (in W. Iberia)
LUTATIUS		FPLA		1	Q. Lutatius, the consul
LUTATIUS	6.687	SIL	1	2	" "
LUX	Capt. 864	PL			"Light" personified
LUXURIA	5.142	PER		1	"Luxury"
LUXURIA	Trin. 8	PL	1	2	"
LUXUS	15.96	SIL			"
LYAEUS		COL		1	ep. of Bacchus (Wine)
LYAEUS		ENN		1	
LYAEUS		FPLR		1	
LYAEUS		HOR		1	
LYAEUS		LUC		1	
LYAEUS		MAN		1	
LYAEUS		MAR		1	
LYAEUS		OV		1	
LYAEUS		PET		1	
LYAEUS		PRIAP		1	
LYAEUS		PROP		1	
LYAEUS		S		1	
LYAEUS		SEN		1	
LYAEUS		SIL		1	
LYAEUS		TIB		1	
LYAEUS		V		1	
LYAEUS		VAL	1	17	
LYAEUS*	A. 1.686	V			Bacchic
LYCABAS		OV	3	3	a Tuscan; an Assyrian; a Centaur
‑ LYCABESOS	T. 12.681	S			mt. in Athens
LYCAEUS		COL		1	mt. in Arcadia (home of Pan)
LYCAEUS		HOR		1	
LYCAEUS		OV		1	
LYCAEUS		S		1	
LYCAEUS		V	1	5	
LYCAEUS*		CAL		1	p. to mt. Lycaeus (and to Pan)
LYCAEUS*		OV		1	
LYCAEUS*		S		1	
LYCAEUS*		VAL	1	4	
LYCAMBES		HOR			a Theban
LYCAMBEUS		MAR		1	p. to Lycambes
LYCAMBEUS		OV	1	2	
LYCAON		GER		1	leg. king of Arcadia
LYCAON		HL		1	
LYCAON		MAN		1	
LYCAON		OV		2	(also his grandson)
LYCAON		S		1	
LYCAON		V	2	8	(+ Cretan bronze worker, A. 9.304)
LYCAONES	pl.	GR			breed of dogs
LYCAONIS	patr.	OV			= Callisto
LYCAONIUS		CAT		1	p. to Lycaon
LYCAONIUS		FPLA		1	
LYCAONIUS		FPLR		1	
LYCAONIUS		MAN		1	
LYCAONIUS		OV		1	

LYCAONIUS		S		1	p. to Lycaon
LYCAONIUS		V	1	7	
- LYCAS	1.71.2	MAR			fict. person
- LYCASTE	T. 5.226	S			Lemnian girl (sister of Hypsipyle)
- LYCCHAEUS	14.434	SIL			a Roman sailor
LYCE		HOR		1	a woman's name
LYCE	6.374	VAL	1	2	a warrior woman
- LYCETUS	M. 5.86	OV		1	Thessalian hero
LYCETUS	T. 9.291	S	1	2	Boeotian hero
LYCEUM		CIC		1	famous school near Athens
LYCEUM		OV	1	2	
LYCIA		HOR		1	country in W. Anatolia
LYCIA		MAN		1	
LYCIA		OV		1	
LYCIA		PL		1	
LYCIA		S		1	
LYCIA		SEN		1	
LYCIA		V	1	7	
LYCIDAS		CAL		1	a shepherd
LYCIDAS		HOR		1	a young man
LYCIDAS		LUC		1	a sailor (at battle of Massilia)
LYCIDAS		OV		1	a Centaur
LYCIDAS		V	1	5	a shepherd
LYCII		V			the people of Lycia
LYCINNA		PROP			a sweetheart of Propertius
LYCISCA		JUV		1	a vile woman
LYCISCA		MAR		1	fict. woman
LYCISCA		V	1	3	a dog
LYCISCE		OV			a dog
LYCISCUS		HOR		1	a young man
LYCISCUS		PL	1	2	a slave
LYCIUS N		JUV		1	a Lycian (boy)
LYCIUS T. 10.344		S	1	2	ep. of Apollo
LYCIUS*		GR		1	p. to Lycia (or to Apollo, etc.)
LYCIUS*		HOR		1	
LYCIUS*		OV		1	
LYCIUS*		PROP		1	
LYCIUS*		S		1	
LYCIUS*		SIL		1	
LYCIUS*		V	1	7	
-LYCO Curc. 341		PL			fict. banker
LYCOMEDIS		S			a king of Scyros
LYCOMEDIUS		PROP			an Etruscan
LYCONIDES		PL			a young man
-LYCOPES or -tas		OV			a Centaur (M.12.350)
LYCOPHON		S			a warrior
LYCOPHRON		OV		1	the Greek poet
LYCOPHRON		S	1	2	" "
-LYCOREA T. 7.715		S			town near Delphi
LYCORIAS		V			sea-nymph
LYCORIS		HOR		1	a girl
LYCORIS		MAR		2	fict. girl; pseud. friend of Gallus
LYCORIS		OV		1	girl-friend of Gallus (the poet)
LYCORIS		PROP		1	" "
LYCORIS		V	1	6	" "
LYCORMAS		OV		2	river of Aetolia; Cephemus
LYCORMAS T. 4.837		S		1	" "

LYCORMAS	HO 591	SEN	1	river of Aetolia
LYCORMAS		SIL	1	
LYCORMAS		VAL	1 6	
LYCOTAS		CAL	1	a pastoral figure
LYCOTAS		PROP	1 2	a man's pseudonym (= Postumius?)
LYCTIUS		OV	1	p. to Lyctus (t. of Crete), Cretan
LYCTIUS		S	1	
LYCTIUS		V	1	
LYCTIUS		VAL	1 4	
LYCURGIDES	patr.	OV		= Ancaeus
LYCURGUS		AET	1	the Spartan lawyer
LYCURGUS	Dirae 8	AV	1	son of Dryas
LYCURGUS		HOR	1	"
LYCURGUS		LUC	1	"
LYCURGUS		MAN	1	the Spartan
LYCURGUS		OV	1	a king of Thrace
LYCURGUS		PL	2	the Spartan; a Thracian
LYCURGUS		PROP	1	son of Dryas
LYCURGUS		S	2	son of Dryas; son of Pheres
LYCURGUS		SEN	1	"
LYCURGUS		SIL	1	the Spartan
LYCURGUS		TR	1	son of Dryas
LYCURGUS		V	1	"
LYCURGUS		VAL	1 16	"
LYCUS		HOR	2	a boy; a surly old man
LYCUS		OV	5	r. in Bithynia; r. in Phrygia; Dirce's mate;
LYCUS		PL	1	a leno comp. of Diomedes; Centaur
LYCUS		PROP	1	brother of Nycteus
LYCUS		S	1	a Theban
LYCUS		SEN	1	a Theban
LYCUS		SIL	1	a Saguntine
LYCUS		V	2	comp. of Aeneas; r. in Paphlagonia
LYCUS		VAL	2 16	a king; a river
LYDA	(nurus) 4.369	VAL		Lydian bride
LYDE		HOR	1	a girl-singer
LYDE		JUV	1	a woman quack-doctor
LYDE		MAR	1	cont. woman
LYDE		OV	1 4	friend of Antimachus (the poet)
LYDI		HOR	1	Lydians, people of Lydia
LYDI		LUCIL	1	"
LYDI	4.719	SIL	1	Etruscans
LYDI		V	1 4	"
LYDIA		AV	2	a girl; ep. of Omphale (queen of Lydia)
LYDIA		FPLB	1	title of poem
LYDIA		GR	1	the country in W. Anatolia
LYDIA		HOR	1	a girl
LYDIA		MAR	2	a dog; Omphale (Lydian queen)
LYDIA	M. 6.146	OV	1	the country
LYDIA		SEN	1	the country
LYDIA		V	1 10	the country
LYDIAE		S		Lydian girls
LYDIUS		CAT	1	Lydian, p. to Lydia; (sometimes) Etruscan
LYDIUS		COL	1	
LYDIUS		FPLA	1	
LYDIUS		MAR	1	
LYDIUS		OV	1	
LYDIUS		PROP	1	

LYDIUS		S		1	Lydian
LYDIUS		SEN		1	
LYDIUS		STL		1	
LYDIUS		TIB		1	
LYDIUS		V	1	11	
LYDUS	(Atilius 4)	COM		1	a man's name?, a Lydian?
LYDUS		PET		1	a Lydian
LYDUS		PL	2	4	2 different slaves
LYDUS*		AV		1	Lydian (or Etruscan)
LYDUS*		HOR		1	
LYDUS*		OV		1	
LYDUS*		PROP		1	
LYDUS*		S		1	
LYDUS*		VAR	1	6	
LYGDAMUS	3.710	LUC		1	name of a Balearic slinger
LYGDAMUS		PROP		1	slave of Cynthia
LYGDAMUS	3.2.29	TIB	1	3	pseudonym of poem in Tibullan corpus
- LYGDUS cf. Ligdus		MAR		2	a shepherd; a homosexual
LYGDUS T. 9.764		S		1	a Theban
LYGDUS 1.438		STL	1	4	a Saguntine
LYGMON or Lucmo		PROP			an Etruscan hero
LYMPHAE		COM		1	water goddesses (equated with Gk. nymphae
LYMPHAE		HOR	1	2	
LYNCESTIUS adj.		OV			Macedonian
LYNCEUS		HOR		1	an Argonaut
LYNCEUS		OV		2	an Argonaut; son of Aegyptus
LYNCEUS		PROP		1	poet-friend
LYNCEUS		SEN		1	Argonaut
LYNCEUS		V		1	comp. of Aeneas
LYNCEUS		VAL	1	7	Argonaut
LYNCĒUS*		OV			p. to the Argonaut
LYNCIDES m.sg.		OV			ep. of Perseus
LYNCUS		OV			king of Scythia
LYRA		COL		1	constellation "Lyre"
LYRA		GER		1	
LYRA		MAN		1	
LYRA F. passim		OV	1	4	
{ LYRCEIUS		VAL			Lyrcean
{ LYRCĒUS		OV			
LYRCIUS		S			a fountain in the Peloponnese
- LYRIS 2.73.1		MAR			a courtesan
LYRNESIS		OV		1	= Briseis
LYRNESIS		SEN	1	2	"
LYRNESIUS adj.		OV		1	p. to Lyrnesos
LYRNESIUS		V	1	2	
{ LYRNESOS fem.		SEN			town in Troad
{ LYRNESUS		V			
- LYSIDAMUS		PL			a senex
LYSIMACHUS		PL			a senex
LYSIPPUS		HOR		1	Greek sculptor
LYSIPPUS		LUCIL		1	
LYSIPPUS		MAR		1	
LYSIPPUS		PROP		1	
LYSIPPUS		S	1	5	
LYSITELES		PL			a young man
MACAREIS patron.		OV			= Isse
MACAREUS		OV	3	3	son of Aeolus; comp. of Ulixes; a Centaur

MACCUS/TITUS	FPLA		1	Plautus, the comedian
MACCUS/TITUS	PL	1	2	
MACEDO	HOR		1	a Macedonian (espec. Alexander)
MACEDO	LUCIL	1	2	
MACEDON	LUC			
MACEDONES	PL			Macedonian
MACEDONIA	PL			the region of Greece
MACEDONIENSIS	PL			Macedonian
MACEDONIUS	OV		1	Macedonian
MACEDONIUS	PL	1	2	
-MACELO or -edo	OV			(unknown) (Ibis 475)
MACER (Roman name)	MAR		3	three contemporaries
MACER	OV		2	Aemilius (poet); Pompeius (poet)
MACER	TIB	1	6	Aemilius
MACES sg. of Macae	SIL			one of the Macae tr. (of N. Africa)
MACETAE	GR		1	Macedonians
MACETAE	LUC		1	
MACETAE	MAN		1	
MACETAE	S		1	
MACETAE	SIL		1	
MACETAE	VAL	1	6	
MACHAERA m.	JUV			an auctioneer
-MACHAERIO Aul. 398	PL			a slave
MACHAON	HL		1	leg. Greek physician
MACHAON as pl.	MAR		1	
MACHAON	OV		1	
MACHAON	PROP		1	
MACHAON	V	1	5	
MACHAONIUS	OV		1	p. to Machaon
MACHAONIUS	S	1	2	
MACIES 13.581	SIL			"Leanness" personified
MACRA	LUC			river of Liguria
MACRINUS	PER			cont. man
MACRONES 5.151	VAL			tribe of Pontus (or of Caucasus?)
MAEANDER cf. -drus	LUC		1	river of Ionia
MAEANDER	PROP		1	
MAEANDER	SEN	1	3	
MAEANDRIUS	OV		1	p. to the Maeander
MAEANDRIUS	PROP	1	2	
MAEANDRUS cf. -der	OV		1	the river of Ionia
MAEANDRUS	SIL	1	2	
MAECENAS	AV		1	famous patron of Augustan poets
MAECENAS	HOR		1	
MAECENAS	JUV		1	
MAECENAS	LP		1	
MAECENAS	MAR		1	
MAECENAS	PROP		1	
MAECENAS	SIL		1	
MAECENAS	V	1	8	
MAECENATES pl.	JUV			type of men of distinction
-MAECILIA em., 113.2	CAT			cont. woman
MAECIUS AP 387	HOR			Sp. Maecius Tarpa
MAEDI	JUV			Thracian tribe
MAENADES	CAT		1	Bacchantes
MAENADES 6.317	JUV		1	(attendants of Priapus)
MAENADES	MAR	1	3	
MAENALA n.pl.	LUC		1	Arcadian mts.

MAENALA n.pl.	OV		1	Arcadian mts.
MAENALA	SEN		1	
MAENALA	SIL		1	
MAENALA	V	1	5	
-MAENALIDES Eins.2.18	MLP			daughters of Maenalus
MAENALIS	OV		1	Arcadian
MAENALIS	S	1	2	
MAENALIUS	AV		1	Arcadian
MAENALIUS	COL		1	
MAENALIUS	FPLB		1	
MAENALIUS	GR		1	
MAENALIUS	MAR		1	
MAENALIUS	OV		1	
MAENALIUS	PROP		1	
MAENALIUS	S		1	
MAENALIUS	SEN		1	
MAENALIUS	V	1	10	
MAENALOS m.	S			mt. range in Arcadia
MAENALUS	GR		1	
MAENALUS	OV		1	
MAENALUS	PRIAP		1	
MAENALUS	SEN		1	
MAENALUS	V	1	5	
MAENAS -ad-, also pl.	CAT		1	a Bacchante (attendant of Cybele)
MAENAS also pl.	OV		1	
MAENAS	PER		1	
MAENAS	PROP		1	
MAENAS	S		1	
MAENAS	SIL	1	6	
MAENIUS Epist.1.3.21	HOR		1	cont. Roman
MAENIUS	LUCIL	1	2	" "
MAEON	S		1	a priest of Apollo
MAEON	V	1	2	a Rutulian
MAEONIA	OV		1	Lydia
MAEONIA	V	1	2	Etruria (by transfer)
MAEONIDAE m.pl.	V			Etrurians
MAEONIDES	MAR		1	Homer
MAEONIDES	OV		1	
MAEONIDES 6.11	PER		1	
MAEONIDES	S		1	
MAEONIDES 6.607	SIL	1	5	Etruscans (coll.sg.)
MAEONIS	OV	2	2	Arachne; Omphale
MAEONIS* (femina)	OV			Lydian (Am. 2.5.40)
MAEONIUS	AV		1	Homeric
MAEONIUS	HOR		1	Lydian/Phrygian
MAEONIUS (senex)	LP		1	Lydian/Phrygian
MAEONIUS	MAR		1	Homeric
MAEONIUS	OV		2	Lydian (Etruscan); Homeric
MAEONIUS	PET		1	Homeric
MAEONIUS	PROP		1	Homeric
MAEONIUS	S		1	Homeric; Lydian
MAEONIUS	SEN		1	Lydian
MAEONIUS	SIL		1	Etruscan; Homeric
MAEONIUS	V	1	12	Lydian
MAEOTICUS	JUV		1	p. to lake Maeotis
MAEOTICUS	PROP	1	2	
MAEOTIS	LUC		1	lake Maeotis (= Azov)

MAEOTIS		MAN	1	lake Maeotis
MAEOTIS also adj.		S	1	
MAEOTIS		SEN	2	(+ an Amazon)
MAEOTIS		VAL	2 7	(+ a nymph)
MAEOTIS*		ENN	1	p. to lake Maeotis
MAEOTIS*		JUV	1	
MAEOTIS*		OV	1	
MAEOTIS*		PROP	1 4	
MAEOTIUS		LUC	1	p. to lake Maeotis
MAEOTIUS		V	1	
MAEOTIUS		VAL	1 3	
MAERA		OV	1	woman changed to dog
MAERA		S	1 2	priestess of Venus
MAEROR 13.582		SIL		"Sorrow" personified
-MAGARIA n.pl.		PL		Punic town (Poen. 86)
-MAGII 4.187		SIL		tribe of Tibur
-MAGNA sc. Mater		MLP		goddess of fertility (Cybele)
-MAGNA/DEA F. 4.194		OV		goddess of fertility
-MAGNA/MATER Prec. 15		MLP		goddess of fertility
MAGNES also adj. & pl.		LUCR		Magnesian
MAGNESIUS		LUCR		p. to Magnesia
MAGNES*		VAL		p. to Magnesia
MAGNESSA*		HOR		p. to Magnesia
MAGNETES pl., 6.385		LUC	1	Thessalian tribe
MAGNETES		OV	1 2	
MAGNETIS adj.		OV		Magnesian
MAGNUS		CAT	1	Pompey the Great
MAGNUS		FPLR	1	
MAGNUS		LUC	2	(+ his son)
MAGNUS		MAN	2	(+ Alexander)
MAGNUS		MAR	1	
MAGNUS		OV	1	
MAGNUS		PET	1	
MAGNUS App. 8		PH	1	
MAGNUS		PROP	1	(a dwarf)
MAGNUS		S	1	
MAGNUS		SIL	1 13	
MAGNUS/POMPEIUS		PH		
MAGO		LUCIL	1	any Punic man
MAGO		SIL	1 2	brother of Hannibal
MAGULLA		MAR		fict. woman
MAGUS em. 90.1		CAT	1	(a name?, dub.)
MAGUS		V	1 2	a Rutulian
-MAGYNI 3.7.146		TIB		a Sarmatian tribe
-MAHALCES 7.599		SIL		a Punic leader
MAHARBAL		SIL		a Punic leader
MAIA		CIC	1	a Pleiad
MAIA		FPLA	1	the mother of Mercury
MAIA		GER	1	Pleiad
MAIA		HOR	1	mother of Mercury
MAIA		MAN	1	"
MAIA		OV	1	" (also as Pleiad)
MAIA		S	1	"
MAIA (Accius)		TR	1	"
MAIA		V	1 9	"
MAIESTAS F. 5.25		OV		"Splendor" personified
MAIOR sc. Arctus		CIC		constell. (Great Bear)

MAIUS sc. mensis	OV		1	the month of May
MAIUS	PROP	1	2	
MALCHIO	MAR			fict. man
MALEA	LUC		1	promontory (in S. Peloponnese)
MALEA	OV		1	
MALEA	PROP		1	
MALEA	S		1	
MALEA	SEN		1	
MALEA	V		1	
MALEA	VAL	1	7	
MALIACUS	LUC			a gulf in W. Aegean
-MALISIANUS 4.6	MAR			fict. man
MALIUS*	CAT			= Maliacus
MALLIUS dub.	CAT			= Manlius (?)
-MALLIUS* (mensa)	FPLR			Manlian (banquet)
MALLOS	LUC			town in Cilicia
MALTINUS S. 1.2.25	HOR			a cognomen
-MALUS	CIC			constell. "Mast"
MAMERCI pl.(of next)	JUV			a Roman family
MAMERCUS	MAR		1	fict.
MAMERCUS Ibis 546	OV		1	(or Mamertus) tyrant of Catania
MAMERCUS	SIL	1	3	a Roman soldier
MAMERTINUS	MAR			p. to the Mamertines (of Sicily)
-MAMURIANUS N, 1.92	MAR			a cont. man
MAMURIUS -rr-	OV			a maker of ancilia
MAMURRA m.	CAT		1	Roman engineer, time of Caesar
MAMURRA	MAR	1	2	
MAMURRAE	HOR			(pl. as type)
MAMURRIUS -r-	PROP			a maker of ancilia
MANCINUS	MAR		1	fict. man
MANCINUS	SIL	1	2	son of Satricus of Sulmo
MANDELA	HOR			Sabine town
MANDONIUS	SIL			Spanish general
MANDUCUS	COM			comic figure
MANES pl.	COL		1	deified souls of the dead
MANES	HOR		1	
MANES	MAR		1	
MANES	OV		1	
MANES	PH		1	
MANES	PROP		1	
MANES	S		1	
MANES	TIB	1	8	
MANILIA	JUV			a courtesan
MANILIUS dub.	LUCIL			(unknown man)
MANILIUS/VOPISCUS	S			a Roman poet
MANIUS Afranius 211	COM		1	comic character
MANIUS	FPLR		1	a cont. of Augustus
MANIUS	MAR		2	a friend; fict. man
MANIUS	PER	1	3	(unknown beggar)
MANIUS/VALERIUS	FPLA			a consul (time of Hannibal?)
MANLIUS	CAT		1	M. Torquatus (consul)
MANLIUS	HOR		1	M. Torquatus
MANLIUS	LUCIL		1	(dub.)
MANLIUS	MAR		1	a Spanish planter
MANLIUS	OV		1	M. Manlius Capitolinus
MANLIUS A. 8.652	V	1	6	" "
-MANNEIA 1.83	MAR			fict. woman

MANTO	OV		1	the daughter of Tiresias (Gk.myth.)
MANTO	S		1	
MANTO	SEN		1	
MANTO	V	1	4	(an Italic nymph)
MANTUA	AV		1	town of North Italy
MANTUA	MAR		1	
MANTUA	MLP		1	
MANTUA	OV		1	
MANTUA	S		1	
MANTUA	SIL		1	
MANTUA	V	1	7	
MANTUANUS	S			p. to Mantua, i.e. Vergilian
MARATHON fem.	MAR		1	town of Attica
MARATHON	OV		1	
MARATHON	S		1	
MARATHON	SEN	1	4	
MARATHONIS adj.	S			p. to Marathon
MARATHONIUS	S		1	p. to Marathon
MARATHONIUS	SIL	1	2	
MARATHUS 1.4.81	TIB			unknown man
– MARAXES 7.324	SIL			Punic leader
– MARCELLA 12.21.3	MAR			friend of MAR
– MARCELLANUM 2.29.5	MAR			a theater
MARCELLI 2.145	JUV			a Roman family
– MARCELLINUS N, 3.6	MAR			friend of MAR
MARCELLUS	HOR		1	C. Claudius Marcellus (at time of Caesar)
MARCELLUS 1.313	LUC		1	" " "
MARCELLUS 1.788	MAN		1	M. Claudius Marcellus
MARCELLUS 10.51.11	MAR		1	" "
MARCELLUS	PET		1	C. Claudius M.
MARCELLUS	S		1	Victorius M.
MARCELLUS	SIL		1	M. Claudius M.
MARCELLUS A.8.855,883	V	1	8	M.Cl.Marc. & the "Young Marcellus"
MARCIA	LUC		1	wife of Cato
MARCIA sc. aqua	MAR		1	aqueduct
MARCIA	OV		1	w. of Paulus Fab. Maximus
MARCIA	S		1	aqueduct
MARCIA	SIL	1	5	w. of Regulus
MARCIANUS	MAR			fict. man
MARCIPOR	PL			title of a lost comedy
MARCIUS	SIL			Roman general
MARCIUS*	PROP		1	aqueduct
MARCIUS* sc. lympha	TIB	1	2	aqueduct
MARCOMANI	S			Germanic tribe
MARCUS	ENN		1	father of M. C. Cethegus
MARCUS	FPLA		1	(unknown)
MARCUS 10.73	MAR		1	M. Antonius (Primus)
MARCUS 5.80	PER	1	4	M. Dama
– MARCUS/ANTONIUS	MAR			M. A. Primus
– MARCUS/DAMA 5.79	PER			(unknown man)
MARCUS/TULLIUS	CAT			Cicero
MAREOTICUM	GR			wine from Mareotis
MAREOTICUS	HOR		1	p. to Mareotis
MAREOTICUS	LUC		1	
MAREOTICUS	MAR		1	
MAREOTICUS	OV		1	
MAREOTICUS	S	1	5	

MAREOTIS sc. palus	LUC		1	lake (near t.) of Egypt
MAREOTIS	MAR	1	2	town of Egypt
MAREOTIS*	LUC		1	Egyptian
MAREOTIS*	S		1	
MAREOTIS*	V	1	3	
MARIANDYNI	VAL			tribe of Bithynia
MARIANUS	MAR			fict. man
MARIANUS*	PROP			p. to C. Marius
MARICA	HOR		1	(poetic term for) Minturnae
MARICA	LUC		1	nymph of river Liris
MARICA	MAR		1	"
MARICA	V	1	4	"
MARII 3.227	LUC		1	the family of Marius
MARII G. 2.169	V	1	2	"
-MARINUS 10.83	MAR			fictional man
MARISCAE	COL			figs
MARIUS	CIC		1	C. Marius
MARIUS	FPLB		1	"
MARIUS	HOR		1	(unknown)
MARIUS	JUV		1	proconsul
MARIUS	LUC		2	C. Marius; M. Gratidianus
MARIUS 4.45	MAN		1	C. Marius
MARIUS	MAR		2	consul; fict.
MARIUS	OV		2	C. Marius; a poet
MARIUS	PROP		1	C. Marius
MARIUS	SIL	3	15	Roman leader; Roman soldier; fr. of Scipio
MARMARICUS	LUC		1	p. to Marmarica (country of N. Africa)
MARMARICUS	SEN		1	
MARMARICUS	SIL	1	3	
MARMARIDAE N, pl.	LUC			tribe of N. Africa
MARMARIDES	OV		1	a Marmarican
MARMARIDES	SIL	1	2	
MARMARIDES*	SIL			Marmarican
MARO	COL		1	Vergil
MARO	ENN		1	
MARO	JUV		1	
MARO	MAR		2	(+ fict.)
MARO	PROP		1	
MARO	S		1	
MARO	SIL	1	8	
MARONEUS	S		1	p. to Maro (Vergil)
MARONEUS	TIB	1	2	p. to Maronea (t. in Thrace)
MARONIANUS	S			p. to Vergil
-MARONILLA 1.10	MAR			fict. woman
MARPESIUS*	TIB		1	p. to Marpesus (t. of Troad)
MARPESIUS*	V	1	2	p. to Marpesus (mt. on Paros)
-MARPESSA T. 3.172	S			a Theban woman
-MARRIUS 10.92	MAR			a friend of MAR
MARRUCINI	COL			tribe of E. Italy
MARRUCINUS	S		1	p. to the Marrucini
MARRUCINUS	SIL	1	2	
-MARRUCINUS/ASINIUS	CAT			brother of Pollio (12.1)
-MARRUS 8.505	SIL			king of the Marsi
MARRUVIUM	SIL			town of Latium
MARRUVIUS	V			p. to Marruvium
MARS	AET		1	Roman god of WAR (cf. Mavors)
MARS	AV		1	

MARS	CAL	1		god of War
MARS	COM	1		
MARS	ENN	1		
MARS	FPLB	1		
MARS	GER	1		
MARS	GR	1		
MARS	HL	1		
MARS	HOR	1		
MARS	JUV	1		
MARS	LUC	1		
MARS	LUCIL	1		
MARS	LUCR	1		
MARS	MAN	2		(+ a planet)
MARS	MAR	1		
MARS	OV	1		
MARS	PET	1		
MARS	PH	1		
MARS	PL	1		
MARS	PRIAP	1		
MARS	PROP	1		
MARS	S	1		
MARS	SEN	1		
MARS	SIL	1		
MARS	TIB	1		
MARS	V	1		
MARS	VAL	1		
MARS	VAR	1	30	
-MARSAEUS S. 1.2.55	HOR			unknown man
MARSI	HOR	1		tribe of Latium
MARSI	JUV	1		
MARSI	LUC	1		
MARSI 4.220	SIL	1		
MARSI	V	1	5	
MARSICA n.pl.	MAR			wines of the Marsi
MARSICUS	SIL			p. to the Marsi
MARSUA cf. Marsyas	MAR			legendary satyr (2.64.8)
MARSUS C. 3.5.9	HOR	1		a Marsian man
MARSUS	LUCIL	1		" "
MARSUS	MAR	1		a poet (Domitius M.)
MARSUS	OV	1	4	"
MARSUS*	COM	1		p. to the Marsi
MARSUS*	ENN	1		
MARSUS*	HOR	1		
MARSUS*	JUV	1		
MARSUS*	LUC	1		
MARSUS*	MAR	1		
MARSUS*	OV	1		
MARSUS*	PER	1		
MARSUS*	S	1		
MARSUS*	SIL	1		
MARSUS*	V	1	11	
MARSYA cf. Marsua	HOR	1		the satyr (or his statue)
MARSYA	JUV	1		
MARSYA	LUC	1		
MARSYA F. 6.705	OV	1		
MARSYA	SIL	1	5	
MARSYAS	MAR	1		

MARSYAS	M. 6.400	OV	1 2	river in Phrygia
MARTIALIS		MAR		M. Valerius Martialis, the poet
MARTIALIS*		HOR		p. to Mars
MARTICOLA	m.	OV		devotee of Mars
MARTIGENA		OV	1	Quirinus
MARTIGENA		SIL	1 2	desc. of Mars
MARTIGENAE	pl.	S		" "
MARTIS/CAMPUS		OV		= Campus Martius in Rome
MARTIUS		AET	1	p. to Mars (god)
MARTIUS		CIC	1	
MARTIUS		COM	1	(month of March)
MARTIUS		GER	1	
MARTIUS		HL	1	
MARTIUS		HOR	2	(+ month)
MARTIUS		LUC	1	
MARTIUS		MAN	1	
MARTIUS		MAR	1	
MARTIUS		MLP	1	
MARTIUS		OV	1	
MARTIUS		PROP	1	
MARTIUS		S	1	
MARTIUS		SIL	1	
MARTIUS		TIB	1	
MARTIUS		V	1	
MARTIUS		VAL	1 18	
MARTIUS/CAMPUS		HOR		the field in Rome
MARULLA		MAR		fict. woman
-MARULLINUS	4.70	MAR		fict. man
MARULLUS		MAR		fict. man
MARUS		SIL		
-MASCLION	5.12.2	MAR		an athlete
MASINISSA	m.	OV	1	king of Numidia
MASINISSA		SIL	1 2	
MASSA		JUV	1	Baebius Massa, informer
MASSA		MAR	1 2	
MASSAGETAE		HOR	1	Scythian tribe
MASSAGETAE		S	1	
MASSAGETAE		VAL	1 3	
MASSAGETES		LUC	1	member of the Massagetae
MASSAGETES		SEN	1	
MASSAGETES		SIL	1 3	
MASSICA	n.pl.	GR	1	famous wines of Massicus
MASSICA		MAR	1	
MASSICA		V	1 3	
MASSICUM		HOR		the wine
MASSICUS		S	1	mt. in Campania
MASSICUS		SIL	2	mt.; a soldier
MASSICUS		V	1 4	an Etruscan
MASSICUS*		MAR	1	p. to mt. Massicus
MASSICUS*		PL	1	
MASSICUS*		SIL	1	
MASSICUS*		V	2 5	
MASSILIA		LUC	1	town in S. Gaul (Marseille)
MASSILIA		MAR	1	
MASSILIA		SIL	1 3	
MASSILIENSES		PL		people of Massilia
MASSILI/TANUS		ENN		p. to Massilia (in tmesis)

MASSILITANUM	MAR			wine of Massilia
MASSILITANUS	MAR			p. to Massilia
MASSYLI	V			tribe of N. Africa
MASSYLIUS	LUC	1		p. to the Massyli
MASSYLIUS	SIL	1	2	
MASSYLUS N	SIL			= Syphax; (as pl.) the people
MASSYLUS*	MAR	1		p. to the Massyli
MASSYLUS*	S	1		
MASSYLUS*	SIL	1		
MASSYLUS*	V	1		
MASSYLUS*	VAL	1	5	
-MASULIS 1.405	SIL			a Punic
MASURIUS	PER			a jurist
MATER sc. magna	AET	1		= Cybele (Anatolian fertility goddess)
MATER	LUCR	1		
MATER	MAR	1		
MATER	MLP	1		
MATER	OV	1		
MATER	SIL	1		
MATER	V	1		
MATER	VAL	1	8	
MATERNUS	MAR			a cont. man (friend & lawyer)
MATER/DEUM	VAR			Cybele
MATHO	JUV	1		a rich man
MATHO	MAR	1	2	
MATINUS	HOR	1		mt. in Apulia
MATINUS	LUC	1	2	
MATRALIA n.pl.	OV			festival of Mater Matuta
-MATRINIA 3.32	MAR			fict. woman
MATTIACUS	MAR			p. to Mattiacum (a German town)
MATUTA	LUCR	1		goddess of morning
MATUTA	OV	1	2	" " (as ep. of Ino)
MATUTINUS (pater)	HOR			Janus
MAURA	JUV			name of a loose woman
MAURI	CAL	1		the Moors
MAURI	JUV	1		
MAURI	LUC	1		
MAURI	S	1		
MAURI	SEN	1	5	
MAURICATIM (Laberius)	COM			(adv.) like a Moor
MAURICUS	MAR			a cont. man
MAURITANIA	MAN			land of the Moors
MAURUS	JUV	1		a Moor
MAURUS	LUC	1		
MAURUS	MAR	1		
MAURUS	OV	1		
MAURUS	PRIAP	1		
MAURUS	SIL	1		
MAURUS	VAL	1	7	
MAURUSIACUS	MAR			Moorish
MAURUSIUS	LUC	1		Moorish
MAURUSIUS	SIL	1		
MAURUSIUS	V	1	3	
MAURUS*	HOR	1		Moorish
MAURUS*	JUV	1		
MAURUS*	MAR	1		
MAURUS*	PRIAP	2		

MAURUS*	S		1	Moorish
MAURUS*	SIL	1	7	
MAUSOLĒA pl., 8.697	LUC			burial vaults (in general)
MAUSOLĒUM	MAR			tomb of Mausolus
MAUSOLĒUS	PROP			p. to Mausolus
MAUSOLUS	MAR			king of Caria
MAVORS cf. Mars	AV		1	god of War
MAVORS	CAT		1	
MAVORS	CIC		1	
MAVORS	COL		1	
MAVORS	COM		1	
MAVORS	ENN		1	
MAVORS	GER		1	
MAVORS	GR		1	
MAVORS	HL		1	
MAVORS	HOR		1	
MAVORS	LUC		2	(+ planet)
MAVORS	LUCR		1	
MAVORS	MAN		2	(+ planet)
MAVORS	OV		1	
MAVORS	PL		1	
MAVORS	PRIAP		1	
MAVORS	PROP		1	
MAVORS	S		1	
MAVORS	SEN		1	
MAVORS	SIL		1	
MAVORS pl. in Accius	TR		1	
MAVORS	V		1	
MAVORS	VAL	1	25	
MAVORTIUS	OV		1	ep. of Meleager
MAVORTIUS	PET	1	2	ep. of Romulus
MAVORTIUS*	GR		1	Martian, p. to Mars
MAVORTIUS*	HL		1	
MAVORTIUS*	MAN		1	
MAVORTIUS*	OV		1	
MAVORTIUS*	PET		1	
MAVORTIUS*	S		1	
MAVORTIUS*	SIL		1	
MAVORTIUS*	V		1	
MAVORTIUS*	VAL	1	9	
-MAXIMINA 2.41	MAR			fict. woman
MAXIMUS	MAR		2	fict.; Vibius Maximus
MAXIMUS	OV		1	Fabius Maximus
MAXIMUS	S		1	Vibius (or Vinius) Maximus
MAXIMUS	V	1	5	Fabius Maximus
MAXIMUS/CIRCUS	OV			the famous Roman race-course
MAXIMUS/COTTA	OV			M. Aur. C. Max. (poet-friend)
MAXIMUS/LOLLIUS	HOR			consul, 21 BC
MAXIMUS/QUINTUS	LUCIL			Q. Fabius Max. Aemilianus, consul 145 BC
-MAZAEUS 4.627	SIL			Punic soldier
-MAZARA 14.273	SIL			town of Sicily
MAZAX	LUC			a Moor
MEDEA	ENN		1	d. of Aeetes & mistress of Jason
MEDEA	HOR		1	
MEDEA	LUC		1	
MEDEA	MAN		1	
MEDEA	OV		2	(+ title of tragedy)

MEDEA	PET	1	d. of Aeetes & mistress of Jason
MEDEA	PH	1	
MEDEA	PL	1	
MEDEA	PROP	1	
MEDEA	SEN	1	
MEDEA	TIB	1	
MEDEA	TR	1	
MEDEA	VAL	1 14	
MEDEIS adj.	OV		Medean, p. to Medea
MEDEŌN	S		town of Boeotia
MEDI	CAT	1	Medes (Persians)
MEDI	LUC	1	
MEDI	PER	1	
MEDI	PROP	1	
MEDI	V	1	
MEDI	VAL	1 6	
MEDIA	V		Persia
MEDICUS	LUC		Median, Persian
MEDON	OV	2	a sailor; a Centaur
MEDON	V	1	a Trojan
MEDON	VAL	1 4	a Cyzican
- MEDORES 6.211, m.sg.	VAL		a Scythian
MEDULLINA	JUV		Livia Medullina
MEDUS sc. canis	GR	1	breed of dogs
MEDUS also pl.	HOR	1	a Persian
MEDUS	JUV	1	= Xerxes
MEDUS T. 602	SEN	1 4	a Persian
MEDUSA	LUC	1	d. of Phorcus & snake-haired Gorgon
MEDUSA	MAN	1	
MEDUSA	OV	2	(+ a girl)
MEDUSA	S	1	
MEDUSA	SEN	1	
MEDUSA	SIL	1	
MEDUSA	VAL	1 8	
MEDUSAEUS	MAR	1	p. to Medusa
MEDUSAEUS	OV	1	
MEDUSAEUS	SIL	1 3	
MEDUS*	HOR	1	Median, Persian
MEDUS*	PRIAP	1	
MEDUS*	V	1 3	
- MEGADORUS Aul. 183	PL		a senex
MEGAERA	LUC	1	one of the three Furies
MEGAERA	PET	1	
MEGAERA	S	1	
MEGAERA	SEN	1	
MEGAERA	SIL	1	
MEGAERA	V	1 6	
MEGALENSIS	MAR		p. to the Magna Mater
MEGALESIA n.pl.	JUV	1	festival for the Magna Mater
MEGALESIA	OV	1 2	
MEGALESIACUS	JUV		p. to the festival of the Magna Mater
MEGALIA	S		island off Campania
- MEGALOBULUS em.	PL		an Ephesian (fict. man)
MEGARA n.pl.	AV	1	town in central Greece
MEGARA	COL	1	
MEGARA	COM	1	
MEGARA fem.	MAR	1	daughter of Creon

MEGARA	n.pl.	OV	1	town of Greece
MEGARA	fem.	SEN	1 6	daughter of Creon
MEGAREA	(sc. arva)	OV		= Megara (< Megarus) of Sicily
MEGAREIUS	adj.	OV	1	p. to Megareus (hero)
MEGAREIUS		S	1 2	p. to Megara (town)
MEGARES	= Megara	PL		Greek town
MEGAREUS		OV	1	son of Neptune & f. of Hippomenes
MEGAREUS		S	1 2	a Theban
−MEGARONIDES	Trin.49	PL		a senex
MEGARUS		V		p. to Megara (in Sicily)
MEGES		HL	1	son of Phyleus
MEGES		S	1 2	
−MEGILLA	C. 1.27.11	HOR		a maiden
−MELAENAE	T. 12.619	S		an Attic deme
−MELAENIS	7.29.8	MAR	1	a friend of Marsus
MELAENIS	Cist. 171	PL	1 2	a lena
MELAMPUS	-od-, m.	OV	1	a dog
MELAMPUS		PROP	1	Greek physician & prophet
MELAMPUS		S	1	
MELAMPUS		TIB	1	
MELAMPUS		V	2 6	(+ a Latin warrior)
MELANCHAETES		OV		a dog
MELANEUS		OV	3 3	dog; Centaur; Cephenus
MELANIPPE		JUV		mother of Boeotus
MELANIPPUS		S	1	leg. figure in the Tydeus story
MELANIPPUS		TR	1 2	
MELANTHEUS	adj.	OV		p. to a Melanthus
−MELANTHION	10.67	MAR		fict. man
MELANTHIUS		OV		goatherd of Ulixes
MELANTHO		OV		sea-nymph
MELANTHUS		OV	2	river in Sarmatia; a sailor
MELANTHUS		VAL	1 3	a Cyzican
MELAS	m.	LUC	1	river in Thessaly
MELAS		OV	2	river in Thrace; river in Sicily
MELAS		S	1	river in Boeotia
MELAS		VAL	1 5	son of Phrixus
MELEAGER	(= -gros)	HOR	1	the leg. hunter (son of Oeneus)
MELEAGER		JUV	1	
MELEAGER		OV	1	
MELEAGER		S	1	
MELEAGER		SEN	1	
MELEAGER		TR	1	
MELEAGER		VAL	1 7	
MELEAGREUS		LUC		p. to Meleager
MELEAGRIUS		S		
MELEAGROS	cf. -ger	MAN	1	son of Oeneus
MELEAGROS		MAR	1 2	
MELES	m.sg.	S		river in Ionia
−MELESIA	em.	COM		a woman's name
MELETEUS		TIB		p. to the Meles, i.e. Homeric
MELIBOEA		LUC	1	town in Thessaly
MELIBOEA		S	1 2	
MELIBOEUS		AV	1	a shepherd
MELIBOEUS		CAL	1	pseudonym of Seneca
MELIBOEUS		V	1 3	a shepherd
MELIBOEUS*		LUCR	1	p. to Meliboea
MELIBOEUS*		V	1 2	

MELICERTA	m.	OV		1	son of Ino
MELICERTA		PER		1	
MELICERTA		V	1	3	
MELICUS	adj. or N	VAR			??
MELIE		OV		1	a nymph
MELIE		VAL	1	2	
MELINUM		PL			a pigment (white of Melos)
- MELIOR	2.69.7	MAR		1	= Atedius, a cont. man
MELIOR	S. 2.1.3	S	1	2	
MELISSUS		OV			a poet
MELITA		FPLA			island near Sicily (modern Malta)
MELITE		OV		1	island off Dalmatia
MELITE		SIL		1	island of Malta
MELITE		V	1	3	a nymph
MELITENSIS		COM		1	p. to Melita, Maltese
MELITENSIS		GR	1	2	
MELLA		CAT		1	river in N. Italy
MELLA		V	1	2	
MELO -ōn-,	m.	ENN			the Nile river (archaic Latin name)
MELPOMENE		HOR		1	the Muse of Tragedy
MELPOMENE		MAR		1	
MELPOMENE		MLP	1	3	
MEMMIADAE	patr.	LUCR			the family of Memmius
MEMMIUS		CAT		1	C. Memmius, the friend of Lucretius
MEMMIUS	Pomp. 15	COM		1	the family
MEMMIUS		LUCR		1	C. Memmius
MEMMIUS		MAR		1	C. Memmius Regulus (?)
MEMMIUS		OV		1	a poet
MEMMIUS		V	1	6	the gens name
MEMNON		CAT		1	leg. king of Ethiopia
MEMNON		HOR		1	
MEMNON		JUV		1	
MEMNON		MAR		1	
MEMNON		OV		1	
MEMNON		PROP		1	
MEMNON		SEN		1	
MEMNON		SIL		1	
MEMNON		V	1	9	
MEMNONIDES	fem. pl.	OV			birds of Memnon
MEMNONIUS		LUC		1	p. to Memnon
MEMNONIUS		OV		1	
MEMNONIUS		PROP	1	3	
MEMOR	11.9.10	MAR			a tragic poet
MEMORIA		COM			goddess of Memory
MEMPHIS		HOR		1	town of Egypt
MEMPHIS		LUC		1	
MEMPHIS		MAR		1	
MEMPHIS		OV		1	
MEMPHIS		PROP		1	
MEMPHIS		S		1	
MEMPHIS		SIL		1	
MEMPHIS		VAL	1	8	
MEMPHITES	adj.	TIB			p. to Memphis
MEMPHITICUS		LUC		1	p. to Memphis
MEMPHITICUS		MAR		1	
MEMPHITICUS		OV	1	3	
MEMPHITIS		JUV		1	p. to Memphis

MEMPHITIS		LUC	1	p. to Memphis
MEMPHITIS		MAR	1	
MEMPHITIS		OV	1	
MEMPHITIS		SIL	1 5	
MENA	Ep. 1.7.55	HOR		Volteius M., a cont.
MENAECHMUS		PL		twin youths in PL's comedy
MENAEUS adj.		SIL		p. to Menae (town on Sicily)
MENALCAS		CAL	1	shepherd
MENALCAS		S	1	a Spartan
MENALCAS		V	1 3	shepherd
- MENALEUS	T. 7.755	S		a Theban
MENANDER		CIC	1	Greek poet
MENANDER		FPLR	1	
MENANDER		HOR	1	
MENANDER		MAN	1	
MENANDER		MAR	1	
MENANDER		OV	1	
MENANDER		PH	1	
MENANDER		S	1	
MENANDER		TER	1 9	
MENANDREUS		PROP		p. to Menander
MENANDROS cf. -der		PL		Greek poet
MENANDRUS		PROP		
MENAPI		MAR		Belgian tribe
- MENARCHUS Capt. 26		PL		fict. doctor
MENDACIUM	A.4.21	PH		"Falsehood"
MENDESIUS	M. 5.144	OV		p. to Mendes (town in Egypt)
MENECRATES		S		Julius Menecrates, a cont.
MENEDEMUS		TER		a senex
MENELAEUS adj.		PROP		p. to Menelaus
MENELAUS		ENN	1	husband of Helen, son of Atreus
MENELAUS		HL	1	
MENELAUS		HOR	1	
MENELAUS		MAR	1	
MENELAUS		OV	1	
MENELAUS		PL	1	
MENELAUS		PROP	1	
MENELAUS		SEN	1	
MENELAUS		TR	1	
MENELAUS		V	1 10	
MENENIUS Roman gens		CAT	1	(unknown)
MENENIUS		HOR	1 2	
MENEPHRON		OV		an immoral person
MENESTHEUS		HL	1	an Athenian
MENESTHEUS		S	1	an Argive
MENESTHEUS		V	1 3	a Trojan (= Mnestheus)
MENINX		SIL		island near Africa
- MENIPPE 6.377		VAL		woman's name
MENOECEUS		JUV	1	son of Creon
MENOECEUS		S	1 2	
MENOECEUS*		S		p. to Menoeceus
MENOETES M. 12.116		OV	1	a Lycian hero
MENOETES		S	1	friend of Argia
MENOETES		V	2 4	two heroes
MENOETIADES m.sg.		OV	1	ep. of Patroclus
MENOETIADES		PROP	1	
MENOETIADES		S	1 3	

MENOETIUS	VAL			an Argonaut
MENOGENES	MAR			fict. man
-MENOPHILUS 7.82.1	MAR			fict. man
MENS F. 6.241	OV			goddess of Thought
MENSIS M. 2.25	OV			personification of Month
-MENS/BONA Am.1.2.31	OV		1	goddess
MENS/BONA 3.24.19	PROP	1	2	
MENTOR	JUV		1	famous silversmith, or cup made by him
MENTOR	MAR		1	
MENTOR	PROP		1	
MENTOR	VAR	1	4	
MENTOREUS	MAR		1	p. to Mentor
MENTOREUS	PROP	1	2	
MENTULA	CAT			ep. of Mamurra
MERCATOR	PL			title of comedy
MERCURIALIS	GER		1	p. to Mercury
MERCURIALIS	HOR		1	
MERCURIALIS	PER	1	3	
MERCURIUS	CIC		1	the Roman god Mercury
MERCURIUS	COM		1	
MERCURIUS	ENN		1	
MERCURIUS	FPLA		1	
MERCURIUS	GER		1	
MERCURIUS	HOR		1	
MERCURIUS	MAN		1	(planet Mercury)
MERCURIUS	MAR		1	
MERCURIUS	OV		1	
MERCURIUS	PER		1	
MERCURIUS	PH		1	
MERCURIUS	PL		1	
MERCURIUS	PRIAP		1	
MERCURIUS	PROP		1	
MERCURIUS	S		1	
MERCURIUS	TR		1	
MERCURIUS	V		1	
MERCURIUS	VAR	1	18	
MERIONES	HL		1	pilot for Idomeneus
MERIONES	HOR		1	
MERIONES	OV	1	3	
MERMEROS	OV			a Centaur
MEROE	JUV		1	island in the Nile
MEROE	LUC		1	
MEROE	OV		1	
MEROE	PROP		1	
MEROE	STL	1	5	
MEROPE	CIC		1	a Pleiad
MEROPE	GER		1	
MEROPE	OV		1	
MEROPE	SEN	1	4	
MEROPS	OV		1	a king of Ethiopia
MEROPS	V	1	2	a Trojan
MESEMBRIACUS	OV			Mesembrian (of a t. in Thrace)
-MESIUS = Maesius	COM			Pappus Maesius
MESSALA cf. Messalla	MAR		1	M. Val. M. Corvinus, a general
MESSALA	PER	1	2	" " " "
MESSALINA	JUV		1	the wife of Claudius
MESSALINA	SEN	1	2	" "

MESSALĪNUS	OV	1		friend of Ovid
MESSALINUS 2.5.17	TIB	1	2	son of Messala
MESSALLA	AV	1		M. Val. Messala
MESSALLA	HOR	1		
MESSALLA also pl.	OV	1		
MESSALLA	TIB	1	4	
MESSANA	LUCIL	1		town of Sicily
MESSANA	MAN	1		
MESSANA	OV	1	3	
MESSAPIUS	OV			Messapian (in S. Italy)
MESSAPUS	ENN	1		leg. prince of the Messapians
MESSAPUS	SIL	1		
MESSAPUS	V	1	3	
-MESSE T. 4.226	S			town of Laconia
MESSEIS*	VAL			p. to a fountain in Thessaly
MESSENA	S	1		town in Messenia (?)
MESSENA	SIL	1	2	town in Sicily
MESSENE	OV			town in Messenia
-MESSENIO Men.passim	PL			a slave
MESSENIUS adj.	OV			Messenian
-MESSIUS S. 1.5.58	HOR			a cont.
METABUS	SIL		1	a Roman soldier
METABUS	V	1	2	king of the Volsci
METAMORPHOSES	MAR			title of Ovid's poem
-METANIRA F. 4.539	OV			mother of Triptolemus
METAURUS	LUC		1	river in Umbria
METAURUS	SIL	2	3	river; a Roman soldier
METAURUS* (flumen)	HOR			p. to the river
METELLA	HOR			wife of P. Cornelius Lentulus
METELLI	FPLA	1		the well-known family
METELLI	LUC	1		
METELLI	LUCIL	1		
METELLI	MAN	1	4	
METELLUS	HOR		2	Q. Caecilius M. Maced.; Q.C.M. Celer
METELLUS	JUV		2	L. Caecil. M.; Q. Caec. M. Pius
METELLUS	LUC		3	Scipio; Q. C. M. Creticus; L.C.M. Cret.
METELLUS	MAR		1	Q.C.M. Creticus
METELLUS	OV		1	the family name
METELLUS	SIL	2	11	a Roman soldier; a Roman general
METEREA (turba)	OV			a tribe on the Black Sea
-METHONE 1.388	VAL			small town in Messenia (?)
METHYMNA	OV		1	town on Lesbos
METHYMNA	S		1	
METHYMNA	SIL	1	3	
METHYMNAEUS	HOR		1	p. to Methymna
METHYMNAEUS	MAR		1	
METHYMNAEUS	OV		1	
METHYMNAEUS	PROP		1	
METHYMNAEUS	V	1	5	
METHYMNIAS adj.	OV			Methymnean
METILIUS 4.43.6	MAR			a poisoner
METIOEUS/FUFETIUS	ENN			an Alban general
METION	OV			father of Phorbas
METISCUS 1.437	SIL		1	a Saguntine
METISCUS	V	1	2	a Rutulian charioteer
METIUS (Celer)	S			general of Domitian
-METROPHANES	LUCIL		1	name of a slave

METROPHANES 11.90.4	MAR	1	2	(quoting Lucilius)
METTUS cf. Metius	OV		1	M. Albanus, the Alban general
METTUS (?)	V	1	2	Metius, the general
METUS 12.6.4	MAR		1	"Fear, Terror" personified
METUS F. 5.29	OV		1	
METUS	S		1	
METUS	SIL		1	
METUS	V	1	5	
MEVANAS	SIL		1	p. to Mevania
MEVANIA	LUC		1	town in Umbria
MEVANIA	PROP		1	
MEVANIA	S		1	
MEVANIA	SIL	1	4	
MEVIA	JUV			a virago
-MEVIUS Epod. 10.2	HOR		1	a bad poet
MEVIUS 10.76	MAR		1	fict. man
MEVIUS (Maevius)	V	1	3	a bad poet (B. 3.90)
MEZENTIUS (or -zz-)	OV		1	Etruscan ally of Turnus
MEZENTIUS	V	1	2	
-MICA 2.59.1	MAR			pleasure palace of Domitian
MICCOTROGUS	PL			a parasite
MICIO	TER			a man's name
MICIPSA m.	SIL			son of Masinissa of Numidia
MICIPSAE pl.	JUV			Numidians in general
MICON	CAL		1	a shepherd
MICON	V	1	2	
-MIDA m.	TER			a slave name
MIDAS	CAT		1	the rich king of Phrygia
MIDAS	MAR		1	
MIDAS (or Mida?)	MLP		1	(shepherd)
MIDAS	OV		1	
MIDAS	S	1	5	
MIDE	S			town in Boeotia
MIDEA	S			town in the Argolid
MILANION m.	OV		1	husband of Atalanta
MILANION	PROP	1	2	
MILESIUS	OV		1	p. to Miletus
MILESIUS	PL		1	
MILESIUS	TER		1	
MILESIUS	V	1	4	
MILETIS	COM		1	Milesian woman
MILETIS	OV	1	2	= Byblis, daughter of Miletus
MILETIS*	OV			Milesian, p. to Miletus
MILETOS fem.	JUV		1	town in Caria
MILETOS	MAR	1	2	
MILETUS	HOR		1	town in Caria
MILETUS fem.; m.	OV		2	town; father of Caunus & Byblis
MILETUS m.	TER	1	4	father of Caunus
MILICHUS	MAR		1	fict.
MILICHUS	SIL	1	2	Spanish king
MILO	JUV		1	tribunus plebis
MILO	LUC		1	" "
MILO	OV		2	k. of Pisa (in Elis); athlete
MILO	SIL	1	5	a Lanuvine
MILONIUS	HOR			a parasite
-MILPHIDIPPA Mil.874	PL			a maid
-MILPHIDISCUS	PL			a slave (Poen. 421)

-MILPHIO	PL			a slave (Poen. 129)
MILVIUS cf. Mulvius	S			bridge on the Tiber
MILVUS	OV			constellation
MIMALLONES fem.pl.	S			the Bacchantes
MIMALLONEUS	FPLR	1		p. to the Mimallones
MIMALLONEUS	PER	1	2	
MIMALLONIS	OV			a Bacchante
MIMANS = Mimas	SEN			a giant
MIMAS	HOR	1		"
MIMAS	LUC	1		mt. range in Ionia
MIMAS	OV	1		" "
MIMAS	S	1		a Theban
MIMAS	SIL	2		mt. range; giant
MIMAS	V	1	7	a Trojan
MIMNERMUS	HOR	1		Greek elegist
MIMNERMUS	PROP	1	2	
MINAE	HOR	1		"Threats" personified
MINAE T. 9.290	S	1	2	
MINCIUS	SIL	1		Roman soldier
MINCIUS	V	1	2	river in N. Italy
MINERVA	AET	1		Roman goddess of Wisdom (spinning, etc.)
MINERVA	AV	1		
MINERVA	ENN	1		
MINERVA	FPLA	1		
MINERVA	FPLR	1		
MINERVA	HL	1		
MINERVA	HOR	1		
MINERVA	JUV	1		
MINERVA	LUC	1		
MINERVA	LUCIL	1		
MINERVA	MAR	1		
MINERVA	OV	1		(spinning)
MINERVA	PH	1		
MINERVA	PL	1		
MINERVA	PRIAP	1		
MINERVA	PROP	1		(spinning)
MINERVA	S	1		
MINERVA	SEN	1		
MINERVA	SIL	1		
MINERVA	TER	1		
MINERVA	TIB	1		
MINERVA	TR	1		
MINERVA	V	1		(spinning)
MINERVA	VAL	1		
MINERVA	VAR	1	25	
MINIO m.	V			river in Etruria
MINOIS patr.	AET	1		Ariadne
MINOIS	AV	1		
MINOIS	CAT	1		
MINOIS	OV	1		
MINOIS	PROP	1		
MINOIS	SEN	1		
MINOIS	TIB	1	7	
MINOIUS	LUC	1		p. to Minos, Minoan
MINOIUS	OV	1		
MINOIUS	PROP	1		
MINOIUS	S	1		

MINOIUS	SIL		1	p. to Minos, Minoan
MINOIUS	V		1	
MINOIUS	VAL	1	7	
MINOS	AET		1	leg. son of Juppiter & king of Crete
MINOS	AV		1	
MINOS	CAT		1	
MINOS	HOR		1	
MINOS	MAN		1	
MINOS	OV		2	(+ the grandson)
MINOS	PH		1	
MINOS	PROP		1	
MINOS	S		1	
MINOS	SEN		1	
MINOS	SIL		1	
MINOS	V	1	13	
MINOTAURUS	CAT		1	the monster of Crete
MINOTAURUS	V	1	2	
MINŌUS	GER		1	Minoan, Cretan
MINOUS	MAR		1	
MINOUS	OV		1	
MINOUS	PROP		1	
MINOUS	S	1	5	
MINTURNAE	HOR		1	town in Latium
MINTURNAE	JUV		1	
MINTURNAE	OV	1	3	
MINTURNENSES	ENN			the people of Minturnae
MINUCI/VIA Ep 1.18.20	HOR			road from Brundisium to Beneventum
MINUCIUS	LUC		1	a soldier of Caesar
MINUCIUS	SIL	1	2	M. Minucius Rufus
MINYAE patr.	LUC		1	the legendary Minyans (Argonauts)
MINYAE	OV		1	
MINYAE	PROP		1	
MINYAE	S		1	
MINYAE	SEN		1	
MINYAE	VAL	1	6	
MINYEIAS	OV			d. of Minyas (k. of Thessaly)
MINYEIDES	OV		1	p. to Minyas
MINYEIDES	SEN	1	2	
MINYEIUS	OV			p. to Minyas
MISARGYRIDES	PL			a loan-shark
MISENA n.pl. (= -um)	PROP			promontory in Campania
MISENENSIS	PH			p. to Misenum
MISENUM	HOR			promontory or town in Campania
MISENUS	PROP		1	comp. of Aeneas
MISENUS	S		1	comp. of Hector
MISENUS = -um	SIL		1	town in Campania
MISENUS	V	2	5	town; promontory
MISTYLLUS	MAR			a cook
MITHRAS	S			sun-god (of the Iranians)
MITHRIDATES	JUV		1	king of Pontus
MITHRIDATES	MAN		1	
MITHRIDATES	MAR	1	3	
MITHRIDATEUS	MAN		1	p. to Mithridates
MITHRIDATEUS	OV	1	2	
MITHRIDATICUS	MAR			p. to Mithridates
MITYLENA = Mytilene	ENN			town on Lesbos
MITYLENAEUS = Mytil.	LUC			p. to Mytilene

- ⎧ MNASYLLOS	B. 6.13	V			a young satyr
⎩ MNASYLLUS		CAL			a shepherd
MNEMONIDES	fem.pl.	OV			the Muses
MNEMOSYNE		OV		1	mother of the Muses
MNEMOSYNE		PH	1	2	
- MNESILOCHUS Bacch.		PL			a young man
MNESTHEUS		V			a Trojan
- MODESTUS 10.21.1		MAR			a grammarian
- MODIA 3.130		JUV			an orphan
- MOERAE em. to Mortes		S			?? (S. 2.7.131)
MOERIS		AV		1	shepherd
MOERIS		V	1	2	shepherd
MOESI		JUV		1	a Balkan tribe
MOESI		VAL	1	2	
MOESIA		LUC			land of the Moesi
- MOESUS*_		VAL			p. to the Moesians
MOLORCHEUS		TIB			p. to Molorchus
MOLORCHUS		MAR		1	leg. host of Hercules
MOLORCHUS		S		1	
MOLORCHUS		V	1	3	
MOLOSSUS		GR		1	breed of dog
MOLOSSUS		HOR		1	"
MOLOSSUS		LUC		1	"
MOLOSSUS		LUCR		1	"
MOLOSSUS		MAR		1	"
MOLOSSUS		OV		1	king Pyrrhus
MOLOSSUS	also pl.	S		1	tribe of Epirus
MOLOSSUS		SEN		1	breed of dog
MOLOSSUS		V	1	9	"
MOLOSSUS*	Culex 33	AV		1	
MOLOSSUS*	(canis)	GR		1	
MOLOSSUS*	(rex)	JUV		1	
MOLOSSUS*	(gens)	OV		1	
MOLOSSUS*	(canis)	PROP		1	
MOLOSSUS*	(canis)	S		1	
MOLOSSUS*	(custos)	SIL	1	7	
- MOLPEUS M. 5.163		OV			a warrior
MONAESES		HOR			Parthian king
MONAESUS 7.604		SIL			Punic soldier
- ⎧ MONESES m.sg., 6.189		VAL			a Colchian
⎩ MONESUS 6.651		VAL			
MONETA	(L. Andr.)	FPLA		1	ep. of Juno
MONETA		LUC		1	
MONETA		OV	1	3	
MONOECUS		LUC		1	promontory in Liguria (modern Monaco)
MONOECUS		SIL		1	
MONOECUS		V	1	3	
MONTANUS	N	JUV		1	poet(-friend of Tiberius)
MONTANUS		OV	1	2	poet
MONYCHUS		JUV		1	a Centaur
MONYCHUS		LUC		1	
MONYCHUS		OV		1	
MONYCHUS		VAL	1	4	
MOPSOPIA		SEN			ep. of Athens
MOPSOPIUS		OV		1	Athenian
MOPSOPIUS		SEN		1	
MOPSOPIUS		TIB	1	3	

MOPSUS		CAL	1	shepherd
MOPSUS		OV	1	Thessalian prophet
MOPSUS		S	1	Argonaut
MOPSUS		SEN	1	Argonaut
MOPSUS		SIL	1	a Cretan
MOPSUS		V	1	shepherd
MOPSUS		VAL	1 7	Argonaut
-MORA	Mil. 1292	PL		"Delay"
MORBI	A. & G.	V		"Diseases"
MORBUS	HF 694	SEN		"Disease"
MORGENTIA		SIL		town of Sicily
MORINI		GR	1	Gaulish tribe
MORINI		V	1 2	
-MORINUS		SIL	2 2	a Punic; a Gaulish soldier (15.723)
MORPHEUS		OV		god of dreams
MORS		HOR	1	"Death" personified
MORS		LUC	1	
MORS		PET	1	
MORS		PL	1	
MORS		S	1	
MORS		SEN	1	
MORS		SIL	1	
MORS		TIB	1	
MORS		V	1 9	
MOSA	10.727	SIL		a Gaulish soldier
MOSCHI		LUC		Scythian tribe
MOSCHIS		COM		a girl
MOSCHUS		HOR	1	a rhetorician
MOSCHUS		PL	1 2	fict. Sicilian
-MOSSYNI	5.151	VAL		tribe in Pontus
-MOTHONE	Tr. 822	SEN		town in Messenia
MOYSES	14.102	JUV		a Jew
MUCIUS	Cul. 365	AV	1	Scaevola
MUCIUS		HOR	1	
MUCIUS		JUV	2	(+ Lucilianus)
MUCIUS		LUCIL	1	
MUCIUS		MAN	1	
MUCIUS		MAR	1	
MUCIUS		PER	1	Lucilianus
MUCIUS	8.386	SIL	1 9	Scaevola
MULCIBER		CIC	1	= Vulcan, god of fire
MULCIBER		FPLA	1	
MULCIBER		LUC	1	
MULCIBER		OV	1	
MULCIBER		PL	1	
MULCIBER		S	1	
MULCIBER		SEN	1	
MULCIBER		SIL	1	
MULCIBER		TR	1	
MULCIBER		V	1	
MULCIBER		VAL	1 11	
MULVIUS	cf. Milvius	HOR	1	bridge on Tiber
MULVIUS		MAR	1 2	
MUNATIUS		HOR		son of L. Mun. Plancus (?)
-MUNATIUS/FBRIA		COM		
-MUNATIUS/GALLUS		MAR		a cont. (10.33.1)
MUNDA		LUC	1	town of Spain

MUNDA	SIL	1	2	town of Spain
-MUNNA 9.82	MAR			fict.
MUNYCHIUS adj.	OV		1	Athenian
MUNYCHIUS	S	1	2	
MURENA m.	HOR			cont. man
MURRANUS	SIL		1	a Roman soldier
MURRANUS	V	1	2	leg. king of Latium
-MURRUS 9.828	LUC		1	soldier of Cato
MURRUS	SIL	2	3	Punic soldier; Saguntine soldier
MUSA also pl.	AV		1	a goddess (one of nine) of the liberal arts
MUSA	CAL		1	
MUSA	COL		1	
MUSA	ENN		1	
MUSA	FPLA		1	
MUSA	HOR		1	
MUSA	MAN		1	
MUSA	MAR		1	
MUSA	OV		1	
MUSA	PER		1	
MUSA	PH		1	
MUSA	PROP		1	
MUSA	S		1	
MUSA	SEN		1	
MUSA	SIL		1	
MUSA	V		1	
MUSA	VAL		1	
MUSA	VAR	1	19	
MUSAE also sg.	CAT		1	
MUSAE	CIC		1	
MUSAE	FPLR		1	
MUSAE	HL		1	
MUSAE	JUV		1	
MUSAE also sg.	LUC		1	
MUSAE	LUCIL		1	(also "song": 564W)
MUSAE	LUCR		1	
MUSAE	PRIAP		1	
MUSAE	TIB	1	10	
MUSAEUS	V			legendary Greek poet
MUSA/ANTONIUS	HOR			physician of Augustus
-MUSCON 1067 W	LUCIL			unknown
-MUSSETIUS 12.95.1	MAR			cont. poet
MUTA	OV			goddess of silence (cf. Tacita)
MUTINA	LUC		1	town in N. Italy (modern Módena)
MUTINA	MAR		1	
MUTINA	OV		1	
MUTINA	PROP		1	
MUTINA	SIL	1	5	
MUTINENSIS	OV			p. to Mutina
-MUTUS Ep. 1.6.32	HOR			name of a nouveau-riche
MUTUSCA	V			Sabine town
MUTYCE	SIL			town of Sicily
MYCALE 5.141	JUV		1	a concubine
MYCALE	OV		2	promontory; mother of Orion
MYCALE	SEN	1	4	female poisoner
MYCALESIUS	S			p. to Mycalesos
MYCALESOS	S			town in Boeotia
MYCENA sg.	PRIAP			town in Argolid

MYCENAE	GR	1		town in the Argolid, ruled by Agamemnon
MYCENAE	HOR	1		
MYCENAE	LUC	1		
MYCENAE	MAR	1		
MYCENAE	MLP	1		
MYCENAE	OV	1		
MYCENAE	PER	1		
MYCENAE	PROP	1		
MYCENAE	S	1		
MYCENAE	SEN	1		
MYCENAE	SIL	1		
MYCENAE	V	1		
MYCENAE	VAL	1	13	
MYCENAEUS	HL	1		p. to Mycenae
MYCENAEUS	LUC	1		
MYCENAEUS	OV	1		
MYCENAEUS	PROP	1		
MYCENAEUS	S	1		
MYCENAEUS	SEN	1		
MYCENAEUS	SIL	1		
MYCENAEUS	V	1		
MYCENAEUS	VAL	1	9	
MYCENE cf. -a, -ae	S	1		town in Argolid
MYCENE	SIL	1		
MYCENE	V	1	3	
MYCENENSES	TR			people of Mycenae
MYCENIS 12.127	JUV	1		ep. of Iphigenia
MYCENIS M. 12.34	OV	1	2	" "
MYCONIUS	TER			p. to Myconos
MYCONOS fem.	LUCIL	1		island in the Cyclades
MYCONOS	OV	1		
MYCONOS	S	1		
MYCONOS	V	1	4	
MYCONUS	SIL			
MYGDON 3.320, sg.	VAL			Mygdonians (coll.sg.)
MYGDONIDES	V			son of Mygdon
MYGDONIS adj.	OV			Mygdonian (Lydian)
MYGDONIUS	HOR	1		Phrygian
MYGDONIUS	OV	2		Phrygian; Thracian
MYGDONIUS	PROP	1		Phrygian
MYGDONIUS	S	1		Phrygian
MYGDONIUS 8.504	SIL	1		Phrygian
MYGDONIUS	VAL	1	7	Phrygian
MYLAE 14.202	SIL			fort in Sicily
MYRACE 6.50	VAL			river in "Scythia"
MYRACES 6.690	VAL			a Parthian
MYRICE	SIL			a nymph
MYRINUS	MAR	2	2	two gladiators
MYRINUS*	MAR			p. to Myrina (town in Aeolia)
MYRMIDONE	S			a Lemnian woman
MYRMIDONES	ENN	1		legendary tribe of Thessaly
MYRMIDONES	GER	1		
MYRMIDONES	HL	1		
MYRMIDONES	OV	1		
MYRMIDONES	V	1	5	
MYRON	AET	1		Greek sculptor
MYRON	JUV	1		

MYRON		MAR	1	Greek sculptor
MYRON		OV	1	
MYRON		PROP	1	
MYRON		S	1 6	
-MYRRHA	Cir. 238	AV	1	d. of Cinyras
MYRRHA		OV	1	
MYRRHA	3.19.16	PROP	1	
MYRRHA	HO 196	SEN	1 4	
MYRRHINA		PL		a matrona
MYRRINA		TER		
MYRTALE		HOR	1	freedman, friend of HOR
MYRTALE		MAR	1 2	fict.
MYRTILOS		GER	1	charioteer
MYRTILOS		S	1 2	son of Mercury
MYRTILUS		SEN	1	" "
MYRTILUS	(Accius)	TR	1 2	charioteer
MYRTŌUM		HOR		part of the Aegean Sea
MYRTŌUS		GER	1	p. to Myrtos island
MYRTOUS		OV	1	
MYRTOUS		SEN	1 3	
MYS		MAR	1	a silversmith
MYS	5, prol. 7	PH	1	" (or Myron?)
MYS		PROP	1 3	"
MYSCELUS		OV		founder of Croton
MYSI		PROP		country of W. Anatolia
MYSIA		LUC	1	
MYSIA		SEN	1	
MYSIA		V	1	
MYSIA		VAL	1 4	
-MYSIS	And. passim	TER		a slave-girl
MYSIUS		TR		p. to Mysia
MYSTES	m.sg.	HOR	1	a young man
MYSTES		MLP	1 2	a shepherd
MYSUS		OV	1	a Mysian
MYSUS		PROP	1 2	"
MYSUS*		HOR	1	p. to Mysia
MYSUS*		OV	1	
MYSUS*		V	1 3	
MYTILENAEUS		LUC		p. to Mytilene
MYTILENE		HOR	1	town on Lesbos
MYTILENE		MAR	1 2	
MYTILINAEUS		MAR		p. to Mytilene
-MYTTHUMBALIS	Poen.	PL		a Punic
NABATAEUS		JUV	1	p. to Nabataea (in Arabia)
NABATAEUS		LUC	1	
NABATAEUS		OV	1	
NABATAEUS		SEN	1 4	
NABATES	m.sg.	SEN		a Nabataean
NABIS	15.672	SIL		priest of Ammon
-NAEVIA	1.68	MAR		fict.
NAEVIUS		FPLA	1	Cn. Naevius, the poet
NAEVIUS		HOR	2	(+ an unknown)
NAEVIUS		TER	1 4	
-NAEVOLUS	9.1	JUV	1	fict.
NAEVOLUS	1.97	MAR	1 2	"
NAIADES	pl.	HOR		a class of water-nymphs
NAIAS	sg.	OV		" " "

NAICUS	PROP			p. to the Naiads
NAIDES	AV	1		water-nymphs
NAIDES	GR	1		
NAIDES	PRIAP	1		
NAIDES	SEN	1		
NAIDES	VAR	1	5	
NAIS also pl.	CAL	1		a water-nymph
NAIS	COL	1		
NAIS	LUC	1		
NAIS also pl.	MAR	1		
NAIS	OV	1		
NAIS	S	1		
NAIS	SIL	1		
NAIS	TIB	1	9	
-NANNEIUS 5.14	MAR			fict.
NAPAEAE pl.	S	1		wood-nymphs
NAPAEAE	V	1	2	
NAPAEUS	COL			p. to the nymphs
NAPE	OV	2	2	a dog; a woman
NĀR (Nāris, m.)	ENN	1		river of central Italy
NAR	LUC	1		
NAR	OV	1		
NAR	SIL	1		
NAR	V	1	5	
NARBO	MAR			town of Gaul
-NARBO/PATERNA 8.72.5	MAR			" " (poetic label)
NARCISSUS	JUV		1	freedman of Claudius
NARCISSUS	OV		2	son of Cephisus; a flower
NARCISSUS	S		1	" "
NARCISSUS	V	1	5	" "
-NARIS 7.598	SIL			soldier of Hannibal
NARNIA	MAR		1	town of Umbria
NARNIA	SIL	1	2	
NARYCIA	OV			town of S. Italy
NARYCIUS	COL		1	p. to Narycion (in Greece)
NARYCIUS	OV		1	
NARYCIUS	V	1	3	
NASAMON	LUC		1	a Nasamonian
NASAMON	SIL	1	2	
NASAMONES	LUC			people of Libya
-NASAMONIA em., 517	GR			region in Libya
NASAMONIACUS	OV		1	p. to Nasamonia or its people
NASAMONIACUS	S		1	
NASAMONIACUS	SIL	1	3	
NASAMONIAS	SIL			Nasamonian
NASAMONIUS	S		1	Nasamonian
NASAMONIUS	SEN		1	
NASAMONIUS	SIL	1	3	
NASAMON*	SIL			Nasamonian
NASICA m.	HOR		1	(unknown Roman)
NASICA	MAR		1	(unknown)
NASICA F. 4.347	OV	1	3	Scipio Nasica
NASIDIANUS	MAR			fict. man
NASIDIENUS	HOR			a nouveau-riche
NASIDIUS 9.790	LUC		1	a Marsian
NASIDIUS 15.450	SIL	1	2	a Spaniard
NASO	CAT		1	cont.

NASO	MAR		1	Ovid, the poet
NASO	OV		1	
NASO	S	1	4	
-NASTA 9.87.5	MAR			a slave
NATALIS	TIB			ep. of Juno
- NATTA m.	CIC		1	unknown
NATTA	HOR		1	cont. (as type)
NATTA	JUV		1	fict.
NATTA	MAR		1	fict.
NATTA	PER	1	5	Horace's Natta
NATURA	MAR		1	"Nature" personified
NATURA	PH		1	
NATURA	S		1	
NATURA	SEN		1	
NATURA	SIL	1	5	
NAUBOLIDES patr.	VAL			ep. of Iphitus
NAUBOLUS	FPLR		1	king of Phocis
NAUBOLUS	S	1	2	
NAUCRATES	PL			character in comedy
NAULOCHA n.pl.	SIL			town in Sicily
NAUPACTOŪS adj.	OV			p. to Naupactus
NAUPACTUS	PL			town in Aetolia
NAUPLIADES patron.	FPLR		1	= Proetus
NAUPLIADES	OV	1	2	= Palamedes
NAUPLIOS	FPLB			legendary king of Euboea
NAUPLIUS	PROP		1	
NAUPLIUS	SEN		1	
NAUPLIUS	VAL	1	3	an Argonaut
NAUSICAA	MAR		1	daughter of Alcinoos
NAUSICAA	PRIAP	1	2	
NAUSISTRATA	TER			a woman
NAUTES	V			a Trojan
NAVALIS	PROP			ep. of Phoebus
NAVIS	CIC			Argo as constellation
NAXIUS	PROP			p. to Naxos
NAXOS fem.	OV		1	island in the Cyclades
NAXOS	PROP		1	
NAXOS	S		1	
NAXOS	SEN		1	
NAXOS	V	1	5	
NEAERA	COM		1	mistress of Mars
NEAERA	HOR		1	" of Horace
NEAERA Am.3.6.28	OV		1	mistress of Xanthus
NEAERA	TIB		1	mistress of Lygdamus
NEAERA	V		1	mistress of shepherd Aegon
NEAERA	VAL	1	6	a Lemnian woman
-NEALCE T. 12.122	S			wife of Hippomedon
- NEALCES 9.226	SIL		1	Punic leader
NEALCES A. 10.753	V		1	a Trojan
NEALCES 3.191	VAL	1	3	a Cyzican
NEAPOLIS	AET		1	Naples, Gk. t. of Campania
NEAPOLIS	HOR		1	
NEAPOLIS	LP		1	
NEAPOLIS	MAR		1	
NEAPOLIS	PH		1	
NEAPOLIS	S		1	
NEAPOLIS	VAR	1	7	

Entry	Source			Description
NEAPOLITANUS	VAR			p. to Naples
NEAPOLITIS (Afranius)	COM			a woman of Naples
NEARCHUS	HOR			a handsome young man
–NEBRISSA 3.393	SIL			town of Spain
NEBRODES m.sg.	GR		1	mt. in Sicily
NEBRODES	SIL	1	2	
NEBROPHONOS	OV			a dog
NECESSITAS	CIC		1	"Necessity" personified
NECESSITAS	HOR	1	2	
–NEDYMNUS M.12.350	OV			a Centaur
NEFAS T. 7.48	S			comp. of Mars, personified
–NEISTA T. 8.354	S			a gate of Thebes
NELEIUS	OV			= Nestor
NELEIUS*	OV		1	p. to Neleus
NELEIUS*	S		1	
NELEIUS*	SIL	1	3	
NELEUS	OV			father of Nestor & king of Pylos
NELEUS*	OV			p. to Neleus
NELIDAE pl., patron.	VAL			desc. of Neleus (or Nestor)
NELIDES m.sg.	OV		1	
NELIDES	VAL	1	2	(= Perichymenus)
NEMEA	AV		1	town of Argolis
NEMEA	PL		1	
NEMEA	S		1	
NEMEA	SEN		1	
NEMEA	SIL		1	
NEMEA	V		1	
NEMEA	VAL	1	7	
NEMEAEUS	CIC		1	p. to Nemea
NEMEAEUS	GER		1	
NEMEAEUS	LUC		1	
NEMEAEUS	LUCR		1	
NEMEAEUS	MAN		1	
NEMEAEUS	MAR		1	
NEMEAEUS	OV		1	
NEMEAEUS	S		1	
NEMEAEUS	SEN	1	9	
NEMEE cf. Nemea	MAR			town in Argolis
–NEMEEIUS = -aeus	MAN			p. to Nemea (3.404)
NEMESE v.l.	OV			town of Bruttium
NEMESIS	CAT		1	mistress of Tibullus
NEMESIS	MAR		1	
NEMESIS	OV		1	
NEMESIS	TIB	1	4	
NEMETES	LUC			Gaulish tribe
NEMORENSIS	PROP			ep. of Diana
NEOBULE	HOR			cont. maiden
NEOCLIDES	OV			= Themistocles
NEOPTOLEMUS	OV		1	= Pyrrhus, son of Achilles
NEOPTOLEMUS	V	1	2	
NEPA	CIC		1	constellation Scorpio
NEPA	COL		1	
NEPA	FPLB		1	
NEPA	MAN	1	4	
NEPESINUS adj.	SIL			p. to Nepete (t. of Etruria)
NEPHELAEUS	VAL			p. to Nephele
NEPHELE	OV		1	comp. of Diana

NEPHELE	SEN	1	2	mother of Nessus by Ixion
NEPHELEIAS metron.	LUC			daughter of Nephele
NEPHELEIS	OV	2	2	Helle; comp. of Diana
NEPOS	MAR			friend of Martial
NEPTUNICOLA	SIL			devotee of Neptune
NEPTUNINE em.	CAT			daughter of Neptune
NEPTUNIUS	AV		1	p. to Neptune
NEPTUNIUS	CAT		1	
NEPTUNIUS	CIC		1	
NEPTUNIUS	FPLR		1	
NEPTUNIUS	HL		1	
NEPTUNIUS	HOR		1	
NEPTUNIUS	LUC		1	
NEPTUNIUS	OV		1	
NEPTUNIUS	PL		1	
NEPTUNIUS	PROP		1	
NEPTUNIUS	S		1	
NEPTUNIUS	SEN		1	
NEPTUNIUS	SIL		1	
NEPTUNIUS	TIB		1	
NEPTUNIUS	V		1	
NEPTUNIUS	VAL	1	16	
NEPTUNUS	AV		1	god of the sea (or the Sea)
NEPTUNUS	CAT		1	
NEPTUNUS	CIC		1	
NEPTUNUS	COL		1	
NEPTUNUS	COM		1	
NEPTUNUS	ENN		1	
NEPTUNUS	FPLA		1	
NEPTUNUS	FPLR		1	
NEPTUNUS	GER		1	
NEPTUNUS	HL		1	
NEPTUNUS	HOR		1	
NEPTUNUS	JUV		1	
NEPTUNUS	LUC		1	
NEPTUNUS	LUCIL		1	
NEPTUNUS	LUCR		1	
NEPTUNUS	MAN		1	
NEPTUNUS	MLP		1	
NEPTUNUS	OV		1	
NEPTUNUS	PET		1	
NEPTUNUS	PL		1	
NEPTUNUS	PRIAP		1	
NEPTUNUS	PROP		1	
NEPTUNUS	S		1	
NEPTUNUS	SEN		1	
NEPTUNUS	SIL		1	
NEPTUNUS	TER		1	
NEPTUNUS	V		1	
NEPTUNUS	VAL		1	
NEPTUNUS	VAR	1	29	
NEREIDES pl., patron.	CAT		1	the sea-nymphs (daughters of Nereus)
NEREIDES	CIC		1	
NEREIDES	GER		1	
NEREIDES	HL		1	
NEREIDES	HOR		1	
NEREIDES	MAR		1	

NEREIDES		PROP	1	the sea nymphs
NEREIDES		SEN	1	
NEREIDES		V	1 9	
NEREIS	sg.	AV	1	a sea nymph
NEREIS		MAN	1	
NEREIS		OV	1	
NEREIS		PET	1	
NEREIS		S	1	
NEREIS		SIL	1	
NEREIS		TIB	1 7	
NEREIUS		GER	1	p. to Nereus
NEREIUS		HL	1	
NEREIUS		HOR	1	
NEREIUS		LP	1	
NEREIUS		OV	1	
NEREIUS		SIL	1	
NEREIUS		V	1 7	
NERETUM		OV		town in Calabria
NEREUS		ENN	1	son of Ocean & a sea-god
NEREUS		FPLR	1	
NEREUS		GER	1	
NEREUS		HL	1	
NEREUS		HOR	1	
NEREUS		LUC	1	(the sea)
NEREUS		MAN	1	
NEREUS		MAR	1	
NEREUS		OV	1	(the sea)
NEREUS		PER	1	
NEREUS		PET	1	
NEREUS		PL	1	
NEREUS		PROP	1	
NEREUS		S	1	
NEREUS		SEN	1	(the sea)
NEREUS		SIL	1	
NEREUS		TIB	1	(the sea)
NEREUS		TR	1	
NEREUS		V	1	
NEREUS		VAL	1 20	(the sea)
NERIENES	fem.sg.	VAR		= Nerio, w. of Mars
NERINE		V		= Nereis (a Nereid)
NERIO = -ienis		COM	1	wife of Mars
NERIO		ENN	1	
NERIO		PL	1 3	
-NERIS T.4.47		S		town in the Argolid
NERITIUS		OV	1	p. to Neritos
NERITIUS		SIL	1 2	
NERITOS		SEN	1	= the island Ithaca
NERITOS		SIL	1	
NERITOS		V	1 3	
NERIUS		HOR	1	a loan-shark
NERIUS	2.14	PER	1	" "
NERIUS		SIL	1 3	a Roman soldier
NERO		FPLR	1	the emperor Nero
NERO		HOR	2	Tiberius; (as pl.) Tiberius & Drusus
NERO		JUV	2	Nero; Domitian
NERO	1.33	LUC	1	Nero
NERO	1.791	MAN	1	C. Claudius Nero (consul 207 BC)

NERO		MAR	2	Nero; Domitian
NERO		S	1	Nero
NERO	Oct. passim	SEN	1	Nero
NERO		SIL	1 12	C. Cl. Nero (consul)
NERONEUS	S. 1.5.62	S		p. to Nero
NERONIANUS		MAR		p. to Nero
NERSAE		V		town of the Aequi
NERVA		MAR		the emperor
NERVIUS	1.429	LUC		member of the Nervii tr. (of Gaul)
NESAEE		PROP	1	one of the Nereids
NESAEE		V	1 2	
NESIS	-id-, fem.	LUC	1	island off Cumae
NESIS		S	1 2	
NESSEUS		OV	1	p. to Nessus (the Centaur)
NESSEUS		SEN	1 2	
NESSUS		HOR	1	the famous Centaur
NESSUS		LUC	1	
NESSUS		MAR	1	
NESSUS		OV	1	
NESSUS		S	1	
NESSUS		SEN	1	
NESSUS		SIL	1	
NESSUS		VAL	1 8	
NESTOR		AV	1	king of Pylos & son of Neleus
NESTOR		FPLA	1	
NESTOR		FPLB	1	
NESTOR		HL	1	
NESTOR		HOR	1	
NESTOR		JUV	1	
NESTOR		MAR	2	(+ a fict. man)
NESTOR		OV	1	
NESTOR		PL	1	
NESTOR		PRIAP	1	
NESTOR		PROP	1	
NESTOR		S	1	
NESTOR		SIL	1	
NESTOR		TIB	1	
NESTOR		TR	1	
NESTOR		VAL	1 17	(an Argonaut)
NESTOREUS		FPLB	1	p. to Nestor
NESTOREUS		LP	1	
NESTOREUS		MAR	1	
NESTOREUS		S	1	
NESTOREUS		SEN	1 5	
–NESTORIDES	patron.	HL	1	Antilochus
NESTORIDES	P. 2.4.22	OV	1 2	"
NETUM		SIL		town in Sicily
NEURUS		VAL		a Scythian
NICAEA		CAT		town in Bithynia
–NICARETUS	And.87	TER		an adulescens
–NICASIO		COM		a slave
NICEROS	-ot-, m.	MAR		a perfumer
NICEROTIANUS		MAR		p. to Niceros
–NICOBULUS	Bac. 174	PL		a senex
–NICODEMUS	Vid. 69	PL		a youth
NICOMEDES		FPLB		son of king of Bithynia
NIGRINA		MAR		wife of Antistius Rusticus

NILEUS		OV		enemy of Perseus
NILIACUS		AV	1	p. to the Nile
NILIACUS		JUV	1	
NILIACUS		LUC	1	
NILIACUS		MAN	1	
NILIACUS		MAR	1	
NILIACUS		OV	1	
NILIACUS		PET	1	
NILIACUS		S	1 8	
NILOTICUS		LUC	1	p. to the Nile
NILOTICUS		MAR	1	
NILOTICUS		SIL	1 3	
NILOTIS		LUC	1	p. to the Nile
NILOTIS		MAR	1 2	
NILUS		AV	1	the river of Egypt
NILUS		CAT	1	
NILUS		ENN	1	
NILUS		FPLR	1	
NILUS		GER	1	
NILUS		HOR	1	
NILUS		JUV	1	
NILUS		LUC	1	
NILUS		LUCR	1	
NILUS		MAN	1	
NILUS		MAR	1	
NILUS		OV	1	
NILUS		PET	1	
NILUS		PH	1	
NILUS		PROP	1	
NILUS		S	1	
NILUS		SEN	1	
NILUS		SIL	1	
NILUS		TIB	1	
NILUS		V	1	
NILUS		VAL	1 21	
NIMBI		S		"Clouds", comp. of Neptune
NINOS		LUC		town of Assyria, Nineveh
NINUS		MAR	1	king of Assyria
NINUS		OV	1 2	king of Assyria
NIOBE		JUV	1	daughter of Tantalus
NIOBE		MAR	1	
NIOBE		OV	1	
NIOBE		PROP	1	
NIOBE		S	1 5	
NIOBEUS		HOR		p. to Niobe
NIOBIDAE	6.39.20	MAR		children of Niobe
NIPHAEUS		V		a Rutulian
NIPHATES		HOR	1	mt. in Armenia
NIPHATES		JUV	1	river in Armenia
NIPHATES		LUC	1	river
NIPHATES		SIL	1	mt.
NIPHATES		V	1 5	mt.
NIREUS		HOR	1	Greek warrior at Troy
NIREUS		OV	1	
NIREUS		PROP	1 3	
-NISA	T. 7.261	S		town in Boeotia
NISAEUS	3.198	VAL		a Cyzican

NISAEUS*	OV			p. to Nisus
NISEIS patr.	OV			Scylla
NISEIUS	AV		1	p. to Nisus
NISEIUS	OV	1	2	
NISIAS	OV			Nisaean, Megarian
NISUS	AV		1	king of Megara & father of Scylla
NISUS	OV		2	(+ friend of Euryalus)
NISUS	PROP		1	
NISUS	S		1	
NISUS	TIB		1	
NISUS	V	2	8	(+ a Trojan)
-NIXAE M. 9.294	OV			birth-deities
NIXUS	CIC		1	constellation (= Engonasi)
NIXUS (genu) M. 8.182	OV	1	2	"
-NOAS or Novas?	VAL			unknown river (4.719)
NOCTIFER	CAL		1	= Hesperus, evening star
NOCTIFER	CAT	1	2	
NOCTILUCA	FPLA		1	epithet of Diana
NOCTILUCA	HOR	1	2	
-NOCTUĪNUS Cat. 6.2	AV			the "Owl", pseudon. of Lucienus
NOCTURNUS Amph. 272	PL			god of night
NODUS	CIC		1	star in Pisces
NODUS	GER	1	2	
-NOEMON M. 13.258	OV		1	a Lycian at Troy
NOEMON Ā. 9.767	V	1	2	a Trojan
NOLA	SIL			town of Campania
NOLANUS	SIL			p. to Nola
NOMADES	MAR		1	wandering Numidians
NOMADES	S		1	
NOMADES	V	1	3	
NOMAS	MAR		1	Numidia
NOMAS	PROP		1	(a slave of Cynthia)
NOMAS	SIL	1	3	Numidia
NOMENTANUM	MAR	2	2	wine; estate (praedium)
NOMENTANUS	HOR		2	p. to Nomentum
NOMENTANUS	MAR	1	3	
NOMENTUM	MAR		1	town of Latium
NOMENTUM	OV		1	
NOMENTUM	PROP		1	
NOMENTUM	V	1	4	
NOMIUS	S			an Argive
NONACRIA	OV			= Atalanta
NONACRINA	FPLA			= Callisto
NONACRĪNUS	OV			Arcadian
NONACRIUS	OV		1	Arcadian
NONACRIUS	S		1	
NONACRIUS	VAL	1	3	
NONAE	OV			fifth day of month (or 7th in some months)
NONIUS	CAT			cont. official
-NORBANA 7.74	MAR			wife of Carpus
NORBANUS	MAR		1	L. Appius Max. Norbanus
NORBANUS	SIL	1	2	a Mantuan soldier
NORICUS	HOR		1	p. to Noricum (region in NE Alps)
NORICUS	MAR		1	
NORICUS	OV		1	
NORICUS	V	1	4	
NORTIA	JUV			(Italic) goddess of fortune

NOSTIUS	LUCIL			a haruspex
− NOTHUS C. 3.15.11	HOR			a young man
NOTUS	AET	1		South Wind
NOTUS	HOR	1		
NOTUS	LUC	1		
NOTUS	MAN	1		
NOTUS	MAR	1		
NOTUS	OV	1		
NOTUS	PROP	1		
NOTUS	S	1		
NOTUS	SEN	1		
NOTUS	SIL	1		
NOTUS	TIB	1		
NOTUS	V	1		
NOTUS	VAL	1	13	
NOVA/VIA F. 6.396	OV			a road in Rome (one of the oldest!)
−NOVAS v.l., 4.719	VAL			a river (?)
NOVI/AGRI 4.8.2	PROP			gardens on the Esquiline
NOVIUS	HOR	1		fict.
NOVIUS	JUV	1		fortune hunter
NOVIUS	MAR	1	3	friend of MAR
NOVUM/COMUM 35.3	CAT			= Comum, t. in N. Italy
NOX	CIC	1		goddess of Night
NOX	HOR	1		
NOX	OV	1		
NOX	PL	1		
NOX	S	1		
NOX	SIL	1		
NOX	TIB	1		
NOX	TR	1		
NOX	V	1		
NOX	VAL	1	10	
NUBAE	SIL			the Nubians (of E. Africa)
NUBA* (populus)	SIL			Nubian
NUBES v.l. of Nephele	SEN			mother of Nessus (HO 492)
NUBIGENAE pl.	OV			ep. of Centaurs
NUBILA n.pl.	S			comp. of Neptune
NUCERIA	LUC	1		town in Campania
NUCERIA	SIL	1	2	
NUCRAE	SIL			town of central Italy
NUCULA 1135W	LUCIL			(obscure pun)
−NUGIEPILOQUIDES	PL			(comic formation) Pers. 703
NUMA	CAL	1		early king of Rome
NUMA	HOR	1		
NUMA	JUV	1		
NUMA	LUC	1		
NUMA	MAR	2		; (fict.)
NUMA	OV	2		; poet
NUMA	PER	1		
NUMA	PROP	1		
NUMA	S	1		
NUMA	V	1	12	
NUMAE/POMPILII pl.	LUCIL			= Numa
NUMANA	SIL			town of Picenum
NUMANTIA	HOR			town of Spain
NUMANTINI	JUV			people of Numantia
NUMANTĪNUS	OV	1		p. to Numantia

NUMANTĪNUS	PROP	1	2	p. to Numantia
NUMANUS	V			a Rutulian
NUMERI	FPLA			"Meters" personified
NUMERIUS	COM			unknown man
NUMICIUS	HOR		1	unknown man
NUMICIUS	OV		1	stream in Latium
NUMICIUS	SIL	1	3	
NUMICIUS	TIB		1	
NUMICUS	V	1	2	
NUMIDA	HOR			a friend of Horace
NUMIDAE	ENN		1	tribe of N. Africa
NUMIDAE	FPLB		1	
NUMIDAE	GR		1	
NUMIDAE	HOR		1	
NUMIDAE	JUV		1	
NUMIDAE	LUC		1	
NUMIDAE	MAN		1	
NUMIDAE	OV		1	
NUMIDAE	PET		1	
NUMIDAE	S		1	
NUMIDAE	SIL		1	
NUMIDAE	V	1	12	
NUMIDICAE sc. gallinae	MAR			breed of fowl
NUMIDICUS	COM		1	p. to Numidia
NUMIDICUS	PET	1	2	
NUMIDUS*	JUV		1	Numidian
NUMIDUS*	OV	1	2	
NUMISIUS	COM			a man's name
NUMITOR	JUV		1	king of Alba
NUMITOR	OV		1	
NUMITOR	SIL		1	
NUMITOR	V	2	5	(+ a Rutulian)
NUMMOSEXPALPONIDES	PL			comic formation (Pers. 704)
NUMQUAMERIPIDES	PL			" " (Pers. 705)
NURSIA	COL		1	town of the Sabines
NURSIA	SIL		1	
NURSIA	V	1	3	
NURSĪNUS	MAR			p. to Nursia
-NUTHA 1.49.18	MAR			river of Spain
NYCTEIS patron.	OV		1	Antiope
NYCTEIS	PROP		1	
NYCTEIS	S	1	3	
NYCTELIUS	AV		1	Bacchus
NYCTELIUS	OV		1	
NYCTELIUS	SEN		1	
NYCTELIUS	VAL	1	4	
NYCTEUS	OV		1	comp. of Diomedes
NYCTEUS	PROP		1	
NYCTEUS	TR	1	3	
-NYCTILUS 6.1	CAL			a shepherd
NYCTIMENE	OV			daughter of Epopeus
NYMPHA	CAT		1	a goddess of nature
NYMPHA	MAR		1	
NYMPHA	OV		1	
NYMPHA	S		1	
NYMPHA	SIL		1	
NYMPHA	VAL	1	6	

NYMPHAE	pl.	CAL	1	goddess of nature
NYMPHAE		CAT	1	
NYMPHAE		HOR	1	
NYMPHAE		LUC	1	
NYMPHAE		LUCR	1	
NYMPHAE		MAN	1	
NYMPHAE		PET	1	
NYMPHAE		PRIAP	1	
NYMPHAE		PROP	1 9	
NYMPHAEUM		LUC		port of Illyria
NYSA		JUV	1	town in India (home of Bacchus)
NYSA		LUC	1	
NYSA		MAR	1	
NYSA		S	1	
NYSA		SEN	1	
NYSA		V	2 7	(+ a girl)
NYSAEUS		LUC	1	p. to Nysa, hence Bacchic
NYSAEUS		PROP	1	
NYSAEUS		S	1	
NYSAEUS		SEN	1	
NYSAEUS		SIL	1 5	
NYSEIS		OV		Bacchic
NYSEIUS		COL	1	Bacchic
NYSEIUS		LUC	1 2	
NYSEUS		OV		ep. of Bacchus
NYSIAS		OV		Bacchic
NYSIGENA		CAT		born in Nysa, ep. of Bacchus
NYSIUS		COL		ep. of Bacchus
OARION = Orion		CAT		constellation
OAXES		V		river in Crete
OBLIVIA em., T. 10.89		S		"Forgetfulness" personified
OBSCĒ adv.		COM		in Oscan (cf. Opscō)
OBSEQUENS		PL		ep. of Fortuna (Asin.716)
OBTRECTATIO		PL		"Calumny" personif. (Pers. 556)
-OCALEA T. 7.260		S		town of Boeotia
OCCIDENS		CAT	1	the West
OCCIDENS		HOR	1 2	
OCEANITIS		V		an Ocean nymph
OCEANUS		AV	1	the encircling sea, often personified
OCEANUS		CAT	1	
OCEANUS		COL	1	
OCEANUS		FPLB	1	
OCEANUS		HL	1	
OCEANUS		HOR	1	
OCEANUS		JUV	1	(adj.? 11.94)
OCEANUS		MAN	1	
OCEANUS		MAR	2	(+ a surname, 3.95.10)
OCEANUS		OV	1	
OCEANUS		PROP	1	
OCEANUS		S	1	
OCEANUS		SEN	1	
OCEANUS		SIL	1	
OCEANUS		TIB	1	
OCEANUS		TR	1	
OCEANUS		V	1	
OCEANUS		VAL	1 19	
OCEANUS* 115.6		CAT		Oceanic

OCEANUS/RUBER	HOR		the Persian Gulf
-OCHEUS 6.200	VAL		a Scythian
OCHUS	VAL		Cyzican
OCNUS	PROP	1	allegorical picture
OCNUS	SIL	1	founder of Mantua
OCNUS	V	1 3	" "
-OCRES 10.32	SIL		Roman soldier
OCRESIA	OV		a slave
-OCREUS 6.251	VAL		a Colchian
OCTAVIA	SEN		daughter of Claudius
OCTAVIUS Cul.;Cat.	AV	2	Augustus; Oct. Musa, the poet
OCTAVIUS S. 1.10.83	HOR	1	a poet
OCTAVIUS	JUV	1	emperor Augustus
OCTAVIUS	LUC	1 5	M. Octavius
OCYRHOE	OV		d. of Chiron
ODESOS	OV		town of Moesia
ODIUM T. 5.73	S		(personification)
-ODIUS	HL		leader of the Halizones
-ODRUSSA 5.594	VAL		a Colchian
ODRYSII	OV		tribe of Thrace
ODRYSIUS	OV	1	= Polymestor
ODRYSIUS	VAL	1 2	= Orpheus
ODRYSIUS*	MAR	1	p. to the Odryssae (-ii), Thracian tr.
ODRYSIUS* (rex)	OV	1	(= Tereus)
ODRYSIUS*	S	1	
ODRYSIUS*	SEN	1	
ODRYSIUS*	SIL	1 5	
ODYSSEA	OV		title of epic
OEA	SIL		town in Africa
OEAGRIUS	AV	1	p. to Oeagrus, Thracian
OEAGRIUS	MAN	1	
OEAGRIUS	OV	1	
OEAGRIUS	S	1	
OEAGRIUS	SIL	1	
OEAGRIUS	V	1 6	
OEAGRUS	OV	1	a king of Thrace
OEAGRUS	PROP	1	
OEAGRUS	VAL	1 3	
-OEAX	TR		brother of Palamedes
OEAXIS adj.	FPLR		p. to Oaxes, Cretan
OEBALIDAE patron.	OV		Castor & Pollux
OEBALIDES	OV	1	Hyacinthos
OEBALIDES	S	1	"
OEBALIDES	VAL	1 3	Pollux
OEBALIS adj.	OV	1	Spartan; Roman
OEBALIS	S	1 2	Spartan
OEBALIUS	MAR	1	p. to Oebalus, Spartan
OEBALIUS	OV	1	" (+ Sabine)
OEBALIUS	S	1	
OEBALIUS	SIL	1	
OEBALIUS	V	1	
OEBALIUS	VAL	1 6	
OEBALUS	OV	1	king of Sparta
OEBALUS	S	1	" "
OEBALUS	V	1 3	king of Caprea
-OEBASUS 6.245	VAL		a Colchian
OECHALIA	OV	1	town in Euboea

OECHALIA		SEN		1
OECHALIA		V	1	3
OECHALIS		OV		an Oechalian woman
OECLIDES	patr.	OV		1 = Amphiaraus
OECLIDES		S	1	2
OEDIPODES	m.sg.	MAR		1 = Oedipus
OEDIPODES		S	1	2
OEDIPODIONIDES patr.		S		= Polyneices
OEDIPODIONIUS		LUC		1 p. to Oedipus
OEDIPODIONIUS		OV		1
OEDIPODIONIUS		S	1	3
OEDIPUS		OV		1 famous king of Thebes
OEDIPUS		PL		1
OEDIPUS		SEN		1
OEDIPUS		TER	1	4
OENEIS	patr.	SEN		= Deianira
OENEIUS	adj.	S		p. to Oeneus
OENEUS		CIC		1 king of Aetolia & father of Meleager
OENEUS		LUC		1
OENEUS		OV		1
OENEUS		S		1
OENEUS		TR	1	5
OENEUS*		S		1 p. to Oeneus
OENEUS*		SIL	1	2
OENIDES	Cat. 9.6	AV		1 Diomedes
OENIDES		OV		2 Meleager; Diomedes (s. of Tydeus)
OENIDES		S		1 Diomedes (and Tydeus)
OENIDES		VAL	1	5 Meleager
OENIUS	(= -eus)	OV		p. to Oeneus
OENOMAUS		ENN		1 king of Elis
OENOMAUS		S		1
OENOMAUS		TR	1	3
OENONE		LUC		1 Paris' sweetheart
OENONE		OV	1	2
OENOPIA		OV		Aegina (island)
OENOPION		CIC		1 king of Chios
OENOPION		GER	1	2
OENOPIUS		OV		p. to Oenopia (Aegina)
OENOTRI	8.46	SIL		= Italians
OENOTRIA		VAL		region of S. Italy
OENOTRIUS		SIL		1 p. to Oenotria
OENOTRIUS		V	1	2
OENOTRUS		V		p. to Oenotria
OETA	cf. Oete	AV		1 mt. of Thessaly (in Hercules story)
OETA		OV		1
OETA		S		1
OETA		SEN		1
OETA		V	1	5
OETAEUS		CAT		1 p. to Oeta
OETAEUS		LUC		1
OETAEUS		MAR		1
OETAEUS	N (Ibis 349)	OV		1 (Hercules)
OETAEUS		PROP		1
OETAEUS		S		1
OETAEUS		SEN		1
OETAEUS		TR	1	8
OETE	cf. Oeta	LUC		1 mt. of Thessaly

OETE	SIL	1	2	mt. of Thessaly
OFELLUS	HOR			a Roman stoic
-OGULNIA 6.352	JUV			a cont. woman
OGYGIAE	S			a gate of Thebes
OGYGIDAE patr.	S			Thebans
OGYGIUS	AET	1		p. to Ogyges, Theban
OGYGIUS	AV	1		
OGYGIUS	LUC	1		
OGYGIUS	OV	1		
OGYGIUS	S	1		
OGYGIUS	SEN	1		
OGYGIUS	TR	1		
OGYGIUS	VAL	1	8	
⎧OILEOS	HL			king of Locris
⎪OILEUS	OV		1	
⎨OILEUS	SEN		1	
⎪OILEUS	V		1	
⎩OILEUS	VAL	1	4	
OILIADES patron.	PROP		1	Ajax
OILIADES	SIL	1	2	
-OLEUS 6.638	VAL			a Colchian
OLEAROS = -iaros	S		1	island in Cyclades
OLEAROS	V	1	2	
OLENIDES patr.	OV		1	son of Olenus
OLENIDES	VAL	1	2	
OLENIE (adj!)	MAN			p. to Achaia
OLENIUS	OV		1	
OLENIUS	S		2	(an Aetolian; a Theban: T. 12.741)
OLENIUS	SEN		1	
OLENIUS	VAL	2	6	Lemnian; Cyzican
OLENOS M. 10.69	OV		1	husband of Lethaea
OLENOS	S		1	town in Aetolia
OLENOS	SEN	1	3	" "
-OLFIUS 9.95.1	MAR			fict. man
OLIAROS cf. Olearus	OV			island in Cyclades
-OLMIUS T. 7.284	S			river of Boeotia
OLOR 1.687	MAN			= Cygnus (constell.)
-OLPAEUS 15.300	SIL			adj. of *Ολπαι
OLUS = Aulus	MAR			fict. man
OLYMPIA n.pl.	ENN		1	Olympic games
OLYMPIA	HOR		1	" "
OLYMPIA fem.	PL	1	3	sacred precinct in Elis
OLYMPIACUS adj.	LUC		1	Olympic
OLYMPIACUS	V	1	2	
OLYMPIAS	MAR		1	Olympiad, i.e. lustrum of 5 years
OLYMPIAS	OV	1	2	"
OLYMPICUS	HOR		1	Olympic
OLYMPICUS	PL		1	
OLYMPICUS	SEN	1	3	
OLYMPIO	PL			a slave-name
OLYMPISCUS	PL			diminutive of Olympio (slave)
OLYMPIUS (ludi)	PL			Olympic
OLYMPUS	AET	1		mt. in Thessaly
OLYMPUS	AV	1		
OLYMPUS	CAL	1		
OLYMPUS	CAT	1		
OLYMPUS	CIC	1		

OLYMPUS	COL	1		mt. in Thessaly
OLYMPUS	ENN	1		
OLYMPUS	FPLᴬ	1		
OLYMPUS	GER	1		
OLYMPUS	GR	1		
OLYMPUS	HL	1		
OLYMPUS	HOR	1		
OLYMPUS	LP	1		
OLYMPUS	LUC	1		
OLYMPUS	MAN	1		
OLYMPUS	MAR	1		
OLYMPUS	OV	2		(+ musician)
OLYMPUS	PET	1		
OLYMPUS	PROP	1		
OLYMPUS	S	1		
OLYMPUS	SEN	1		
OLYMPUS	SIL	1		
OLYMPUS	TIB	1		
OLYMPUS	V	1		
OLYMPUS	VAL	1	26	
OLYNTHUS fem.	JUV		1	town of Thrace
OLYNTHUS	S	1	2	
-OMBI 15.35	JUV			a place in Egypt
OMNIPOTENS 7.372	SIL			ep. of Juppiter
OMPHALE	PROP	1		queen of Lydia
OMPHALE	SEN	1		
OMPHALE	TER	1	3	
ONAGUS	PL			title of a (lost) comedy
ONCHESMITES	CIC			a wind (from Onchesmus)
ONCHESTIUS	OV		1	p. to Onchestos
ONCHESTIUS	S	1	2	
ONCHESTOS	S			town of Boeotia
-ONCHEUS 6.256	VAL			a Scythian
-ONETOR M. 11.348	OV			Phocian herdsman
-ONITES A. 12.514	V			Rutulian warrior
OPHELTES	OV		1	Etruscan sailor
OPHELTES	S		1	son of Lycurgus
OPHELTES	V		1	Trojan warrior
OPHELTES	VAL	1	4	a Cyzican
OPHIAS	OV			daughter of Ophius
OPHIONIDES	OV			= Amychus
OPHIUCHUS	CIC		1	constellation (cf. Anguitenens)
OPHIUCHUS	MAN	1	2	
OPHIUCUS	GER			
OPHIUSA 6.85	VAL			town (uncertain location)
OPHIUSIUS adj.	OV			Cyprian
OPIMIANUM	MAR			a wine
OPIMIANUS	MAR			p. to Opimius
OPIMIUS	HOR		1	a consul (121 BC)
OPIMIUS	LUCIL		1	
OPIMIUS	MAR	1	3	
OPIS	V			a nymph of Diana
OPITER	SIL			a Roman soldier
OPITERGINUS	LUC			p. to Opitergium (t. in N.E. Italy)
-OPORINOS 9.13.1	MAR			fict. man
OPPIA 10.220	JUV			wife of L. Mindius
-OPPIANUS 6.42; 6.62	MAR	2	2	two contemporaries

OPPIUS	CIC		1	a quaestor
OPPIUS	FPLA	1	2	"
OPPIUS* Curc. 485	PL			??
OPPORTUNITAS	PL			goddess of Opportunity
OPS	OV		1	goddess of Wealth
OPS (nom. opis)	PL		1	
OPS	TIB	1	3	
OPSCUS cf. Obsce	ENN			Oscans, tr. of Central Italy
-OPTATUS S. 5.2.152	S			a cont.
OPUNTIUS adj.	HOR			p. to Opus
OPŪS -nt- fem.	OV			town in Greece
ORATIUS = Horatius	ENN			
ORBILIA	LUCIL			unknown woman
ORBILIUS	FPLR		1	grammarian, O. Publius
ORBILIUS	HOR	1	2	"
ORBIS/SIGNIFER	CIC			the Zodiac
ORBIUS	HOR			rich cont.
ORCADES	JUV			the Orkneys
ORCHAMUS	OV			k. of Babylonia & f. of Leucothoe
ORCHOMENOS	OV		1	town of Arcadia
ORCHOMENOS	S	1	2	town of Boeotia
ORCHOMENUS	OV			town of Arcadia
ORCHUS	FPLA			= Orcus
ORCINIANUS	MAR			p. to Orcus
ORCUS	CAT		1	the Underworld
ORCUS	COM		1	
ORCUS	ENN		1	
ORCUS	GR		1	
ORCUS	HL		1	
ORCUS	HOR		1	
ORCUS	LUC		1	
ORCUS	LUCIL		1	
ORCUS	LUCR		1	
ORCUS	OV		1	
ORCUS	PET		1	
ORCUS	PL		1	
ORCUS	PROP		1	
ORCUS	S		1	
ORCUS	TIB		1	
ORCUS	V		1	
ORCUS	VAL		1	
ORCUS	VAR	1	18	
OREAS	CAL		1	a class of mountain nymphs
OREAS	OV		1	
OREAS	V	1	3	
ORESITROPHOS	OV			one of Actaeon's dogs
ORESTAE or Oretae	LUC			tribe of W. India
ORESTES	ENN		1	famous son of Agamemnon
ORESTES	HOR		1	
ORESTES	JUV		1	(title of tragedy)
ORESTES	LUC		1	
ORESTES	LUCIL		1	
ORESTES	MAN		1	
ORESTES	MAR		1	
ORESTES*	OV		1	
ORESTES	PER		1	
ORESTES	PL		1	

ORESTES		PROP	1	the son of Agamemnon
ORESTES		S	1	
ORESTES		SEN	1	
ORESTES		SIL	1	
ORESTES		TR	1	
ORESTES		V	1	
ORESTES		VAL	1 17	
ORESTEUS		OV		p. to Orestes
-ORFITUS 5.166		SIL		a Roman soldier
ORIBASUS		OV		one of Actaeon's dogs
ORICIUS	adj.	PROP	1	p. to Oricus
ORICIUS		V	1 2	
ORICOS	fem.	LUC	1	town of Illyria
ORICOS		PROP	1	
ORICOS		SIL	1 3	
ORICUM	n.	HOR		town of Illyria
ORIENS		AV	1	the East, the Orient
ORIENS		HOR	1	
ORIENS		OV	1	
ORIENS		V	1 4	
ORIGO		HOR		a woman mime
ORION		AET	1	constellation
ORION		AV	1	
ORION		CIC	1	
ORION		FPLR	1	
ORION		GER	1	
ORION		HOR	2	(= the hunter)
ORION		LUC	1	
ORION		MAN	1	
ORION		OV	1	
ORION		PROP	1	
ORION		S	1	
ORION		SEN	1	
ORION		TR	1	
ORION		V	1	
ORION		VAL	1 16	
-ORIOS M. 12.262 bis		OV		a Lapith
ORITHYIA		OV	1	daughter of Pandion
ORITHYIA		PROP	1	
ORITHYIA		SIL	1	
ORITHYIA		V	1	
ORITHYIA		VAL	1 5	
-ORITHYIUS T. 12.630		S		p. to Orithyia
ORMENIS	patron.	OV		= Astydamia
-ORMENUS T. 10.515		S		an Argive
ORNEUS		OV		a Centaur
ORNYTOS	14.478	SIL		Punic soldier
ORNYTUS		CAL	1	a shepherd
ORNYTUS		HOR	1	a young man
ORNYTUS	T. 12.142	S	1	an Argive
ORNYTUS		V	1	an Etruscan
ORNYTUS		VAL	1 5	a Cyzican
ORODES		V		Trojan warrior
ORONTES		JUV	1	river of Syria
ORONTES		LUC	1	
ORONTES		OV	1	
ORONTES		PROP	1	

ORONTES	S		1	river of Syria
ORONTES	V	1	6	(comp. of Aeneas)
ORONTĒUS	PROP			p. to the Orontes, i.e. Syrian
-OROPS 4.1.77	PROP			an astrologer
ORPHEUS	AV		1	legendary bard
ORPHEUS	FPLR		1	
ORPHEUS	HOR		1	
ORPHEUS	MAN		1	
ORPHEUS	MAR		1	
ORPHEUS	OV		1	
ORPHEUS	PH		1	
ORPHEUS	PROP		1	
ORPHEUS	S		1	
ORPHEUS	SEN		1	
ORPHEUS	SIL		1	
ORPHEUS	V		1	
ORPHEUS	VAL	1	13	
ORPHĒUS*	LUC		1	p. to Orpheus, Orphic
ORPHEUS*	MAR		1	
ORPHEUS*	OV		1	
ORPHEUS*	PROP		1	
ORPHEUS*	S		1	
ORPHEUS*	VAL	1	6	
ORPHNE	OV			a nymph
ORSES	V			a Trojan warrior
ORSILOCHUS	V			a Trojan warrior
- ORTALUS 65.2	CAT			a cont. (Q. Hortensius Hortalus)
ORTHRUS	SIL			Geryon's dog
ORTYGIA	OV		2	Delos; Syracusan island
ORTYGIA	PROP		1	Delos
ORTYGIA	S		1	Delos
ORTYGIA	V	1	5	island at Syracuse
ORTYGIE	SIL			" "
ORTYGIUS	V			a Rutulian
ORTYGIUS*	OV			p. to Delos
OSCI cf. Opsci, Obsce	HOR		1	the Oscans, Italic tr. of Central Italy
OSCI	SIL		1	
OSCI	V	1	3	
- OSCULANUS	COM			man's name
OSCUS	FPLR		1	Oscan
OSCUS	PROP		1	
OSCUS	SIL	1	3	
OSINIUS	V			king of Clusium
OSIRIS	HOR		1	Egyptian god, husband of Isis
OSIRIS	JUV		1	
OSIRIS	LUC		1	
OSIRIS	OV		1	
OSIRIS	S		1	
OSIRIS	TIB		1	
OSIRIS	V	1	7	(Rutulian warrior)
OSSA fem.	AET		1	mt. in Thessaly
OSSA	LUC		1	
OSSA	MAR		1	
OSSA m., M. 1.155	OV		1	
OSSA	PROP		1	
OSSA	S		1	
OSSA	SEN		1	

OSSA	SIL		1	
OSSA	V		1	
OSSA	VAL	1	10	
OSSAEUS	AV		1	p. to Ossa
OSSAEUS	LUC		1	
OSSAEUS	OV		1	
OSSAEUS	PROP		1	
OSSAEUS	S		1	
OSSAEUS	VAL	1	6	
OSTIA fem.sg.	ENN		1	port of Rome
OSTIA	JUV		1	
OSTIA	OV	1	3	
- OTACES 6.121	VAL			a Scythian (?)
OTACILIUS	MAR			fict.
- OTAXES 6.529	VAL			a Scythian
OTHO	CAT		1	cont.
OTHO	FPLR		1	the emperor (69 AD)
OTHO	HOR		1	Roman tribune
OTHO	JUV		2	the emperor; a knight
OTHO	MAR	1	6	emperor
OTHRYADES	OV		1	Spartan general
OTHRYADES	V	1	2	Panthus
OTHRYS	LUC		1	mt. in Thessaly
OTHRYS	OV		1	
OTHRYS	S		1	
OTHRYS	SEN		1	
OTHRYS	SIL		2	(+ an African)
OTHRYS	V		1	
OTHRYS	VAL	1	8	
OTIA pl., T. 10.91	S			(personification)
OTOS	AV			a giant
- OTREUS 4.162	VAL			a man's name
OUFENS (= Ufens)	LUCIL			river in Latium
OUFENTINUS	LUCIL			p. to Oufens
OVIDIUS	MAR	2	2	Ov. Naso (the poet); a friend
PACCIUS	JUV			a poet
PACCIUS 14.78.2	MAR	1	2	a doctor
- PACENIUS	LUCIL			(unknown)
PACHYNUM	LUC			promontory of Sicily
PACHYNUS fem.	AV		1	promontory of Sicily
PACHYNUS	OV		1	
PACHYNUS	SIL		1	
PACHYNUS	V	1	4	
PACIDEIANUS	HOR		1	a gladiator
PACIDEIANUS	LUCIL	1	2	
- PACILIUS	LUCIL			(unknown)
- PACIUS 12.99	JUV			cont.
PACORUS	HOR		1	king of the Parthians
PACORUS	MAR	1	2	
PACTOLIS adj.	OV			p. to the Pactolos
PACTOLOS	LUC		1	river of Lydia
PACTOLOS	SEN		1	
PACTOLOS	V	1	3	
PACTOLUS	HOR		1	
PACTOLUS	JUV		1	
PACTOLUS	MAN		1	
PACTOLUS	OV		1	

PACTOLUS	PROP		1	river of Lydia
PACTOLUS	SIL		1	
PACTOLUS	VAR	1	7	
PACTUMEIUS	HOR			bastard son of Canidia
PACUUS dub.	FPLA			= Pacuvius (?)
PACUVIANUS	LUCIL			p. to Pacuvius
PACUVIUS	COM		1	early Roman tragic poet
PACUVIUS	HOR		1	
PACUVIUS	JUV		1	
PACUVIUS	MAR		1	
PACUVIUS	PER		1	
PACUVIUS	SIL	1	6	
PACUVIUS/MARCUS	FPLA			the tragic poet
PADAEUS	TIB			Indian tribe
-PADUA 95.7	CAT			tributary of the Po (cf. Gk. Παδόα)
PADUS	FPLB		1	river Po in N. Italy
PADUS	GER		1	
PADUS	HOR		1	
PADUS	LUC		1	
PADUS	MAR		1	
PADUS	OV		1	
PADUS	S		1	
PADUS	SIL		2	(+ Gaulish soldier)
PADUS	V		1	
PADUS	VAL	1	11	
PADUSA	FPLB		1	canal in N. Italy
PADUSA	V	1	2	
PAEAN 224	COL		1	ep. of Apollo
PAEAN	FPLB		1	" " (said of Nero in jest)
PAEAN 426	GR		1	" "
PAEAN 880	HL		1	hymn to Apollo
PAEAN	JUV		1	ep. of Apollo
PAEAN	LUC		1	" "
PAEAN	OV		1	Apollo (also exclamation)
PAEAN 3 prol. 20; em.	PH		1	"
PAEAN	S		1	" ; hymn to Apollo
PAEAN HO 92	SEN		1	ep. of Apollo
PAEAN A. 6.657	V	1	11	hymn to Apollo
PAEGNIUM	PL			a slave-boy
PAELIGNI = Pel-	MAR		1	tribe of central Italy
PAELIGNI	OV	1	2	
-PAELIGNUM	MAR			wine of the Paeligni
PAELIGNUS (Pel-)	HOR		1	p. to the Peligni
PAELIGNUS	MAR		1	
PAELIGNUS	OV	1	3	
PAEONES	OV		1	tribe of Macedonia
PAEONES	S		1	
PAEONES	VAL	1	3	
PAEONIS	OV			a female Paeonian
PAEONIUS	HL		1	p. to the Paeonians
PAEONIUS	OV		1	
PAEONIUS	S		1	
PAEONIUS	SIL		1	
PAEONIUS	V	1	5	
PAESTANUS	MAR		1	p. to Paestum
PAESTANUS	OV	1	2	
PAESTUM	COL		1	town of Lucania

PAESTUM	MAR	1		town of Lucania
PAESTUM	OV	1		
PAESTUM	PROP	1		
PAESTUM	SIL	1		
PAESTUM	V	1	6	
PAETUS	MAR	2		cont. man; fict. man
PAETUS 3.7 passim	PROP	1	3	a friend of PROP
⎧PAGASA	PROP			town of Thessaly
⎩PAGASAE	VAL			
PAGASAEUS	LUC	1		p. to Pagasa
PAGASAEUS	OV	1		
PAGASAEUS	S	1		
PAGASAEUS	SIL	1	4	
PAGASEIUS	VAL			p. to Pagasa
-PAGASUS A. 11.670	V			an Etruscan
-PAGO dub.	PL			title of lost comedy
PALAEMON	AV	1		sea-god
PALAEMON	JUV	1		Roman grammarian
PALAEMON	MAR	1		" "
PALAEMON M. 13.919	OV	1		sea-god
PALAEMON	PL	1		
PALAEMON	S	1		
PALAEMON	SEN	1		
PALAEMON	V	2	9	(+ shepherd)
PALAEMONIUS	S			p. to Palaemon (god)
-PALAEPAPHIUS Cir.88	AV			ep. of Venus
PALAESTINI	OV			residents of Palestine
PALAESTINUS 5.460	LUC	1		p. to Palaeste
PALAESTINUS F. 2.464	OV	1		p. to Palestine (also to Palaeste, F. 4.236).
PALAESTINUS S. 2.1.1615		1		" "
PALAESTINUS	SIL	1		
PALAESTINUS 1.7.18	TIB	1	5	
PALAESTRA	PL			a girl
-PALAESTRIO Mil. 161	PL			a slave
PALAMEDES	MAR	1		Greek hero at Troy
PALAMEDES	OV	1		p. to Palamedes
PALAMEDES	SEN	1		
PALAMEDES	TR	1		
PALAMEDES	V	1	5	
PALAMEDEUS	MAN			p. to Palamedes
-PALANTINUS adj.	LUCIL			reference to a region or place in Spain
PALATIA n.pl.	MAR	1		the Palatine Hill (with the palace)
PALATIA	SIL	1		
PALATIA	V	1	3	
PALATINUS	CAL	1		p. to the Palatine
PALATINUS	HOR	1		
PALATINUS	JUV	1		
PALATINUS	MAR	1		
PALATINUS	OV	1		
PALATINUS	PROP	1		
PALATINUS	S	1		
PALATINUS	V	1	8	
PALATIUM	JUV	1		the Palatine Hill
PALATIUM	OV	1		
PALATIUM	PET	1		
PALATIUM	PROP	1		
PALATIUM	S	1		

PALATIUM	TIB	1	6	the Palatine Hill
PALATUALIS	ENN			p. to Palatua (goddess of Palatine)
PALES fem.	AV		1	Italic pastoral goddess
PALES	CAL		1	
PALES	COL		1	
PALES	OV		1	
PALES	S		1	
PALES	TIB		1	
PALES	V		1	
PALES	VAR	1	8	
-PALFURIUS 4.53	JUV			cont.
PALICI pl.	OV		1	sons of Juppiter
PALICI	SIL	1	2	
PALICUS	OV		1	a god (s. of Juppiter)
PALICUS	V	1	2	
PALILIA n.pl.	PER		1	festival of Pales (cf. Parilia)
PALILIA	TIB	1	2	
PALILIS	OV			p. to Pales
PALINURUS	HOR		1	the pilot of Aeneas
PALINURUS	LUC		1	
PALINURUS	LUCIL		1	
PALINURUS	MAR		1	
PALINURUS	OV		1	
PALINURUS	PL		1	
PALINURUS	V	1	7	
PALLADIOS cf. -ius	SEN			p. to Pallas (Minerva)
PALLADIUM	AV		1	the statue of Pallas Minerva
PALLADIUM	LUCR		1	
PALLADIUM	SIL		1	
PALLADIUM	V	1	4	
PALLADIUM/FORUM	MAR			= Forum Romanum
PALLADIUS	AV		1	p. to Pallas (Minerva)
PALLADIUS	COL		1	
PALLADIUS	GER		1	
PALLADIUS	LUC		1	
PALLADIUS	MAR		1	
PALLADIUS	OV		1	
PALLADIUS	PH		1	
PALLADIUS	PROP		1	
PALLADIUS	S		1	
PALLADIUS	SIL		1	
PALLADIUS	V		1	
PALLADIUS	VAL	1	12	
PALLANTEUS	V			p. to Pallas (k. of Arcadia)
PALLANTIAS	OV			Aurora
PALLANTIS M. 15.700	OV		1	Aurora; day (F. 6.567)
PALLANTIS	VAL	1	2	"
PALLANTIUS	OV			p. to Pallas (ancestor of Evander)
PALLAS -ad-	AET		1	Minerva, goddess of learning
PALLAS	AV		1	
PALLAS	CIC		1	
PALLAS	FPLR		1	(promontory)
PALLAS	HL		1	
PALLAS	HOR		1	
PALLAS -nt-, m.	JUV		1	freedman of Claudius
PALLAS -ad-	LUC		1	goddess Minerva
PALLAS	LUCR		1	

PALLAS		MAN	1	goddess Minerva (+ olive: 2.21)
PALLAS		MAR	1	(+ oil: 7.28.3)
PALLAS	-ad-, -nt-	OV	3	goddess (+ olive, oil); son of Pandion;
PALLAS		PET	1	goddess son of Evander.
PALLAS		PH	1	
PALLAS		PRIAP	1	
PALLAS		PROP	1	(+ Vesta: 4.4.45)
PALLAS	-ad-, -nt-	S	2	goddess; son of Evander
PALLAS		SEN	1	"
PALLAS		SIL	1	"
PALLAS	-nt- (Accius)	TR	1	a giant
PALLAS	-ad-, -nt-	V	3	goddess; s. of Evander; k. of Arcadia
PALLAS		VAL	1	goddess.
PALLAS		VAR	1 28	"
PALLENAEUS		LUC	1	p. to Pallene
PALLENAEUS		S	1 2	
PALLENE		OV	1	a town of Thrace
PALLENE		V	1	
PALLENE		VAL	1 3	
PALLOR	M. 8.790	OV	1	god of Fear
PALLOR	13.582	SIL	1 2	
-PALMA	12.9, m.	MAR		A. Corn. Palma, consul
-PALMUS	A. 10.697	V		an Etruscan
PALUDA		ENN		ep. of Minerva
PAMPHAGUS		OV		a dog
-PAMPHILA		FPLA	1	mistress of Val. Aedituus
PAMPHILA		PL	1	a matrona
PAMPHILA		TER	2 4	virgo; meretrix
-PAMPHILIPPUS		PL		a youth (Stichus 527)
PAMPHILUS		LUCIL	1	a youth
PAMPHILUS		PL	1	"
PAMPHILUS		TER	1 3	"
PAMPHYLIA		S		country of S. Anatolia
PAMPHYLIUS		LUC		p. to Pamphylia
PAN	(cf. pl. Panes)	CAL	1	Greek woodland god (cf. Faunus)
PAN		LUCR	1	
PAN		MAN	1	
PAN		MAR	1	
PAN		OV	1	
PAN		PROP	1	
PAN		S	1	
PAN		SIL	1	
PAN		TIB	1	
PAN		V	1	
PAN		VAL	1 11	
PANAETIUS		FPLA	1	(unknown)
PANAETIUS		HOR	1 2	the stoic philosopher of Rhodes
-PANARETUS	6.98	MAR		fict.
PANCHAEUS		LUCR	1	p. to Panchaia
PANCHAEUS		OV	1	
PANCHAEUS		V	1 3	
PANCHAIA		TIB	1	legendary island in Persian gulf
PANCHAIA		V	1	
PANCHAIA		VAL	1 3	
PANCHAIUS		AV	1	p. to Panchaia
PANCHAIUS		OV	1 2	
-PANCHATES	16.348	SIL		name of a horse

PANDARUS	HL		1	a Trojan (s. of Lycaon)
PANDARUS	V	2	3	a Trojan; a Lycian
PANDA/CELA	VAR			an Italic deity
PANDATARIA	SEN			island in the Tyrrhene Sea
PANDION	LP		1	father of Philomela & k. of Athens
PANDION	LUCR		1	
PANDION	MAR		1	
PANDION	OV	1	4	
PANDIONIUS	AV		1	p. to Pandion
PANDIONIUS	OV		1	
PANDIONIUS	PROP		1	
PANDIONIUS	S		1	
PANDIONIUS	SEN	1	5	
PANDROSOS	OV			daughter of Cecrops
-PANEGYRIS Stichus 247	PL			a matrona
-PANEMUS T. 9.293	S			a Theban
PANES pl. of Pan	AV		1	woodland deities
PANES	COL		1	
PANES	LUC		1	
PANES	OV		1	
PANES	S		1	
PANES	SEN	1	6	
PANGAEA n.pl., 1.679	LUC		1	mt. of Thrace
PANGAEA	OV		1	
PANGAEA	S		1	
PANGAEA	V		1	
PANGAEA	VAL	1	5	
PANGAEUS m., Med.721	SEN			mt. of Thrace
PANGAEUS*	LUC		1	p. to Pangaeus
PANGAEUS* 2.73	SIL		1	
PANGAEUS*	VAL	1	3	
PANHORMOS =Panormus	SIL			town in Sicily
PANICEUS	PL			a character (comic formation)
PANNICULUS	MAR			a mime
PANNONIA	OV		1	a region in Central Europe (=Hungary)
PANNONIA	S	1	2	
PANNONICUS	MAR		1	p. to Pannonia
PANNONICUS	MLP	1	2	
PANNONIS adj.	LUC			p. to Pannonia
PANNONIUS	LUC		1	
PANNONIUS	S		1	
PANNONIUS	TIB	1	3	
-PANNYCHUS 2.36	MAR			fict. man.
PANOMPHAEUS	OV			ep. of Juppiter
PANOPE	GER		1	town of Phocis
PANOPE	OV		2	" ; a Nereid
PANOPE	S		1	"
PANOPE	VAL	1	5	a Nereid
PANOPEA	V			"
PANOPES	V			a Sicilian
-PANOPEUS M. 8.312	OV		1	hero at Calydonian boar-hunt
-PANOPEUS T. 10.497	S	1	2	Spartan
PANSA	JUV		1	C. V. Pansa
PANSA	TIB	1	2	
-PANTAENIS 7.69.7	MAR			friend of Sappho
-PANTAGATHUS 6.52	MAR			a slave
PANTAGIAS m.	SIL			river in Sicily

PANTAGIES	OV			river in Sicily
PANTAGYAS	V			
-PANTALEO/PISATILIS	COM			(unknown; Naevius 113)
PANTHOIDES	HOR		1	Pythagoras' reincarnation
PANTHOIDES	OV	1	2	
PANTHUS	PROP		1	lover of Cynthia
PANTHUS	V	1	2	Trojan priest
-PANTILIUS S.1.10.78	HOR			a malicious critic
PANTOLABUS	HOR			parasite
PAPHIA	AET			ep. of Venus
PAPHIE	MAR		1	
PAPHIE	S	1	2	
PAPHIUS	COL		1	p. to Paphus
PAPHIUS	LUC		1	
PAPHIUS	MAR		1	
PAPHIUS	OV		1	
PAPHIUS	S		1	
PAPHIUS	SEN		1	
PAPHIUS	V	1	7	
PAPHLAGONES	HL		1	people of Paphlagonia (in Anatolia)
PAPHLAGONES	PL	1	2	
PAPHOS	AV		1	town on Cyprus
PAPHOS	MAR		1	"
PAPHOS	OV		2	" ; son of Pygmalion
PAPHOS	PRIAP		1	
PAPHOS	S		1	
PAPHOS	SIL		1	
PAPHOS	V	1	8	
PAPHUS	HOR			
PAPIRIA (sc. tribus)	LUCIL			a Roman "tribe" (1132W)
PAPIRIANUS	MAR			fict. man
PAPIRIUS 1.786	MAN			member of the Papirii
-PAPYLUS 7.94	MAR			fict. man
-PARAETONICUS AA 3.390	OV			p. to Paraetonium
PARAETONIUM	OV			town of Africa (Libya)
PARAETONIUS	FPLR		1	p. to Paraetonium (or Africa)
PARAETONIUS	LUC		1	
PARAETONIUS	MAR		1	
PARAETONIUS	S		1	
PARAETONIUS	SIL	1	5	
PARCA also pl.	OV		1	a Fate
PARCA	PER		1	
PARCA also pl.	S	1	3	
PARCAE	AV		1	the (three) Fates
PARCAE	CAT		1	
PARCAE	FPLR		1	
PARCAE	HOR		1	
PARCAE	JUV		1	
PARCAE	LUC		1	
PARCAE	MAR		1	
PARCAE	PROP		1	
PARCAE	SEN		1	
PARCAE	SIL		1	
PARCAE	TIB		1	
PARCAE	V		1	
PARCAE	VAL	1	13	
-PARDALISCA Cas. 631	PL			a maid(-servant)

PARENTALIS	OV			p. to Parentalia (festival)
PARILIA cf. Palilia	CAL		1	festival of Pales
PARILIA	OV		1	
PARILIA	PROP	1	3	
PARIS	AV		1	the famous son of Priam
PARIS	CAT		1	
PARIS	ENN		1	
PARIS	HL		1	
PARIS	HOR		1	
PARIS	JUV		2	(+ an actor)
PARIS	MAR		2	(+ a pantomime)
PARIS	OV		1	
PARIS	PROP		1	
PARIS	S		1	
PARIS	SEN		1	
PARIS	TR		1	
PARIS	V	1	15	
PARIUM	VAL			town of Mysia
PARIUS	HOR		1	p. to Paros
PARIUS	MAR		1	
PARIUS	OV		1	
PARIUS	SEN		1	
PARIUS	V		1	
PARIUS	VAL	1	6	
PARMA	MAR			town of N. Italy
-PARMENO	COM		1	(uncertain)
PARMENO	PL		1	a slave
PARMENO	TER	1	3	a slave
PARMENSIS	MAR			p. to Parma
PARNASIS adj.	OV			p. to Parnassus
PARNASIUS	AV		1	p. to Parnassus (or Delphi)
PARNASIUS	OV		1	
PARNASIUS	S		1	
PARNASIUS	SIL		1	
PARNASIUS	V		1	
PARNASIUS	VAL	1	6	
PARNASOS cf. -us	LUC		1	mt. in Phocis, behind Delphi
PARNASOS	PER		1	
PARNASOS	SEN	1	3	
PARNASSIUS =-s-	SEN			p. to Parnassus
PARNASSUS	VAL			mt. in Phocis
PARNASUS	CAT		1	
PARNASUS	COL		1	
PARNASUS	OV		1	
PARNASUS	PH		1	
PARNASUS	PROP		1	
PARNASUS	S		1	
PARNASUS	SIL		1	
PARNASUS	TR		1	
PARNASUS	V	1	9	
PARNES -eth-, m.	S		1	mt. in Attica
PARNES	SEN	1	2	
PAROS cf. -us	AV		1	island in Cyclades
PAROS	OV		1	
PAROS	S		1	
PAROS	V	1	4	
PARRHASIS N	OV		1	Callisto

PARRHASIS N	S	1	2	Callisto
PARRHASIS*	LUC		1	Arcadian
PARRHASIS*	OV		1	
PARRHASIS*	SEN	1	3	
PARRHASIUS	HOR		1	painter of Ephesus
PARRHASIUS	JUV		1	" "
PARRHASIUS	PROP	1	3	" "
PARRHASIUS*	CAL		1	Arcadian
PARRHASIUS*	LUC		1	
PARRHASIUS*	MAR		1	(p. to the North, to the Palatine)
PARRHASIUS*	OV		1	
PARRHASIUS*	S		1	
PARRHASIUS*	SEN		1	
PARRHASIUS*	SIL		1	
PARRHASIUS*	V		1	
PARRHASIUS*	VAL	1	9	
PARTHAON	OV		1	king of Calydon
PARTHAON	S	1	2	
PARTHAONIDES	VAL			Meleager
PARTHAONIUS	MAR		1	p. to Parthaon
PARTHAONIUS	OV		1	
PARTHAONIUS	S	1	3	
PARTHENIANUS adj.	MAR			p. to Parthenius (the chamberlain)
─ PARTHENIE 4.7.74	PROP			Cynthia's nurse
PARTHENIUS	JUV		1	a silversmith
PARTHENIUS	MAR		1	Domitian's chamberlain
PARTHENIUS	OV		1	river in Paphlagonia
PARTHENIUS	V		1	a Trojan
PARTHENIUS	VAL	1	5	river in Paphlagonia
PARTHENIUS*	OV		1	p. to mt. in Arcadia
PARTHENIUS* 1.1.11	PROP		1	
PARTHENIUS*	S		1	
PARTHENIUS*	SEN		1	
PARTHENIUS*	V	1	5	
PARTHENOPAEUS	MAR		2	son of Meleager
PARTHENOPAEUS	S		1	
PARTHENOPAEUS	TR		1	
PARTHENOPAEUS	V	1	5	
PARTHENOPE	COL		1	old name for Naples
PARTHENOPE	OV		1	
PARTHENOPE	PET		1	
PARTHENOPE	S		1	
PARTHENOPE	SIL		2	(+ a siren)
PARTHENOPE	V	1	7	
PARTHENOPEIUS	OV			p. to Naples
PARTHI	CAT		1	the Parthians (an Iranian people)
PARTHI	GR		1	
PARTHI	LUC		1	
PARTHI	MAN		1	
PARTHI	MAR		1	
PARTHI	OV		1	
PARTHI	PROP		1	
PARTHI	S		1	
PARTHI	VAL	1	9	
PARTHIA	LUC		1	country of the Parthians, SE of Caspian
PARTHIA	MAR	1	2	
PARTHICUS	LUC		1	p. to Parthia (the Parthians)

PARTHICUS		SEN	1	2	p. to Parthia (the Parthians)
-PARTHIS em., 4.803		MAN			p. to Parthia
PARTHUS		FPLB		1	a Parthian
PARTHUS	also pl.	HOR		1	
PARTHUS		LUC		1	
PARTHUS		OV		1	
PARTHUS		PER		1	
PARTHUS		PET		1	
PARTHUS		PROP		1	
PARTHUS	also pl.	SEN		1	
PARTHUS		SIL		1	
PARTHUS	also pl.	V	1	10	
PARTHUS*		AV		1	Parthian
PARTHUS*		JUV		1	
PARTHUS*		LUC		1	
PARTHUS*		MAR		1	
PARTHUS*		OV		1	
PARTHUS*		PROP		1	
PARTHUS*		S		1	
PARTHUS*		V	1	8	
-PARTICULO 4, pr.10		PH			friend of Phaedrus
PARUS cf. -os		ENN			island in the Cyclades
-PASIBULA And. 945		TER			a virgo
PASICOMPSA		PL			a meretrix
PASIPHAË		MAR		1	wife of Minos
PASIPHAE		OV		1	
PASIPHAE		PROP		1	
PASIPHAE		SEN		1	
PASIPHAE		SIL		1	
PASIPHAE		V	1	6	
PASIPHAEIA		OV			= Phaedra
PASITHEA		CAT		1	one of the Graces
PASITHEA		S	1	2	
-PASSER 6.42.6		MAR			a fountain
PASSERINUS		MAR			a circus horse
-PASTOR 9.22		MAR			a friend (Junius Pastor)
PATAREUS		HOR		1	ep. of Apollo
PATAREUS		OV		1	p. to Patara (town in Lycia)
PATAREUS		S	1	3	" " "
PATAVINUS		MAR			p. to Patavium
PATAVIUM		V			town in N. Italy (modern Padua)
PATER		AET		1	ep. of Juppiter
PATER		SIL	1	2	
PATERCLIANUS (sellae)		MAR			p. to a man (unknown) 12.77.9
PATERNUS 12.53		MAR			fict. man
PATRAE		OV		1	town in Achaia
PATRAE		SIL	1	2	
PATRENSIS		MAR			p. to Patrae
PATRES 3.11.32		PROP			Roman senators
PATRICOLES		ENN			= Patroclos
-PATROBAS 2.32.3		MAR			fict. (freedman of Nero?)
PATROCLOS		PROP			the friend
PATROCLUS		FPLA		1	
PATROCLUS		HL		1	
PATROCLUS		OV		1	
PATROCLUS		S	1	4	
PATRON		V			comp. of Evander

PATULCIUS		OV		ep. of Janus
PAULA		COM	1	a girl
PAULA		MAR	1 ?	cont. girl
PAULINUS		MAR	2 2	two cont. men
PAULLUS cf. Paulus		HOR	2	L. Aemilius P.; Fabius Maximus P.
PAULLUS		PROP	2	L. Aemilius P.; his son
PAULLUS S. 1.1.30		S	1 5	L. Aemilius P.
PAULLUS/MAXIMUS		HOR		the consul
PAULUS cf. -11-		JUV	?	a lawyer; a noble type
PAULUS 9.824		LUC	1	L. Aemilius (?)
PAULUS 236W		LUCIL	1	unknown
PAULUS		MAR	?	a lawyer; fict. man
PAULUS		SIL	1 7	L. Aemilius P.
PAUPERTAS 4.156		CAL		"Poverty" personified
PAUSIACUS		HOR		p. to Pausias, the painter
PAUSIAS		COM		a man's name
PAVOR M. 4.485		OV	1	god of "Dread"
PAVOR T. 3.425		S	1	
PAVOR		SIL	1	
PAVOR		VAL	1 4	
PAX		HOR	1	goddess of Peace
PAX		JUV	1	"
PAX 1.2.8		MAR	1	temple of Peace
PAX F. 1.121 et al.		OV	1	goddess & temple
PAX		PET	1	goddess
PAX		PL	1	name of a slave
PAX		S	1	temple of Peace
PAX Med. 63		SEN	1	the goddess
PAX 6.692		SIL	1	"
PAX		TIB	1	"
PAX G. 2.425		V	1 11	"
PECULATUS Pers. 555		PL		"Embezzlement" personified
PECUNIA		HOR	1	"Profit" personified
PECUNIA		JUV	1 2	
PEDANUS		HOR		p. to Pedum (t. in Latium)
— PEDASUS M. 5.115		OV		comp. of Phineus
— PEDIANUS 12.212		SIL		a Roman soldier
PEDIATIA		HOR		nickname of J. Pediatius
PEDIUS 1.85		PER		P. Blaesius (?)
PEDIUS/POPLICOLA		HOR		consul/lawyer
PEDO		JUV	1	Albinovanus Pedo, the poet
PEDO		MAR	1	
PEDO		OV	1 3	
PEGAE		PROP		fountain in Bithynia
— PEGASAEUS M. 8.349		OV		= Pagasaeus
PEGASEIUS		PER		p. to Pegasus (i.e. poetic)
PEGASEUS		CAT	1	p. to Pegasus or to the Muses
PEGASEUS		OV	1	
PEGASEUS		PROP	1	
PEGASEUS		SEN	1 4	
PEGASIDES		AV	1	the Muses
PEGASIDES		COL	1	
PEGASIDES		OV	1	
PEGASIDES		PROP	1 4	
PEGASIS		OV		fountain nymph, Muse
PEGASIS*		MAR	1	p. to Pegasus
PEGASIS*		OV	1 2	

PEGASUS		GER	1	the winged horse
PEGASUS		HOR	1	
PEGASUS		JUV	1	(a jurist)
PEGASUS		OV	1	
PEGASUS		SIL	1 5	(a ship)
- PELAGON	M. 8.360	OV	1	hero at Calydonian boar-hunt
PELAGON	Bacc. 262	PL	1 2	a senex
PELASGI		HL	1	the legendary pre-Greeks
PELASGI		OV	1	
PELASGI		S	1	
PELASGI		SEN	1	
PELASGI		SIL	1	
PELASGI		VAL	1 6	
PELASGIAS		OV		Grecian
PELASGIS		OV		Grecian
PELASGUS		OV		king of the Argives
PELASGUS*		AV	1	Pelasgian, Greek
PELASGUS*		ENN	1	
PELASGUS*		OV	1	
PELASGUS*		PROP	1	
PELASGUS*		S	1	
PELASGUS*		V	1	
PELASGUS*		VAL	1 7	
- PELATES	M. 5.124	OV	2 2	comp. of Phineus; a Lapith (12.255)
PELEIUS		S	1	p. to Peleus (f. of Achilles)
PELEIUS		SIL	1 2	
PELETHRONIUS		LUC	1	Thessalian
PELETHRONIUS		OV	1	
PELETHRONIUS		PRIAP	1	
PELETHRONIUS		S	1	
PELETHRONIUS		V	1 5	
PELEUS		AV	1	king of Thessaly & father of Achilles
PELEUS		CAT	1	
PELEUS		HL	1	
PELEUS		HOR	1	
PELEUS		JUV	1	
PELEUS		MAR	1	
PELEUS		OV	1	
PELEUS		PROP	1	
PELEUS		S	1	
PELEUS		SEN	1	
PELEUS		TIB	1	
PELEUS		TR	1	
PELEUS		VAL	1 13	
PELIACUS		CAT	1	p. to Pelion
PELIACUS		LUC	1	
PELIACUS		OV	1	
PELIACUS		PROP	1	
PELIACUS		S	1	
PELIACUS		SEN	1	
PELIACUS		SIL	1	
PELIACUS		VAL	1 8	
PELIADES	fem.pl.	PH		daughters of Pelias
PELIAS	m.	ENN	1	legendary king of Thessaly
PELIAS	fem.	LP	1	a spear
PELIAS	m.	MAR	1	king of Thessaly
PELIAS		OV	1	"

PELIAS		PET	1	king of Thessaly
PELIAS		PH	1	
PELIAS	**Pseud**. 869	PL	1	
PELIAS		SEN	1	
PELIAS	A. 2.435	V	1	(a Trojan)
PELIAS		VAL	1 10	king of Thessaly
PELIAS*	(hasta)	OV	1	p. to Pelion
PELIAS*		S	1 2	
PELIDES	m.sg., patr.	HL	1	Achilles
PELIDES		HOR	1	
PELIDES		JUV	1	
PELIDES		OV	1	
PELIDES		PROP	1	
PELIDES		S	1	
PELIDES		SEN	1	
PELIDES		V	2 9	(+ Neoptolemus)
PELIGNUS	cf. Pael-	SIL		a Paelignian
PELIGNUS*		CAL	1	p. to the Paelignians (Peligni)
PELIGNUS*		ENN	1	
PELIGNUS*		SIL	1 3	
PELION	n.	AET	1	mountain in Thessaly
PELION		CAT	1	
PELION		HOR	1	
PELION		LUC	1	
PELION		MAR	1	
PELION		OV	1	
PELION		PH	1	
PELION		PROP	1	
PELION		S	1	
PELION		SEN	1	
PELION		SIL	1	
PELION		TR	1	
PELION		V	1	
PELION		VAL	1 14	
PELIUS		ENN		p. to Pelion
PELLA		LUC	1	town of Macedonia
PELLA		MAN	1	
PELLA		SIL	1	
PELLA		VAL	1 4	
PELLAEUS		GR	1	Macedonian
PELLAEUS		JUV	1	Pellan
PELLAEUS		LUC	2	Pellan (Macedonian); Alexandrian (Egyptian)
PELLAEUS		MAR	2	Pellan; Alexandrian
PELLAEUS	M. 5.302	OV	1	Macedonian
PELLAEUS	Asin. 333	PL	1	Pellan
PELLAEUS		S	1	Macedonian
PELLAEUS		SIL	2	Pellan; Egyptian
PELLAEUS		V	1 12	Egyptian
PELLENE	HF 979	SEN		town of Achaia
-PELLIO	Bacch. 215	PL		an actor
PELOPEA		JUV	1	title of tragedy ("D. of Thyestes")
PELOPEA	Ibis 359	OV	1 2	daughter of Thyestes
PELOPEIA	Ep. 8.81	OV		fem. desc. of Pelops
PELOPEIAS	adj.	OV		Pelopian
PELOPEIDES	fem.pl.	S		Argive women
PELOPEIS	adj.	OV		Pelopian
PELOPEIUS		HL	1	p. to Pelops, Pelopian

PELOPEIUS	OV	1	2	p. to Pelops
PELOPEUS	LUC		1	p. to Pelops
PELOPEUS	PROP		1	
PELOPEUS	S		1	
PELOPEUS	SEN		1	
PELOPEUS	SIL		1	
PELOPEUS	V	1	6	
PELOPIDAE m.pl., patr.	TR			desc. of Pelops
PELOPIUS	SEN		1	p. to Pelops
PELOPIUS	TR	1	2	
PELOPONNESUS fem.	LUCR		1	southern Greece
PELOPONNESUS	MAN	1	2	
PELOPS	CAT		1	legendary king of Phrygia
PELOPS	ENN		1	
PELOPS	GER		1	
PELOPS	HOR		1	
PELOPS	LUC		1	
PELOPS	MAR		1	
PELOPS	OV		1	
PELOPS	S		1	
PELOPS	SEN		1	
PELOPS	SIL		1	
PELOPS	TIB		1	
PELOPS	TR		1	
PELOPS	V		1	
PELOPS	VAL	1	14	
PELORIAS fem.	OV			a promontory of Sicily
PELORUS	AV		1	a promontory of Sicily
PELORUS	LUC		1	
PELORUS	OV		1	
PELORUS	S		1	
PELORUS	SEN		1	
PELORUS	SIL		3	(+ a horse; a soldier of Hannibal)
PELORUS	V		1	
PELORUS	VAL	1	10	
PELUSIACUS	COL		1	p. to Pelusium
PELUSIACUS	LUC		1	
PELUSIACUS	S		1	
PELUSIACUS	SIL		1	
PELUSIACUS	V	1	5	
PELUSIUM	PROP			fortress-town on Nile
PELUSIUS	LUC		1	p. to Pelusium
PELUSIUS	MAR		1	
PELUSIUS	PH	1	3	
PENATES	CAT		1	Italic household gods
PENATES	COL		1	
PENATES	HOR		1	
PENATES	LP		1	
PENATES	OV		1	
PENATES	PER		1	
PENATES	PL		1	
PENATES	PROP		1	
PENATES	SEN		1	(= domus)
PENATES	TIB	1	10	
PENEIS	OV			Daphne
PENEIS*	OV			p. to the Peneus river
PENEIUS	LUC		1	p. to the Peneus

PENEIUS	OV		1	p. to the Peneus
PENEIUS	S		1	
PENEIUS	V		1	
PENEIUS	VAL	1	5	
⎰PENELEOS	HL			a suitor of Helen
⎱PENELEUS	V			
PENELOPA	PL			wife of Ulixes
PENELOPE	HOR		1	
PENELOPE	JUV		1	
PENELOPE	MAR		1	(any chaste woman)
PENELOPE	OV		1	
PENELOPE and -ēa	PRIAP		1	
PENELOPE	PROP		1	
PENELOPE	S		1	
PENELOPE	SEN	1	8	
PENELOPEUS	CAT		1	p. to Penelope
PENELOPEUS	OV		1	
PENELOPEUS	PRIAP	1	3	
PENĒUS	GR		1	river of Thessaly
PENEUS	LUC		1	
PENEUS also adj.	OV		1	
PENEUS	V	1	4	
PENICULUS	PL			comic name of a parasite
PĒNĪOS (= Peneus)	CAT			river of Thessaly
PENĬUS	OV			river in Colchis
-PENTETRONICUS adj	PL			(obscure pun, Poen. 471)
PENTHEIUS = -ēus	S			p. to Pentheus
-PENTHELIDES dub.	OV			(or Pentheides) (Ibis 607)
PENTHESILEA	OV		1	queen of the Amazons
PENTHESILEA	PROP		1	
PENTHESILEA	V	1	3	
PENTHEUS	HOR		1	legendary king of Thebes
PENTHEUS	LUC		1	
PENTHEUS 11.84.11	MAR		1	
PENTHEUS	OV		1	
PENTHEUS	PL		1	
PENTHEUS	PROP		1	
PENTHEUS	S		1	
PENTHEUS	SEN		1	
PENTHEUS	V		1	
PENTHEUS	VAL	1	10	
PENTHĒUS* M. 4.429	OV		1	p. to Pentheus
PENTHEUS*	S		1	
PENTHEUS*	SEN		1	
PENTHEUS*	VAL	1	4	
PENTIDES dub., Ibis	OV			male desc. of Pentheus
⎰PEPARETHOS	SEN			island in the Cyclades
⎱PEPARETHUS	OV			
PERBIBESIA em.	PL			(comic formation)
PERCOSIUS	VAL			p. to the king of Cyzicus
PERCOTE	VAL			town in Mysia
-PERELLIUS S. 2.3.75	HOR			a loan-shark
PERENNA F. 3.673	OV			= Anna Perenna
PERFIDIA Pers. 555	PL			"Treachery" personified
PERGAMA n.pl.	HL		1	Troy
PERGAMA	HOR		1	
PERGAMA	LUC		1	

PERGAMA	n.pl.	LUCR	1	Troy
PERGAMA		MAN	1	
PERGAMA		OV	1	
PERGAMA		PROP	1	
PERGAMA		S	1	
PERGAMA		SEN	1	
PERGAMA		SIL	1	(= Lavinium)
PERGAMA		V	1	
PERGAMA		VAL	1 12	
PERGAMĒNUS		S		p. to Pergamum (in Mysia)
PERGAMĒUS		MAR	1	p. to Pergamum
PERGAMEUS		PROP	1	Trojan
PERGAMEUS		S	1	p. to Pergamum
PERGAMEUS		SIL	1	Trojan (also 1.47: Roman)
PERGAMEUS		V	1 5	Trojan
PERGAMON	cf. -um	MAR		town in Mysia
-PERGAMOS	fem. (= -us)	AET		Troy
PERGAMUM		ENN	1	Troy
PERGAMUM	Bacch. 723	PL	1	
PERGAMUM		SEN	1	
PERGAMUM	also -a	TR	1 4	
-PERGAMUS	fem.	S		Troy (S. 1.4.100)
PERGUS		OV		lake in Sicily
PERIBOMIUS		JUV		fict. man
PERICLES	4.3	PER		Athenian statesman
PERICLYMENUS		OV	1	an Argonaut (son of Neleus)
PERICLYMENUS		VAL	1 2	
-PERIDIA	A. 12.515	V		mother of Onites
PERILLA		OV	2 2	a poetess; = Metella, mistress of Ticida
PERILLĒUS		OV		p. to Perillus
PERILLUS		OV	1	Greek metal-worker
PERILLUS		PROP	1 2	
PERIMEDĒUS		PROP		p. to Perimede (witch)
PERIMELE		OV		a nymph
PERINTHIA		TER		title of Menander's comedy
PERINTHUS	T. 11.199	S		an Argive warrior
-PERIPHANES	Epid.	PL		a senex
PERIPHAS		OV	2	king of Attica; a Lapith
PERIPHAS		S	1	a Theban
PERIPHAS		V	1 4	comp. of Pyrrhus
-PERIPLANES	Curc. 636	PL		a father in comedy
-PERIPLECTOMENUS	MG	PL		a senex
PERITHOUS	cf. Piri-	SEN		son of Ixion
PERJURIUM	Pers. 557	PL		"Perjury"
PERMESSIS		MAR		p. to the Permessus
PERMESSUS		PROP	1	river of Boeotia
PERMESSUS		S	1	
PERMESSUS		V	1 3	
PERO		PROP		daughter of Neleus
PERRHAEBUS		OV	1	p. to Perhaebi (tr. of Thessaly)
PERRHAEBUS		PROP	1 2	
PERSA		HOR	1	a Persian
PERSA	also pl.	PL	1	
PERSA		PROP	1 3	
PERSAE		AV	1	Persians
PERSAE		CAT	1	
PERSAE		FPLA	1	

PERSAE		LUC	1	Persians
PERSAE		PET	1	
PERSAE		SEN	1	
PERSAE		VAR	1 7	
PERSEIS		GER	1	Hecate
PERSEIS		OV	1	title of epic
PERSEIS		S	1	Hecate
PERSEIS	M. 814	SEN	1	"
PERSEIS	7.238	VAL	1 5	"
PERSEIS*		OV		p. to Hecate
PERSEIUS		OV	1	p. to Perseus
PERSEIUS		S	1	p. to Persa (d. of Ocean)
PERSEIUS		VAL	1 3	" " "
PERSEPHONE		AV	1	Proserpina, goddess of Underworld
PERSEPHONE		LUC	1	
PERSEPHONE		OV	1	(+ death)
PERSEPHONE		PROP	1	
PERSEPHONE		S	1	
PERSEPHONE	3.5.5	TIB	1 6	
PERSES		FPLB	1	king of Macedonia
PERSES	(sc. canis)	GR	1	breed of dog
PERSES		LUC	2	k. of Macedonia; Xerxes
PERSES		PROP	1	k. of Macedonia
PERSES		S	1	a Persian (king)
PERSES		VAL	1 7	son of Sol and Persa
PERSEUS		CAT	1	son of Juppiter & Danaë and a leg. hero
PERSEUS		CIC	1	constellation
PERSEUS		GER	1	"
PERSEUS		LUC	1	hero
PERSEUS		MAN	2	hero; const.
PERSEUS		OV	1	hero
PERSEUS		PROP	1	hero
PERSEUS		S	1	hero
PERSEUS		SEN	1	hero; const.
PERSEUS		SIL	2	hero; const.
PERSEUS		TR	1	hero
PERSEUS		VAL	2 15	hero; const.
PERSEUS*		LUC	1	p. to Perseus
PERSEUS*		PROP	1	
PERSEUS*		S	1 3	
PERSIA		PL		the country Persia
PERSICA	(sc. poma)	FPLA	1	peaches
PERSICA		MAR	1 2	"
PERSICUS		COL	1	peach-tree
PERSICUS		JUV	2 3	a Persian (man); a poet-friend
PERSICUS*		CAT	1	Persian
PERSICUS*		HOR	1	
PERSICUS*		JUV	1	
PERSICUS*		MAN	1	
PERSICUS*		OV	1	
PERSICUS*		PL	1	
PERSICUS*		SEN	1 7	
PERSIS		COL	1	Persia
PERSIS		FPLB	1	
PERSIS		LUC	1	
PERSIS		MAN	1	
PERSIS		OV	1	

PERSIS	S		1	Persia
PERSIS	SEN		1	
PERSIS	V	1	8	
PERSIS*	OV			Persian
PERSIUS	HOR		1	name of a merchant
PERSIUS	LUCIL		1	C. Persius, the orator
PERSIUS	MAR	1	3	the satirist
PERSPECTUS Pr. 1.2	TIB			personif. (dub.)
PERUSINUS	SIL			son of Crista
PERUSINUS*	LUC		1	p. to Perusia
PERUSINUS*	PROP		1	
PERUSINUS*	SIL	1	3	
-PETALE 6.9	CAL		1	a shepherdess
PETALE 4.7.43	PROP	1	2	slave of Cynthia
-PETASUS 6.51	CAL			name of a horse
PETELIA	V			town in Bruttium
PETEON fem.	S			town in Boeotia
-PETERIS 4.55.18	MAR			town in Spain
PETILIA = Petelia	SIL			town in Bruttium
PETILIANUS adj.	MAR			belonging to Q. P. Cerealis (?)
PETOSIRIS	JUV			an Egyptian astrologer
PETRA	LUC			a hill at Dyrrhachium
-PETRAEA 14.248	SIL			town of Sicily
PETRAEUS	OV			a Centaur
PETREIUS	LUC			M. Petreius, a Pompey-man
PETRINUS (sc. vicus)	HOR			a villa near Sinuessa
PETRONIUS*	GR			a breed of dog
-PETRULLUS	VAR			a man's name
-PETTIUS Epod. 11.1	HOR			a young man (friend)
PEUCE	LUC		1	island in the lower Danube
PEUCE	MAR		1	"
PEUCE	S		1	goddess of the island
PEUCE	VAL	2	5	goddess; island
PEUCETIUS adj.	OV			p. to Peucetia (in Apulia)
-PEUCON 6.564	VAL			a Scythian
PHACELINA	SIL			ep. of Diana (cf. Facelinus)
PHAEACES	JUV		1	the Phaeacians (tr. of Scheria)
PHAEACES	OV		1	
PHAEACES	V	1	3	
PHAEACIA	TIB			land of the Phaeacians
PHAEACIS	OV			title of poem (on Ulixes)
PHAEACIUS	OV			Phaeacian
PHAEACUS	LUC		1	"
PHAEACUS	SIL	1	2	
PHAEAX	HOR			a Phaeacian
PHAEAX* 15.23	JUV		1	Phaeacian
PHAEAX* 3.2.13	PROP	1	2	" (or -acus?)
-PHAEDIMUS M. 6.239	OV		1	a son of Niobe
PHAEDIMUS T. passim	S	1	2	a Theban
PHAEDRA	OV		1	daughter of Minos
PHAEDRA	PRIAP		1	
PHAEDRA	PROP		1	
PHAEDRA	SEN		1	
PHAEDRA	V	1	5	
-PHAEDRIA Aul. IV.7	PL		1	a girl
PHAEDRIA m.	TER	1	2	a young man
-PHAEDROMUS Curc. 2	PL			a young man

PHAEDRUS		MAR	1	the writer of fables
PHAEDRUS	3 Prol. 1	PH	1	the writer of fables (himself)
PHAEDRUS		TER	1 3	fict. young man
-PHAEOCOMES	M. 12.431	OV		a Centaur
PHAESTIUS		OV		Cretan
PHAESTUS		HL		a Lydian hero
PHAETHON		AV	1	son of Sun (Helios) and Clymene
PHAETHON		CAT	1	
PHAETHON		CIC	1	
PHAETHON		FPLR	1	
PHAETHON		GER	1	
PHAETHON		HOR	1	
PHAETHON		LUC	1	
PHAETHON		LUCR	1	
PHAETHON		MAN	1	
PHAETHON		MAR	1	
PHAETHON		OV	1	
PHAETHON		S	1	
PHAETHON		SEN	1	
PHAETHON		V	1	
PHAETHON		VAL	2 16	Sun; his son
PHAETHONTEUS		MAR	1	p. to Phaethon
PHAETHONTEUS		OV	1	
PHAETHONTEUS		S	1 3	
PHAETHONTIADES		SEN	1	the sisters of Phaethon
PHAETHONTIADES		V	1 2	
PHAETHONTIDES		GER		sisters of Phaethon
PHAETHONTIS		MAR	1	p. to Phaethon
PHAETHONTIS		OV	1 2	
PHAETHONTIUS		S	1	p. to Phaethon
PHAETHONTIUS		SIL	1 2	
PHAETHUSA		OV		sister of Phaethon
PHAETON (= -th -)		SIL		= Phaethon
PHALAECEUS		OV		p. to Phalaecus (Gk. poet)
PHALANTEUS		SIL		p. to Phalanthus
PHALANTHINUS	5.37.2	MAR		p. to Phalanthus, i.e. Tarentine
PHALANTHUS		HOR	1	the founder of Tarentum
PHALANTHUS		MAR	1	
PHALANTHUS		S	1 3	
PHALANTUS		SIL		
PHALARIS		JUV	1	tyrant of Agrigentum
PHALARIS		OV	1 2	
- PHALCES	6.88	VAL		a Scythian
PHALEREUS		PH		Demetrius Phalereus, the orator
- PHALERIS	A. 9.762	V		a Trojan
- PHALERUS	1.398	VAL		an Argonaut
PHALISCI	= Falisci	S		a brand of sausages
PHANAEUS adj.		V		p. to Phanae in Chios
- PHANIA	m.	TER		senex
- PHANISCUS	Most. 883	PL		a boy
- PHANIUM	Ph. 201	TER		a virgo
- PHANOCRATES	H. 1061	TER		a senex
- PHANOSTRATA	Cist.	PL		a matrona
PHANTASOS		OV		son of Somnus
PHAŌN		MAR	1	friend of Sappho
PHAON		OV	1	
PHAON		PL	1 3	

PHARIS **fem.**	S		1	town of Messenia
PHARIS	SEN	1	2	
PHARIUS **adj.**	GER		1	p. to Pharos, hence Egyptian
PHARIUS	GR		1	
PHARIUS	JUV		1	
PHARIUS	LUC		1	
PHARIUS	MAR		1	
PHARIUS	OV		1	
PHARIUS	PROP		1	
PHARIUS	S		1	
PHARIUS	SEN		1	
PHARIUS	SIL		1	
PHARIUS	TIB		1	
PHARIUS	VAL	1	12	
PHARNACES	LUC			son of Mithridates
PHAROS cf. -us	JUV		1	island at Alexandria (or its lighthouse)
PHAROS	LUC		1	(at 8.433: Egypt)
PHAROS	PROP	1	3	
PHARSALIA	CAT		1	area around Pharsalus
PHARSALIA	LUC		2	" ; title of his poem (9.985)
PHARSALIA	OV	1	4	"
PHARSALICUS **adj.**	LUC		1	Pharsalian
PHARSALICUS	S	1	2	
PHARSALIUS	CAT			p. to Pharsalos
{ PHARSALOS **fem.**	LUC			town in Thessaly
{ PHARSALUS	S	2	2	" " ; a Theban (T, 9.312)
PHARUS cf. -os	MAR		1	island at Alexandria (or its lighthouse)
PHARUS	OV		1	
PHARUS	S		1	(S. 3.2.102: Egypt)
PHARUS	V		1	(a Rutulian)
PHARUS	VAL	1	5	island
PHASELIS	LUC			town in Judaea
PHASIACUS	OV		1	p. to the Phasis (in Colchis)
PHASIACUS	PET		1	
PHASIACUS	SEN	1	3	
PHASIADES 6.640	VAL			(patron.) ep. of Thydrus
PHASIANA 3.77.4	MAR			a pheasant ("bird from the Phasis")
PHASIANUS	MAR			p. to the Phasis
PHASIAS*	OV			Medea
PHASIAS*	OV			p. to the Phasis
PHASIDES as adj.	MAR			p. to the Phasis
PHASIS **m.**	CAT		1	river in Colchis
PHASIS 2.585	LUC		1	
PHASIS	MAN		1	
PHASIS	MAR		2	(+a fict. man)
PHASIS	OV		2	Medea; river
PHASIS	PET		1	river
PHASIS	PROP		1	
PHASIS	S		1	
PHASIS	SEN		1	
PHASIS	V		1	
PHASIS	VAL	2	14	(+ the river-god)
PHASMA **n.**	JUV		1	title of a mime-farce
PHASMA	TER	1	2	title of a comedy
PHATNE sg. fem.	AET		1	part of constell. Cancer
PHATNE	CIC	1	2	
- PHEDULIUM (frag.)	PL			a meretrix

PHEGEIUS (= -ēus)	OV			p. to a Phegeus
PHEGEUS	HL	1		a Trojan
PHEGEUS	S	1		a Theban
PHEGEUS	V	1	3	a Trojan
PHEGEUS* (a per)	OV			p. to Phegeus (H. 9.37)
- PHEGIACUS M. 2.244	OV			Arcadian
PHEGIS patron.	OV			= Alphesiboea (daughter of Phegeus)
PHEMIUS	OV			any good citharist
PHEMONOE	LUC	1		daughter (& priestess) of Apollo
PHEMONOE	S	1	2	
-PHENE M. 7.399	OV			legendary Athenian woman
PHENEOS	OV		1	town of Arcadia
PHENEOS	S	1	2	
PHENEUS	CAT		1	
PHENEUS	V	1	2	
PHERAE	GR			town of Thessaly
PHERAEUS N, Ibis 319	OV			Alexander the Great
PHERAEUS*	OV		1	p. to Pherae
PHERAEUS*	S		1	
PHERAEUS*	SEN		1	
PHERAEUS*	VAL	1	4	
PHERECLEUS	OV			p. to Phereclus
- PHERECLUS T. 11.199	S			legendary ship-builder
PHERES -et-	S		1	a Trojan (also a Theban)
PHERES	TR		1	"
PHERES	V	1	3	"
PHERETIADES m. sg.	OV		1	= Admetus
PHERETIADES pl.	SIL	1	2	inhabitants of Naples
PHIALE 10.238	JUV		1	a meretrix
PHIALE	OV	1	2	a nymph (comp. of Diana)
PHIDIACUS	JUV		1	p. to Phidias
PHIDIACUS	MAR		1	
PHIDIACUS	OV		1	
PHIDIACUS	PRIAP		1	
PHIDIACUS	PROP		1	
PHIDIACUS	S	1	6	
PHIDIAS	MAR			the Greek sculptor
- PHIDIPPUS Hec. 246	TER			a senex
- PHIDYLE C. 3.23.2	HOR			a maiden
- PHIGALESIUS em.	OV			p. to Phigalia (t. in Arcadia) (Ibis 327)
PHILAE	LUC			island in the Nile
PHILAENI 15.701	SIL			Punic brothers
- PHILAENIS 2.33	MAR		1	fict. woman
PHILAENIS 63.17	PRIAP	1	2	a poetess (?)
- PHILAENIUM Asin. 53	PL			a meretrix
PHILAMMON	OV			son of Apollo & a leg. singer
- PHILEMATIUM Most.253	PL			a meretrix
PHILEMO Trin. 19	PL			Greek comic poet
PHILEMON	OV			legendary husband of Baucis
- PHILENUS or -inus	MAR			fict. man (10.102.2)
- PHILEROS	FPLA		1	fict. man
PHILEROS 10.43	MAR	1	2	fict. man
PHILETAEUS adj.	PROP			p. to Philetas
PHILETAS	PROP		1	Greek poet of Cos
PHILETAS	S	1	2	
PHILETOS S. 2.6.81	S			slave
PHILETUS 2.44.8	MAR		1	fict.

PHILETUS	5.10.10	PH	1	2	friend of Phaedrus (?)
-PHILIPPA	Epid.636	PL			a woman
PHILIPPEUS		MAN		1	p. to Philippi
PHILIPPEUS		PL		1	p. to king Philippus
PHILIPPEUS		PROP	1	3	" " "
PHILIPPI		AV		1	town in Macedonia
PHILIPPI		CAL		1	
PHILIPPI		HOR		2	(+ coins: Epist. 2.1.234)
PHILIPPI		LUC		1	
PHILIPPI		OV		1	
PHILIPPI		PET		1	
PHILIPPI		PROP		1	
PHILIPPI		S		1	
PHILIPPI		SEN		1	
PHILIPPI		V	1	11	
PHILIPPICA	fem.	JUV		1	title of an oration (10.125)
PHILIPPUS		ENN		1	king of Macedonia
PHILIPPUS		FPLB		1	" "
PHILIPPUS		HOR		1	L. M. Philippus (consul 91 BC)
PHILIPPUS	13.125	JUV		1	a doctor
PHILIPPUS		LUC		2	king of Macedon; another king
PHILIPPUS		MAR		1	fict. man
PHILIPPUS		OV		1	Lucius Marcius
PHILIPPUS		PL		1	k. of Macedon (+ a coin: Bacch. 272)
PHILIPPUS		SIL	1	10	" "
PHILISTIO		MAR		1	a pantomime
PHILLYRIDES	m.	MAR		1	Chiron (son of Philyra, the nymph)
PHILLYRIDES		OV		1	
PHILLYRIDES		PROP		1	
PHILLYRIDES		V	1	4	
PHILO		MAR			fict.
PHILOCOMASIUM		PL			a girl
-PHILOCRATES	Capt.	PL			a young man
PHILOCTETES		MAN		1	the Thessalian hero
PHILOCTETES		OV		1	
PHILOCTETES		PROP		1	
PHILOCTETES		SEN		1	
PHILOCTETES		V	1	5	
-PHILODAMUS	Asin.444	PL			a man's name
PHILODEMUS	S. 1.2.121	HOR			Epicurean philosopher
-PHILOLACHES	Most.	PL			a young man
PHILOMELA		AET		1	daughter of Pandion (as nightingale)
PHILOMELA		JUV		1	(title of play)
PHILOMELA		MAR		1	daughter of Pandion
PHILOMELA		OV		1	"
PHILOMELA		PL		1	
PHILOMELA		S		1	
PHILOMELA	HO 199	SEN		1	
PHILOMELA		V	2	9	(+ nightingale)
-PHILOMELUS	93.22	MAR			a rich old man
-PHILOMUSUS	3.10	MAR			fict.
-PHILOPOLEMUS	Capt.95	PL			a youth
-PHILOSTRATUS	11.82	MAR			fict.
-PHILOTIS	Hec. 81	TER			a meretrix
PHILOXENUS	Bacch.451	PL			a senex
-PHILTERA	Heaut. 662	TER			an uxor
-PHILTO	Trin. 432	PL			a senex

–PHILUMENA	PL		1	a matrona (v.l. of Panegyris)
PHILUMENA	TER	1	2	a virgo
PHILUS em.	FPLA			= L. Furius Philus (?)
PHILYRA	VAL			a nymph
PHILYREIUS	OV			p. to Philyra
PHINEIUS	OV		1	p. to Phineus
PHINEIUS	V		1	
PHINEIUS	VAL	1	3	
PHINEUS em.	HL		1	(dub.; should be Guneus?)
PHINEUS	MAR		1	k. of Salmydessus (or 'blind man')
PHINEUS	OV		2	k. of Salmydessus; brother of Cepheus
PHINEUS 3.5.41	PROP		1	k. of Salmydessus
PHINEUS	S		1	" "
PHINEUS	VAL	1	7	" "
PHINĒUS*	OV		1	p. to Phineus
PHINEUS*	PET		1	
PHINEUS*	SEN	1	3	
PHINIDES patron.	OV			male desc. of Phineus
PHINTIA **Men**. 410 (m.)	PL			king of Syracuse
PHLEGETHON	AV		1	fiery river in Underworld
PHLEGETHON	S		1	
PHLEGETHON	SEN		1	
PHLEGETHON	SIL		1	
PHLEGETHON	V		1	
PHLEGETHON	VAL	1	6	
PHLEGETHONTIS adj.	OV			p. to Phlegethon
PHLEGON	OV			a Sun-horse
PHLEGRA	AV		1	region in Macedonia
PHLEGRA	LUC		1	
PHLEGRA	S		1	
PHLEGRA	SEN		1	
PHLEGRA	VAL	1	5	
PHLEGRAEUS **M**. 12.378	OV			a Centaur
PHLEGRAEUS*	AET		1	p. to Phlegra
PHLEGRAEUS*	LUC		1	
PHLEGRAEUS*	MAR		1	
PHLEGRAEUS*	OV		1	
PHLEGRAEUS*	PROP		1	
PHLEGRAEUS*	S		1	
PHLEGRAEUS*	SEN		1	
PHLEGRAEUS*	SIL		1	
PHLEGRAEUS*	VAL	1	9	
PHLEGYAE	OV			tribe of Thrace or Thessaly
PHLEGYAS **M**. 5.87	OV		1	son of Mars & king of the Lapiths
PHLEGYAS	S		1	
PHLEGYAS	V		1	
PHLEGYAS	VAL	2	5	(a Cyzican; an Argonaut)
–PHLIAS 1.412	VAL			an Argonaut
–PHLIŪS **T**. 4.45, fem.	S			island or town (?)
–PHLOGIS 11.60	MAR			fict. person
–PHLOGIUS 5.114	VAL			an Argonaut
–PHLYUS **P**. 29	SEN			son of Earth (?)
PHOBETOR	OV			son of Morpheus
PHOCAEI	HOR			people of Phocaea (t. in Ionia)
PHOCAEUS*	SEN			Phocaean (p. to Phocis)
PHOCAICUS	LUC		1	p. to Phocis
PHOCAICUS	OV		1	p. to Phocis; p. to Phocae

PHOCAICUS		SIL	1 3	(Massiliote)
PHOCAIS		LUC	1	Phocaean (or Massiliote)
PHOCAIS		SIL	1 2	"
⌈PHOCEUS		HOR	1	(See: Xanthias)⌋
PHOCEUS	3.697	LUC	1	a Phocean
PHOCEUS		OV	1	= Pylades
PHOCEUS	9.127	S	1	a Cydonian
PHOCEUS	3.204	VAL	1 5	a Cyzican
PHOCIS		LUC	1	= Phocaea
PHOCIS	M. 1.313	OV	1	a region of Central Greece
PHOCIS		S	1	
PHOCIS		SEN	1 4	
PHOCIS*	4.256	LUC		p. to Phocis (not Phocaea)
PHOCUS		OV		son of Aeacus
PHOEBAS		LUC	1	priestess of Apollo
PHOEBAS		OV	1	(= Cassandra)
PHOEBAS		SIL	1 3	priestess of Apollo
PHOEBE		AET	1	Luna (Diana)
PHOEBE		AV	1	
PHOEBE		COL	1	
PHOEBE		FPLA	1	
PHOEBE		FPLB	1	
PHOEBE		GER	1	
PHOEBE		LUC	1	
PHOEBE		MAN	1	
PHOEBE		OV	3	Luna; sister of Helen; d. of Leucippus
PHOEBE		PET	1	Luna
PHOEBE		PROP	1	d. of Leucippus
PHOEBE		S	1	Diana (Luna)
PHOEBE		SIL	1	
PHOEBE		V	1	
PHOEBE		VAL	1 17	
PHOEBEIUS		HL	1	p. to Phoebus (Apollo)
PHOEBEIUS		LUC	1	
PHOEBEIUS		MAN	1	
PHOEBEIUS		OV	1	
PHOEBEIUS		PET	1	
PHOEBEIUS		S	1	
PHOEBEIUS		VAL	1 7	
PHOEBEUS		GER	1	p. to Phoebus (Apollo)
PHOEBEUS		LP	1	
PHOEBEUS		LUC	1	
PHOEBEUS		LUCR	1	
PHOEBEUS		MAN	1	
PHOEBEUS		OV	1	
PHOEBEUS		S	1	
PHOEBEUS		SEN	1	
PHOEBEUS		SIL	1	
PHOEBEUS		V	1	
PHOEBEUS		VAL	1 11	
PHOEBIGENA m., patr.		V		ep. of Aesclapius
- PHOEBI/VADA		MAR		aqueduct in Etruria (Aquae Apollinares)
PHOEBUS		AET	1	Apollo, god of Sun (etc.)
PHOEBUS		AV	1	
PHOEBUS		CAL	1	
PHOEBUS		CAT	1	
PHOEBUS		CIC	1	

PHOEBUS		COL	1	Apollo, god of Sun
PHOEBUS		FPLA	1	
PHOEBUS		FPLR	1	
PHOEBUS		GER	1	
PHOEBUS		GR	1	
PHOEBUS		HL	1	
PHOEBUS		HOR	1	
PHOEBUS		JUV	1	
PHOEBUS		LP	1	
PHOEBUS		LUC	1	
PHOEBUS		LUCR	1	
PHOEBUS		MAN	2	(+the Sun)
PHOEBUS		MAR	2	(+a loan-shark)
PHOEBUS		MLP	1	
PHOEBUS		OV	1	
PHOEBUS		PET	1	
PHOEBUS		PH	1	
PHOEBUS		PRIAP	1	
PHOEBUS		PROP	2	(+ the Sun)
PHOEBUS		S	1	
PHOEBUS		SEN	1	
PHOEBUS		SIL	1	
PHOEBUS		TIB	1	
PHOEBUS		V	1	
PHOEBUS		VAL	1 33	
PHOENICES		CIC	1	the Phoenicians (or Carthaginians)
PHOENICES		GER	1	
PHOENICES	3.220	LUC	1	
PHOENICES		OV	1	
PHOENICES		PROP	1	
PHOENICES		V	1 6	
-PHOENICIUM	Ps. 41	PL		a meretrix
PHOENISSA		SIL	1	Carthage
PHOENISSA		V	1 2	Dido, queen of Carthage
PHOENISSA*	fem.adj.	OV	1	Phoenician
PHOENISSA*		S	1	Theban
PHOENISSA*		SIL	1 3	Carthaginian
PHOENIX		AV	1	father of Carme (?)
PHOENIX		LUC	2	fabulous bird; river of Thessaly
PHOENIX	M.15.393;8.307	OV	2	fabulous bird; son of Amyntor
PHOENIX	Bacch. 156	PL	1	friend of Achilles
PHOENIX		PROP	1	" "
PHOENIX		S	2	the bird; friend of Achilles
PHOENIX	also pl.	SIL	2	a Phoenician; (1.89) eponymous ancestor
PHOENIX		TR	1	friend of Achilles
PHOENIX	A. 2.762	V	1 13	" "
PHOLOE		HOR	1	a maiden
PHOLOE		LUC	1	mt. in Thessaly
PHOLOE		OV	1	mt. in Arcadia
PHOLOE		S	2	mt. in Thessaly; a nymph
PHOLOE		TIB	1	a girl
PHOLOE		V	1	a slave-woman
PHOLOE		VAL	1 8	a mt.
PHOLUS		JUV	1	a Centaur
PHOLUS		LUC	1	
PHOLUS		OV	1	
PHOLUS		S	1	

PHOLUS	1.437	SIL		1	(a Saguntine)
PHOLUS		V		2	a Centaur; a Trojan
PHOLUS		VAL	1	8	Centaur
PHORBAS		OV		3	comp. of Phineus; k. of Phlegyae; Lapith
PHORBAS		S		1	attendant of Laius
PHORBAS	Oed. 840	SEN		1	an old shepherd
PHORBAS		V	1	6	a Trojan
PHORCIS	patr.	OV		1	desc. of Phorcus (i.e. a Gorgon)
PHORCIS	cf. Phorcys	PROP	1	2	" "
PHORCUS		HL		1	son of Neptune & f. of the Gorgons
PHORCUS		MAN		1	
PHORCUS		S		1	
PHORCUS		V	2	5	(+ a Latin warrior)
PHORCYNIS		LUC		1	Medusa
PHORCYNIS		OV		1	
PHORCYNIS	2.59	SIL	1	3	
PHORCYS = Phorcus		LUC		1	sea-god (9.646)
PHORCYS		SIL		1	Spanish leader
PHORCYS	3.727	VAL	1	3	sea-god
PHORMIO		TER	2	2	a parasite; a comedy-title
PHORONĚUS		S			son of Inachus of Argos
PHORONĚUS*		S			p. to Phoroneus
PHORONIS	patr.	OV			= Io
PHORONIS*		SEN			Phoronean, Argive
PHOSPHOROS		GER		1	the Morning-star
PHOSPHOROS		SEN	1	2	
PHOSPHORUS		MAR		1	
PHOSPHORUS		S	1	2	
PHRAATES		HOR			king of Parthia
PHRADMON		COL			Greek sculptor
PHRIXEUS		GER		1	p. to Phrixus
PHRIXEUS		LUC		1	
PHRIXEUS		MAN		1	
PHRIXEUS		MAR		1	
PHRIXEUS		OV		1	
PHRIXEUS		S		1	
PHRIXEUS		SEN		1	
PHRIXEUS		VAL	1	8	
PHRIXUS		GER		1	son of Athamas
PHRIXUS		MAN		1	
PHRIXUS		MAR		1	
PHRIXUS		OV		1	
PHRIXUS		PL		1	
PHRIXUS		S		1	
PHRIXUS		SEN		1	
PHRIXUS		VAL	2	9	(+ a Scythian)
-PHRONESIUM	Truc. 12	PL			a meretrix
-PHRONTIS	5.460	VAL			son of Phrixus
-PHRUGIA	Aul. 333	PL			a girl flutist
PHRYGES		AET		1	the Phrygians, of NW Anatolia
PHRYGES		COM		1	
PHRYGES		HL		1	
PHRYGES		HOR		1	
PHRYGES		JUV		1	
PHRYGES		LUC		1	
PHRYGES		OV		1	(M. 12.70: "Trojans")
PHRYGES		PET		1	

PHRYGES		SEN	1	Phrygians
PHRYGES		SIL	1	
PHRYGES		TR	1	(Romans 1.106)
PHRYGES		VAL	1 12	
PHRYGIA		AV	1	country of NW Anatolia
PHRYGIA		CAT	1	
PHRYGIA		HL	1	
PHRYGIA		HOR	1	
PHRYGIA		MAN	1	
PHRYGIA		OV	1	
PHRYGIA		PL	1	
PHRYGIA		PROP	1	
PHRYGIA	cf. Phrug-	TER	1	(a slave-girl)
PHRYGIA	also pl.	V	1	country; (in pl.) Phrygian women
PHRYGIA		VAL	1 11	
PHRYGIUS		AV	1	Phrygian (sometimes: Trojan)
PHRYGIUS		CAT	1	
PHRYGIUS		COL	1	
PHRYGIUS		GER	1	
PHRYGIUS		HL	1	
PHRYGIUS		HOR	1	
PHRYGIUS		JUV	1	
PHRYGIUS		LUC	1	
PHRYGIUS		LUCR	1	
PHRYGIUS		MAR	1	
PHRYGIUS		OV	1	
PHRYGIUS		PET	1	
PHRYGIUS		PROP	1	
PHRYGIUS		S	1	
PHRYGIUS		SEN	1	
PHRYGIUS		SIL	1	
PHRYGIUS		TIB	1	
PHRYGIUS		V	1	
PHRYGIUS		VAL	1	
PHRYGIUS		VAR	1 20	
PHRYNE		HOR	1	a Roman courtesan
PHRYNE		LUCIL	1	
PHRYNE		PROP	1	
PHRYNE		TIB	1 4	
PHRYX	also adj.	JUV	1	a Phrygian
PHRYX		MAR	2	a cont. man; adj.
PHRYX		OV	1	a Phrygian; (also adj)
PHRYX	3 Prol. 52	PH	1	a Phrygian
PHRYX	also adj.	PROP	1	"
PHRYX		S	1	"
PHRYX	A. 12.99	V	1 8	" (also pl.)
PHRYXĒUS	= Phrix.	COL		p. to Phryxus
PHRYX*	63.22	CAT	1	Phrygian
PHRYX*		LUC	1	
PHRYX*	13.64	SIL	1 3	
PHRYXUS		COL		= Phrixus
PHTHIA H̲. 7.165		OV	2 2	a Phthian woman; concubine of Amyntor
PHTHIE = -ia, T̲r̲. 817		SEN		town of Thessaly (A̲A̲ 1.337)
PHTHIOTES as pl.		OV		people of Phthia
PHTHIOTICUS adj·		CAT		p. to Phthia (i.e. Thessalian)
PHTHIUS		HOR	1	p. to Phthia
PHTHIUS		OV	1	

PHTHIUS	PROP	1	3	p. to Phthia
PHTIA frag. 23	CIC			= Phthia
-PHYCUNS (-ūs) -nt-	LUC			a promontory in Cyrene (9.40)
PHYLACE	LUC		1	town in Thessaly
PHYLACE	VAL	1	2	
PHYLACEIS	S			= Laodamia
PHYLACEIS*	OV			p. to Phylace
PHYLACEIUS adj.	OV			p. to Phylace
PHYLACIDES	OV		1	= Protesilaus
PHYLACIDES	PROP	1	2	"
-PHYLEUS M. 8.308	OV		1	Calydonian hunter
PHYLEUS T. 12.745	S	1	2	a Theban
PHYLLEIUS M., AA	OV			p. to Phyllus in Thessaly
-PHYLLEUS M.12. 479	OV		1	ep. of Caeneus
PHYLLEUS T. 3.173	S	1	2	a Theban
PHYLLIS	CAL		1	a shepherdess
PHYLLIS	HOR		1	a girl
PHYLLIS	MAR		1	fict. girl
PHYLLIS	OV		3	shepherdess; d. of Sithon; title of poem
PHYLLIS	PER		1	d. of Sithon
PHYLLIS	PROP		2	a heroine; a meretrix
PHYLLIS	V	1	10	a shepherdess
PHYLLIUS M. 7.378	OV			friend of Cycnus
PHYLLODOCE	V			a sea-nymph
-PHYTO 2.5.68	TIB			a Sibyl
-PIACCHES P. 4.10.43	OV			a Thracian
PICANUS	SIL			mt. in Picenum
PICENS	JUV		1	a Picentine
PICENS	MAR		1	fictional
PICENS	SIL	1	3	Roman soldier
PICENTES	SIL			people of Picenum
PICENTIA	SIL			town of Campania
PICENTINUS N	MAR			a fict. person
PICENTINUS*	MAR			p. to Picenum
PICENUM	SIL			region of Italy
PICENUS	HOR		1	p. to Picenum
PICENUS	JUV		1	
PICENUS	MAR		1	
PICENUS	PRIAP		1	
PICENUS	SIL	1	5	
-PICES Aul. 701	PL			"qui aureos montes colunt."
PICUMNUS	FPLR			a primitive Roman god
PICUS	JUV		1	son of Saturn
PICUS	OV		1	
PICUS	SIL		1	
PICUS	V		1	
PICUS	VAL	1	5	
PIERIDES fem.pl.	AV		1	the Muses
PIERIDES	COL		1	
PIERIDES	HL		1	
PIERIDES	JUV		1	
PIERIDES	LUC		1	
PIERIDES	LUCR		1	
PIERIDES	MAN		1	
PIERIDES	MAR		1	
PIERIDES	MLP		1	
PIERIDES	OV		1	

PIERIDES		PROP	1	the Muses
PIERIDES		S	1	
PIERIDES		TIB	1	
PIERIDES		V	1	
PIERIDES		VAR	1 15	
PIERIS	patr., sg.	HOR	1	a Muse
PIERIS	F. 4.222	OV	1 2	
PIERIUS		AET	1	p. to the Muses
PIERIUS		AV	1	
PIERIUS		COL	1	
PIERIUS		GER	1	
PIERIUS		GR	1	
PIERIUS		HOR	1	
PIERIUS		JUV	1	
PIERIUS		LP	1	
PIERIUS		LUCR	1	
PIERIUS		MAR	1	
PIERIUS		OV	1	
PIERIUS		PET	1	
PIERIUS		PH	1	
PIERIUS		PRIAP	1	
PIERIUS		PROP	1	
PIERIUS		S	1	
PIERIUS		SEN	1	
PIERIUS		SIL	1	
PIERIUS		TIB	1 19	
PIEROS	M. 5.302	OV		k. of Emathia, f. of the Muses
PIETAS	personif.	OV	1	goddess of Piety
PIETAS	Curc. 639	PL	1	
PIETAS	T. 5.3	S	1	
PIETAS		TR	1 4	
PILUMNUS	A. 9.4	V		primitive Roman deity
PIMPLEA	S. 1.4.26	S		a fountain
-PINACIUM	St. 270	PL		name of a slave-boy
PINARIUS		V		p. to Pinarii (Roman priestly family)
PINDARICUS		HOR	1	p. to Pindar
PINDARICUS		MAR	1	
PINDARICUS		OV	1	
PINDARICUS		PROP	1	
PINDARICUS		S	1 5	
PINDARUS		HOR	1	the Greek poet
PINDARUS		S	1 2	
PINDUS		HOR	1	mt. range in Epirus-Thessaly
PINDUS		LUC	1	
PINDUS		OV	1	
PINDUS		PROP	1	
PINDUS		SEN	1	
PINDUS		SIL	1	
PINDUS		V	1	
PINDUS		VAL	1 8	
-PINNA	8.517	SIL		town of Picenum
PIPLEIS	(or -ea)	HOR	1	a muse (C. 1.26.9)
PIPLEIS		MAR	1 2	p. to Pipleis (of the Muses)
PIPLEIUS		CAT		p. to the Muses
PIPLEUS		MAR		p. to the Muses
PIRAEA	n.pl.	OV		harbor of Athens
PIRAEEUS		AV	1	harbor of Athens

PIRAEEUS		S	1	2	harbor of Athens
PIRAEUS		CAT		1	harbor of Athens
PIRAEUS		COM		1	
PIRAEUS		OV		1	
PIRAEUS		PL		1	
PIRAEUS		TER	1	5	
PIRAEUS*		OV		1	p. to Piraeus
PIRAEUS*	3.21.23	PROP		1	
PIRAEUS*		SIL	1	3	
PIRENA		PL			a fountain at Corinth
PIRENE		PER		1	
PIRENE		S	1	2	
PIRENIS adj.		OV		1	p. to Pirene
PIRENIS		SEN	1	2	
-PIRESIUS	1.356	VAL			p. to Peiresia in Thessaly
PIRITHOUS		HOR		1	legendary hero (son of Ixion)
PIRITHOUS		MAR		1	
PIRITHOUS		OV		1	
PIRITHOUS		PROP		1	
PIRITHOUS		S		1	
PIRITHOUS		V	1	6	
-PIRRIA Ep. 1.13.14		HOR			legendary maid in comedy
PISA 7.56.4		MAR		1	town of Elis
PISA M.5.494; Ibis 323		OV		1	town of Elis; town of Etruria
PISA		S		1	town of Elis
PISA		V		1	
PISA		VAL	1	5	
PISAE		LUC		1	town of Etruria
PISAE		SEN		1	
PISAE		TR		1	
PISAE		V	1	4	
PISAEA		OV			Hippodamia
PISAEUS		JUV		1	p. to Pisa in Elis
PISAEUS		LUC		1	
PISAEUS		OV		1	
PISAEUS		S		1	
PISAEUS		SEN		1	
PISAEUS		SIL		1	
PISAEUS		TR	1	7	
PISANDER		OV			suitor of Penelope
PISAURUM		CAT			town in Umbria
PISCES pl.		CIC		1	constellation
PISCES		FPLB		1	
PISCES		GER		1	
PISCES		LUC		1	
PISCES		MAN		1	
PISCES		PROP	1	6	
PISCIS sg.		MAN		1	constellation (same?)
PISCIS		OV		1	
PISCIS		V	1	3	
PISCIS/AUSTRALIS		CIC			constellation (same as above)
-PISENOR M. 12.303		OV			a Centaur
PISISTRATUS		PH			tyrant of Athens
PISO 28.1		CAT		1	L. Calp. P. Caesoninus
PISO		JUV		1	Calpurnius Piso
PISO also pl.		LP		1	Calpurnius Piso
PISO 8.463		SIL	1	4	an Umbrian leader

PISONES	HOR		1	Piso family
PISONES	MAR	1	2	" "
-PISTOCLERUS Bac.109	PL			a young man
-PISTORENSES Capt.160	PL			(comic ethnic formation)
PISTRIX	CIC			constell. "Whale"
-PISTUS Merc. 278	PL			an overseer
PITANE	LUC		1	town of Aeolia
PITANE	OV	1	2	"
PITHECIUM fem.	PL			a maid
PITHECUSAE	OV			island off Naples
-PITHO Am. 3.7.23	OV			"Persuasion" < Πειθώ
-PITHOLEON S. 1.10.22	HOR			cont. of Caesar
PITTACOS	JUV			one of the wise men
PITTHEIS	OV			= Aethra
PITTHEIUS	OV			p. to Pittheus
PITTHEUS	OV			son of Pelops
PITTHEUS*	OV			p. to Pittheus
-PITYA 2.623	VAL			town (uncertain)
PLACENTIA	SIL			town in N. Italy
PLACENTINI	PL			people of Placentia (in a pun)
PLANCI (pl.)	FPLA			a Roman family
PLANCTUS 2.550	SIL			"Grief" personified
PLANCUS	HOR			a friend, L. Munatius P. (consul 42 BC)
-PLANESIUM Curc. 159	PL			a girl
PLATAEAE T. 4.373	S			town of Boeotia
-PLATAGIDORUS	PL			a miles (Curc. 408)
-PLATEA 4.55.13	MAR			town of Spain
-PLATENIUS Epid. 438	PL			??
PLATO	HOR		1	the Greek philosopher
PLATO	LUC		1	
PLATO	MAR		1	
PLATO	PROP	1	4	
PLATON	MAN			
PLAUSTRA n.pl.	GER			const. (Big Dipper)
PLAUSTRUM	LUC		1	"
PLAUSTRUM	S	1	2	
PLAUTINUS	HOR		1	p. to Plautus
PLAUTINUS	PL	1	2	
PLAUTIUS/MARCUS	FPLA			(unknown)
PLAUTUS	FPLA		1	the Roman comic poet
PLAUTUS	HOR		1	
PLAUTUS	PL		1	
PLAUTUS	SEN		1	
PLAUTUS	TER	1	5	
- PLECUSA (or Phl.)	MAR			fict. (2.66.4)
PLEIADES fem.pl.	GER		1	the constell. of 7 stars
PLEIADES	HOR		1	
PLEIADES	MAN		1	
PLEIADES	PROP		1	
PLEIADES	S		1	
PLEIADES	SEN		1	
PLEIADES	VAL	1	7	
PLEIAS also pl.	OV			
PLEIONE	OV		1	wife of Atlas (and a constell.)
PLEIONE	VAL	1	2	
-PLEMINIUS 17.458	SIL			a Roman soldier
PLEMYRIUM	V			promontory of Sicily

-PLESIDIPPUS Rud.339	PL			a young man
PLEURŌN fem.	OV	1		town in Aetolia
PLEUROŃ	S	1		
PLEURON	SEN	1		
PLEURON	SIL	1	4	
PLEURONIUS	OV			p. to Pleuron
-PLEUSICLES Mil. 7	PL			a young man
PLEXIPPUS M. 8.440	OV			son of Thestius
PLIAS cf. Pleias	GER	1		a Pleiad
PLIAS	GR	1		
PLIAS	LUC	1		
PLIAS	S	1		
PLIAS	V	1		
PLIAS	VAL	1	6	
PLINIUS	FPLR		1	Pliny the Younger
PLINIUS	MAR	1	2	" "
PLISTHENES	SEN			son of Thyestes
PLISTHENIUS	OV			p. to Plisthenes
-PLOCINUS dub.	PL			title of a lost comedy (?)
-PLOTIUS S. 1.5.40	HOR			a friend, P. Tucca
-PLUTIA = Plotia	MAR			fict.
⎧PLUTO	HOR		1	Greek god of the Underworld
⎪PLUTO	TIB	1	2	
⎨PLUTON	JUV		1	
⎪PLUTON	SEN		1	
⎩PLUTON	V	1	3	
PLUTONIUS	HOR			p. to Pluto
PLUTUS	PH			god of Wealth
-PODAETUS 14.492	SIL			a Siculian warrior
PODALIRIUS	HL		1	Trojan doctor
PODALIRIUS	MAR		1	(typical doctor)
PODALIRIUS	OV		1	Trojan doctor
PODALIRIUS	V	1	4	" "
-PODARCES	HL		1	the horse of Thoas
PODARCES T. 6.444	S	1	2	" "
POEANS = Poeas	SEN			father of Philoctetes
POEANTIADES	OV			= Philoctetes
POEANTIUS	OV		1	= Philoctetes
POEANTIUS	VAL	1	2	
POEANTIUS*	MAR		1	p. to Poea(n)s
POEANTIUS*	OV		1	
POEANTIUS*	VAL	1	3	
POEAS	HL		1	father of Philoctetes
POEAS	OV		1	
POEAS	TR	1	3	
POEMENIS fem.	OV			a dog
POENA personif.	HOR		1	goddess of Vengeance
POENA	S		1	
POENA	TIB		1	
POENA	VAL	1	4	
POENAE pl.	AV		1	Vengeance
POENAE	LUC		1	
POENAE	SIL		1	
POENAE	VAR	1	4	
POENI	ENN		1	Phoenicians (usually as Carthaginians)
POENI	LUC		1	
POENI	LUCR		1	

POENI		MAN	1	Phoenicians (or Carthaginians)
POENI		MAR	1	
POENI		S	1	
POENI		SIL	1	
POENI		V	1 8	
POENICEUS = Phoen-		OV		Punic
POENICUS	adj.	FPLA		"
POENUS	N	FPLA	1	Punic, Carthaginian man
POENUS	also pl.	HOR	1	
POENUS		LUC	1	
POENUS		MAR	1	
POENUS		OV	1	
POENUS	also pl.	PL	1	(note: Poenior, Poen. 991)
POENUS		SIL	1 7	Hannibal
POENUS*		AV	1	Punic, Carthaginian
POENUS*		FPLB	1	
POENUS*		GER	1	
POENUS*		JUV	1	
POENUS*		LUC	1	
POENUS*		MAR	1	
POENUS*		OV	1	
POENUS*		PROP	1	
POENUS*		S	1	
POENUS*		SEN	1	
POENUS*		SIL	1	
POENUS*		V	1 12	
POLEMON		HOR	1	Greek philosopher
POLEMON	822W	LUCIL	1 2	
POLIO =	Pollio	V		P. Asinius
POLITES		HL	1	son of Priam
POLITES	M. 14.251	OV	1	
POLITES		S	1	a Theban
POLITES		V	1 4	son of Priam
POLLA		MAR	2	w. of the poet Lucan; fict. woman
POLLA		S	2 4	" " " ; w. of P. Fabia
POLLENTIA		SIL		town of Liguria
POLLENTINUS		MAR	1	p. to Pollentia
POLLENTINUS		S	1 2	
POLLIO		CAT	1	Asinius Pollio, friend of Augustus
POLLIO		HOR	1	" "
POLLIO		JUV	1	a cont.
POLLIO		MAR	2 5	two cont.
- POLLITTA 2.68		JUV	.	unknown woman
- POLLIUS S. 2.2.96		S		P. Felix, a cont.
POLLUCES = Pollux		PL		demi-god, brother of Castor
POLLUX		CAT	1	
POLLUX		HOR	1	
POLLUX		MAR	1	
POLLUX		OV	1	
POLLUX		PROP	1	
POLLUX		S	1	
POLLUX		SEN	1	
POLLUX		SIL	1	
POLLUX		V	1	
POLLUX		VAL	1 10	
{ POLOS		GER		North Pole (?)
{ POLUS		CIC		

-POLYBADISCUS frag.	PL			??
POLYBIUS	MAR			an athlete
-POLYBOTES <u>A</u>. 6.484	V			a Trojan
POLYBUS	OV	1		king of Corinth
POLYBUS	S	1		
POLYBUS	SEN	1	3	
-POLYCHARMUS 8.37	MAR			fict. man
⎰POLYCLETĒUS	S			p. to Polyclitus
⎱POLYCLITĒUS	COL			
POLYCLITUS	JUV	1		Greek sculptor
POLYCLITUS	MAR	1	2	
POLYDAMANTĒUS	SIL			p. to Polydamas
POLYDAMAS	HL		1	a Trojan, friend of Hector
POLYDAMAS	OV		1	
POLYDAMAS 1.4	PER		1	
POLYDAMAS	PROP	1	4	
POLYDECTES	OV			king of Seriphus
-POLYDEGMON <u>M</u>. 5.85	OV			(or Polydaemon) desc. of Semiramis
POLYDORĒUS	OV			p. to Polydorus
POLYDORUS	OV	1		a son of Priam
POLYDORUS	PROP	1		
POLYDORUS	TR	1		
POLYDORUS	V	1	4	
POLYHYMNIA	AV	1		one of the nine Muses
POLYHYMNIA	HOR	1		
POLYHYMNIA	MAR	1		
POLYHYMNIA	OV	1	4	
-POLYIDON	HL			son of Eurydamas
POLYIDOS em., <u>Cir</u>.112	AV			a priest
POLYMACHAEROPLAGIDES	PL			fict. soldier
POLYMESTOR (-mn-)	OV		1	legendary king of Thrace
POLYMESTOR	PROP	1	2	
POLYMNIA	MLP			= Polyhymnia
POLYNICES	S		1	son of Oedipus
POLYNICES	SEN	1	2	
-POLYPEMON <u>M</u>., <u>Ibis</u>	OV			legendary thief, friend of Procrustes
POLYPHEMOS	MAR			a slave
POLYPHEMUS	JUV	1		the one-eyed Cyclops
POLYPHEMUS	LUCIL	1		
POLYPHEMUS	MAR	1		
POLYPHEMUS	OV	1		
POLYPHEMUS	PROP	1		
POLYPHEMUS	S	1		
POLYPHEMUS	SIL	2		(+ Punic soldier)
POLYPHEMUS	V	1		
POLYPHEMUS	VAL	2	11	(+ an Argonaut)
POLYPLUSIUS	PL			comic name of a gens
-POLYTIMUS 12.75.1	MAR			a homosexual
POLYXENA	JUV	1		a daughter of Priam
POLYXENA	OV	1		
POLYXENA	SEN	1	3	
POLYXENIUS adj.	CAT			p. to Polyxena
-POLYXENUS	HL			a hero of Elis
POLYXO fem.	S		1	a prophetess of Lemnos
POLYXO	VAL	1	2	
POMETII	V			Volscian town
POMONA	CAL		1	old Italic goddess of orchards

POMONA	MAR		1	goddess of orchards
POMONA	OV	1	3	
POMONALIS	ENN			p. to Pomona
POMPEI	LUC		1	sons of Pompey
POMPEI	S	1	2	family of Pompey
POMPEIA 2.32.11	PROP			colonnade
POMPEIANI also sg.	LUC			partisan(s) of Pompey
POMPEIANUM	MAR			theater
POMPEIANUS N, adj.	LUC		2	(p. to) Pompey the Great
POMPEIANUS	MAR		1	p. to Pompey
POMPEIANUS	S	1	4	
POMPEIUS	CAT		1	Pompey the Great
POMPEIUS	HOR		1	P. Varus (cf. Grosphus)
POMPEIUS	JUV		2	" " (+ friend of Domitian)
POMPEIUS	LUC		2	two sons of Pompey
POMPEIUS	MAN		2	Pompey the Great (+ Sextus Pompeius)
POMPEIUS	MAR		1	" "
POMPEIUS	OV		1	Pompeius Sextus (a friend)
POMPEIUS	PH		1	Pomp. the Great
POMPEIUS	PROP		1	" "
POMPEIUS & pl.	S	1	13	" "
POMPEIUS*	COL		1	p. to Pompey or his family
POMPEIUS*	MAN		1	
POMPEIUS*	MAR		1	
POMPEIUS*	OV		1	
POMPEIUS*	PROP	1	5	
POMPEIUS/AUCTUS	MAR			friend of Martial
POMPEIUS/GROSPHUS	HOR			(unknown)
POMPILIUS	FPLA		1	early Roman poet
POMPILIUS	HOR		1	Numa P., second k. of Rome
POMPILIUS	OV	1	3	"
POMPILIUS*	HOR			p. to Numa Pomp.
POMPONIA	SIL			mother of Scipio Africanus
POMPONIUS	HOR		1	unknown man
POMPONIUS 6.48	MAR	1	2	fict.
POMPTINUS adj.	JUV		1	p. to a district in Latium
POMPTINUS	LUC		1	
POMPTINUS	MAR		1	
POMPTINUS	SIL	1	4	
-POMPULLA 4.61.5	MAR			fict.
-POMPULLUS 6.61	MAR			fict.
PONTIA	JUV		1	notorious poisoner
PONTIA	MAR	2	3	" " (+ another woman)
-PONTICA n.pl.	S			countries around the Black Sea
PONTICUS	JUV		1	a poet
PONTICUS	MAR		1	fict.
PONTICUS	OV		1	poet-friend
PONTICUS	PROP	1	4	poet-friend
PONTICUS*	CAT		1	p. to Pontus (sea or province)
PONTICUS*	HOR		1	
PONTICUS*	JUV		1	
PONTICUS*	LUC		1	
PONTICUS*	OV		1	
PONTICUS*	S		1	
PONTICUS*	SEN		1	
PONTICUS*	VAL	1	8	
-PONTILIANUS 5.66	MAR			fict. man

PONTIUS	88W	LUCIL		(unknown man)
PONTOS	cf. Euxinus	LUCR		Black Sea
PONTUS		JUV	2	Sea; the Roman province
PONTUS		LUC	1	Sea
PONTUS		OV	2	Sea; region around Sea
PONTUS		PER	1	Sea
PONTUS		PET	1	Sea
PONTUS	4.7.10	PH	1	Sea
PONTUS		PL	1	region around Sea
PONTUS		SEN	1	Sea
PONTUS	13.477	SIL	1	region
PONTUS		TR	1	Sea
PONTUS		V	2	Sea; Roman province
PONTUS		VAL	1 15	Sea
PONTUS/EUXINUS		OV		Black Sea
POPILIUS		LUCIL		P. Laenas, a general
POPPAEA		SEN		wife of Nero
POPPAEANA		JUV		a cosmetic
POPULONIA		V		town of Etruria
PORCIA		MAR		wife of M. J. Brutus
PORCIUS		CAT	1	a cont.
PORCIUS		HOR	1 2	a cont.
PORPHYRION		HOR	1	king of the giants
PORPHYRION		MAR	1 2	
PORRIMA	F. 1.633	OV		Roman goddess (conn. with Carmenta)
PORSENA		HOR	1	king of Etruria
PORSENA		MAR	1	
PORSENA	13.477	SIL	1 3	
PORSENNA		V		
PORTA/CAPENA		OV		gate of Rome
-PORTHAON	(or Parth.)	PL		grandfather of Deianira (Men. 745)
PORTHMEUS		PET		ep. of Charon
PORTICUS/PHILIPPI		MAR		colonnade of temple to Hercules (5.49.12)
PORTUNUS		OV	1	god of ports
PORTUNUS		V	1 2	
PORUS	Tr. 3.5.39	OV		king of India(n tribe ?)
POSIDES	m.	JUV		freedman of Claudius
-POSTUMA		COM		fict. woman
POSTUMIA		CAT		(unknown woman)
POSTUMIANUS		MAR		fict.
-POSTUMILLA	12.49	MAR		fict.
POSTUMIUS		CAT	1	a native of Brescia
POSTUMIUS		LUCIL	1	L. P. Albinus
POSTUMIUS		OV	1 3	L. P. Albinus
POSTUMUS		HOR	1	unknown friend
POSTUMUS		JUV	1	Ursidius Postumus
POSTUMUS		MAR	1	P. Tubertus
POSTUMUS		OV	1	king (Silvius) Postumus
POSTUMUS		PL	1	a child's name
POSTUMUS		PROP	1 6	friend of PROP
POSTVERTA	F. 1.633	OV		goddess (Carmenta)
POTESTAS	12.6.3	MAR		"Power" personified
POTHINUS	N	LUC	1	Pompey's assassin
POTHINUS		MAR	1 2	
POTITIUS		V		eponymous ancestor of P. gens
POTITUS		MAR		cont. scholar
POTNIAS	adj.	OV	1	p. to Potniae (t. in Boeotia)

POTNIAS		V	1 2	p. to Potniae (t. in Boeotia)
–POTONUS	or -ius	FPLA		an unknown Roman
PRAENESTE	n.	HOR	1	town of Latium
PRAENESTE		JUV	1	
PRAENESTE		LUC	1	
PRAENESTE		MAR	1	
PRAENESTE		PROP	1	
PRAENESTE		S	1	
PRAENESTE		SIL	1	
PRAENESTE		V	1 8	(fem.: A. 8.561)
PRAENESTINUS		COM	1	p. to Praeneste
PRAENESTINUS		HOR	1	
PRAENESTINUS		JUV	1	
PRAENESTINUS		MAR	1	
PRAENESTINUS		OV	1	
PRAENESTINUS		PL	1	(also N pl.)
PRAENESTINUS		S	1	
PRAENESTINUS		V	1 8	
PRAETUTIUS	adj.	SIL		p. to the Praetutii (tr. of Picenum)
PRAXITELES		MAR	1	Greek sculptor
PRAXITELES		PH	1	
PRAXITELES		PRIAP	1	
PRAXITELES		PROP	1	
PRAXITELES		S	1 5	
PRIAMEIS	patron.	OV		Cassandra
PRIAMEIUS		HL	1	p. to Priam
PRIAMEIUS		LP	1	
PRIAMEIUS		OV	1	
PRIAMEIUS		V	1 4	
PRIAMIDAE	patr., pl.	PET	1	sons of Priam
PRIAMIDAE	13.68	SIL	1 2	
PRIAMIDES	m.sg.	HL	1	ep. of Hector
PRIAMIDES		HOR	1	" "
PRIAMIDES	also pl.	OV	2	Paris; Helenus
PRIAMIDES		S	1	Hector
PRIAMIDES		V	2 7	Helenus; Deiphobus
PRIAMUS		CIC	1	king of Troy
PRIAMUS		ENN	1	
PRIAMUS		FPLR	1	
PRIAMUS		HL	1	
PRIAMUS		HOR	1	
PRIAMUS		JUV	1	
PRIAMUS		MAN	1	
PRIAMUS		MAR	1	
PRIAMUS		OV	1	
PRIAMUS		PL	1	
PRIAMUS		PRIAP	1	
PRIAMUS		PROP	1	
PRIAMUS		S	1	
PRIAMUS		SEN	1	
PRIAMUS		TR	1	
PRIAMUS		V	2	(+ his grandson)
PRIAMUS		VAL	1 18	
PRIAPUS		AV	1	god of fertility (sometimes: phallic device)
PRIAPUS		CAL	1	
PRIAPUS		CAT	3	(+ a lustful man; t. of Mysia)
PRIAPUS		COL	1	

PRIAPUS		COM	1	god of fertility
PRIAPUS	as pl.	FPLB	1	
PRIAPUS		HOR	1	
PRIAPUS		JUV	1	
PRIAPUS		MAR	1	
PRIAPUS		OV	1	
PRIAPUS		PET	1	
PRIAPUS		PRIAP	1	
PRIAPUS		TIB	1	
PRIAPUS		V	1 16	
PRINCEPS	5.7.4	PH		a flute-player
-PRION	6.619	VAL		a Getic hero
-PRISCILLA	S. 5.1.3	S		wife of Abascantus
PRISCI/LATĪNI		V		the prehistoric Latins
PRISCUS		HOR	1	fict. man
PRISCUS		MAR	5	five cont. men
PRISCUS		OV	1 7	poet
PRISTIS	fem.	GER	1	constellation "Whale"
PRISTIS		MAN	1	
PRISTIS		V	1 3	name of a ship (in Aeneas' fleet)
PRIVERNAS	adj.	SIL		p. to Privernum
PRIVERNUM		LUCIL	1	town of Latium
PRIVERNUM		SIL	1	
PRIVERNUM		V	1 3	
PRIVERNUS		V		a Rutulian warrior
PROBUS		MAR		a grammarian
PROCA	m.	OV		king of Alba
PROCAS		V		
PROCHYTA		JUV	1	an island off Campania
PROCHYTA		S	1	
PROCHYTA		V	1 3	
PROCHYTE		OV	1	
PROCHYTE		SIL	1 2	
-PROCILLUS	1.27	MAR		fict. man
PROCNE	cf. Progne	AV	1	d. of Pandion, wife of Tereus (or: a swallow
PROCNE		HOR	1	
PROCNE		JUV	1	
PROCNE		MAR	1	
PROCNE		OV	1	
PROCNE		PER	1	
PROCNE		PET	1	
PROCNE		SEN	1 8	
-PROCNESSUS	3.34	VAL		an island
PROCRIS		OV	1	daughter of Erechtheus
PROCRIS		V	1 2	
PROCRUSTES		OV	1	legendary robber
PROCRUSTES		SEN	1 2	
PROCULA		JUV		unknown Roman woman
-PROCULEIA	10.41	MAR		fict. woman
PROCULEIUS		HOR	1	C. Proculeius, friend of Augustus
PROCULEIUS		JUV	1 2	
-PROCULINA	6.22	MAR		fict.
PROCULUS	1.70	MAR	1	C. J. Proculus (friend of MAR)
PROCULUS	P. 4.16.32	OV	1 2	Augustan poet (Iulius Proculus)
PROCULUS/JŪLIUS		OV		" " (F. 2.499)
PROCYON		CIC	1	constellation (= Antecanis)
PROCYON		GER	1	

PROCYON	HOR		1	constellation
PROCYON	MAN	1	4	
PROETIDES fem.pl.	OV		1	daughters of Proetus
PROETIDES	S		1	
PROETIDES	SEN		1	
PROETIDES	V	1	4	
PROETUS	FPLR		1	mythological king of Tiryns
PROETUS	HOR		1	
PROETUS	OV		1	
PROETUS	S	1	4	
PROGNE cf. Procne	PL		1	sister of Philomela
PROGNE	S		1	
PROGNE	V	1	3	(as swallow)
–PROMACHUS	HL			a Boeotian
PROMETHEUS	CAT		1	the demi-god, son of Iapetus
PROMETHEUS	CIC		1	
PROMETHEUS	HOR		1	
PROMETHEUS	JUV		1	(and a skillful potter)
PROMETHEUS	MAR		1	
PROMETHEUS	OV		1	
PROMETHEUS	PH		1	
PROMETHEUS	PROP		1	
PROMETHEUS	S		1	
PROMETHEUS	TR		1	
PROMETHEUS	V		1	
PROMETHEUS	VAL	1	12	
PROMETHEUS*	COL		1	p. to Prometheus
PROMETHEUS*	MAR		1	
PROMETHEUS*	OV		1	
PROMETHEUS*	PROP		1	
PROMETHEUS*	S		1	
PROMETHEUS* HF 1207	SEN		1	
PROMETHEUS*	VAL	1	7	
PROMETHIDES patr.	OV			Deucalion
– PROMOLUS A. 9.574	V			a Trojan
PROPERTIUS	MAR		1	Sextus Aurel. Prop., the poet
PROPERTIUS	OV		1	
PROPERTIUS	PROP		1	
PROPERTIUS	S	1	4	
PROPOETIDES	OV			Cyprian girls
PROPONTIACUS	OV		1	p. to the Propontis
PROPONTIACUS	PROP	1	2	
PROPONTIS	CAT		1	Sea of Marmora at Byzantium
PROPONTIS	LUC		1	
PROPONTIS	MAN		1	
PROPONTIS	OV		1	
PROPONTIS	SIL		1	
PROPONTIS	VAL		1	
PROPONTIS	VAR	1	7	
– PRORA	CIC			constellation
PROREUS M. 3.634	OV			a sailor (<πρωρεύς)
PROSERPINA	COL		1	Greek goddess of Underworld; cf. Persephone
PROSERPINA	ENN		1	
PROSERPINA	FPLA		1	
PROSERPINA	GR		1	
PROSERPINA	HOR		1	
PROSERPINA	MAR		1	

PROSERPINA		OV	1	Greek goddess of the Underworld
PROSERPINA		S	1	
PROSERPINA		SEN	1	
PROSERPINA		SIL	1	
PROSERPINA		V	1	
PROSERPINA		VAL	1° 12	
PROSPICIENS M.14.761		OV		ep. of Venus
PROSYMNA		S		town of Argolis
PROTESILAEUS		CAT		p. to Protesilaus
PROTESILAUS		HL	1	a Greek (Thessalian) against Troy
PROTESILAUS		OV	1	
PROTESILAUS		S	1 3	
PROTEUS		HL	1	a sea-god (the "old man of the sea")
PROTEUS		HOR	1	(said of a tricky person)
PROTEUS		LUC	1	
PROTEUS		OV	1	
PROTEUS		PET	1	
PROTEUS		S	1	
PROTEUS		SEN	1	
PROTEUS		SIL	1	
PROTEUS		V	1	
PROTEUS		VAL	1 10	
PROTHOENOR		HL	1	a Boeotian warrior
PROTHOENOR		OV	1 2	a guest at Perseus' wedding
-PROTHOUS T. 6.367		S	1	an Argive
PROTHOUS Tr. 829		SEN	1 2	a Magnesian leader
-PROTIS em. 3.158		VAL		a Cyzican
PROTOGENES 3.120		JUV		(unknown)
PROVINCIA		CAT		Cisalpine Gaul
PRUSIACUS		FPLR	1	p. to Prusias, king of Bithynia
PRUSIACUS		SIL	1 2	
-PRYTANIS M. 13.258		OV	1	comp. of Sarpedon
PRYTANIS A. 9.767		V	1 2	a Trojan
PSAMATHE		OV	2	d. of Crotopus; nymph (m. of Phocus)
PSAMATHE		VAL	1 3	a spring in Laconia
PSECAS		JUV	1	woman slave (hairdresser)
PSECAS		OV	1 2	a nymph
PSEUDOLUS		PL		a slave (in comedy of same name)
PSOPHIS fem.		OV	1	town of Arcadia
PSOPHIS		S	1 2	
PSYLLI pl.		LUC		tribe of Marmarica
PSYLLUS sg.		FPLR	1	
PSYLLUS		LUC	1 2	
PTELEON		S		town of Elis
PTELEOS fem.		LUC		port of Thessaly
PTERELA m.		PL		king of the Teleboae
PTERELAS		OV	2	a dog; king of the Taphians
PTERELAS		S	1 3	an Argive
PTHIA = Phthia		V		town of Thessaly
- PTOLEMOCRATIA		PL		a priestess (Rud. 481)
PTOLOMAEEUS		PROP		p. to Ptolemy
PTOLOMAEUS		LUC	1	one of the kings of Egypt
PTOLOMAEUS		SIL	1 2	" " "
PTOLOMAIS patron.		LUC		Cleopatra
PUBLICIUS as pl.		OV		a Roman gens
PUBLICIUS*		OV		p. to a hill in Rome
PUBLICOLA (Poplic-)		AV	1	cognomen of the Messallae (Cat. 9.40)

PUBLICOLA	SIL	1	2	P. Val. Publicola
PUBLIUS	HOR		1	a praenomen
PUBLIUS	LUCIL		1	"
PUBLIUS	MAR	2	4	two cont.
PUBLIUS/SCIPIO	FPLA			Scipio Africanus
{PUDENS	MAR			A. Pudens of Sassina, friend of MAR
{PUDENS/AULUS	MAR			" "
PUDICITIA personif.	JUV		1	goddess of Chastity
PUDICITIA	MAR		1	
PUDICITIA	PL		1	
PUDICITIA	PROP	1	4	
PUDOR personif.	HOR		1	goddess of Decency
PUDOR	OV	1	2	
-PULFENIUS v.l., 5.190	PER			a centurion
-PULLIA C. 3.4.10	HOR			friend of Horace (nurse)
PUNICE adv.	PL			in Punic (language)
PUNICEUS	OV		1	Carthaginian, Punic
PUNICEUS	S	1	2	
PUNICUS	COL		1	Carthaginian, Punic
PUNICUS	HOR		1	
PUNICUS	JUV		1	
PUNICUS	LUC		1	
PUNICUS	MAN		1	
PUNICUS	MAR		1	
PUNICUS	OV		1	
PUNICUS	PL		1	
PUNICUS	SIL		1	
PUNICUS	V	1	10	
PUPIUS	HOR			a tragic poet
PUPPIS	CIC		1	constell. "Ship"
PUPPIS	GER	1	2	
-PURPUREUS	FPLA			son of Earth
PUSILLA	HOR			a woman's name
PUTEAL n.	HOR		1	a curb-stone in Rome
PUTEAL	OV		1	
PUTEAL	PER	1	3	
PYGMAEUS adj.	JUV		1	p. to the Pygmies
PYGMAEUS	OV		1	
PYGMAEUS	PRIAP	1	3	
PYGMALION	OV		1	legendary sculptor, grandson of Agenor
PYGMALION	SIL		1	son of Belus (of Tyre)
PYGMALION	V	1	3	" "
PYGMALIONEUS	SIL			p. to Pygmalion
PYLADES	HOR		1	the friend of Orestes
PYLADES	JUV		1	
PYLADES	MAN		1	
PYLADES	MAR		1	
PYLADES	OV		1	
PYLADES	S		1	
PYLADES	SEN	1	7	
PYLENE	S			town of Aetolia
PYLII	S			the people of Pylos
PYLIUS also adj.	AV		1	Nestor, king of Pylos
PYLIUS	MAN		1	
PYLIUS	OV		1	
PYLIUS	S	1	4	
PYLIUS*	FPLR		1	p. to Pylos or Nestor

PYLIUS*	HOR		1	p. to Pylos (or Nestor)
PYLIUS*	JUV		1	
PYLIUS*	MAR		1	
PYLIUS*	OV		1	
PYLIUS*	S		1	
PYLIUS*	SEN		1	
PYLIUS*	SIL		1	
PYLIUS*	TIB		1	
PYLIUS*	VAL	1	10	
PYLOS fem.	S		1	town in Messenia, ruled by Nestor
PYLOS	SEN		1	
PYLOS	TIB	1	3	
PYLUS	FPLA		1	
PYLUS	OV	1	2	
PYRACMON cf. -gm-	S			a Cyclops
-PYRACTES M.12.460	OV			a Centaur (em.)
PYRAETHUS M. 12.449	OV			a Centaur
PYRAGMO	VAL			a Cyclops
PYRAGMON	V			"
PYRAMIDES	PROP		1	the Pyramids of Egypt
PYRAMIDES	S	1	2	
PYRAMUS	OV			lover of Thisbe
PYRENAEUM N, n.	JUV			the Pyrenees mts.
PYRENAEUS	LUC		1	p. to the Pyrenees
PYRENAEUS	SIL	1	2	the mt. range
PYRENE	GR		1	
PYRENE	LUC		1	
PYRENE	SEN		1	
PYRENE	SIL		2	(+ a Gaulish princess)
PYRENE	TIB	1	6	
PYRENEUS N	OV			king of Thrace
PYRGENSIS	LUCIL			p. to Pyrgi
PYRGI	MAR		1	town in Etruria
PYRGI	V	1	2	
PYRGO fem.	V			a Trojan nurse
PYRGOPOLYNICES	PL			a comic miles
-PYRNUS 3.112	VAL			a Cyzican
PYROIS -ent-, m.	COL		1	the planet Mars
PYROIS	OV		1	a sun-horse
PYROIS	VAL	1	3	" "
PYRRHA	HOR		2	wife of Deucalion; a hetaira
PYRRHA 1.84	JUV		1	" "
PYRRHA	MAR		1	
PYRRHA	OV		1	
PYRRHA	S		1	
PYRRHA	SEN		1	
PYRRHA B. 6.41	V		1	
PYRRHA 6.390	VAL	1	9	
PYRRHAEUS	S			p. to Pyrrha
PYRRHIAS adj.	OV			Pyrrhian (of t. in Lesbos)
PYRRHUS	HL		1	son of Achilles
PYRRHUS	HOR		2	king of Epirus; a young man
PYRRHUS	JUV		1	
PYRRHUS	LUC		1	
PYRRHUS em.	MAN		1	
PYRRHUS	OV		1	son of Achilles
PYRRHUS	PROP		1	king of Epirus

PYRRHUS	S		1	king of Epirus
PYRRHUS	SEN		1	son of Achilles
PYRRHUS	SIL		1	king of Epirus
PYRRHUS	V	1	12	son of Achilles
PYRRUS = Pyrrhus	TER			king of Epirus
PYTHAGORAS	HOR		1	the Greek philosopher
PYTHAGORAS	JUV		1	
PYTHAGORAS	MAR		2	(+ a libertus)
PYTHAGORAS	OV	1	5	
PYTHAGOREI	JUV			followers of Pythagoras
PYTHAGOREUS	COM		1	p. to Pythagoras
PYTHAGOREUS	HOR		1	
PYTHAGOREUS	PER	1	3	
PYTHIA n.pl.	HOR		1	games at Delphi
PYTHIA	LUC		1	" "
PYTHIA fem.	LUCR		1	priestess of Apollo
PYTHIA n.pl.	OV	1	4	games
PYTHIAS	COM		1	a female slave
PYTHIAS	HOR		1	" "
PYTHIAS	TER	1	3	" "
PYTHIUS	HOR		1	ep. of Apollo
PYTHIUS	PRIAP		1	
PYTHIUS	S	1	3	
PYTHIUS*	FPLA		1	Pythian, Delphic, p. to Apollo
PYTHIUS*	JUV		1	
PYTHIUS*	LUC		1	
PYTHIUS*	PROP	1	4	
PYTHO A. 6.6	PH		1	the priestess at Delphi
PYTHO fem.	TIB	1	2	Delphi
-PYTHODICUS Aul.II.7	PL			a slave
PYTHON fem.; m.	LUC		2	Delphi; dragon at Delphi
PYTHON m., M.1.438	OV		1	dragon
PYTHON	PROP		1	
PYTHON	S		1	
PYTHON	SEN		1	
PYTHON 14.572	SIL	1	7	ship's name
QUADRIPES Ar. 34.211	CIC			unknown constell.
-QUERCENS 10.151	SIL		1	an Umbrian
QUERCENS A. 9.684	V	1	2	a Rutulian
QUIES S. 1.6.91	S			"Rest" personified
QUINQUATRIA n.pl.	PL			festival of Minerva
QUINQUATRUS fem.pl.	HOR		1	" "
QUINQUATRUS	OV	1	2	
-QUINTIA 86.1	CAT			a cont. woman
QUINTIA 27.2	PRIAP	1	2	unknown woman (a saltatrix)
-QUINTIANUS 1.52	MAR			a friend (= Pompeius Q. ?)
QUINTILIA	CAT		1	mistress of Calvus
QUINTILIA	PROP	1	2	
QUINTILIANUS	JUV		1	M. Fabius Q., the rhetorician
QUINTILIANUS	MAR	1	2	" " "
QUINTILII F. 2.378	OV			a class of Luperci (priests)
QUINTILIS	OV			the month of July
QUINTILIUS	HOR			a poet-friend
-QUINTILLA 7.75	JUV			a cont.
QUINTIUS Cat. 10.8	AV		1	(or Quinctio) fict.
QUINTIUS	CAT		1	a cont.
QUINTIUS	MAR		1	Cincinnatus, the hero

QUINTIUS		PER	1	4	Cincinnatus, the hero
QUINTUS	Ann. 295	ENN	1		Fabius Pictor (pater)
QUINTUS		HOR	1		Quintus Arrius
QUINTUS		MAR	1		unknown (see Pollius)
QUINTUS		PER	1		Q. Ennius
QUINTUS	Amph. 305	PL	1	5	fict.
QUINTUS/ARRIUS		HOR			a friend of Cicero
QUINTUS/ENNIUS		ENN			himself, the poet
QUINTUS/OPIMIUS		LUCIL			father of L. Opimius
QUINTUS/OVIDIUS		MAR			an unknown cont.
QUIRINALIS		MAR	1		p. to Quirinus
QUIRINALIS		OV	1		
QUIRINALIS		S	1		
QUIRINALIS		V	1	4	
QUIRINI		JUV			Romulus & Remus
_QUIRINIUS	4.192	SIL			a Roman soldier
QUIRINUS		ENN	1		Romulus
QUIRINUS		HOR	2		(+ Janus)
QUIRINUS		JUV	1		
QUIRINUS		LUC	1		
QUIRINUS		LUCIL	1		
QUIRINUS		MAN	1		
QUIRINUS		MAR	1		
QUIRINUS		OV	1		
QUIRINUS		PROP	1		(4.6.21: Augustus)
QUIRINUS		S	1		
QUIRINUS		SIL	1		
QUIRINUS		V	2	14	(+ Augustus)
QUIRIS	sg.	HOR	1		a resident of Cures (Sabine t.)
QUIRIS		LUC	1		
QUIRIS		PROP	1	3	
QUIRITES	pl.	COM	1		residents of Cures (also: Romans)
QUIRITES		FPLR	1		
QUIRITES		JUV	1		
QUIRITES		LP	1		
QUIRITES		LUC	1		
QUIRITES		MAN	1		
QUIRITES		OV	1		
QUIRITES		PER	1		
QUIRITES		PET	1		
QUIRITES		PRIAP	1		
QUIRITES		PROP	1		
QUIRITES		SEN	1		
QUIRITES		SIL	1		
QUIRITES		V	1	14	
QUIRITIS	Ann. 107V	ENN			Romans (pl.)
QUODSEMELARRIPIDES		PL			a comic man's name (Pers. 705)
RABIES	2.206	VAL			"Frenzy" personif.
RABIRIUS	7.56	MAR	1		an architect
RABIRIUS	P. 4.16.5	OV	1	2	a poet
RAETI		HOR			an Alpine tribe
RAETICUS		CAT	1		Raetian
RAETICUS		MAR	1		
RAETICUS		OV	1		
RAETICUS		V	1	4	
RAETUS		MAR			a Raetian (of the Alps)
RAETUS*		HOR			Raetian

RAMNENSES	ENN			one of the three early Roman "tribes"
RAMNES	HOR	1		" " "
RAMNES F. 3.132	OV	1		
RAMNES	PROP	1	3	
RAMNUSIUS (Rham-)	AV	1		p. to Rhamnus (t. in Attica)
RAMNUSIUS	CAT	1	2	
-RANIS M. 3.171	OV			a nymph
- RAPO A. 10.748	V			a Rutulian
- RASINA 3.67.2	MAR			a stream in Forum Cornelii
RATIO	GR			"Reason" personified
RATIS	MAN			constell. Argo
RAVENNA	MAR	1		town in NE Italy
RAVENNA	SIL	1	2	
RAVENNAS adj.	MAR			p. to Ravenna
- RAVIDUS 40.1	CAT			a rival for Lesbia
- RAVOLA 9.4	JUV			cont. (a pervert)
REATE n.	SIL			a Sabine town
REGĪNUS	LUCIL			p. to Region in Calabria
REGION M. 14.48	OV			t· of S. Italy (Calabria)
REGIUM	OV			t. of Cisalpine Gaul
REGULUS	HOR	1		legendary Roman general
REGULUS	MAR	1		M. Aquilius Regulus, a lawyer
REGULUS 1.4.88	S	1		the general
REGULUS	SIL	1	4	
REMORA	ENN			the "Rome" of Remus
REMULUS	OV		1	king of Alba
REMULUS	SIL		1	minor warrior
REMULUS	V	1	3	" "
- REMURIA pl., F.5.479	OV			= Lemuria (festival)
REMUS	CAT		1	brother of Romulus
REMUS	ENN		1	
REMUS	HOR		1	
REMUS	JUV		1	
REMUS	LUC		1	
REMUS	MAR		1	
REMUS	OV		1	
REMUS	PER		1	
REMUS	PRIAP		1	
REMUS	PROP		1	
REMUS	S		1	
REMUS	TIB		1	
REMUS	V	2	14	(+ a Rutulian)
RESTITUTUS 10.87	MAR			a lawyer (Claudius R.)
REVERENTIA F.5.23	OV			personification
-REX/RUPILIUS	HOR			P. Rupilius Rex, of Praeneste
-RHADALUS 6.69	VAL			a Scythian
RHADAMANTHUS	JUV		1	son of Juppiter & a judge in Underworld
RHADAMANTHUS	OV		1	
RHADAMANTHUS	SEN		1	
RHADAMANTHUS	SIL		1	
RHADAMANTHUS	V	1	5	
RHADAMAS Trin. 928	PL			fict. name
-RHAEBUS A. 10.861	V			the horse of Mezentius
-RHAMBELUS 6.529	VAL			a Scythian (?)
- RHAMNES Ibis 629	OV		1	a Rutulian
RHAMNES A. 9.325	V	1	2	"
RHAMNŪS -nt-, fem.	LUC			town of Attica (cf. Ram.)

RHAMNUSIA	OV		1	Nemesis
RHAMNUSIA	S	1	2	
RHAMNUSIS	OV			Nemesis
RHAMNUSIUS	TER			p. to Rhamnus (cf. Ram.)
–RHASCYPOLIS 5.55	LUC			a Balkan prince
–RHAUCUS em., Cir. 384	AV			town in Crete
RHEA F. 4.201	OV		1	wife of Saturn (cf. Silvia)
RHEA	S		1	
RHEA A. 7.659	V	1	3	a priestess
–RHEBAS 4.698	VAL			a stream
RHENANUS adj.	MAR			p. to Rhenus (the Rhine)
RHENUS	CAT		1	the Rhine river
RHENUS	HOR		1	
RHENUS	JUV		1	
RHENUS	LUC		1	
RHENUS	MAR		1	
RHENUS	OV		1	
RHENUS	PER		1	
RHENUS	PET		1	
RHENUS	PROP		1	
RHENUS	S		1	
RHENUS	SEN		1	
RHENUS	SIL		2	(+ stream in N. Italy)
RHENUS	V	1	14	
RHENUS*	HOR			p. to the Rhine
RHESUS	AV		1	legendary king of Thrace
RHESUS	CAT		1	
RHESUS	HL		1	
RHESUS	OV		1	
RHESUS	SEN		1	
RHESUS	SIL		1	
RHESUS	V	1	7	
–RHEXENOR M. 14.504	OV			comp. of Diomedes
RHIPAEUS –ph–	PROP			p. to mt. in Scythia
–RHIPE T. 4.286	S			town of Arcadia
RHIPHAEUS	S			p. to mt. in Scythia
RHIPHEUS (Ri.)	OV			a Centaur
RHODANUS	HOR		1	the Rhone river
RHODANUS	LUC		1	
RHODANUS	OV		1	
RHODANUS	SEN		1	
RHODANUS	SIL		1	(= the Gauls)
RHODANUS	TIB	1	6	
RHODANUS*	SIL			p. to the Rhone
–RHODE C. 3.19.27	HOR			a girl
RHODIACUS	MAR			p. to Rhodos, Rhodian
RHODIENSIS	COM			p. to Rhodos
RHODII	JUV			the people of Rhodos
RHODIUS	HL		1	p. to Rhodos
RHODIUS	HOR		1	
RHODIUS	MAR		1	
RHODIUS	OV		1	
RHODIUS	PL		1	
RHODIUS	TER		1	
RHODIUS	V	1	7	
RHODOPE	HOR		1	mt. range in Thrace
RHODOPE	JUV		1	

RHODOPE	LUC		1	mt. range in Thrace
RHODOPE	MAR		1	
RHODOPE	OV		1	
RHODOPE	S		1	
RHODOPE	SEN		1	
RHODOPE	SIL		1	
RHODOPE	V		1	
RHODOPE	VAL	1	10	
RHODOPEIUS	MAR		1	p. to Rhodope, i.e. Thracian
RHODOPEIUS	OV		1	
RHODOPEIUS	S		1	
RHODOPEIUS	SIL		1	
RHODOPEIUS	V	1	5	
RHODOPEUS	LUC			p. to Rhodope, Thracian
RHODOS	HOR		1	island, SW of Anatolia
RHODOS	JUV		1	
RHODOS	LUC		1	
RHODOS	MAN		1	
RHODOS	MAR		1	
RHODOS	OV		2	(a nymph; a city)
RHODOS	PRIAP		1	island
RHODOS	S	1	9	
RHODUS	CAT		1	island
RHODUS	FPLR		1	
RHODUS	LUCIL		1	
RHODUS	PL		1	
RHODUS	TER	1	5	
RHOECUS (-tus)	V			a Centaur (G. 2.456)
RHOETEIUS 2.51	SIL			a Roman (in general)
RHOETEIUS*	LUC		1	p. to Rhoeteum, Trojan
RHOETEIUS*	SIL		1	
RHOETEIUS*	V	1	3	
RHOETEUM	OV			promontory in the Troad
RHOETEUS N	V			a Rutulian
RHOETEUS*	AV		1	p. to Rhoeteum, Trojan
RHOETEUS*	CAT		1	
RHOETEUS*	S		1	
RHOETEUS*	SEN		1	
RHOETEUS*	SIL		1	
RHOETEUS*	TR		1	
RHOETEUS*	V	1	7	
RHOETION = -eum	LUC			promontory in Troad
RHOETUS	HOR		1	a giant
RHOETUS	LUC		1	a Centaur
RHOETUS	MAR		1	giant
RHOETUS	OV		2	Centaur; comp. of Phineus
RHOETUS	V		2	a Rutulian; a Marsian
RHOETUS	VAL	1	8	a Centaur
RHONDES dub.	LUCIL			a pirate
RHUNDACUS	VAL			a river in W. Anatolia
RHYNDACUS	SIL		1	king of Spain
RHYNDACUS	VAL	1	2	a Scythian
-RHYTIEUS adj.	HL			p. to Rhytium (town in Crete)
-RIGAE 4.55.19	MAR			town of Spain
RIPAEUS Rh-, adj.	ENN			p. to mt. range of "Scythia"
RIPHAEUS adj.	COL		1	" " "
RIPHAEUS	LUC		1	

RIPHAEUS		SEN		1	p. to mt. range of "Scythia"
RIPHAEUS		SIL		1
RIPHAEUS		V		1
RIPHAEUS		VAL	1	6
RIPHEUS	(Rh-)	OV		1	a Centaur
RIPHEUS		V		1	a Trojan
RIPHEUS		VAL	1	3	a Scythian
RISUS	personif.	FPLA			god of Laughter
-RIXAMAE	4.55.16	MAR			town of Spain
ROBIGO	F. 4.907, fem.	OV			goddess of Rust-prevention (on wheat)
ROMA		AV		1	the city of Rome
ROMA		CAL		1
ROMA		CAT		1
ROMA		CIC		1
ROMA		ENN		1
ROMA		FPLA		1
ROMA		FPLB		1
ROMA		GR		1
ROMA		HOR		1
ROMA		JUV		1
ROMA		LUC		1
ROMA		LUCIL		1
ROMA		MAN		1
ROMA		MAR		1
ROMA		MLP		1
ROMA		OV		1
ROMA		PER		1
ROMA		PET		1
ROMA		PH		1
ROMA		PROP		1
ROMA		S		1
ROMA		SEN		1
ROMA		SIL		1
ROMA		TIB		1
ROMA		V		1
ROMA		VAR	1	26
ROMANĒ	adverb	ENN			in the Roman way
ROMANI		FPLA		1	the Romans
ROMANI		FPLB		1
ROMANI		LUC		1
ROMANI		LUCR		1
ROMANI		MAN		1
ROMANI		MAR		1
ROMANI		PET		1
ROMANI		TIB	1	8
ROMANUM/FORUM		MAR		1	the Roman Forum, chief civic center
ROMANUM/FORUM		OV		1
ROMANUM/FORUM		PROP	1	3
ROMANUS & pl.		ENN		1	a Roman; Romans
ROMANUS		HOR		1
ROMANUS		JUV		1
ROMANUS		LUC		1
ROMANUS	& -a	MAR		1
ROMANUS		OV		1
ROMANUS		SIL		1
ROMANUS		V		1
ROMANUS		VAR	1	9

ROMANUS*	AV	1	p. to Rome, Roman
ROMANUS*	CAL	1	
ROMANUS*	COL	1	
ROMANUS*	COM	1	
ROMANUS*	ENN	1	
ROMANUS*	FPLA	1	
ROMANUS*	FPLB	1	
ROMANUS*	GER	1	
ROMANUS*	HOR	1	
ROMANUS*	JUV	1	
ROMANUS*	LP	1	
ROMANUS*	LUC	1	
ROMANUS*	LUCIL	1	
ROMANUS*	MAN	1	
ROMANUS*	MAR	1	
ROMANUS*	MLP	1	
ROMANUS*	OV	1	
ROMANUS*	PET	1	
ROMANUS*	PH	1	
ROMANUS*	PL	1	
ROMANUS*	PROP	1	
ROMANUS*	S	1	
ROMANUS*	SEN	1	
ROMANUS*	SIL	1	
ROMANUS*	TIB	1	
ROMANUS*	TR	1	
ROMANUS*	V	1	
ROMANUS*	VAL	1 28	
-ROMETHIUM v.l.	OV		a promontory (M. 15.705)
ROMULEUS	CAL	1	p. to Romulus
ROMULEUS	JUV	1	
ROMULEUS	MAR	1	
ROMULEUS	OV	1	
ROMULEUS	S	1	
ROMULEUS	SIL	1	
ROMULEUS	V	1 7	
ROMULIDAE patron.	LUCR	1	desc. of Romulus, i.e. the Romans
ROMULIDAE	PER	1	
ROMULIDAE	V	1 3	
ROMULUS	CAT	1	legendary founder of Rome, brother of Remus
ROMULUS	ENN	1	
ROMULUS	FPLA	1	
ROMULUS	FPLB	1	
ROMULUS	HOR	1	
ROMULUS	LUC	1	
ROMULUS	MAR	2	(+ a vintner)
ROMULUS	OV	1	
ROMULUS	PER	1	
ROMULUS	PROP	1	
ROMULUS	S	1	
ROMULUS	TIB	1	
ROMULUS	V	1 14	
ROMULUS*	HOR	1	p. to Romulus
ROMULUS*	OV	1	
ROMULUS*	PROP	1	
ROMULUS*	SIL	1	
ROMULUS*	V	1 5	

ROSCIUS	FPLA		1	cont. of Q. Catulus
ROSCIUS	HOR	2	3	Q. Roscius (a friend); unknown man
ROSCIUS* (lex)	HOR			a Roscian law
ROSEUS	V			p. to Rosea (area near Reate)
- ROTHUS 2.165	SIL			a Punic soldier
ROTUNDA line 435	AET			island in the Lipari group
- RUBELLIUS/BLANDUS	JUV			husband of Julia (8.39-40)
RUBER/PONTUS	MAN		1	Arabian Gulf
RUBER/PONTUS	SIL	1	2	
RUBI	HOR			town in Apulia
{ RUBICO	SIL			river in NE Italy
{ RUBICON	LUC			
RUBIGO fem.	COL			goddess of Rust (in wheat); cf. Robigo
RUBRAE = Saxa Rubra	MAR			a place on the Flaminian Way
- RUBRENUS/LAPPA 7.72	JUV			cont. poet
- RUBRIUS 4.105	JUV			R. Gallus (unknown)
RUBRUM sc. mare	PROP			Arabian Gulf
RUBRUM/MARE	LUC		1	"
RUBRUM/MARE	TIB	2	3	
RUDIAE	SIL			town of Calabria
RUDINI Ann. 377V	ENN			people of Rudiae
- RUFA 59.1	CAT		1	cont. woman
RUFA S. 2.3.216	HOR	1	2	fict. woman
- RUFILLUS S. 1.2.27	HOR			unknown cont.
- RUFINUS 3.31	MAR		1	fict. man
RUFINUS P. 1.3.1	OV	1	2	friend of Ovid
RUFRAE	SIL		1	town of Samnium
RUFRAE	V	1	2	
RUFULUS	CAT			cont. man
RUFUS	CAT		1	cont. man
RUFUS	FPLA		1	L. Plancus Rufus
RUFUS	FPLR		1	L. Verginius Rufus
RUFUS	HOR		1	R. Nasidienus
RUFUS	JUV		1	cont. of Cicero
RUFUS	MAR		4	four cont.
RUFUS	OV	2	11	a poet; Ovid's relation
RULLUS	SIL			a Roman soldier
RUMINUS adj.	OV			= Ruminalis (p. to goddess Rumina)
RUMOR F. 6.527	OV		1	god of Rumor
RUMOR 3.20.1	TIB	1	2	
-RUNCUS dub.	FPLA			(for Roscus ? cf. Gk. 'Poῖκος)
RUSO	HOR		1	a loan-shark
RUSO pl.	MAR	1	2	cont.
RUSPINA	SIL			town in N. Africa (Tunis)
-RUSTICUS 8.23.2	MAR			Antistius Rusticus, a cont.
RUTENI	LUC			tribe of Aquitania
-RUTILA 10.294	JUV			cont. woman
-RUTILIA	COM			a woman
RUTILIUS	OV			P. Rutilius Lupus
RUTILIUS/GALLICUS	S			R. G. Valens (poet and politician)
RUTILUS	JUV		2	two cont.
RUTILUS	SIL	1	3	a Roman soldier
RUTUBA m.	HOR		1	a gladiator
RUTUBA	LUC	1	2	a river in Liguria
RUTULI	OV		1	Ardeates
RUTULI	SIL	3	4	Ardeates; Romani; Saguntines
RUTULUS	JUV		1	Turnus, the Italic hero

RUTULUS		OV		1	Turnus
RUTULUS		SIL		1	a Roman soldier
RUTULUS		V	1	4	a Rutulian
RUTULUS*		JUV		1	p. to the Rutuli of Latium
RUTULUS*		OV		1	
RUTULUS*		SIL		1	
RUTULUS*		TIB		1	
RUTULUS*		V	1	5	
RUTUPĪNUS		JUV		1	p. to Rutupiae (t. in Britain)
RUTUPĪNUS		LUC	1	2	
SABAEA sc. terra		HOR			South Arabia ("Arabia Felix")
SABAEI		GR		1	the Sabaeans of S. Arabia
SABAEI		LUC		1	
SABAEI		MAR		1	
SABAEI		S		1	
SABAEI		VAL	1	5	
SABAEUS		COL		1	Arabian
SABAEUS		LUC		1	
SABAEUS		OV		1	
SABAEUS		S		1	
SABAEUS		SEN		1	
SABAEUS		V		1	
SABAEUS		VAL	1	7	
SABATIUS		SIL			p. to a lake (of Sabate in Etruria)
SABBURA cf. Sabura		LUC			soldier of Juba
SABELLA		MAR			fict. woman
SABELLI		COL			the Sabines
SABELLICUS adj.		V			Sabine
SABELLUS		HOR		1	a Sabine (= Horace)
SABELLUS		LUC		1	a soldier of Cato
SABELLUS		MAR		1	fict. person(s)
SABELLUS		SIL	1	4	a Roman soldier
SABELLUS*		HOR		1	Sabine
SABELLUS*		JUV		1	
SABELLUS*		LUC		1	
SABELLUS*		SIL		1	
SABELLUS*		V	1	5	
-SABIDIUS 1.32		MAR			fict. man
SABĪNA		JUV		1	a Sabine woman
SABINA		MAR		1	
SABINA		OV		1	
SABINA		S	1	4	
SABINAE pl.		LUC		1	Sabine women
SABINAE		PROP	1	2	
-SABINEIUS 3.25		MAR			fict. man
SABĪNI C. 2.18.14		HOR		1	HOR's Sabine farm (fundus)
SABINI		JUV		1	the Sabines
SABINI		MAR		1	
SABINI		PROP		1	
SABINI		SIL		1	
SABINI		V	1	6	
SABĪNUM C. 1.20.1		HOR		1	a wine
SABINUM		MAR	1	2	
SABĪNUS Cat.10.1		AV		1	a mule-driver
SABINUS		CAT		1	a Sabine man
SABINUS Epist.1.5.27		HOR		1	a friend; (also: any Sabine)
SABINUS		LUCIL		1	a Sabine

SABĪNUS		MAR	1	fict. man
SABĪNUS		OV	1	poet-friend
SABĪNUS		SIL	1 7	a Sabine man
SABĪNUS*	(Culex 404)	AV	1	Sabine
SABĪNUS*		CAT	1	
SÁBĪNUS*		HOR	1	
SABĪNUS*		JUV	1	
SABĪNUS*		LUC	1	
SABĪNUS*		MAR	1	
SABĪNUS*		OV	1	
SABĪNUS*		PER	1	
SABĪNUS*		PROP	1	
SABĪNUS*		V	1 10	
SABRATHA		SIL	2 2	town of N. Africa; a soldier
SABURA	cf. Sabb.	SIL		soldier of Juba
SABUS		SIL		eponymous ancestor of Sabines
SACAE		CAT		an Iranian people
SACER/MONS	5.123	MAN	1	a hill near Rome
SACER/MONS		OV	1 2	
SACES	nom.sg., 2.161	SIL	1	a Moor
SACES	" A.12.651	V	1 2	a Rutulian
SACRANUS		V		p. to the Sacrani (tribe of Latium)
SACRA/VIA		HOR	1	street in Rome
SACRA/VIA		OV	1	
SACRA/VIA		PROP	1 3	
SACRATOR		V		Rutulian warrior
SACRI/PORTUS		LUC		town in Latium
SADALA	m.	LUC		a king of Thrace
-SAENIA	12.26	MAR		fict. woman
SAEPTA	n.pl., (Julia)	MAR	1	part of Rome
SAEPTA		S	1 2	
-SAETABES		GR		people of Saetabis
SAETABIS		SIL		town of Spain
SAETABUS	adj.	CAT		p. to Saetabis
-SAFRONIUS	11.103.1	MAR		fict. man
-SAFRONIUS/RUFUS		MAR		cont. man (4.71)
SAGANA		HOR		a witch
SAGARIS		MAR	1	river in Phrygia
SAGARIS		OV	1	" "
SAGARIS		V	1 3	a Trojan
-SAGARISTIO	Pers. 16	PL		slave
SAGARITIS		OV		
-SAGES	T. 7.714	S	1	a Theban
SAGES		VAL	1 2	a Cyzican
SAGITTA		CIC	1	constell. (Arrow)
SAGITTA		GER	1	
SAGITTA		MAN	1 3	
SAGITTARIUS		CIC	1	constellation (Archer)
SAGITTARIUS		MAN	1 2	
SAGITTIFER		GER	1	constell. (Archer)
SAGITTIFER		MAN	1 2	
SAGITTIPOTENS		CIC	1	constell. (Archer)
SAGITTIPOTENS		FPLR	1 2	
SAGUNTĪNUS		JUV	1	p. to Saguntum
SAGUNTĪNUS		MAR	1	
SAGUNTĪNUS		SIL	1 3	
SAGUNTOS	fem.	SIL		town in Spain

SAGUNTUM	LUC		1	town in Spain
SAGUNTUM	MAR		1	
SAGUNTUM	S		1	
SAGUNTUM	SIL	1	4	
SAIS -is, fem.	LUC			town of Egypt
SALACIA	TR			ep. of the Sea
SALAMIN fem.	S			island in Saronic Gulf
SALAMINA	SEN			
SALAMINIACUS	LUC		1	p. to Salamis
SALAMINIACUS	SIL	1	2	
SALAMINIUS	AV		1	p. to Salamis
SALAMINIUS	HL		1	
SALAMINIUS	HOR	1	3	
SALAMIS cf. Salamin	HOR		2	island; town on Cyprus
SALAMIS	JUV		1	
SALAMIS	LUC		1	
SALAMIS	MAN		1	
SALAMIS	OV		1	
SALAMIS	TR		1	
SALAMIS	V	1	8	
-SALANUS (Sil-), 6.62	MAR		1	fict. man
SALANUS P. 2.5.1	OV	1	2	friend of Ovid
SALARIA	MAR			highway from Rome to Ancona
-SALEIANUS 2.65	MAR			fict. man
SALEIIUS	JUV			S. Bassus, a poet
SALENTINUS (-11-)	OV			p. to a tribe of Calabria
SALERNUM	HOR		1	town of the Picenti
SALERNUM	LUC	1	2	
SALERNUS	LUCIL		1	a resident of Salernum
SALERNUS	SIL	1	2	
SALES pl., S.1.6.6	S			"Wit"
SALIARIS	HOR			p. to the Salii
SALII	HOR		1	an order of priests at Rome
SALII	OV		1	
SALII	S		1	
SALII	V	1	4	
SALISUBSALUS em.	CAT			= Salii (a comic formation)
SALIUS	LUC		1	a priest (of Mars)
SALIUS	V	2	3	two different heroes
SALLENTINUS	SIL		1	p. to a tribe of Calabria
SALLENTINUS	V	1	2	
SALMACIS	ENN		1	type of sissy
SALMACIS	MAR		1	nymph & fountain
SALMACIS	OV		1	"
SALMACIS	S	1	4	"
SALMONEUS	MAN		1	myth. son of Aeolus
SALMONEUS	V		1	
SALMONEUS	VAL	1	3	
SALMONIS patr.	OV		1	Tyro, d. of Salmoneus
SALMONIS	PROP		1	
SALMONIS	VAL	1	3	
SALO m.	MAR			river of Spain
SALONAE	LUC		1	town of Illyria
SALONAE	MAR	1	2	
-SALONINUS N, 6.18	MAR			friend of Priscus
SALPINUS adj.	LUC			p. to Salapia (t. of Apulia)
SALUBRITAS	PL			"Health"(personification)

SALUS F. 3.882	OV		1	"Health"
SALUS	PL		1	
SALUS	TER	1	3	
SAME	SIL		1	island near Cephallenia
SAME	V	1	?	
SAMERAMIS (Semir.)	JUV			queen of Assyria
SAMII H. 1.87	OV			residents of Samos
SAMIOLUS dim. adj.	PL			Samian, of Samos
SAMIRAMIS	MAR			queen of Assyria
SAMIRAMIUS	MAR			p. to Samiramus
SAMIUS	OV		1	Pythagoras
SAMIUS	SIL	1	2	a Macedonian
SAMIUS*	HOR		1	p. to Samos
SAMIUS*	JUV		1	
SAMIUS*	LUCIL		1	
SAMIUS*	MAR		1	
SAMIUS*	OV		1	
SAMIUS*	PER		1	
SAMIUS*	PL		1	
SAMIUS*	TER		1	
SAMIUS*	TIB	1	9	
SAMNIS	LUC		1	the Samnites
SAMNIS	LUCIL		1	a kind of gladiator
SAMNIS	SIL	1	3	a Samnite
SAMNIS*	SIL			p. to the Samnites
SAMNITES	HOR			gladiators
SAMOS cf. -us, fem.	HOR		1	island in the E. Aegean
SAMOS	JUV		1	
SAMOS	LUC		1	
SAMOS	OV		2	(+ Cephallenia)
SAMOS	PRIAP		1	
SAMOS	S	1	7	
SAMOTHRACA	VAL			island near Thrace
SAMOTHRACES	JUV		1	people of Samothraca
SAMOTHRACES	S	1	2	" "
SAMOTHRACIA (= -ca)	V			island near Thrace
SAMOTHRACIUS	LUCR			p. to the island
SAMUS cf. Samos	PL		1	island in East Aegean
SAMUS	V	1	2	
{SANCTUS F. 6.214	PROP			a Sabine god
{SANCUS	OV		1	
{SANCUS	SIL	1	2	
-SANGA m. Eun. 776	TER			a slave
-SANGARINUS Stich.433	PL			slave
-SANGARIO Trin.1105	PL			slave
SANGARIUS (Sag-)	S			p. to Sagaris river
-SANNIO Ad. & Eun.	TER	2	2	slave; leno
SANTONICUS	JUV		1	p. to the Santoni (in Aquitania)
SANTONICUS	MAR		1	
SANTONICUS	TIB	1	3	
SANTONUS	LUC			tribe in Aquitania
SANTRA m.	MAR	2	2	cont.; fict.
SAPAEI	OV			Thracian tribe
-SAPHARUS 7.604	SIL			Punic soldier
SAPIENTIA personif.	COM			"Wisdom"
SAPIS m.	LUC		1	river in N. Italy
SAPIS	SIL	1	2	

SAPPHICUS	CAT			p. to Sappho, the poetess
SAPPHO	HOR	1		poetess of Lesbos
SAPPHO	MAR	1		
SAPPHO	OV	1		
SAPPHO	S	1	4	
SARAPIS m.	CAT	1		Egyptian god
SARAPIS	MAR	1	2	
SARDANAPALLUS	JUV	1		king of Assyria
SARDANAPALLUS	MAR	1		
SARDANAPALLUS	OV	1	3	
SARDI	PL			people of Sardinia
SARDIANUS	FPLA			p. to Sardis
SARDINIA	HOR	1		the island
SARDINIA	MAN	1		
SARDINIA	MAR	1	3	
SARDINIENSIS	LUCIL			p. to Sardinia
SARDĪS fem.pl.	HOR	1		town of Lydia
SARDIS	OV	1		
SARDIS	VAR	1	3	
SARDONIUS	V			p. to Sardinia
SARDŌUS	LUC	1		p. to Sardinia
SARDOUS	MAR	1		
SARDOUS	OV	1		
SARDOUS	SIL	1	4	
SARDUS 12.359	SIL			name of a Libyan man
SARDUS*	FPLR	1		p. to Sardinia
SARDUS*	HOR	1	2	
SARMATA m.sg.	JUV		1	a Sarmatian (of Central Europe)
SARMATA	LUC		1	
SARMATA	MAR		1	
SARMATA also pl.	SEN	1	4	
SARMATAE pl.	S		1	the Sarmatians (cf. Sauromatae)
SARMATAE	VAL	1	2	
SARMATICĒ adverb	OV			in Sarmatian language
SARMATICUS	LUC		1	p. to the Sarmatians
SARMATICUS	MAR		1	
SARMATICUS	OV		1	
SARMATICUS	S		1	
SARMATICUS	SEN		1	
SARMATICUS	SIL		1	
SARMATICUS	VAL	1	7	
SARMATIS adj.	OV			Sarmatian
- SARMENS 4.200	SIL			a Gaulish soldier
- SARMENTUS	FPLR		1	an Etruscan
SARMENTUS S. 1.5.56	HOR		1	a freedman
SARMENTUS 5.3	JUV	1	3	a cont. dandy
SARNUS	LUC		1	river in Campania
SARNUS	S		1	
SARNUS	SIL		1	
SARNUS	V	1	4	
SARPEDON	HL		1	legendary king of Lycia
SARPEDON	OV		1	
SARPEDON	V	1	3	
SARRA	ENN			town of Tyre (in Phoenicia)
SARRANUS	COL		1	Tyrian
SARRANUS	JUV		1	
SARRANUS	SIL		2	; Punic

SARRANUS	V	1	5	Tyrian
SARRASTES pl.	SIL		1	tribe of Campania
SARRASTES	V	1	2	
SARSINATIS nom.fem.	PL			a woman of Sarsina (<u>Most</u>. 770)
SASON	LUC		1	island off Illyria
SASON	SIL	1	2	
SASSINA	MAR		1	town of Umbria
SASSINA	SIL	1	2	
SASSINAS adj.	MAR			p. to Sassina
-SATARCHAE 6.144	VAL			unknown tribe
SATICULUS N	V			a man from Saticula (Samnite town)
SATOR	CIC		1	"Father", ep. of Juppiter
SATOR	PROP	1	2	
-SATRACHUS 95.5	CAT			river of Cyprus
SATRICUS	SIL			warrior
-SATTIA 3.93.20	MAR			a crone
SATURA	LUCR		1	a girl
SATURA	SIL		1	lake in Latium
SATURA	V	1	3	" "
SATUREIANUS adj.	HOR			Apuleian
SATURIO	PL			name of a parasite
SATURITAS	PL			(comic) name of goddess of Full Belly
SATURNALIA n.pl.	CAT		1	festival of Saturn in late December
SATURNALIA	COM		1	
SATURNALIA	HOR		1	
SATURNALIA	MAR		1	
SATURNALIA	S	1	5	
SATURNALICIUS	MAR			p. to the Saturnalia
SATURNIA fem. sg.	OV		2	Juno; town on Capitoline hill
SATURNIA	S		1	Juno
SATURNIA	SIL		1	
SATURNIA	TIB		1	
SATURNIA	V		1	(also the town: <u>A</u>. 8.358)
SATURNIA	VAL	1	7	
SATURNINUS N	MAR			Antonius Saturninus, a tribune
SATURNIUS N, Spur. 8W	ENN		1	Juppiter
SATURNIUS <u>M</u>.	OV	2	3	Juppiter; Pluto
SATURNIUS*	CIC		1	Saturnian (i.e. p. to Saturn, Juppiter)
SATURNIUS*	ENN		1	
SATURNIUS*	FPLA		1	
SATURNIUS*	GER		1	
SATURNIUS*	HL		1	
SATURNIUS*	HOR		1	
SATURNIUS*	LUC		1	
SATURNIUS*	OV		1	
SATURNIUS*	PER		1	
SATURNIUS*	PET		1	
SATURNIUS* (parens)	S		1	
SATURNIUS*	SIL		1	
SATURNIUS*	V		1	
SATURNIUS*	VAL	1	14	
SATURNUS	AET		1	old Italic god (of farming & culture)
SATURNUS	CAL		1	
SATURNUS	ENN		1	
SATURNUS	FPLA		1	
SATURNUS	FPLR		1	
SATURNUS	GER		1	

SATURNUS		HOR	2	old Italic god; the planet
SATURNUS		JUV	1	the god
SATURNUS	1.652	LUC	1	planet
SATURNUS		LUCIL	1	god
SATURNUS		LUCR	1	
SATURNUS		MAN	2	(+ planet)
SATURNUS		MAR	1	
SATURNUS		MLP	1	
SATURNUS		OV	1	
SATURNUS		PER	1	
SATURNUS		PL	1	
SATURNUS		PROP	1	
SATURNUS		S	1	
SATURNUS		SEN	1	
SATURNUS		SIL	1	
SATURNUS		TIB	1	
SATURNUS		TR	1	
SATURNUS		V	1	
SATURNUS		VAL	1 27	
SATYRI		AV	1	myth. forest-gods, half-goat
SATYRI		CAL	1	
SATYRI		CAT	1	
SATYRI		COL	1	
SATYRI		HOR	2	(+ a satyr-play)
SATYRI		MAR	1	
SATYRI		OV	1 8	
SATYROS	sg.	LUCR		a satyr
SATYRUS		OV	1	Marsyas
SATYRUS		PER	1	
SATYRUS	also pl.	S	1	Marsyas
SATYRUS		SIL	1 4	
SAUFEIA		JUV	1	priestess of the Bona Dea
SAUFEIA		MAR	1 2	fict.
SAUFEIUS		MAR		fict.
SAUREA	m.	PL		a male slave
SAUROCTONOS		MAR		Greek ep. of Apollo
SAUROMATAE		JUV	1	tribe of Russia (cf. Sarmatae)
SAUROMATAE		MAR	1	
SAUROMATAE		OV	1	
SAUROMATAE		S	1	
SAUROMATAE		VAL	1 5	
SAUROMATES		OV		the same tribe (-es = -ae)
-SAVO	S. 4.3.66	S		river of Campania
SAXETANUS		MAR		p. to Sex (t. in Spain)
SAXUM	sc. sacrum	OV		a place on the Aventine hill
SCAEAE		PROP		gate of Troy
SCAEAE/PORTAE		V		
SCAEA/PORTA		SIL		
SCAEVA	m.	HOR	2	two unknown contemporaries
SCAEVA		LUC	1 3	a centurion of Caesar
-SCAEVINUS	3.70	MAR		fict. man
SCAEVOLA	m.	LUC	1	cognomen of legendary C. Mucius
SCAEVOLA		MAN	1	
SCAEVOLA		MAR	1	
SCAEVOLA		SIL	1 4	
SCAMANDER		CAT	1	river of Troy
SCAMANDER		ENN	1	

SCAMANDER	HOR	1	3	river of Troy
SCAMANDRIUS	TR			p. to Scamander
SCANTINIA (lex)	JUV			a law
-SCAPHA Most. 158	PL			a maid
SCAPTENSULA	LUCR			town of Thrace
SCAPTIUS adj.	SIL			p. to Scaptia (t. in Latium)
-SCARPHE Tr. 848	SEN			town in Locris
SCAURI	HOR		1	Roman family
SCAURI 2.35	JUV	1	2	
SCAURUS	SIL			Roman general
-SCELEDRUS Miles 276	PL			a slave
SCELERATUS/VICUS	OV			a place on the Esquiline hill
SCELUS Pers. 558	PL			"Crime" personified
-SCEPARNIO Rud. 97	PL			a slave
SCEPSIUS	OV			Metrodorus Scepsius, a philosopher
-SCETANUS S. 1.4.112	HOR			fict. man
-SCHEDIA Vid. 6	PL			title of a comedy
-SCHEDIUS	HL			Greek hero
SCHOENEIA	OV			Atalanta
SCHOENEIS	OV		1	Atalanta
SCHOENEIS	PRIAP	1	2	"
SCHOENEIUS	OV			p. to Schoeneus (k. of Boeotia)
-SCHOENOS T. 7.268	S			town of Boeotia
SCIATHOS fem.	VAL			island in Thermaic Gulf
SCIPIADAE m.pl.	AV		1	desc. of Scipio, the Scipio family
SCIPIADAE	JUV		1	
SCIPIADAE	LUCR		1	
SCIPIADAE	V	1	4	
SCIPIADAS nom.sg.	LUCIL		1	a Scipio
SCIPIADAS	MAN	1	2	
SCIPIADES nom.sg.	HOR		1	a Scipio
SCIPIADES	PROP		1	
SCIPIADES	SIL	1	3	
SCIPIŎ	ENN		1	Sc. Africanus
SCIPIO	LUC		2	Africanus; Metellus
SCIPIO	MAR		1	Africanus
SCIPIO AA 3.410	OV		1	"
SCIPIO	S		1	"
SCIPIO	SIL	5	11	P. C. Scipio (consul 218 BC)
SCIRON	AV		1	legendary robber
SCIRON	OV		1	
SCIRON	PROP		1	
SCIRON	S		1	
SCIRON	SIL	1	5	
SCIRONIS adj.	SEN			p. to Attic coast (where Sciron lived)
SCIRONIUS adj.	SEN			
-SCIRTUS Hec. 78	TER			a slave
SCOLOS fem.	S			town of Boeotia
SCOPAS	HOR		1	Greek sculptor
SCOPAS	MAR		1	
SCOPAS	PRIAP	1	3	
SCORPIOS	AV		1	sign of the Zodiac "Scorpion"
SCORPIOS	CIC		1	
SCORPIOS	GER		1	
SCORPIOS	HOR		1	
SCORPIOS	LUC		1	
SCORPIOS	MAN		1	

SCORPIOS		OV		1	sign of the Zodiac
SCORPIOS		V	1	8	
-SCORPUS	passim	MAR			cont. charioteer
SCORTUM	Capt. 69	PL			cognomen of a parasite
SCRIBONIA		PROP			mother of Cornelia
-SCYBALE	Mor. 31	AV			a slave-girl
⎧SCYLACEON		VAL			Greek town in Bruttium
⎩SCYLACEUM		V			" "
SCYLACEUS	adj.	OV			p. to Scylaceus
SCYLLA	also pl.	AV		1	rock; d. of Nisus
SCYLLA		CAT		1	rock-monster
SCYLLA		HOR		1	
SCYLLA		JUV		1	
SCYLLA		MAN		1	
SCYLLA		MAR		2	(+ a slave-woman)
SCYLLA		OV		2	d. of Nisus; d. of Phorcys
SCYLLA		PROP		2	rock-monster; d. of Nisus
SCYLLA		SEN		1	rock-monster
SCYLLA		SIL		1	"
SCYLLA		TIB		1	daughter of Phorcys
SCYLLA		V	3	17	rock; d. of Nisus; a ship
SCYLLAE	4.730, 5.890	LUCR		1	a class of monsters
SCYLLAE	T. 4.533	S	1	2	" "
SCYLLAEUS		AV		1	p. to Scylla (rock)
SCYLLAEUS		LUC		1	
SCYLLAEUS		S		1	p. to d. of Nisus, Megarean
SCYLLAEUS		SIL		1	p. to Scylla (rock)
SCYLLAEUS		V	1	5	
-SCYLLEIUS	Maec. 107	AV			p. to the rock of Scylla
SCYREIDES	fem.pl.	S			maidens of Scyros
SCYRIADES	fem.pl.	S			
SCYRIAS	adj.	OV			p. to Scyros
SCYRIUS	adj.	OV		1	p. to Scyros
SCYRIUS		PROP		1	
SCYRIUS		S		1	
SCYRIUS		SEN		1	
SCYRIUS		V	1	5	
SCYROS	fem.	CAT		1	Aegean island
SCYROS		S	1	2	
SCYRUS		OV		1	
SCYRUS		SEN	1	2	
SCYTHA	m.	LUC		1	a Scythian
SCYTHA		MAR	1	2	
SCYTHAE		VAR			Scythians
SCYTHA*	(Pontus)	S			p. to Scythia
SCYTHES	m.sg.	HOR		1	a Scythian
SCYTHES		PH		1	
SCYTHES		SEN	1	3	
SCYTHIA		LUC		1	large, indefinite region of E. Europe
SCYTHIA		MAN		1	
SCYTHIA		OV		1	
SCYTHIA		PROP		1	
SCYTHIA		S		1	
SCYTHIA		SEN		1	
SCYTHIA		TIB		1	
SCYTHIA		V		1	
SCYTHIA		VAL	1	9	

SCYTHICUS	HOR	1		Scythian
SCYTHICUS	JUV	1		
SCYTHICUS	LUC	1		
SCYTHICUS	MAN	1		
SCYTHICUS	MAR	1		
SCYTHICUS	MLP	1		
SCYTHICUS	OV	1		
SCYTHICUS	PROP	1		
SCYTHICUS	S	1		
SCYTHICUS	SEN	1		
SCYTHICUS	SIL	1		
SCYTHICUS	VAL	1	12	
SCYTHIDES fem.pl.	VAL			Scythian women
SCYTHIS	OV			a Scythian woman
-SCYTHOLATRONIA Mil.43	PL			an implausible country (comic formation)
SEBETHIS*	COL	1		p. to the Sebethos
SEBETHIS*	V	1	2	
SEBETHOS m.	S			river near Naples
-SECUNDILLA 2.65	MAR			fict. woman
SECUNDUS	MAR	4	4	four cont. men
SECUNDUS/CARRINAS	JUV			a rhetorician (time of Caligula)
SEDES/SCELERATA	OV			torture-place in Underworld
-SEDETANUS adj. (?)	SIL			p. to a Spanish tribe (3.372)
SEDITIO personific.	OV			attendant of Fama (M. 12.61)
-SEGIUS 4.21	MAR			fict. person
SEIIUS 4.13	JUV			fict. person
SEJANUS 10.63	JUV	1		L. Aelius Sejanus, minister of Tiberius
SEJANUS 3, prol. 41	PH	1	2	" " "
-SELENIUM Cist. 22	PL			a meretrix
SELEUCIA Trin. 771	PL			a town in Near East (uncertain)
SELEUCUS	JUV		1	a citharist
SELEUCUS	PL	1	2	king of Syria
SELINUS -nt-	LUC		1	river of Sicily
SELINUS	SIL		1	town in Sicily
SELINUS	V	1	3	" "
-SELIUS Cat. 5.3	AV		1	rhetorician
SELIUS 2.11	MAR		1	fict.
SELIUS 17.429	SIL	1	3	a Roman soldier
-SELLOE Gk. pl., 3.180	LUC			tribe of Epirus
SEMELA	PROP		1	daughter of Cadmus & m. of Bacchus
SEMELA	TR	1	2	
SEMELE	AV		1	
SEMELE	HOR		1	
SEMELE	MAR		1	
SEMELE	OV		1	
SEMELE	S		1	
SEMELE	SEN		1	
SEMELE	TIB	1	7	
SEMELEIUS	HOR		1	p. to Semele
SEMELEIUS	OV		1	
SEMELEIUS	S	1	3	
SEMELEUS	S			p. to Semele
SEMIGRAECEI adv.?	LUCIL			in half-Greek fashion (391W)
SEMIRAMIS cf. Same-	OV		1	queen of Assyria
SEMIRAMIS	PROP	1	2	
SEMIRAMIUS adj.	OV			p. to Semiramis
SEMO F. 6.214	OV			ep. of Sancus

SEMPRONIA 12.52	MAR			cont. woman (w. of Rufus?)
SEMPRONIUS/TUCCA	MAR			a cont. man (7.41)
SENA	LUC	1		river of Umbria
SENA	SIL	1	2	
SENECA	JUV		1	Seneca the Younger, Stoic philosopher
SENECA	MAR		1	
SENECA	S		1	
SENECA Oct. 589	SEN	1	4	"Old Age" (13.583)
SENECTUS personif.	SIL		1	
SENECTUS A. 6.275	V	1	2	
SENONES	JUV		1	a Gaulish tribe
SENONES	LUC		1	
SENONES	S		1	
SENONES	SIL	1	4	
SEPIAS	VAL			promontory of Magnesia
SEPLASIA fem.	COM			street in Capua
SEPTEMBER adj.	COM		1	the month
SEPTEMBER	HOR		1	
SEPTEMBER	JUV	1	3	
SEPTEM/TRIONES	CIC		1	constellation (Great Dipper)
SEPTEM/TRIONES	OV	1	2	
SEPTENTRIONES	PL		1	
SEPTENTRIONES	VAR	1	2	
-SEPTICIANUS 11.107	MAR			fict. man
SEPTICIANUS*	MAR			p. to a Septicius in Roman legend
-SEPTICIUS Ep. 1.5.26	HOR			friend of Horace
-SEPTIMILLUS (dimin.)	CAT			unknown (45.13)
SEPTIMIUS	CAT		1	" (45.1: same person)
SEPTIMIUS	HOR		1	a friend
SEPTIMIUS	S	1	3	S. Severus, a friend
SEQUANICUS	MAR			p. to the Sequani
SEQUANUS	LUC			" " "
SER also pl.	SEN			a Chinese
SERAPIS cf. Sarapis	VAR			Egyptian god
SERENUS	MAR			Annaeus Serenus (friend of Seneca)
SERES	FPLB		1	the Chinese
SERES	GR		1	(Tibetan?: breed of dog)
SERES	HOR		1	
SERES	JUV		1	
SERES	LUC		1	
SERES	MAR		1	
SERES	OV		1	
SERES	PET		1	
SERES	S		1	
SERES	SIL		1	
SERES	V	1	11	
SERESTUS	V			a Trojan
SERGESTUS	V			"
-SERGIOLUS 6.105	JUV			a gladiator
SERGIUS	JUV			(same man)
SERGIUS* A. 5.121	V			p. to the Sergii family
SERICA n.pl.	MAR			Chinese silks
SERICUS	HOR		1	p. to the Seres (often: 'silken)
SERICUS	MAR		1	
SERICUS	PROP		1	
SERICUS	S	1	4	
SERIPHOS fem.	JUV		1	island in the Cyclades

⎧ SERIPHOS	S	1	2	island in the Cyclades
⎨ SERIPHUS	AV		1	
⎩ SERIPHUS	OV	1	2	
SERMO Bacch. 116	PL			"Chitchat" personified
SERPENS	CIC		1	constellation
SERPENS	GER		1	
SERPENS	MAN		1	
SERPENS	OV	1	4	
SERRANUS	GR		1	C. Atilius Regulus, legendary consul
SERRANUS	JUV		1	a poet
SERRANUS 4.148, pl.	MAN		1	(as type)
SERRANUS	MAR		1	fict.
SERRANUS	SIL		1	C. Atilius Regulus
SERRANUS	V	2	7	C. Atil. Reg.; a Rutulian
SERTORIUS 6.142	JUV		1	unknown
SERTORIUS	LUC		1	Q. Sertorius (general of Marius)
SERTORIUS	MAR	1	3	fict. man
SERVILIA	JUV			a lustful woman
SERVILIUS	ENN		1	Serv. Geminus (consul 217 BC)
SERVILIUS	SIL	1	2	Gn. Servilius
-SERVILIUS/BALATRO	HOR			parasite of Maecenas (S. 2.8.21)
SERVITUS personif.	PL			"Slavery" (Asin. 306)
SERVIUS	COM		1	fict.
SERVIUS	HOR		1	Serv. Sulpicius (?)
SERVIUS 4.213	MAN		1	" "
SERVIUS	OV		1	poet
SERVIUS	PET		1	lawyer
SERVIUS	TIB	1	6	cont.
-SERVIUS/OPPIDIUS	HOR			a cont. (from Canusium) (S. 2.3.168)
SESCENTOPLAGUS	PL			comic name of a slave (Capt. 726)
SESOSTRIS	LUC		1	a king of Egypt
SESOSTRIS 5.418	VAL	1	2	" "
SESTIACUS adj.	S			p. to Sestos
SESTIANUS	CAT			
SESTIAS adj.	S			p. to Sestos
SESTIUS	CAT		1	P. Sestius, trib.plebis 56 BC
SESTIUS	HOR	1	2	L. S. Quirinus, a consul
⎧ SESTOS	LUC		1	town in Thrace
⎪ SESTOS	S		1	
⎨ SESTOS	SEN		1	
⎪ SESTOS	VAL	1	4	
⎩ SESTUS	OV			
SETIA	COM		1	town of Latium
SETIA	MAR		1	
SETIA	S		1	
SETIA	SIL	1	4	
SETĪNUM	JUV		1	wine of Setia
SETINUM	MAR	1	2	
SETĪNUS (Titin. 121)	COM		1	p. to Setia
SETINUS	JUV		1	
SETINUS	LUCIL		1	
SETINUS	MAR	1	4	
-SETUS = Zethus (?)	TR			myth. personage
SEVERUS	MAR		2	two cont.
SEVERUS	OV		1	Cornelius Severus, poet friend
SEVERUS	S		1	Septimius Severus
SEVERUS	V	1	5	a mt. (in Sabine territory)

−SEVIUS/NICANOR	FPLA			a freedman
SEXTILIANUS N	MAR			a cont.
SEXTILIS	HOR			month of August
−SEXTILLUS 2.28	MAR			fict. man
SEXTUS	COM	1		fict.
SEXTUS	JUV	1		fict.
SEXTUS	LUC	1		Sextus Pompeius
SEXTUS	MAR	?		two cont.
SEXTUS P. 4.1.2	OV	1	6	S. Pompeius
−SEXTUS/SABINUS	AV			a young man (Cat. 5.7)
−SIBOTES 6.249	VAL			a Colchian
SIBULLA Pseud. 25	PL			a prophetess
SIBYLLA	GR	1		
SIBYLLA	JUV	1		
SIBYLLA	LUC	1		
SIBYLLA	MAR	1		
SIBYLLA	OV	1		
SIBYLLA	PRIAP	1		
SIBYLLA	PROP	1		
SIBYLLA	S	1		
SIBYLLA	SIL	1		
SIBYLLA	TIB	1		
SIBYLLA	V	1	11	
SIBYLLĪNUS (versus)	HOR			books of the Sibyl
SICANI	V			a tribe of Sicily
SICANIA 6.66	LUC	1		Sicily
SICANIA	OV	1		
SICANIA	SIL	1		
SICANIA	V	1	4	
SICANIS adj.	OV			p. to Sicania, Sicilian
SICANIUS	COL	1		Sicanian, Sicilian
SICANIUS	LUC	1		
SICANIUS	MAR	1		
SICANIUS	OV	1		
SICANIUS	PET	1		
SICANIUS	S	1		
SICANIUS	SEN	1		
SICANIUS	SIL	1		
SICANIUS	V	1		
SICANIUS	VAL	1	10	
SICANUS	HOR	1		Sicanian, Sicilian
SICANUS	OV	1		
SICANUS	PROP	1		
SICANUS	S	1		
SICANUS	SIL	1		
SICANUS	V	1	6	
SICCA	COL			town in Numidia
−SICCHA 9.385	SIL			a Punic man
SICELIDES 14.467	SIL	1		Sicilian women (Muses)
SICELIDES	V	1	2	
SICELIS	OV			a Sicilian woman
SICILIA	ENN	1		island of Sicily
SICILIA	PL	1	2	
SICILIENSES	FPLA			people of Sicily
SICILIENSIS	PL			Sicilian
SICORIS	LUC	1		river in Spain
SICORIS	SIL	2	3	(+ a man's name)

SICULI	AET	1	people of Sicily
SICULI	GR	1	
SICULI	LUCR	1	
SICULI T. 3.11.55	OV	1 4	
SICULUS	PL	1	a Sicilian
SICULUS	SIL	2 3	" ; a Ligurian chief
SICULUS*	AET	1	Sicilian
SICULUS*	FPLB	1	
SICULUS*	HOR	1	
SICULUS*	JUV	1	
SICULUS*	LUC	1	
SICULUS*	LUCIL	1	
SICULUS*	MAN	1	
SICULUS*	MAR	1	
SICULUS*	OV	1	
SICULUS*	PER	1	
SICULUS*	PET	1	
SICULUS*	PH	1	
SICULUS*	PROP	1	
SICULUS*	S	1	
SICULUS*	SEN	1	
SICULUS*	SIL	1	
SICULUS*	V	1	
SICULUS*	VAL	1 18	
SICYON	JUV	1	town in N. Peloponnese
SICYON	OV	1	
SICYON	PL	1	
SICYON	S	1 4	
SICYONIA n.pl.	AV	1	brand of shoes
SICYONIA n.pl.	LUCIL	1	" " (1156W)
SICYONIA	LUCR	1	" "
SICYONIA fem.sg.	PL	1 4	a girl from Sicyon (Cist. Arg.1.2)
SICYONIUS M. 3.216	OV	1	p. to Sicyon
SICYONIUS	S	1	
SICYONIUS	V	1 3	
SIDE AA 1.731, conj.	OV		town in Pamphylia
SIDICĪNUS	SIL	1	p. to Sidicini (tribe in Campania)
SIDICĪNUS	V	1 2	
SIDON	LUC	1	town in Phoenicia
SIDON	LUCR	1	
SIDON	MAR	1	
SIDON	OV	1	
SIDON	SIL	1	
SIDON	V	1	
SIDON	VAL	2 8	(+ a Scythian)
SIDONES	VAL		Scythian tribe
SIDONII F. 3.108	OV	1	Phoenicians
SIDONII	S	1	(Thebans)
SIDONII	SEN	1 3	Phoenicians
SIDONIS	OV	3	Dido; Anna; Europe
SIDONIS	S	1	Europa
SIDONIS	SIL	1 5	Anna
SIDONIS*	OV		Phoenician
SIDONIUS N	OV	1	
SIDONIUS	SIL	2 3	Hasdrubal; Hannibal
SIDONIUS*	AV	1	Phoenician, hence Punic
SIDONIUS*	GER	1	

SIDONIUS*	HOR	1	Phoenician; Punic
SIDONIUS*	LUC	1	
SIDONIUS*	MAR	1	
SIDONIUS*	PROP	1	
SIDONIUS*	S	2	(+ Theban)
SIDONIUS*	SEN	1	
SIDONIUS*	SIL	1	
SIDONIUS*	TIB	1	
SIDONIUS*	V	1	
SIDONIUS*	VAL	1 13	
SIGĒON = -um	SEN		promontory in Troad
-SIGERUS 4.78.8	MAR		valet of Domitian
SIGĒUS	AV	1	p. to Sigeum, i.e. Trojan
SIGEUS	LUC	1	
SIGEUS or -eius	OV	2	
SIGEUS	S	1	
SIGEUS	SEN	1	
SIGEUS	SIL	1	
SIGEUS	V	1	
SIGEUS	VAL	1 9	
SIGNIA	COL	1	town in Latium
SIGNIA Capt. 882	PL	1	
SIGNIA	SIL	1 3	
SIGNIFER sc. Orbis	CIC		the Zodiac
SIGNĪNUM	MAR		wine of Signia
SIGNĪNUS	JUV		p. to Signia
SILA 11.23	MAR	1	fict. girl
SILA	V	1 2	forest in Bruttium
-SILAI 4.55.20	MAR		tribe of Spain
SILANUS	JUV	1	fict.
SILANUS Oct. 148	SEN	1	a Roman
SILANUS	SIL	1 3	a Roman general
SILAR m., cf. Siler	LUCIL		river in Campania
SILARUS	SIL	2	" (+ a soldier)
SILARUS	V	1 3	"
-SILENA 4.1169	LUCR		a girl
SILENI	CAT		satyrs
SILENTIA T. 10.91	S		
SILENUS	HOR	1	a satyr, comp. of Bacchus
SILENUS	OV	1	
SILENUS	PROP	1	
SILENUS	SEN	1	
SILENUS	V	1 5	
SILER cf. Silar	COL	1	river in Campania
SILER	LUC	1 2	
SILIUS	MAR		Silius Italicus, the poet
SILO	CAT		a cont.
SILVANI	LUC	1	woodland gods
SILVANI M. 1.193	OV	1 ?	
SILVANUS	CAL	1	a god of the woods
SILVANUS	GR	1	
SILVANUS	HOR	1	
SILVANUS	JUV	1	
SILVANUS	MAR	1	
SILVANUS	PL	1	
SILVANUS	PROP	1	
SILVANUS	S	1	

SILVANUS	TR		1	a god of the woods
SILVANUS	V	1	10	
SILVIA	MAR		1	daughter of Numitor, legendary priestess
SILVIA	OV		1	
SILVIA	V	1	3	
-SILVINUS	COL			a friend of Columella
SILVIUS	OV		1	Silvius Postumus, k. of Alba
SILVIUS	V	1	2	son of Aeneas
-SILVIUS/AENEAS	V			king of Alba (A. 6.769)
-SIMAETHUS Sym-	AET			river in Sicily
-SIMALIO Eun. 772	TER			a slave
SIMBRUVIUM	SIL			part of Latium
SIMIA m.	PL			a male slave
SIMO	COM		1	a senex
SIMO	HOR		1	"
SIMO	PL		2	two senes
SIMO	TER	1	5	a senex
SIMOIS -nt-, m.	AV		1	river in the Troad
SIMOIS	HOR		1	
SIMOIS	LUC		1	
SIMOIS	OV		1	
SIMOIS	PROP		1	
SIMOIS	S		1	
SIMOIS	SEN		1	
SIMOIS	SIL		1	
SIMOIS	V	1	9	
SIMONIDES 4.22.2	PH			the Greek poet
SIMONIDEUS	CAT			p. to Simonides
SIMULUS Ad. 352	TER			a senex
SIMUS Heaut. 498	TER			a senex
-SIMYLUS Mor. 3	AV			a farmer
SINDI	VAL			the people of India
SINIS	OV		1	the bandit of Corinth
SINIS	PROP		1	
SINIS	S		1	
SINIS	SEN	1	4	
SINO Bacch. 937	PL			a fict. Achaean
SINON	PET		1	the treacherous Trojan
SINON 3, Prol. 27	PH		1	
SINON Tr. 39	SEN		1	
SINON	V	1	4	
SINOPE	VAL			town of Paphlagonia
SINOPES pl., Curc.443	PL			tribe (?)
SINOPEUS	OV			p. to Sinope
-SINTIUS* or Sintus	OV			?? (T. 4.1.21)
SINUESSA	HOR		1	town in Campania
SINUESSA	MAR		1	
SINUESSA	OV		1	
SINUESSA	SIL	1	4	
SINUESSANUS	HOR		1	p. to Sinuessa
SINUESSANUS	MAR	1	2	
SIPUS -nt-, fem.	LUC		1	= Sipuntum (t. in Apulia)
SIPUS	SIL	1	2	
SIPYLEIUS	S			p. to Sipylus
SIPYLOS	S			mt. in Lydia
SIPYLUS	OV		2	mt.; son of Niobe
SIPYLUS	PROP		1	mt. in Lydia

SIPYLUS	SEN	1	4	mt. in Lydia
SIREN	FPLR		1	mythical bird-woman
SIREN	HOR		1	
SIREN	JUV		1	
SIREN	S		1	
SIREN	SEN		1	
SIREN	SIL	2	7	(+ a ship)
SIRENES	MAR		1	bird-women
SIRENES	OV		1	
SIRENES	PET		1	
SIRENES	PROP		1	
SIRENES	TIB		1	
SIRENES	V	1	6	
-SIRĪNUS M. 15.52	OV			p. to Siris (t. in Lucania)
SIRIUS	AET		1	the dog-star (Canicula)
SIRIUS	GER		1	
SIRIUS	LUC		1	
SIRIUS	MAR		1	
SIRIUS	PRIAP		1	
SIRIUS	S		1	
SIRIUS	SIL		1	
SIRIUS	TIB		1	
SIRIUS	V		1	
SIRIUS	VAL	1	10	
SIRIUS*	COL		1	p. to the dog star
SIRIUS*	V	1	2	
SIRMIO	CAT			peninsula in lake Benacus
-SIRON Cat. 5.9	AV			Epicurean philosopher
SISENNA	HOR		1	cont. slanderer
SISENNA	OV	1	2	L. Cornelius Sisenna (historian)
SISYPHIDES patron.	OV			ep. of Ulixes
SISYPHIUS	OV		1	p. to Sisyphus (hence: Corinthian)
SISYPHIUS	PROP		1	
SISYPHIUS	S		1	
SISYPHIUS	SEN		1	
SISYPHIUS	SIL	1	5	
SISYPHUS	HOR		2	legendary king of Corinth; (a dwarf)
SISYPHUS	LUCR		1	king
SISYPHUS	MAR		1	
SISYPHUS	OV		1	
SISYPHUS	PH		1	
SISYPHUS	PROP		1	
SISYPHUS	SEN	1	8	
SITHONES	OV			Thracian tribe
SITHONIS	OV			a Thracian woman
SITHONIS*	OV			Sithonian (Thracian)
SITHONIUS	HOR		1	p. to Sithon in Thrace, Thracian
SITHONIUS	OV		1	
SITHONIUS	S		1	
SITHONIUS	SEN		1	
SITHONIUS	V	1	5	
SMILAX M. 4.283	OV			a legendary girl
SMINTHEUS cf. Zm-	OV			ep. of Apollo
SMYRNA	FPLR		1	a girl
SMYRNA	HOR		1	town in Ionia
SMYRNA P. 1.3.65	OV		1	"
SMYRNA	S	1	4	"

SMYRNAEUS	SIL			p. to Smyrna (town)
SOCRATES	LUCIL	1		the Greek philosopher
SOCRATES	MAR	1		
SOCRATES pl.	MLP	1		
SOCRATES	PH	1		
SOCRATES	PL	1		
SOCRATES	VAR	1	6	
SOCRATICI	LUCIL			followers of Socrates
SOCRATICUS	HOR	1		p. to Socrates
SOCRATICUS	JUV	1		
SOCRATICUS	OV	1		
SOCRATICUS	PER	1		
SOCRATICUS	PET	1		
SOCRATICUS	PROP	1	6	
-SOCRATION 47.1	CAT			a cont. (nickname)
SOL	AV	1		the Sun (= Apollo, Phoebus)
SOL	CAL	1		
SOL	CAT	1		
SOL	CIC	1		
SOL	FPLA	1		
SOL	FPLB	1		
SOL	GER	1		
SOL	HL	1		
SOL	HOR	1		
SOL	JUV	1		
SOL	LUCR	1		
SOL	MAN	2		(+ the star)
SOL	MAR	1		
SOL	OV	1		
SOL	PH	1		
SOL	PL	1		
SOL	PRIAP	1		
SOL	PROP	1		
SOL	S	1		
SOL	SEN	1		
SOL	TIB	1		
SOL	TR	1		
SOL	V	1		
SOL	VAL	1	25	
-SOLA 4.25.4	MAR			a nymph
SOLIGENA 5.317	VAL			(born of the Sun): Aeetes
SOLIMOS 9.75	SIL			founder of Sulmo
-SOLIMUS	SIL	2	2	two heroes (s. of Satricus; a Phrygian)
SOLON	JUV	1		Athenian statesman
SOLON	MAN	1		
SOLON	PL	1	3	
SOLONES pl.	PER			(as type of philosophers)
SOLYMA n.pl.	MAR			= Jerusalem
SOLYMUS cf. Solimus	OV			comp. of Aeneas
SOLYMUS* 6.544	JUV	1		p. to Jerusalem
SOLYMUS* S. 5.2.138	S	1	2	
SOMNIA n.pl.	S		1	Dreams
SOMNIA	TIB		1	
SOMNIA	V	1	3	
SOMNUS	CAT		1	God of Sleep
SOMNUS	HL		1	
SOMNUS 1.71.4	MAR		1	

SOMNUS	M. 11.593	OV		1	God of Sleep
SOMNUS		S		1	
SOMNUS	HF 1066	SEN		1	
SOMNUS	4.89 et al.	SIL		1	
SOMNUS		TIB		1	
SOMNUS		V	1	9	
SOPHENE		LUC			a part of Armenia
SOPHIA	Afran. 299	COM			"Wisdom" personif.
SOPHOCLES		HOR			the Greek tragic poet
SOPHOCLĒUS		JUV		1	p. to Sophocles
SOPHOCLEUS		MAR		1	
SOPHOCLEUS		OV		1	
SOPHOCLEUS		V	1	4	
SOPHOCLIDISCA		PL			a maid (Pers. 201)
SOPHRON		S			Greek mime-writer
SOPHRONA		TER			nurse of Pamphila
SOPOR	personif.	S		1	= Somnus
SOPOR		SIL		1	
SOPOR		V	1	3	
SORA		JUV		1	town in Latium
SORA		SIL	1	2	
SORACTE		HOR		1	mt. in Etruria
SORACTE		SIL		1	
SORACTE		V	1	3	
SOROR		PROP			= Parca
SORORES		CAT		1	= Parcae
SORORES		MAR		1	" (but 4.14.1: Musae)
SORORES	H. 12.3, 14.15	OV		2	Parcae; Danaids
SORORES		PROP		1	Musae
SORORES		S		1	Parcae
SORORES		SIL	1	7	"
SORTIENTES	Cas. 32	PL			title of his lost comedy
SOSIA	m.	PL		1	male slave
SOSIA		TER	1	2	" "
-SOSIBIANUS	1.81	MAR			fict.
-SOSICLES	Men. 1123	PL			a young man
SOSII		HOR			booksellers
-SOSIO	(fr.inc. 29)	PL			a slave
SOSPITA		OV			ep. of Juno
_SOSTRATA	passim	TER			an uxor
SOSTRATUS		JUV			cont.
SOTADES		MAR	2	2	Greek comic poet; fict. (6.26)
-SOTAS	4.9.1	MAR			a doctor
-SOTERO	Vid. 17	PL			a girl
-SPANIUS	2.41.10	MAR			fict.
SPARAX		PL			slave
SPARSUS		MAR			friend of MAR
SPARTA	cf. Sparte	AET		1	chief town of Laconia
SPARTA		CIC		1	
SPARTA		GR		1	
SPARTA		MAN		1	
SPARTA		OV		1	
SPARTA		PL		1	
SPARTA		SIL		1	
SPARTA		TR		1	
SPARTA		V	1	9	
SPARTACUS		HOR		1	famous slave-rebel

SPARTACUS	LUC	1	2	famous slave-rebel
SPARTANA	LUC			= Helen (wife of Menelaus)
SPARTANI	LUC			a breed of dogs
SPARTANUS	JUV		1	Spartan
SPARTANUS	MAR		1	
SPARTANUS	OV		1	
SPARTANUS	PL		1	
SPARTANUS	PROP		1	
SPARTANUS	S		1	
SPARTANUS	SEN		1	
SPARTANUS	SIL		1	
SPARTANUS	V	1	9	
SPARTE = Sparta	PROP		1	
SPARTE	S		1	
SPARTE	SEN	1	3	
[SPARTI ref. Oed.731ff.	SEN			the dragons' progeny]
SPARTIATICUS	PL			Spartan
SPARTIATUS (or -es)	PL			a Spartan (Poen. 780)
SPARTICUS Cul. 400	AV			Spartan
SPATALE 2.52	MAR			a nymph (or fict.?)
-SPENDOPHOROS 9.56	MAR			a boy (slave)
SPERCHEIS adj.	OV			p. to Spercheos
SPERCHEOS	LUC		1	river in Thessaly
SPERCHEOS	S		1	
SPERCHEOS	V	1	3	
SPERCHIONIDES	OV			dweller by the Spercheos
SPERCHIOS = -eos	OV			r. in Thessaly
SPES	HOR		1	"Hope" personified
SPES Am. 1.445	OV		1	
SPES Most. 350 et al.	PL		1	
SPES	S		1	
SPES	TIB	1	5	
-SPHAERIO Most. 419	PL			a slave
SPHINX	OV		1	myth. monster at Thebes
SPHINX Poen. 444	PL		1	
SPHINX	S		1	
SPHINX	SEN		1	
SPHINX	SIL	1	5	
SPICA	GER		1	star in Virgo
SPICA 5.269	MAN	1	2	
SPIO -ūs, fem.	V			a sea-nymph
SPOLETINUM	MAR			wine of Spoletum (town of Umbria)
SPOLETINUS	MAR			p. to Spoletum
STABERIUS	HOR			a greedy man
STABIAE	COL		1	town near Pompeii
STABIAE	OV		1	
STABIAE	S		1	
STABIAE	SIL	1	4	
-STAIUS 7.83	PER			type of average Roman
STALAGMUS	PL			name of a slave
-STALITIO Cas. 347	PL			(false name for Lysidamus)
STAPHYLA Aul. 269	PL			an old woman
STASIMUS Trin. 404	PL			a slave
STATIUS	JUV			P. Papinius S. (the poet)
STATOR	OV			ep. of Juppiter
-STELLA m., passim	MAR		1	L. Aruntius Stella (the poet)
STELLA S. 1.2.17	S	1	2	" "

STENTOR	JUV			legendary Greek hero
STEPHANIO	COM		1	fict. man
STEPHANIO	TER	1	2	fict. man (cook)
- STEPHANISCIDIUM	PL			a maid (Stich. 740)
STEPHANIUM	PL			a maid
STEPHANUS	MAR			a bath-owner
STEROPE	OV		1	a Pleiad
STEROPE	TR	1	2	
STEROPES	OV		1	a Cyclops
STEROPES	S		1	
STEROPES	V	1	3	
STERTINIUS	HOR			a Stoic philosopher
STESICHORUS	HOR		1	Greek lyric poet
STESICHORUS	S	1	2	
STHENEBOEA	JUV			daughter of Iobates (k. of Lydia)
STHENELEIUS adj.	OV	2	2	p. to Sthenelus (f. of Eurystheus; f. of
STHENELUS	HL		1	son of Capaneus Cycnus)
STHENELUS	HOR		1	an epigonus (Gk. hero)
STHENELUS	S		1	son of Capaneus
STHENELUS	V	2	5	an epigonus; a Trojan
STHENIUS	SIL		1	Roman soldier
STHENIUS	V	1	2	Rutulian
STICHUS	PL			a slave (& the comedy named from him)
STICTE	OV			a dog
STILPO	TER			a senex
-{STIMICHON B. 5.55	V			a shepherd
{STIMICON 6.84	CAL			
STIMULA	OV			a goddess (who goads to action)
STOECHADES fem. pl.	LUC			islands off S. Gaul
STOICIDAE m. pl.	JUV			bogus Stoics
STOICUS	HOR		1	Stoic
STOICUS adj. & N	JUV		2	
STOICUS	PER	1	4	
-STORAX Ad. 26	TER			a slave
- STRABAX Truc. 297	PL			a young man
STRATIE T. 4.286	S			town of Arcadia
- STRATILAX⁻(em.)	PL			(false name in ms.)
STRATIPPOCLES	PL			a young man
STRATO	TER			a slave
STRATOCLES	JUV			Greek comedian
STRATON	PL			a slave
STRATONICUS	PL			fict.
STRATOPHANES	PL			a soldier
STROBILUS	PL		1	a slave
STROBILUS	VAR	1	2	a slave (?)
STROPHADES	OV		1	islands off Messenia
STROPHADES	V		1	
STROPHADES	VAL	1	3	
STROPHIUS	HL		1	king of Phocis & f. of Pylades
STROPHIUS	OV		1	
STROPHIUS	SEN	1	3	
- STRUTHUS Trin. 1020	PL			(?)
{STRYMO	SIL			river of Thrace
{STRYMON	LUC		1	
{STRYMON	OV		1	
{STRYMON	S		2	(+ Thrace itself)
{STRYMON	SEN		1	

STRYMON	V		1	river of Thrace
STRYMON	VAL	1	7	(a Scythian)
STRYMONIS	PROP			an Amazon
STRYMONIUS ✗	V			a Trojan
STRYMONIUS*	AV		1	p. to Strymon, i.e. Thracian
STRYMONIUS*	GR		1	
STRYMONIUS*	MAR		1	
STRYMONIUS*	OV		1	
STRYMONIUS*	S		1	
STRYMONIUS*	SEN		1	
STRYMONIUS*	V	1	7	
STYGIUS	AET		1	p. to the Styx, Stygian
STYGIUS	AV		1	
STYGIUS	COL		1	
STYGIUS	FPLB		1	
STYGIUS	GR		1	
STYGIUS	HL		1	
STYGIUS	HOR		1	
STYGIUS	JUV		1	
STYGIUS	LUC		1	
STYGIUS	MAR		1	
STYGIUS	OV		1	
STYGIUS	PET		1	
STYGIUS	PROP		1	
STYGIUS	S		1	
STYGIUS	SEN		1	
STYGIUS	SIL		1	
STYGIUS	TIB		1	
STYGIUS	V		1	
STYGIUS	VAL	1	19	
STYMPHALA n.pl.	LUCR			region in Arcadia, with fabulous lake
STYMPHALICUS	PL			p. to Stymphala (-os)
STYMPHALIDES fem.pl.	MAR		1	the birds of Stymphala
STYMPHALIDES	PET		1	
STYMPHALIDES HF 244	SEN	1	3	
STYMPHALIS	SEN			a bird
STYMPHALIS*	OV			p. to Stymphala
STYMPHALIUS	CAT			p. to Stymphala, -os
STYMPHALOS cf. -a	S			region of Arcadia
STYMPHALUS	FPLA			
STYPHELUS	OV			a Centaur
-STYRUS 3.497	VAL			a Scythian
STYX	HOR		1	myth. river of Underworld (or the Under-
STYX	LUC		1	world itself)
STYX	MAR		1	
STYX	OV		1	(+ a nymph: F 3.802)
STYX	S		1	
STYX	SEN		1	
STYX	SIL		1	
STYX	V		1	
STYX	VAL	1	9	
SUADELA personific.	HOR			goddess of Persuasion (cf. Pitho)
-SUASISAVIATIO Ba.116	PL			"Sweet-kiss" (comic personification)
SUBBALLIO Ps. 607	PL			fict. name
SUBURA	JUV		1	a section of Rome
SUBURA	MAR		1	
SUBURA	PER		1	

SUBURA	PROP	1	4	a section of Rome
SUBURANUS	HOR		1	p. to the Subura
SUBURANUS	MAR		1	
SUBURANUS	PRIAP	1	3	
SUCRO 3.372	SIL		1	town & river in Spain
SUCRO A. 12.505	V	1	2	a Rutulian
-SUEBAE Med. 713	SEN			Swabian women
SUESSA	SIL			a town of Latium
SUESSONES	LUC			tribe of Gaul
-SUETES m.sg., 6.550	VAL			a Scythian
SUEVI	LUC			German tribe (Swabians)
SUEVUS*	PROP		1	p. to the Suevi
SUEVUS*	SIL	1	2	
SUFFENUS	CAT			cont. poet
-SUFFICIUS em., 54.5	CAT			cont.
-SUILLIUS P. 4.8.1	OV			a relative of Ovid
-SULCIUS s. 1.4.65	HOR			cont.
SULLA	CAT		1	L. Corn. Sulla, the dictator
SULLA	FPLB		1	
SULLA	HOR		1	
SULLA	JUV		1	
SULLA	LUC		2	(+ his son)
SULLA	MAR		1	
SULLA	MLP		1	
SULLA	OV		1	
SULLA	S		1	
SULLA	SEN		1	
SULLA	SIL	2	13	(+ a Roman general, 8.393)
SULLANUS	LUC		1	p. to Sulla
SULLANUS	PET	1	2	
SULMO	OV		1	Pelignian town, home of Ovid
SULMO	SIL		1	
SULMO	V	1	3	(a Rutulian hero)
SULMONENSIS	JUV			p. to Sulmo (a S. woman)
SULPICIA	MAR		1	a Roman poetess
SULPICIA	TIB	1	2	
SULPICIUS	ENN			P. Sulp. Galba
SULPICIUS*	HOR			p. to a Sulpicius
-SUMMANIS adj., 5.521	LUCR			p. to Summanis
SUMMANUS (Subm-)	OV		1	an old god of the Night
SUMMANUS	PL	1	2	
-SUMMENIANUS em.	MAR			p. to Summanus (3.82.2)
-SUMMENIUM (Submen-)	MAR			a place in Rome (1.34.6 dub.)
{SUNION	OV		1	promontory of S. Attica
SUNION	S		1	
SUNION	SEN	1	3	
SUNIUM	TER			
SUPERBI 8.479	SIL			the Tarquinii
SUPERBUS	OV			ep. of Tarquin the Younger
SUPERBUS/TARQUINIUS	HOR			the last k. of Rome
SURA fem., Truc. 405	PL			a slave (cf. Syra)
SURIA =Syria	PL			the country or province of Syria
SURISCUS Syr., adj.	AV			Syrian
SURRENTĪNUM	JUV		1	the wine of Surrentum
SURRENTINUM	MAR		1	
SURRENTINUM	PER	1	3	
SURRENTĪNUS	AV		1	p. to Surrentum

SURRENTĪNUS	HOR		1	p. to Surrentum
SURRENTINUS	MAR		1	
SURRENTINUS	OV		1	
SURRENTINUS	S	1	5	
SURRENTUM	ENN		1	town of Campania
SURRENTUM	HOR		1	
SURRENTUM	SIL	1	3	
SUSA n.pl.	LUC		1	chief town of Persia
SUSA	MAN	1	2	
SUSURRI M. 12.61	OV			"Whispers" (attendants of Fama)
SUTRIUS	SIL			p. to Sutrium (t. of Etruria)
SYBARIS	HOR		1	(a young man)
SYBARIS	JUV		1	town in Magna Graecia
SYBARIS M. 15.51	OV		1	"
SYBARIS	S		1	a Theban
SYBARIS	V	1	5	"
SYBARITICA T. 2.417	OV			title of a poem of Hemitheon
SYBARITICUS	MAR			p. to Sybaris (town)
SYCAMBRI = Syg-	GR		1	breed of dogs
SYCAMBRI	PROP	1	2	Germanic tribe
SYCHAEUS Ep. 7.97	OV		1	Dido's husband
SYCHAEUS	SIL		2	two Punics
SYCHAEUS	V	1	4	Dido's husband
SYCHAEUS*	V			p. to Sychaeus
SYENE	GR		1	town of Egypt
SYENE	JUV		1	
SYENE	LUC		1	
SYENE	MAR		1	
SYENE	OV		1	
SYENE	S	1	6	
SYENES	VAL			a Scythian
SYENITES adj.	OV			p. to Syene
SYGAMBRA (Syc.)	OV			Sycambrian woman
SYGAMBRI	HOR		1	Germanic tribe
SYGAMBRI	JUV		1	
SYGAMBRI	MAR	1	3	
- SYHEDRA n.pl., 8.259	LUC			a harbor in Cilicia
SYLLAE = Sullae	SIL			young soldiers of Fabius' army (7.618)
SYMAETHEUS	OV			p. to Symaethus
SYMAETHIS	OV			p. to Symaethus
SYMAETHIUS	OV		1	p. to Symaethus
SYMAETHIUS	V	1	2	
SYMAETHUS	SIL			the river in Sicily
SYME em.	HL			an Aegean island
SYMMACHUS	LUCIL		1	a plowman
SYMMACHUS	MAR	1	2	a doctor
SYMPLEGADES	OV			leg. rocky islands in the Black Sea
SYMPLEGAS	LUC		1	one of these islands
SYMPLEGAS	MAR		1	
SYMPLEGAS	SEN		1	
SYMPLEGAS	VAL	1	4	
SYNAPOTHNESCONTES	TER			title of comedy by Diphilus
-SYNCERASTUS Poen.821	PL			a slave
-SYNHALUS 5.352	SIL			a physician
SYNNAS	MAR		1	a town in Phrygia
SYNNAS	S	1	2	
SYPHAX	FPLB		1	king of Numidia

SYPHAX	JUV		1	king of Numidia
SYPHAX	OV		1	
SYPHAX	PROP		1	
SYPHAX	SIL	1	5	
SYRA	PL		1	an old woman
SYRA	TER	1	2	" " "
SYRACOSIUS	AV		1	p. to Syracuse
SYRACOSIUS	OV		1	
SYRACOSIUS	SIL		1	
SYRACOSIUS	V	1	4	
SYRACUSAE	LUCIL		1	town of Sicily
SYRACUSAE	MAN		1	
SYRACUSAE	OV		1	
SYRACUSAE	PL		1	
SYRACUSAE	SIL	1	5	
SYRACUSANUS	PL			p. to Syracuse
SYRI	HOR		1	the Syrians
SYRI	JUV		1	
SYRI	LUC		1	
SYRI	OV		1	
SYRI	PL		1	
SYRI	S	1	6	
SYRIA	CAT		1	the country or province
SYRIA	GER		1	
SYRIA	JUV		1	
SYRIA	LUC		1	
SYRIA	LUCR		1	
SYRIA	MAN		1	
SYRIA	MAR	1	7	
SYRIACUS	S			p. to Syria
SYRINX	OV			a nymph
SYRISCUS N, 5.70	MAR		1	fict.
SYRISCUS N	TER	1	2	a slave
SYRIUS adj.	AV		1	Syrian
SYRIUS	CAT		1	
SYRIUS	HOR		1	
SYRIUS	JUV		1	
SYRIUS	MAN		1	
SYRIUS	MAR		1	
SYRIUS	PROP		1	
SYRIUS	TIB		1	
SYRIUS	V	1	9	
SYROPHOENIX	JUV		1	a resident of the Syro-Phoenician border
SYROPHOENIX	LUCIL	1	2	
SYROS M. 7.464	OV			island in the Cyclades
SYRTES pl.	HOR		1	the two reefs on coast of N. Africa
SYRTES	MAN		1	
SYRTES	OV		1	
SYRTES	PROP		1	
SYRTES	V		1	
SYRTES	VAL	1	6	
SYRTICUS	LUC		1	p. to these reefs
SYRTICUS	SIL	1	2	
SYRTIS sg.	AV		1	one of the reefs
SYRTIS	CAT		1	
SYRTIS	LUC		1	
SYRTIS	PET		1	

SYRTIS	S		1	
SYRTIS	SEN		1	
SYRTIS	SIL		1	
SYRTIS	TIB	1	8	
SYRUS	HOR		1	a gladiator
SYRUS	LUCIL		1	a Syrian
SYRUS	MAR		1	
SYRUS	PL		2	(+ a slave's name)
SYRUS	TER		1	a slave's name
SYRUS	TIB	1	7	a Syrian
SYRUS*	COM		1	Syrian
SYRUS*	HOR		1	
SYRUS*	MAR		1	
SYRUS*	OV	1	4	
-TABAS 14.272	SIL			town of Sicily
TABURNUS	GR		1	mt. in N. Campania
TABURNUS	SIL		1	
TABURNUS	V	1	3	
TACITA	OV			goddess of Silence (cf. Muta)
TADIUS	PER		1	a type (?)
TADIUS	SIL	1	2	a Roman soldier
-TAENARA n.pl. (= -os)	SEN			promontory in Laconia (Tr. 402)
TAENARIDES	OV			ep. of Hyacinth
TAENARIS	OV			Spartan
TAENARIUS	LUC		1	p. to Taenaros (i.e. Spartan)
TAENARIUS	OV		1	
TAENARIUS	PRIAP		1	
TAENARIUS	PROP		1	
TAENARIUS	S		1	
TAENARIUS	SEN		1	
TAENARIUS	V		1	
TAENARIUS	VAL	1	8	
TAENAROS cf. -a	LUC		1	promontory in Laconia
TAENAROS	PRIAP		1	
TAENAROS	S		1	
TAENAROS	VAL	1	4	
TAENARUM	HOR			
TAENARUS	SEN		1	
TAENARUS	TIB		1	
TAENARUS	TR	1	3	
TAGES	COL		1	an Etruscan god (of divination)
TAGES	LUC		1	
TAGES	OV		1	
TAGES	S		1	
TAGES	VAL	1	5	(a Scythian)
TAGUS	AV		1	river of Lusitania
TAGUS	CAT		1	
TAGUS	JUV		1	
TAGUS	LUC		1	
TAGUS	MAR		1	
TAGUS	OV		1	
TAGUS	S		2	(+ an Argive)
TAGUS	SEN		1	
TAGUS	SIL		2	(+ a Spaniard)
TAGUS	V	1	12	
TALAIONIDES patr.	S			= Adrastus
TALAIONIUS AA 3.13	OV			descended from Talaus

TALASIO		AV		(a cry of good wishes to a bride)
TALASIUS		CAT		
TALASSIO		MAR		
TALASSUS = -io		MAR		
TALAUS		OV	1	an Argonaut
TALAUS		S	1	
TALAUS		VAL	1 3	
-TALOS A. 12.513		V		a Rutulian
TALTHUBIUS		PL		a herald
TALTHYBIUS		OV		"
-TAMASENUS M. 10.644		OV		Cretan
-TAMYRIS 3.7.143		TIB		queen of Armenia
TANAGER m.		V		river in Lucania
TANAGRA		S		town in Boeotia
TANAGRAEUS		S		p. to Tanagra
TANAIS -is, m.		HOR	2	the river Don in Russia; a spado
TANAIS		LUC	1	
TANAIS		MAN	1	
TANAIS		OV	1	
TANAIS		PROP	1	
TANAIS		S	1	
TANAIS		SEN	1	
TANAIS		TIB	1	
TANAIS		V	2	
TANAIS		VAL	1 12	(+ a Rutulian)
TANAQUIL		JUV	1	(type of proud woman)
TANAQUIL F. 6.629		OV	1	wife of Tarquin
TANAQUIL		SIL	1 3	
TANTALEUS		AV	1	
TANTALEUS		PROP	1	p. to Tantalus
TANTALEUS		S	1	
TANTALEUS		SEN	1 4	
-TANTALICUS adj.		SEN		p. to Tantalus (Th. 229)
TANTALIDAE patr.		SEN	1	desc. of Tantalus
TANTALIDAE		TR	1 2	
TANTALIDES m.sg.		OV	5	Pelops; Atreus & Thyestes; Agamemnon;
TANTALIDES		PRIAP	1 6	Agamemnon ⌐ Menelaus; Orestes.
TANTALIS		OV	3	Niobe; Hermione; desc. of Tantalus
TANTALIS		PROP	1	Niobe
TANTALIS		S	1 5	"
TANTALUS		AET	1	son of Juppiter & k. of Phrygia
TANTALUS		ENN	1	
TANTALUS		HOR	1	
TANTALUS		LUCIL	1	
TANTALUS		LUCR	1	
TANTALUS		OV	2	;(son of Niobe)
TANTALUS		PET	1	
TANTALUS		PH	1	
TANTALUS		S	1	
TANTALUS		SEN	1	
TANTALUS		TIB	1	
TANTALUS		TR	1 13	
-TAPPO 104.4		CAT		cont. man
TAPPULUS* (lex)		LUCIL		a fict. law (named from Tappo?)
TAPROBANE		OV		Ceylon
TARANIS m.		LUC		the Gaulish Jove
-TARANS S. 1.1.103		S		founder of Tarentum

TARAS	LUC		1	Tarentum
TARAS	VAL	1	2	(unknown river)
TARATALLA	MAR			a cook (comic name)
TARBELLICUS	LUC			p. to a Gaulish tribe
TARBELLUS	TIB			" " "
⎧TARCHO	V			a leg. Etruscan leader
⎨TARCHON	COL		1	
⎩TARCHON	SIL	1	2	
TARCHONDIMOTUS 9.219	LUC			a Cilician king
TARDIPES	COL			ep. of Vulcan: "Slow-foot"
TARENTINUM 13.125	MAR			wine of Tarentum
TARENTINUS	CAL		1	p. to Tarentum
TARENTINUS	COM		1	
TARENTINUS	HOR		1	
TARENTINUS	MAR		1	
TARENTINUS	PL	1	5	
-TARENTOS 1.69.2	MAR		1	a place in the Campus Martius
⎧TARENTOS 12.434, m.	SIL	1	2	town in S. Italy
⎪TARENTUM	ENN		1	town in S. Italy
⎪TARENTUM	HOR		1	
⎪TARENTUM	JUV		1	
⎨TARENTUM	LUCIL		1	
⎪TARENTUM	OV		2	(+ place in Campus Martius)
⎪TARENTUM	PL		1	
⎪TARENTUM	S		1	
⎩TARENTUM	V	1	9	
-TARIUS 4.252	SIL			name of a Roman soldier
TARPA m.	HOR			= Sp. Maecius T.
TARPEIA	OV		1	legendary Roman maiden
TARPEIA	PROP		1	
TARPEIA	SIL		1	
TARPEIA	V	1	4	
TARPEIUS	CAL		1	p. to Tarpeian rock
TARPEIUS	FPLR		1	
TARPEIUS	JUV		1	
TARPEIUS	LUC		1	
TARPEIUS	MAR		1	
TARPEIUS	OV		1	
TARPEIUS	PROP		1	
TARPEIUS	S		1	
TARPEIUS	SIL		1	
TARPEIUS	V	1	10	
TARQUINII Cat. 9.36	AV			the Tarquin family of Etruria
TARQUINIUS	HOR		1	T. Superbus, k. of Rome
TARQUINIUS 1.778	MAN		1	
TARQUINIUS F. passim	OV		1	
TARQUINIUS 3.11.47	PROP		1	
TARQUINIUS Oct. 305	SEN		1	
TARQUINIUS A. 8.646	V	1	6	
TARQUINIUS* A. 6.817	V			p. to Tarquin
TARQUITIUS N, Cat.5.3	AV			a rhetorician
-TARQUITUS A. 10.550	V			a Rutulian warrior
TARRACINENSIS	FPLA			p. to Tarracina (town in Latium)
TARRACO fem.	MAR		1	town in Spain
TARRACO	SIL	1	2	" "
TARRACONENSIS	MAR			p. to Tarraco
TARSOS fem., 3.225	LUC			town of Cilicia

TARTARA	n.pl.	AET	1	the Lower World, Underworld
TARTARA		AV	1	
TARTARA		COL	1	
TARTARA		GER	1	
TARTARA		HL	1	
TARTARA		HOR	1	
TARTARA		LUC	1	
TARTARA		LUCR	1	
TARTARA		OV	1	
TARTARA		PET	1	
TARTARA		SEN	1	
TARTARA		SIL	1 12	
TARTAREUS		CAL	1	p. to the Lower World
TARTAREUS		LUC	1	
TARTAREUS		MAR	1	
TARTAREUS		OV	1	
TARTAREUS		S	1	
TARTAREUS		SEN	1	
TARTAREUS		SIL	1	
TARTAREUS		V	1	
TARTAREUS		VAL	1 9	
TARTAROS	m.	MAN	1	the Lower World, Underworld
TARTAROS		S	1 2	
TARTARUS		HOR	1	
TARTARUS		LUCR	1	
TARTARUS		V	1	
TARTARUS		VAL	1 4	
TARTESIACUS		COL	1	p. to Tartessos, Tartessian
TARTESIACUS		MAR	1 2	
TARTESIS		COL		p. to Tartessos
TARTESIUS		SEN		p. to Tartessos
TARTESSIACUS		SIL		p. to Tartessos
TARTESSIUS		OV	1	p. to Tartessos
TARTESSIUS		SIL	1 2	
TARTESSOS		SIL	2 2	town of Spain; a Spaniard
TARTESUS		COL		town of Spain
TATIUS		JUV	1	king of the Sabines
TATIUS		MAR	1	
TATIUS		OV	1	
TATIUS		PROP	1	
TATIUS		V	1 5	
TATIUS*		PROP		p. to Tatius
TAULANTIUS		LUC	1	p. to the Taulantii (tr. of Illyria)
TAULANTIUS		SIL	1 2	
-TAULAS 6.221		VAL		a Scythian
-TAURANUS N, 5.472		SIL		a Roman soldier
-TAUREA m., 13.143		SIL		a Campanian
TAURI		GER	1	a tribe of Scythia (Crimea)
TAURI		LUC	1	
TAURI		OV	1	
TAURI		VAL	1 4	
TAURICUS		JUV	1	p. to the Tauri
TAURICUS		OV	1 2	
TAURINUS F. 6.197		OV	1	p. to the Taurini (tr. of N. Italy)
TAURINUS		SIL	1 2	
TAUROMENITANUS		JUV	1	p. to Tauromen(i)um
TAUROMENITANUS		LUC	1	

TAUROMENITANUS	SIL	1	3	p. to Tauromen(i)um
TAUROMENUM (= -ium)	OV			town in Sicily
TAURUBULAE	S			island near Naples
TAURUS	CAT	1		mt. range in SE Anatolia
TAURUS	CIC	1		constell. "Bull"
TAURUS	FPLR	1		
TAURUS	GER	1		
TAURUS	HOR	1		T. Statilius T., cos. 26 BC
TAURUS	LUC	2		constell.; mt.
TAURUS	MAN	2		constell.; mt.
TAURUS	OV	2		constell.; mt. (M. 2.217)
TAURUS	S	1		constell.
TAURUS	SEN	1		mt.
TAURUS	SIL	2		mt.; a pilot
TAURUS	TIB	1		mt.
TAURUS	V	1		constell.
TAURUS	VAL	1	18	constell.
-TAXES 6.252	VAL			a Scythian
TAYGETA n.pl., cf.-os	SIL		1	mt. range in Laconia
TAYGETA	V		1	
TAYGETA	VAL	1	3	
TAYGETE fem.	CIC		1	a Pleiad, d. of Atlas
TAYGETE	GER		1	
TAYGETE	OV		1	
TAYGETE	V	1	4	
TAYGETOS m., (= -a)	VAL			mt. range in Laconia
TAYGETUS	LUC		1	
TAYGETUS	MAR		1	
TAYGETUS	PROP		1	
TAYGETUS	S		1	
TAYGETUS	SEN		1	
TAYGETUS	V	1	6	
TEANUM	HOR			town in Campania
TEATE n.	S		1	town in Apulia
TEATE	SIL	1	2	
⎧ TECMESA	TR			daughter of King Teuthras
⎨ TECMESSA	HOR		1	
⎩ TECMESSA	OV	1	2	
-TECTA (sc. via)	MAR			portico in Campus Martius (3.5.5)
-TECTAPHOS M. 12.433	OV			a Lapith
-TECTA/VIA F. 6.192	OV			a portico
-TEDIA em., 2.49	JUV			a cont.
TEGEA	S			town of Arcadia
TEGEAEA	OV	2	2	Atalanta; Carmenta
TEGEAEUS	OV		1	p. to Tegea, i.e. Arcadian
TEGEAEUS	PROP		1	
TEGEAEUS	S		1	
TEGEAEUS	V		1	
TEGEAEUS	VAL	1	5	
TEGEATICUS	S			Arcadian
TEGEATIS	S		1	Arcadian
TEGEATIS	SIL	1	2	
-TEGIA conj., Pac. 56	TR			= Tegea (t. of Arcadia)
-TEIA 4.8.31	PROP			a courtesan
TEIUS	HOR		1	p. to Teos (t. of Ionia)
TEIUS	OV	1	2	
TELAMO	ENN		1	an Argonaut & father of Ajax & Teucer

TELAMO	TR	1	2	an Argonaut
TELAMON	HL		1	
TELAMON	HOR		1	
TELAMON	JUV		1	
TELAMON	OV		1	
TELAMON	S		1	
TELAMON	VAL	1	6	
TELAMONIADES m.sg.	OV			= Ajax
TELAMONIUS patr.	AV		1	= Ajax
TELAMONIUS	HL		1	
TELAMONIUS	OV	1	3	
TELCHINES m.pl.	OV		1	Rhodian priests
TELCHINES	S	1	2	
TELEBOAE m.pl.	S		1	robber band of Acarnania
TELEBOAE	SIL		1	
TELEBOAE	V	1	3	
TELEBOAS m.sg.	OV			a Centaur
-TELECOON 3.140	VAL			a Cyzican
TELEGONI pl.	OV			title of his poems
TELEGONUS	HOR		1	son of Ulixes & Circe
TELEGONUS	OV		1	
TELEGONUS	PROP		1	
TELEGONUS	S		1	
TELEGONUS	SIL	1	5	
TELEMACHUS	CAT		1	son of Ulixes & Penelope
TELEMACHUS	HOR		1	
TELEMACHUS	OV		1	
TELEMACHUS	SEN	1	4	
TELEMUS	OV			a prophet
TELEPHUS	HOR		2	k. of Mysia; a cont. young man
TELEPHUS	JUV		1	king of Mysia
TELEPHUS	OV		1	
TELEPHUS	PET		1	
TELEPHUS	S		1	
TELEPHUS	SEN	1	7	
-TELESILLA 6.7 et al.	MAR			fict. woman
-TELESINA 2.49	MAR		1	fict. woman
TELESINA 40.1	PRIAP	1	2	a prostitute
-TELESINUS N, 7.25	JUV		1	epic poet
TELESINUS 3.41 etc.	MAR		1	fict.
TELESINUS 10.148	SIL	1	3	a son of Crista
-TELESPHORUS 10.83.7	MAR			a homosexual
TELESTES m.	OV			father of Ianthe
-TELESTIS fem.	PL			a fict. girl (Epid. 568)
TELETHUSA 6.71	MAR		1	fict. girl
TELETHUSA	OV		1	myth. wife of Ligdus
TELETHUSA	PRIAP	1	3	a prostitute
-TELEUS or Tereus	OV			father of Itys (Ibis 434)
TELLŪS fem., personif.	COL		1	Earth (= Gk. Gê); cf. Terra
TELLUS	HOR		1	
TELLUS	LUC		1	
TELLUS	MAN		1	
TELLUS	MLP		1	
TELLUS	OV		1	
TELLUS	PET		1	
TELLUS	PROP		1	
TELLUS	S		1	

TELLŪS	SEN		1	Earth
TELLUS	SIL		1	
TELLUS	V	1	12	
TELMESSIS adj.	LUC			p. to Telmessus (town in Lycia)
-TELO (-on-) 3.592	LUC			a sailor
TELOBOAE = Teleboae	PL			robber band of Acarnania
-TELON 14.443, 8.541	SIL		2	sailor of Marcellus; k. of the Teleboae
TELON A. 7.734	V	1	3	hero of Capri
-TELPHUSIACUS T. 9.847	S			Arcadian
TEMESAEUS	OV		1	p. to Temese
TEMESAEUS	S	1	2	
TEMESE fem.	OV		1	town of Bruttium
TEMESE	S	1	2	
-TEMISUS 1.431	SIL			a Spaniard
TEMO	S			constell. (Big Dipper)
TEMPE	CAT		1	valley in Thessaly
TEMPE	COL		1	
TEMPE	HOR		1	
TEMPE	LUC		1	
TEMPE	OV		1	
TEMPE	S		1	
TEMPE	SEN		1	
TEMPE	V		1	
TEMPE	VAL	1	9	
TEMPESTAS personif.	OV		1	goddess of Weather
TEMPESTAS	S	1	2	
TEMPESTATES pl.	HOR		1	goddesses of Weather
TEMPESTATES	PL		1	
TEMPESTATES	V	1	3	
TEMPUS 5.8.7	PH			"Time" personified
TEMPYRA n.pl.	OV			town in Thrace
TENEDOS fem.	OV		1	island in N. Aegean
TENEDOS	PET		1	
TENEDOS	S		1	
TENEDOS	SEN		1	
TENEDOS	V	1	5	
TENEDUS	MAN			
TENOS fem.	OV			island in the Cyclades
TENTHREDON m.	HL			father of Prothous
TENTURA n.pl.	JUV			town of Egypt
TEREIDES m., patr.	OV			= Itys
TERENTIA	LUCIL			fict. woman
TERENTIANUS	MAR			cont. man
TERENTIUS	CIC		1	Terentius Afer, the comic poet
TERENTIUS	COM		1	
TERENTIUS	FPLA		1	
TERENTIUS	FPLR		1	
TERENTIUS	HOR		1	
TERENTIUS	OV	1	6	
-TERENTIUS/PRISCUS	MAR			friend of Martial (8.45)
-TERESIA cf. Tir., m.	PL			a senex (Amph. 1128)
TERESIAS cf. Tir.	JUV			any blind man (a type)
-TERETEUS em., T.2.191	OV			Thracian tribe (?)
TEREUS	AET		1	legendary king of Thrace
TEREUS	JUV		1	
TEREUS	MAR		1	
TEREUS	OV		1	

TEREUS		PL	1	king of Thrace
TEREUS		S	1	
TEREUS		SEN	1	
TEREUS		TR	1	
TEREUS		V	2 10	(+ a Trojan)
TERMINALIA	n.pl.	HOR		festival of Terminus
TERMINUS	personif.	HOR	1	god of Boundaries
TERMINUS		OV	1 2	
TERPSICHORE		JUV	1	muse of Dance (also poetry)
TERPSICHORE		MAR	1	
TERPSICHORE		MLP	1 3	
TERRA	personif.	FPLA	1	Earth-goddess (cf. Tellus)
TERRA		HOR	1	
TERRA		JUV	1	
TERRA		MAN	1	
TERRA		OV	1	
TERRA		SEN	1	
TERRA		V	1 7	
TERROR	M. 4.485	OV	1	god of Fear
TERROR	4.325	SIL	1	
TERROR	3.89	VAL	1 3	
TESSALA	(= Th.)	LUCTL		Thessalian mare
TETHYS	fem.	AV	1	goddess of the Sea (also the Sea)
TETHYS		CAT	1	
TETHYS		COL	1	
TETHYS		FPLA	1	
TETHYS		GER	1	
TETHYS		LUC	1	
TETHYS		MAR	1	
TETHYS		OV	1	
TETHYS		S	1	
TETHYS		SEN	1	
TETHYS		SIL	1	
TETHYS		V	1	
TETHYS		VAL	1 13	
TETRICA	fem.	V		mt. in Sabine area
-TETRICUS	adj., 8.417	SIL		p. to Tetrica
-TETTIUS		CIC	1	unknown contemporary
TETTIUS		FPLA	1 2	" "
-TETTIUS/CABALLUS		MAR		a clown type (1.41.17)
TEUCER		HL	1	Trojan hero
TEUCER		HOR	1	son of Telamon
TEUCER		MAN	1	" "
TEUCER		OV	2	brother of Ajax; king of Troy
TEUCER		SIL	2	a Greek; a Punic
TEUCER		TR	1	son of Telamon
TEUCER		V	2	son of Telamon; king of Troy
TEUCER		VAL	1 11	son of Telamon
TEUCRI		HL	1	the Trojans
TEUCRI		JUV	1	
TEUCRI		OV	1	
TEUCRI		S	1	
TEUCRI		SEN	1	
TEUCRI		SIL	1	
TEUCRI		V	1	
TEUCRI		VAL	1 8	
TEUCRIA	fem.	V		Troy

TEUCRIUS	adj.	AV	1	Trojan
TEUCRIUS		SIL	1 2	
TEUCRUS	adj.	CAT	1	Trojan
TEUCRUS		HOR	1	
TEUCRUS		OV	1	
TEUCRUS		PROP	1 4	
-TEUMESIUS	adj.	S		Theban
-TEUMESUS	T. 4.85	S		mt. in Boeotia
-TEUTAGONUS	6.97	VAL		a Scythian
-TEUTALUS	4.199	SIL		a Gaulish soldier
TEUTATES		LUC		a Gaulish deity
TEUTHRANTEUS		OV		p. to Teuthras (= Mysian)
TEUTHRANTIUS		OV		p. to Teuthras
TEUTHRAS		PROP	1	river in Campania
TEUTHRAS		SIL	1	a Cumaean
TEUTHRAS	A. 10.402	V	1 3	an Arcadian ally of the Trojans
TEUTONICUS	adj.	JUV	1	Germanic
TEUTONICUS		LUC	1	
TEUTONICUS		MAR	1	
TEUTONICUS		PROP	1	
TEUTONICUS		V	1 5	
TEUTONUS	sg.	LUC		a German (or Germany)
-TEUXIMARCHA	Men.1131	PL		mother of the Menaechmi
THABRACA		JUV		town of Numidia
-THAEMON	A. 10.126	V		a Lycian
THAIS		COM	1	fict. woman
THAIS		JUV	1	" "
THAIS		MAR	2	courtesan; a comedy
THAIS		OV	1	courtesan
THAIS		PROP	1	"
THAIS		TER	1 7	" (in comedy)
-THALAMUS	8.52.2	MAR		the barber of Nero
THALEA		V		a sea-nymph
THALES	-etis	JUV	1	Greek philosopher
THALES		PL	1 2	
THALEUS	adj.	CAL		Sicilian
THALIA	Culex 1	AV	1	muse of Comedy (?)
THALIA		HOR	1	muse of lyric poetry
THALIA		MAR	1	muse of comedy
THALIA	Florus 14.3	MLP	1	" "
THALIA	F. 5.54	OV	1	" of lyric poetry
THALIA	S. 2.1.116	S	1	" of comedy
THALIA		V	2 8	muse of comedy; a sea-nymph
THALIARCHUS		HOR		pseudonym of unknown friend
THALLUS		CAT	1	cont.
THALLUS		MAR	1 2	a cook
THAMYRAS		MLP	1	legendary Thracian bard
THAMYRAS		OV	1	
THAMYRAS		PROP	1 3	
THAMYRIS	m.	S	1	(the same bard)
THAMYRIS		SIL	1	a Saguntine warrior
THAMYRIS	3.128	VAL	1 3	king of the Pelasgi
-THAMYRUS	A. 12.341	V		a Rutulian
THAPSOS	fem.	SIL		town in Sicily
THAPSUS		OV	1	" "
THAPSUS		SIL	2	" in Africa; a soldier
THAPSUS		V	1	" in Sicily

THAPSUS		VAL	1	5	(a Cyzican)
-THARSIMACHUS em.		JUV			cont. rhetorician (7.204)
THASIUS adj.		COM		1	p. to Thasos
THASIUS Poen. 699		PL		1	
THASIUS		V	1	3	
THASOS fem.		PET		1	island in N. Aegean
THASOS		S	1	2	
THAUMANTEUS		OV			p. to Thaumas
THAUMANTIAS fem.patr.		COL		1	Iris
THAUMANTIAS		OV		1	
THAUMANTIAS		S		1	
THAUMANTIAS		V		1	
THAUMANTIAS		VAL	1	5	
THAUMANTIS patr.		OV		1	Iris
THAUMANTIS		S	1	2	
THAUMAS		OV			a Centaur
-THEANO A. 10.703		V			a Trojan woman
THEBAE		AET		1	town of Boeotia
THEBAE		HOR		1	
THEBAE		JUV		2	(+ a tragedy)
THEBAE		LUC		2	(+ t. of Egypt)
THEBAE 3.16		MAN		1	
THEBAE		MAR		1	
THEBAE		OV		2	(+ town in Mysia)
THEBAE		PL		1	
THEBAE		PROP		1	
THEBAE		S		2	(+ title of poem: S 1.5)
THEBAE		SEN		1	
THEBAE 1.276		SIL		1	
THEBAE Att. 584		TR		1	
THEBAE A. 4.470		V		1	
THEBAE		VAL	2	20	(+ town of Egypt)
THEBAEUS T. 9.291		S			p. to Thebes (in Boeotia)
THEBAGENES adj.		VAR			Theban
THEBAICAE		S			palm-dates
THEBAIS		JUV		1	title of Statius' poem
THEBAIS also pl.		OV		1	Theban woman
THEBAIS		S	1	3	title of his poem
THEBAIS* (Alcmene)		FPLB		1	Theban
THEBAIS*		S		1	
THEBAIS*		SEN	1	3	
THEBANA T.4.3.29		OV	2	2	Andromache; Antigone (3.3.69)
THEBANI		PL			people of Thebes
THEBANUS		HOR		1	Theban (of Boeotia)
THEBANUS		LUC		1	
THEBANUS		LUCR		1	
THEBANUS		MAN		1	
THEBANUS		MAR		1	
THEBANUS		OV		1	
THEBANUS		PL		1	
THEBANUS		PROP		1	
THEBANUS		S		1	
THEBANUS		SEN		1	
THEBANUS		TR		1	
THEBANUS		V	1	12	
THEBE = Thebae, 15.6		JUV		1	town in Egypt
THEBE		OV		2	town of Boeotia; a nymph

THEBE		S	1	town of Boeotia
THEBE	3.678	SIL	1	" "
THEBE	6.118	VAL	1 6	town of Egypt
-THEIODAMANTEUS adj.		PROP		p. to Theiodamas (1.20.6)
-THELGON	4.628	SIL		a Pyrenean
THELIS		ENN		= Thetis
-THELYS	10.52	MAR		a eunuch
-THEMILLAS A. 9.576		V		a Rutulian
THEMIS		CAL	1	Greek goddess of Justice
THEMIS		CAT	1	
THEMIS		LUC	1	
THEMIS		OV	1 4	
THEMISON		JUV	1	a doctor (of Syria)
THEMISON	12.20	MAR	1 2	fict. man
THENSAURUS		PL	1	title of a comedy
THENSAURUS		TER	1 2	
-THEODOROMEDES		PL		a fict. Elean (Capt. 635)
THEODORUS		JUV	1	cont.
THEODORUS		MAR	1 2	cont.
-THEODOTUS		COM		Greek painter
THEONĪNUS		HOR		p. to Theon (the poet)
-THEOPHILA 7.69.1		MAR		cont. woman
THEOPOMPUS		MAR		a slave
-THEOPROPIDES		PL		a senex (Most. 447)
-THEOTIMUS		FPLA	1	unknown man
THEOTIMUS		PL	1 2	fict. Ephesian
THERAEUS		TIB		p. to Thera (island)
THERAPNAE		S		town in Laconia
THERAPNAEUS		MAR	1	p. to Therapnae, i.e. Spartan
THERAPNAEUS		OV	1	
THERAPNAEUS		S	1	
THERAPNAEUS		SIL	1 4	
THERAPNE sg., = -ae		SIL		town in Laconia
-THERAPONTIGONUS		PL		fict. soldier (Curc. 408)
-THEREUS M. 12.353		OV		a Centaur
-THERINOS 9.13.3		MAR		fict. name (Gk. θερινός 'summertime')
THERMAE		SIL		town in Sicily
THER(M)ODAMANTEUS		OV		p. to Ther(m)odamas (Ibis 385)
THERMODON -nt-, m.		OV	1	a river of Pontus
THERMODON		PROP	1	
THERMODON		SIL	1	
THERMODON		V	1	
THERMODON		VAL	1 5	
THERMODONTIACUS		OV	1	p. to the Thermodon
THERMODONTIACUS		PROP	1	
THERMODONTIACUS		S	1	
THERMODONTIACUS		SEN	1	
THERMODONTIACUS		SIL	1 5	
THERMODONTIUS		SEN		p. to the Thermodon
THERMOPULAE		LUCIL		a pass in Thessaly
THERMOPYLAE		CAT		
THERMUS		LUC		Q. Minucius Thermus, a follower of Pompey
THERODAMAS M. 3.233		OV		a dog
-THEROMEDON P. 1.2.119		OV		a king of Scythia
-THERON M. 3.211		OV	1	a dog
THERON T. 2.572		S	1	a Theban
THERON		SIL	2	a Spaniard; a Saguntine

THERON	A. 10.312	V	1	5	a Rutulian
-THERSANDER	T. 3.683	S			son of Polynices
-THERSES	M. 13.682	OV			Theban guest of Anius
-THERSILOCHUS	A.6.483	V	2	2	two Trojan warriors
THERSITES		HL		1	the ugly Greek at Troy
THERSITES		JUV		1	" " (or any grouch)
THERSITES		OV	1	3	" "
-THESCELUS	M. 5.182	OV			comp. of Phineus
THESEIS		JUV			title of poem
THESEIUS		OV		1	p. to Theseus
THESEIUS		S	1	2	
THESEUS		AET		1	legendary king of Athens
THESEUS		AV		1	
THESEUS		CAT		1	
THESEUS		HOR		1	
THESEUS		LUC		1	
THESEUS		MAR		1	
THESEUS		OV		1	
THESEUS		PRIAP		1	
THESEUS		PROP		1	
THESEUS		S		1	
THESEUS		SEN		1	
THESEUS		V		1	
THESEUS		VAL	1	13	
THESEUS*		MAR		1	p. to Theseus
THESEUS*		OV		1	
THESEUS*		PROP		1	
THESEUS*		S		1	
THESEUS*		SEN		1	
THESEUS*		TIB	1	6	
THESIDAE	patron.	V			Athenians
THESIDES	"	OV			Hippolytus
THESPIACUS		S		1	p. to Thespiae in Boeotia
THESPIACUS		VAL	1	2	
THESPIADAE		S			Thebans
THESPIADES	m.sg.	S		1	a Theban
THESPIADES	fem.pl.	SEN		1	the Muses (HO 369)
THESPIADES	11.19	SIL		1	" "
THESPIADES	m.sg.	VAL		2	Argus the Thespian; Tiphys
THESPIADES	fem.pl.	VAR	1	6	the Muses
THESPIAS	adj.	OV			Thespian
THESPIS		HOR			the Greek dramatist
THESPIUS	61.29	CAT		1	p. to Thespiae (in Boeotia)
THESPIUS		VAL	1	2	" "
-THESPRIO	Epid. 3	PL			name of a slave
THESPROTI		LUC			tribe of Epirus
THESPROTIUS		SIL			p. to the Thesproti
THESPROTUS		PROP		1	a king of Puteoli
THESPROTUS		TR	1	2	" "
THESSALA	sc. maga	LUC		1	a Thessalian witch
THESSALA		PL	1	2	a slave-girl of Alcmene
THESSALIA		CAT		1	region of Central Greece
THESSALIA		GER		1	
THESSALIA		JUV		1	
THESSALIA		LUC		1	
THESSALIA		MAN		1	
THESSALIA		OV		1	

THESSALIA	PET	1	region of central Greece
THESSALIA	PROP	1	
THESSALIA	S	1	
THESSALIA	VAL	1 10	
THESSALICUS	HL	1	p. to Thessaly
THESSALICUS	LUC	1	
THESSALICUS	LUCR	1	
THESSALICUS	MAR	1	
THESSALICUS	OV	1	
THESSALICUS	PET	1	
THESSALICUS	PROP	1	
THESSALICUS	S	1	
THESSALICUS	SEN	1	
THESSALICUS	VAL	1 10	
THESSALIDES 6.492	LUC		Thessalian witches
THESSALIS 6.451	LUC	1	a witch
THESSALIS N & adj.	OV	1	Thessalian
THESSALIS N & adj	S	1	
THESSALIS 1.737	VAL	1 4	Thessalian woman
THESSALIUS	GR		Thessalian
THESSALUS sc. equus	GR	1	Thessalian horse-breed
THESSALUS N, M.8.768	OV	1	the Thessalian (= Erysichthon)
THESSALUS 1.19.10	PROP	1	a Thessalian
THESSALUS 7.40	VAL	1 4	"
THESSALUS*	CAT	1	Thessalian, p. to Thessaly
THESSALUS*	COL	1	
THESSALUS*	HOR	1	
THESSALUS*	JUV	1	
THESSALUS*	LP	1	
THESSALUS*	LUC	1	
THESSALUS*	OV	1	
THESSALUS*	PET	1	
THESSALUS*	PH	1	
THESSALUS*	PL	1	
THESSALUS*	PROP	1	
THESSALUS*	S	1	
THESSALUS*	SEN	1	
THESSALUS*	SIL	1	
THESSALUS*	TIB	1	
THESSALUS*	TR	1	
THESSALUS*	VAL	1 17	
-THESSANDRUS A. 2.261	V		a Greek
THESTIADES	OV	2 2	Plexippus & Toxeus; Meleager
THESTIAS	LUCIL	1	Leda
THESTIAS	OV	1 2	Althaea
THESTIUS	OV	1	mythical king of Aetolia
THESTIUS	S	1 2	"
THESTORIDES	HL	1	son of Thestor, i.e. Calchas
THESTORIDES	OV	1	
THESTORIDES	S	1 3	
-THESTYLIS 8.55.18	MAR	1	a shepherdess
THESTYLIS B. 2.10	V	1 2	
-THESTYLUS 7.29	MAR		a slave
-THETIDEIUS adj.	HL		p. to Thetis
THETIS	CAT	1	a sea-nymph, mother of Achilles
THETIS	HL	1	
THETIS	HOR	1	

THETIS	MAR	1	a sea-nymph
THETIS	PL	1	
THETIS	PROP	1	
THETIS	S	1	
THETIS	SEN	1	
THETIS	SIL	1	
THETIS	TIB	1	
THETIS	V	1	
THETIS	VAL	1 12	
—THEUDOTUS Ibis 465	OV		myth. name (see scholiast on passage)
THIA	CAT		wife of Hyperion
THIODAMAS (Theo-)	OV	1	(unspecified) hero (Ibis 488)
THIODAMAS T. 8.279	S	1 2	son of Melampus
THISBAEUS	OV	1	p. to Thisbe (town)
THISBAEUS	S	1 2	" "
THISBE	OV	1	beloved by Pyramus
THISBE	S	1 2	town in Boeotia
—THOACTES M. 5.147	OV		armor-bearer of Cepheus
THOANTEUS	OV	1	p. to Thoas
THOANTEUS	SIL	1	
THOANTEUS	VAL	1 3	
THOANTIAS patron.	OV		=Hypsipyle
THOANTIS patron.	S		"
THOAS	HL	1	an Aetolian hero
THOAS	OV	2	king of Lemnos; k. of Thracian Chersonese
THOAS	S	1	king of Lemnos
THOAS	SIL	1	an Aetolian
THOAS Inc.Fab. 138	TR	1	(unspecified) hero
THOAS	V	2	an Aetolian at Troy; a Trojan
THOAS 2.418	VAL	1 9	king of Lemnos
—THOE T. 6.440	S	1	horse of Admetus
THOE 6.375	VAL	1 2	a woman's name (an Amazon)
—THOON M. 13.259	OV		a Trojan hero
—THOOS M. 3.220	OV		a dog
⌠THRACA	HOR	1	Thrace
⟨THRACA	V	1 2	
⟨THRACE	OV	1	
⟨THRACE	S	1	
⌡THRACE	SIL	1 3	
THRACES pl.	HOR	1	Thracians, people of Thrace
THRACES	JUV	1	
THRACES	MAR	1	
THRACES	S	1	
THRACES	V	1	
THRACES	VAL	1 6	
THRACIA	CAT	1	Thrace
THRACIA	LUC	1	
THRACIA	LUCR	1	
THRACIA	MAN	1	
THRACIA	OV	1 5	
THRACIUS	HOR	1	Thracian
THRACIUS	LUC	1	
THRACIUS	OV	1	(Tereus: M. 6.661)
THRACIUS	S	1	(Orpheus)
THRACIUS	SEN	1	
THRACIUS	SIL	1	
THRACIUS	V	1	

THRACIUS		VAL	1 8	Thracian
THRACIUS*		OV		Thracian
-THRAECA = Thraca		ENN		Thrace
THRAECES pl.		HL		Thracians
THRAECIA		MAN		Thrace
THRAEISSA 2.147		VAL		Thracian woman
THRAESSUS adj.& N		VAL		Thracian
THRAEX		HOR		a gladiator
THRAEX* (Dirae 37)		AV		Thracian
THRASEA m.		JUV	1	a Roman stoic
THRASEA		MAR	1 2	" "
-THRASIUS AA 1.6.48		OV		a seer
THRASO		TER		braggart soldier
THRASYLLUS		JUV	1	astrologer of Tiberius
THRASYLLUS Ibis 329		OV	1 2	a Greek, brother of Symus
THRAX collective sg.		JUV	1	the Thracians
THRAX M. 9.194		OV	1	ep. of Diomedes
THRAX HF 1170		SEN	1 3	" "
THRAX*		GER	1	Thracian
THRAX*		HOR	1	
THRAX*		OV	1	
THRAX*		PROP	1	
THRAX*		SEN	1	
THRAX*		SIL	1 6	
THRECE = Thrace		MAN	1	Thrace
THRECE "		OV	1 2	"
-THRECIUS = Thracius*		OV		Thracian (Am. 1.14.21)
THREICIUS		GER	1	Thracian
THREICIUS		GR	1	
THREICIUS		HOR	1	
THREICIUS		LUC	1	
THREICIUS		OV	1	
THREICIUS		PROP	1	
THREICIUS		SEN	1	
THREICIUS		SIL	1	
THREICIUS		V	1	
THREICIUS		VAL	1 10	
THREISSA also adj.		V		Thracian (woman)
THREISSA*		PH		" "
THRESSA*		HOR	1	" "
THRESSA*		OV	1	
THRESSA*		SEN	1 3	
-THRIASIUS Ph. 5		SEN		p. to Thria (Attic deme)
- THRONIUS A. 10.753		V		a Trojan
- THRYON T. 4.180		S		town in Elis
THUCYDIDES Cat. 2.3		AV		the Greek historian
THULE		S	1	an island of NW Europe
THULE		SEN	1	
THULE		V	1 3	
-THULIS m., 7.602		SIL		Punic soldier
THURINUS		HOR		p. to Thurii (town of Lucania)
-THURIS 7.598		SIL		Punic soldier
THYADES = Thyiades		CAT		Bacchantes
THYBRINUS		V		p. to Tiber river
THYBRIS m.		AV	1	Tiber river (cf. Tiberis)
THYBRIS		GR	1	
THYBRIS		LUC	1	

THYBRIS	MAR		1	the Tiber river
THYBRIS	OV		1	
THYBRIS	S		1	
THYBRIS	SIL		1	
THYBRIS	V		3	(+ river-god; k. of Etruria)
THYBRIS	VAL	1	11	
-THYDRUS 6.639	VAL			a Colchian
THYESTES	HOR		1	son of Pelops
THYESTES	JUV		1	
THYESTES	LUC		1	
THYESTES	MAR		1	
THYESTES	OV		1	
THYESTES	PER		1	
THYESTES	PL		1	
THYESTES	SEN		1	
THYESTES	TR	1	9	
THYESTEUS	HOR		1	p. to Thyestes
THYESTEUS	LUC		1	
THYESTEUS	OV		1	
THYESTEUS	SEN	1	4	
THYESTIADES patron.	OV			Aegisthus
THYIADES fem.pl.	OV		1	Bacchantes
THYIADES	VAL	1	2	
THYIAS	HOR		1	a Bacchant
THYIAS	S		1	
THYIAS	V		1	
THYIAS	VAL	1	4	
-THYLACUS	COM			a slave
THYLE = Thule	JUV		1	island in NW Europe
THYLE	SIL	1	2	
-THYMBER A. 10.391	V			a Rutulian
THYMBRA	S			town in the Troad
THYMBRAEUS	S		1	ep. of Apollo
THYMBRAEUS	V	1	2	a Trojan
THYMBRAEUS*	S		1	p. to Thymbra
THYMBRAEUS*	V	1	2	
THYMELE	JUV		1	woman mime
THYMELE	MAR	1	2	
-THYMOETES A. 2.32	V			a Trojan
-THYNEIUS M. 8.719	OV			p. to Thyni
THYNEUS 4.424	VAL			p. to the Thyni
THYNI	CAT			tribe of Bithynia
THYNIA	CAT			chief town of the Thyni
THYNIACUS	OV			p. to the Thyni
THYNIAS	PROP			p. to the Thyni
THYNUS	HOR			p. to the Thyni
THYONE	OV			a Hyad
THYONEUS	HOR		1	son of Thyone (Bacchus)
THYONEUS	OV		1	Bacchus
THYONEUS	S		1	"
THYONEUS	VAL	1	4	"
THYONIANUS	CAT			Bacchus = wine
THYOTES	VAL			a priest
THYREA T. 4.48	S			district of Laconia (or t.?)
THYREATIS adj.	OV			p. to Thyrea
-THYRMIS 15.724	SIL			name of a Gaul
THYRSAGETAE m.pl.	VAL			tribe of E. Central Europe

THYRSIS	CAL		1	a shepherd
THYRSIS	PROP		1	
THYRSIS	V	1	3	
-THYRUS 2.110	SIL			Punic soldier
-THYSDRUS 15.448	SIL			" "
TIBARENI	VAL			tribe of Anatolia
TIBEREIUS adj.	S			p. to Tiberius
TIBERINIS adj.	OV			p. to Tiber river
TIBERINUS N	FPLA		1	river-god
TIBERINUS	JUV		1	river; (also a fish)
TIBERINUS	OV		2	river; king of Alba
TIBERINUS	PROP		1	river
TIBERINUS	SIL		1	ship-pilot
TIBERINUS	V		1	the Tiber
TIBERINUS	VAL	1	8	river-god
TIBERINUS*	COM		1	p. to the Tiber
TIBERINUS*	ENN		1	
TIBERINUS*	HOR		1	
TIBERINUS*	LUC		1	
TIBERINUS*	LUCIL		1	
TIBERINUS*	MAR		1	
TIBERINUS*	OV		1	
TIBERINUS*	PER		1	
TIBERINUS*	PROP		1	
TIBERINUS*	S		1	
TIBERINUS*	SIL		1	
TIBERINUS*	V	1	12	
TIBERIS cf. Thybris	COM		1	river Tiber
TIBERIS	ENN		1	
TIBERIS	FPLA		1	
TIBERIS	HOR		1	
TIBERIS	JUV		1	
TIBERIS	MAR		1	
TIBERIS	OV		1	
TIBERIS	PROP		1	
TIBERIS	S		1	
TIBERIS (Tibris)	V	1	10	river-god
TIBERIUS	COM		1	an unknown man
TIBERIUS	HOR	1	2	Tiberius Oppidius
-TIBISENUS adj., 6.50	VAL			p. to a river in Thrace
TIBULLUS	FPLA		1	Albius Tibullus, the poet
TIBULLUS	MAR		1	
TIBULLUS	OV		1	
TIBULLUS	S		1	
TIBULLUS	TIB	1	5	
TIBUR n.	COL		1	town of Latium (Tivoli)
TIBUR	HOR		1	
TIBUR	JUV		1	
TIBUR	MAR		1	
TIBUR	OV		1	
TIBUR	PRIAP		1	
TIBUR	PROP		1	
TIBUR	S		1	
TIBUR	SIL		1	
TIBUR	V	1	10	
-TIBURNA 2.554	SIL			wife of Murrus, a Saguntine
TIBURNUS	S			founder of Tibur

TIBURNUS*	HOR		1	p. to Tibur
TIBURNUS*	PROP		1	
TIBURNUS*	S	1	3	
TIBURS	CAT		1	p. to Tibur
TIBURS	HOR		1	
TIBURS	S		1	
TIBURS	SIL		1	
TIBURS	TIB		1	
TIBURS also N	V	1	6	
-TIBURTĪNA/PILA	MAR			columns on the Quirinal
TIBURTĪNUM (praedium)	MAR			a villa
TIBURTĪNUS	JUV		1	p. to Tibur
TIBURTINUS	MAR		1	
TIBURTINUS	PROP		1	
TIBURTINUS	S	1	4	
TIBURTUS	V			founder of Tibur
TICIDA m.	OV			a Roman poet
TICĪNUS	SIL			a river in N. Italy
TICINUS*	SIL			p. to the Ticinus
TIFATA n.pl.	SIL			mt. in Campania
TIGELLIUS	FPLB		1	Hermogenes Tigellius, cont. of Horace
TIGELLIUS	HOR	1	2	" "
TIGILLĪNUS N	JUV		1	cont. of Nero
TIGILLINUS	MAR	1	2	
TIGRANES	LUC			king of Armenia
TIGRIS m.	FPLB		1	river of Mesopotamia
TIGRIS	HOR		1	
TIGRIS	LUC		1	
TIGRIS	MAN		1	
TIGRIS	MAR		1	(a circus-horse)
TIGRIS	OV		2	river; dog
TIGRIS	PROP		1	
TIGRIS	SEN		1	
TIGRIS	V	2	11	(+ ship, fem.)
TILLIUS	HOR			cont. of Caesar
TIMAGENES	HOR			a rhetorician
TIMARCHIDES	PL			a senex
TIMAVUS	LUC		1	river in Istria
TIMAVUS	MAR		1	
TIMAVUS	S		1	
TIMAVUS	SIL		1	
TIMAVUS	V	1	5	
TIMOLUS (also SEN HO)	OV			mt. in Lydia (= Tmolus)
TIMOR	HOR		1	"Fear" personified
TIMOR	V	1	2	
TIMORES M. 12.60	OV			"Fear"
TINGI fem., 3.258	SIL			town of Mauretania
-TINIA 8.452	SIL			river of Umbria
TIPHYS	FPLB		1	pilot of the Argo
TIPHYS	MAN		1	
TIPHYS	OV		1	
TIPHYS	S		1	
TIPHYS	SEN		1	
TIPHYS	V		1	
TIPHYS	VAL	1	7	
TIRESIA m.	LUCIL		1	blind prophet of Thebes
TIRESIA	SEN	1	2	

TIRESIAS m.		HOR	1	blind prophet of Thebes
TIRESIAS		OV	1	
TIRESIAS		PROP	1	
TIRESIAS		S	1 4	
TIRIDATES		HOR		king of Armenia
TIRO		CIC	1	Cicero's freedman
TIRO		FPLR	1 2	" "
-TIRRIUS adj.		COM		= Tyrius (?)
TIRYNS T. 4.147		S		town in Argolis
TIRYNTHIA		OV		Alcmene
TIRYNTHIUS		MAR	1	Hercules
TIRYNTHIUS		OV	1	
TIRYNTHIUS		PET	1	
TIRYNTHIUS		S	1	
TIRYNTHIUS		SIL	1	
TIRYNTHIUS		V	1	
TIRYNTHIUS		VAL	1 7	
TIRYNTHIUS*		GR	1	p. to Tiryns or to Hercules
TIRYNTHIUS*		JUV	1	
TIRYNTHIUS*		OV	1	
TIRYNTHIUS*		S	1	
TIRYNTHIUS*		SIL	1 5	
TISAEUS m.		VAL		mt. of Thessaly
TISAMENUS		OV		son of Orestes
TISIPHONE		AV	1	a Fury
TISIPHONE		HOR	1	
TISIPHONE		JUV	1	
TISIPHONE		LUC	1	
TISIPHONE		LUCIL	1	
TISIPHONE		OV	1	
TISIPHONE		PET	1	
TISIPHONE		PROP	1	
TISIPHONE		S	1	
TISIPHONE		SEN	1	
TISIPHONE		SIL	1	
TISIPHONE		TIB	1	
TISIPHONE		V	1	
TISIPHONE		VAL	1 14	
TISIPHONEUS		OV		p. to Tisiphone
TISSE fem.		SIL		town in Sicily
TITAN		CIC	1	Sol (Phoebus)
TITAN		COL	1	
TITAN	also Titanus	ENN	1	
TITAN		GER	1	
TITAN		HL	1	
TITAN	14.35	JUV	1	(Prometheus)
TITAN		LP	1	Sol
TITAN		LUC	2	" (+ Atlas)
TITAN	8.21.7	MAR	1	"
TITAN		OV	2	" (+ ancestor of Titans)
TITAN	em.	PET	1	
TITAN		S	1	
TITAN		SEN	1	
TITAN		SIL	1	
TITAN		TIB	1	
TITAN		V	1	
TITAN		VAL	2 20	Sol; Prometheus

TITANES pl.	CIC		1	the Titans (anti-Olympian gods)
TITANES	HOR		1	
TITANES	MAN		1	
TITANES	PROP		1	
TITANES	SIL	1	5	
TITANI =-es, Pers.26	PL			Titans
TITANIA patron.	OV		4	Latona; Diana; Circe; Pyrrha
TITANIA	SIL	1	5	Luna
TITANIACUS	OV			p. to Titan(s)
TITANIS	ENN		1	Luna (Diana)
TITANIS	OV		3	Latona; Circe; Tethys
TITANIS	S		1	Luna
TITANIS	VAL	1	6	Circe
TITANIS*	JUV			p. to the Titans
TITANIUS	GER		1	p. to the Titans
TITANIUS	MAN		1	
TITANIUS	SIL		1	
TITANIUS	V		1	
TITANIUS	VAL	2	6	p. to Sol; p. to Prometheus
TITANUS and pl. -i	FPLA			a Titan
TITARESOS	LUC			river of Thessaly
TITARESSUS Tr.846	SEN			
TITHONIA patr.	OV		1	Aurora
TITHONIA	S		1	
TITHONIA	VAL	1	3	
TITHONIS fem.patr.	S			Aurora
TITHONIUS	GER		1	p. to Tithonus
TITHONIUS	OV		1	
TITHONIUS	S		1	
TITHONIUS	SIL		1	
TITHONIUS	V	1	5	
TITHONUS	AV		1	husband of Aurora & s. of Laomedon
TITHONUS	HOR		1	
TITHONUS	OV		1	
TITHONUS	PL		1	
TITHONUS	PRIAP		1	
TITHONUS	PROP		1	
TITHONUS	SIL		1	
TITHONUS	V	1	8	
TITI 1.20	PER			= Titiens, the primitive Roman tribe
TITIENS pl.	PROP			"
TITIENSES = Titiens	OV			" (F. 3.131)
TITIUS Novius 67	COM		1	Sextus Titius (?)
TITIUS	HOR		1	cont. poet
TITIUS	JUV		1	fict.
TITIUS	MAR		1	fict.
TITIUS	TIB	1	5	unknown (a type)
TITIUS* (sodales)	LUC			p. to the Titiens(es)
-TITULLUS 8.44	MAR			fict.
TITUS	LUCIL		1	fict.
TITUS	MAR		2	the emperor; a cont.
TITUS	PL	1	4	= Plautus
TITUS/TATIUS	ENN			legendary Sabine king
TITYOS cf. -us	AET		1	mythical giant, son of Juppiter
TITYOS	AV		1	
TITYOS	HOR		1	
TITYOS	LUC		1	

TITYOS	LUCR	1	mythical giant
TITYOS	OV	1	
TITYOS	PH	1	
TITYOS	S	1	
TITYOS	SEN	1	
TITYOS	TIB	1	
TITYOS	V	1 11	
TITYRUS	CAL	1	a shepherd
TITYRUS	FPLR	1	
TITYRUS	MAR	1	(esp. of V's Bucolics)
TITYRUS	OV	2	a shepherd; ep. of V's Bucolics
TITYRUS 2.34.72	PROP	1	= Virgil
TITYRUS	V	1 7	a shepherd
TITYUS = Tityos	PROP	1	the giant
TITYUS	VAL	1 2	
TLEPOLEMUS M. 12.537	OV	1	son of Hercules
TLEPOLEMUS	SIL	1 2	
TLEPOLOMUS	HL		
TMARIUS A. 5.620	V		p. to Tmaros
TMAROS	V		a mt. in Epirus
TMOLIUS	AV	1	
TMOLIUS	OV	1	
TMOLIUS as N	V	1 3	the Tmolus mt.
TMOLOS cf. Timolus	S	1	mt. in Lydia
TMOLOS	V	1 2	
TMOLUS	OV	1	mt. in Lydia (& its god)
TMOLUS also Timolus	SEN	1	
TMOLUS	SIL	1	
TMOLUS	TR	1 4	
-TOLENUS or Telonum?	OV		r. in Marsian territory (F. 6.565)
TOLETANUS	GR		p. to Toletum (t. in Spain)
TOLOSA	MAR		town of Gaul
TOLOSAS adj.	MAR		p. to Tolosa
TOLUMNIUS	PROP	1	king of Veii
TOLUMNIUS	V	1 2	Rutulian prophet
TOMI = Tomis	S		port-town of Moesia (S. 1.2.258)
TOMIS fem.	OV		" "
TOMITAE	OV		residents of Tomi
TOMITANUS	OV		p. to Tomi
TONANS	GER	1	ep. of Juppiter
TONANS	HL	1	
TONANS	JUV	1	
TONANS	LUC	1	
TONANS	MAN	1	
TONANS	MAR	3	(+ Saturn; Domitian)
TONANS	OV	1	
TONANS	PH	1	
TONANS	S	1	
TONANS	SIL	1	
TONANS	VAL	1 13	
-TONGILIANUS 3.52	MAR		fict. man
-TONGILIUS 7.130	JUV	1	cont. lawyer
TONGILIUS 2.40	MAR	1 2	fict.
TORANIUS	MAR		cont. man (a friend of MAR)
TORQUATUS	CAT	1	son of M. Torquatus
TORQUATUS	CIC	1	consul
TORQUATUS	HOR	2	consul; a friend of HOR

TORQUATUS	LUC		1	T. Manlius Torquatus
TORQUATUS	MAN		1	friend of Horace
TORQUATUS	MAR		1	(unknown)
TORQUATUS	SIL		2	T. Manlius T.; a Roman soldier
TORQUATUS	V	1	10	T.M.T.
TORQUATUS* 7.584	LUC			p. to the T. family
TORYNI (-ini)	VAL			tribe of Scythia
-TOXEUS M. 8.441	OV		1	son of Thestius
TOXEUS HO 214	SEN	1	2	mythical youth killed by Hercules
-TOXILUS Pers. passim	PL			name of slave
TRABEA m.	FPLA			a Roman comic poet
-TRACHALIO Rud. passim	PL			name of a slave
TRACHAS -nt-, fem.	OV			= Terracina (t.)
TRACHIN fem.	LUC		1	town of Thessaly
TRACHIN	OV		1	
TRACHIN	SEN	1	3	
TRACHINIUS	OV			= Ceyx
TRACHINIUS*	LUC		1	p. to Trachin
TRACHINIUS*	OV		1	
TRACHINIUS*	S	1	3	
TRAECI em.,Pac.209	TR			(a reading discarded by Warmington)
TRAGOEDIA	OV			Tragedy personified
TRAIANUS	MAR			the emperor Trajan
TRALLES fem.pl.	JUV			town of Lydia
TRANIO Most. passim	PL			a slave-name
TRANSPADANUS N	CAT			a person from beyond the Po
TRANSTIBERINUS	MAR			p. to region across the Tiber
/TRASIMENNUS	MAN			lake in Etruria
\TRASIMENUS	S			
TRASIMENUS* F.6.765	OV			p. to the lake
TRASUMENNUS	SIL	3	3	lake; god of lake; a hero
-TRASUS or Thasos	OV			(uncertain meanings) Ibis 476
TRAUSIUS	HOR			cont. man
TREBATIUS	HOR			cont. of Cicero
TREBELLIUS/LUCIUS	LUCIL			(perhaps) the L. Tr. mentioned in Cicero
TREBIA m., 2.46	LUC		1	river in N. Italy
TREBIA	MAN		1	
TREBIA	SIL	1	3	
TREBIUS	JUV			fict. man
TREBONIUS	HOR			cont.
TREBULA	MAR			Sabine town
TREBULANUS	MAR			p. to Trebula
TREMOR M. 8.790	OV			"Tremor" personified
TREVIR 1.441	LUC			one of the Belgian Treviri
-TRICASTINUS 3.466	SIL			p. to a Gaulish tribe
TRICCE	SEN			town of Thessaly
-TRICRENE em., F.2.276	OV			mt. in Arcadia
TRIFOLINUM	MAR			wine of mt. Trifolium
TRIFOLINUS	JUV			p. to mt. Trifolium
TRIGEMINA/PORTA	PL			an old gate at Rome (Capt. 90)
TRIGONUM	MAN			constell. (Triangle)
TRINACRIA fem.	AV		1	Sicily
TRINACRIA	MAN		1	
TRINACRIA	OV		1	
TRINACRIA	SIL		1	
TRINACRIA	V		1	
TRINACRIA	VAL	1	6	

TRINACRIS	OV		Sicily
TRINACRIUS	AET	1	p. to Sicily
TRINACRIUS	CAT	1	
TRINACRIUS	GR	1	
TRINACRIUS	OV	1	
TRINACRIUS	S	1	
TRINACRIUS	SIL	1	
TRINACRIUS	V	1	
TRINACRIUS	VAL	1 8	
TRINUMMUS	PL		title of his comedy
TRIONES pl.	OV	1	constell. (Big & Little Dippers)
TRIONES	V	1 2	
TRIOPEIS patr.	OV		Mestra, d. of Erysichthon (M. 8.872)
TRIOPEIUS m., N	OV		Erysichthon
TRIPHALLUS	JUV	1	ep. of Priapus
TRIPHALLUS	PRIAP	1	
TRIPHALLUS	TIB	1 3	
TRIPTOLEMUS	AV	1	mythical king of Eleusis
TRIPTOLEMUS	OV	1	
TRIPTOLEMUS	S	1	
TRIPTOLEMUS	SEN	1 4	
TRIQUETRUS adj.	HOR	1	Sicilian
TRIQUETRUS	SIL	1 2	
TRITANUS	LUCIL		a gladiator
TRITON	AET	1	s. of Neptune & a god of the sea
TRITON 64.395	CAT	1	mythical river
TRITON	LUC	1	r. in N. Africa (and lake)
TRITON	MAR	1	son of Neptune
TRITON	OV	1	"
TRITON	PROP	1	"
TRITON	S	1	river in N. Africa
TRITON	SIL	2	son of Neptune; a ship-name
TRITON	TR	1	"
TRITON	V	2	" ; a ship (A. 10.209)
TRITON 1.679	VAL	1 13	
TRITONES pl.	HL	1	sea-gods (in brother)
TRITONES	SEN	1 2	
TRITONIA	HL	1	ep. of Minerva
TRITONIA	LUC	1	
TRITONIA	OV	1	
TRITONIA	S	1	
TRITONIA	SIL	1	
TRITONIA	VAL	1 6	
TRITONIACUS adj.	OV		p. to Minerva
TRITONIS	LUC	1	Minerva
TRITONIS	MAR	1	
TRITONIS	OV	1	
TRITONIS	PET	1	
TRITONIS	S	2	Minerva's olive tree; lake Triton
TRITONIS	SIL	2	wife of Iarbas; lake Triton
TRITONIS	V	1 9	Minerva
TRITONIS*	LUCR	1	p. to Minerva
TRITONIS*	OV	1 2	
TRITONIUS	SIL	1	p. to lake Triton
TRITONIUS	V	1 2	
-TRIUMPHUS (Sp. 20)	MAR	1	beast-fighter
TRIUMPHUS P. 3.4.3	OV	1	title of Ovid's poem on Tiberius

TRIUMPHUS	15.100	SIL	1 3	"Triumph" personified
TRIVIA		CAT	1	ep. of Diana
TRIVIA		ENN	1	
TRIVIA		LUCR	1	
TRIVIA		MAR	1	
TRIVIA		OV	1	
TRIVIA		PET	1	
TRIVIA		PROP	1	
TRIVIA		S	1	
TRIVIA		SEN	1	
TRIVIA		SIL	1	
TRIVIA		TIB	1	
TRIVIA		V	1	
TRIVIA		VAL	1 13	
TRIVICUM		HOR		town in Apulia
TROADES	fem.pl.	OV	1	Trojan women
TROADES		S	1	
TROADES		SEN	1	
TROADES		V	1 4	
TROAS	M. 13.566	OV		a Trojan woman (Hecuba)
TROAS*		OV		Trojan
TROES	pl. of Tros	AV	1	Trojans
TROES		PET	1	
TROES		SEN	1 3	
-TROESMIS	fem.	OV		town of Moesia (P. 4.9.79)
TROEZEN	fem.	OV	1	town of the Argolid
TROEZEN		S	1	
TROEZEN		SEN	1 3	
TROEZENIUS	adj.	OV		p. to Troezen
-TROGILOS	14.259	SIL		town of Sicily
-TROGINUS	1021 W	LUCIL		a (Celtic?) soldier
TROIA		AET	1	the famous town (cf. Ilium etc.)
TROIA		AV	1	
TROIA		CAT	1	
TROIA		CIC	1	
TROIA		ENN	1	
TROIA		FPLA	1	
TROIA		GER	1	
TROIA		HL	1	
TROIA		HOR	1	
TROIA		JUV	1	
TROIA		LUC	1	
TROIA		LUCR	1	
TROIA		MAN	1	
TROIA		MAR	1	
TROIA		MLP	1	
TROIA		OV	2	(+ t. in Epirus: M. 13.721)
TROIA		PET	1	
TROIA		PL	1	
TROIA		PROP	1	
TROIA		S	1	
TROIA		SEN	1	
TROIA		SIL	1	
TROIA		TIB	1	
TROIA		TR	1	
TROIA		V	3	(+ t. in Epirus; game of Troy)
TROIA		VAL	1 29	

TROIADES	fem.pl.	PER			Trojan women (1.4)
TROIANI		HL		1	residents of Troy
TROIANI		OV		1	
TROIANI		SIL		1	
TROIANI		TIB	1	4	
TROIANUS		OV		1	a Trojan
TROIANUS	& pl.	V	1	2	"
TROIANUS*		ENN		1	Trojan
TROIANUS*		HL		1	
TROIANUS*		HOR		1	
TROIANUS*		JUV		1	
TROIANUS*		LUC		1	
TROIANUS*		MAN		1	
TROIANUS*		OV		1	
TROIANUS*		PL		1	
TROIANUS*		PROP		1	
TROIANUS*		S		1	
TROIANUS*		SIL		1	
TROIANUS*		V	1	12	
-TROICA	n.pl., 8.221	JUV			title of an epic
TROICUS		CAT		1	p. to Troy
TROICUS		HL		1	
TROICUS		HOR		1	
TROICUS		OV		1	
TROICUS		PRIAP		1	
TROICUS		PROP		1	
TROICUS		S		1	
TROICUS		SEN		1	
TROICUS		TIB	1	9	
TROIIANI	= Troiani	LUCR			Trojans
TROIIUGENAE		LUCR			Trojans
TROILOS		HOR			a son of Priam
TROILUS		PL		1	
TROILUS		S		1	
TROILUS		SEN		1	
TROILUS		V	1	4	
TROIUGENA		FPLA		1	a Roman
TROIUGENA		V	1	2	a Trojan
TROIUGENAE		CAT		1	Trojans
TROIUGENAE		JUV		1	Romans
TROIUGENAE		SIL	1	3	"
TROIUS		AV		1	p. to Troy
TROIUS		CAT		1	
TROIUS		HL		1	
TROIUS		OV		1	
TROIUS		PET		1	
TROIUS		S		1	
TROIUS		SIL		1	
TROIUS		V	1	8	
TROS	also pl.	HL		1	a Trojan
TROS	v.l. (Troas?)	HOR		1	
TROS	also pl.	OV		1	
TROS		SIL		1	a king of Phrygia
TROS		V	2	6	a k. of Phrygia; a Trojan
-TROUS	= Tros	TR			a king in Phrygia
TRUCULENTUS		PL			a title of play
TRUENTĪNUS	adj.	SIL			p. to Truentum (t. of Picenum)

TRUTHUS	or Struthus	PL			?? (Trin. 1020)
TRYPHERUS		JUV			a Roman carver
TRYPHON	Cat. 10.6	AV		1	a muleteer
TRYPHON		MAR	1	2	a publisher
TUBERTUS/POSTUMUS		OV			Postumus, dictator(430 BC)
TUBILUSTRIA n.pl.		OV			festival of trumpets
TUBULUS/LUCIUS		LUCIL			L. Tubulus, praetor in 142 BC
-TUCCA	Cat. 1.1	AV		1	fict. or unknown
TUCCA	1.18	MAR	1	2	"
TUCCIA	6.64	JUV			unknown girl of Apulia
TUCCIUS		MAR			fictional
TUDER (-er-) n.		SIL			town of Umbria
TUDERS	as N	SIL			a resident of Tuder
TUDITANUS	dub.	ENN			a Roman name]
-TULLA	A. 11.656	V			attendant of Camilla
TULLIA	6.307	JUV		1	unknown cont. woman
TULLIA		OV		1	Tullia minor, d. of Servius Tullius
TULLIA	Oct. 305	SEN		1	
TULLIA	13.835	SIL	1	4	
TULLIUS		HOR		1	Servius Tullius, king of Rome
TULLIUS		JUV		1	
TULLIUS	7.63	LUC		1	M. T. Cicero
TULLIUS	1.794	MAN		1	Servius T. (?)
TULLIUS		MAR		1	Cicero
TULLIUS	F. 6.581	OV		1	Servius T.
TULLIUS	8.404	SIL		1	a leader of the Arpinates
TULLIUS	Att., pr. 40	TR	1	8	Servius T.
TULLIUS/QUINTUS		LUCIL			(unknown)
TULLUS	(anon.mim. 10)	COM		1	(unknown)
TULLUS		HOR		2	a king of Rome; a consul 66 BC.
TULLUS	5.57	JUV		1	Hostilius Tullus
TULLUS	9.806	LUC		1	(unknown young man)
TULLUS		MAR		1	Cn. Domitius T., cont.
TULLUS		PROP		1	a friend of Tullus
TULLUS		SIL		2	a king; a soldier
TULLUS		V	1	10	a king of Rome
TUNGER	sg.	SIL			a member of the Tungri (Belgian tribe)
-TUNNICUS	= Thyn. (?)	FPLB			Bithynian
-TURASIA	4.55.21	MAR			town of Spain
-TURBALIO	Rud. 657	PL			slave-name
TURBO		HOR			a gladiator
TURDETANI		PL			a tribe of Spain (pun on turdus)
-TURGONTUS	4.55.21	MAR			lake in Spain
TURIBULUM		GER			constell. "Censer" (cf. Ara)
TURIUS		HOR			C. Turius, praetor
TURNUS		COL		1	king of the Rutuli & opponent of Aeneas
TURNUS		JUV		1	
TURNUS		MAR		1	
TURNUS		OV		1	
TURNUS		S		1	
TURNUS		TIB		1	
TURNUS		V	1	7	
TURPILIUS		FPLA			the comic poet
TURRANIUS		OV			a poet
TUSCA		JUV			any Italic woman
TUSCI	pl. m.	COM		1	Etruscans
TUSCI		GR		1	

TUSCI	LUCIL	1		Etruscans
TUSCI	MAR	1		
TUSCI	PROP	1		
TUSCI	V	1	6	
TUSCULANUM (praedium)	FPLR			an estate at Tusculum
TUSCULANUS	MAR			p. to Tusculum
TUSCULI 7.31.11	MAR			an estate or farm at Tusculum
-TUSCULIDAE m.pl.	LUCIL			people of Tusculum
TUSCULUM	HOR			town of Latium
TUSCULUS	MAR	1		p. to Tusculum
TUSCULUS	S	1		
TUSCULUS	SIL	1		
TUSCULUS	TIB	1	4	
TUSCUS N	JUV		2	= Sejanus
TUSCUS sg., 1.637	LUC		1	the Etruscans (collectively)
TUSCUS	OV	1	4	a poet
TUSCUS*	COL		1	Etruscan
TUSCUS*	HOR		1	
TUSCUS*	JUV		1	
TUSCUS*	LUC		1	
TUSCUS*	MAR		1	
TUSCUS*	OV		1	
TUSCUS*	PER		1	
TUSCUS*	PH		1	
TUSCUS*	PL		1	
TUSCUS*	PRIAP		1	
TUSCUS*	PROP		1	
TUSCUS*	S		1	
TUSCUS*	SIL		1	
TUSCUS*	TIB		1	
TUSCUS*	V		1	
TUSCUS*	VAL	1	16	
TUTANUS N	VAR			a Roman protective deity
-TUTIA 13.5	SIL			stream in Latium
TUTICANUS	OV			poet-friend
TUTILIUS	MAR			a Roman rhetorician
-TVETONISSA 4.55.22	MAR			town of Spain
TYCHIUS	OV			a shoe-maker of Boeotia
-TYDE 3.367	SIL			a fort in Spain
-TYDEIUS adj., 453	HL			p. to Tydeus (and to Diomedes)
TYDEUS m., dissyll.	OV		1	legendary father of Diomedes
TYDEUS	PRIAP		1	
TYDEUS	S		1	
TYDEUS	V		1	
TYDEUS	VAL	1	5	(an Argonaut)
TYDIDES patron.	HL		1	Diomedes
TYDIDES	HOR		1	
TYDIDES	JUV		1	
TYDIDES	MAN		1	
TYDIDES	OV		1	
TYDIDES	S		1	
TYDIDES	SIL		1	
TYDIDES	V	1	8	
-TYMBRENUS 2.633	SIL			a Saguntine soldier
TYNDAREUS	OV		1	legendary king of Sparta
TYNDAREUS	SIL		1	
TYNDAREUS	TR		1	

TYNDAREUS		VAL	1	4	legendary king of Sparta
TYNDARIDAE	Cir. 399	AV		1	Castor & Pollux (Dioscuri)
TYNDARIDAE		HOR		1	the children of Tyndareus
TYNDARIDAE		OV		1	Castor & Pollux
TYNDARIDAE		PROP	1	4	" "
TYNDARIDES	sg.	S		1	Pollux
TYNDARIDES		VAL	1	2	"
TYNDARIS	Cat. 9.27	AV		1	Helen
TYNDARIS		HOR		1	woman friend of HOR
TYNDARIS	6.657	JUV		1	Clytemnestra
TYNDARIS	1.464	LUCR		1	Helen
TYNDARIS		MAR		1	"
TYNDARIS		OV		2	" ; Clytemnestra
TYNDARIS		PROP		1	Clytemnestra
TYNDARIS	A. 1.946	S		1	Helen
TYNDARIS		SEN		2	" ; Clytemnestra
TYNDARIS	14.208	SIL		1	town of Sicily
TYNDARIS		V	1	13	Helen
- TYNDARUS	Capt. 36	PL			a slave-name
TYPHOEUS		HOR		1	the Titan-giant of Aetna
TYPHOEUS		LUC		1	
TYPHOEUS		MAN		1	
TYPHOEUS		OV		1	
TYPHOEUS		SEN		1	
TYPHOEUS		SIL		1	
TYPHOEUS		V		1	
TYPHOEUS		VAL	1	8	
TYPHOEUS*	or -oius	V			p. to Typhoeus
TYPHOIS	adj.	OV			p. to Typhoeus
TYPHON		AV		1	= Typhoeus, the giant
TYPHON		LUC		1	
TYPHON		MAN		1	
TYPHON		OV		1	
TYPHON		SEN		1	
TYPHON		VAL	1	6	
TYPHONIDES	fem.pl.	VAL			daughters of Typhon
TYPHONIS		MAN			an astrological position
TYRAS	m.	OV			river in Russia (Dniester?)
- TYRES m.sg.,	6.44	SIL		1	a Nasamonian
TYRES	A. 10.403	V		1	an Arcadian
TYRES	4.719, 6.201	VAL	2	4	a river (?); a Scythian
TYRIAE	sc. lacernae	MAR			Tyrian purple (4.28.2)
TYRII		FPLB		1	(Tyrians), Carthaginians
TYRII		LUC		1	
TYRII	AA. 2.297	OV		1	
TYRII		S		1	
TYRII		SIL		1	
TYRII		V	1	6	
TYRIUS	N, 1.301	MAN		1	a Tyrian, a Phoenician
TYRIUS	N, 15.433	SIL	1	2	= Hannibal
TYRIUS*		CAT		1	Tyrian, Phoenician
TYRIUS*		COM		1	
TYRIUS*		GER		1	
TYRIUS*		HOR		1	
TYRIUS*		JUV		1	
TYRIUS*		LUC		1	
TYRIUS*		MAN		1	

TYRIUS*	MAR	1	Tyrian, Phoenician
TYRIUS*	OV	1	
TYRIUS*	PROP	1	
TYRIUS*	S	1	
TYRIUS*	SEN	1	
TYRIUS*	SIL	1	
TYRIUS*	TIB	1	
TYRIUS*	V	1	
TYRIUS*	VAL	1 16	
TYRO Ep. 18.132	OV	1	daughter of Salmoneus
TYRO	PROP	1 ?	" "
TYROS fem.	LUC	1	town in Phoenicia (cf. Sarra)
TYROS	MAR	1	
TYROS	PROP	1	
TYROS	S	1	
TYROS	SIL	1	
TYROS	TIB	1	
TYROS	V	1 7	
TYRRHENIA M. 14.452	OV		Etruria
TYRRHENUS N, 3.709	LUC	1	a soldier of Caesar
TYRRHENUS	SIL	3	three different warriors
TYRRHENUS & pl.	V	1	an Etruscan
TYRRHENUS	VAL	1 6	the Tyrrhene Sea
TYRRHENUS*	CIC	1	Etruscan, p. to Etruria
TYRRHENUS*	COL	1	
TYRRHENUS*	HOR	1	
TYRRHENUS*	JUV	1	
TYRRHENUS*	LUC	1	
TYRRHENUS*	LUCR	1	
TYRRHENUS*	OV	1	
TYRRHENUS*	PROP	1	
TYRRHENUS*	S	1	
TYRRHENUS*	SEN	1	
TYRRHENUS*	SIL	1	
TYRRHENUS*	V	1	
TYRRHENUS*	VAL	1 13	
TYRRHIDAE m.pl.	V		sons of Tyrrhus
TYRRHUS	V		a legendary shepherd of k. Latinus
TYRTAEUS AP 402	HOR		the Greek elegiac poet
TYRUS = Tyros	OV	1	town in Phoenicia
TYRUS	VAL	1 ?	
UCALEGON -ont-, 3.199	JUV	1	(Virgil's Ucalegon)
UCALEGON A. 2.312	V	1 2	a Trojan
UFENS -nt-, m.	SIL	2	river in Latium; a man
UFENS cf. Oufens	V	2 4	river
-ULIUS em. (Julius)	HOR		a cont. (S. 1.8.39)
ULIXES	AV	1	the heroic king of Ithaca
ULIXES	CIC	1	
ULIXES	ENN	1	
ULIXES	FPLA	1	
ULIXES	HL	1	
ULIXES	HOR	1	
ULIXES	JUV	1	
ULIXES	LUCIL	1	
ULIXES	MAR	1	
ULIXES	OV	1	
ULIXES	PET	1	

ULIXES	PL		1	king of Ithaca
ULIXES	PRIAP		1	
ULIXES	PROP		1	
ULIXES	S		1	
ULIXES	SEN		1	
ULIXES	SIL		1	
ULIXES	TIB		1	
ULIXES	TR		1	
ULIXES	V		1	
ULIXES	VAR	1	21	
ULTOR	JUV		1	ep. of Mars
ULTOR	OV	1	2	
ULUBRAE	HOR		1	town of Latium
ULUBRAE	JUV	1	2	
UMBER	CAT		1	an Umbrian
UMBER	GR		1	breed of dog
UMBER	MAR		1	fict. man
UMBER	S		1	Umbrian boar
UMBER	SEN		1	dog breed
UMBER	SIL		1	" "
UMBER	V		1	" "
UMBER	VAL	1	8	" "
UMBER* (aper)	HOR		1	Umbrian
UMBER*	MAR		1	
UMBER*	OV		1	
UMBER*	PROP		1	
UMBER*	SIL	1	5	
UMBRA	PL			an Umbrian woman (pun)
UMBRENUS	HOR			a soldier of Octavian
UMBRI	LUC		1	the people of Umbria
UMBRI	PER		1	
UMBRI	SIL	1	3	
UMBRIA	LUC		1	region of Italy
UMBRIA	MAR		1	
UMBRIA	OV		1	
UMBRIA	PROP	1	4	
UMBRICIUS N	JUV			a poet-friend
UMBRICUS adj.	GR			
-UMBRO A. 10.544	V			a Marsian warrior
-UMMIDIUS S. 1.1.95	HOR			a cont.
-UNDA 2.542	MAN			constell. (Aquarius)
-UNICUS 12.44	MAR			a cont. poet
UNOMAMMIA	PL			"Amazonia" (comic formation)
URANIA	CAT		1	Muse of Astronomy
URANIA or -ie	OV	1	2	
URANIE	MLP		1	
URANIE T. 8.551	S	1	2	
URBANAE/PORTAE	OV			uncertain gate (Nux 137)
URBICUS	JUV		1	a poet
URBICUS	MAR	2	3	a poet; a child
URBS m.	AV		1	Rome
URBS	OV		1	
URBS	PROP	1	3	
-URII 36.12	CAT			town in Apulia
-URION F. 5.535	OV			= Orion
URNA 9.537	LUC		1	constell. "Aquarius"
URNA	MAN	1	2	

URSA		GER	1	constell. "Bear"
URSA		LUC	1	
URSA		MAN	1	
URSA		OV	1	
URSA		S	1	5	
-URSIDIUS	6.38	JUV		a moechus
-URSUS	S. 2.6.60	S		Flavius Ursus, a cont.
USIPI		MAR		a Germanic tribe
USTĪCA		HOR		mt. in Sabine territory
USUS	Afran. 298	COM		"Enjoyment" personified
UTICA		HOR	1	town of N. Africa
UTICA		LUC	1	
UTICA		SIL	1	3	
UXAMA		SIL		a town in Spain
-VACERRA	8.69	MAR		a fict. person
VACUNA		HOR	1	a Sabine goddess
VACUNA		OV	1	2	
VACUNALIS		OV		p. to Vacuna
-VADAVERO	1.49.6	MAR		place (or stream?) in Spain
VAGA or Vacca		SIL		town in Numidia
-VAGELLIUS	16.23	JUV		a declamator
VAGENNI		SIL		Alpine tribe
-VALA m., Epist.1.15.1		HOR		a friend of HOR
VALERIANUS/POLLIUS		MAR		Q. Poll. Val., a book-dealer
VALERIUS		HOR	1	P. P. Valerius
VALERIUS		LUCIL	1	2	Val. Valentinus
VALERIUS/MARTIALIS		MAR		himself, the epigrammatist
-VALERUS A. 10.752		V		an Etruscan
VALGIUS		HOR	1	T. Valgius Rufus, the poet
VALGIUS		TIB	1	2	
VANGIONES	1.431	LUC		German tribe
VANILOQUIDORUS		PL		comic name
-VANUS em., 6.115		VAL		a priest (?)
VARENUS	4.543	SIL		an Umbrian man
VARIA fem.		HOR		town of the Sabines
-VARILLUS	2.22	JUV		a cont.
VARIUS		AV	1	L. Varius, the poet
VARIUS		HOR	1	
VARIUS		LP	1	
VARIUS		MAR	1	
VARIUS		OV	1	
VARIUS		V	1	6	
VARRO		AV	1	the poet Atacinus
VARRO		FPLA	1	the scholar
VARRO		MAN	1	the consul
VARRO		MAR	1	(unknown cont. poet)
VARRO		OV	1	P. T. Varro Atacinus
VARRO		PROP	1	the poet Atacinus
VARRO		SIL	1	7	the consul
VARRO/ATACINUS		HOR		poet
VARUS		CAT	1	Quintilius Varus (the general)
VARUS		HOR	1	" "
VARUS		LUC	2	P. Attius Varus; r. in S. Gaul (1.404)
VARUS		MAN	1	Quintilius Varus
VARUS		MAR	2	a centurion; fict.
VARUS B. 6.7		V	1	8	Alfenus Varus (consul 39 BC)
VASCO (sg. of next)		SIL		a Basque of Spain

VASCONES	JUV			the Basques
-VATERNUS (Vatrenus?)	MAR			a stream (in N. Italy?) 3.67.2
VATICANA n.pl.	MAR			wines from the Vatican hill
VATICANUS mons	HOR	1		Vatican hill in Rome
VATICANUS	JUV	1		
VATICANUS	MAR	1	3	
-VATIENA	FPLA			a Roman woman
VATINIANUS adj.	CAT			p. to Vatinius
VATINIUS	CAT	1		P. Vatinius
VATINIUS	MAR	1	2	a shoemaker
-VATIVESCA 4.55.26	MAR			a place in Spain
VEI = Veii	PROP			town of Etruria
VEIA Epod. 5.29	HOR			name of a sorceress
-VEIANIUS Epist.1.1.4	HOR			a gladiator
VEIENS -nt-, adj.	HOR	1		p. to Veii
VEIENS	PROP	1		
VEIENS	S	1		
VEIENS	TR	1	4	
VEIENTANUM	HOR	1		wine of Veii
VEIENTANUM	MAR	1	2	
VEIENTANUS	MAR			p. to Veii
VEIENTES	OV	1		people of Veii
VEIENTES	SIL	1	2	
VEII cf. Vei	FPLR	1		town of Etruria
VEII	LUC	1	2	
VEIIENTANUM	PER			wine of Veii
VEIIENTO (-on-), m.	JUV			A. Fabricius V., cont. of Nero
VEIUS adj.	PROP			p. to Veii
VEJOVIS	OV			Etruscan god of the Underworld
VELABRENSIS	MAR			p. to Velabrum
VELABRUM	HOR	1		a street in Rome
VELABRUM	OV	1		
VELABRUM	PL	1		
VELABRUM as pl.	PROP	1		
VELABRUM	TIB	1	5	
VELEDA S. 1.4.90	S			a German prophetess
VELIA	HOR			a town in Lucania
VELIE	S			
VELINA (tribus)	HOR			a Latian tribe
VELINA/PUBLIUS	PER			a freedman
VELINUS 4.183	SIL	1		a Sabine lake (and river)
VELINUS	V	1	2	" "
VELINUS*	V			p. to Velinus
VELITERNUS	SIL			p. to Velitrae
VELITRAE	SIL			Volscian town
-VELIUS 9.31	MAR			cont.
VELOX 1.110	MAR			fict.
VENAFRANUM	JUV			olive-oil from Venafrum
VENAFRANUS	HOR			p. to Venafrum
VENAFRUM	HOR	1		town of Campania
VENAFRUM	MAR	1		
VENAFRUM	SIL	1	3	
VENERES	CAT	1		"Charm" personified
VENERES	MAR	1		
VENERES	PROP	1	3	
VENERIUM Asin.905	PL			a throw (in dice)
VENERIUS	COM	1		p. to Venus

VENERIUS	ENN	1	p. to Venus
VENERIUS	PL	1 3	
VENETI	SIL		a tribe in NE Italy
VENETUS N. 4.134	LUC	1	the Veneti (collective sg.)
VENETUS	MAR	1 2	
VENETUS*	JUV	1	p. to the Veneti
VENETUS*	MAR	1	
VENETUS*	PROP	1	
VENETUS*	SIL	1 4	
VENILIA	OV	1	wife of Janus
VENILIA	V	1 2	mother of Turnus
VENTIDIUS	JUV		Ventidius Bassus
-VENULEIUS 4.82.1	MAR		a consul
VENULUS M. 14.457	OV	1	Rutulian emissary of Turnus
VENULUS 4.181	SIL	1	a Roman soldier
VENULUS A. 8.9	V	1 3	Rutulian hero
VENUS	AV	1	Roman goddess of Love
VENUS	CAL	1	
VENUS	CAT	1	
VENUS	COL	1	
VENUS	COM	1	
VENUS	ENN	1	
VENUS	FPLA	1	
VENUS	FPLR	1	
VENUS	GER	1	(planet Venus)
VENUS	GR	1	
VENUS	HL	1	
VENUS	HOR	1	(C. 2.7.25: dice-throw)
VENUS	JUV	1	
VENUS	LUC	2	(+ planet)
VENUS	LUCR	1	
VENUS	MAN	2	(+ planet)
VENUS	MAR	1	
VENUS	MLP	1	
VENUS	OV	1	
VENUS	PER	1	
VENUS	PET	1	
VENUS	PH	1	
VENUS	PL	1	
VENUS	PRIAP	1	
VENUS	PROP	1	(4.8.45: dice-throw)
VENUS	S	1	
VENUS	SEN	1	
VENUS	SIL	1	
VENUS	TER	1	
VENUS	TIB	1	
VENUS	V	1	
VENUS	VAL	1	
VENUS	VAR	1 35	
VENUSINUS	HOR	1	p. to Venusia (town of Apulia)
VENUSINUS	JUV	1 2	
VENUSTAS Bacch. 115	PL		"Grace" personified
-VENUSTINA (ms. variant)	JUV		cont. man (6.167)
VER 5.735	LUCR	1	youthful Spring
VER M. 2.27	OV	1 2	" "
-VERANIOLUS 12.17	CAT		friend of Catullus
-VERANIUS 9.1	CAT		" " (same man)

VERCELLAE	MAR		1	town in N. Italy
VERCELLAE	SIL	1	2	
VERGILIAE	CIC		1	the Pleiades (constell.)
VERGILIAE	PL		1	
VERGILIAE	PROP	1	3	
VERGILII pl.	MAR			Vergils (as a type)
VERGILIUS	COL		1	P. Vergilius Maro, Roman epic poet
VERGILIUS	FPLR		1	
VERGILIUS	HOR		2	(+ a merchant)
VERGILIUS	JUV		1	
VERGILIUS	LP		1	
VERGILIUS	MAR		1	
VERGILIUS	OV		1	
VERGILIUS	PROP		1	
VERGILIUS	SIL		1	
VERGILIUS	TIB		1	
VERGILIUS G. 4.563	V	1	12	
-VERGINIA 10.294	JUV		1	legendary Roman girl
VERGINIA 13.824	SIL	1	2	
-VERGINIUS 8.221	JUV			Verg. Rufus (consul 63 AD)
VERITAS C. 1.24.7	HOR		1	"Truth, Integrity" personified
VERITAS 10.72.11	MAR		1	
VERITAS Ap. 4.2	PH		1	
VERITAS	VAR	1	4	
VERONA	CAT		1	town of N. Italy
VERONA	MAR		1	
VERONA	OV		1	
VERONA	SIL	1	4	
VERONENSIS	CAT			p. to Verona
VERRES	JUV			C. Cornel. V., the praetor of Sicily
VERTRAHA	GR			greyhound (a Celtic breed of dog)
VERTUMNUS cf. Vort-	HOR		1	Italic god of the Year & of Commerce
VERTUMNUS	OV		1	
VERTUMNUS	PROP		1	
VERTUMNUS	TIB	1	4	
-VERUS Sp. 29	MAR			a gladiator
VESAEVUS	V			mt. Vesuvius
VESBIUS	MAR		1	
VESBIUS	SIL	1	2	
VESEVUS	S		1	
VESEVUS	VAL	1	2	
VESPER m.	AV		1	Evening Star or the West
VESPER	CAT		1	
VESPER	GR		1	
VESPER	HOR		1	
VESPER	OV		1	
VESPER	S		1	
VESPER	V	1	7	
VESPERUGO Amph. 275	PL			Evening Star
VESPERUS m.	ENN			" " (a variant form)
VESTA	AV		1	Italic goddess of the Hearth, d. of Saturn
VESTA	ENN		1	
VESTA	HOR		1	
VESTA	JUV		1	
VESTA	MAN		1	
VESTA	MAR		1	
VESTA	OV		2	(+ mother of Saturn)

VESTA	PRIAP	1		Italic goddess of the Hearth
VESTA	PROP	1		
VESTA	S	1		
VESTA	SIL	1		
VESTA	V	1	13	
VESTALIS N	OV	2	2	man (friend of Ovid); vestal virgin
VESTALIS*	LUC	1		p. to Vesta
VESTALIS*	OV	1		
VESTALIS*	PER	1		
VESTALIS*	SIL	1		
VESTALIS*	TIB	1	5	
VESTĪNUS	MAR	1		a cont. (friend of N. Vindex)
VESTINUS	S	1	2	
VESTĪNUS*	ENN	1		p. to the Vestini (tribe of E. Italy)
VESTĪNUS*	JUV	1		
VESTĪNUS*	LUC	1		
VESTĪNUS*	MAR	1		
VESTĪNUS*	SIL	1	5	
VESUĪNUS (= -uvi-)	S			p. to Vesuvius
VESULUS	SIL		1	mt. in NW in Italy
VESULUS	V	1	2	
VESUVĪNUS	SIL			p. to Vesuvius
⟨VESUVIUS	S			volcanic mt. near Naples (in Campania)
⟨VESVIUS	VAL			
VESVIUS*	COL			p. to Vesuvius
-VETTIDIUS 4.25	PER			a rich man
VETTIUS 7.150	JUV			a rhetor
VETTONES	LUC		1	tribe of Lusitania
VETTONES	SIL	1	2	
-VETTUS	CIC			unknown contemporary
VETULONIA	SIL			town of Etruria
VETUSTAS S. 1.6.39	S			"Old Age" personified
-VETUSTILLĀ 3.93	MAR			fict.
-VETUSTINA 2.28.4	MAR			fict.
VIA/LACTEA M. 1.169	OV			the Milky Way
-VIBE m.	TR			an Etruscan
-VIBENNIUS 33.2	CAT			unknown cont.
-VIBIDIUS S. 2.8.22	HOR			a dandy
VIBIUS	MAR			V. Maximus, prefect of Egypt (104 AD)
-VICTIUS 98.1	CAT			cont.
VICTOR 80.7	CAT			unknown cont.
VICTORIA personif.	FPLA	1		a Roman goddess, "Victory"
VICTORIA	HOR	1		
VICTORIA	JUV	1		
VICTORIA	MAR	1		
VICTORIA	OV	1		
VICTORIA	PL	1		
VICTORIA	S	1		
VICTORIA	SIL	1		
VICTORIA	TIB	2		
VICTORIA	V	1	11	
VICUS/TUSCUS 4.2.50	PROP			a street in Rome
VIDULARIA fem.	PL			title of his comedy
VIENNA	MAR			town in Gaul
VILLIUS S. 1.2.64	HOR			a cont. (Sextus Villius ?)
VINALIA n.pl.	OV			a festival of wine
⟨VINCLA n.pl.	CIC			constellation

VINCULA	n.pl.	GER		constellation
VINDELICI		HOR		an Alpine tribe
VINDELICUS	adj.	MAR		p. to the Vindelici
VINDEMITOR		OV		a star in Virgo
-VINDEX		FPLR	1	G. Julius Vindex
VINDEX	8.222	JUV	1	Julius Vindex
VINDEX	9.43	MAR	1	Novius Vindex
VINDEX	S. 4.6.4	S	1 4	Novius Vindex, a friend
-VINNIUS Epist.1.13.2		HOR		unknown friend
-VIOLENTILLA S 1.2.25		S		wife of Stella
VIPSANUS	adj.	MAR		p. to Vipsanius Agrippa
VIRBIUS	M. 15.544	OV	1	ep. of Hippolytus
VIRBIUS		PER	1	a hill near Aricia
VIRBIUS		SIL	1	a group of triplets from Aricia
VIRBIUS		V	2 5	Hippolytus; his son
VIRDOMARUS		PROP		Gaulish chief
VIRGINES pl.		PROP		the Muses
VIRGINESVENDONIDES		PL		comic name of a man (Pers. 702)
VIRGINEUS adj., 2.627		MAN	1	p. to constell. Virgo
VIRGINEUS	P. 1.8.38	OV	1 2	p. to Virgo Aqua
VIRGO		AV	1	ep. of Astraea
VIRGO		CAT	1	constellation
VIRGO		CIC	1	
VIRGO		FPLR	1	
VIRGO		GER	1	
VIRGO	2.691	LUC	1	
VIRGO		MAN	1	
VIRGO		MAR	1	aqueduct (fountain of Trevi)
VIRGO		OV	3	const.; aqueduct; Minerva
VIRGO		S	1	aqueduct
VIRGO		SIL	1	Minerva
VIRGO		V	1 14	Astraea
VIRGO/AQUA	T. 3.12.220	V		fountain of Trevi
-VIRIASIUS 5.551		SIL		leader of the Sidicini (in Campania)
⟨VIRIATHUS		SIL		Spanish (Lusitanian?) general
⟨VIRIATUS		LUCIL		" "
-VIRRIUS 11.65		SIL		a Campanian man
-VIRRO em., 71.1		CAT	1	a cont. (?)
VIRRO	5.39	JUV	1 2	a cont.
VIRTUS	Culex 299	AV	1	"Courage, Valor" personified
VIRTUS	C. 2.2.19	HOR	1	Stoic "Virtue"
VIRTUS	1.115	JUV	1	Valor
VIRTUS	AA 3.23	OV	1	Valor
VIRTUS	Amph. 42	PL	1	Valor
VIRTUS	T. 7.51	S	1	Valor
VIRTUS	15.22	SIL	1 7	Virtue
-VISCUS 1.9.22		HOR		a friend of HOR
VISCUS/THURINUS		HOR		" "
-VISELLIUS S. 1.1.105		HOR		unknown man
VITELLIANI 2.6.6		MAR		a kind of writing tablet
VITELLIUS P. 4.7.27		OV		P. Vitellius, friend of Germanicus
-VOBERCA 1.49.14		MAR		town of Spain
-VOCONIUS/VICTOR 7.29		MAR		poet & friend
VOCONTIUS	3.467	SIL		p. to Vocontii (Gaulish tribe)
-VOLANERIUS S. 2.17.15		HOR		a dandy
VOLCAE	m.pl.	SIL		a Gaulish tribe
VOLCANIUS cf. Vul-		GR	1	p. to Vulcan

VOLCANIUS		JUV	1	p. to Vulcan
VOLCANIUS		TR	1	
VOLCANIUS		V	1 4	
VOLCANUS	cf. Vul-	FPLA	1	Roman god of fire
VOLCANUS		GR	1	
VOLCANUS		JUV	1	
VOLCANUS		MAR	1	
VOLCANUS		PL	1	(fire: Amph. 341)
VOLCANUS		TIB	2	
VOLCANUS		TR	1	
VOLCANUS		V	1 9	(fire: A. 2.311)
-VOLCENS	or -lsc-	V		a Latin warrior (A. 9.375)
VOLESI	8.182	JUV		two Sabine heroes named Volesus
VOLESUS		OV	1	a Sabine hero
VOLESUS		SIL	2 3	a Roman soldier; eponymous ancestor of
VOLSCE	adv.	COM		in Volscian language the Valerii.
VOLSCI		JUV	1	a tribe of Latium
VOLSCI	F. 6.721	OV	1	
VOLSCI		SIL	1 3	
VOLSCUS	adj.	SIL	1	p. to the Volscians
VOLSCUS		V	1 2	
VOLSINII		JUV		town in Etruria
VOLSINIUS		PROP		p. to Volsinii
VOLSO	10.143	SIL		son of Crista
VOLTEIUS	1.7.64	HOR		freedman
VOLTEIUS/MENA		HOR		(the same: Epist. 1.7.55)
VOLTURNUS	cf. Vul-	LUCR	1	SE wind
VOLTURNUS	M.15.715	OV	1	river in Campania
VOLTURNUS	S. 4.3.69	S	1	
VOLTURNUS	A. 7.729	V	1 4	
VOLUCRES		CIC		two stars "Birds"
VOLUMNIUS		VAR		a Roman gens
-VOLUNX	5.261	SIL		an African soldier
VOLUPTAS	Bacch. 115	PL	1	"Pleasure" personified
VOLUPTAS	S. 1.3.9	S	1	
VOLUPTAS	15.95	SIL	1 3	
VOLUSIUS		CAT		Roman poet
-VOLUSIUS/BITHYNICUS		JUV		a friend of JUV (15.1)
-VOLUSUS	A. 11.463	V		a Rutulian
-VOMANUS	8.437	SIL		river of Picenum
VOPISCUS	S. 1.3.1	S		Manilius Vopiscus, a poet
-VORANUS	S. 1.8.39	HOR		a thief
-VORAPTUS	6.288	VAL		a Scythian
VORTUMNUS = Vert-		COL		god of changing seasons
VORTUMNUS		HOR	1 2	
VOSEGUS	1.397	LUC	1	mt. range in E. Gaul (Vosges)
VOSEGUS	4.213	SIL	1 2	a Gaulish soldier
-VOTIENUS	8.72.5	MAR		V. Montanus, the rhetorician (?)
VULCANIUS	cf. Vol-	AV	1	p. to Vulcan
VULCANIUS		HL	1	
VULCANIUS		LUCIL	1	
VULCANIUS		OV	1	
VULCANIUS		S	1	
VULCANIUS		SIL	1	
VULCANIUS		VAL	1 7	
VULCANUS	cf. Vol-	AET	1	Roman god of fire
VULCANUS		AV	1	

VULCANUS	ENN	1		Roman god of fire
VULCANUS	FPLR	1		
VULCANUS	HL	1		
VULCANUS	HOR	1		
VULCANUS	MAN	1		
VULCANUS	OV	1		
VULCANUS	SEN	1		
VULCANUS	SIL	1		
VULCANUS	VAL	1	11	
-VULSCULUS (coll.sg.)	ENN			the Volscians (An. 162)
-VULTEIUS 4.465	LUC			a ship's captain
VULTUR m.	HOR	1		mt. in Apulia
VULTUR	LUC	1	2	mt. in Apulia
VULTURNALIS adj.	ENN			p. to Vulturnus (or -um) (An. 112)
VULTURNUM	SIL			town in Campania
VULTURNUS	LUC		1	river in Campania
VULTURNUS	SIL	1	2	SE wind
VULTURNUS*	SIL			p. to the river in Campania
-XANTHIAS/PHOCEUS	HOR			a made-up name for a doctor (C. 2.4.2)
XANTHIPPUS	SIL	2	2	a Spartan & his son
XANTHO fem.	V			a sea-nymph
XANTHUS	AV	1		river in Lycia
XANTHUS	FPLR	1		(a river)
XANTHUS	HL	2		two different rivers
XANTHUS	HOR	1		river in Lycia
XANTHUS	LUC	1		river in the Troad (Homeric)
XANTHUS 8.21.7	MAR	1		horse of the Sun
XANTHUS	OV	1		river in the Troad
XANTHUS A. 1.927	S	1		
XANTHUS	SEN	1		
XANTHUS	SIL	1		
XANTHUS	V	3	14	(+ r. in Lycia; r. in Epirus)
XERXES	LUC	1		king of Persia
XERXES	MAN	1		
XERXES	PROP	1	3	
XUTHUS AA 3.6.31	OV			husband of Creusa
XYSTILIS Pseud. 210	PL			a meretrix
-ZACORUS 6.554	VAL			a Scythian
ZACYNTHIUS Merc. 945	PL			p. to Zacynthos
ZACYNTHOS v.l.	JUV	1		= Saguntum (15.114)
ZACYNTHOS	SIL	2		Ionian island; friend of Hercules
ZACYNTHOS	V	1	4	
ZACYNTHUS	OV	1		
ZACYNTHUS Merc. 647	PL	1		
ZACYNTHUS	SEN	1	3	
-ZALACES 2.164	JUV			a cont. Armenian (v.l.: Zelates)
ZAMA 3.261	SIL			town in Numidia
ZANCLAEUS	AV	1		p. to Zancle
ZANCLAEUS M. 13.729	OV	1		
ZANCLAEUS or -eius	SIL	1	3	
ZANCLE M. 14.5	OV		1	= Messana (t. in Sicily)
ZANCLE 1.662	SIL	1	2	
ZANCLEIUS M.14.47	OV			p. to Zancle
-ZELYS 3.152	VAL			a Cyzican
ZENO	JUV	1		a Greek stoic philosopher
ZENO pl.	MAR	1	2	(as type of philosopher)
-ZENODOTUS	FPLR			Alexandrian librarian

ZEPHRITIS		CAT		ep. of Arsinoë
ZEPHYRUS		AV	1	god of the West Wind
ZEPHYRUS		CAT	1	
ZEPHYRUS		COL	1	
ZEPHYRUS		FPLR	1	
ZEPHYRUS		GER	1	
ZEPHYRUS		HOR	1	
ZEPHYRUS	also pl.	LUC	1	
ZEPHYRUS		LUCR	1	
ZEPHYRUS		MAN	1	
ZEPHYRUS	pl.	MAR	1	
ZEPHYRUS		OV	1	
ZEPHYRUS		PROP	1	
ZEPHYRUS		S	1	
ZEPHYRUS		SEN	1	
ZEPHYRUS		SIL	1	
ZEPHYRUS		V	1	
ZEPHYRUS		VAL	1 17	
ZERYNTHIUS		OV		p. to Zerynthus (t. in Thrace)
ZETES	m.	OV	1	son of Boreas & an Argonaut
ZETES		PROP	1	
ZETES		SEN	1	
ZETES		VAL	2 5	(+ a Colchian)
ZETHUS		HOR	1	son of Zeus & Antiope
ZETHUS		PL	1	
ZETHUS		PROP	1	
ZETHUS		SEN	1 4	
ZEUGMA	n.	LUC	1	town in Syria
ZEUGMA		S	1 2	
-ZEUSIS	7.665	SIL		son of Phalantus
ZEUXIS	5, prol. 7	PH	1	Greek painter
ZEUXIS		PL	1 2	
ZMINTHEUS	cf. Sm-	SEN		ep. of Apollo (A. 176)
ZMYRNA	cf. Sm-	CAT		title of an epic poem
ZMYRNAEUS	cf. Sm-	LUC		p. to Smyrna (town in Ionia)
ZODIACUS		CIC		the Zodiac
ZOILUS		MAR	1	fict. person
ZOILUS		OV	1 2	(type of critical person)
ZOPYRION		LUCIL 2 2		a slave-name

DIFFERENT NAMES: 7906; FREQUENCY: 20687

CORRECTIONS

Caspius to Caspius* for LUC,
   MAN, OV, S, SEN, V
Cressa to * for HOR, PROP, SEN
Evadne OV: 1 to 2
Gallicus PROP to *
Germanicus* MAR: change 2 to 1
Indiges TIB: change 2 to 1
Liger TIB: change 2 to 1
Lyda VAL to Lydus (adj.)
Maurus* PRIAP: 2 to 1
Metioeus: change to Metius

Oebalius OV: 1 to 2
Pansa TIB: delete
Parthenopaeus MAR 2: change to
   1 and add adj.*.
Phocaicus OV: 1 to 2
Pisa OV: 1 to 2
Rubrum Mare TIB: 2 to 1
Sidonius N (OV) to adj.*
Tiburnus* HOR to noun
Venetus (N) MAR: delete
Victoria TIB: 2 to 1
Volcanus TIB: 2 to 1

THE
REVERSE
INDEX

NAUSICAA
GABBA
CYBEBA
ALBA
GALBA
IARBA
ARISBA
HECUBA
CORDUBA
JUBA
NUBA
RUTUBA
ITHACA
THABRACA
THRACA
SAMOTHRACA
ACCA
SICCA
TUCCA
SEMPRONIUS/TUCCA
THRAECA
SENECA
EURYDICA
DELPHICA
MICA
LUCANICA
HERNICA
TROICA
PHILIPPICA
SPICA
MARICA
SERICA
AFRICA
TETRICA
NASICA
MARSICA
PERSICA
CORSICA
MASSICA
BAETICA
SYBARITICA
PONTICA
USTICA
ATTICA
UTICA
AURUNCA
PROCA
PARCA
VOBERCA
CIRCA
DIRCA
CASCA
VATIVESCA
LYCISCA
SOPHOCLIDISCA

PARDALISCA
HALISCA
AMPELISCA
TUSCA
MUTUSCA
LEUCA
LUCA
NOCTILUCA
BAGRADA
PHOEBI/VADA
LEDA
VELEDA
ANDROMEDA
IDA
AEACIDA
TICIDA
APULIDA
MIDA
NUMIDA
LEONIDA
ATRIDA
ALABANDA
UNDA
MUNDA
ROTUNDA
EMODA
ILERDA
ALAUDA
PALUDA
LYDA
AEA
SABAEA
NICAEA
JUDAEA
AEAEA
TEGEAEA
PANGAEA
APHAEA
LETHAEA
ALTHAEA
ASTYPALAEA
LILAEA
POPPAEA
GRAEA
PIRAEA
PETRAEA
ASTRAEA
PISAEA
HYPSAEA
TRABEA
CEA
DICEA
CYMODOCEA
DEA
LEBADEA

MEDEA
MIDEA
ARDEA
MAGNA/DEA
BONA/DEA
HEGEA
ELEGEA
TEGEA
LIGEA
RHEA
PASITHEA
AMALTHEA
LEUCOTHEA
ERYTHEA
OCALEA
THALEA
MALEA
ANTICLEA
PENTHESILEA
MAUSOLEA
PIMPLEA
HIPPODAMEA
DEMEA
NEMEA
AENEA
CYDONEA
ALBUNEA
OEA
STHENEBOEA
MELIBOEA
ALPHESIBOEA
EUBOEA
EUPLOEA
CLIPEA
DEIOPEA
CALLIOPEA
CASSIOPEA
PELOPEA
PANOPEA
CLUPEA
BAREA
MEGAREA
ALEXANDREA
CHAEREA
CYTHEREA
METEREA
LYCOREA
CALAUREA
SAUREA
TAUREA
THYREA
THRASEA
ODYSSEA
GALATEA
PLATEA

VIA/LACTEA
ADRASTEA
RUFA
VAGA
AURIGA
BELGA
SANGA
CINGA
ALBA/LONGA
LARGA
FUGA
VERTRAHA
ANDROMACHA
BACCHA
SICCHA
NAULOCHA
TEUXIMARCHA
SCAPHA
NYMPHA
CIRRHA
CYRRHA
MYRRHA
PYRRHA
SABRATHA
LAPITHA
JUGURTHA
NUTHA
SCYTHA
SCYTHA
ACHAIA
PANCHAIA
MAIA
FABIA
ARABIA
TREBIA
LESBIA
CIA
PHAEACIA
SALACIA
AMBRACIA
THRACIA
SAMOTHRACIA
TUCCIA
CALLAECIA
GRAECIA
THRAECIA
CILICIA
SULPICIA
ARICIA
PROVINCIA
CAPPADOCIA
MARCIA
PORCIA
GLAUCIA
FIDUCIA

SELEUCIA
LYCIA
NARYCIA
BEBRYCIA
DIA
ARCADIA
LEUCADIA
SCHEDIA
MEDIA
TRAGOEDIA
COMOEDIA
TEDIA
PERFIDIA
AUFIDIA
CANIDIA
PERIDIA
INVIDIA
INDIA
FACUNDIA
CLODIA
MODIA
CONCORDIA
DISCORDIA
GAUDIA
CLAUDIA
LYDIA
IAPYDIA
PASIPHAEIA
SAUFEIA
ELEGEIA
LIGEIA
AQUILEIA
AURUNCULEIA
PROCULEIA
SCHOENEIA
MANNEIA
POMPEIA
PELOPEIA
TARPEIA
CYTHEREIA
TEIA
CARTEIA
VEIA
AVEIA
FROEGIA
TEGIA
LANGIA
ARGIA
PHRUGIA
HYGIA
IAPYGIA
PHRYGIA
ORTYGIA
CHIA
BATRACHOMACHIA

CENTAUROMACHIA
BATRACHOMYOMACHIA
INACHIA
DULICHIA
PAPHIA
SOPHIA
THIA
EMATHIA
AEMATHIA
PHTHIA
HYACINTHIA
PERINTHIA
CYNTHIA
BERECYNTHIA
TIRYNTHIA
PTHIA
PARTHIA
SCYTHIA
PYTHIA
ERYTHIA
FORNACALIA
ACIDALIA
CEREALIA
MEGALIA
OECHALIA
THALIA
BACCHANALIA
AGNALIA
TERMINALIA
VINALIA
SATURNALIA
LIBERALIA
FERALIA
FLORALIA
MATRALIA
PHARSALIA
THESSALIA
ITALIA
COMPITALIA
LARENTALIA
CASTALIA
CONSUALIA
AELIA
CAELIA
LAELIA
DELIA
CORNELIA
CLOELIA
AURELIA
PETELIA
VELIA
ILIA
ORBILIA
MAECILIA
SICILIA

PALILIA
MANILIA
VENILIA
PARILIA
HERSILIA
MASSILIA
PETILIA
QUINTILIA
RUTILIA
SERVILIA
ALLIA
GALLIA
GELLIA
CAERELLIA
PULLIA
TULLIA
AEOLIA
FOLIA
AETOLIA
CAPITOLIA
JULIA
AUGUSTA/JULIA
APULIA
GAETULIA
PAMPHYLIA
DEIDAMIA
LAODAMIA
HIPPODAMIA
LAUDAMIA
INFAMIA
LAMIA
ACADEMIA
SIMIA
UNOMAMMIA
EUNOMIA
BROMIA
POSTUMIA
LAECANIA
SICANIA
HYRCANIA
LUCANIA
DARDANIA
PHANIA
ATHAMANIA
GERMANIA
CAMPANIA
HISPANIA
URANIA
INSANIA
LALETANIA
MAURITANIA
TITANIA
MEVANIA
SAENIA
IPHIGENIA

AMPHIGENIA
TYRRHENIA
ARMENIA
ANAGNIA
SIGNIA
GABINIA
DINIA
SARDINIA
CARFINIA
FULGINIA
VERGINIA
CLINIA
FLAMINIA
MATRINIA
TINIA
SCANTINIA
LAVINIA
OGULNIA
LEMNIA
SOMNIA
LICYMNIA
POLYHYMNIA
POLYMNIA
BRITANNIA
FESCENNIA
CELENNIA
CAESENNIA
AONIA
CHAONIA
SCRIBONIA
COSCONIA
MACEDONIA
ALCEDONIA
CALIDONIA
HERDONIA
CYDONIA
CALYDONIA
MAEONIA
AGONIA
TITHONIA
IONIA
COLONIA
POPULONIA
VETULONIA
NASAMONIA
HAEMONIA
HARMONIA
PANNONIA
BONONIA
POMPONIA
LARONIA
FERONIA
CORONIA
SEMPRONIA
SCYTHOLATRONIA

CAESONIA
AUSONIA
LATONIA
TRITONIA
BISTONIA
SICYONIA
NARNIA
AESERNIA
SATURNIA
CERAUNIA
ACROCERAUNIA
PECUNIA
JUNIA
THYNIA
BITHYNIA
TROIA
CASSIEPIA
LAMPIA
OLYMPIA
COPIA
BONA/COPIA
AETHIOPIA
OENOPIA
INOPIA
CECROPIA
MOPSOPIA
APPIA
EPPIA
OPPIA
CARIA
ICARIA
MAGARIA
SALARIA
VIDULARIA
AENARIA
ASINARIA
PANDATARIA
ARGENTARIA
VARIA
BOVARIA
CALABRIA
MUNATIUS/FBRIA
FIMBRIA
UMBRIA
TRINACRIA
NONACRIA
TEUCRIA
ADRIA
HADRIA
FAEDRIA
PHAEDRIA
ANDRIA
ALEXANDRIA
HIBERIA
CELTIBERIA

LUCERIA	MYSIA	CANDAVIA
NUCERIA	DIONYSIA	IGNAVIA
EGERIA	CATIA	OCTAVIA
CASPERIA	PEDIATIA	LAEVIA
HESPERIA	CALATIA	NAEVIA
HYPERIA	PALATIA	MEVIA
FABRATERIA	ELATIA	LIVIA
PAPIRIA	COLLATIA	OBLIVIA
GLORIA	DALMATIA	TRIVIA
MEMORIA	GNATIA	SILVIA
ANEMORIA	PTOLEMOCRATIA	FULVIA
VICTORIA	GRATIA	CLODIA/VIA
LAETORIA	AETIA	AEMILIA/VIA
CYPRIA	LUCRETIA	FLAMINIA/VIA
ARRIA	SETIA	APPIA/VIA
PIRRIA	PHTIA	LATIA/VIA
EQUIRRIA	PUDICITIA	SACRA/VIA
BYRRIA	ANGITIA	TECTA/VIA
ATRIA	AVARITIA	NOVA/VIA
QUINQUATRIA	LAETITIA	MINUCI/VIA
ERETRIA	JUSTITIA	CLUVIA
OENOTRIA	NUMANTIA	BRIXIA
TUBILUSTRIA	LUBENTIA	IDYIA
CURIA	PLACENTIA	ILITHYIA
FURIA	LICENTIA	ORITHYIA
INIURIA	PICENTIA	ILYTHYIA
LEMURIA	CONFIDENTIA	HARPYIA
REMURIA	DIGENTIA	SADALA
ETRURIA	INDILIGENTIA	GALA
SURIA	MORGENTIA	BURDIGALA
LUXURIA	SAPIENTIA	STYMPHALA
ILLYRIA	EXPERIENTIA	MAENALA
SYRIA	SILENTIA	THESSALA
ASSYRIA	POLLENTIA	MESSALA
ASIA	CLEMENTIA	TESSALA
SEPLASIA	LARENTIA	VALA
TURASIA	TERENTIA	HYBLA
PERBIBESIA	REVERENTIA	VINCLA
MEGALESIA	DRUENTIA	ARBELA
MELESIA	FAVENTIA	PANDA/CELA
MOESIA	PHINTIA	SUADELA
OCRESIA	QUINTIA	MANDELA
TERESIA	PONTIA	GELA
TIRESIA	ACERUNTIA	SEMELA
APHRODISIA	OTIA	PHILOMELA
ALIDENSIA	BOEOTIA	PTERELA
EBOSIA	NORTIA	NUBILA
LEUCOSIA	KARISTIA	ANTIPHILA
GNOSIA	OSTIA	PAMPHILA
SOSIA	SATTIA	THEOPHILA
PERSIA	COTYTTIA	TIBURTINA/PILA
NURSIA	PLUTIA	SILA
BANDUSIA	TUTIA	RUTILA
AMATHUSIA	ASTUTIA	AQUILA
RHAMNUSIA	COTYTIA	GALLA

AELIA/GALLA	APENNINICOLA	AMEANA
MESSALLA	APPENNINICOLA	ALLIFANA
TARATALLA	LEMNICOLA	SAGANA
BELLA	JUNONICOLA	DIANA
ABELLA	NEPTUNICOLA	CAPELLIANA
DOLABELLA	MARTICOLA	PHASIANA
SABELLA	GRADIVVICOLA	GRATIANA
MARCELLA	NOLA	ATELLANA
MELLA	SOLA	NUMANA
HIMELLA	RAVOLA	MESSANA
PELLA	SCAEVOLA	ECBATANA
APELLA	PAULA	CERRETANA
CAPELLA	TREBULA	SPARTANA
ATELLA	BIBULA	ARIADNA
METELLA	PASIBULA	ECHIDNA
ENTELLA	ALBULA	APHIDNA
STELLA	CLEOBULA	CALYDNA
CILLA	CANICULA	LACAENA
FLACCILLA	VINCULA	LACAENA
ATTICILLA	PROCULA	LEAENA
PRISCILLA	ARBUSCULA	DAMASCENA
GADILLA	NUCULA	MYCENA
SECUNDILLA	AEFULA	FIDENA
MEGILLA	ANIMULA	PHOEBIGENA
IPSITHILLA	STIMULA	SOLIGENA
CAMILLA	APULA	JANIGENA
CASMILLA	FAESULA	APENNINIGENA
POSTUMILLA	SCAPTENSULA	JUNONIGENA
MARONILLA	MENTULA	LATONIGENA
PERILLA	EPISTULA	FAUNIGENA
TELESILLA	HYLA	NYSIGENA
PUSILLA	STAPHYLA	BAETIGENA
VIOLENTILLA	ERIPHYLA	MARTIGENA
QUINTILLA	DAMA	CADMOGENA
CHRESTILLA	MARCUS/DAMA	GRAIUGENA
VETUSTILLA	FAMA	TROIUGENA
POLLA	PERGAMA	CATIENA
FABULLA	UXAMA	VATIENA
LABULLA	ZAMA	HELENA
SIBULLA	ZEUGMA	AUFILENA
MAGULLA	PORRIMA	SILENA
POMPULLA	ARA/MAXIMA	MITYLENA
HISPULLA	PALMA	MENA
MARULLA	ROMA	CAMENA
SULLA	PARMA	ALCMENA
TULLA	PHASMA	VOLTEIUS/MENA
CATULLA	NUMA	ALCUMENA
ARETULLA	BRUMA	PHILUMENA
ANTULLA	POSTUMA	POENA
SIBYLLA	DINDYMA	CAPENA
SCYLLA	SOLYMA	PORTA/CAPENA
BOLA	THEBANA	PIRENA
PUBLICOLA	NORBANA	MURENA
PEDIUS/POPLICOLA	VATICANA	SENA
ANIENICOLA	POPPAEANA	MISENA

PORSENA	LAEVINA	SMYRNA
MESSENA	CALVINA	ZMYRNA
POLYXENA	CELEMNA	AETNA
HAGNA	ANTEMNA	VACUNA
MAGNA	CROMNA	LUNA
SABINA	METHYMNA	FORTUNA
ALBINA	PROSYMNA	BONA/FORTUNA
CLOACINA	ANNA	FORS/FORTUNA
LUCINA	CANNA	DICTYNA
JUNO/LUCINA	ANNA/PERANNA	GORTYNA
ERYCINA	ENNA	COA
CLAUDIA/RUFINA	ERGENNA	HYPAEPA
AEGINA	HENNA	NEPA
MYRRHINA	VIENNA	ARGYRIPA
MESSALINA	PERENNA	CALLIOPA
PHACELINA	ANNA/PERENNA	ANTIOPA
VELINA	SISENNA	PENELOPA
CATILINA	PORSENNA	EUROPA
GALLINA	RAVENNA	RUBRENUS/LAPPA
MEDULLINA	CINNA	MILPHIDIPPA
PROCULINA	LYCINNA	PHILIPPA
SALAMINA	PINNA	AGRIPPA
MAXIMINA	CORINNA	DORIPPA
FLUMINA	MUNNA	TARPA
CAENINA	GARUNNA	ARA
AGRIPPINA	DICTYNNA	BACCARA
PROSERPINA	DIVA/BONA	MEGARA
RUSPINA	MENS/BONA	GARGARA
LARINA	DODONA	CANTHARA
CAMARINA	ANTIGONA	LARA
NONACRINA	ILIONA	ISMARA
LUCRINA	HESIONA	TAENARA
HIBERINA	BELLONA	CINARA
INSULA/TIBERINA	CREMONA	ISARA
AMERINA	ARTEMONA	TARTARA
CAMERINA	POMONA	LATTARA
CLAUDIA/PEREGRINA	ANNONA	GYARA
NIGRINA	EPONA	MAZARA
MYRRINA	VERONA	LIBRA
ASINA	SOPHRONA	SYGAMBRA
CASINA	CORONA	UMBRA
RASINA	LATONA	THYMBRA
TELESINA	CORTONA	MACRA
SASSINA	ARNA	ASCRA
CANUSINA	CARNA	PHAEDRA
ATINA	LERNA	SYHEDRA
CATINA	NARBO/PATERNA	CASSANDRA
LATINA	AVERNA	HYDRA
LIBITINA	LAVERNA	NEAERA
CHRESTINA	JUVERNA	MEGAERA
JUSTINA	URNA	MACHAERA
VENUSTINA	LIBURNA	IAERA
VETUSTINA	TIBURNA	MAERA
MUTINA	JUTURNA	CHIMAERA
FLAVINA	AGATHYRNA	LIBERA

ARCERA	SURA	CILISSA
GLYCERA	CYNOSURA	PHOENISSA
ABDERA	LICINIUS/SURA	PHOENISSA
CYTHERA	NATURA	MASINISSA
CREMERA	SATURA	TVETONISSA
HIMERA	TENTURA	NEBRISSA
CRATERA	HECYRA	ANTISSA
PHILTERA	ANTICYRA	OSSA
AFRA	CORCYRA	ODRUSSA
TANAGRA	GLAPHYRA	LIBYSSA
PHLEGRA	LYRA	PLECUSA
AETHRA	PHILYRA	PADUSA
IRA	CINYRA	MEDUSA
HILAIRA	TEMPYRA	CREUSA
DEIANIRA	SYRA	PHAETHUSA
METANIRA	COSYRA	TELETHUSA
CORA	COSSYRA	ARETHUSA
AESCHRODORA	PAGASA	OPHIUSA
HORA	HALAESA	MUSA
FLORA	TECMESA	ANTONIUS/MUSA
MORA	ANCHISA	ICHNUSA
REMORA	AMPHISA	DONUSA
PRORA	NISA	SUSA
AURORA	PISA	NYSA
SORA	LARISA	DONYSA
CAPRA	PANSA	LEUCATA
CUPRA	TOLOSA	FATA
SARRA	MOSA	TIFATA
ACERRA	MICIPSA	AMATA
VACERRA	HYEMPSA	DALMATA
TERRA	PASICOMPSA	COMATA
LIGURRA	HYPSA	SARMATA
MAMURRA	PERSA	SEDES/SCELERATA
CLEOPATRA	URSA	ARCHESTRATA
BACTRA	BYRSA	NAUSISTRATA
ELECTRA	BASSA	CLEOSTRATA
PETRA	MASSA	PHANOSTRATA
SANTRA	IPHIANASSA	SOSTRATA
AMASTRA	DEMONASSA	ARTAXATA
PALAESTRA	BESSA	TECTA
CLYTAEMESTRA	TECMESSA	GETA
CLYTEMESTRA	MAGNESSA	TAYGETA
HYPERMESTRA	GONOESSA	CAIETA
CLYTAEMNESTRA	MARPESSA	MONETA
CLYTEMNESTRA	CRESSA	OETA
PLAUSTRA	CRESSA	CLEARETA
BUTRA	THRESSA	CRETA
AURA	BIS/COMPRESSA	IARBITA
MAURA	SINUESSA	CALYBITA
SABURA	SUESSA	TACITA
SABBURA	ISSA	DERCEITA
SUBURA	THRAEISSA	MELITA
CURA	THREISSA	SOSPITA
AMPSIGURA	THREISSA	EMERITA
BANIURA	ELISSA	BISALTA

ATALANTA
JUVENTA
CLAUDIA/QUINTA
ACROTA
EPIROTA
EUROTA
SAEPTA
SPARTA
LACERTA
MELICERTA
POSTVERTA
CIRTA
SCAEA/PORTA
COLLATIA/PORTA
FENESTELLA/PORTA
ALBANA/PORTA
COLLINA/PORTA
TRIGEMINA/PORTA
CARMENTIS/PORTA
IOCASTA
NASTA
ACESTA
GELESTA
VESTA
NEISTA
CRISTA
FAUSTA
LUCUSTA
AUGUSTA
ATTA
NATTA
SAGITTA
GALLITTA
POLLITTA
COTTA
LUCIUS/COTTA
MAXIMUS/COTTA
BUTA
CICUTA
MUTA
MATUTA
PROCHYTA
HIPPOLYTA
PADUA
DITIS/JANUA
CAPUA
AQUA
VIRGO/AQUA
MARSUA
MANTUA
SCAEVA
BONA/DIVA
ILVA
NERVA
MINERVA

LIBYA
MARSYA
PITYA
GAZA
THEBAE
SUEBAE
NUBAE
SACAE
THEBAICAE
NUMIDICAE
CARICAE
VOLCAE
CAPPADOCAE
PARCAE
CAUDINAE/FURCAE
MARISCAE
GRAVISCAE
AENEADAE
EPHYREIADAE
BACCHIADAE
MEMMIADAE
SCIPIADAE
CASPIADAE
THESPIADAE
ABANTIADAE
BATTIADAE
DANAIDAE
NIOBIDAE
AEACIDAE
STOICIDAE
OGYGIDAE
ADYRMACHIDAE
INACHIDAE
TYRRHIDAE
OEBALIDAE
TANTALIDAE
BELIDAE
NELIDAE
AEOLIDAE
TUSCULIDAE
ROMULIDAE
PRIAMIDAE
NUMIDAE
AENIDAE
BORYSTHENIDAE
MAEONIDAE
IXIONIDAE
HAEMONIDAE
IASONIDAE
AUSONIDAE
ALOIDAE
PELOPIDAE
CECROPIDAE
TYNDARIDAE
GANGARIDAE

MARMARIDAE
AGENORIDAE
ACTORIDAE
ATRIDAE
THESIDAE
KALENDAE
SCAEAE
NAPAEAE
PLATAEAE
DIOMEDEAE
HERACLEAE
CYANEAE
CENCHREAE
CAPREAE
ALLIFAE
AEGAE
PEGAE
RIGAE
DAHAE
BACCHAE
SATARCHAE
PASIPHAE
LYMPHAE
NYMPHAE
CARRHAE
LAPITHAE
SCYTHAE
BAIAE
AQUAE/BAIAE
STABIAE
INSIDIAE
RUDIAE
LYDIAE
OGYGIAE
FICELIAE
ENCHELIAE
VERGILIAE
ESQUILIAE
ESQUILLIAE
LAMIAE
FORMIAE
CAUNIAE
EMPORIAE
FURIAE
ILLYRIAE
TYRIAE
ETESIAE
GRATIAE
BLANDITIAE
HARPYIAE
AMYCLAE
CHELAE
PHILAE
GALLAE
VERCELLAE

FREGELLAE	LIPARAE	NIXAE
CERILLAE	ULUBRAE	PHLEGYAE
BOVILLAE	RUBRAE	MINYAE
SCYLLAE	ACRAE	HECABE
SYLLAE	NUCRAE	CYBEBE
TAURUBULAE	PHERAE	HEBE
AMUNCULAE	MOERAE	THEBE
JUGULAE	RUFRAE	BOEBE
THERMOPULAE	ERYTHRAE	PHOEBE
MYLAE	IRAE	VIBE
THERMOPYLAE	DIRAE	COMBE
RIXAMAE	HORAE	DEIPHOBE
THERMAE	ACERRAE	NIOBE
CUMAE	ACHERRAE	THISBE
DANAE	MAMURRAE	ARISBE
APHIDNAE	CHOATRAE	CALYBE
CELAENAE	PATRAE	ITHACE
MELAENAE	ELECTRAE	PHYLACE
MYCENAE	VELITRAE	CANACE
FIDENAE	ISAURAE	THRACE
FREGENAE	CURAE	MYRACE
NUBIGENAE	PAGASAE	TRICCE
MARTIGENAE	PISAE	GRAECE
GRAIUGENAE	COSAE	THRECE
GRAIIUGENAE	MICIPSAE	ARABICE
TROIIUGENAE	NERSAE	LAUDICE
TROIUGENAE	PERSAE	EURYDICE
ATHENAE	SYRACUSAE	DELPHICE
CAMENAE	PITHECUSAE	HELICE
CLAZOMENAE	MUSAE	BERONICE
EURYMENAE	AUCHATAE	PUNICE
POENAE	GALATAE	MYRICE
CRENAE	SAUROMATAE	SARMATICE
CYRENAE	EXOMATAE	GETICE
SABINAE	SARMATAE	ALCE
MINAE	MACETAE	NEALCE
CARINAE	GETAE	IMILCE
LATINAE	THYRSAGETAE	PHYLLODOCE
ANTEMNAE	MASSAGETAE	CYMODOCE
CANNAE	COELALETAE	BARCE
CEBENNAE	AREOPAGITAE	CIRCE
CINNAE	DICARCHITAE	DIRCE
CLEONAE	TOMITAE	OBSCE
SALONAE	BISALTAE	LYCISCE
NONAE	CELTAE	VOLSCE
THERAPNAE	BAPTAE	LEUCE
ACHARNAE	SCAEAE/POPTAE	PEUCE
BATARNAE	URBANAE/PORTAE	LYCE
BASTERNAE	CERASTAE	CALYCE
LIBURNAE	ORESTAE	HARPALYCE
MINTURNAE	ATRIUM/VESTAE	MUTYCE
TELEBOAE	HYPSISTAE	ALCIMEDE
TELOBOAE	COTTAE	ANDROMEDE
CENTURIPAE	ARGONAUTAE	IDE
ARAE	CARDUAE	CHLIDE

MIDE
SIDE
RHODE
LYDE
TYDE
LIMNAEE
NESAEE
NEMEE
CYANEE
LALAGE
GORGE
AUGE
ISCHOMACHE
DINOMACHE
ANDROMACHE
CANACHE
HENIOCHE
ASTYOCHE
ANAPHE
SCARPHE
PSAMATHE
LETHE
IANTHE
EUANTHE
AGLAIE
ARTACIE
ORTYGIE
GARGAPHIE
PAPHIE
PHTHIE
IDALIE
MELIE
VELIE
HERSILIE
URANIE
PARTHENIE
OLENIE
DAEMONIE
HESPERIE
ASTERIE
ANACTORIE
HYRIE
STRATIE
LAMPETIE
CLYTIE
SCYBALE
HECALE
CROCALE
MYCALE
OMPHALE
AEGIALE
ANCHIALE
PHIALE
SPATALE
PETALE

MYRTALE
HYALE
EURYALE
ZANCLE
AMYCLE
CYBELE
NEPHELE
SEMELE
PERIMELE
THYMELE
AEGLE
HEROPHILE
HELLE
AGYLLE
IOLE
HOMOLE
NEOBULE
THULE
PHIDYLE
HYLE
ERIPHYLE
THYLE
DEIPYLE
HYPSIPYLE
HIPPODAME
SAME
ACME
INARIME
ITHOME
HYLONOME
EURYNOME
CARME
IDUME
CYME
DYME
IDYME
DIDYME
SYME
TAPROBANE
ROMANE
DREPANE
HISPANE
CRANE
CATANE
PITANE
CYANE
PROCNE
EUHADNE
EUADNE
EVADNE
MYCENE
PHENE
SOPHENE
HELENE
MYTILENE

PALLENE
PELLENE
CYLLENE
PYLENE
ALCMENE
NYCTIMENE
MELPOMENE
ISMENE
DINDYMENE
CLYMENE
ARENE
TRICRENE
HIPPOCRENE
PIRENE
CYRENE
PYRENE
MESSENE
SYENE
PROGNE
LACHNE
ARACHNE
DAPHNE
ORPHNE
CYTAEINE
NEPTUNINE
BARINE
NERINE
ASINE
LATINE
AEETINE
CALYMNE
CONE
MYRMIDONE
DODONE
ERIGONE
ANTIGONE
PERSEPHONE
TISIPHONE
METHONE
MOTHONE
DIONE
PLEIONE
CHIONE
ILIONE
HERMIONE
HESIONE
ACRISIONE
DEXIONE
LIMONE
AMYMONE
OENONE
ITONE
ALCYONE
THYONE
THERAPNE

ARNE	ENISPE	GRAECI
PHATNE	RUBRUM/MARE	TRAECI
PHRYNE	LIPARE	DECI
MNEMOSYNE	CAERE	LABICI
ADELPHOE	HERE	ALLOBROGICI
CALLIRHOE	CAMERE	PALICI
ALEXIRHOE	AGRE	VINDELICI
CALLIRRHOF	TERPSICHORE	CYNICI
OCYRHOE	HYPERMESTRE	SOCRATICI
THOE	EPHYRE	PLANCI
ALCATHOE	LIMYRE	AURUNCI
ALCITHOE	NEMESE	MAMERCI
LEUCOTHOE	TEMESE	LUPERCI
CYMOTHOE	HERSE	FALISCI
CHLOE	MESSE	PHALISCI
SELLOE	ISSE	VOLSCI
PHOLOE	TISSE	OSCI
CLERUMENOF	CHRYSE	ETRUSCI
IPHINOE	HECATE	TUSCI
ARSINOE	LEUCATE	CAYCI
LEUCONOE	REATE	LIBYCI
PHEMONOE	TEATE	HAEDI
AUTONOE	CALACTE	MAEDI
BEROE	SORACTE	MEDI
MEROE	STICTE	LEPIDI
ARCTOE	TAYGETE	INDI
NAPE	OETE	SINDI
RHIPE	ARETE	FUNDI
CALPE	ANAXARETE	SARDI
TEMPE	CRETE	LYDI
RHODOPE	CLITE	SABAEI
IOPE	MELITE	PHOCAEI
CHALCIOPE	AMPHITRITE	BARCAEI
CALLIOPE	PERCOTE	CHALDAEI
LIRIOPE	SPARTE	JUDAEI
CASSIOPE	ACASTE	ACHAEI
ANTIOPE	LYCASTE	ITONAEI
PENELOPE	PRAENESTE	SAPAEI
PANOPE	ASBYTE	ITYPAEI
PARTHENOPF	PROCHYTE	CYTAEI
SINOPE	HIPPOLYTE	SEMIGRAECFI
AEROPE	AGAUE	CIRCEI
MEROPE	LIBYE	ARGEI
STEROPE	SILAI	POMPEI
ASTEROPE	DANAI	PYTHAGOREI
EUROPE	GRAI	VEI
DRYOPE	ARABI	LOTOPHAGI
ALCIPPE	NIMBI	CETHEGI
CYDIPPE	OMBI	GOLGI
AGANIPPE	SUPERBI	TINGI
MELANIPPE	MORBI	ARGI
MENIPPE	RUBI	PYRGI
EUIPPE	DACI	PELASGI
HARPE	FLACCI	GRACCHI
EUTERPE	CALLAECI	COLCHI

HENIOCHI
MOSCHI
DELPHI
PARTHI
GRAII
FABII
GABII
DECII
FABRICII
LYCII
RHODII
CIRCEII
VEII
MAGII
SALII
VERGILII
NUMAE/POMPILII
QUINTILII
PYLII
SAMII
DARDANII
ARMENII
VOLSINII
TARQUINII
AONII
CALEDONII
SIDONII
CHALCODONII
AUSONII
BOII
MARII
CIMMERII
URII
CURII
AQUA/MERCURII
ILLYRII
ASSYRII
TYRII
SOSII
ELYSII
ODRYSII
ATII
LATII
POMETII
GRAVII
CURVII
ITALI
FORUM/CORNELI
GALLI
CORALLI
SABELLI
MARCELLI
METELLI
CAMILLI
PSYLLI

CARSEOLI
AETOLI
BAULI
SICULI
TUSCULI
IULI
APULI
FORULI
RUTULI
MASSYLI
TOMI
THEBANI
AFRICANI
SICANI
HYRCANI
LUCANI
POMPEIANI
TROIIANI
AEMILIANI
VITELLIANI
TROIANI
CAESARIANI
JANI
ALANI
MARCOMANI
ROMANI
GERMANI
CAMPANI
HISPANI
LATERANI
TURDETANI
CRETANI
CERRETANI
TITANI
SPARTANI
SILVANI
PHILAENI
SILENI
POENI
TIBARENI
RUTENI
PAELIGNI
SABINI
MARRUCINI
RUDINI
CAPITOLINI
GEMINI
IRPINI
CAMERINI
QUIRINI
MORINI
LATINI
PRISCI/LATINI
NUMANTINI
PLACENTINI

LEONTINI
AEGYPTINI
PALAESTINI
CORVINI
BRITANNI
BRITTANNI
VAGENNI
CHAONI
EDONI
TELEGONI
GELONI
CORONI
ARVERNI
LIBURNI
FAUNI
GENAUNI
BREUNI
MARIANDYNI
MAGYNI
THYNI
TORYNI
MOSSYNI
MENAPI
USIPI
FORUM/APPI
PHILIPPI
PORTICUS/PHILIPPI
ARPI
ARINASPI
SYCAMBRI
SYGAMBRI
CIMBRI
UMBRI
LOCRI
TEUCRI
HIBERI
NUMERI
CRUSTUMERI
AFRI
NOVI/AGRI
CABIRI
SUSURRI
OENOTRI
HISTRI
SCAURI
MAURI
TAURI
CENTAURI
SYRI
SATYRI
VOLESI
MOESI
MARSI
AGATHYRSI

CRASSI
BESSI
DRUSI
MYSI
RAETI
CALETI
VENETI
BALLONITI
TITI
BUTUNTI
BOEOTI
THESPROTI
SPARTI
FASTI
CHATTI
BRUTI
CASTRUM/INUI
AEQUI
BATAVI
SUEVI
ARGIVI
ACHIVI
ANNIBAL
HANNIBAL
MAHARBAL
HASDRUBAL
LUPERCAL
PUTEAL
BACCHANAL
HISPAL
HIEMPSAL
TANAQUIL
SOL
MAURICATIM
CAECUBUM
BEBRIACUM
LABICUM
LEUCONICUM
ORICUM
MASSICUM
ADRIATICUM
GETICUM
MAREOTICUM
TRIVICUM
LIBYCUM
BOTERDUM
LILYBAEUM
AEGAEUM
LECHAEUM
NYMPHAEUM
PYRENAEUM
SCYLACEUM
LYCEUM
MATER/DEUM
MAUSOLEUM

RHOETEUM
LESBIUM
MENDACIUM
PINACIUM
PITHECIUM
PHOENICIUM
DORCIUM
CORYCIUM
PALLADIUM
LAMPADIUM
STEPHANISCIDIUM
ODIUM
CAUDIUM
GAUDIUM
CRURIFRAGIUM
AEGIUM
REGIUM
CHIUM
DURRACHIUM
DYRRACHIUM
DULICHIUM
ASTAPHIUM
DELPHIUM
ROMETHIUM
IDALIUM
CONDALIUM
ILIUM
AUXILIUM
CAPITOLIUM
PHEDULIUM
CRUSTUMIUM
PHANIUM
STEPHANIUM
PHILAENIUM
SELENIUM
SUMMENIUM
PAEGNIUM
LACINIUM
CORFINIUM
LAVINIUM
CYDONIUM
AGONIUM
IONIUM
DAEMONIUM
PARAETONIUM
SUNIUM
CASPIUM
BARIUM
ICARIUM
PARIUM
GLYCERIUM
VENERIUM
ANACTORIUM
PERJURIUM
PLEMYRIUM

ADELPHASIUM
PHILOCOMASIUM
GYMNASIUM
PLANESIUM
PHRONESIUM
BRUNDISIUM
ALSIUM
ELEUSIUM
CLUSIUM
PELUSIUM
CANUSIUM
ELYSIUM
LATIUM
PALATIUM
PHILEMATIUM
ERGETIUM
ARRETIUM
ANTIUM
LEONTIUM
CROCOTIUM
EROTIUM
ACROTELEUTIUM
HEDYTIUM
PATAVIUM
IGUVIUM
LANUVIUM
SIMBRUVIUM
MARRUVIUM
GUBERNACLUM
ASCLUM
CAELUM
BELLUM
HISPELLUM
GAULUM
TURIBULUM
JANICULUM
TUSCULUM
BATULUM
ASYLUM
PERGAMUM
CATAGELASIMUM
COMUM
NOVUM/COMUM
ALBANUM
FUNDANUM
TEANUM
POMPEIANUM
OPIMIANUM
COSMIANUM
MARCELLANUM
TUSCULANUM
DREPANUM
HADRANUM
VENAFRANUM
CAERETANUM

MASSILITANUM	NERETUM	ANCON
VEIENTANUM	NOMENTUM	MUSCON
VEIIENTANUM	TARENTUM	LAUCON
NOMENTANUM	FORENTUM	LEUCON
PICENUM	SURRENTUM	PEUCON
CALENUM	LAURENTUM	GLYCON
TAUROMENUM	BENEVENTUM	ADON
MISENUM	SAGUNTUM	LADON
PAELIGNUM	BUTHROTUM	CELADON
SABINUM	SCORTUM	MACEDON
MELINUM	PAESTUM	CHALCEDON
TRIFOLINUM	SAXUM	CALCHEDON
ARIMINUM	PAEAN	ANTHEDON
SIGNINUM	EUHAN	MEDON
CASINUM	ATHAMAN	CREMEDON
SPOLETINUM	ALCMAN	ALCIMEDON
SETINUM	ACARNAN	AMPHIMEDON
ALTINUM	ACARNAN	LAOMEDON
TARENTINUM	PAN	HIPPOMEDON
FERENTINUM	TITAN	THEROMEDON
SURRENTINUM	EUAN	AUTOMEDON
TIBURTINUM	AZAN	EURYMEDON
AQUINUM	ANIEN	SARPEDON
LAVINUM	FLUMEN	TENTHREDON
TRIGONUM	HYMEN	MYGDON
FALERNUM	SIREN	SIDON
SALERNUM	TROEZEN	POLYIDON
LITERNUM	TRACHIN	THERMODON
PRIVERNUM	DELPHIN	CYDON
VULTURNUM	SALAMIN	CALYDON
CERAUNUM	ENGONASIN	AMYDON
PACHYNUM	ELEUSIN	CORYDON
COUM	AON	LILYBAEON
MYRTOUM	HELICAON	AEGAEON
TAENARUM	LYCAON	MAEON
VELABRUM	CHAON	HECATAEON
RUBRUM	MACHAON	ACTAEON
VENAFRUM	DOLICHAON	SCYLACEON
AD/PIRUM	PHAON	MEDEON
FORUM	LAPITHAON	SIGEON
CORNELI/FORUM	PARTHAON	ANDROGEON
PALLADIUM/FORUM	PORTHAON	PTELEON
LATIUM/FORUM	AMYTHAON	DEILEON
ROMANUM/FORUM	IMAON	PITHOLEON
AUGUSTUM/FORUM	DIDYMAON	DEMOLEON
CAESARIS/FORUM	CREMETAON	ALCIMEON
CASTRUM	HYPETAON	CREON
PLAUSTRUM	LACON	ANACREON
PISAURUM	LACON	PETEON
LISSUM	RUBICON	PELAGON
FATUM	HELICON	AEGON
LETUM	MICON	UCALEGON
ARGILETUM	STIMICON	PHLEGON
NETUM	ATTICON	THELGON
ERETUM	ALCON	LANGON

GORGON
LAESTRYGON
IAHON
STIMICHON
TARCHON
LYCOPHON
COLOPHON
BELLEROPHON
BELLOROPHON
TRYPHON
TYPHON
MARATHON
AETHON
PHAETHON
PHLEGETHON
LETHON
DAMASICHTHON
ERYSICHTHON
COTHON
PYTHON
ION
ICADION
PANDION
AEGION
REGION
ECHION
AMPHION
EMATHION
AETHION
MELANTHION
DEUCALION
DAEDALION
AETHALION
PYGMALION
MASCLION
PELION
ILION
GONGYLION
ENDYMION
MILANION
CHARMENION
SUNION
OENOPION
ARION
OARION
HYPERION
ASTERION
AGRION
ORION
DORION
PRION
URION
PORPHYRION
ZOPYRION
IASION

SOCRATION
EETION
METION
RHOETION
BYZANTION
EROTION
EURYTION
IXION
TELON
DOLON
SOLON
AULON
CAULON
BABYLON
DERCYLON
DAMON
PERGAMON
TELAMON
NASAMON
NASAMON
ACMON
HALIACMON
PYRACMON
ADMON
PHRADMON
IDMON
LACEDAEMON
HAEMON
THAEMON
EUHAEMON
PALAEMON
ANDRAEMON
ITHEMON
ALEMON
PHILEMON
POLEMON
NOEMON
POLYPEMON
CHAEREMON
AGMON
PYRAGMON
POLYDEGMON
LYGMON
LIMON
AUXIMON
AMMON
HAMMON
PHILAMMON
ECHEMMON
DINDYMON
STRYMON
HAGNON
AELINON
SINON
MEMNON

AGAMEMNON
HANNON
CRANNON
CONON
TELECOON
LAOCOON
DEMOCOON
HIPPOCOON
DEMOPHOON
THOON
LAMPON
ARON
GARGARON
CHARON
ACRON
ANDRON
CITHAERON
ACHERON
THERON
HIERON
MENEPHRON
LYCOPHRON
SOPHRON
IRON
SCIRON
CHIRON
SIRON
PATRON
BRAURON
PLEURON
MYRON
IASON
SASON
AESON
THEMISON
ELISSON
BATON
PLATON
STRATON
PHAETON
CRITON
TRITON
CROTON
DELTOTON
PLUTON
SICYON
PROCYON
CERCYON
ENGYON
CROMYON
GERYON
THRYON
AMPHITRYON
ALAZON
AMAZON

GORTYN	CLOTHO	SOSIO
LIBO	PYTHO	TALASSIO
CARBO	IO	SUASISAVIATIO
NARBO	MICIO	RATIO
TURBO	LAMPADIO	OBTRECTATIO
HISBO	HEGIO	AMBITIO
DRACO	MALCHIO	SEDITIO
TARRACO	MILPHIO	STALITIO
BUCCO	ACANTHIO	PHILISTIO
RUBICO	TURBALIO	SAGARISTIO
HIMILCO	CORDALIO	CEPHALO
VASCO	TRACHALIO	CARTHALO
LYCO	CEPHALIO	SALO
BURADO	SIMALIO	CHARICLO
MACEDO	CLIO	MACELO
PEDO	EUCLIO	MELO
DIDO	BALLIO	TELO
FORMIDO	SUBBALLIO	PHILO
CUPIDO	GALLIO	MILO
CERDO	PELLIO	SILO
LABEO	POLLIO	AQUILO
DECEO	CREPEREIUS/POLLIO	AELLO
LEO	POLIO	GILLO
CREO	CURCULIO	APOLLO
CALLIFO	ANTHEMIO	CAULO
CARTHAGO	HERMIO	CORBULO
KARTHAGO	SIRMIO	PARTICULO
MAGO	PHORMIO	EPULO
PAGO	GRUMIO	CASTULO
ROBIGO	ANIO	BABYLO
RUBIGO	STEPHANIO	TELAMO
ORIGO	TRANIO	ARTAMO
ARGO	MESSENIO	PHILEMO
VIRGO	MINIO	SEMO
GORGO	SANNIO	TEMO
PYRGO	SCEPARNIO	ARTEMO
GISGO	SCIPIO	PYRAGMO
VESPERUGO	PUBLIUS/SCIPIO	BRIMO
ECHO	OLYMPIO	DRIMO
TARCHO	SPIO	SIMO
CALLIPHO	CARIO	ALMO
DEMIPHO	SANGARIO	SULMO
CTESIPHO	LUCRIO	DROMO
CLITIPHO	MACHAERIO	SERMO
ANTIPHO	SPHAERIO	STRYMO
SAPPHO	NERIO	THEANO
MATHO	CONGRIO	CELAENO
GNATHO	DORIO	PARMENO
ERICTHO	THESPRIO	ZENO
CRETHO	CITRIO	INO
ERICHTHO	PALAESTRIO	SINO
PITHO	CURIO	FRUSINO
MELANTHO	SATURIO	AGAMEMNO
XANTHO	NICASIO	HANNO
OTHO	TALASIO	JUNO

RAPO
STILPO
TAPPO
HIPPO
HISPO
BLEPHARO
MARO
LIPARO
UMBRO
SUCRO
CYDRO
CICERO
HERO
HIERO
NERO
CLAUDIUS/NERO
PERO
SOTERO
VADAVERO
CHIRO
TIRO
VARRO
VIRRO
BALATRO
SERVILIUS/BALATRO
TYRO
NASO
THRASO
CAESO
PISO
CALPURNIUS/PISO
COTISO
VOLSO
HYPSO
CALYPSO
RUSO
BATO
CATO
PLATO
ERATO
STRATO
ALECTO
ALLECTO
CETO
CAPITO
BRITO
CRITO
PHILTO
MANTO
DENTO
FABIUS/VEIENTO
VEIIENTO
ALUMENTO
FRONTO
DOTO

CALLISTO
BITTO
PLUTO
PHYTO
COTYTO
AMPHITRUO
CUPAVO
SAVO
POLYXO
CERCYO
ENYO
GABAR
BOCCAR
HAMILCAR
LAR
SILAR
NAR
ARAR
AESAR
CAESAR
AUGUSTUS/CAESAR
GESTAR
BOSTAR
CALABER
CALABER
CANTABER
IBER
MULCIBER
HIBER
LIBER
CELTIBER
CELTIBER
DECEMBER
SEPTEMBER
CIMBER
UMBER
UMBER
THYMBER
OCEANUS/RUBER
FALACER
MACER
CANCER
TEUCER
IADER
ALCANDER
MAEANDER
SCAMANDER
MENANDER
GESANDER
PISANDER
THERSANDER
EUANDER
ALEXANDER
TUDER
AFER

AFER
CADUCIFER
LUCIFER
SIGNIFER
ORBIS/SIGNIFER
CHIMAERIFER
NOCTIFER
SAGITTIFER
MELEAGER
TANAGER
LIGER
LANIGER
CORNIGER
BICORNIGER
CLAVIGER
TUNGER
AETHER
CELER
SILER
APER
CAPER
ASPER
VESPER
SER
ANSER
PASSER
MATER
MAGNA/MATER
PATER
CRATER
OPITER
JUPPITER
DIESPITER
JUPITER
ISTER
HISTER
AUSTER
CAYSTER
DEXTER
VER
ACIR
TREVIR
LABOR
DECOR
ARDOR
PUDOR
MAIOR
MELIOR
CALOR
PALLOR
OLOR
DOLOR
AMOR
MEMOR
TREMOR

TIMOR	PAVOR	GIGAS
RUMOR	LIVOR	TRACHAS
SEVIUS/NICANOR	TIBUR	LICHAS
ALCANOR	LIGUR	CALCHAS
BIANOR	VULTUR	PERIPHAS
EUPHRANOR	ASTUR	ATHAS
LEXANOR	ASTUR	EURYTHAS
AGENOR	ANXUR	IAS
ALPHENOR	ATHYR	ACHAIAS
BIENOR	ASTYR	NAIAS
HELENOR	ABAS	LESBIAS
PROTHOENOR	LYCABAS	GLAUCIAS
AGAPENOR	TABAS	CEPHALOEDIAS
ELPENOR	RHEBAS	PHIDIAS
HYPERENOR	PHOEBAS	ALPHEIAS
PISENOR	LIBAS	NEPHELEIAS
ANTENOR	PATROBAS	PLEIAS
RHEXENOR	IARBAS	PELOPEIAS
CAMPUS/MINOR	HIARBAS	CYTHEREIAS
HONOR	PHORBAS	MINYEIAS
MARCIPOR	ARISBAS	PANTAGIAS
SOPOR	CORYBAS	PELASGIAS
MAEROR	PSECAS	IPHIAS
SOROR	CALCAS	OPHIAS
ERROR	MENALCAS	PYRRHIAS
TERROR	ISALCAS	ERYMANTHIAS
FUROR	PROCAS	PYTHIAS
MERCATOR	ARCAS	EUHIAS
DOMATOR	ARCAS	ELIAS
SACRATOR	BARCAS	BELIAS
SATOR	LEUCAS	PELIAS
CUNCTATOR	LUCAS	PELIAS
STATOR	LYCAS	PHLIAS
ACTOR	CLEADAS	ILIAS
HYLACTOR	SCIPIADAS	CALLIAS
HECTOR	LADAS	PLIAS
VICTOR	AGELADAS	DAULIAS
VOCONIUS/VICTOR	IDAS	DAULIAS
PHOBETOR	LYCIDAS	ISMENIAS
ONETOR	APHIDAS	LEMNIAS
CLITOR	MIDAS	METHYMNIAS
VINDEMITOR	CYDAS	NASAMONIAS
NUMITOR	AEAS	POTNIAS
JANITOR	AENEAS	DAUNIAS
ULTOR	SILVIUS/AENEAS	THYNIAS
CRANTOR	POEAS	ACHELOIAS
MENTOR	OREAS	SEPIAS
STENTOR	BOREAS	OLYMPIAS
AMYNTOR	BROTEAS	APPIAS
CASTOR	FAS	CASPIAS
ALASTOR	NEFAS	THESPIAS
PASTOR	BAGAS	LYCORIAS
POLYMESTOR	ACRAGAS	DORIAS
NESTOR	AGRAGAS	PELORIAS
FAVOR	SYMPLEGAS	SCYRIAS

PHASIAS
PHASIAS
TERESIAS
TIRESIAS
CEPHISIAS
NISIAS
GNOSIAS
GNOSIAS
PAUSIAS
NYSIAS
ACTIAS
AEETIAS
BITIAS
CRITIAS
PALLANTIAS
ATLANTIAS
THAUMANTIAS
THOANTIAS
THESTIAS
SESTIAS
THYIAS
CYCLAS
AMYCLAS
GELAS
MELAS
PTERELAS
ASILAS
ARCESILAS
PALLAS
HELLAS
HISPELLAS
ACHILLAS
THEMILLAS
IOLLAS
ATLAS
TAULAS
HYLAS
DORYLAS
ACAMAS
RHADAMAS
ALCIDAMAS
IPHIDAMAS
AMPHIDAMAS
CHERSIDAMAS
ANTIDAMAS
THIODAMAS
HIPPODAMAS
THERODAMAS
POLYDAMAS
EURYDAMAS
ATHAMAS
GARAMAS
MIMAS
NOMAS
DROMAS

LYCORMAS
THAUMAS
DYMAS
ERYMAS
MEVANAS
LAENAS
MAENAS
MAECENAS
CAPENAS
ECHINAS
ARPINAS
LARINAS
LARINAS
SECUNDUS/CARRINAS
CASINAS
SASSINAS
ATINAS
ALTINAS
AQUINAS
RAVENNAS
SYNNAS
PRIVERNAS
TELEBOAS
THOAS
NOAS
TROAS
TROAS
SCOPAS
IOPAS
TARAS
HERAS
MITHRAS
TEUTHRAS
CORAS
PYTHAGORAS
ATHENAGORAS
ANDRAGORAS
HAMPSAGORAS
ARISTAGORAS
ANAXAGORAS
THAMYRAS
CINYRAS
TYRAS
APESAS
GLISAS
BARISAS
TOLOSAS
DIPSAS
CHRYSAS
IETAS
PIETAS
EBRIETAS
PHILETAS
DAMOETAS
COMMODITAS

CREDULITAS
OPPORTUNITAS
SALUBRITAS
VERITAS
SATURITAS
NECESSITAS
FAUSTITAS
JUVENTAS
AMYNTAS
LYCOTAS
EUROTAS
SOTAS
VOLUPTAS
LIBERTAS
PAUPERTAS
LABYRTAS
CYRTAS
AESTAS
EGESTAS
MAIESTAS
TEMPESTAS
POTESTAS
VENUSTAS
VETUSTAS
ARCHYTAS
ALEUAS
NOVAS
GYAS
PANTAGYAS
PHLEGYAS
HYAS
DRYAS
ADRYAS
HAMADRYAS
BERYAS
MARSYAS
ARABS
URBS
ARABES
SAETABES
LYCAMBES
ADHERBES
NUBES
CHALYBES
PHAEACES
AIACES
ZALACES
MACES
PHARNACES
DRACES
THRACES
SAMOTHRACES
MYRACES
SACES
EURYSACES

OTACES
THRAECES
CILICES
PHOENICES
POLYNICES
PYRGOPOLYNICES
PICES
NEALCES
MAHALCES
PHALCES
DRANCES
CAPPADOCES
PODARCES
PISCES
CAUDINAE/FAUCES
POLLUCES
ARCADES
ORCADES
AENEADES
CARNEADES
GADES
SYMPLEGADES
STOECHADES
STROPHADES
LAIADES
NAIADES
PLEIADES
AMPHIAREIADES
HELIADES
PELIADES
ILIADES
LUCILIADES
OILIADES
NAUPLIADES
DAULIADES
HAGNIADES
CLINIADES
HELICONIADES
ACRISIONIADES
TELAMONIADES
AMPHITRYONIADES
TROIADES
SCIPIADES
ASOPIADES
CROTOPIADES
THESPIADES
SCYRIADES
PHASIADES
ANCHISIADES
MENOETIADES
PHERETIADES
ABANTIADES
POEANTIADES
ATALANTIADES
ATLANTIADES

ATHAMANTIADES
DRYANTIADES
LAOMEDONTIADES
PHAETHONTIADES
BERECYNTIADES
AMYNTIADES
LAERTIADES
THESTIADES
THYESTIADES
BATTIADES
THYIADES
LADES
CYCLADES
PYLADES
NOMADES
MAENADES
ECHINADES
TROADES
HIPPOTADES
SOTADES
HYADES
THYADES
DRYADES
AMADRYADES
HAMADRYADES
OTHRYADES
PALAMEDES
NICOMEDES
DIOMEDES
THEODOROMEDES
EUMEDES
GANYMEDES
NAIDES
DANAIDES
LABDACIDES
AEACIDES
PHYLACIDES
ATRACIDES
ARSACIDES
HYRTACIDES
ASTACIDES
APOECIDES
ALCIDES
LYNCIDES
AMARYNCIDES
AMPYCIDES
CORYCIDES
THUCYDIDES
TYDIDES
ELELEIDES
CADMEIDES
PELOPEIDES
NEREIDES
TEREIDES
SCYREIDES

MINYEIDES
FIDES
POLYMACHAEROPLAGIDES
HARPAGIDES
AEGIDES
LYCURGIDES
BUMBOMACHIDES
INACHIDES
COLCHIDES
TIMARCHIDES
SISYPHIDES
EMATHIDES
PROMETHIDES
CRETHIDES
ERECHTHIDES
ATTHIDES
SCYTHIDES
OEBALIDES
COCALIDES
STYMPHALIDES
AETHALIDES
MAENALIDES
THESSALIDES
ITALIDES
TANTALIDES
OECLIDES
NEOCLIDES
EUCLIDES
AMYCLIDES
BELIDES
SICELIDES
PENTHELIDES
NELIDES
PELIDES
CYPSELIDES
ACHILLIDES
NAUBOLIDES
AEOLIDES
ARGOLIDES
ASTYLIDES
PRIAMIDES
PYRAMIDES
ARCHIDEMIDES
CALLIDEMIDES
CHARMIDES
EURYMIDES
DARDANIDES
AENIDES
OLENIDES
ACHAEMENIDES
IALMENIDES
EUMENIDES
OENIDES
PHINIDES
AONIDES

PARTHAONIDES
HELICONIDES
LYCONIDES
MYGDONIDES
ARGENTUMDONIDES
VIRGINESVENDONIDES
CALYDONIDES
MAEONIDES
ARCHONIDES
TYPHONIDES
TALAIONIDES
OEDIPODIONIDES
DEIONIDES
CHIONIDES
ECHIONIDES
SPERCHIONIDES
OPHIONIDES
HYPERIONIDES
IAPETIONIDES
IXIONIDES
ANTAMONIDES
ACMONIDES
HAEMONIDES
ALEMONIDES
MNEMONIDES
SIMONIDES
MEMNONIDES
AGAMEMNONIDES
NUMMOSEXPALPONIDES
MEGARONIDES
HOMERONIDES
CORONIDES
AESONIDES
BISTONIDES
AMAZONIDES
PANTHOIDES
ACHELOIDES
HOMOLOIDES
INOIDES
HEROIDES
LETOIDES
LEOPREPIDES
NUMQUAMERIPIDES
QUODSEMELARRIPIDES
EURIPIDES
CECROPIDES
THEOPROPIDES
TYNDARIDES
LARIDES
MARMARIDES
MARMARIDES*
TAENARIDES
BASSARIDES
CAPHERIDES
PIERIDES

HESPERIDES
LIBETHRIDES
AGENORIDES
ANTENORIDES
ACTORIDES
AMYNTORIDES
THESTORIDES
NESTORIDES
ARESTORIDES
ATRIDES
MISARGYRIDES
PHILLYRIDES
PEGASIDES
PHASIDES
IASIDES
HIPPASIDES
IMBRASIDES
THESIDES
POSIDES
ALCETIDES
PROPOETIDES
PROETIDES
LAMPETIDES
IPHITIDES
ATLANTIDES
PENTIDES
PHAETHONTIDES
ACROPOLISTIDES
ARISTIDES
AEPYTIDES
EURYTIDES
NUGIEPILOQUIDES
RHONDES
GYNDES
OEDIPODES
NEBRODES
HERODES
ORODES
ILERDES
LAUDES
HAGES
SAGES
TAGES
ASTYAGES
LELEGES
MEGES
INDIGES
CIZIGES
GANGES
ALLOBROGES
BRUGES
FRUGES
GYGES
PHRYGES
IAZYGES

LACHES
PHILOLACHES
PIACCHES
ARABARCHES
LETHES
LAPITHES
CLEANTHES
EUANTHES
SCYTHES
RABIES
MACIES
OIES
PANTAGIES
ARIES
QUIES
ALES
CALES
THALES
ANNALES
PALES
FLORALES
SALES
CALLICLES
PERICLES
SOSICLES
PLEUSICLES
COCLES
EMPEDOCLES
ETEOCLES
SOPHOCLES
AGATHOCLES
STRATIPPOCLES
STRATOCLES
AGORASTOCLES
MELES
HEDYMELES
LYSITELES
PRAXITELES
ARISTOTELES
TRALLES
APELLES
ACHILLES
PATRICOLES
AUTOLOLES
HERCULES
HYLES
FAMES
HIEMES
CHREMES
ARIMES
PHAEOCOMES
ARMES
HERMES
PERIPHANES
METROPHANES

STRATOPHANES
ARISTOPHANES
CEPHALLANES
PERIPLANES
MANES
ATHAMANES
PANES
TIGRANES
TITANES
THEBAGENES
TIMAGENES
ARCHIGENES
ANTIGENES
HERMOGENES
MENOGENES
PROTOGENES
CEPHENES
PLISTHENES
DEMOSTHENES
BORYSTHENES
NERIENES
CEPHALLENES
ACHAEMENES
HIPPOMENES
SIRENES
SYENES
MAGNES
MAGNES
CUPIDINES
VIRGINES
GORGINES
TELCHINES
AMNES
RHAMNES
RAMNES
AONES
HELICAONES
LYCAONES
LACONES
CICONES
VASCONES
EDONES
MACEDONES
MYRMIDONES
SIDONES
CYDONES
PAEONES
PAPHLAGONES
LINGONES
LAESTRYGONES
SITHONES
IONES
VANGIONES
MERIONES
TRIONES

SEPTENTRIONES
SEPTEM/TRIONES
MIMALLONES
SOLONES
NASAMONES
DAEMONES
GEMINEI/LENONES
SENONES
MACRONES
PISONES
SUESSONES
AUSONES
CATONES
ANTICATONES
CAPITONES
TRITONES
BISTONES
VETTONES
BRITTONES
HALCYONES
GERYONES
AMAZONES
PARNES
TROES
TARDIPES
QUADRIPES
ALPES
CERCOPES
LYCOPES
AETHIOPES
CYCLOPES
DOLOPES
PANOPES
SINOPES
STEROPES
DRYOPES
SPES
HYDASPES
CHOASPES
DRYASPES
ARES
CARES
DARES
MEGARES
CHARES
LARES
CAESARES
CRES
OCRES
VOLUCRES
CAERES
HIBERES
CERES
HELVINA/CERES
LUCERES

PHERES
VENERES
SERES
BYZERES
MEDORES
DIORES
AMORES
TIMORES
SORORES
ANTORES
CENTORES
APRES
VERRES
PATRES
CURES
LIGURES
LEMURES
TYRES
MONAESES
MONESES
ANCISES
ANCHISES
SICILIENSES
MASSILIENSES
ATHENIENSES
TITIENSES
FICEDULENSES
MYCENENSES
RAMNENSES
MINTURNENSES
PISTORENSES
CRETENSES
METAMORPHOSES
CYNAPSES
ARSES
HERSES
THERSES
PERSES
ORSES
CAMBYSES
MOYSES
CHRYSES
PHRAATES
NABATES
ICHNOBATES
EURYBATES
MITHRIDATES
TIRIDATES
AEGATES
ACHATES
PANCHATES
NIPHATES
ANTIPHATES
PELATES
CALLIDAMATES

SAUROMATES	OPHELTES	ERINYES
MAECENATES	CORYBANTES	BYZES
PENATES	GIGANTES	THEBAIS
CRATES	BRIGANTES	THEBAIS
ECHECRATES	BACCHANTES	PHOCAIS
MENECRATES	ATLANTES	ACHAIS
PHILOCRATES	GARAMANTES	ACHAIS
HERMOCRATES	DOROZANTES	THAIS
PHANOCRATES	PICENTES	LAIS
HIPPOCRATES	VEIENTES	CALAIS
HARPOCRATES	COMMORIENTES	PTOLOMAIS
SOCRATES	SORTIENTES	NAIS
ARISTOCRATES	LAURENTES	DANAIS
NAUCRATES	SYNAPOTHNESCONTES	TANAIS
EUPHRATES	BELLEROPHONTES	SAIS
TEMPESTATES	ARISTOPHONTES	ALABIS
TEUTATES	BRONTES	NABIS
THOACTES	ORONTES	SAETABIS
PYRACTES	ERIBOTES	IBIS
POLYDECTES	SIBOTES	ALBIS
CURICTES	POLYBOTES	CARAMBIS
MELANCHAETES	PHTHIOTES	LACTEUS/ORBIS
ERICETES	APHELIOTES	LESBIS
AEETES	BOOTES	LESBIS
GETES	HIPPOTES	ANUBIS
GETES	BROTES	ACIS
MASSAGETES	THYOTES	PHAEACIS
ALETES	IAXARTES	SALMACIS
HECATEBELETES	LAERTES	ATRACIS
NEMETES	IERTES	ATRACIS
COMETES	ILERTES	BERENICIS
MAGNETES	AGYRTES	CHALCIS
ACOETES	SYRTES	PHOCIS
THYMOETES	COASTES	PHOCIS
MENOETES	SARRASTES	PHORCIS
CRETES	ACESTES	PISCIS
CURETES	ARGESTES	BAUCIS
PHILOCTETES	TELESTES	GLAUCIS
SUETES	AULESTES	DIS
ZETES	ORESTES	CARYBDIS
HODITES	THYESTES	CHARYBDIS
MEMPHITES	PROCRUSTES	LYCOMEDIS
COCLITES	MYSTES	SARDIS
POLITES	ALYATTES	CRATAEIS
ONCHESMITES	NAUTES	CYTAEIS
SYENITES	BUTES	BOEBEIS
SAMNITES	ASBYTES	PHYLACEIS
ONITES	COLAXES	PHYLACEIS
ATARNITES	OAXES	MEDEIS
CHARITES	ARAXES	LELEGEIS
ABDERITES	MARAXES	BACCHEIS
QUIRITES	TAXES	SPERCHEIS
THERSITES	OTAXES	CEPHEIS
AQUITES	ULIXES	PITTHEIS
EPHIALTES	XERXES	ERYTHEIS

RANIS	SCIRONIS	APOLLINARIS
TARANIS	CORONIS	APOLLINARIS
TITANIS	PHORONIS	LUNARIS
TITANIS	PHORONIS	PARIS
PRYTANIS	AUSONIS	HIPPARIS
CAENIS	TRITONIS	DYSPARIS
MELAENIS	TRITONIS	BASSARIS
PHILAENIS	BISTONIS	THYBRIS
PANTAENIS	BISTONIS	TRINACRIS
MYCENIS	AMAZONIS	LOCRIS
GIDDENIS	PHORCYNIS	PROCRIS
LEMNISELENIS	BITHYNIS	LUCRIS
CYLLENIS	GORTYNIS	HIBERIS
POEMENIS	EREBOIS	TIBERIS
ORMENIS	EUBOIS	PIERIS
ISMENIS	DEOIS	PHALERIS
ISMENIS	TYPHOIS	NERIS
EUMENIS	ACHELOIS	MOERIS
CEBRENIS	SIMOIS	PETERIS
PIRENIS	MINOIS	ASTERIS
JUVENIS	PYROIS	TIGRIS
DAPHNIS	LATOIS	IRIS
TIBERINIS	LETOIS	CIRIS
SINIS	APIS	LIRIS
AMNIS	SARAPIS	OSIRIS
SAMNIS	SERAPIS	PETOSIRIS
SAMNIS	SAPIS	BUSIRIS
HYMNIS	OPIS	QUIRIS
AONIS	INOPIS	SICORIS
LYCAONIS	CECROPIS	LYCORIS
CHAONIS	CECROPIS	DORIS
LACONIS	ASOPIS	DORIS
HELICONIS	ASOPIS	CHLORIS
ADONIS	LEUCIPPIS	CYPRIS
EDONIS	AGANIPPIS	LATRIS
MYGDONIS	PUPPIS	AMASTRIS
SIDONIS	ASPIS	SESOSTRIS
SIDONIS	LEUCASPIS	BURIS
DODONIS	THESPIS	THURIS
CALYDONIS	ARIS	CYNOSURIS
MAEONIS	ABARIS	CYRIS
MAEONIS	FABARIS	PANEGYRIS
PAEONIS	SYBARIS	LYRIS
TYPHONIS	ICARIS	ILLYRIS
MARATHONIS	TYNDARIS	THAMYRIS
SITHONIS	BALEARIS	TAMYRIS
SITHONIS	SAGARIS	ASIS
TITHONIS	PHARIS	BUBASIS
HYPERIONIS	BALIARIS	PEGASIS
CLONIS	BALIARIS	PEGASIS
MIMALLONIS	SALIARIS	PHASIS
HAEMONIS	LATIARIS	PARRHASIS
SALMONIS	PHALARIS	PARRHASIS
STRYMONIS	NARIS	IASIS
PANNONIS	TAENARIS	AMASIS

ENGONASIS
PARNASIS
AESIS
ALBESIS
LACHESIS
ATHESIS
NEMESIS
NESIS
LYRNESIS
TARTESIS
ISIS
CEPHISIS
ENSIS
ITHACENSIS
LUCENSIS
ALIDENSIS
PYRGENSIS
RHODIENSIS
CORINTHIENSIS
SICILIENSIS
HISPANIENSIS
ATHENIENSIS
SARDINIENSIS
CARTHAGINIENSIS
EPIDAMNIENSIS
LEMNIENSIS
MACEDONIENSIS
BABYLONIENSIS
BONONIENSIS
MEGALENSIS
MENSIS
PARMENSIS
CASSIUS/PARMENSIS
CYRENENSIS
MISENENSIS
TARRACINENSIS
ARIMINENSIS
CATINENSIS
MUTINENSIS
CANNENSIS
TARRACONENSIS
SULMONENSIS
VERONENSIS
LUGUDUNENSIS
LUNENSIS
VELABRENSIS
NEMORENSIS
PATRENSIS
CURENSIS
MELITENSIS
GNOSIS
GNOSIS
ANACHARSIS
PERSIS
PERSIS

THYRSIS
CYPASSIS
TELMESSIS
PERMESSIS
ANAUSIS
ZEUSIS
ARETHUSIS
RHAMNUSIS
ACHERUSIS
MYSIS
CHRYSIS
DATIS
TEGEATIS
THYREATIS
SARMATIS
SARSINATIS
FERENTINATIS
RATIS
ATRIUM/LIBERTATIS
BAETIS
DERCETIS
DIRCETIS
AEETIS
GANGETIS
THETIS
MILETIS
MILETIS
MAGNETIS
CRETIS
CURETIS
DITIS
MEMPHITIS
NEAPOLITIS
OCEANITIS
SAGARITIS
ZEPHRITIS
QUIRITIS
BISALTIS
ELEPHANTIS
PALLANTIS
ATLANTIS
ATLANTIS
ATHAMANTIS
GARAMANTIS
THAUMANTIS
DYMANTIS
THOANTIS
CARMENTIS
LAURENTIS
PHAETHONTIS
PHLEGETHONTIS
PROPONTIS
PHRONTIS
MAEOTIS
MAEOTIS

MAREOTIS
MAREOTIS
ICARIOTIS
ICARIOTIS
LOTIS
PHILOTIS
NILOTIS
PROTIS
LEPTIS
BRITOMARTIS
SYRTIS
BUBASTIS
ADRASTIS
ALCESTIS
TELESTIS
PRISTIS
LIBYSTIS
ATTIS
BITTIS
CARNUTIS
EURYTIS
ANGUIS
AVIS
NAVIS
CIVIS
JOVIS
VEJOVIS
AXIS
OEAXIS
ALEXIS
ZEUXIS
HIEMS
POEANS
BACCHANS
ADVOLANS
ATLANS
ACAMANS
GARAMANS
MIMANS
TONANS
CAMPANS
TARANS
PICENS
VOLCENS
ARCENS
QUERCENS
OCCIDENS
PUDENS
UFENS
OUFENS
PROSPICIENS
VEIENS
ORIENS
TITIENS
MENS

CLEMENS	TECTAPHOS	APIDANOS
SARMENS	SERIPHOS	COERANOS
CANENS	ORESITROPHOS	OLENOS
ARCITENENS	ATHOS	ORCHOMENOS
ANGUITENENS	SCIATHOS	EPIDICAZOMENOS
ARQUITENENS	SEBETHOS	ACONTIZOMENOS
SERPENS	PEPARETHOS	ISMENOS
LAURENS	CORINTHOS	DIADUMENOS
LAURENS	LEBYNTHOS	HEAUTON/TIMORUMENOS
BELLIPOTENS	CYNTHOS	SCHOENOS
ARMIPOTENS	ZACYNTHOS	TENOS
IGNIPOTENS	COCYTHOS	EUENOS
OMNIPOTENS	PALLADIOS	CYTHNOS
SAGITTIPOTENS	CHIOS	CARCINOS
OBSEQUENS	SPERCHIOS	LINOS
AVENS	EUCHIOS	MINOS
FONS	ILIOS	NINOS
SACER/MONS	NAUPLIOS	EIARINOS
PHYCUNS	PENIOS	THERINOS
ACHERUNS	IXIONIOS	CHIMERINOS
ARRUNS	SCORPIOS	OPORINOS
TIRYNS	ORIOS	EPIDAMNOS
CHAOS	ALATRIOS	LEMNOS
LABOS	EPITRAPEZIOS	MYCONOS
GENABOS	DAEDALOS	ETEONOS
LESBOS	STYMPHALOS	HONOS
AESACOS	AETHALOS	NEBROPHONOS
PITTACOS	MAENALOS	IONOS
ORICOS	PHARSALOS	SAUROCTONOS
CYZICOS	TALOS	AORNOS
IOLCOS	PATROCLOS	CAUNOS
DAMASCOS	ICELOS	HYDROCHOOS
ENCELADOS	DELOS	THOOS
TENEDOS	HELOS	LEPOS
CNIDOS	AMPELOS	NEPOS
GNIDOS	TROGILOS	ENCOLPOS
POLYIDOS	TROILOS	CANOPOS
RHODOS	MYRTILOS	ATROPOS
ABYDOS	MALLOS	ASOPOS
EOS	MNASYLLOS	OLEAROS
ANDROGEOS	SCOLOS	PHAROS
SPERCHEOS	TMOLOS	OLIAROS
ALPHEOS	POLOS	CLAROS
PENELEOS	PACTOLOS	CYLLAROS
PTELEOS	PYLOS	TMAROS
OILEOS	SIPYLOS	TAENAROS
DEMOLEOS	ASTYLOS	PAROS
PHENEOS	PERGAMOS	TARTAROS
EUNEOS	SAMOS	GYAROS
EPEOS	POLYPHEMOS	LABROS
AREOS	ISTHMOS	IMBROS
CRAGOS	SOLIMOS	ANDROS
ARGOS	HIPPALMOS	LEANDROS
EUTYCHOS	ENNOMOS	MENANDROS
PAPHOS	PANHORMOS	ANTANDROS

HYDROS	ARCTOS	LAUS
EROS	CETOS	TALAUS
NICEROS	TAYGETOS	AGELAUS
AEGOCEROS	ASCHETOS	MENELAUS
PIEROS	PHILETOS	ARCESILAUS
PHILEROS	MILETOS	PROTESILAUS
HERMEROS	NERITOS	IOLAUS
MERMEROS	TARENTOS	OENOMAUS
HESPEROS	PONTOS	DANAUS
MELEAGROS	SAGUNTOS	DANAUS
ANIGROS	OTOS	AMPHIARAUS
EPIROS	CROTOS	COLLABUS
HOROS	BUTHROTOS	PANTOLABUS
SPENDOPHOROS	COPTOS	ARABUS
BOSPHOROS	AEGYPTOS	ARABUS
PHOSPHOROS	HALIARTOS	SABUS
EMPOROS	ABSYRTOS	SAETABUS
BOSPOROS	CESTOS	METABUS
CYTOROS	ONCHESTOS	RHAEBUS
CYPROS	SESTOS	PERRHAEBUS
TROS	CARYSTOS	PHOEBUS
BACTROS	HYMETTOS	COROEBUS
CAYSTROS	COCYTOS	EREBUS
AGLAUROS	CLYTOS	BALBUS
ANAUROS	ORNYTOS	OLBUS
EPICUROS	DAVOS	EXAERAMBUS
SCYROS	NAXOS	CERAMBUS
AMYROS	TITYOS	CORYMBUS
SYROS	LAELAPS	DEIPHOBUS
TYROS	DARAPS	PROBUS
SATYROS	PRINCEPS	SUPERBUS
CAUCASOS	HIEMPS	EUPHORBUS
THASOS	OPS	MORBUS
PARNASOS	AETHIOPS	POLYBUS
HIPPASOS	AETHIOPS	ARBACUS
PHANTASOS	CYCLOPS	CACUS
LYCABESOS	HELOPS	DACUS
HERBESOS	PELOPS	DACUS
ODESOS	DOLOPS	LABDACUS
EPHESOS	CHAROPS	RHUNDACUS
MYCALESOS	CECROPS	RHYNDACUS
LYRNESOS	MEROPS	AEACUS
TITARESOS	OROPS	PHAEACUS
AEGISOS	DRYOPS	ITHACUS
CEPHISOS	CINYPS	ITHACUS
ELISOS	ARS	IOLCIACUS
ILISOS	LARS	PHIDIACUS
GNOSOS	MARS	RHODIACUS
PANDROSOS	TUDERS	ZODIACUS
THAPSOS	CAMERS	EPHYREIACUS
TARSOS	FORS	PHEGIACUS
TARTESSOS	FORTUNA/FORS	ARCHIACUS
CYPARISSOS	MORS	CORINTHIACUS
AMPHRYSOS	MAVORS	MALIACUS
ABATOS	TIBURS	DELIACUS

HELIACUS
PELIACUS
ILIACUS
NILIACUS
ISTHMIACUS
TITANIACUS
SALAMINIACUS
LEMNIACUS
COLOPHONIACUS
ARGANTHONIACUS
IONIACUS
BABYLONIACUS
NASAMONIACUS
AMMONIACUS
TRITONIACUS
DAUNIACUS
THYNIACUS
GORTYNIACUS
OLYMPIACUS
CASPIACUS
THESPIACUS
MESEMBRIACUS
ADRIACUS
HADRIACUS
HIBERIACUS
CYTHERIACUS
HOMERIACUS
CYTORIACUS
AMASTRIACUS
SYRIACUS
PHASIACUS
MEGALESIACUS
TARTESIACUS
ISIACUS
GNOSIACUS
TARTESSIACUS
PAUSIACUS
TELPHUSIACUS
AMATHUSIACUS
PELUSIACUS
PRUSIACUS
MAURUSIACUS
AMPHRYSIACUS
ACTIACUS
ATLANTIACUS
BYZANTIACUS
THERMODONTIACUS
PROPONTIACUS
HELLESPONTIACUS
SESTIACUS
MATTIACUS
THYLACUS
BENACUS
ASSARACUS
LAMPSACUS

SPARTACUS
HYRTACUS
ASTACUS
FLACCUS
GRACCUS
ECUS
GRAECUS
GRAECUS
DECUS
RHOECUS
MONOECUS
AGROECUS
CAICUS
PHOCAICUS
BARDAICUS
JUDAICUS
ACHAICUS
CALLAICUS
NAICUS
LABICUS
ARABICUS
URBICUS
DACICUS
ARCADICUS
CAEDICUS
MEDICUS
CHALCIDICUS
NUMIDICUS
EPIDICUS
INDICUS
PYTHODICUS
BELGICUS
BACCHICUS
COLCHICUS
DELPHICUS
DELPHICUS
SAPPHICUS
PARTHICUS
SCYTHICUS
STYMPHALICUS
PALICUS
PHARSALICUS
THESSALICUS
ITALICUS
ITALICUS
TANTALICUS
ATTALICUS
VINDELICUS
MELICUS
COELICUS
GALLICUS
GALLICUS
RUTILIUS/GALLICUS
SABELLICUS
TARBELLICUS

ARGOLICUS
AETOLICUS
APULICUS
GAETULICUS
NUMICUS
DARDANICUS
GERMANICUS
GERMANICUS*
CAESAR/GERMANICUS
CAMPANICUS
GRANICUS
SEQUANICUS
POENICUS
CALLINICUS
BRITANNICUS
BRITANNICUS
TUNNICUS
LESBONICUS
LACONICUS
LEUCONICUS
LINGONICUS
GNATHONICUS
IONICUS
BABYLONICUS
PANNONICUS
PENTETRONICUS
STRATONICUS
PARAETONICUS
SANTONICUS
TEUTONICUS
AMAZONICUS
HERNICUS
LIBURNICUS
UNICUS
PUNICUS
CYNICUS
CYNICUS
BITHYNICUS
VOLUSIUS/BITHYNICUS
EUTHYNICUS
EUBOICUS
TROICUS
STOICUS
PICUS
GLYMPICUS
OLYMPICUS
PINDARICUS
BALEARICUS
MARMARICUS
BASSARICUS
CANTABRICUS
UMBRICUS
HIBERICUS
HOMERICUS
SERICUS

AFRICUS
AFRICUS
DORICUS
NORICUS
GARRICUS
SATRICUS
TETRICUS
CASTRICUS
MAURICUS
ARAURICUS
TAURICUS
CENTAURICUS
HILURICUS
ASTURICUS
ILLYRICUS
HAMPSICUS
MARSICUS
PERSICUS
PERSICUS
CORSICUS
CLASSICUS
MASSICUS
MASSICUS
MITHRIDATICUS
TEGEATICUS
ASIATICUS
SPARTIATICUS
DALMATICUS
DELMATICUS
SARMATICUS
SOCRATICUS
CIBYRATICUS
BAETICUS
BAETICUS
RAETICUS
GETICUS
GANGETICUS
CRETICUS
CRETICUS
CURETICUS
MEMPHITICUS
SYBARITICUS
CELTICUS
ATLANTICUS
GARAMANTICUS
PONTICUS
PONTICUS
LEPONTICUS
ACHERUNTICUS
MAEOTICUS
MAREOTICUS
PHTHIOTICUS
NILOTICUS
EPIROTICUS
SPARTICUS

CLAUDIA/PORTICUS
LIVIA/PORTICUS
SYRTICUS
LIGUSTICUS
RUSTICUS
ANTISTIUS/RUSTICUS
ATTICUS
ATTICUS
CHATTICUS
SCELERATUS/VICUS
CYZICUS
ANCUS
PLANCUS
SANCUS
CUPENCUS
JUNCUS
RUNCUS
AURUNCUS
LYNCUS
CAPPADOCUS
LEODOCUS
DEMODOCUS
PHOCUS
JOCUS
ARCILOCUS
CROCUS
ARCUS
MARCUS
PLAUTIUS/MARCUS
PACUVIUS/MARCUS
MAMERCUS
LUPERCUS
CIRCUS
MAXIMUS/CIRCUS
ORCUS
PHORCUS
DAMASCUS
COLLYBISCUS
LYCISCUS
DISCUS
POLYBADISCUS
LAMPADISCUS
MILPHIDISCUS
FALISCUS
PHANISCUS
OLYMPISCUS
VOPISCUS
MANILIUS/VOPISCUS
PRISCUS
TERENTIUS/PRISCUS
SURISCUS
SYRISCUS
METISCUS
VISCUS
VOLSCUS

OSCUS
OPSCUS
FUSCUS
AUFIDIUS/LUSCUS
ETRUSCUS
ETRUSCUS
TUSCUS
TUSCUS
VICUS/TUSCUS
LIBYSCUS
RHAUCUS
GLAUCUS
MANDUCUS
LEUCUS
SELEUCUS
BREUCUS
OPHIUCUS
LUCUS
CAYCUS
IBYCUS
LIBYCUS
LYCUS
HARPALYCUS
AUTOLYCUS
AMYCUS
AMPYCUS
FADUS
CLADUS
CELADUS
ENCELADUS
PADUS
ARADUS
GARADUS
HAEDUS
LEBEDUS
CONGEDUS
MEDUS
MEDUS
TENEDUS
LIGDUS
LYGDUS
IDUS
CANDIDUS
AUFIDUS
AUFIDUS
ALGIDUS
ALGIDUS
NUMIDUS
CNIDUS
LEPIDUS
RAVIDUS
RUBELLIUS/BLANDUS
INDUS
INDUS
LINDUS

PINDUS	PYRRHAEUS	ZMYRNAEUS
SECUNDUS	LETHAEUS	AETNAEUS
RHODUS	LAPITHAEUS	EUNAEUS
ARGIODUS	CARTHAEUS	CORYNAEUS
HESIODUS	ALAEUS	NAPAEUS
NODUS	HYBLAEUS	RHIPAEUS
SARDUS	ZANCLAEUS	RIPAEUS
SARDUS	AMYCLAEUS	OLPAEUS
CORDUS	NEPHELAEUS	PARTHENOPAEUS
LUDUS	MENELAEUS	EUROPAEUS
ABYDUS	LILAEUS	LIPARAEUS
LYDUS	PROTESILAEUS	HEBRAEUS
LYDUS	PELLAEUS	THYMBRAEUS
SABAEUS	SCYLLAEUS	THYMBRAEUS*
THEBAEUS	HYLAEUS	ASCRAEUS
THISBAEUS	HYLAEUS	ASCRAEUS
LILYBAEUS	ERIPHYLAEUS	PHERAEUS
ALCAEUS	CADMAEUS	PHERAEUS
ANCAEUS	PYGMAEUS	THERAEUS
DRANCAEUS	PTOLOMAEUS	TANAGRAEUS
PHOCAEUS	CUMAEUS	PHLEGRAEUS
BARCAEUS	IDUMAEUS	PHLEGRAEUS*
CIRCAEUS	EUMAEUS	ERYTHRAEUS
DIRCAEUS	CYMAEUS	PIRAEUS
LYCAEUS	IDYMAEUS	PIRAEUS
LYCAEUS	DIDYMAEUS	PETRAEUS
PADAEUS	PHANAEUS	ASTRAEUS
LEDAEUS	ARIADNAEUS	ASTRAEUS
IDAEUS	CELAENAEUS	ITURAEUS
IDAEUS	CENAEUS	CORCYRAEUS
CHALDAEUS	MYCENAEUS	EPHYRAEUS
JUDAEUS	ATHENAEUS	CINYRAEUS
JUDAEUS	LENAEUS	ITYRAEUS
AEAEUS	LENAEUS	PAGASAEUS
TEGEAEUS	MYTILENAEUS	PEGASAEUS
NEMEAEUS	PALLENAEUS	TEMESAEUS
LAGAEUS	MITYLENAEUS	ISAEUS
AEGAEUS	MENAEUS	NISAEUS
ENNOSIGAEUS	ALALCOMENAEUS	NISAEUS
PANGAEUS	HYMENAEUS	PISAEUS
PANGAEUS	HYMENAEUS	LARISAEUS
GYGAEUS	CRENAEUS	BRISAEUS
ACHAEUS	CYRENAEUS	TISAEUS
ACHAEUS	PYRENAEUS	MARSAEUS
LYCCHAEUS	ARACHNAEUS	CESSAEUS
LECHAEUS	MYTILINAEUS	ELISSAEUS
PANCHAEUS	METHYMNAEUS	LARISSAEUS
SYCHAEUS	ENNAEUS	OSSAEUS
SYCHAEUS	HENNAEUS	MEDUSAEUS
RHIPHAEUS	DODONAEUS	MUSAEUS
NIPHAEUS	CLEONAEUS	NYSAEUS
RIPHAEUS	DIONAEUS	NABATAEUS
PANOMPHAEUS	THERAPNAEUS	HECATAEUS
CORYPHAEUS	LERNAEUS	ACTAEUS
CIRRHAEUS	SMYRNAEUS	DICTAEUS

DICTAEUS
AEETAEUS
PHILETAEUS
GENETAEUS
OETAEUS
CRETAEUS
ANTAEUS
ATALANTAEUS
TYRTAEUS
ARISTAEUS
CYTAEUS
LYAEUS
LYAEUS
MAZAEUS
PHOEBEUS
AMOEBEUS
EREBEUS
LYCAMBEUS
NIOBEUS
CEUS
SCYLACEUS
GERYONACEUS
PHALAECEUS
MENOECEUS
MENOECEUS
PANICEUS
POENICEUS
BERONICEUS
PUNICEUS
LYNCEUS
LYNCEUS
PHOCEUS
XANTHIAS/PHOCEUS
HERCEUS
DORCEUS
LYRCEUS
DEUS
PALAMEDEUS
PERIMEDEUS
DIOMEDEUS
GANYMEDEUS
SIMONIDEUS
TYDEUS
PTOLOMAEEUS
PIRAEEUS
LAGEUS
AEGEUS
AEGEUS
PHEGEUS
PHEGEUS
SIGEUS
ARGEUS
AUGEUS
BACCHEUS
ONCHEUS

OCHEUS
DICARCHEUS
DICARCHEUS*
LEARCHEUS
MOLORCHEUS
CEPHEUS
CEPHEUS
RHIPHEUS
RIPHEUS
ALPHEUS
ORPHEUS
ORPHEUS
MORPHEUS
ERECTHEUS
SYMAETHEUS
PROMETHEUS
PROMETHEUS*
CRETHEUS
ERECHTHEUS
ERECHTHEUS*
ANTHEUS
CLEANTHEUS
MELANTHEUS
ERYMANTHEUS
PENTHEUS
PENTHEUS
SMINTHEUS
ZMINTHEUS
LABYRINTHEUS
MENESTHEUS
MNESTHEUS
EURYSTHEUS
EURYSTHEUS*
PITTHEUS
PITTHEUS
HYRIEUS
HYRIEUS
RHYTIEUS
AGYIEUS
ALEUS
DAEDALEUS
AEGALEUS
THALEUS
AEGIALEUS
MENALEUS
TANTALEUS
PHERECLEUS
SOPHOCLEUS
AGATHOCLEUS
ELEUS
CELEUS
ELELEUS
SEMELEUS
NELEUS
NELEUS

PENELEUS
PELEUS
TELEUS
NILEUS
OILEUS
APELLEUS
ACHILLEUS
PERILLEUS
AGYLLEUS
HYLLEUS
PHYLLEUS
MAUSOLEUS
PIPLEUS
HOPLEUS
HERCULEUS
ASCULEUS
IULEUS
ROMULEUS
HYLEUS
HYLEUS
AESCHYLEUS
PHYLEUS
HYPSIPYLEUS
PERGAMEUS
CADMEUS
PORTHMEUS
ALCUMEUS
EUGANEUS
MELANEUS
HERCULANEUS
CAPANEUS
CAPANEUS
CYANEUS
ARIADNEUS
ECHIDNEUS
CAENEUS
CELAENEUS
PHENEUS
CYLLENEUS
IDOMENEUS
CLYMENEUS
OENEUS
OENEUS
PENEUS
PYRENEUS
DAPHNEUS
CUPIDINEUS
VIRGINEUS
CHINEUS
PHINEUS
PHINEUS
APOLLINEUS
AMINNEUS
ADONEUS
CYDONEUS

CALYDONEUS
ANDROGEONEUS
GORGONEUS
TISIPHONEUS
BIONEUS
DEUCALIONEUS
PYGMALIONEUS
ILIONEUS
HERMIONEUS
ACRISIONEUS
EETIONEUS
MIMALLONEUS
SALMONEUS
MARONEUS
NERONEUS
CORONEUS
PHORONEUS
PHORONEUS
HALCYONEUS
CERCYONEUS
THYONEUS
ACHARNEUS
ORNEUS
CYRNEUS
EUNEUS
GUNEUS
THYNEUS
GRYNEUS
GRYNEUS
MELIBOEUS
MELIBOEUS
ALPHESIBOEUS
EUBOEUS
COEUS
TYPHOEUS
TYPHOEUS
ALOEUS
EPEUS
ENIPEUS
MOLPEUS
RHODOPEUS
CYCLOPEUS
PENELOPEUS
PELOPEUS
PANOPEUS
SINOPEUS
EPOPEUS
PHILIPPEUS
AGANIPPEUS
MACAREUS
DAREUS
TYNDAREUS
MEGAREUS
APHAREUS
CAPHAREUS

CAPHAREUS
AMPHIAREUS
BRIAREUS
AESAREUS
CAESAREUS
BASSAREUS
PATAREUS
TARTAREUS
GYAREUS
IMBREUS
OCREUS
MENANDREUS
CASSANDREUS
CHIMAEREUS
CERBEREUS
CAPHEREUS
THEREUS
CYTHEREUS
PHALEREUS
HOMEREUS
NEREUS
CAPEREUS
TEREUS
AGREUS
MELEAGREUS
CENCHREUS
NIREUS
BOREUS
HYPERBOREUS
ACOREUS
POLYDOREUS
PYTHAGOREUS
CHLOREUS
AGENOREUS
ANTENOREUS
PROREUS
HECTOREUS
MENTOREUS
CASTOREUS
NESTOREUS
ATREUS
LATREUS
ALATREUS
OTREUS
ASTREUS
CENTAUREUS
PURPUREUS
EPHYREUS
CINYREUS
CAUCASEUS
PEGASEUS
THESEUS
THESEUS
ANCHISEUS
CRISEUS

ROSEUS
HYPSEUS
PERSEUS
PERSEUS
NESSEUS
CISSEUS
NYSEUS
MITHRIDATEUS
ARATEUS
CAERATEUS
LACTEUS
ARECTEUS
NYCTEUS
POLYCLETEUS
MELETEUS
RHOETEUS
RHOETEUS
TERETEUS
POLYCLITEUS
ABANTEUS
GIGANTEUS
PHALANTEUS
ATALANTEUS
PALLANTEUS
ATLANTEUS
THEIODAMANTEUS
THERMODAMANTEUS
POLYDAMANTEUS
ATHAMANTEUS
THAUMANTEUS
THOANTEUS
TEUTHRANTEUS
HYANTEUS
ACONTEUS
LAOMEDONTEUS
LEONTEUS
BELLEROPHONTEUS
PHAETHONTEUS
ORONTEUS
PROTEUS
ADRASTEUS
ORESTEUS
THYESTEUS
CARYSTEUS
PHRIXEUS
TOXEUS
PHRYXEUS
ENYEUS
RUFUS
JULIUS/RUFUS
CANIUS/RUFUS
CAMONIUS/RUFUS
SAFRONIUS/RUFUS
INSTANTIUS/RUFUS
LUCAGUS

PAMPHAGUS
LAGUS
GLAGUS
SESCENTOPLAGUS
MAGUS
ONAGUS
CRAGUS
ARVIRAGUS
TAGUS
LATAGUS
CETHEGUS
CORNELIUS/CETHEGUS
VOSEGUS
LIGUS
LIGUS
FRIGUS
JUNIUS/CONGUS
BOGUS
EULOGUS
MICCOTROGUS
ARTOTROGUS
ARGUS
ARGUS
LARGUS
PERGUS
AMORGUS
LYCURGUS
PELASGUS
PELASGUS
TELEMACHUS
AMPHIMACHUS
CALLIMACHUS
THARSIMACHUS
LYSIMACHUS
ANTIMACHUS
SYMMACHUS
CLEOMACHUS
PROMACHUS
EUMACHUS
EURYMACHUS
INACHUS
INACHUS
SATRACHUS
BACCHUS
IACCHUS
GRACCHUS
BOCCHUS
MILICHUS
STICHUS
COLCHUS
COLCHUS
BRANCHUS
OCHUS
HENIOCHUS
HENIOCHUS

ANTIOCHUS
ARCHELOCHUS
DEILOCHUS
ARCHILOCHUS
AMPHILOCHUS
MNESILOCHUS
THERSILOCHUS
ORSILOCHUS
ANTILOCHUS
EURYLOCHUS
DICARCHUS
LEARCHUS
NEARCHUS
THALIARCHUS
DINIARCHUS
DEMARCHUS
CALLIMARCHUS
ALCESIMARCHUS
HERMARCHUS
MENARCHUS
ARISTARCHUS
EUARCHUS
ANAXARCHUS
ORCHUS
MOLORCHUS
MOSCHUS
AUCHUS
OPHIUCHUS
EUNUCHUS
PANNYCHUS
MONYCHUS
EUTYCHUS
ASCALAPHUS
COLAPHUS
PAPHUS
EPAPHUS
TELEPHUS
SERIPHUS
ANTIPHUS
TRIUMPHUS
EPISTROPHUS
GROSPHUS
POMPEIUS/GROSPHUS
SISYPHUS
PYRRHUS
TYRRHUS
PANTAGATHUS
VIRIATHUS
AMATHUS
MARATHUS
SIMAETHUS
SYMAETHUS
PYRAETHUS
BOETHUS
PEPARETHUS

ZETHUS
BITHUS
CANTHUS
ARGANTHUS
PHALANTHUS
MELANTHUS
RHADAMANTHUS
ERYMANTHUS
CLOANTHUS
PANTHUS
XANTHUS
ARACINTHUS
HYACINTHUS
CERINTHUS
PERINTHUS
CORINTHUS
ACROCORINTHUS
CYNTHUS
ARACYNTHUS
ZACYNTHUS
OLYNTHUS
NOTHUS
ROTHUS
PARTHUS
PARTHUS
AEGISTHUS
TRUTHUS
STRUTHUS
XUTHUS
CORYTHUS
BAIUS
CAIUS
GAIUS
CASSIUS/GAIUS
ACHAIUS
PANCHAIUS
LAIUS
MAIUS
GRAIUS
GRAIUS
STAIUS
FABIUS
FABIUS
GURGES/FABIUS
ARABIUS
BAEBIUS
TREBIUS
VIBIUS
ALBIUS
VIRBIUS
ORBIUS
LESBIUS
VESBIUS
EUBIUS
TALTHUBIUS

DANUBIUS	LUCIUS	LYRCEIUS
TALTHYBIUS	TREBELLIUS/LUCIUS	AEACIDEIUS
POLYBIUS	TUBULUS/LUCIUS	THETIDEIUS
CIUS	MUCIUS	TYDEIUS
LABDACIUS	MINUCIUS	NEMEEIUS
AEACIUS	ERUCIUS	SAUFEIUS
PHAEACIUS	LYCIUS	PHEGEIUS
PACIUS	LYCIUS	LELEGEIUS
AMBRACIUS	NARYCIUS	BACCHEIUS
THRACIUS	BEBRYCIUS	CEPHEIUS
THRACIUS	CORYCIUS	CRETHEIUS
SAMOTHRACIUS	ARCADIUS	LAPITHEIUS
ATRACIUS	LEUCADIUS	PENTHEIUS
LAMPSACIUS	PALLADIUS	CARTHEIUS
ARSACIUS	TADIUS	PITTHEIUS
BYZACIUS	EXADIUS	ALEIUS
ACCIUS	SCHEDIUS	ASTYPALEIUS
PACCIUS	ALLEDIUS	ZANCLEIUS
ICCIUS	LYCOMEDIUS	CYBELEIUS
TUCCIUS	PEDIUS	SEMELEIUS
MAECIUS	SABIDIUS	NELEIUS
DECIUS	VIBIDIUS	NELEIUS
THRECIUS	DIDIUS	STHENELEIUS
CAEDICIUS	FIDIUS	PELEIUS
THREICIUS	DIUS/FIDIUS	SCYLLEIUS
SUFFICIUS	AUFIDIUS	PHYLLEIUS
CORNIFICIUS	FUFIDIUS	PIPLEIUS
SATURNALICIUS	UMMIDIUS	PROCULEIUS
FLORALICIUS	CNIDIUS	VENULEIUS
PUBLICIUS	GNIDIUS	SIPYLEIUS
PUBLICIUS	SERVIUS/OPPIDIUS	PRIAMEIUS
ELICIUS	NASIDIUS	CADMEIUS
CILICIUS	FAESIDIUS	CARMEIUS
NUMICIUS	URSIDIUS	PACTUMEIUS
APICIUS	VENTIDIUS	CAPANEIUS
SULPICIUS	VETTIDIUS	CYCNEIUS
SULPICIUS	BRUTTIDIUS	AENEIUS
FABRICIUS	HELVIDIUS	CLYMENEIUS
FABRICIUS	OVIDIUS	OENEIUS
UMBRICIUS	QUINTUS/OVIDIUS	SCHOENEIUS
ORICIUS	ALABANDIUS	PENEIUS
CRASSICIUS	ISINDIUS	SABINEIUS
SEPTICIUS	ODIUS	PHINEIUS
SULCIUS	RHODIUS	NANNEIUS
PATULCIUS	CLODIUS	ERIGONEIUS
MINCIUS	CLAUDIUS	THYNEIUS
MARCIUS	CLAUDIUS	AUTONOEIUS
MARCIUS	LYDIUS	POMPEIUS
PORCIUS	DANAEIUS	POMPEIUS
LYRCIUS	BOEBEIUS	MAGNUS/POMPEIUS
ROSCIUS	PHOEBEIUS	RHODOPEIUS
ROSCIUS	CHALYBEIUS	TRIOPEIUS
LUSCIUS	LILYBEIUS	PELOPEIUS
DAUCIUS	PHYLACEIUS	DOLOPEIUS
ALBUCIUS	COCCEIUS	PARTHENOPEIUS

CHAROPEIUS	SISYPHIUS	ACILIUS
TARPEIUS	EMATHIUS	PACILIUS
MEGAREIUS	CARPATHIUS	OTACILIUS
APHAREIUS	SYMAETHIUS	CAECILIUS
TIBEREIUS	PHTHIUS	LUCILIUS
CYTHEREIUS	MELANTHIUS	TONGILIUS
NEREIUS	ERYMANTHIUS	GARGILIUS
PETREIUS	CORINTHIUS	VERGILIUS
EPHYREIUS	CYNTHIUS	AEMILIUS
PHILYREIUS	CYNTHIUS	AEMILIUS
CINYREIUS	ZACYNTHIUS	MANILIUS
PAGASEIUS	BERECYNTHIUS	POMPILIUS
PEGASEIUS	ZERYNTHIUS	POMPILIUS
THESEIUS	TIRYNTHIUS	POPILIUS
NISEIUS	TIRYNTHIUS*	TURPILIUS
PERSEIUS	PYTHIUS	REX/RUPILIUS
NYSEIUS	PYTHIUS	SILIUS
TEIUS	ERYTHIUS	ATILIUS
HECATEIUS	EUHIUS	METILIUS
ELATEIUS	SALEIIUS	PANTILIUS
RHOETEIUS	SEIIUS	QUINTILIUS
RHOETEIUS	OEBALIUS	HOSTILIUS
VOLTEIUS	DAEDALIUS	RUTILIUS
VULTEIUS	IDALIUS	TUTILIUS
FONTEIUS	ACIDALIUS	DUILIUS
CAPITO/FONTEIUS	HALIUS	ESQUILIUS
VEIUS	STYMPHALIUS	SERVILIUS
MINYEIUS	MALIUS	ALLIUS
ALFIUS	MAENALIUS	GALLIUS
OLFIUS	SALIUS	MALLIUS
FUFIUS	PHARSALIUS	MALLIUS
SEGIUS	THESSALIUS	CASCELLIUS
VALGIUS	CASTALIUS	DELLIUS
PHLOGIUS	CASTALIUS	GELLIUS
SERGIUS	PUBLIUS	VAGELLIUS
SERGIUS	VELINA/PUBLIUS	TIGELLIUS
BRUGIUS	CORNELIUS/PUBLIUS	HERMOGENES/TIGELLIUS
OGYGIUS	ELIUS	ARELLIUS
IAPYGIUS	AELIUS	PERELLIUS
PHRYGIUS	CAELIUS	VISELLIUS
ORTYGIUS	LAELIUS	VITELLIUS
ORTYGIUS	DELIUS	TILLIUS
STYGIUS	DELIUS	CAPITOLINUSPETILLIUS
CHIUS	HELIUS	SUILLIUS
CHIUS	CORNELIUS	VILLIUS
INACHIUS	CLOELIUS	LOLLIUS
BACCHIUS	PELIUS	MAXIMUS/LOLLIUS
DULICHIUS	AURELIUS	POLLIUS
MUNYCHIUS	SELIUS	VALERIANUS/POLLIUS
TYCHIUS	NYCTELIUS	TULLIUS
PAPHIUS	VELIUS	MARCUS/TULLIUS
PALAEPAPHIUS	PHLIUS	PHYLLIUS
AMPHIUS	ILIUS	MANLIUS
STROPHIUS	ILIUS	AEOLIUS
CINYPHIUS	ORBILIUS	TMOLIUS

AETOLIUS
NAUPLIUS
ULIUS
JULIUS
JULIUS
LUCIUS/JULIUS
PROCULUS/JULIUS
AMULIUS
PAMPHYLIUS
PYLIUS
PYLIUS
MASSYLIUS
SAMIRAMIUS
SEMIRAMIUS
SAMIUS
SAMIUS
PHEMIUS
ISTHMIUS
OPIMIUS
QUINTUS/OPIMIUS
SEPTIMIUS
OLMIUS
MEMMIUS
PERIBOMIUS
NOMIUS
BROMIUS
BROMIUS
CHROMIUS
LATMIUS
POSTUMIUS
CRUSTUMIUS
ANIUS
CANIUS
SICANIUS
VOLCANIUS
VULCANIUS
HYRCANIUS
ASCANIUS
FUNDANIUS
DARDANIUS
DARDANIUS
DIANIUS
VEIANIUS
BOVIANIUS
CLANIUS
MANIUS
SPANIUS
VERANIUS
AFRANIUS
GRANIUS
TORANIUS
TURRANIUS
TITANIUS
MAENIUS
PACENIUS

PULFENIUS
GENIUS
PARTHENIUS
PARTHENIUS*
STHENIUS
PLISTHENIUS
BORYSTHENIUS
CYLLENIUS
CYLLENIUS
OLENIUS
ACHAEMENIUS
ARMENIUS
ARMENIUS
ISMENIUS
MENENIUS
OENIUS
PENIUS
MESSENIUS
PLATENIUS
CENTENIUS
POLYXENIUS
TROEZENIUS
LACINIUS
LICINIUS
LICINIUS
VERGINIUS
TRACHINIUS
TRACHINIUS*
PLINIUS
SALAMINIUS
FLAMINIUS
FLAMINIUS
PLEMINIUS
CIMINIUS
COMINIUS
HERMINIUS
CANINIUS
QUIRINIUS
CERRINIUS
MARRUCINUS/ASINIUS
VOLSINIUS
OSINIUS
VATINIUS
STERTINIUS
TARQUINIUS
TARQUINIUS*
SUPERBUS/TARQUINIUS
LAVINIUS
FLAVINIUS
CILNIUS
EPIDAMNIUS
LEMNIUS
LEMNIUS
CONTEREBROMNIUS
TOLUMNIUS

VOLUMNIUS
LICYMNIUS
ANNIUS
FANNIUS
ENNIUS
VIBENNIUS
CUPIENNIUS
QUINTUS/ENNIUS
VINNIUS
AONIUS
AONIUS
HELICAONIUS
LYCAONIUS
CHAONIUS
MACHAONIUS
PARTHAONIUS
AMYTHAONIUS
HICETAONIUS
TREBONIUS
HELICONIUS
COSCONIUS
MYCONIUS
MACEDONIUS
CARCHEDONIUS
ANTHEDONIUS
CALEDONIUS
ESSEDONIUS
ISSEDONIUS
MYGDONIUS
CHELIDONIUS
SIDONIUS
SIDONIUS
MANDONIUS
SARDONIUS
CYDONIUS
CALYDONIUS
MAEONIUS
ALCMAEONIUS
PAEONIUS
GARGONIUS
LAESTRYGONIUS
COLOPHONIUS
MARATHONIUS
ERICTHONIUS
CHTHONIUS
ERICHTHONIUS
ERICHTHONIUS
SITHONIUS
TITHONIUS
IONIUS
TALAIONIUS
PANDIONIUS
OEDIPODIONIUS
ECHIONIUS
AMPHIONIUS

BALLIONIUS	DAUNIUS	AQUARIUS
DOLIONIUS	JUNIUS	VARIUS
CURCULIONIUS	NEPTUNIUS	RUBRIUS
ARIONIUS	CORTYNIUS	TRINACRIUS
HYPERIONIUS	GORTYNIUS	NONACRIUS
IXIONIUS	BOIUS	TEUCRIUS
CLONIUS	DEOIUS	ANDRIUS
MILONIUS	ACHELOIUS	MAEANDRIUS
AQUILONIUS	MINOIUS	LEANDRIUS
GALLONIUS	TROIUS	SCAMANDRIUS
BABYLONIUS	LATOIUS	EUANDRIUS
TELAMONIUS	LETOIUS	LABERIUS
NASAMONIUS	AESCULAPIUS	STABERIUS
IDMONIUS	MESSAPIUS	TIBERIUS
LACEDAEMONIUS	EPIUS	CAESAR/TIBERIUS
HAEMONIUS	ASCLEPIUS	HERIUS
PALAEMONIUS	AESEPIUS	PIERIUS
STRYMONIUS	OLYMPIUS	VALERIUS
STRYMONIUS*	CYCLOPIUS	MANIUS/VALERIUS
NONIUS	PELOPIUS	CAMERIUS
MEMNONIUS	CANOPIUS	CIMMERIUS
AGAMEMNONIUS	OENOPIUS	NUMERIUS
PANNONIUS	CECROPIUS	CAELIUS/NUMERIUS
JUNONIUS	ASOPIUS	NERIUS
POMPONIUS	AESOPIUS	VOLANERIUS
HIPPONIUS	MOPSOPIUS	VENERIUS
CRONIUS	APPIUS	HESPERIUS
SAFRONIUS	OPPIUS	AGRIUS
THRONIUS	OPPIUS	MELEAGRIUS
PELETHRONIUS	CASPIUS	OEAGRIUS
SCIRONIUS	CASPIUS	RABIRIUS
LATRONIUS	THESPIUS	PODALIRIUS
CAETRONIUS	PUPIUS	PAPIRIUS
PETRONIUS	ARIUS	SIRIUS
PLEURONIUS	ICARIUS	SIRIUS
IASONIUS	ICARIUS	DORIUS
AESONIUS	ANCARIUS	BOSPHORIUS
AUSONIUS	DUCARIUS	HELORIUS
AUSONIUS	DARIUS	ANACTORIUS
LATONIUS	SANGARIUS	LAETORIUS
PARAETONIUS	PHARIUS	CLITORIUS
TRITONIUS	CORINTHIARIUS	ARTORIUS
ANTONIUS	LARIUS	SERTORIUS
MUSA/ANTONIUS	LARIUS	CYTORIUS
MARCUS/ANTONIUS	CLARIUS	CAPRIUS
BISTONIUS	CLARIUS	CYPRIUS
PLUTONIUS	MARIUS	ARRIUS
FAVONIUS	ISMARIUS	MARRIUS
SICYONIUS	TMARIUS	QUINTUS/ARRIUS
AMAZONIUS	TAENARIUS	BIRRIUS
FURNIUS	GALLINARIUS	TIRRIUS
CALPURNIUS	PINARIUS	VIRRIUS
CALPURNIUS*	PARIUS	MAMURRIUS
SATURNIUS	TARIUS	BACTRIUS
SATURNIUS	SAGITTARIUS	ELECTRIUS

DEMETRIUS
FERETRIUS
OENOTRIUS
CAYSTRIUS
SUTRIUS
EPIDAURIUS
EPIDAURIUS*
CURIUS
MERCURIUS
DURIUS
FURIUS
PALFURIUS
HILURIUS
MAMURIUS
MASURIUS
TURIUS
ASTURIUS
SCYRIUS
SYRIUS
ASSYRIUS
ASSYRIUS
TYRIUS
TYRIUS
ASIUS
ASIUS
CASIUS
CAUCASIUS
DASIUS
PARRHASIUS
PARRHASIUS*
THASIUS
IASIUS
IASIUS
THRIASIUS
VIRIASIUS
TALASIUS
PARNASIUS
THRASIUS
CAESIUS
ITHACESIUS
ARCESIUS
LEUCESIUS
MENDESIUS
EPHESIUS
MYCALESIUS
PHIGALESIUS
MILESIUS
MESIUS
TEUMESIUS
MAGNESIUS
LYRNESIUS
MARPESIUS
CRESIUS
PIRESIUS
TARTESIUS

CEPHISIUS
NUMISIUS
ACRISIUS
HORTENSIUS
SYRACOSIUS
PERCOSIUS
CNOSIUS
GNOSIUS
AMBROSIUS
SCEPSIUS
PERSIUS
CASSIUS
CLASSIUS
PARNASSIUS
MESSIUS
CRESSIUS
TARTESSIUS
TRAUSIUS
ARETHUSIUS
OPHIUSIUS
ARIUSIUS
CLUSIUS
PELUSIUS
VOLUSIUS
POLYPLUSIUS
RHAMNUSIUS
RAMNUSIUS
ACHERUSIUS
MAURUSIUS
IALYSIUS
ELYSIUS
MYSIUS
NYSIUS
DIONYSIUS
ODRYSIUS
ODRYSIUS
AMPHRYSIUS
SABATIUS
TREBATIUS
CATIUS
CURIATIUS
LATIUS
BULLATIUS
EGNATIUS
MUNATIUS
EISOCRATIUS
ORATIUS
HORATIUS
HORATIUS
TATIUS
TATIUS
TITUS/TATIUS
STATIUS
CAECILIUS/STATIUS
LUTATIUS

ACTIUS
VICTIUS
HIRPINUS/QUINCTIUS
LYCTIUS
PANAETIUS
ARCETIUS
PEUCETIUS
LUCETIUS
AEETIUS
METIOEUS/FUFETIUS
METIUS
MENOETIUS
LUCRETIUS
MUSSETIUS
DOMITIUS
NERITIUS
TITIUS
TITIUS
POTITIUS
TARQUITIUS
ANTIUS
ANTIUS
ABANTIUS
CORYBANTIUS
POEANTIUS
POEANTIUS
PALLANTIUS
TAULANTIUS
TEUTHRANTIUS
HYANTIUS
BYZANTIUS
GENTIUS
TERENTIUS
LAURENTIUS
CLUENTIUS
JUVENTIUS
BUXENTIUS
MEZENTIUS
SINTIUS
QUINTIUS
ACONTIUS
VOCONTIUS
LAOMEDONTIUS
THERMODONTIUS
PHAETHONTIUS
PONTIUS
DIAPONTIUS
HELLESPONTIUS
OPUNTIUS
BERECYNTIUS
MAEOTIUS
BOEOTIUS
PLOTIUS
THESPROTIUS
SCAPTIUS

AEGYPTIUS
LARTIUS
MARTIUS
LAERTIUS
LAERTIUS
PROPERTIUS
MAVORTIUS
MAVORTIUS
CURTIUS
CURTIUS
BUBASTIUS
PHAESTIUS
BESTIUS
LYNCESTIUS
ONCHESTIUS
THESTIUS
SESTIUS
ARISTIUS
FUSCUS/ARISTIUS
NOSTIUS
CRISPUS/SALLUSTIUS
ATTIUS
GRATTIUS
GARGETTIUS
HYMETTIUS
PETTIUS
TETTIUS
VETTIUS
BRUTTIUS
BRUTTIUS
BRUTIUS
PRAETUTIUS
COCYTIUS
CLYTIUS
AEPYTIUS
BAVIUS
FLAVIUS
FLAVIUS
OCTAVIUS
LAEVIUS
NAEVIUS
MEVIUS
LIVIUS
LIVIUS
MILVIUS
SILVIUS
FULVIUS
MULVIUS
NOVIUS
CERVIUS
NERVIUS
SERVIUS
VESVIUS
VESVIUS
PACUVIUS

HISTER/PACUVIUS
DANUVIUS
MARRUVIUS
VESUVIUS
NAXIUS
ORITHYIUS
OEBALUS
COCALUS
RHADALUS
DAEDALUS
CORDALUS
DORDALUS
CEFALUS
SYNHALUS
CEPHALUS
STYMPHALUS
CROBIALUS
ANCIALUS
ANCHIALUS
MALUS
MAENALUS
HARPALUS
BUPALUS
SALUS
SALISUBSALUS
CRUCISALUS
PHARSALUS
THESSALUS
THESSALUS
CHRYSALUS
ITALUS
ITALUS
TANTALUS
ORTALUS
ATTALUS
TEUTALUS
EURYALUS
ECHECLUS
PHERECLUS
IPHICLUS
PATROCLUS
DORYCLUS
CAELUS
BELUS
RHAMBELUS
CYBELUS
SCELUS
THESCELUS
MYSCELUS
DELUS
STYPHELUS
PHILOMELUS
CARMELUS
EUMELUS
CYMELUS

STHENELUS
EUTRAPELUS
CANCHLUS
ILUS
STROBILUS
PHILUS
DIPHILUS
PAMPHILUS
DEMOPHILUS
MENOPHILUS
NILUS
TROILUS
ZOILUS
CHOERILUS
ASILUS
ASILUS
BASILUS
ERGASILUS
CATILUS
NYCTILUS
COTILUS
MYRTILUS
RUTILUS
TOXILUS
TETTIUS/CABALLUS
GALLUS
GALLUS
MUNATIUS/GALLUS
TRIPHALLUS
THALLUS
SARDANAPALLUS
SABELLUS
SABELLUS
TARBELLUS
MARCELLUS
FISCELLUS
OFELLUS
GEMELLUS
ASELLUS
TELLUS
METELLUS
CAECILIUS/METELLUS
ENTELLUS
PROCILLUS
RUFILLUS
AMILLUS
CAMILLUS
HAMILLUS
SEPTIMILLUS
VARILLUS
PERILLUS
CATILLUS
CURTILLUS
CHRESTILLUS
SEXTILLUS

PAULLUS	CERCOBULUS	LYSIDAMUS
FABULLUS	MEGALOBULUS	PHILODAMUS
LABULLUS	CAECULUS	HIPPODAMUS
TIBULLUS	GRAECULUS	PERGAMUS
LUCULLUS	PENICULUS	ORCHAMUS
JULLUS	PANNICULUS	PRIAMUS
POMPULLUS	SICULUS	LAMUS
RULLUS	SICULUS	THALAMUS
MARULLUS	SATICULUS	CINNAMUS
PETRULLUS	AQUICULUS	GARAMUS
TULLUS	AEQUICULUS*	PYRAMUS
CATULLUS	PROCULUS	SAMUS
TITULLUS	JULIUS/PROCULUS	CYAMUS
HYLLUS	VULSCULUS	CADMUS
BATHYLLUS	TUSCULUS	LADMUS
GRYLLUS	RUFULUS	HAEMUS
MNASYLLUS	REGULUS	ACADEMUS
THRASYLLUS	FIGULUS	MENEDEMUS
PSYLLUS	CINGULUS	ARCHIDEMUS
MISTYLLUS	IULUS	CHARIDEMUS
OLUS	REMULUS	NICODEMUS
DIABOLUS	SIMULUS	PHILODEMUS
ASBOLUS	ROMULUS	EUPHEMUS
NAUBOLUS	ROMULUS	POLYPHEMUS
BAETICOLUS	VENULUS	TELEMUS
AEQUICOLUS	APULUS	TLEPOLEMUS
DOLUS	APULUS	PHILOPOLEMUS
PSEUDOLUS	TAPPULUS	TRIPTOLEMUS
AEOLUS	CAERULUS	NEOPTOLEMUS
LAUREOLUS	HERULUS	PANEMUS
PHOLUS	VESULUS	REMUS
SERGIOLUS	CATULUS	STALAGMUS
SAMIOLUS	GAETULUS	MENAECHMUS
VERANIOLUS	GAETULUS	ISTHMUS
ANCHEMOLUS	GETULUS	DECIMUS
CIMOLUS	LENTULUS	ALCIMUS
TIMOLUS	FAUSTULUS	PHAEDIMUS
PROMOLUS	RUTULUS	CYDIMUS
TMOLUS	RUTULUS	SOLIMUS
POLUS	HEDYLUS	SIMUS
MAUSOLUS	CONDYLUS	GELASIMUS
PACTOLUS	AESCHYLUS	STASIMUS
AETOLUS	SIMYLUS	ENAESIMUS
AETOLUS	PYLUS	ALCESIMUS
NAEVOLUS	PAPYLUS	THEOTIMUS
AULUS	SIPYLUS	POLYTIMUS
DIAULUS	EURYPYLUS	MAXIMUS
PAULUS	CERYLUS	CAESONIUS/MAXIMUS
PUDENS/AULUS	ASYLUS	PAULLUS/MAXIMUS
CASCELLIUS/AULUS	MASSYLUS	PALMUS
ATABULUS	MASSYLUS	TRINUMMUS
BIBULUS	ITYLUS	TLEPOLOMUS
ARCHIBULUS	ASTYLUS	EPIGNOMUS
CHAERIBULUS	THESTYLUS	AMPHINOMUS
NICOBULUS	LYGDAMUS	EURYNOMUS

BROMUS	STEPHANUS	ATRIANUS
PHAEDROMUS	BAIANUS	MAMURIANUS
EPICHARMUS	CAIANUS	ASIANUS
POLYCHARMUS	TRAIANUS	PHASIANUS
HERMUS	FABIANUS	BLAESIANUS
THERMUS	SOSIBIANUS	MALISIANUS
MIMNERMUS	DECIANUS	CHARISIANUS
HORMUS	CAEDICIANUS	CASSIANUS
COSMUS	SEPTICIANUS	CATIANUS
LAELIUS/DECUMUS	SEPTICIANUS	DOMITIANUS
POSTUMUS	MARCIANUS	TERENTIANUS
TUBERTUS/POSTUMUS	PEDIANUS	QUINTIANUS
DIDYMUS	NASIDIANUS	NICEROTIANUS
DIDYMUS	SARDIANUS	SESTIANUS
DINDYMUS	CLAUDIANUS	BRUTTIANUS
ELYMUS	PACIDEIANUS	PACUVIANUS
HELYMUS	SALEIANUS	JANUS
SOLYMUS	POMPEIANUS	SEJANUS
SOLYMUS	SATUREIANUS	ALANUS
ERYMUS	PATERCLIANUS	SALANUS
ANUS	AELIANUS	SILANUS
THEBANUS	CAECILIANUS	SULLANUS
LIBANUS	TONGILIANUS	BOLANUS
ALBANUS	GARGILIANUS	CARSEOLANUS
NORBANUS	AEMILIANUS	NOLANUS
CANUS	PETILIANUS	TREBULANUS
LABICANUS	QUINTILIANUS	CORNICULANUS
GALLICANUS	PONTILIANUS	OSCULANUS
PICANUS	SEXTILIANUS	TUSCULANUS
AFRICANUS	GELLIANUS	AEFULANUS
AFRICANUS	CATULLIANUS	AMANUS
SICANUS	JULIANUS	SUMMANUS
VATICANUS	OPIMIANUS	ROMANUS
TUTICANUS	AMMIANUS	ROMANUS
VOLCANUS	FORMIANUS	VOMANUS
VULCANUS	COSMIANUS	CARMANUS
CONCANUS	POSTUMIANUS	GERMANUS
ARCANUS	PARTHENIANUS	GERMANUS
HYRCANUS	SUMMENIANUS	FIRMANUS
LUCANUS	LICINIANUS	CUMANUS
LUCANUS	ORCINIANUS	NUMANUS
TRANSPADANUS	VATINIANUS	GENUMANUS
PEDANUS	ANNIANUS	RHENANUS
APIDANUS	MARONIANUS	AMENANUS
ERIDANUS	NERONIANUS	AMENANUS
FUNDANUS	CATONIANUS	CAMPANUS
RHODANUS	THYONIANUS	CAMPANUS
RHODANUS	TROIANUS	HISPANUS
DARDANUS	TROIANUS	CLARANUS
DARDANUS	OPPIANUS	SACRANUS
OCEANUS	MARIANUS	GLYCERANUS
OCEANUS	MARIANUS	LATERANUS
ALLIFANUS	CAESARIANUS	VENAFRANUS
GARGANUS	HADRIANUS	CORANUS
GARGANUS	PAPIRIANUS	VORANUS

SARRANUS	AENUS	TAMASENUS
SERRANUS	AMBENUS	TIBISENUS
MURRANUS	PICENUS	MISENUS
CASTRANUS	ABYDENUS	EUENUS
GAURANUS	ABYDENUS	VENUS
TAURANUS	SUFFENUS	AXENUS
SUBURANUS	ALFENUS	PHILOXENUS
VIPSANUS	COMMAGENUS	POLYXENUS
SINUESSANUS	GARGENUS	MAGNUS
SYRACUSANUS	CEPHENUS	PAELIGNUS
SCETANUS	RHENUS	PELIGNUS
SEDETANUS	RHENUS	PELIGNUS
CAIETANUS	TYRRHENUS	CYGNUS
LALETANUS	TYRRHENUS	CYTHNUS
ARGILETANUS	LABIENUS	GABINUS
TOLETANUS	NASIDIENUS	SABINUS
CALPETANUS	ANIENUS	SABINUS
CAERETANUS	ANIENUS	CAESIUS/SABINUS
SAXETANUS	CATIENUS	SEXTUS/SABINUS
GADITANUS	VOTIENUS	ALBINUS
GADITANUS	CLUVIENUS	BALBINUS
TUDITANUS	CALENUS	CORACINUS
MASSILITANUS	CALENUS	VARRO/ATACINUS
NEAPOLITANUS	HELENUS	GRAECINUS
ANTIPOLITANUS	AUFILENUS	SIDICINUS
TOMITANUS	PHILENUS	LICINUS
TAUROMENITANUS	SILENUS	ARICINUS
ABDERITANUS	TOLENUS	TICINUS
TRITANUS	FUFICULENUS	TICINUS
LUSITANUS	PERGAMENUS	MANCINUS
LUSITANUS	TISAMENUS	PLOCINUS
TITANUS	DEXAMENUS	FUSCINUS
AQUITANUS	TRASIMENUS	FUCINUS
VEIENTANUS	TRASIMENUS*	MARRUCINUS
NOMENTANUS	IALMENUS	ERYCINUS
FRENTANUS	ORCHOMENUS	AEACIDINUS
BENEVENTANUS	PERIPLECTOMENUS	CAUDINUS
FONTANUS	ORMENUS	CAUDINUS
MONTANUS	IDASMENUS	RUFINUS
SPARTANUS	ARIASMENUS	REGINUS
MASSILI/TANUS	ISMENUS	LONGINUS
PAESTANUS	CLYMENUS	TROGINUS
TUTANUS	PERICLYMENUS	ERGINUS
AEQUANUS	AMOENUS	OPITERGINUS
AEQUANUS	POENUS	HYGINUS
SEQUANUS	POENUS	AESCHINUS
MANTUANUS	CAPENUS	DELPHINUS
VANUS	LONGARENUS	AGATHINUS
SILVANUS	VARENUS	PHALANTHINUS
ALBINOVANUS	FIBRENUS	POTHINUS
CELSUS/ALBINOVANUS	UMBRENUS	JUGURTHINUS
OCNUS	TYMBRENUS	LINUS
CYCNUS	SERENUS	CHALINUS
APHIDNUS	ANNAEUS/SERENUS	MESSALINUS
CYDNUS	AMASENUS	FACELINUS

SELINUS	ALEXANDRINUS	SALLENTINUS
VELINUS	TIBERINUS	POLLENTINUS
VELINUS	TIBERINUS	TARENTINUS
CASILINUS	TRANSTIBERINUS	FERENTINUS
ESQUILINUS	AMERINUS	SURRENTINUS
MARCELLINUS	CAMERINUS	LAURENTINUS
TIGILLINUS	PASSERINUS	TRUENTINUS
COLLINUS	SIRINUS	AVENTINUS
COLLINUS	QUIRINUS	AVENTINUS
FABULLINUS	MORINUS	FAVENTINUS
MARULLINUS	CENSORINUS	LEONTINUS
SIBYLLINUS	PETRINUS	FRONTINUS
AGYLLINUS	CAURINUS	SAGUNTINUS
TRIFOLINUS	TAURINUS	POMPTINUS
CAPITOLINUS	LIGURINUS	MAMERTINUS
CAPITOLINUS	LIGURINUS	HORTINUS
PAULINUS	THURINUS	TIBURTINUS
GEMINUS	VISCUS/THURINUS	JUGURTINUS
CIMINUS	AGYRINUS	TRICASTINUS
TERMINUS	MYRINUS	CRASTINUS
RUMINUS	MYRINUS	PALAESTINUS
NINUS	CASINUS	PRAENESTINUS
CAENINUS	CASINUS	ATESTINUS
EUENINUS	ERASINUS	ATESTINUS
SIGNINUS	ACESINUS	VESTINUS
FESCENNINUS	TELESINUS	VESTINUS
APENNINUS	NEPESINUS	FAUSTINUS
APPENNINUS	NURSINUS	JUSTINUS
THEONINUS	ELEUSINUS	LIBYSTINUS
SALONINUS	CLUSINUS	PLAUTINUS
AESERNINUS	CANUSINUS	MATUTINUS
AMITERNINUS	VENUSINUS	LANUINUS
SATURNINUS	PERUSINUS	AQUINUS
LEPINUS	PERUSINUS	VESUINUS
ALPINUS	LATINUS	NOCTUINUS
SALPINUS	LATINUS	LAVINUS
CHAROPINUS	PALATINUS	PATAVINUS
ARPINUS	COLLATINUS	SCAEVINUS
IRPINUS	MATINUS	LAEVINUS
IRPINUS	CRATINUS	CALVINUS
HIRPINUS	LAETINUS	SILVINUS
HIRPINUS	SPOLETINUS	CORVINUS
CRISPINUS	ARRETINUS	LANUVINUS
ARUPINUS	SETINUS	VESUVINUS
RUTUPINUS	MALTINUS	EUXINUS
EARINUS	BANTINUS	EUXINUS
SANGARINUS	ACRAGANTINUS	PONTUS/EUXINUS
CHARINUS	PALANTINUS	EPIDAMNUS
MARINUS	NUMANTINUS	RHAMNUS
THYBRINUS	PICENTINUS	CERAMNUS
MACRINUS	PICENTINUS*	LEMNUS
DAMACRINUS	FIDENTINUS	SOMNUS
NONACRINUS	OUFENTINUS	PICUMNUS
LUCRINUS	AGRIGENTINUS	PILUMNUS
LUCRINUS	SALENTINUS	CLITUMNUS

CLITUMNUS	ALBURNUS	LEPUS
VERTUMNUS	TURNUS	CIPUS
VORTUMNUS	SATURNUS	OEDIPUS
AUTUMNUS	NOCTURNUS	ARGIPUS
NEDYMNUS	VOLTURNUS	GRIPUS
ANNUS	VULTURNUS	EURIPUS
LEMANNUS	VULTURNUS	SIPUS
BRITANNUS	CYRNUS	CALPUS
DERCENNUS	PYRNUS	EUMOLPUS
TRASIMENNUS	AUNUS	CAMPUS
TRASUMENNUS	CAUNUS	MARTIS/CAMPUS
BRENNUS	DAUNUS	MARTIUS/CAMPUS
DOSSENNUS	FAUNUS	LAMPUS
CRINNUS	LIGAUNUS	MELAMPUS
DONNUS	CERAUNUS	TEMPUS
ARGYNNUS	NEPTUNUS	THEOPOMPUS
MYCONUS	PORTUNUS	OLYMPUS
EDONUS	PACHYNUS	OPUS
TEUTAGONUS	THYNUS	AETHIOPUS
TELEGONUS	BITHYNUS	CANOPUS
THERAPONTIGONUS	LESBOUS	INOPUS
LINGONUS	COUS	ASOPUS
CHRYSOGONUS	COUS	AESOPUS
TITHONUS	SARDOUS	CROTOPUS
CLONUS	EOUS	LEUCIPPUS
GELONUS	EOUS	PHIDIPPUS
APONUS	BAGOUS	PLESIDIPPUS
ITONUS	ARGOUS	ARCHIPPUS
SANTONUS	ALCATHOUS	XANTHIPPUS
POTONUS	PERITHOUS	EUHIPPUS
TEUTONUS	PIRITHOUS	PHILIPPUS
HYPNUS	GESSITHOUS	PAMPHILIPPUS
ARNUS	HIPPOTHOUS	CALLIPPUS
SARNUS	PROTHOUS	GYLIPPUS
LAERNUS	GELOUS	MELANIPPUS
FALERNUS	ACHELOUS	CHAERIPPUS
FALERNUS	INOUS	ARGYRIPPUS
SALERNUS	ALCINOUS	DAMASIPPUS
HELERNUS	IPHINOUS	LYSIPPUS
MATERNUS	MINOUS	CHRYSIPPUS
PATERNUS	ARSINOUS	ARISTIPPUS
VATERNUS	ANTINOUS	PLEXIPPUS
LITERNUS	HIPPONOUS	DIOXIPPUS
VELITERNUS	EUTHYNOUS	CARPUS
AMITERNUS	HEROUS	SCORPUS
AVERNUS	TROUS	ARIMASPUS
AVERNUS	LATOUS	CRISPUS
PRIVERNUS	LATOUS	ERIGDUPUS
CAPRICORNUS	NAUPACTOUS	LUPUS
BURNUS	ARCTOUS	GRYPUS
TABURNUS	LETOUS	LABARUS
LIBURNUS	MYRTOUS	CARUS
LIBURNUS	PRIAPUS	ICARUS
TIBURNUS	ANAPUS	PANDARUS
TIBURNUS	MESSAPUS	PINDARUS

TYNDARUS	SEVERUS	CAURUS
FARFARUS	OEAGRUS	SCAURUS
MEGARUS	EUAGRUS	EPIDAURUS
PHARUS	ORTHRUS	GAURUS
SAPHARUS	IRUS	LAURUS
CANTHARUS	EPIRUS	MAURUS
LARUS	CORUS	MAURUS
BALARUS	PACORUS	ISAURUS
CLARUS	ZACORUS	THENSAURUS
HILARUS	DORUS	TAURUS
SILARUS	MEGADORUS	METAURUS
CYLLARUS	PLATAGIDORUS	METAURUS
MARUS	CALIDORUS	CENTAURUS
VIRDOMARUS	ARTEMIDORUS	MINOTAURUS
ISMARUS	VANILOQUIDORUS	EPICURUS
TAENARUS	THEODORUS	EURUS
PARUS	DIODORUS	NEURUS
DEIOTARUS	HELIODORUS	PALINURUS
TARTARUS	CALLIODORUS	ATURUS
BATTARUS	APOLLODORUS	ARCTURUS
VARUS	POLYDORUS	ANXURUS
HEBRUS	ACHORUS	CYRUS
IMBRUS	CALLICHORUS	SCYRUS
TEUCRUS	STESICHORUS	GLAPHYRUS
CHARADRUS	CARPOPHORUS	ZEPHYRUS
PHAEDRUS	TELESPHORUS	THYRUS
SCELEDRUS	FAENIUS/TELESPHORUS	THAMYRUS
ANDRUS	BOSPHORUS	LAMYRUS
MAEANDRUS	PHOSPHORUS	SYRUS
MENANDRUS	HELORUS	SYRUS
THESSANDRUS	PELORUS	TYRUS
CORIENDRUS	FLORUS	SATYRUS
CYLINDRUS	JULIUS/FLORUS	TITYRUS
CODRUS	ARCHEMORUS	STYRUS
THYSDRUS	PORUS	OEBASUS
CYDRUS	BOSPORUS	ORIBASUS
HYDRUS	CYTISORUS	CASUS
THYDRUS	CYTORUS	CAUCASUS
CAERUS	AZORUS	PEDASUS
HIBERUS	CUPRUS	BAGASUS
HIBERUS	CYPRUS	PAGASUS
CERBERUS	BARRUS	PEGASUS
GERUS	MARRUS	DAMASUS
SIGERUS	CICIRRUS	PARNASUS
TRYPHERUS	HIRRUS	HIPPASUS
HIERUS	BURRUS	IMBRASUS
PHALERUS	MURRUS	TRASUS
VALERUS	PYRRUS	PETASUS
PISTOCLERUS	QUINQUATRUS	GALAESUS
HOMERUS	ELECTRUS	HALAESUS
HESPERUS	TRIQUETRUS	BLAESUS
VESPERUS	OENOTRUS	MONAESUS
CYPERUS	AMASTRUS	HERBESUS
CRATERUS	HISTRUS	BAGESUS
VERUS	CAYSTRUS	HESUS

EPHESUS
RHESUS
GALESUS
HALESUS
VOLESUS
TEUMESUS
PELOPONNESUS
MONESUS
LYRNESUS
MOESUS
CROESUS
CAMPESUS
CARESUS
CORESUS
TARTESUS
CEPHISUS
TEMISUS
NISUS
CRINISUS
RISUS
ALSUS
CELSUS
CONSUS
APSUS
THAPSUS
DIPSUS
MOPSUS
MARSUS
MARSUS
SPARSUS
CORSUS
URSUS
BASSUS
TALASSUS
PARNASSUS
CRASSUS
THRAESSUS
BESSUS
PERMESSUS
NESSUS
PROCNESSUS
TITARESSUS
CALOCISSUS
NARCISSUS
AMPHISSUS
MELISSUS
CYPARISSUS
COSSUS
MOLOSSUS
MOLOSSUS
USUS
LAUSUS
CLAUSUS
EBUSUS
VOLUSUS

PHILOMUSUS
GENUSUS
DRUSUS
MYSUS
MYSUS
GENYSUS
DIONYSUS
AMPHRYSUS
BATUS
CATUS
VIRIATUS
SPARTIATUS
ARMILLATUS
PECULATUS
DALMATUS
CANUSINATUS
FORTUNATUS
ARATUS
CHAERESTRATUS
CALLISTRATUS
PISISTRATUS
PHILOSTRATUS
SOSTRATUS
INCITATUS
OPTATUS
TORQUATUS
TORQUATUS
JUVATUS
NAUPACTUS
SENECTUS
PERSPECTUS
ATRECTUS
PLANCTUS
SANCTUS
AMPSANCTUS
ARCTUS
POMPEIUS/AUCTUS
EUCTUS
LUCTUS
PODAETUS
ACHAETUS
PAETUS
RAETUS
RAETUS
LYCETUS
TAYGETUS
FLETUS
PHILETUS
MILETUS
METUS
ADMETUS
DEMAENETUS
VENETUS
VENETUS
RHOETUS

PROETUS
CAPETUS
IAPETUS
CALPETUS
IMPETUS
NICARETUS
PANARETUS
SETUS
HERMAPHRODITUS
LEITUS
CATAMEITUS
ORFITUS
IPHITUS
HERACLITUS
POLYCLITUS
CATAMITUS
DEMOCRITUS
TITUS
POTITUS
MACCUS/TITUS
TARQUITUS
AVITUS
SERVITUS
ABASCANTUS
PHALANTUS
ADIMANTUS
TRUCULENTUS
SARMENTUS
HYACINTUS
QUINTUS
TULLIUS/QUINTUS
MAXIMUS/QUINTUS
TURGONTUS
PONTUS
RUBER/PONTUS
EUXINUS/PONTUS
HELLESPONTUS
COTUS
THEODOTUS
APOLLODOTUS
ZENODOTUS
THEUDOTUS
BOEOTUS
BOEOTUS
TARCHONDIMOTUS
NOTUS
CROTUS
THESPROTUS
VORAPTUS
AEGYPTUS
GLYPTUS
SCIRTUS
VIRTUS
SACRI/PORTUS
TIBURTUS

ABSYRTUS	ARGIVUS	ANTHRAX
ACASTUS	ARGIVUS	CORAX
ADAMASTUS	ACHIVUS	STORAX
ADRASTUS	ACHIVUS	ATAX
SYNCERASTUS	CALVUS	BRUTTAX
PHAESTUS	MILVUS	MAZAX
GERAESTUS	CORVUS	THRAEX
MODESTUS	CHARAXUS	THRAEX
FESTUS	LIXUS	VINDEX
SERGESTUS	NIXUS	LELEX
SERESTUS	CRIXUS	CULEX
CHRESTUS	PHRIXUS	FELIX
SESTUS	EUDOXUS	HELIX
CACISTUS	LUXUS	CILIX
CALLISTUS	PHRYXUS	CILIX
PISTUS	PHLYUS	PHOENIX
HOSTUS	CARYUS	SYROPHOENIX
FAUSTUS	TITYUS	PISTRIX
AUGUSTUS	LIBYS	BITURIX
AUGUSTUS	LIBYS	SPHINX
CAESAR/AUGUSTUS	PHORCYS	MENINX
CARYSTUS	TIPHYS	SYRINX
BATTUS	TETHYS	VOLUNX
CATTUS	HALYS	CAPPADOX
METTUS	THELYS	VELOX
HYMETTUS	ZELYS	NOX
VETTUS	MYS	ALLOBROX
PLAUTUS	ERINYS	ALLOBROX
PLUTUS	ERINNYS	LUX
MUTUS	CAPYS	POLLUX
CORNUTUS	IAPYS	CEYX
BRUTUS	OTHRYS	IAPYX
RESTITUTUS	ATYS	IAPYX
SEXTUS	DICTYS	AMPYX
AELIUS/SEXTUS	ITYS	BEBRYX
COCYTUS	COTYS	ERYX
CLYTUS	STRABAX	PHRYX
HIPPOLYTUS	PHAEAX	PHRYX
ANYTUS	PHAEAX	STYX
ORNYTUS	OEAX	IAZYX
EPYTUS	SYPHAX	AEPY
AEPYTUS	AIAX	
ERYTUS	SMILAX	
BERYTUS	STRATILAX	
EURYTUS	COLAX	
PACUUS	ARCTOPHYLAX	
DAVUS	ASTYANAX	
FLAVUS	DONAX	
TIMAVUS	FORNAX	
BATAVUS	PAX	
LAEVUS	HARPAX	
VESAEVUS	SPARAX	
VESEVUS	LABRAX	
SUEVUS	THRAX	
GRADIVUS	THRAX	

APPENDICES

APPENDIX I

Dubious Readings, Emendations, Conjectures

LIST OF VARIANTS

This is a selection of some 160 notable manuscript variants or emendations. The items involved are unique each in its text, and some of them are *hapax legomena*, created by editors' corrections. Many are insoluble cruces, because they denote obscure, out-of-the-way places or personages. Ovid has the largest number, thirty-four, of which twelve are found in the *Ibis*.

Acir is Madvig's em. for ager S
  S. 2.6.64
Adimantus em. to Aphidantus OV
  Ibis 325 (327)
Admon: (H)idmon VAL 3.167
Adryas: mss. Adriacus PROP
  1.20.12
Aeaea should be Aea (= Colchis)
  acc. to Warmington; TR Pac. 218
Afer em. from era PROP 4.11.30
Africus em. to acrius PROP
  4.3.49
Alpis conj. from valde CAT 68.59
Amaryncides em. from mare egeum
  HL 377
Amunculae: ms. Anyclae COM
Andron: ms. Andrius LUCIL 1104
Anthemio conj. from Amphione HL
  463
Antius em. from avia S S. 1.3.89
Apsus: Hapsus LUC 5.462
Apulicus: publicus HOR *C*. 3.24.4
Arabius ms.: Arabia PL *Trin*. 933

Aretulla: Aratulla MAR 8.32
Arimes em. to Arines VAL 6.638
Arna em. of Alma AV *Culex* 14
Arretium em. from Arretinus PL (frag.)
Asina: Sasinae LUC 8.195
Aspasius conj. PL *Vid*. 17 *et passim*
Asturius em. from Assyrii LUC 4.298
Azanis em. from mss. OV *F*. 3.658
Azorus em. from Acirus GR 183
Brotes em. to Brontes VAL 3.152
Byzes: Byces VAL 6.68
Caesennia: Censennia (etc.) JUV
  6.136
Caleti em. from Calleti TR Accius
  Pr. 10
Calyce em. from ceuce, celice OV
  H. 18.133
Canchlus: Cancer GER 665
Carthaeus: -eus OV *Met*. 10.109
Caspias: Casetas SEN *HO* 145
Celadus: Enceladus JUV 7.215
Cercobulus: Cerconicus PL *Trin*.
  1020

Phigalesius : Phylacesius OV *Ibis*
327; both are emendations.
Philaenus : Philenus MAR 10.102.2
Philotis : Philotium TER *Hec.*
passim
Philus em. from fixus FPLA p. 45
(Morel)
Pices or Pici PL *Aul.* 701
Pimplea : Piplea S *S.* 1.4.26
Pipleis : Piplea HOR *C.* 1.26.9
Pirena em. from Pirineum PL *Aul.*
559
Plecusa em. from Phlegusa MAR
2.66.4
Polyidos em. from hipolidosa AV
Ciris 112
Protalides : Lycastus OV *Ibis* 605
Protis : Prothis (etc.) VAL 3.158
Pulfenius : many variants PER 5.190
Pulidamas : Poly– PROP 3.1.29
Pyractes em. from Pyraechmes OV
Met. 12.460
Pyrrhus em. to furtum by Housman
MAN 1.786
Rhaucus em. from raucus AV
Ciris 384
Romethium : Rhymetium OV *Met.*
15.705
Sacae : Sagae CAT 11.6
Salisubsalus : –il(i)us CAT 17.6
Scamander conj. PROP 3.1.27
Sestus : Sesta OV *H.* 17.2
Side em. from lince (etc.) OV *AA*
1.731
Sinopes dub. PL *Cur.* 443
Sintus or Sintius OV *Ibis* 431
Sirinus em. from Thurinos OV
Met. 15.52

Solonium conj. from coloni PROP
4.1.31
Stalitio : Stalino PL *Cas.* II.3
(see G. Lodge's Lexicon)
Sufficius : Fuficius (conj.) CAT
54.5
Summenianus : Submemmianus
MAR *passim*
Sylla : Sulla mss. HOR *S.* 1.2.64
Syme em. from –sumptis HL 195
Teleus : Tereides OV *Ibis* 434
Tenthredon em. from voces nihili
HL 199
Tereteus em. from Metereus OV *Tr.*
2.191
Tharsymachus or Thrasymachus (?)
JUV 7.204
Thesides : –eides OV *H.* 4.65
Thyrea or Thyre S *Th.* 4.48
Tiresia : Teresia HOR *S.* 2.5.1
Traeci em. from extraxerim TR
Pacuv. 209
Trasus : Thasus OV *Ibis* 476
Triops em. from propria PROP
3.9.16
Tros : Troas HOR *C.* 4.6.15
Truthus : Struthus PL *Tr.* 1020
Turasia : Turgantum MAR 4.55.21
Tyres : Tyra (river), Lyces VAL
4.719; 6.84
Ulius conj. for Julius HOR *S.*
1.8.39
Vanus : Vannus : Varus VAL 6.115
Venustina : Venusina JUV 6.167
Victius : Vectius : Vettius CAT 98.1
Virro em. from vir of mss. CAT
71.1
Zacynthos : Saguntum JUV 15.114

CRITICAL REMARKS ON TEXT

Since the present work has been based on indices nominum prepared
largely by other people, it is ostensibly a tertiary product. However,
several steps have been taken to make this a critical and, in a sense,
also a secondary work. First of all, six indices of lesser texts were
prepared by me, and twelve indices were redone from those of other work-
ers in the field. Second, all names about which there was some doubt
have been examined in context, and attention paid to the manuscript

readings. Well-known names, problematic in one or more passages, but which otherwise occur in a given author, are not discussed here.

I give a slightly longer discussion of the following special problems in textual criticism or grammatical interpretation.

1. *Athaman* (PROP 4.6.15) is so read as an adjective, following E. A. Barber, but Harpers' Dictionary suggests *Athamanus*, and this is probably right.

2. *Bruttax* seems to be a *hapax legomenon*, but cf. *Bruttates* in earlier editions. The form *Bruttace* (in ENN, LUCIL) is evidently an ablative.

3. *Caere* (town of Etruria) seems to have this (Etruscan) nominative, but some editors make *Caeres* the nominative, e.g. in Vergil, by Wetmore and Janell.

4. *Cephalio* in OV *Am*. 1.13.31 is either an ablative of *Cephalius* or a nominative subject.

5. *Ceraunum*. The genitive in GR 532 is converted into an indexed nominative *Ceraunus* by the editor, erroneously, since *Ceraunum* is universally a neuter in prose texts.

6. *Colchi*. In ENN *Tr*. 259 (Warmington) the form *Colchis* is to be taken as ablative or locative of *Colchi*. Warmington's translation is non-committal on the lexical form.

7. *Cressus* (adj.) was coined by me for HOR and PROP, and I note that Barber's index does the same for PROP, but *Cressa* is the proper adjectival form, occurring, of course, only with feminine nouns. (Similarly, the Ovid concordance created an imaginary *Phoenissus*.)

8. *Dindymene* (gen. *-ae*) but not adj. *Dindymenus*, in CAT 63.16; Schuster (BT) and Lafay (Budé) correctly read as noun.

9. *Eurota* is read by Ribbeck (*Fab. inc. Trag.* #207), quoted from Cicero. The name occurs before *sol*, and although old Latin often does not spell (or pronounce?) final *-s*, this instance could be explained as a sandhi loss of final *-s* before initial *s-*.

10. *Janiculum* seems to be a neuter everywhere, but in MAR three indices make it a masculine *Janiculus*. The sole occurrence of the name in MAR (4.64.3) is a genitive. R. Conway (*Italic Dialects*, I, 340) lists only a neuter. But H. Kiepert (in his *Manual of Ancient Geography* of 1881, pp. 232 f.) speaks of *Janiculus*.

11. *Lissum* or *-us* (t. of Illyria, in LUC 3.719) occurs only in the genitive. Following the editor I make the nominative *Lissum*; in prose both genders occur.

12. *Lydia* in PROP 1.6.32 is taken by Barber as a noun, but Schuster and I take it as an adjective modifying neuter *arata*. *Aratum* then becomes a new *hapax legomenon* meaning "field"(= arvum). *Lydia* cannot construe as a nominative subject.

13. *Meninx* (SIL 3.318) is indexed by several editors as *Meninge*, but this latter form must be a third declension ablative.

14. *Oceanus* could be an adjective (by zero-change) in JUV 11.94 and 113, and there is good manuscript authority for this; it is rejected, however, by Clausen and others. In CAT 115.6 the phrase *mare ad oceanum* must use *oceanum* as adjective, separated from *mare* by normal poetic "interpositional" *ad*.

15. *Oebali nympha* OV *Ep*. 15.128. Upon whether this form is vocative or genitive depends our setting up an adjective *Oebalis* or a noun *Oebalus*.

16. *Pale*, read as a name in S twice (*Th*. 6.870 and *Ach*. 2.155) by one or more editors, is inexplicable to me.

17. *Phlegra* is taken by Harpers' Dictionary as an adjective in AV *Culex* 28 in the phrase *Phlegra ... tellus*, but more likely this is a case of two nouns in apposition. The Teubner and Oxford texts punctuate *Phlegra* as a noun.

18. *Syra* in COM Caecil. 223 is taken here as an adjective, but the passage is brief and faulty and perhaps it is the name of a girl slave as in PL and TER.

19. *Thalea* in CAL 6.78 is preferred here rather than an adjective *Thaleus*.

APPENDIX II

Sources of the Data

The principal sources have been the indices nominum of the poets and collections of verse fragments, where these indices existed in published form. One index furnished the basis in most cases, and other indices (of the same text) were used for verification. The published indices have some errors, and conflicting notions of interpretation, presentation, and spelling have been a major problem. The best index of names known to me is that of A. E. Housman's Manilius. The present lexicon itself is not without errors, of course, but many dozens of published errors have been tacitly corrected in the process of sifting and verifying.

A more subtle problem lies in the varied practice of editorial arrangement and spelling. I have tried to normalize many aberrations, preserving those, however, which have some authenticity as archaisms, vulgarisms, etc. The original verse texts were checked in innumerable cases. The most harassing problem is illustrated by these two examples:

INDI pl. (the people)	PHRYGES pl. 'the Phrygians'
INDUS a member of the people *or*	PHRYX 'a Phrygian'
INDUS* 'Indian'	PHRYX* 'Phrygian'

I have tried to separate such clusters into three different entries, and many editors have so indexed them. But other editors have not, and for these texts I may not have been entirely successful in ferreting out the separate forms.

Complete indices verborum (i.e., of the ordinary vocabulary along with names) for some authors have been useful. In the identification of rare names, many translations and commentaries were brought into service, and in fact much of the literature of Roman poetry and of Latin linguistics has been consulted for method and information.

Twenty edited texts provide usable and available indices (and often more than one for some authors); I have indexed six other texts for the first time (see Appendix III). For the remaining twelve texts, the published indices were awkward or unsuitable, and I was forced to edit them for my own purposes, but I do not publish these reworkings now. The twelve texts are: Cicero's verse, Columella, Comic fragments, Ennius, Germanicus (but see No. 7 below), Grattius, the *Homerus Latinus*, Lucilius, Lucretius, Ovid, Petronius, Varro. The editing consisted primarily in the deletion of ineligible forms and in normalization.

TEXTS USED

1. *Appendix Vergiliana* (AV) Edited by Fr. Vollmer (2nd ed.; BT, 1932) and R. Ellis (OCT, 1907). The basis was Ellis, whose text includes these nine poems:

Culex	*Dirae* (with *Lydia*)	*Est et Non*
Ciris	*Copa*	*Vir Bonus*
Moretum	*Catalepton*	*Maecenas*

   Vollmer's text gives also the *Aetna* (see No. 33 below) but omits *Est et Non*, which has no proper names, and *Vir Bonus*, which has three (Apollo, Cancer, Capricornus). The Loeb Vergil (Vol. II) gives some of these texts, and its index identifies most names. The *Index Vergilianus* of M. N. Wetmore (2nd ed.; New Haven, 1930) records all the names of the *Appendix* along with those of the major (authentic) works of Vergil.

2. Catullus (CAT) The edition of R. Mynors (OCT, 1958) was the basis; M. Schuster's Teubner text (1954) and the Budé text served for checking.

3. Cicero (CIC) The fragments of the *Aratea* and of the other poems have been edited by A. Traglia (Roma, 2 vols., 1950–52). His two indices I have conflated into one list of 174 items.[1] The *Aratea* and the miscellaneous fragments have only eight names in common. W. Ewbank's edition (London, 1933) was useful.

4. Columella (COL) The tenth book of the *Res Rustica*, subtitled *de cultu hortorum*, consists of 436 hexameters. Harrison B. Ash edited this text separately for a University of Pennsylvania dissertation in 1930, and his index is the basis for the Columella content in the present work. Some of the forms have been normalized.

5. Comic Fragments (COM) The fragments of lost comedies were edited and indexed by Otto Ribbeck (2nd ed.; *Comicorum Romanorum Fragmenta*, 1873). I have normalized and otherwise edited his index. The principal lost writers of comedy are Caecilius, Novius, Turpilius, and Afranius. Of these, only Caecilius is found in E. H. Warmington's *Remains of Old Latin* I (Loeb Library, 1935).

6. Ennius (ENN) The fragments of the *Annales* and the plays have been edited (2nd ed.; 1903) by J. Vahlen, and his index (normalized) has

---

1. There are 116 names in the *Aratea* and 65 in Cicero's other fragments. The eight names common to the two groups of fragments are: Aurora, Centaurus, Graeci, Grai, Hydra, Juppiter, Musae, Titan(es).

been the basis, with occasional reference to E. H. Warmington (*Remains* I, 1935). I have omitted names only quoted in the prose summaries or in ancient comments, but not actually found in extant lines of Ennius.

7. Germanicus Caesar (GER) The *Aratea* were edited by A. Breysig (2nd ed.; BT, 1899), in whose index names are included with the common vocabulary, and the names of stars and constellations have not been specially marked. In the text most such names are printed with spaced letters at their first appearance. In order to bring Germanicus into line with the astronomical nomenclature of the Manilius index and Cicero's fragments, I have excerpted from the text these fifty-six names:

Aegoceros	Corona	Lyra
Amnis	a. north	Ophiucus
Anguis	b. south	Pisces
Aquarius	Corvus	Plaustra
Ara	Crater	Polos
Arctos	Cycnus	Pristis (Pistris)
Arctophylax	Delphin	Procyon
Arcturus	Delphinus	Puppis
Arcus	Deltoton	Sagitta
Aries	Gemini	Sagittifer
Auriga	Haedi	Scorpios
Avis	(double star)	Serpens
Axis	Hyades	Sol
Bootes	Hydra	Sonipes (?)
Cancer	Hydrochoos	Taurus
Canis	Hydros	Turibulum
Capra	Lacteus Orbis	Ursa
(star)	Leo	Vincula (pl.)
Capricornus	Lepus	Virgo
Chelae (pl.)	Libra	Zephyrus

8. Grattius Faliscus (GR) The *Cynegeticon* is extant in 541 defective hexameters, dated at the time of Ovid. Edited and inexpertly indexed by Fr. Vollmer (*Poetae Latini Minores* II.1, BT, 1911); checked occasionally with the Duff *Minor Latin Poets* (Loeb Library, 1934) 150-204.

9. *Homerus Latinus* (HL) Edited by Fr. Vollmer (*PLM* II.3, BT, 1913); the text is in bad shape, and I have deleted fifty-four dubious items from the index and also normalized it. The author is supposed to be Baebius Italicus, and the defective acrostic of ITALICxS is found at the head of the first eight lines of the poem.

10. Horace (HOR) F. Klingner's Teubner edition (2nd ed.; 1950) was the basis, and D. Bo's Index of his Paravia Horace (Vol. 3, Torino, 1960) was useful, as was also an article[2] by Niall Rudd.

---

2. Niall Rudd, "The Names in Horace's Satires" *Classical Quarterly* 54 (1960) 161-78.

11. Juvenal (JUV) The W. Clausen edition (OCT, 1959) was made the basis of the index, checked with V. Knoche's edition (Heidelberg, 1950) and with L. Friedländer's annotated edition (1895). A fragment of Juvenal, known only since 1900, called 0.1–33 and placed after line 365 of Book Six in Clausen's edition, has been taken into account.

12. Lucan (LUC) Karl Hosius' Teubner edition (3rd ed.; Leipzig, 1913) was the basis, checked with A. E. Housman's edition (2nd ed.; Oxford, 1927) and with G. W. Mooney's index verborum to Lucan.

13. Lucilius (LUCIL) Edited and indexed by Fr. Marx (1904); I have normalized his index and checked this with E. H. Warmington's edition (*Remains* III, 1938).

14. Lucretius (LUCR) Joseph Martin's index (4th ed.; BT, Leipzig, 1959) was the basis, checked occasionally with J. Paulson's *Index Lucretianus*. I have also consulted my *Formal Analysis of Lucretius' Vocabulary* (Minneapolis, 1962).

15. Manilius (MAN) Edited and well indexed by A. E. Housman, editio minor (Cambridge, 1932). The editio major was useful for difficult readings.

16. Martial (MAR) The edition of C. Giarratano (2nd ed.; Paravia, 1951) was the basis, and this was checked with L. Friedländer's index in his annotated edition. Identifications have been taken in part from H. J. Izaac's Budé edition, 1961 (2nd ed.).

17. Ovid (OV) Roy Deferrari's *Concordance to Ovid* (Washington, 1939) has, despite its deficiencies and lack of critical notes, provided a convenient basis for the onomastic element in Ovid. Separate indices to different poems and collections have been important as supplements and corrective guides:

   a) *Tristia, Ex Ponto, Ibis, Halieuticon*; ed. S. Owen (OCT, 1915).
   b) *Fasti*; editions of F. Paley and F. Bömer, and the index in the Paravia edition of C. Landi (1928).
   c) *Amores, Epistulae, Medicamina Faciei Femineae, Ars Amatoria, Remedia Amoris*; indices in the editions of R. Ehwald (BT, Vol. I, 1888) and of E. J. Kenney (OCT, 1961).
   d) *Metamorphoses*; index by Paul Klink in H. Magnus' edition (Berlin, 1914) 723–66.
   e) fragments of lost works are given in Owen's *Tristia* (above) and indexed in the *Concordance*.
   f) the *Nux*, an apocryphal little poem often ascribed to Ovid; edited by E. Baehrens (*PLM*, BT, I, 1879) 90–96. The fourteen names in the *Nux* are all standard, but *Deus* (line 145) is dubious.

18. Persius (PER) The index in W. Clausen's OCT text (1959) was the basis, with identifications taken from B. Gildersleeve's edition.

19. Petronius (PET) Only those names which are found in the verses have been included. See on this subject my *Formal Analysis of Petronius'*

Vocabulary (Minneapolis, 1963) pp. xviii f. The index in Fr. Buecheler's editio major (Berlin, 1862, pp. 237–42) has been the basis, and this was checked with the complete *Index Verborum Petronianus* of J. Segebade and E. Lommatzsch (Leipzig, 1898).

20. Phaedrus (PH) The *Fabulae*, including the Appendix Perottina and the *Fabulae Novae*; edited by J. Postgate (OCT, 1919).

21. Plautus (PL) Plays and fragments edited by Fr. Leo (Berlin, 1896), whose index in Vol. II is the only separate index nominum in Plautus editions of the past hundred years or more. G. Lodge's *Lexicon Plautinum* (2 vols., Leipzig, 1901–24) was used as a check.[3] The material of the argumenta and the prologi has been included. Since many names in the plays are casual allusions, otherwise unimportant, I have simply labelled them as "comic characters."

22. *Priapeia* (PRIAP) This is a collection of erotic poems, eighty to eighty-five in number, depending on the editor; in three meters: elegiac distichs, choliambics, hendecasyllabics. The collection was made in the first century A.D., after the time of Ovid and Tibullus, who contributed one and two poems respectively (Vergil has three). Fr. Buecheler provided the convenient edition of the *Priapeia* in his editio minor of Petronius (Berlin, 1882; 4th ed., 1904) 138–62; with index nominum. I have used this edition as well as the recent one of Egn. Cazzaniga, *Carmina Ludicra* (Torino, Paravia, 1959) text pp. 23–53, index pp. 53–55.

23. Propertius (PROP) E. A. Barber's edition (OCT, 1953; 2nd ed., 1960) was the basis; M. Schuster's excellent Teubner edition (1958) was used as a corrective and as a source of identification of rare items.

[Publilius Syrus, edited by R. Bickford-Smith (London, 1895). The text contains only three names (Fortuna, Neptunus, Venus); included with Minor Latin Poets, No. 37 below.]

24. Seneca (SEN) The ten tragedies (including the *Octavia* of uncertain authorship) edited and indexed by R. Peiper and G. Richter (BT, 1902). The index is an awkward maze of cross-references and enigmatic concordance-like entries. I have consulted also the *Index Verborum* of W. Oldfather *et al.* (Urbana, 1918).

25. Silius Italicus (SIL) The basis for material has been L. Bauer's edition (BT, 1892), whose second volume gives a full listing with identifications of rare items. Norma D. Young's *Index Verborum Silianus* (Iowa City, 1939) was useful.

26. Statius (S) The three poems (*Thebais*, *Achilleis*, *Silvae*, abbreviated *Th.*, *A.*, *S.*) have been indexed together in Ph. Kohlmann's text (BT, 1884). I have also used the index of names in A. Marastoni's edition

---

3. K. Schmidt classifies the ingredients of the Plautine onomasticon in his "Die griechischen Personennamen bei Plautus" in *Hermes* 37 (1902) 173–211, 353–90, 608–26.

of the *Silvae* (BT, 1961), and made my own checklist for the *Achilleid* on the basis of O. A. W. Dilke's excellent edition of this text (Cambridge, 1954).

27. Terence (TER) The critical edition of Sesto Prete (Heidelberg, 1954) has a good index, the basis for the present work. Identifications and other data were secured from M. Slaughter's Johns Hopkins dissertation of 1891: "The Substantives of Terence" (pp. 8–10), which gives a semantic classification and a comparison with Plautine usage.

28. Tibullus (TIB) The Tibullan corpus includes the *Panegyricus Messallae*, Lygdamus, and Sulpicia. J. Postgate's Oxford text of 1914 and F. Lenz's edition (Leiden, Brill, 1959) were used. The Concordance of Tibullus by Edward N. O'Neill (Ithaca, 1963) was occasionally useful.

29. Tragic Fragments (TR) The fragments have been edited and indexed by Otto Ribbeck. Names occurring in Ennius' tragedies have been deleted (see No. 6 above), and I have normalized the whole list. The chief remaining authors (Pacuvius and Accius) are also presented in E. H. Warmington (*Remains* II, 1936).

30. Valerius Flaccus (VAL) The *Argonautica* in eight books was edited and indexed by E. Baehrens (BT, 1875); this index has been my basis, along with W. Schulte's *Index Verborum* (1931). J. H. Mozley's Loeb index has provided a useful check and also some identifications of rare names.

31. Varro (VAR) The verse parts of the *Menippean Satires* of M. Terentius Varro of Reate have been edited by Alexander Riese (Leipzig, 1865); his index contains also the material from prose parts. I have edited the verse names, which total eighty forms. His prose parts alone have 123 names.

32. Vergil (V) W. Janell's Teubner edition (2nd ed.; 1930) has been my basis; I have also used M. Wetmore's *Index Vergilianus*, R. Sabbadini's Paravia edition (1919) of the *Aeneid*, W. Richter's *Georgica* (München, 1957), and de Saint Denis' Budé edition of the *Bucolics*, as well as several school texts for identifications. There is need for a complete *catalogue raisoné* of Vergilian onomastics.[4]

The following indices were compiled by the author for this work (see Appendix III):

33. *Aetna* (AET) This anonymous work of the first century A.D., in 646 dactylic hexameters, is conveniently edited by the Duffs (*MLP*, 1934, pp. 358–418). From this text I have constructed an index and have checked this with the one in J. Vessereau's edition (Paris, 1905). Since the latter has a few errors and is also relatively unavailable, I have decided to present my version.

---

4. Angel Montenegro-Duque has studied the Rutulian and Etruscan personal names in great detail in his *La onomástica de Virgilio . . .* (Salamanca, 1949).

34. Calpurnius Siculus (CAL) The text consists of seven pastoral eclogues in 759 dactylic hexameters, dated mid-first century A.D. I have indexed this text from the Duff edition (*MLP*, pp. 218–84) and checked the result with C. Giarratano's edition (Torino, Paravia, 1924).

35. Fragments of Classical Latin Poets (FPLA, FPLB) These are the quoted fragments contained in Willy Morel's *Fragmenta Poetarum Latinorum* (BT, 1927). I have deleted Cicero from Morel's text because he is handled separately (see No. 3 above). The remaining text has been divided chronologically into three periods. The first two periods I have indexed as:

> FPLA: archaic fragments to Cicero; pp. 1–66, addenda 171–75;
> FPLB: classical fragments from time of Cicero to Hadrian; pp. 79–136, addenda 175–79; Ovid omitted (see No. 17 above).

There are twenty-eight names in common to these two lists. The third chronological period lies outside of the scope of this volume.[5] W. Morel provides material from this Late Latin period on pp. 137–71 and 179–86. The new edition of the *Poetae Novi* by A. Traglia (Roma, 1962) covers Morel pp. 48–66, 80–99.[6]

36. *Laus Pisonis* (LP) This anonymous poem (*c*. 65 A.D.) of 261 dactylic hexameters has been indexed from the Duff edition (*MLP*, pp. 289–315).

37. Minor Latin Poets (MLP) I refer to five short, obscure items (published in Duff) which otherwise would be neglected. To these I have added Publilius Syrus. See Appendix III for particulars.

Note that several outstanding archaic poets were not extensive enough to merit separate indices. Writers like Naevius, L. Andronicus, and others are indeed indexed here but in general collections like TR and FPLA.

A supplementary checklist, covering the period known as Late Latin, would deal with several Christian poets, many minor pagan poets and fragments, and include such worthies as Ausonius, Prudentius, Claudian, and the like. This is a desirable but separate project.

TEXTS ARRANGED CHRONOLOGICALLY

The fragment collections (like FPLA) cover several generations, and certain anonymous texts cannot be dated exactly. This arrangement is tentative.

Ennius	Terence	Catullus
Tragici	Lucilius	Cicero—fr.
Comici	FPLA	Varro—*Menipp. Sat.*
Plautus	Lucretius	Vergil

---

5. In addition the authors are very minor or even unknown.

6. Traglia's edition follows Morel very closely, but he adds a commentary and index nominum for the texts covered.

Horace	Phaedrus	Persius
Appendix	Seneca—*Tr.*	Lucan
Vergiliana	Grattius	Statius
Propertius	Columella	Juvenal
Tibullus	*Priapeia*	Martial
Manilius	*Homerus Latinus*	*Aetna*
Ovid	Petronius	MLP
Germanicus	Valerius Flaccus	FPLB
Calp. Siculus	Silius Italicus	*Laus Pisonis*

TEXTS OMITTED

1. C. Rabirius A papyrus fragment of a Latin poem found at Herculaneum has been tentatively identified by some as a part of Rabirius' epic on the battle of Actium. So thinks Joannes Garuti in his edition, *C. Rabirius. Bellum Actiacum (e pap. Herculanensi 817)* (Bologna, 1958), index pp. 88–104. I reproduce without further comment the twenty-four names indexed by the editor:

Actiacus	Caesar	Musa
Aegyptus	Indi	Nilus
Alexander	Indicus	Parthi
Antonius	Italus	Pelusius
Anubis	Julius	Pharius
Araxes	Latius	Proculeii (conj.)
Atropos	Laurentes	Venus
Bactra	Mars	Z[ephyri] (pl., conj.)

All these names occur in the List. Note that the quoted fragments of Rabirius are listed under the cover label of FPLB (Morel's *FPL*, pp. 120 f.); four names occur in these five extant lines.

2. *Pervigilium Veneris* This late text, dated variously from second to fifth century A.D. (and usually toward the later date) has, despite the classical tone of the poem, been omitted. I repeat here, however, the twenty-eight names from the index of the latest editor, Cazzaniga (see No. 22 above, under *Priapeia*); all the names occur in the List.

Aether	Favonius	Phoebus
Aetna (city)	Gratiae	Quirites
Amor (6x)	Hybla (2x)	Ramnes
Amyclae	Hyblaeus	Romuleus
Bacchus	Latini	Romulus (?)
Caesar	Laurens	Sabini
Ceres	Mars	Tereus
Cupido	Musa	Trojanus
Delia (2x)	Nymphae (3x)	Venus (2x)
Dione (4x)		

3. The *Fabulae* of Hyginus This practically anonymous (Hyginus is unidentified) prose handbook on mythology is an important adjunct to

the poets for the study of myths and legends. Except for two brief quotations[7] the entire work is in prose, usually very dry, compressed and unadorned. Many of the paragraphs are merely lists. But obviously the sources of the information are the poets—Greek and Roman. Four Greek poets and two Romans (Cicero, Ovid) are mentioned by name. The standard edition is by H. I. Rose: *Hygini Fabulae* (Leiden, 1934, revised 1964); the translation by Mary Grant, *The Myths of Hyginus* (Lawrence, 1960), includes the stories of the *Poetica Astronomica*. The date of the *Fabulae* is "before 207."

Rose's index of proper names totals around 1,800 items and is very complete.[8] This mass of names fits in very well with the mythic content of my List, but in many cases the meanings of names are different; one of Hyginus' specialties is giving several variants of myths or of characters in the stories. Harpers' Latin Dictionary has entered many names from Hyginus.

---

7. A fragment of Cicero's *Aratea* is quoted in story No. 14. An anonymous quotation is given in No. 177.

8. I have noted only the following omissions: *Atthis* 14.8, *Graece* (adv. *passim*), *Gyrto* 14.3, *Latine* 192, *Marathon* 38.7, *Tegeates* 14.14. (Most of these are excluded from Miss Grant's index.) Other errors in Rose's index: *Aigialeus* should read *Aegialus*; *Delos*: add *lii*; *Iphimele*: read *Iphimede*; *Tityus*: add *14.13*.

APPENDIX III

Indices Nominum Compiled for This Work

INDEX NOMINUM TO CALPURNIUS SICULUS (CAL)

(Based on C. Giarratano and Duff, *MLP*; 105 items)

Analysis of Calpurnius' Names

Nouns

shepherds 25, shepherdesses 8, pastoral gods 12 (viz., Dryades, Faunus, Flora, Nais, Nymphae, Oreas, Pales, Pan, Pomona, Priapus, Satyri, Silvanus), other gods 15
winds: Africus, Eurus
personifications: Clementia, Discordia, Paupertas
time names: [December (adj.)], Kalendae, Parilia
animal: Petasus (horse)
river: Baetis
cities: Philippi, Roma
miscellaneous: 8 items; dubious: Thalea

Adjectives

a) zero-change: Augustus, Brūtius, Hiberus, Lucanus, Lycaeus, Palatinus, Pelignus, Tarpeius
b) suffixes:

-aeus 2 items	-eus 3 items	-icus 1 item
-alis 1 item	-ēus 1 item	-inus 1 item
-anus 1 item	-iacus 1 item	-ius 2 items

INDEX NOMINUM TO MINOR LATIN VERSE TEXTS (MLP)

AND PUBLILIUS SYRUS

This Index lists the names in five short poems or collections of poems as printed in the Duff *MLP*. To this is added Publilius Syrus. All other poems in the collection are indexed in various other places. The pieces (containing 56 names) are abbreviated:

E Einsiedeln Eclogues, 2 poems, totalling 87 lines; 25 names; *MLP*, pp. 324—34

F Florus, 14 poems, 56 lines; 22 names; *MLP*, pp. 426—35

H Hadrian, 4 poems, 26 lines; 6 names; *MLP*, pp. 444—46

POH Precatio Omnium Herbarum, 21 lines; one name (Mater); pp. 342—44

PS Publilius Syrus, ed. Bickford-Smith; 3 names

PT Precatio Terrae, 32 lines, 4 names; pp. 344—46

INDEX NOMINUM TO THE *LAUS PISONIS*

(Based on the Duff *MLP*, pp. 294–314)

Acidalius (adj.) 91 (-a ales: 'a dove'; reference to fountain)
Achilles 173
Aeneius (adj.) 230
Aonius (adj.) 165
Apollinĕus (adj.) 167
Atrides 61 (= Menelaus)
Ausonius (adj.) 230, 242
Caesarĕus (adj.) 71
Calliope 81
Calpurnius (adj.) 15
Calpus 3, 15
Cecropius (adj.) 90
Cicero 35
Euboicus (adj.) 92
Ganymedēus (adj.) 153
Gnosius 142 (a Cretan)
Graecia 90
Graius (adj.) 240
Horatius 242 (the poet)
Laertiades 61 (= Ulixes)

Maecenas 235, 238, 239, 248
Maeonius (adj.) 232
Neapolis 92
Nereius (adj.) 176
Nestoreus (adj.) 64
Olympus 209, 231
Pandion 77 (f. of Philomela)
Pelias (N) 177 (a spear)
Penates 218
Phoebēus (adj.) 171
Phoebus 168
Pierius (adj.) 244
Piso 2, 16, 25, 37 (pl.), 65, 75, 82, 129, 253 (= Calpurnius Piso)
Priameius (adj.) 174
Quirites 23
Romanus (adj.) 4, 89, 232, 241
Thessalus (adj.) 49
Titan 209 (= Sun)
Varius 239 (= L. V. Rufus, the poet)
Vergilius 237

Summary

40 different forms, 57 repetitions; 19 adjectives, 19 nouns, and 2 adjectives used absolutely (Pelias, Gnosius). Of the nouns 16 are people, 3 are places. The adjectives are formed as follows: 7 by zero-change from nouns; suffixation by -ēus (3), -ius (2), -eius (2), -icus (1) [all these being Greek], and the Latin suffixes -eus and -anus (Romanus). Note the poetic substitution of -ĕus for -(i)anus in Caesarĕus, and of -ĕus for -aris in Apollinĕus.

INDEX NOMINUM TO FRAGMENTS OF LATIN POETS TO CICERO (FPLA)

(Edited by W. Morel, *FPL*, Part I, pp. 1–66, excluding Cicero, and 171–75; references are to pages of the Morel text.)

Accius 41
Aenea(s) 21
Aesopus 54
Afer (= Terence) 45, 47
Africanus 45 (= Scipio)
Agroecus 37 (a comedy)
Albanum 45 (*sc.* praedium)
Alexander 53

Amulius 21
Anchisa (nom.) 17
Andromacha 56
Anus 37 (a comedy)
Apollo 22, 23
Arcadia 45
Ardea 32
Asia 32, 47

Phoebe 66
Phoebus 49, 64
Planci (pl.) 175
Plautius/Marcus 32
Plautus 32, 37, 46
Poenicus (adj.) 44
Poenus (N) 25
Pompilius 42 (poet)
Pōtōnus 42
Proserpina 22
Publius/Scipio 40, 45
Purpureus 20 (= Πορφυρίων)
Pylus 8
Pythius 22, 64 (adj.)
Risus 32 (personif.)
Roma 28
Romanus (adj.) 24; Romani 64 bis
Romulus 44
Roscius 43
Rufus 175
Runcus 20 (= 'Ροῦκος)
Sardianus (adj.) 59
Saturnius (adj.) 28

Saturnus 7, 10, 34
Sevius/Nicanor 63
Sicilienses 26
Sol 62
Stymphalus 45 (t. of Arcadia)
Tarracinensis 40
Terentius 46 (em. 47) (poet)
Terra 20 (gen. -as), 31
Tethys 172
Tettius 172
Theotimus 43 (unknown)
Tiberinus 5 (N, Tiber?)
Titanus, -i 20, 52
Trabea 47 (comic poet)
Troia 18 bis, 21 (abl. -ad)
Troiugena 63 (a Roman)
Turpilius 47
Ulixes 10, 12
Varro 55 (of Reate)
Vatiena 62 (cont. woman)
Venus 43 ter, 60, 61
Victoria 48
Volcanus 15

INDEX NOMINUM TO FRAGMENTS OF LATIN POETS FROM THE TIME OF CICERO TO HADRIAN, OMITTING OVID (FPLB)

Based on W. Morel's *FPL*, pp. 79–136, 175–79. About 46 authors are represented, as well as anonymous verses, from the time of Cicero to the time of Apuleius.

Academia 80
Achelous 102 (god)
Acilius 134 (consul)
Aegon 104 (shepherd)
Aeneas 132
Aetnaeus 175
Alcmene 130
Alpes 83
Alpinus 90, 106
Anchiale 94 (a woman)
Antonius 103, 118, 122
Aonides 178
Aonius (adj.) 117
Apenninus 118; Appenninus 131
Aquarius 79
Aratēus 89
Arcera 79 (const.)
Arctous (adj.) 123

Aries 79 (const.)
Attis 131
Aurora 81
Auster 123
Bacchus 106; 126 ter
Bassareus 126 (= Bacchus)
Bassaris 131
Bavius 110
Belides 87
Berecynthius 131
Bithynia 86
Bootes 79, 123
Boreas 123
Brennus 130
   (or Brennius?)
Bromia 127 (girl)
Brutus 92 (first consul)
Cadmus 87

Caesar 86, 92 (5x, Julius); 103
(Augustus); 122 (Tiberius)
Caesarĕus 134 *bis*
Calenus 134 (husband of Sulpicia)
Calliope 126
Calvus 135 (poet)
Cancer 79 (const.)
Capricornus 79, 177
Caralis 98 (town)
Castalia 105
Catilina 118
Catina 81
Cato 80, 81, 83 (Valerius C.), 90
(Valerius); Catones (pl.) 135
Catullus 135
Cecrops 87
Cethegus 118
Cicero 80, 118, 119, 135 *bis*
Cinna 105
Clytemestra 175
Clytius 93 (an Argonaut)
Cnosius 123
Codrus 105
Corinthiarius 104 (worker in
bronze)
Corycius 95 (corr. from ms.
Ortygiae)
Crassicius 111 *bis* (ms. -itius)
Crates 81
Crisēus 105 (= Phocean)
Crispus 134
Cumanus 81
Cupra 99 (= Cyprus?)
Curius 84 (a dice-player)
Cybebe 102
Cyclops 175
Cynthia 123
Cytheriacus 131
Damoetas 104 (shepherd)
Danaus 93 *bis* (king); Danai 120,
176 (Greeks)
Demodocus 105
Dictynna 90 (a title)
Draco 79
Elius 125 (adj. of Elis)
Elysius (adj.) 111
Emathius 119 (= Macedonian)
Eous 88 (N); 123 (adj.)
Epirota 111 (Q. Caecilius Ep.)

Erucius 121 (gate-keeper)
Eurus 123
Eurydice 128
Fabius Veiento 134
Flaccus 101 (= Horace)
Fortuna 123
Fulvia 103 *bis*
Gaetulicus 133
Galba 133 (emperor)
Gallia 92; Galliae (pl.) 92 *bis*
Gallus 81 (poet), 93 (a Gaul), 135
(poet); Galli 92 *bis*, 93 (Gauls)
Gemini 79 (const.)
Genumanus 89 (= Cenomanus?)
Germani 127
Germanicus (Caesar) 122
Glaphyra 103
Gortynius 100 (-a canis)
Graeci 91
Hannibal 119
Hecatebeletes 133
Hector 120
Helena 129
Hesperius 84, 123, 177
Hesperus 88, 130 (-on)
Horatius 102 (Flaccus)
Hyperion 123
Idaeus (adj.) 120
Indicus (adj.) 98
Jugurtha 119
Juppiter 83, 101, 103, 126, 133, 176
Laernus 93 (= Lernus, an Argonaut?)
Latinus (adj.) 83, 104
Latium 100
Latius 118, 119
Leo 79 (const.)
Libra 79
Libycus 98
Libye 96
Lucifer 130
Lucusta 134 (woman)
Luna 79 (goddess)
Lyaeus 126 (= Bacchus)
Lycaonius (adj.) 123
Lydia 91 (title)
Maenalius 126
Magnus 86 (= Pompey)
Mallius (adj.) 103
Manius 103 (cont. of Augustus)